W9-BZM-164

THE
JUNIOR BOOK
OF AUTHORS

THE AUTHORS SERIES

Edited by *Stanley J. Kunitz and Howard Haycraft*

AMERICAN AUTHORS: 1600-1900
BRITISH AUTHORS BEFORE 1800
BRITISH AUTHORS OF THE NINETEENTH CENTURY
THE JUNIOR BOOK OF AUTHORS
TWENTIETH CENTURY AUTHORS

Edited by *Stanley J. Kunitz*
TWENTIETH CENTURY AUTHORS: FIRST SUPPLEMENT

THE H. W. WILSON COMPANY
950-972 University Avenue
New York 52, N. Y.

THE
JUNIOR BOOK
OF AUTHORS

Second Edition, Revised

EDITED BY
STANLEY J. KUNITZ
AND
HOWARD HAYCRAFT

ILLUSTRATED WITH 232 PHOTOGRAPHS AND DRAWINGS

NEW YORK
THE H. W. WILSON COMPANY
1951

Preface

THIS is the Second Edition, Revised, of THE JUNIOR BOOK OF AUTHORS. The First Edition, published in 1934, has become so well known in schools and libraries that the main function of this Preface will be to describe the principal differences between the two editions.

The former edition included biographical or autobiographical sketches of some 268 individuals, chosen by a poll of representative librarians and specialists in juvenile literature. The new edition contains 289 sketches. Of these, 160 are repeated, with appropriate revisions, from the previous edition. The remaining 129 are brand new names: authors and illustrators who have come into prominence since 1934—also selected for us by specialists in the field.

At one time the editors cherished the vain hope that the new edition might be able to include all the sketches of the old; plus an ample representation of new names; and—most important of all—still sell at a price within reach of the smallest school and library. But the enormous increase in costs which followed the second world war made it sharply evident that economy in some area would be imperative, if the selling price were to be kept at the level desired. Concurrently, librarians and teachers were pressing us to include in the new edition the greatest possible number of hard-to-find "contemporary" authors and illustrators.

As the upshot of these twin pressures, the decision was reluctantly reached to eliminate two principal but dispensable categories of names which appeared in the old edition, on the grounds that material about them could be readily located by young readers in other sources. These were the "classics," e.g. Louisa M. Alcott and Lewis Carroll; and that often closely related group, the "border-liners" between adult and juvenile literature, of whom Mark Twain and Booth Tarkington will serve as examples. Without these excisions—painful as they were—it would have been impossible to find room for the 129 newcomers to the present volume.

No name, however, was dropped unless it occurs in one of the following volumes, all of them in print, compiled by the present editors under The H. W. Wilson Company imprint and found in nearly all libraries: *American Authors: 1600-1900; British Authors of the Nineteenth Century;* and *Twentieth Century Authors.* It is further suggested that libraries and individuals owning the older edition of THE JUNIOR BOOK OF AUTHORS may wish to retain it on their shelves for collateral reference.

Three lesser steps were taken to keep the price of the new edition within reason. The sketches in the new volume are somewhat shorter, on the average, than those in the old; use of a more compact type face reduced the total number of pages required; and a number of out-of-date portraits which could not be replaced have been dispensed with. None of these measures, we believe, will seriously impair the usefulness of the book.

Like its predecessor, the new JUNIOR BOOK OF AUTHORS is really the work of many minds. We do not have space to thank individually everybody who helped or advised us, but in a number of cases the contributions were such that we wish to make special acknowledgment.

For their conscientious voting, which determined the new authors and illustrators to be included, we are happy to acknowledge our indebtedness to the following 51 librarians and specialists in children's literature, representing all sections of the country:

Siri M. Andrews, Young People's Librarian, Concord Public Library, Concord, N.H.; Mrs. May Lamberton Becker, *New York Herald Tribune Weekly Book Review,* New York; Mrs. Lola B. Bellinger, Washington, D.C.; Elizabeth D. Briggs, Director of Work with Children, Cleveland Public Library, Cleveland, O.; Jasmine Britton, Supervising Librarian, City Schools Library, Los Angeles, Cal.; Alice E. Brown, Head, Children's Department, Duluth Public Library, Duluth, Minn.; M. Ethel Bubb, Assistant Director, Department of Work with Children, Public Library of the District of Columbia, Washington, D.C.; Ellen L. Buell, *New York Times Book Review,* New York; Virginia Chase, Head, Boys and Girls Department, Carnegie Library of Pittsburgh, Pittsburgh, Pa.; Agnes Cowing, Yorktown Heights, N.Y.; Carolyn Crawford, Children's Librarian, Ohio State University Library, Athens, O.; Mary Gould Davis, *Saturday Review of Literature,* New York; Josephine K. Dillon, Librarian, Hazeldell School, Cleveland, O.; Anne T. Eaton, New York; Gladys English, Head, Department of Work with Children, Los Angeles Public Library, Los Angeles, Cal.; Helen Fuller, Supervisor, Work with Boys and Girls, Long Beach Public Library, Long Beach, Cal.; Christine B. Gilbert, Librarian, Munsey Park School, Manhasset, N.Y.; Margaret R. Greer, Librarian, Board of Education Library, Minneapolis, Minn.; Elizabeth A. Groves, Assistant Professor, School of Librarianship, University of Washington, Seattle, Wash.; Alice I. Hazeltine, New York; Marian Herr, Head, Children's and School Department, Portland Library Association, Portland, Ore.; Ruth E. Hewitt, Superintendent of Children's Work, Seattle Public Library, Seattle, Wash.; H. Carolyn Howard, Assistant Professor, Department of Librarianship, New York State College for Teachers, Albany, N.Y.; Clara Whitehill Hunt, Boonton, N.J.; Alice M. Jordan, Cambridge, Mass.; Elizabeth Hooks Kelly, Head, Boys and Girls Department, El Paso Public Library, El Paso, Tex.; Marguerite Kirk, Director, Department of Library and Visual Aids, Board of Education, Newark, N.J.; Marcella G. Klein, Children's Librarian, Oak Park Public Library, Oak Park, Ill.; Sarah Malcolm Krentzman, Assistant Dean, School of Library Training and Service, State Department of Education, Tallahassee, Fla.; Jennie D. Lindquist, *The Horn Book,* Boston, Mass.; Harriet G. Long, Associate Professor, School of Library Science, Western Reserve University, Cleveland, O.; Josephine Lynch, Supervisor, Children's Department, San Diego Public Library, San Diego, Cal.; Isabel McLaughlin, Coordinator of Work with Children, Minneapolis Public Library, Minneapolis, Minn.; Anne Carroll Moore, New York; Elizabeth Nesbitt, Associate Professor, Carnegie Institute of Technology Library School, Pittsburgh, Pa.; Mary Helen Pooley, Librarian, Withrow High School, Cincinnati, O.; Effie L. Power, Acting Librarian, Public Library, Pompano Beach, Fla.; Vera J. Prout, Supervisor, Children's Work, Kansas City Public Library, Kansas City, Mo.; Rosette Reese, Librarian, Skokie Junior High School, Winnetka, Ill.; Dorothy C. Robinson, School of Library Service, Columbia University, New York; Mrs. Frances Clarke Sayers, Superintendent of Work with Children, New York Public Library, New York; Velma Ruth Shaffer, Head, Department of Library Service, University of Tennessee, Knoxville, Tenn.; Evelyn Ray Sickels, Supervisor of Work with Children, Indianapolis Public Library, Indianapolis, Ind.; Elva S. Smith, Concord, N.H.; Irene Smith, Superintendent of Work with Children, Brooklyn Public Library, Brooklyn, N.Y.; Lillian H. Smith, Head, Boys and Girls Division, Toronto Public Library, Toronto, Ont., Canada; Miriam B. Snow, Librarian, Campus School Library, Western Washington College of Education, Bellingham, Wash.; Marjorie H. Van Deusen, Los Angeles, Cal.; Margaret J. Ward, Young People's Librarian, Denver Public Library, Denver, Colo.; Adah Frances Whitcomb, Supervisor, Schools Department, Chicago Public Library, Chicago, Ill.; Mabel Williams, Superintendent of Work with Schools, New York Public Library, New York.

For preparation of material in both the old and new editions, we are deeply grateful to these present or sometime members of The H. W. Wilson Company staff: Mrs. Alfred B. Moore, Julia E. Johnsen, the late Wilbur C. Hadden, and the late Frances J. Wallace.

We wish also to acknowledge the assistance of children's book editors and publishers' publicity departments too numerous to list individually, without whose generous cooperation in supplying information, photographs, and pronunciations this book could not have been put together; and to thank as well the individual authors and artists, so large a proportion of whom supplied the stories of their lives in autobiographical form. To Mrs. Margaret C. Reid, Librarian of the Colorado Springs Public Library, a special word of thanks for locating the portrait of Andy Adams in the Pioneer Museum of that city. And a grateful obeisance to Dorothy E. Cook and Dorothy H. West, editors of the *Standard Catalog* series, for their patience in listening to our problems and for their always helpful advice.

A few notes on the style and plan of the volume may be useful. The sketches are arranged in alphabetical order, by surnames. The subjects are generally listed under the names by which junior readers know them best—that is, the names which appear on the title-pages of their books. Cross-references are provided from other name forms and spellings. Bold-face running heads, of the style used in the leading children's encyclopedias, are provided at the top of each page, so that sketches may be located easily and quickly. Pronunciations of difficult names are indicated phonetically in the bottom margins.

One note of sincere regret in conclusion: that there were so many authors and illustrators of merit whom we did not have space to include. If the reception of the present volume warrants, perhaps there will be further editions to remedy the deficiency and also represent the writers and artists of the future.

THE EDITORS

In the present fourth printing of the Second Edition, Revised, we have inserted on page viii a list of death dates of authors who have died since the first printing of the book in 1951.

THE EDITORS

July 1961

List of Death Dates

The authors listed below have died since the first printing of THE JUNIOR BOOK OF AUTHORS, Second Edition, Revised, in 1951. The date of death follows the name.

Merritt Parmelee Allen, December 26, 1954

Nina Brown Baker, September 1, 1957

Jerrold Beim, March 2, 1957

Lorraine Beim, June 15, 1951

John Bennett, December 28, 1956

Walter R. Brooks, August 17, 1958

Margaret Wise Brown, November 13, 1952

Paul Brown, December 25, 1958

Arthur Bowie Chrisman, February 1953

Mary Gould Davis, April 15, 1956

Walter De La Mare, June 22, 1956

Edmund Dulac, May 25, 1953

C. B. Falls, April 16, 1960

Marjorie Flack, August 29, 1958

Rose Fyleman, August 4, 1957

Gertrude Hartman, May 12, 1955

Hildegarde Hawthorne, December 10, 1952

William Heyliger, January 15, 1955

Rupert Sargent Holland, May 3, 1952

Clara Whitehill Hunt, January 11, 1958

Clara Ingram Judson, May 24, 1960

Eric P. Kelly, January 3, 1960

Jim Kjelgaard, July 12, 1959

Emilie Benson Knipe, October 25, 1958

Robert Lawson, May 26, 1957

Elizabeth Foreman Lewis, August 7, 1958

A. A. Milne, January 31, 1956

Anne Carroll Moore, January 20, 1961

Helen Nicolay, September 12, 1954

Helen Fuller Orton, February 16, 1955

Edith M. Patch, September 28, 1954

Miska Petersham, May 15, 1960

Willy Pogány, July 30, 1955

Tom Robinson, November 21, 1954

Helen Sewell, February 24, 1957

Caroline Dale Snedeker, January 22, 1956

Gudrun Thorne-Thomsen, 1956

Laura Ingalls Wilder, February 10, 1957

Ella Young, July 23, 1956

The Junior Book of Authors

Andy Adams

May 3, 1859-September 26, 1935

AUTHOR OF

*The Log of a Cowboy, Cattle Brands, The
Ranch on the Beaver, The Wells
Brothers, Etc.*

Autobiographical sketch of Andy Adams,
written for THE JUNIOR BOOK OF AU-
THORS shortly before his death:

THE subject of this sketch was born in
Whitley County, Indiana. My mother
was a native American, of Scotch parents;
my father was born in Ireland.

I was raised on a stock farm, the youngest of three boys. The years of my youth
are hazy. No doubt but we had good teachers with a perfect confidence in the use of
the rod or hickory switch that a boy might
walk uprightly. Lessons were easy, with
mathematics my favorite, but the dread of
whippings, nurturing a vagabond nature to
burn the bridges behind me, was ever present. Another incentive to leave home was
the misfortune of being the youngest of the
family, with no sisters. With a stern father
and two brothers outranking me on the
farm, it frequently fell to me to churn—
and wash the dishes after meals! My mother
was a favorite of every boy for miles
around; with Scotch thrift, she kept bees
and won all comers with thick slices of
bread and butter and honey.

The environment of my native soil possessed a charm. It was heavy forest interspersed with lakes, huckleberry marshes, and
swamps. The lakes teemed with fish. After
the corn was planted, the dogwood in
bloom, my father allowed his boys a day off,
usually going along himself, when we all
fished as earnestly as the Apostles. We also
fished at night, with a light in the bow of
the boat to blind the fish, using a spear, an
art in which my brothers became proficient.

The early '80's found me in Texas. My
knowledge of domestic cattle and horses was
of very little use to me, but I quickly
blended into the occupation. Great herds
of cattle were trailing out for the upper
country, the Yellowstone River and even
Canada. I fitted into the exodus, a good

From a portrait by Don Jones
ANDY ADAMS

horseman always, a favorite with my em-
ployers, and a hail fellow with my vagabond cronies. The bivouac of a thousand
nights under the stars, the herd asleep, is a
memory still.

The boom in cattle ended in the summer
of 1884. A single decade passed and with
it the trail ended. Other occupations opened
and, with the passing of free range, I
drifted to the mines of Cripple Creek, Colorado, and Goldfield, Nevada. While a camp
follower in the former mining district, I
tried my hand at writing short stories. An
editor of the Houghton Mifflin Company,
Boston, after reading some of my earlier
efforts, encouraged me to undertake a continued narrative. Inviting me to occupy a
pulpit or accept the presidency of a college
would have seemed quite as possible. However, the itch and the material blended, and
without chart or compass, *The Log of a
Cowboy* was the result. After scaling the
mountain, the hills were easier.

* * *

Andy Adams holds a high place among
writers of and about the American West. As
May Lamberton Becker has said, "His books
belong to the honorable and none too large

group of real and reliable cowboy stories.
. . . They are honest, straightforward records of a passing America that now is past."

Still in print in two editions, almost half
a century after its first publication in 1903,
his faithful and absorbing *Log of a Cowboy* is a classic in its field. It has been
acclaimed by J. Frank Dobie, authority on
Western history and literature, as "the best
book ever written on cowboy life." Other
critics have praised Adams' naturalness, simplicity, and sincerity.

A lifelong bachelor, Adams spent his
early and middle age as a wanderer. In
later years he made his home at Colorado
Springs, in the heart of his beloved West.
There he died at seventy-six.

Julia Davis Adams

See *Davis, Julia*

Katharine Adams

AUTHOR OF
*Red Caps and Lilies, Wisp: A Girl
of Dublin, Mehitable,
Grey Eyes, Etc.*

Autobiographical   sketch   of   Katharine
Adams:

I WAS born in Elmira, New York. When
I was still young I went to live in Stockholm, Sweden, where my father was appointed Consul General. I was educated in
France. Later my father was sent to Dublin, Ireland, and I have always devotedly
loved Ireland, its beauty and mystery making a great appeal.

I married an Irishman, Percy Alexander
Walker, in 1926, and we have a daughter
named Sally Caroline. We live in an old
world house in Surrey in England. It has a
lovely garden and my window at the top of
the house overlooks bowers of roses and a
great cedar tree, and on across Surrey towards Epsom Downs.

I am devoted to cats and love all animals.
I have blue eyes and generally wear blue.
I am interested in all my girl readers and
wish I knew them all. I am happiest in my
own home and garden.

* * *

Since the above sketch was written Katharine Adams has returned to the United
States, where she now makes her home. In
their varied and colorful backgrounds her
well-liked books for girls reflect her own
life and extensive travels. Typical of the
praise her work has received is Anne Carroll
Moore's summing-up: "Miss Adams has the
gift of creating atmosphere that girls like,
wherever the story is set." Others have
found her characters "vividly portrayed."
A strong thread of mystery runs through
most of her tales. She has published little
in recent years.

Dorothy Aldis

March 13, 1897-
AUTHOR OF
*Everything and Anything, Seven ι.
Seven, The Magic City,
Dark Summer, Etc.*

Autobiographical notes by Dorothy Keeley
Aldis:

I BEGAN writing and raising a family at
the same time. The score is now four
children and sixteen books, the latest addition being a book.

Naturally, a housewife has to devise ways
and means of getting privacy. One system
I have in summer is to go out in the car to
a deserted subdivision, bringing a squirter
of flit along to ward off flies and mosquitoes.
There I dangle my typewriter on my knee
and have a very fine private office, invaded

DOROTHY ALDIS

Aldis: *AWL dis*

only by occasional lovers, chipmunks, and children being taught how to drive.

I have had stories in women's magazines, verse in *Poetry* magazine and *Harper's*.

* * *

Dorothy Keeley Aldis was born in Chicago, where both her father and mother were newspaper reporters. When she was fourteen the Keeleys moved to a farm near Wheaton, Illinois. Dorothy had two sisters, but they were "so much younger than I that they weren't much good as companions and I was very much alone on the farm."

At sixteen Dorothy was sent away to school and a year later to college, "where I never did any work except in one writing course." Accordingly, she left college in her junior year. A series of jobs followed, including one as editor of women's departments for a Chicago newspaper. At about this time she had her first verse published in *Poetry*.

In 1922 she married Graham Aldis. They have three daughters (two of them twins) and a son. The Aldises live in Lake Forest, Illinois.

Best known of Dorothy Aldis' earlier books for children are her collections of verse for the very small; Anne T. Eaton has spoken of her "happy faculty of catching in her rhymes everyday happenings and the small child's reaction to them." Beginning with *Dark Summer*, however, she turned her talents to teen-age fiction with marked success.

Marjorie Hill Allee

June 2, 1890-April 30, 1945

AUTHOR OF

Susanna and Tristram, The Great Tradition, Judith Lankester, The House, Etc.

Autobiographical sketch of Marjorie Hill Allee, written for THE JUNIOR BOOK OF AUTHORS a few years before her death:

I WAS born on June 2, 1890, which has always seemed to me an admirable date; in the first place, June is the best possible month for birthday celebrations, and in the second place I can always remember how old I am without elaborate mathematical calculations.

MARJORIE HILL ALLEE

I grew up on the farm my great-grandfather had bought in the early days of the state, near Carthage, Indiana, in a community of self-respecting Quakers, most of whose ancestors, like mine, had migrated up from the Carolinas. My sister and I walked a mile to a one-room district school which had been called the "Rabbit Hash School" for three generations, and there were still rabbits in the brush piles of the surrounding woods. When it was time for high school we drove our horse and buggy four miles to town and back every day. My first two college years were spent at Earlham College in Richmond, Indiana; my great-aunt had been one of the first two graduates of that coeducational institution. Then I had a year off, at the age of eighteen, and taught all eight grades that winter at "Rabbit Hash," where the same Great-aunt Luzena had taught in her day.

So far I had been following the trail of those past generations, but at that point I left it to go to a university younger than I was myself, in a great new city; and there at the University of Chicago I found another Quaker, Warder Clyde Allee, who had also migrated from his ancestral farm, and we were married and have lived happily ever afterward in various parts of the country wherever he happened to be teaching zoology: in the New England of Woods Hole and Williamstown; Utah; Oklahoma; the corn country of Champaign and the bluffs of Lake Forest; and since 1921, at the University of Chicago again.

Sometimes I particularly like the flavor of these newer scenes, and then I write *Jane's Island*, about Woods Hole, or *Ann's Surprising Summer*, about the Lake Michigan dunes; but oftener I hark back to old stories and scenes and the accustomed speech of my childhood, and the result is *Susanna and Tristram, Judith Lankester, The Road to Carolina*, and *A House of Her Own*.

My two daughters are Barbara Elliott Allee and Mary Newlin Allee. They both suspect me of using them as models for certain characters in my stories.

*   *   *

Marjorie Hill Allee's books have been warmly praised for their contribution to racial tolerance and understanding among young people. In 1945 her next-to-last novel *The House* received the annual award of the Child Study Association of America with this citation: "A book which faces with honesty and courage real problems in our children's world; a realistic picture translating democratic ideals into everyday terms in a story that will be read for its own sake." And another Quaker author, Elizabeth Janet Gray, has characterized her books as "full of life and color and interest."

In a memorial article in *Horn Book* magazine, Mrs. Allee's lifelong friend Amy Winslow wrote of her: "The contrast between the world as it is and the world as she believed it could be imbued in her a deep seriousness." But "she loved a good joke and a good story" and "she found time to be always warmly human." She never forgot a friendship, and after her death many acts of unheralded kindness came to light.

Merritt Parmelee Allen

July 2, 1892-

AUTHOR OF

*Red Heritage, Spirit of the Eagle,
The Green Cockade, Etc.*

Autobiographical sketch of Merritt Parmelee Allen:

IT is easier to write a book about someone else than a paragraph about myself. It is so hard to remember anything that may be mentioned to my advantage. For ex-

ample, there was the last examination in school; it was in math and the teacher decorated it with a big red D. That D did *not* mean "distinguished." As far as future academic activities went it meant finis. There is no D in finis, of course, but there may be, and there was, a decided finis in D.

So, being firmly established as a scholastic flop, I turned to writing classics. It was a wrong turn. I searched for seven years and couldn't find a classic on that road. Literary immortality was beyond the horizon, therefore I set out to make money. And I made it—two and a half dollars in three years. That was good, considering the quality of the material.

But I was encouraged and felt I had something that would jolt the juvenile publications. It did. One story and *American Boy* folded up. Another single effort put *Youth's Companion* over the dam. A series of baseball yarns finished old *St. Nicholas*. *The Open Road for Boys* absorbed a few punches and then wisely closed the road to further traffic of that kind. *Boys' Life* still survives, thanks to the Scouts' knowledge of self-preservation.

I have written about twenty books, ranging from sheer nonsense to serious biography. American historical novels predominate because I like history and am deeply interested in the men, especially the vigorous outdoor men, who helped build the United States. They are the finest company of heroes that ever marched under any flag. Up here on the farm, far back in the crowd of little people, it is a joy to throw my hat in the air and applaud as they pass in retrospect.

*   *   *

Merritt Parmelee Allen was born and still lives in Bristol, Vermont. Since the above sketch was written he has moved into town from the ancestral farm and lives in a charming house with wide lawns and beautiful trees.

Mr. Allen has made an intensive study of history, particularly American history, and his historical books have been warmly praised. He has written many other successful books also, countless short stories, and a number of sketches which have been used by the National Broadcasting Company.

Merritt: *MAIR it*
Parmelee: *PARM a lee*

Hans Christian Andersen

April 2, 1805-August 4, 1875

AUTHOR OF

Andersen's Fairy Tales

HANS CHRISTIAN ANDERSEN

"**H**E'LL have better luck than he deserves," said the village fortune teller, looking at lanky little Hans Christian Andersen; "a wild, high-flying bird he'll be, something great and fine in the world—the time will come when all of Odense will be illuminated for him!"

The boy Hans was secretly thrilled and his mother wept for joy, but his father only laughed and said the fortune teller was a fake.

Hans Christian was a queer, ugly child, subject to fits, who lived in a dream world of his own. He played with dolls. He made up plays. He hungered for books. When he told the other children that he talked with God's angels at night, they made fun of him. "He's mad like his grandfather," they said. His grandfather, half-crazy, went singing through the village streets.

The village of Odense, in Denmark, was Hans' birthplace and childhood home. The family lived in a little one-room cottage. His mother was a superstitious, illiterate washerwoman, who sent for the witchwoman when he was sick. His father, a poor cobbler, read to him from the plays of Holberg and from the *Thousand and One Nights*.

When Hans was eleven his father died. He was put to work in a cloth factory and later in a tobacco factory, where he charmed the workers with his songs and recitations. His mother soon married again, leaving Hans to shift for himself. The Prince Governor of Fyn, the future King Christian VIII, who lived in Odense, offered to help him if he would take up cabinet-making. But his only desire was to be an actor, and he graciously declined. How thrilled he was when the players from the Royal Theatre in Copenhagen came to Odense on tour and gave him a one-word part in the show!

At fourteen he cracked the clay pig that held his savings and went alone to Copenhagen to seek his fortune in the theatre. Many disappointments followed. The di-

rector of the Royal Theatre would not have him: Hans was too thin. He studied dancing and singing, while apprenticed to a shoemaker, but was discharged from the ballet because he was gawky, and lost a chance in a boys' chorus when his voice changed. Eventually an influential friend persuaded the King to grant him a scholarship and he was sent to a country school.

At twenty-four, having passed the examination which would lead to a degree, he began a career of writing poems and novels and plays. Sometimes they were successful, more often they failed. In his thirtieth year, to bring in a little needed money, he scribbled four fairy tales for children and published them in a pamphlet. The pamphlet sold quite well, so he produced another and another. He continued to issue these fairy tales at intervals the rest of his life and they brought him world fame.

Before he was forty, he had achieved the recognition he so passionately desired. Praise was heaped upon him wherever he went. Proudly he mingled with kings and princes, who feted him at dinners and called him their friend. Once the Queen of Denmark asked him to dance, but he declined. For he knew that his movements were awkward. Tall and lean, he had enormous hands and feet, a small head with high forehead, and a very large nose. Yet he was vain of his personal appearance. He curled his hair and dressed in fashionable clothes, usually appearing on the street in a top hat and frock coat, carrying a stick.

The cultured nobility invited him to their luxurious country manors, for they found him a charming companion who could tell amusing stories. One summer, while staying at one of these manors, his mind went back to his boyhood in Odense and he marveled at the tremendous leap he had made. He who had been looked upon as an ugly duckling was now like one of the petted swans that floated majestically in the moat around the manor. And so he wrote "The Ugly Duckling," a simple fairy tale for young people but really an autobiography in disguise, as were many of his other fairy tales.

At sixty-two came the proudest day of his life; the village of Odense was illuminated for him—just as the fortune teller had predicted. Two years later Copenhagen celebrated the fiftieth anniversary of his arrival in the capital as a penniless lad.

During all these years Andersen traveled restlessly throughout Europe. Not until old age did he make a home and then it was with some friends named Melchior near Copenhagen. He never married. He was repeatedly disappointed in love, notably in his courtship of Jenny Lind, the famous Swedish singer.

He was a child all his life, it was said— and often a spoiled child. When a sculptor planned a statue of him surrounded by dancing children, he said angrily that his stories were for grown-ups as well as children and that he never read with a child behind him or on his lap. So a statue was erected of Andersen in solitary dignity.

He died in his sleep at the age of seventy. To the end, he regarded his fairy tales as "trifles" and refused to believe they were his most important works. The world has disagreed with him, placing his fairy tales among the greatest ever written and ignoring the novels and plays he thought to be his masterpieces. His fairy tales have been translated into many foreign tongues, including Eskimo and Japanese.

In the city of Odense there is a Hans Christian Andersen Museum, built around the cottage where it is believed he was born.

C. W. Anderson

1891-

AUTHOR AND ILLUSTRATOR OF
*Heads Up—Heels Down,
Thoroughbreds, Etc.*

Autobiographical sketch of Clarence William Anderson:

I WAS born in Wahoo, Nebraska. In Indian that means burying ground. It was all of that. Finished local high school and taught country school for two years, then went to Chicago Art Institute for several years. Came to New York around 1925 and did commercial work, painting, and so forth. Did first book called *Billy and Blaze*. Then did two others of the series. Next tried two for teen age.

By this time I decided to retire to New Hampshire, where I had three acres of land a friend had traded me for a portfolio of etchings. Built a stone studio there and another friend gave me a fine thoroughbred horse that served as model for me for many years. Name was Bobcat. Then did *Black Bay and Chestnut,* a large book of profiles of horses. It was well received, so did another.

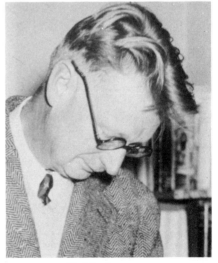

C. W. ANDERSON

Following that I did a book called *Thoroughbreds* in a similar format, explaining the history of the breed and giving other general information. Then went to Kentucky to get material for a life of Man o' War, and did *Big Red*. After that came *Heads Up—Heels Down*, a book for beginners, on riding and taking care of horses. Next came *A Touch of Greatness*, stories of horses that were not quite tops but had color and quality. Next, a book on breeding, raising, and training horses. The last one to date is *Sketchbook*. It's about drawing horses, with suggestions for the student first attempting the subject. Have had a one-man show in New York, of paintings, drawings, and lithographs.

All my illustrations are drawn on stone, for I find lithography the most satisfactory reproduction I know of, for you are in reality your own engraver when you work in lithography. The problem is that it permits no changes or corrections but it gets a brilliance and clarity not found in half tone.

I like horses better than any other subject, finding them perfect for the draughtsman, and they are equally interesting as study for text. As a result I follow breeding, racing, horse shows, hunter trials with great interest. Have qualified as a hunter and jumper judge with the American Horse Show Association and have judged in a number of shows.

Am married and we live in Mason, New Hampshire, most of the year, with two horses, one coach dog, and one cat. I am groom to all of them. Usually spend part of the spring in the horse country gathering material, either Maryland, Pennsylvania, Virginia, Kentucky, or the Carolinas.

* * *

C. W. Anderson has written more than a dozen books. In addition, his lithographs have gained a national reputation and are sought after by both collectors of fine prints and horse enthusiasts. His pictures are exhibited in leading art galleries throughout the country.

Marguerite de Angeli

See de Angeli, Marguerite

Valenti Angelo

1897-

AUTHOR AND ILLUSTRATOR OF
Nino, Hill of Little Miracles, Etc.

Autobiographical sketch of Valenti Angelo:

I WAS born in Massarosa, Tuscany, Italy, and spent eight years of my childhood in this little village nestled on a richly foliaged slope of the Tuscan hills. As a child I remember going to the rice and corn fields in the lowlands with my mother while she worked along with other women and men. Those were the happy days, lying in the shade of willow trees that bordered a canal near by, watching the red, green, and purple dragonflies whirling overhead.

My early school days in the village were interesting too. A solemn, shaven-headed monk taught the village children. In one corner of our schoolroom the teacher kept a good supply of switches. It was seldom, however, that the kind, patient monk used one.

I first became interested in drawing when the village woodcarver found me making ducks of mud beside a puddle. From that time on I was allowed to go to his shop and mold anything I wished out of modeling clay. He was a fine artist. And I can remember him always saying, "Do it over and over again. Do it until there's nothing more to do to it. Do your best."

In 1905 I came to America and lived in a small town in California. Two years were spent at school and then I had to go out into the field to earn money. At fifteen I worked in a paper mill and learned the art of making paper. Other jobs followed in rapid succession. Chemical works, rubber, glass, and steel mills, all claimed a part of my time. My greatest enjoyment in all these branches of labor was in drawing the things around me. This took up all of my lunch hours and most of my time after work.

At nineteen I left home and lived in San Francisco, where I did ordinary labor. I haunted the library at night and the museums on Sundays, and learned a great deal that my few school years had failed to provide. After much struggle I was hired by a photoengraving firm, where I did any sort of art work that came into the shop. I worked there for three years and learned all about reproduction. In 1926 I made my first

Valenti Angelo: *val EN tee AN jel oh*

VALENTI ANGELO

Laura Adams Armer

January 12, 1874-

AUTHOR OF

Waterless Mountain, Dark Circle of Branches, Forest Pool, Etc.

Autobiographical sketch of Laura Adams Armer:

EVERYONE gets born of course, and doesn't know much about it. His parents mark the date for him if he is civilized, so called, and record a certificate of birth in the city hall of his village. Mine was recorded in Sacramento, California, U.S.A.

My parents soon moved to San Francisco, and there I went to public school, private school, and home school—the last for the reason that I was not very strong, and couldn't stand the daily contact with forty-nine husky children of every nationality. San Francisco has always been known as a cosmopolitan center, and of necessity its children came from Italian, Irish, German, French, Jewish, Chinese, and Japanese families.

Very early in life I became interested in a Chinese family who ran a laundry near where I lived. I liked the little children, dressed with bright colored aprons, over their padded coats. When I grew up and studied Chinese art and literature with its legends and symbolism, I always recalled the two almond-eyed, smooth-skinned babies of the laundryman. Come to think of it, those little children may have started me on the study of Indian children, long after I had raised my own son, Austin.

I must tell you about Austin. Of course he was the most beautiful and interesting child ever, and many of the pretty things he did on his way to being a man have been recorded in *Waterless Mountain*. All the other dream happenings came from my own childhood. I believe that every boy and girl born into the world "comes trailing clouds of glory," which most grown-ups have forgotten. I remembered the beautiful visions of another world, and I saw them come true in my own child, who loved all beauty. We had such a glorious time together learning about birds, butterflies, flowers, and ferns, rocks, and even stars. When Austin was not quite three he said to me one night, "I want a paper bag and a ladder. I'm going to

illustrations and this very first illustrated book received the gold medal awarded by the American Institute of Graphic Arts. I felt very honored. Since then I have devoted most of my time to decorating books. During the past twenty years I have illustrated a hundred and twenty, and all have been a source of inspiration to do many more; each is more fun than the last. In my spare time I like to paint and do sculpture. As a matter of fact, I like to do anything that gives me enjoyment and keeps me happy. And the arts keep me very happy

Not until 1937 did I turn my hand to writing. All through the years I had wanted to make some record of my childhood in Italy for American children to read. The result was *Nino*. The book was well received. I was so thrilled I decided to write a sequel. Writing this was even more fun than the first one because I drew from experiences and memories dear to my early days in America.

I intend to keep on writing books for children. I think good books are necessary in children's lives. They help give wings to their imagination and enrich their minds, bring them closer to a clearer understanding of their own lives and the lives of others. Printed words and pictures help them realize noble things in the past and noble things within our own time. And some books help them visualize and catch a glimpse into their future lives—tomorrow.

LAURA ADAMS ARMER

climb to the sky and get a bagful of stars for you, mumsey."

He did get me a bagful of stars, which shine for me this minute while I am telling you about them. His father, Sidney Armer, who married me, so the records say, in San Francisco in 1902, considers Austin the brightest star of all.

Perhaps there are some children who dream as I dreamed when a very little girl, about all the things grown-ups laugh at. I am sure that everyone has dreamed of flying, of soaring so easily in the air and being sure that he could teach others how to do it. There were no flying machines when I was a child, but men were trying to invent them. There were no horseless carriages, but men did make them. So I have seen many dreams of the impossible come true. That is why I still hope that men will learn how not to go to war, how not to be so greedy for money that they enslave their brothers to toil and grow sick with producing for profit instead of making what they need for happiness.

I have the hope of that dream coming true for all the people of the earth, because so many beautiful things have happened in the sixty years that I have been "walking to and fro and up and down the earth."

Of course I know the terrible things that have happened. I do not close my eyes to war and poverty. I can talk about tragedy first hand because I have lived through as much sorrow as anyone, but I do not wish to talk about those bad things, simply because I am much more interested in the "clouds of glory" that all little children know about. Younger Brother knew about them and he sprinkled pollen on them when he sought the gods on their summits, with a prayer within his heart.

"In your heart are secrets you cannot name, songs you cannot hear, and words that you must not speak." I will speak them for you, I will sing them for you, for I know all about those secrets deep in your hearts, those beautiful, unnamable dreams which have come with you out of the long past. They are born through all the experience of all the people who walked the earth before you. They are precious and not to be wasted. You are happiest when you hear them singing in your heart.

> A bag of stars and a ladder to climb,
> A merry hunt for rainbow's end,

and then a book which makes you sure that dreams of beauty are more real than acts that are ugly and sorrowful.

*   *   *

Mrs. Armer was well known as an artist before she began writing books, and her husband is also an artist. All of her books are illustrated by herself or by her husband or by both of them. Her first novel, *Waterless Mountain,* the imaginative story of Younger Brother, a Navaho boy, published when she was fifty-seven, was awarded the Newbery Medal as the best children's book of its year. The Armers make their home at Fortuna, a small town in northern California, just a few miles inland from the Pacific Ocean.

Boris Artzybasheff

1899-

ILLUSTRATOR AND AUTHOR OF
Seven Simeons, Etc.

Autobiographical sketch of Boris Artzybasheff:

I WAS born in Kharkov, Russia. Why, I don't know. I was told that on that day the flags were flying and there was great celebration in the land, but then again, it might have been because of the centennial

Artzybasheff: *art zee BASH eff*

of the birth of Pushkin, Russia's greatest poet.

My father was Michael Artzybasheff, Russian novelist and playwright, probably best known in this country for his novel *Sanine*.

When I was eight I was taken to St. Petersburg (known to you now as Leningrad) and placed in Prince Tenisheff's School, where I spent the next nine years of my life.

I became addicted to the drawing of pictures at the age of three and have been at it ever since. Naturally, during the school years the general studies hindered my inclination seriously and it took a great deal of effort and ingenuity on my part to avoid them, especially the mathematics. Alas! I realize the fallacy of that aversion now as I nobly try to balance my bank book at the end of each month.

Art, as I have said, being my chief interest, I was planning as soon as I finished college in 1919 to go to France to continue my art studies. But it was that very year the Revolution broke out and all thought of "Art for Art's Sake" had to give way before the necessity of learning the far more arduous art of keeping alive.

As I look back upon those two wretched years of Russian civil war it seems to me like ten. I was tossed about from one end of the country to another and in this respect my experiences were similar to those of many other Russians. In 1918, for some unknown reason, I found myself serving as a machine gunner in one of the countless armies that overran the face of Russia. This particular one was a Ukrainian force trying to get a slice of the best part of Russia in order to establish an independent republic. As I was Russian I didn't have much sympathy with the movement and was happy indeed when my noble host was defeated.

Then, in the spring of 1919 I drifted farther south and sat on the shores of the Black Sea, watching longingly for the ships that were sailing to faraway lands; lands where, I thought, the people did not shoot at each other but knew better and lived in peace. At the very first opportunity I shipped as a sailor on a boat bound for Ceylon and India. I had always wanted to travel, and who wouldn't want to go to India? As a boy I had read Kipling. . . . However, such was not to be my fate for at the last moment the boat's destination was changed and we set out for America. But that suited me, because as a boy I also had read James Fenimore Cooper and consequently had a great desire to see the Indians! Thus, in the summer of 1919 at the age of nineteen and full of ambition, I sailed up New York harbor.

I did not see any Indians but the skyscrapers fascinated me and I wrote my mother, from whom I had been separated two years, that I should stay in America about a year as I felt that would be adequate time in which to learn all about the Americans and their habits.

As I had no money and as I didn't speak English, to find a job was a big job in itself. I succeeded in getting into an engraver's shop doing odds and ends. One morning the chief "artist" failed to show up and I was told to draw a bottle. It was an immediate success and for months afterward I drew bottles, big and little, pill bottles and hot-water bottles and what have you, from morning till night. Encouraged, I asked for a raise of three dollars a week; this being refused, I resigned.

As I was known to the New York port authorities at that time as a seaman (and who knows but they may still have my name in their files as such) I pulled out my A.B. certificate and found a berth on an oil tanker bound for Mexico and South America. Five months later I was back in New York greatly refreshed and still determined to be

BORIS ARTZYBASHEFF

an artist. As I had enlarged my English vocabulary through my association with the sailors, most of whom were Swedes and Spaniards, the rest was comparatively easy.

* * *

Boris Artzybasheff is one of the best known of contemporary artists. Besides illustrating a multitude of other authors' books for young people, he illustrates his own stories for children. He does work for adults, as well, especially portraits of persons currently in the news, for magazine covers.

Margaret Ashmun

AUTHOR OF

Isabel Carleton's Year, No School Tomorrow, School Keeps Today, Etc.

Autobiographical sketch of Margaret Ashmun, written for THE JUNIOR BOOK OF AUTHORS a few years before her death:

WHEN my book for boys, *David and the Bear Man*, was published, several people said to me: "How did you come to write about a bear? What do you know about bears, anyhow?"

And I could truthfully answer, "I know quite a lot about bears. In fact, when I was a little girl, we had a bear in our back yard."

It seems that my mother's brother, who was living with us in a little village in central Wisconsin, went out on some adventure in the North Woods. Here someone made him a present of a small bear cub, which he shipped in a crate to my father. So poor Chuck lived in our yard, occasionally getting loose and terrorizing the neighborhood children, and growing bigger and crosser every day.

At last he became so large and fierce that he had to be sent away; but he left some very vivid memories in my little mind. The iron ring to which he was chained may still be seen in the white-oak tree on the lawn. I now own the house and the five acres of land around it. This house, which was once a tavern, was the earliest house to be built (1852) in the village of Rural, Waupaca County, Wisconsin.

About 1858, when my father was a small boy, my grandfather, Orson Branch Ashmun, moved his family from Champlain, New York, to settle in Rural, and there have been Ashmuns in the village ever since. My native village I have accurately described under the name of Belleville in my two books for children, *No School Tomorrow*, and *School Keeps Today*. Many of the incidents in these books were transferred from my own childhood.

My elder sister and I went to the village school. From time to time, younger brothers and sisters arrived in the home, until there were seven children. I went to Waupaca, to attend the high school, and to Stevens Point to attend the state college. Beginning young, I taught in various towns in the state, and then I went to the University of Chicago, and to the University of Wisconsin at Madison, receiving the degress of Ph.B. and A.M.

It was while I was teaching in the high school at Marshfield, Wisconsin, that I learned enough about girls to store up material for a number of books, published later under the titles *Marian Frear's Summer, Including Mother, Brenda Stays at Home, Mother's Away*, and so forth. I spent a year in Montana, and while I was there I was asked to visit on a horse ranch in the Smith River Valley. Afterwards I wrote a book, *Stephen's Last Chance*, which has this ranch for a background.

For several years I taught in the department of English in the University of Wisconsin, and while there I began writing textbooks. Four were published: *Prose Literature for Secondary Schools, Modern Prose and Poetry for Secondary Schools, Modern Short-Stories*, and *The Study and Practice of Writing English* (jointly written with Dr. G. R. Lomer). In 1912, I left the University to engage in literary work in New York City. I lived there for nine years, writing books, poetry, and magazine articles. Among my publications were four novels, *The Lake, Support, Topless Towers*, and *Pa, the Head of the Family*; and a number of books for young people, including the *Isabel Carleton* series of five volumes, which have the scene laid in the university town of Madison, Wisconsin.

Tiring of city life, I bought an old house in Connecticut, and lived there for a while, and then removed to New Haven and to Northampton, Massachusetts. During the years in New York and New England, I went abroad to England and the Continent four or five times. In 1928, I adopted a little girl, Mary Louise, and in 1930 I took her to England, where we stayed a year. My more recent books are *The Singing Swan,* a biography for grown-up people, and *Susie Sugarbeet,* a story for little girls. In all, I have published nearly twenty-five books.

With Mary Louise, I am now back in the village of Rural, where we live in the old family home. We spend our winters in a city, where Mary Louise can go to school, and then we come back to enjoy country life during the summer and autumn. My sister lives in the village, too, and other relatives come and go; and so there are still Ashmuns in Rural as there have been ever since they came from Champlain in 1858.

* * *

Miss Ashmun subsequently made her home at Springfield, Massachusetts, and it was there that she died in 1940, presumably in her late fifties. She wrote little in the last ten years of her life.

Ingri & Edgar Parin d'Aulaire

AUTHORS AND ILLUSTRATORS OF

Ola, Abraham Lincoln, Don't Count Your Chicks, Leif the Lucky, Children of the Northlights, Etc.

Autobiographical sketch of Ingri and Edgar Parin d'Aulaire:

TOGETHER with our son, Per Ola, cats and dogs and sheep and chickens, we live on Lia Farm in Wilton, Connecticut. When we first met we used to roam the world, but now we have become domesticated. When we don't paint and draw and write, we till the soil and train animals and children, and our only complaint is that the days are too short.

As very serious-minded young art students we met in an art school in Paris many, many years ago. A year later we were married in Norway, having found out that the one did not in the least interfere with the other's work.

For several years we had Paris for our headquarters, making exploring trips in all directions between Norway in the north and Africa in the south. We were painting and drawing, Edgar dividing his time between doing murals and illustrations, Ingri between portraits and landscapes.

EDGAR & INGRI D'AULAIRE

Following the principle that every well-bred European has to see America, we went across in 1929. New York proved to be a place of a new beauty and a great inspiration. So we went to Europe again, got our immigration papers, and came back to New York as settlers.

To begin with we did not think of making children's books. But one day a wise old lady put the idea into our heads to start making our own books for children.

Till then we had been strictly separated in our work, two absolute individuals, but now we found out that we might make a happy combination of Ingri's knowledge of children and children's psychology, and Edgar's dramatic sense.

To begin with we had quite some difficulties. We had each our distinct way of expression and were as different as the countries we came from. We worked hard and quarreled a lot, and after a while we started to forget the I and You and became one unity with two heads, four hands and one handwriting — when working on our children's books. When we paint we still manage to be ourselves, and we take care to keep this.

* * *

Edgar d'Aulaire was born in Switzerland September 30, 1898, the only son of a half-Swiss father and an American mother. His father was a noted portrait painter, and as a result he spent his childhood in the various

Aulaire: *oh LAIR*

art centers of Europe, speaking every language, all with an accent, and never feeling completely at home any place. Upon his parents' insistence he had to submit to a rigorous European academic training. But as soon as he became of age he revolted and started out on his career as an artist. He studied in Munich, Florence, and Paris, painting frescoes and illustrating books.

In the last art school Edgar attended, he met Ingri Mortenson, who was just beginning her art training as he was finishing his. She was born in Norway and was as thoroughly Norwegian as Edgar was cosmopolitan. After their marriage Edgar fell in love with Norway. Since then they have spent most of their summers and vacations there. Their winters they mainly spent in Paris until they moved to America.

Their first book for children was *The Magic Rug,* a storybook built on their sketches during a painting trip to Northern Africa. Next they decided to try a story about Norway. The result was their best-known work, *Ola,* the story of a small Norwegian boy's wintertime adventures in his own country in the land of the Lapps, which instantly captured the affection of American boys and girls. Other books have followed in rapid succession, including *Abraham Lincoln,* which won the American Library Association's Caldecott Medal as the best picturebook of the year 1939. All of the d'Aulaires' drawings and stories have won high praise for distinction, authenticity, and imaginative appeal to children.

Esther Averill

AUTHOR OF
*The Voyages of Jacques Cartier,
Flash, Adventures of Jack
Ninepins, Etc.*

Autobiographical sketch of Esther Holden Averill:

I WAS born in Bridgeport, Connecticut, attended the public schools, and graduated from Vassar in 1923. The day after graduation I went to New York to look for a job, and I knocked first at the editorial door of *Life,* which was not the *Life* magazine of today but a humorous publication somewhat like the English *Punch.* I showed one of the editors a few caricatures I had drawn in college. They were caricatures of Shakespeare, Charles Lamb, and other literary gentlemen of olden times. The editor told me that although I had a good feeling for pattern, I would have to learn more about life itself before he could use any of my work.

I laid aside my caricatures and took a job on the trade paper, *Women's Wear Daily,* where I was put in charge of the art work. I greatly enjoyed my associations with the artists and editors of this paper, as well as my excursions into the composing room, with its smell of linotype machines and printer's ink.

In 1925 I did what many of my generation did: I went to Paris. And there I remained for ten years. My first real Paris job was in the office of the well-known journalist-photographer, M. Thérèse Bonney. There I helped write reports on fashions and all that pertained to the new decorative art movement. I also had much to do with staging the photographs, although I did not actually take them.

My special interests led me eventually into the field of the graphic arts and in 1931 I became a publisher of children's illustrated books. I knew many artists in Paris and my aim was to use their illustrations in books that would be designed and printed as well as possible. In that spirit I produced *Daniel Boone* and five other books, some of which were later imported and published by bigger

ESTHER AVERILL

firms in England and the United States. The first four were produced in France, the last two in the United States after I returned here to live. All were illustrated by Feodor Rojankovsky, except one which was illustrated by Emile Lahner. I was the author, or co-author with Lila Stanley, of all the texts, except one, a New Caledonian legend I translated from the French of Jean Mariotti.

My active life as a publisher ended with the Second World War, but my interest in all that concerns children and their books and reading has steadily increased.

In 1946 Harper published a new revised edition of the old Paris edition of Rojankovsky's *Daniel Boone*, and for this I amplified the earlier text. I have also written, as well as illustrated, three juvenile books of my own.

Arni

CAROLYN SHERWIN BAILEY

Carolyn Sherwin Bailey

1875-

AUTHOR OF

*Miss Hickory, Children of the Handcrafts,
Pioneer Art in America, Etc.*

Autobiographical sketch of Carolyn Sherwin Bailey:

I BEGAN to make up stories before I could write; so I dictated to my mother, who was herself a writer for children. At five I won a twenty-five dollar award for *Write Your Own Stories*, a book of pictures and blank pages issued by a publisher to encourage boys and girls to invent stories. But I did no serious writing for publication until I was nineteen, when I began to have verse and fiction accepted by *St. Nicholas* and *Youth's Companion*. Since then I have written more than thirty-five books which are in libraries, schools, and homes, many of them in Braille.

My home life began this interest in story-writing. I was born in Hoosick Falls, New York, and lived my first years in Auburn and in Lansingburg, New York, the latter a sleepy little town on the Hudson River where we could go bobsledding down a hill onto the river, and look for wild berries and nuts through the seasons.

I learned geography from my father, who was a metallurgist and established successful blast furnaces in South America, Can-

ada, and our southern states. He charted ore deposits, often traveling on mule back, and when he came home he told me stories of far places.

My mother was a teacher of mathematics as well as a writer. My sister and I studied with our mother at home, receiving a foundation in education that gave us the power to learn from experience and life later.

I traveled in Europe, the Caribbean Islands, and this country. I taught, did social and editorial work, research in Americana, and at last wrote the books by which I am perhaps the best known. They are hitherto untold stories of boys and girls who helped make us a great nation. There are also country stories about Temple, New Hampshire, where my husband, Dr. Eben Clayton Hill of Johns Hopkins University, and I spent our happiest years. One of these books, *Miss Hickory*, was awarded the Newbery Medal for 1946.

Today I live six months of the year in our hundred-and-fifty-year-old house in Temple with mountains close by, and a secret staircase and six fireplaces to make it interesting. There are more than a hundred acres of forest and an orchard of Wealthy, McIntosh, and Baldwin apples that extends the length of the village. In the winter I live in New York on old Gramercy Park, where there are children playing all the time, a great Christmas tree, and many flower beds. In the center of

Gramercy Park is a statue of Edwin Booth, the Shakespearean actor, looking across to the Players' Club, that used to be his home.

But the country is best of all, for boys and girls, and for anyone who likes to write.

Margaret & Mary Baker

AUTHOR AND ILLUSTRATOR OF

The Black Cats and the Tinker's Wife, The Lost Merbaby, The Tinker Tailor, Lady Arabella's Birthday Party, Etc.

MARGARET and MARY BAKER are two English sisters. Margaret writes stories and Mary illustrates them.

Here is Margaret Baker's own story of her life:

Not many miles from Birmingham there is a little town called Langley Green; this is where I was born on April 8, 1890. I only lived there for five years, and the most exciting thing that happened was the arrival of a baby brother who was called Henry Wright. In 1896 the chemical works with which my father was connected was moved to Runcorn in Cheshire, and of course we had to go there too; but between leaving the old home and settling in the new, I was taken for my one and only visit to the United States. I cannot remember much about it, but I remember Adeline, the Negro cook at the house where we stayed in Virginia, because she let me play at cooking and made a feather bed for my doll. I remember, too, that I did not like maple syrup.

A year after we went to Runcorn a baby sister was born, she was called Mary; two years later the last of the family arrived, a boy who was given the name of Wilson. We used to feel very sorry for Wilson because he was born just three weeks after the beginning of 1900, and so unless he lived to be nearly a hundred years old he could not live in two centuries as we had done.

The parts of our Runcorn home which we loved the most were the big concrete yard and the nursery. The yard had a sand-pile and a good wall on which to play ball, and in the shed at the end there were old planks and boxes and cricket stumps and broom handles and all sorts of useful things like that. We had a go-cart, too, and several hoops and an old kitchen table that we used

MARGARET BAKER
MARY BAKER

upside down as a boat. Any child can understand what a delightful yard it was, and what exciting games we used to invent.

I decided to be an author when I was very small, and began to write stories long before I could spell half the words correctly. The first story I can remember was about a mouse called Algernon, and on page number two I drew a picture of him in a hat and carrying a bag as he set out on his adventures. I do not remember what the adventures were to have been, except that in the end he was to marry a charming young lady mouse called Dorothy, whose portrait in a long, frilled skirt was also given.

After reading *Little Women* I wrote a tiny newspaper for a week or two, and one number still lies in my mother's treasure drawer, and begins with a very bad piece of poetry about Henry the Eighth and his six wives! When I was fourteen, however, I began writing in earnest, for I became editor and principal contributor to a family magazine called "Attempts." For several years the magazine came out regularly every month; after that, as we grew more occupied with other things, it only came out once a quarter, and finally, once a year. It was probably the best training I could have had for my present work. The first eight or nine of my stories and verses that were accepted by real editors for real magazines made their first appearance in "Attempts."

Besides writing fairy stories, I write stories and articles to teach the reason for total abstinence and these I illustrate myself. The drawings are very bad, but they help to explain what I want to say.

We left Runcorn in 1928 and went to live in the quaint old town of Leominster in Herefordshire, and eleven years later, after my father's death, my mother, sister and myself came to the tiny Cotswold village of Sutton-under-Brailes. We have a garden and orchard on the slope of a hill and I like to spend part of every day working there.

Wright and Wilson married long ago and we have two nephews and three nieces. They spend part of every holiday with us and when they come I always read them the last fairy tales I have written to see if other children are likely to enjoy them.

*   *   *

Here is Mary Baker's autobiography:

I was born at Runcorn, Cheshire, England, on July 25, 1897. One of the first things I can remember was leaning against the keyboard of the nursery piano arguing with our governess because I did not see why I should not learn to play it when my sister and elder brother both had lessons. The governess said she would begin to teach me after my third birthday, and I can remember how much I looked forward to that time, which could not have been far off, and how exciting I found the first lessons.

We always stayed on farms for our summer holidays, and there was one where we stayed for several years when we were quite small which we especially loved. There was a little wooded hill at the back of it and there we played at being Red Indians having been fascinated by Ernest Thompson Seton's *Two Little Savages.* Mother made us three younger ones Indian-looking clothes of sacking trimmed with fringes of red and yellow wool, and the boys had head dresses into which they could fix the turkey feathers which were the reward of deeds of prowess, such as finding where the hens laid astray, spotting new birds, and heaps of other things. I was the Princess Pocahontas and only wore one large curly feather stuck in the side of my head band. Father and Mother made us a wigwam out of reeds one year, and the next a bigger one of sacking which lasted till we wanted more grown-up holidays and went climbing and tramping and camping.

I have always loved drawing and the animals I liked watching and drawing best were horses—not just standing still ones, but ones running and doing all sorts of things. I think one reason I was so fond of drawing horses in motion was because I loved Randolph Caldecott's books so much and used to look for hours at his pictures of horses prancing and running and galloping in such lively ways that I was thrilled with wonder and admiration. I would probably never have thought of illustrating children's books if I had not had so many ourselves and been so fond of them.

Except for a few special lessons I was educated at home and I have never had any art school training except one term of life classes, I took a long correspondence course of press illustrating before I began to do that type of work, and it was part of one of these lessons which led to my using the silhouette illustration so much. It is a means of working which especially appeals to me as it can express movement and form without the distraction of unnecessary details.

In the summer when there is not so much illustrating to do as in the winter, I often sketch out of doors in water colors; and quite often use parts of the sketches later in the pictures for the books.

Our present house overlooks the village green, with its tall old elm trees, where there are always hens and geese and often cows going to be milked, or the farm horses pulling red and yellow wagons piled with hay or wheat or roots. Some of the farmers use tractors—but we like to see the horses best.

Nina Brown Baker

December 31, 1888-

AUTHOR OF

Juarez, Garibaldi, William the Silent, Etc.

Autobiographical sketch of Nina Brown Baker:

I WAS born in Galena, Kansas, of pioneer covered-wagon stock. I went to public school in Galena, and then to the University of Colorado just long enough to get the credits I needed for a teacher's certificate.

I thought it would be fun to teach a rural school in western Colorado. I was engaged by letter, and arrived to find that the tiny mountain town consisted of a school, a general store, and a blacksmith shop. The pupils rode in on horseback from ranches as much as twelve miles away. The first day of school was also my first day on a horse. I rode seven miles from the ranch that had taken me in, but I walked home, leading the creature. I didn't know how to get on him by myself, and I thought it would impair my dignity to ask the children for help. I'd thought the Western life

NINA BROWN BAKER

would be fun, and after I got used to it, it was. But it took some getting used to.

When I left Colorado I went to Kansas City, where I met my husband. We've lived in several Midwestern cities, and came to New York in 1938. We have two daughters, both married now.

I'd always meant to be a writer some day, but I didn't begin very early. It's so much easier just to talk about it! Then one Christmas my husband gave me a portable typewritter, and I had no more excuses. So I started, as almost everyone does, with short stories and rejections and tears. If there's an easier way, I didn't find it. I sold my first story to a church school magazine, and after that I had pretty good luck. But I found I liked writing books better than short stories, so I concentrated on them. I wrote seven mystery stories for young people before I began the series of biographies I'm doing now.

I like biographies best of all. I particularly like the subjects I've chosen, heroes of other lands. I think it's really necessary, if we're to have One World, for us to know how other nations got the way they are, what their people are like, and what they want. To me the most interesting way to acquire this knowledge is through the lives of their great men, because that way you get a good story too.

Olaf Baker

AUTHOR OF

Shasta of the Wolves, Thunder Boy, Dusty Star, Bengey and the Beast, Etc.

Autobiographical sketch of Olaf Baker:

ONE often hears of the "Naughty Nineties." I was born in Birmingham, England, in the "Sober Seventies," and my moral character is therefore beyond reproach. The Seventies were not only sober; they were slow. When we wanted to go quickly we rode a horse or a high bicycle. Really reckless persons traveled by train. As a small child, knowing nothing of motor cars, this failed to depress me.

Because Longfellow had written a poem about Scandinavian kings, my English Quaker grandfather insisted upon my being called "Olaf." Otherwise, my father, who had himself visited Norway, wanted me to

OLAF BAKER

be called after *his* father, "George." But the impact of Longfellow upon my grandparent proved stronger than that of the fjords upon my father. Who the eminent poet was who wrote that clangorous and massy line, "My name is Norval. On the Grampian hills my father tends his sheep," I do not know. For me, my name is Olaf.

On Norwegian fjords, my erring father fed the herring. My mother came from the south of Ireland. This, coupled with my father's Norse tendencies, kept me from becoming unduly British. It is true that Birmingham bordered upon the so-called Black Country where the reek of smelting furnaces darked the Midlands for miles. But the smuts gathered upon my small person in my grandfather's extensive shrubberies were negligible beside the glintings of fairyland in my pseudo-Norse-Celtic soul.

Little did I then guess that my future mental habitat lay five thousand miles due west in a Blackfoot territory that was anything but black. But there it is. "Brumajem"-born I was. "Brumajem" I remain—a transatlantic *faux pas*! [Ed. note: "Brumajem" is a nickname for residents of Birmingham, England.]

I think it must have been somewhere about 1902 that, in company with my mother and my step-father (my own father having died when I was only twelve months old) I migrated to America, where our adventurous footing in that colossal wilderness was only arrested by the Pacific. One of my most vivid memories is of our all three sleeping uneasily on pine branches in a log cabin to which Uncle Tom's must have been a Broadway luxury hotel, and of a stove which filled every crevice, including our eyes, with blinding smoke. It was not even a proper stove, but one coal-oil tin set upon another, without pipe or chimney, only a hole in the roof. I trust that my youthful readers have never wept over my stories such painful tears as were· forced from my eyes by the activities of that detestable stove.

That was the real beginning of my education. The slight deposit of syntax, spelling, and geography which settled upon me before and after was as nothing by comparison. And there was the forest, lying league upon league about us; and the great beasts. Even though you might not see them, you felt their invisible presence.

My so-called "American" animal books (two of which have been translated into German) beginning with *Shasta of the Wolves* and ending with *Buffalo Barty* form a blood-and-thunder series which no self-respecting American child's bookshelf should be without. And here I may perhaps be permitted to remark that I did *not* borrow the idea of my first from that of the admirable work *Tarzan of the Apes*. The wolves suckled my "Shasta" serially in the pages of *Little Folks* several years before Edgar Rice Burroughs' apes enriched, with Tarzan, the reading world.

The scene of my latest book, entitled *Bengey and the Beast*, is laid in England, in one of those out-of-the-way corners, which railroads have not yet invaded, where there are no roads for motors, and where, consequently, anything may happen. Nothing in your great America could, I'm convinced, be stranger than what happens in this funny book of mine. You see, Bengey makes the discovery that the forest near his house is a world to itself altogether different from what his home people believe it to be, but which is every bit as real as *their* world, only far more exciting and delightful. But you will not get the right feeling if you try to read the book when walking down Broadway, or while crossing over Woodward Avenue in Detroit. You simply won't believe it, if you do! What you *will* believe is being badly run over, and waking up afterwards in a hospital!—So, don't!

To descend from these lofty regions to sordid personal details, I may mention that I am five feet eleven inches in height, and that the color of my eyes is a greenish gray. I have two innocent hobbies—horse riding and sketching—and no vices. Neither—being a bachelor—have I any children. This being the case, my one passionate desire, coupled with an inordinate craving for barley sugar, is that other people's children should rise up and call me blessed.

* * *

After his American odyssey, Mr. Baker returned to England. He now lives in a country cottage in South Devon. Anne T. Eaton has spoken of "the strangeness and beauty, the feeling for wild creatures, the sense of the ancient world breaking through," that gives *Bengey and the Beast* "its distinctive and fascinating flavor." May Lamberton Becker called *Bengey* "More than a mere 'children's book'—an addition to children's literature." Similar tributes have been paid to *Shasta of the Wolves*, published almost two decades earlier, and still a modern childhood classic.

James Baldwin

December 15, 1841-August 30, 1925

AUTHOR OF

The Story of Siegfried, The Story of Roland, The Story of the Golden Age, Etc.

LITTLE "Towhead" sprawled upon the floor of the rough log cabin with a book before him. A fire of hickory bark blazed in the huge fireplace. Two elderly Friends of the New Settlement in the Indiana backwoods had come to call upon his mother.

"Laws a me!" cried the elder of the two neighbors, an ancient maiden. "If that ain't that booky boy that we've heard so much about. Now, it don't seem possible that sich a leetle feller as him can read, does it?"

"Well, it surely ain't nateral," answered her companion. "It ain't nateral, and I reckon it ain't right, nother."

Once the mother of James Baldwin said he was not born with a silver spoon under his tongue, but with a book in his hand. When other babies would cry for their bottles he would cry for books. The very feel of paper, its smoothness and thinness, would magically soothe his wailings. For a time he was a great bother, for whenever he saw a new word he would point to it and say "What's this? What's this? What's this?" And when he was told he never forgot. Reading seemed to come to him as naturally as eating comes to others.

Baldwin has told us the story of his boyhood in his book *In the Days of My Youth*, written under the pen name of Robert Dudley. In real life his father was Isaac, and his mother Sarah. Owing to his almost complete isolation from the world in a Quaker colony in his early years his ignorance of outside life was very great. Although his first contacts were those of a "greenhorn of the deepest dye," his wide-awake, independent mind soon led him far along the ways of usefulness and honor. He was largely self-educated although he had a little instruction in the district schools. At the age of twenty-four he commenced teaching. After a few years he became superintendent of the graded schools in Indiana, and remained there for eighteen years. Soon afterwards he received an honorary degree of doctor of philosophy from De Pauw University. The last thirty-seven years of his life he was connected with publishers, Harper and Brothers, and the American Book Company, remaining with the latter for thirty years as editor of school books. Meanwhile he had commenced writing books. He wrote the *Story of Siegfried* at forty-one, and followed it with the *Story of Roland* and other books—in all more than fifty volumes. It was said at one time that more than half the school readers then used in the United States were either edited or written by him. His books were known and read in every part of the world, including the schools of such far-away countries as China, Japan, and the Philippine Islands.

Baldwin married Mary S. Taylor at the age of twenty-three. When a little boy he had first seen her in the Friends' meeting house, and to his unaccustomed eyes she had seemed so strange and beautiful that he had at first believed her to be and called her "the angel of the facin' bench." They had fifty happy years together. He survived her and himself passed away at his home in South Orange, New Jersey, at the age of eighty-three.

Helen Bannerman

AUTHOR OF
Little Black Sambo, Etc.

HELEN BANNERMAN

THE creator of one of the childhood's best loved characters, Little Black Sambo, British writer Helen Watson Bannerman became an author by chance. She was the daughter of an army chaplain, Robert Boog Watson, whose work took him to many parts of the British Empire. Born in Edinburgh in the 1860's, she went to live in Madeira when she was two. The child was taught by her father until the age of ten, when she was sent back to Scotland to be educated. There she attended "a small private school of the old-fashioned 'Dame School' kind," later going abroad to study French and German. When her continental studies were finished she returned to Edinburgh, continuing her education by means of correspondence courses until she was able to take an L.L.A. degree from St. Andrew's University.

In 1889 Helen Watson was married to William Burney Bannerman, a surgeon in the Indian medical service of the British army. For the next thirty years she lived in India. Arriving there as a bride, she was separated from her husband almost at once, for he had to march to his station with the regiment, while she proceeded alone by "bullock wagon." In one place, the bullocks, unused to the sight of a white woman, became so frightened that Mrs. Bannerman had to walk about until they could be harnessed. Later she accompanied her husband on his frequent travels around India to inspect hospitals, but her efforts to learn the language were frustrated because whenever she had made a little progress her husband was transferred to another station where the dialect was different.

It was in 1898 while returning from a trip to Scotland, where she had left her two little girls to be educated, that Mrs. Bannerman, who had had lessons in water-color sketching as a young woman, wrote a "picture letter" to her daughters to while away the tedium of the journey and, as she said, to comfort herself for the absence of her family. Friends who were charmed with the story of the little black boy who lost his red coat and purple shoes to the tiger, but who eventually was restored to his home with all his finery intact to devour 169 pancakes of tiger butter, persuaded the young matron to have the story published. Small in size—"because as a child, she had always wanted a book she could hold in her own tiny hands"—*Little Black Sambo* has never been out of print since it first appeared in 1899.

Other books followed but *Little Black Sambo* has remained the favorite and has become a children's classic. It has been translated into many foreign languages, including Indian dialects.

Mrs. Bannerman ceased to write about 1910, devoting herself to her husband's work in stamping out the plague in Madras and Bombay. After his death in 1924, she returned to Edinburgh to live with one of her daughters. In 1936 she was visited by her American publisher who tried to persuade her to write a sequel to *Little Black Sambo*. But with her four children grown, Mrs. Bannerman had no incentive to write. Her reply was, "Sambo's grown up now. He's a middle-aged man, and no fun for children." However, a few weeks later she sent *Sambo and the Twins* to her publisher with the comment: "You must remember that this is your own children's book. If it had not been for them I should never have written it at all."

Helen Bannerman was described as "a small, quiet, gray-haired Scotchwoman, with a kind face and what might be called a dignified twinkle in her eyes." She was about eighty-three years old when she died on October 13, 1946.

Ralph Henry Barbour

November 13, 1870-February 19, 1944

AUTHOR OF

*The Half-Back, The Crimson Sweater,
For the Honor of the School,
Behind the Line, Etc.*

Autobiographical sketch of Ralph Henry Barbour, written for THE JUNIOR BOOK OF AUTHORS a few years before his death:

I WAS born in Cambridge, Massachusetts, November 13, 1870. My father, James Henry Barbour, was of Colonial and Revolutionary stock, his forebears having been, I gather, an extremely Puritanical lot with morbid consciences, painfully honest, and opposed to all frivolities of the flesh or spirit. Those qualities, however, waned somewhere short of me.

My mother was Elizabeth Middleton Morgan, whose parents arrived from Derbyshire, England, just in time for her to be born in Massachusetts. She was a painter of considerable talent and that fact provided a distinctly artistic atmosphere for my boyhood. I was educated in the public schools of Cambridge, the New Church School at Waltham, and the Highland Military Academy at Worcester, Massachusetts.

At about the age of seventeen, in spite of earlier inclination to become an artist, I broke out with rhymes and jests which, over the *nom de plume* of Richard Stillman Powell, were published in such flippant journals as *Life, Puck,* and *Truth,* and convinced me that it would be a waste of time and opportunity to bother further with an education when editors' checks were so astoundingly easy to obtain. My mother, however—my father had died when I was twelve—was dubious of verse-writing as a life's occupation and I consented to try real work and so condescendingly accepted a position as reporter on a Boston evening paper.

Underwood & Underwood
RALPH HENRY BARBOUR

Six months later, having been discharged for cause, I went to Denver, Colorado, and for several years found employment on the papers there. Again out of a job, I yearned for the open spaces and found them in the Grand Valley in western Colorado. I ranched there four years, at odd times pounding out short stories on a decrepit typewriter. Back in Denver, and at work on the *Times,* I collaborated with a brother newspaper man, L. H. Bickford, and produced my part of a first book.

Subsequently I went to Chicago and read copy on the *Inter-Ocean*; and from there to Philadelphia. In the latter city, at the age of twenty-eight, I finally succeeded in tearing myself away from newspapers, ending a career in which I had variously served as leg-man, court reporter, literary editor, columnist, correspondent, rewrite man, cartoonist, and city editor.

My release was largely fortuitous, for it happened that a story of mine for boys published in *St. Nicholas Magazine* caught the attention of Ripley Hitchcock, literary adviser for D. Appleton & Company. It was Ripley Hitchcock who had seen possibilities in Edward Noyes Westcott's *David Harum,* after the manuscript had been declined by a dozen others, and it was Ripley Hitchcock who thought he saw possibilities in a doubting and timorous young man named Barbour. The immediate result of our meeting

Barbour: *BAR ber*

in the old building on Fifth Avenue was *The Half-Back* (published 1899) which, well received then, is now still selling.

Some one hundred and forty other books have followed that, all but a score or so stories for boys; or boys and girls if you like. It has required fourteen publishers to cope with that production, although the Appleton-Century Company is responsible for the bulk of it. I have, too, contributed at least my share of short stories to the magazines; most of them for the younger generation—since, having accustomed myself to viewing life from the juvenile point, I find it difficult to see it from the grown-ups' angle. I live in Tampa, Florida, and am happily married to a lady who corrects my spelling, reads my proofs, beats me at tennis, and doesn't mind it when I tramp sand into the house after my gardening activities.

Although, as this is written, I seem to have arrived at nowhere in particular, the journey has been on the whole very pleasant. Perhaps if I could make it again I'd choose a different and more lucrative route, but—well, I don't know. Maybe not. After all it has been a lot of fun.

* * *

Ralph Henry Barbour has been called "the dean of sport story writers for boys." His more than 150 books have been favorites with three generations of growing Americans. *The Half-Back* alone averaged a printing a year for more than thirty years and is still in steady demand—a truly remarkable testimonial to the book's popularity when the changes in manners and customs that occurred within the time are considered. As one writer has pointed out, "Football, as it was played when *The Half-Back* was written, would scarcely be recognized if seen today. And yet, so fundamentally attuned to boy life and the boy heart is this tale of school activities and athletics that the reader, his interest compelled, brushes aside the elements of time and the game regulations of yesterday."

In his later years Ralph Henry Barbour made his home at Pass Christian, Mississippi, on the Gulf of Mexico. It was there that he died at the age of seventy-three, survived by his wife.

Kitty Barne

1883-

AUTHOR OF
She Shall Have Music, In the Same Boat, We'll Meet in England, Etc.

Autobiographical sketch of Kitty Barne, English playwright and writer for children:

I WONDER whether any of you have that itch to write—write something, anything. It shows itself very early sometimes. I can never remember when I wasn't thrashing round looking for either something to write about or a way of making music.

When I was six I purchased an exercise book and started on—of all things—what I called a "Bible Educator." (I think the title cannot have been mine.) It was a compilation of hard little arid facts having to do with the Bible: the shortest verse, the longest, the largest family, the total number of persons mentioned, and so on. Where I got these horrible little grains of sand I have no idea, but there they were, put down in a large round hand; it all came, I imagine, from our North Ireland Protestant nurse.

Not long afterwards I was given as a birthday present a violin in a case, complete with bow and book of instructions. At the sight of that the passion for dry facts instantly left me (mercifully, or I suppose by now I should be compiling reference books), the writing urge took a back seat, and music was everything.

Then at eleven off I went to school armed with my violin and was allowed to play second violin in the orchestra. That orchestra was the thrill of thrills! I was so busy listening to the others I could hardly play myself.

Then a little later but when I was still in Lower Fourth (in English schools Lower Fourth contains all the newest, worst behaved, most raw of children), I wrote a play about Guy Fawkes blowing up the Houses of Parliament and, wonderful to relate for those days, it was performed by my proud form. Those of you who know what it feels like to see your own play acted and to hear yourself cheered by your own supporters will know just how I felt. I resolved to let everything else go and devote

Barne: *BARN*

myself to the drama. I didn't want only to write the play, I wanted to produce it, give it music, dress it, rake in the audience, to do everything for it in fact except act. To that end I started a junior dramatic society in the holidays and we did very well—but with other people's plays, not mine as yet.

That only whetted my appetite for more. When I went to study music I started a dramatic society in the hostel where I lived; I roped in clever friends and spent every holidays "getting up" plays, now written by myself, for sixty or seventy children of all ages. We even had the temerity to take London theatres and persuade real critics to come to see them. They were always fantastic: the little boy who tied up the winds with the equator (a wet looking rope covered with seaweed and barnacles and shells carried in by small and melancholy Doldrums—geographers will know why).

But time passes; we grew up and got married and the world became a ferociously serious place. I turned to writing books for children about children, real children in dead earnest. By that time I had learned something about them, how they talked and what they were after; I knew they were sensible, critical, and not at all romantic about their own affairs. *She Shall Have Music*, the story of a girl absolutely determined to play the piano, started off the new "line." Whether the heroes and heroines of my books are running a dogs' hotel,

escaping from the Gestapo in Norway, getting up a play, helping a Polish girl find her feet in an English school, or persuading a returned P.O.W. father to change his mind about their future careers, they are all independent energetic people, making up their minds what they want to do with their lives and going all out to do it. "Nice types," as they say; I enjoy them and I often wish I knew them in real life.

* * *

Kitty Barne, Mrs. Eric Streatfeild in private life, lives in Sussex, England, where she writes novels and plays as well as stories for young people. The novels and plays, however, are for the most part published only in England.

Ernest Harold Baynes

May 1, 1868-January 21, 1925

AUTHOR OF

My Wild Animal Guests, Jimmie: The Story of a Black Bear Cub, The Sprite, Polaris, Etc.

AT the English seaside a small boy one day became absorbed in the strange creatures that he found along the shore. He placed two crabs in his pocket and took them back to boarding school, but they were soon found crawling in his desk and he was sent to bed without any supper. Another time he received a beating for bringing a hedgehog to school.

The boy, Ernest Harold Baynes, had been born in far-away Calcutta, India, and brought to England as a young child. His parents were English. They presently went to America, leaving him in a boarding school.

Harold, at the age of eleven, joined his parents in America. They made their home in the country, just north of New York City, and he came to know the birds and beasts of the vicinity intimately. He was valedictorian of his high school class and he distinguished himself at the College of the City of New York as a champion long-distance runner. On leaving college he was for a while reporter on the New York *Times*; then he served several years as assistant to his father, John Baynes, an inventor of photographic processes.

When it became apparent that his father's dream of forming a company would not be

KITTY BARNE

realized, Harold decided to devote his life to nature study. He was then thirty-one. The sale of a series of nature stories to the New York *Herald* enabled him to marry the girl to whom he had been engaged for seven years, Louise Birt O'Connell. They went to live at Beaver Lodge, Stoneham, Massachusetts, on the edge of Middlesex Fells. And after three years they settled near the Blue Mountain Forest Reservation, in Sullivan County, New Hampshire, where their white house stood on a knoll at Sunset Ridge, two miles from the village of Meriden and a half mile from the nearest neighbor.

Hundreds of animals, large and small, were part of the Baynes household at various times. There were notably Actaeon, the fawn; Romulus, the young coyote; Dauntless, a young timber wolf; Polaris, an Eskimo dog; and Jimmy, the black bear cub, who did more mischief than any of his companions. He would break into the house and destroy everything in sight in his search for jam and sugar. It was the Sprite, a little red fox, that Baynes loved best of all.

Baynes carefully observed the habits and development of his animal friends, cramming a big notebook with minute details. He and his wife took thousands of photographs. The animals never injured him. He had a way with them which won their confidence. He kept them as nearly as possible in their natural environment and when his observations were finished set them free. The keeping of pets he regarded as a cruelty and it saddened him to see wild creatures imprisoned in cages.

He supported himself by writing and lecturing. His biography of Jimmy brought hundreds of strangers to Sunset Ridge to see the mischievous little bear. On the platform Baynes talked about wild animals and championed the cause of the birds, forming bird clubs and promoting bird sanctuaries. He was active in saving the North American bison from extinction and one time broke a pair of them to yoke and harness to stir up interest in the movement. After the first World War he went to Europe to gather first-hand lecture material on the work done by animals in the War.

Baynes' beardless face was weather beaten, his body muscular, his movements swift. He would walk sometimes forty miles in a day. He always dressed neatly, with a flower in his buttonhole, and he was quiet of manner. He loved to tell amusing stories.

When Baynes learned that he had only a few months to live, he accepted the verdict calmly and went about the task of completing his writings. He worked until the day before his death. He died in Meriden at the age of fifty-six, and his ashes were scattered over the tree tops of his favorite retreat on the side of Croydon Mountain. A bronze tablet was placed there.

Among Ernest Harold Baynes' biographies of his animal friends, some of the most popular are: *Polaris: The Story of an Eskimo Dog, Jimmie: The Story of a Black Bear Cub, The Sprite: The Story of a Red Fox, Three Young Crows and Other Stories,* and *My Wild Animal Guests.*

Jerrold Beim

1910-

AUTHOR OF

Andy and the School Bus, The Smallest Boy in the Class, Etc.

Autobiographical sketch of Jerrold Beim:

WOULD you like to know how I became a writer? It was way back when I was in the fourth grade in Newark, New Jersey, where I was born. We had to write a theme on "The Life of a Christmas Seal." I guess I did a pretty good job because my teacher said, "Jerry, you ought to be a writer." I remembered those words and kept at it.

The first story I ever sold went to *Scholastic* magazine. They used to run a contest on "Your Favorite Character in Fiction." I wrote about Cinderella's stepsisters. I said Cinderella was a ninny, always complaining and needing a fairy godmother to help her. At least the stepsisters stepped out and did things for themselves. Was I surprised to win the five-dollar prize in that contest!

When I graduated from high school I couldn't afford to go to college and went to work in a Newark bank. I didn't like that and got a job as office boy in the advertising department of a big store. I still wanted to write and did bits of advertisements and was given a chance at writing the home furnishing ads. Then I became advertising manager for a department store in Syracuse, New York. But it still wasn't the kind of

Beim: *rhymes with "time"*

JERROLD BEIM

Lorraine Beim

1909-1951

AUTHOR OF

Triumph Clear, Hurry Back, Alice's Family, Etc.

Autobiographical sketch of Lorraine Beim:

WHEN I was growing up I never expected to be a writer. I loved to swim and hoped I would become a champion swimmer. Everywhere I went I always looked for a good place to swim. In Syracuse, New York, where I was born there were many lakes. Later in Chicago we had Lake Michigan. Once we lived in California on the beach near Los Angeles. You can see my family was always moving around!

I really loved all kinds of sports, tennis, horseback riding, swimming, skating, and there was nothing I loved better than going to camp in the summer, which I did for eight years.

When I graduated from Syracuse University I went to Europe. I traveled all over, visiting many different countries. I liked France so much I got myself a job and stayed for two years. As a matter of fact I had several jobs, one as research secretary for an American writer and another that was very glamorous and exciting, doing publicity work for a Paris dressmaking establishment. I learned to speak French and I still look forward to the day I can return to France for a long visit.

When I came back to the United States I returned to Syracuse for a while to be with my family. That summer, 1931, I took a group of young children out every day for swimming, tennis, and horseback riding. We had wonderful fun I realized I liked doing things with young people more than anything else. But before I could decide just what kind of work I wanted to do I had an accident. I fell off my horse. I broke my back and had to spend the next four years getting better and learning to walk again.

Perhaps you know of a book I wrote called *Triumph Clear*. In it I tell the story of a girl who had infantile paralysis and thought she would never be able to walk again. Though I didn't have infantile paralysis that story is based on my own experiences. I went to Warm Springs, Georgia,

writing I wanted to do. So I quit my job one summer and went to the island of Nantucket, Massachusetts, to try to write short stories for magazines. I didn't eat much that summer but sold a few stories.

Then I married a girl I knew in Syracuse. One day I sold a story to a big magazine, *Cosmopolitan.* We bought a car and drove to Mexico. We lived there for two years and loved it! While there we wrote a children's book together called *The Burro That Had a Name.* That started us on writing books for boys and girls. We kept writing them when we returned to live in New York City.

We liked children so much we wanted to have some and chose a little girl whom we named Alice. Then we chose red-headed twin boys whom we called Andy and Seth. By that time we were too crowded in our little New York apartment and decided to move to the country. We found a big old house that no one had lived in for ten years. The windows were broken, the doors off, the porch falling, but we enjoyed having it fixed up. The children used to call it the Broken House but now it looks like new and it's Our House.

My wife, Lorraine, and I have written lots of books together and separately. We like to write about the real things that happen to boys and girls. I go to work every day in a regular business office because writing is a business, too!

LORRAINE BEIM

too, and one of the greatest thrills of my life came when I met President Roosevelt. We used to go swimming with him and play water games together! Like Marsh Evans, the girl in my book, I learned to find new values in life. I learned to walk again too, though I did have to give up active sports.

In Syracuse in 1935 I met and married my husband. I guess from here on my story is much like his. We lived in Mexico, settled finally in Yorktown Heights, New York, have three adorable children of our own. I think I've solved a problem for myself which lots of girls are facing these days: can you have a home and a career, too? Believe me, running a big household, loving and taking care of your children, and then writing books is a lot of work, but I love almost every moment of it! I try to put things about my experiences and my children into my books and to portray problems all of us have to face.

Laura Benét

AUTHOR OF
*The Boy Shelley, Enchanting
Jenny Lind, Etc.*

Autobiographical sketch of Laura Benét:

I WAS born on a Friday, June thirteenth, and in a house, Number 13, at Fort Hamilton, New York harbor. Yet I've al-

ways been lucky! Our father and his father before him were army officers and my brother, William Rose Benét, and I came into the world in adjacent sets of quarters at this post. Our childhood was a singularly happy one, since our parents had a love of books and games and were both poetic and imaginative.

Moving about with the army we began our first lessons with our mother as a delightful teacher. In the evenings there were long readings aloud from Dickens, Scott, Thackeray, and *St. Nicholas*. Father specialized in ballads and *The Rose and the Ring*. William and I amused ourselves by acting out the stories we heard. He had a love of real plays, in which he and other children performed, while I sat as audience, with my dolls.

When our father was sent to Bethlehem, Pennsylvania, I was ten. We went to Moravian schools and absorbed the atmosphere of a picturesque old town. The Moravian church with its quaint festivals and trombone music made a great impression on us and I described the school life later in several stories. It was there that a third child, our small brother, Stephen Vincent, joined the group.

When our father's post lay between Troy and Albany, we went for four years to good schools in these cities. William Rose graduated at the Albany Academy and I at the Emma Willard, and then went to Vassar College where I did my first scribbling in essay and verse for our college paper, *The Miscellany*. Unlike William and Stephen, I never wrote in childhood. Mine was a case of arrested development: everything came to me late.

College ended, California, where the family had already gone, was my goal. The joys of post life, of riding and swimming and exploring an outdoor land were numerous. Yet I hankered for some kind of career all my own. So I took up social work in New York with the Spring Street Settlement. Except for selling an occasional verse I did no writing. The days were spent in scrubbing Italian babies, listening to complaining Irish, and calling on old people. This was one of the most vivid periods in my life and I enjoyed every minute.

It was after my brother William lost his wife, and his children needed me at home

Benét: *ben AY*

that I began to see writing as my job. At the MacDowell Colony I met Lola Ridge. Because of her encouragement I decided to write. For a year or two I was on the book page of two newspapers and while there fell in with Rachel Field, who became a close friend.

Not until 1930 did I devote myself to my pen. By that time I had published a tiny first book of poems, *Fairy Bread*, a second, *Noah's Dove*, one book of fantastic short stories, and had written a novel or two, but with little success. Then I discovered I had a flair for writing and selling children's stories. A friend urged me to show an editor the manuscript of *The Hidden Valley*. The editor took it at once, also my *Boy Shelley*. Other biographies and stories quickly followed. *Roxana Rampant* was a truthful account of my first experience as a struggling writer.

Once Henry Canby, of the *Saturday Review of Literature*, made me an offer through William. He said, "Tell your sister to write a juvenile after the manner of *Little Women* and I will give her an advance on it." At the time I refused, saying to myself, "I shall be a novelist." But Fate took my hand and led me straight back to the path where I was intended to walk, as she has a way of doing. Since then except for my poetry, I have been a children's author—of nine books!

LAURA BENÉT

John Bennett

May 17, 1865-

AUTHOR AND ILLUSTRATOR OF
Master Skylark, Barnaby Lee, The Pigtail of Ah Lee Ben Loo, Etc.

Autobiographical sketch of John Bennett:

I WAS born in Chillicothe, Ohio. As far back as I can remember I wished to be an illustrator. I loved pictures. I began to draw when I was four years old. I drew on all the blank white paper I could get. I loved humorous drawings, and copied the caricatures of the great English humorists, Gilray, Rowlandson, and Cruikshank, and the cartoons of Thomas Nast in *Harper's Weekly*. I covered every scrap of paper I could get with drawings. I set my heart on being an artist.

I had not much education. I attended the public schools, and got as far as the second year in the high school. I was not a good student; I spent far too much of my time drawing pictures. This was good for my drawing, but bad for my learning. My parents wisely concluded to encourage my drawing and to omit an education for which I showed no aptitude. I was sent to Cincinnati to learn to draw properly. But my father's business, after many misfortunes, failed. I was compelled to leave drawing to find work.

It so happened that I had begun to tell stories to amuse the boys of the neighborhood when I was a very little chap. This came about in an odd way. The stable boy at my best friend's home was a pleasant Irish lad named Peter Dunn. It was Peter's duty, when evening came, to feed, water, and bed down the horses, to cut and carry firewood to the kitchen. We helped him with his chores, throwing down hay, fetching corn from the crib, and carrying in the firewood he had split. His tasks done, he repaid us by telling us stories, Irish fairy legends and tales from the Arabian Nights. We gathered around Peter, astraddle of a big horse block, and for half an hour were in fairyland. He told his stories well. A better place offered, which he took. So we lost our story teller. We bewailed our loss; twilights were as empty of delight as an old tin can. One evening, I do not know just how it came about, I found myself in Peter's place, astride the horse block, telling stories

JOHN BENNETT

to the boys. I thought them all my own. Years afterward I realized where I had found them: in the African explorations of Paul B. Du Chaillu and an account of the buried cities of Herculaneum and Pompeii. All that summer and fall, until frost sent us shivering from the horse block, I told stories to the boys; I had become official story teller to the boys of the neighborhood. By accident. I still meant to be an artist.

It chanced through odd circumstances that the neighbor's boys came into possession of a complete small printing-office outfit, type and press. We all learned the rudiments of printing; and during the summer vacations for several years we printed an amateur paper, on which I was a typesetter. The newspapers of the town regarded the enterprise with amusement; but when the editor of the weekly paper looked about for a cub reporter, he selected me as measurably fitted for the place. Thus I became a reporter, a newspaper writer, editor, and correspondent for greater papers. Then I lost my place. It was my own fault. It seemed a catastrophe. Yet that apparent catastrophe proved in the end to have been good fortune. Misfortune was heaped upon misfortune; I was shabby and poor; I almost wished I had never been born. I did everything I could for a living. Then good fortune came at last. I sent a story to *St. Nicholas*, with my own illustrations. Mrs. Dodge, the editor, asked me to become a

regular contributor of stories, verses and drawings to *St. Nicholas*. For her I wrote *Master Skylark*, the story of *Barnaby Lee*, and almost all the whimsical tales contained in *The Pigtail of Ah Lee Ben Loo*. After many misadventures I had become a successful writer of stories for boys and girls.

Besides these books, I have written for older readers *The Treasure of Peyre Gaillard, Madame Margot, Blue Jacket: War Chief of the Shawnees* and *Doctor to the Dead*.

As a boy I loved the world out of doors, to sail a boat, to shoot with a rifle, and every sport boys know.

Once, being very ill, I was ordered South for the winter, married a wise and charming girl, recovered my health, and have dwelt in Charleston, South Carolina, ever since.

My brother, Henry Holcomb Bennett, also a successful newspaper man and writer, as well as an excellent draughtsman, wrote "Hats Off; the Flag Goes By!" which most young Americans know.

My son, John Bennett III, is also a writer, author of the historical novel, *So Shall They Reap*.

Richard Bennett

1899-

ILLUSTRATOR AND AUTHOR OF
Skookum and Sandy, Hannah Marie, Mister Ole, Etc.

Autobiographical sketch of Richard Bennett:

I WAS born in southern Ireland but came to America with my parents when I was six. Instead of settling in the densely populated cities of the east coast my father bought a little ranch in a wild and unsettled part of the state of Washington, about thirty miles from Seattle.

After attending the local grammar and high schools I went to the University of Washington in Seattle and graduated from the department of art.

For ten years I taught drawing and painting in the Far West, Middle West, and finally New York. During the summer I took trips to Europe and visited many times my birthplace in Ireland. Here I collected folk tales that have since appeared in children's magazines from time to time.

In 1934 I decided once and for all to devote my complete attention to book illus-

RICHARD BENNETT

trating and the writing of stories for children. My first book, *Skookum and Sandy*, was published in that year and in the following five years three more were published. The settings of these books are either Ireland, where I was born, or the American Northwest, where I was raised.

Since 1930 I have illustrated about thirty books, the most important, perhaps, a collection of Hans Andersen's stories and a very fine anthology of Paul Bunyan tales of the tall timber.

My winters are usually spent in New York City, but when the warm weather comes, I like to go to the mountains of western Washington where I live a simple life and devote my time to painting and working on my next book.

"Erick Berry"

1892-

AUTHOR AND ILLUSTRATOR
The Winged Girl of Knossos, Honey of the Nile, Lock Her Through, Harvest of the Hudson, Etc.

Autobiographical sketch of "Erick Berry" (Mrs. Allena Champlin Best):

THE writing habit came on me rather late in life. Long before my first published book, with Erick Berry on the green and magenta jacket, I had been illustrating juvenile books; and my first venture into fiction flowered from my fascination with the pictorial quality of African folk tales.

To go back a number of years: my people were ship builders, clipper-ship builders . . . I've used that in a story . . . in New England, and I was born in New Bedford, the home of whaling ships. On the other side of the family my mother's people pioneered from New Bedford to western New York state. And I've used them in a story too. Father was reference librarian in the State Library in Albany, New York, and I had free access to the big files at almost any time; a wonderful library to grow up in. Because my eyes were not strong my reading was cut down to an hour a day, and so between reading I started copying the book illustrations; from this the family decided that I had ability as an artist and so, a little later, I went off to Boston to study with Eric Pape. That was a delightful year. . . . Some day I mean to put it into a story. Next year I went down to the Pennsylvania Academy of the Fine Arts. And I *have* put *that* into a story. It was at Pennsy, because of my devotion to Eric Pape that I won the nickname of Erick, a far more comfortable handle than the Evangel Allena with which I had been christened.

Then on to New York with a portfolio under my arm. That too went into a later story. Some years of fashion drawing led into greeting cards and into my first juvenile illustrating, and saving my pennies for that first trip to Europe. But I resolved that the first should not be my last, and soon I found that if I informed publishers that I was off to Yucatan, or West Africa, or by mail plane down to Montenegro they would save a job for me along my line of travel.

West Africa wasn't the wild goose chase it seemed. I fell in love with it immediately; the color and the blaze, the drums and mystery and pageantry. And when I married Herbert Best [see autobiographical sketch in this book], then an officer in the Nigerian Government Service, a whole new field of adventure opened up for me. Together we began to experiment with writing, as, together, we explored; strange little bush villages up the tributaries of the Niger, or towns along the desert, mud walled and sun baked; wherever his job took him. And after some six years of this double life, with me running back and forth from Nigeria to New York, or meeting H. B. when he was

"ERICK BERRY"

on leave, to wander around Europe, my husband retired and we settled on writing as a serious business.

We bought a sweet old stone mill in the heart of the English Devonshire country and remodeled it. And got a story out of it too. But then the war came and I returned to the States, and after a time my husband followed me. Looking around for a new home we finally purchased a deserted and overgrown farm adjoining the log cabin and strip of timberland which I had long owned in the heart of the Adirondack mountains. We began to farm. We knew nothing about farming, but we read the Cornell leaflets, and asked questions and experimented. We now have a good subsistence farm, bees and cows and chickens and fruit trees; we even experimented with goats. But our real cash crop has been our books, of course. For down-to-earth reality I recommend farm life; it gives you a contact with people and with animals and with problems that man has had since he first scratched the soil and shoved in a seed to grow. We made the farm our war contribution, since food was needed everywhere. And to date we have pulled some fifty books out of our combined experiences, from H. B.'s *Young'un,* to my *The Little Farm in the Big City.*

Nearly all our work is done in collaboration, the more fun for that and, I think, the richer. I still continue to illustrate the ju-

veniles. My husband says that my pictorial and plot sense are a help, just as I know that his better vocabulary and ability to portray character are important in our combination. Our widely varied backgrounds, mine of a small city life, finishing school, and art classes are an amusing contrast to his English public school, university, and army experience. And our varied interests, from cooking to underwater goggle fishing, tennis, travel, and farm life, give us a broad scope for background material, and local color. And of course the collaboration is fun too. Some day I'll write a story about that.

Elsa Beskow

February 11, 1874-

AUTHOR AND ILLUSTRATOR
*Aunt Green, Aunt Brown and Aunt
Lavender, Pelle's New Suit,
The Adventures of Peter
and Lotta, Etc.*

Autobiographical sketch of Elsa Beskow:

WHEN trying to tell something about oneself, one's thoughts invariably turn back to childhood. For it is then one receives the strongest and most lasting impressions, impressions which form and shape one's personality.

I have almost without exception bright and happy memories from my childhood. I was born in Stockholm. My father was Norwegian, a businessman living in Stockholm, but my mother was Swedish. I recollect that as children we used to say with a certain amount of pride that we were *both* Norwegian and Swedish, and this seemed much more interesting than being only one of the two. Of course, we knew that Norway was a wonderland, with high, snow-covered mountains and deep fjords. We were six brothers and sisters, one boy and five girls, and I was the eldest of the girls.

In summer we led an extremely happy life in our country home, close to a small, idyllic lake surrounded by birch trees and dark pines. The house was old, with a tile roof under whose eaves the swallows built their nests, and was surrounded by a garden with big apple trees. There we children lived a glorious outdoor life, bathing, rowing, picking berries and wild flowers, and inventing all sorts of amusing games. It was a great day of joy, a red-letter day, every spring when we were ready to move to this paradise, and it was very unwillingly we returned to town in the autumn.

As far back as I can remember I loved to sketch. I still recollect the girls with stiffly extended arms and rows of buttons down the backs of their dresses, which I sketched when I was four years old. I have been told that I also began at a very early age to make up stories and tell them to my brother who was one year older than I. I cannot remember this, but I can remember that I was allowed to begin school when I was four, and that it was with the greatest joy I learned to read. This was at a small kindergarten kept by two dear aunts of mine.

Every now and then I used to run in to my grandmother's room in the same house, and pay her a visit. She was the best and kindest grandmother in the world, and I sat on a stool at her feet while she taught me to crochet and told me many amusing stories. How well I remember grandmother's gilt clock under its glass shade, and the big carpet with roses and forget-me-nots embroidered in cross-stitch on a dark background.

As soon as I had learned to read I spent all my time reading fairy tales. Needless to say, Hans Christian Andersen played a very important part in my childhood. I also

sketched with intense pleasure and enthusiasm, and when I was seven years old I secretly made the daring resolution that I would "make picture books" when I was grown up.

After some years I left my aunts' school and entered a girls' grammar school, where I became a very interested pupil. But then my father died when I was fifteen. This was a severe blow. At the same time we found ourselves in rather poor economic circumstances. I had to leave school and begin instead at the Technical School in Stockholm. I made up my mind to learn drawing as soon as possible so I should be able to earn my living as an illustrator. My grandmother had already died by that time, but we moved, together with my two aunts and my bachelor uncle. We had a kind of collective household, and everyone did his or her share and we had everything in common. I remember how happy I felt the first time I succeeded in earning some money for a drawing and was able to run home with the money for the joint household. My sisters also began to earn their living at a very early age. In spite of economic difficulties we were a very happy family, and there was plenty of fun in our home.

My first picture book, *The Wee Little Old Woman,* was published in 1892. In the same year I married and moved to Djursholm, a charming suburb near Stockholm, where my husband had his work, *inter alia,* as headmaster of a school. My husband is both artist and theologian, and a good counselor in my work.

We are still living in Djursholm. There our five boys have grown up, and there many picture books have seen the light of day and then spread out over the world. My sons sat model for me when they were small, and they have also been expert critics of my work. Now they are grown up, and it will soon be my grandchildren's turn to become models for their grandmother, and be her counselors. Life flies so rapidly. I can scarcely believe it is so many years since that little girl decided to "make picture books" when she grew up.

Allena Best

ELSA BESKOW

See "Berry, Erick"

Herbert Best

March 25, 1894-

AUTHOR OF

*Garram the Hunter, Garram the Chief,
Border Iron, Young'un, Etc.*

Autobiographical sketch of Herbert Best:

DO you want to see my passport? Here it is; in a wandering life one learns to keep it handy. Born, you see, in Chester, England. An ancient city, with its ramparts and still more ancient Roman remains. Education? Henry VIII had something to do with that, founding a school which taught me the formal elements; and naked pagans in Africa, who cannot count above five, carried on the training. German shells, Flanders mud, desert thirst, courtly Emirs, insect pests, unhoped for successes, barely endurable failures, surgeons, malaria, critics, Erick Berry, and hosts of other influences have taken a kindly interest in me. The strictly formal result of my education was crystallized long ago with a Cambridge B.A., LL.B., and a London F.R.G.S. My training still goes on.

One summer I was reading for the Law Tripos in a little ghost-haunted room in a suite of chambers in Queen's College, with my future tidily mapped out for me. That was in August 1914. Then a complete stranger killed another complete stranger in a town I had never heard of, and before the

HERBERT BEST

month was ended I had volunteered as a soldier. I suddenly found myself one of the most inefficient members of what was then one of the best trained armies of the world. I had to learn from the bottom up, all those things which the common soldier took for granted, from discipline to shaving, when I would have given the world for just five minutes' sleep. In a year I was sent home as an N.C.O. instructor, so I must have learned something. Shortly afterwards I was commissioned and sent east. I though it a comedown; anyone could be a pampered officer!

As a civilian, when that war was over, I went to West Africa and was posted as administrative officer in Nigeria to a most backward area, where the Hillmen looked upon a good murderous fight as healthy manly sport. They sandwiched in this pastime with my other duties as judge, tax collector, road maker, bridge builder, surveyor, sheriff, coroner, and even executioner. Spare time went into the study of native languages, customs, and folklore.

Twelve years of what is known as the White Man's Grave was broken by another sort of adventure. I met and after a long chase through parts of Africa, Europé and America, married the writer, artist, and traveler, Erick Berry [see autobiographical sketch in this book]. From her illustrations and our combined stories you can gather a more vivid picture of the natives, the country, and our life in tropical Africa than there is space for here.

Our stories grow out of our own experience and first-hand information of many different occupations and many different kinds of people. But when necessary we supplement this, particularly in our historical stories, with a good deal of library research. My first group of books arose from my life in Africa, both juveniles and adult novels. I have written nothing directly as a result of my soldiering experience, though *The Twenty-Fifth Hour* comes nearest to it.

My next group has grown out of our farming, near Lake Champlain. At the moment we have seven cattle, three hundred hens, six hives of bees, garden, orchard, and experimental trees of many sorts, and handle all this ourselves, without hired labor. The place has historical association with the

French Indian wars and the Revolution, for Baron Dieskau, Robert Rogers, Israel Putnam, and some of Burgoyne's army passed this way. *Gunsmith's Boy, Border Iron,* and *Young'un* (which was a Book-of-the-Month-Club choice) along with many other tales, grew out of our own soil and our experiences and research here.

As writers Erick Berry and I are a team of two, though generally we publish under separate names. This gives us two sets of knowledge to draw on, two checks for accuracy—and plenty of scope for heated argument. So far we have published around fifty books, not counting various editions such as book clubs, foreign translations, reprints, etc. So we're getting nicely into our stride.

Henry Beston

June 1, 1888-

AUTHOR OF

The Firelight Fairy Book, The Sons of Kai, The Starlight Wonder Book, Five Bears and Miranda, Etc.

Autobiographical sketch of Henry Beston:

MY father was a doctor, and my boyhood memories center around a doctor's house in a New England seacoast town. To the east of us lay the salt meadows, the tidal creeks, and the whaleback islands of the harbor. To the west and a mile or two inland, the rocky uplands of the granite quarries with their derricks which stood black against the sunsets of our Massachusetts fall. The town itself lay in a valley between two ragged, woodsy uplands, and from it a lowland plain and a drumlin peninsula spread out towards the sea. Now and then a boy would hear a muffled boom, and that was a blast in one of the quarries.

Across a field and a fence was a blacksmith's shop with its day-long sound of clanging hammer and anvil, and across from this was the fire station with "the steamer" and the hook and ladder, and the great horses whose unquiet, dancing hoofs pounded the floors of their stalls when the station gong clanged its occasional alarm.

It was a pleasant place to grow up in. It called itself a "city," even then, but being a small boy, given to wandering about with other small boys, I privately knew better. City we might be, according to what was still called the town report, but to a boy's mind the place was a pleasant inheritance of village, prospering town, and dubious "city," these elements not being superimposed like layers in a cake but existing side by side like countries in a map. Beyond a neighbor's back yard and orchard was a great green meadow with an old barn, elm trees, a brook, and muskrats—that was village; the wooden shops, churches, the library, and the postoffice—that was town; the two new "blocks," one with a real passenger elevator—that was city indeed. Boy-like we knew all three, going in twenty minutes from the brook and the muskrats to the glories of the main street and the white oilcloth tabletops of the rather solemn ice cream parlor.

Then the world suddenly began to gather momentum, catching us all up with it. The automobile came in, and presently unoccupied stores turned into queer "theatres" where you could sit in uncomfortable wooden chairs and look at "moving pictures." Nine tenths of them were about chases, groups of people, dozens, hundreds, chasing a funny man down streets, round corners, through buildings, through rooms—all wild, full of action, and meaningless like a troubled yet comic dream.

Presently came a pleasant August afternoon, and the Sunday papers brought along on a family picnic at the beach, and great headlines, a picture of Kaiser Wilhelm and the War. My own recollections here turn into something of an old film. I find myself with the French in Lorraine at the wood of the Bois le Prêtre; I remember a long, long winter, the great melancholy sound of distant cannon in the night, a bombarded town and the arriving whizz 'and rending crash of the big shells, an air shell at Verdun which all but got me.

Then the film changes to the sea, and blue uniforms and the American ensign and the gray shape of an American submarine in the waters off the Irish coast, and a flicker or two of the control room and one's eye on the depth gauges, and the swing of the great wheels, and an accompanying sound of the roar of compressed air, and the other roar of water and air. Shipmates all, where are you now?

And then comes civilian life and parades, and writing and traveling and seeking many things. Afoot in the fortress mountains of

HENRY BESTON

Spain, following a path in the Central American tropics, a winter in the Indian country, the quiet of a parlor fire in an inn beside a great and lonely moor, the great beach of Cape Cod. These are some memories and pictures.

Since 1932 I have lived on a farm in Maine. My wife—whose picture you will find in this book—is Elizabeth Coatsworth; she wrote *The Cat Who Went To Heaven*, the *Sally* books, and a lot of other grand things. At the farm, I have tried to make a way of life out of writing and a little old-fashioned farming. Though I write on various topics, what has always interested me most is nature in America and American history, and at the farm I have a chance to study nature and live within the boundaries of her changing world. The great snowfalls and occasional low temperatures of our state can seem rather Arctic to those used to milder climates, but I do not mind them, being something of a born polar bear. Indeed, I thoroughly enjoy our beautiful crystalline winter with its dazzling light and snow-covered fields and woods.

Speaking as a naturalist, few things have given me so great a pleasure as being named an honorary editor of the national *Audubon Magazine*. Another pleasure is a weekly column of Nature and the Farm which appears in *The Progressive* under the head of "County Chronicle." I am glad to be able to say that I still often "play hookey"

from this more grown-up world and wander back into the world of my earlier fairy tales. "The Chimney Farm Stories" for children which began some years ago in the *Christian Science Monitor* are still going strong, and are still favorites, bringing me letters from all over the world. And there has been time to write *Five Bears and Miranda* and *The Runaway Tree*.

Since the publication of *The Outermost House* I have written but one long adult book, *The St. Lawrence River*, in the Rivers of America Series.

I am glad to be able to set down that my two books of fairy tales, written twenty-five years ago, seem to stay very much alive. "The Seller of Dreams" and a number of other tales have become a part of the radio story teller's program and are often on the air. If you read or hear these tales, I would like to have you find three things in them. These three things are courage, kindness, and a sense of the wonder and mystery of life.

I write these notes on a winter morning at the farm, with great snow clouds blowing over from the inland hills and the northwest. Now they mass together and send down a squall of driving snow, now they break open and let wild splendors of sunlight take over the wintry land while a fierce wind blows the new snow from the trees. Time to bring in another armful of wood, I guess, and get another pail of drinking water from the spring.

Margery Williams Bianco
July 22, 1881-September 4, 1944

AUTHOR OF
The Velveteen Rabbit, The Little Wooden Doll, All About Pets, Winterbound, Etc.

Autobiographical sketch of Margery Williams Bianco, written for THE JUNIOR BOOK OF AUTHORS a few years before her death:

T O be the youngest of a family by as much as six years is almost like being an only child, and that is what happened in my case.

I was born in London and my earliest recollections are of being taken for walks along the Thames Embankment and in the Chelsea Pensioners' Gardens, where one

MARGERY WILLIAMS BIANCO

could pick daisies on the lawns under pink and white hawthorn trees, and where the pensioners, nice old men in scarlet coats and peaked caps, who had fought in the Crimean War, would cut one big bunches of mixed flowers for twopence from their little garden plots. The smell of Southernwood—"Old Man" we called it—always brings back the Chelsea Gardens, and to this day I love it.

My father, a barrister and a distinguished classical scholar of his day, believed that children should be taught to read early and then have no regular teaching until they were ten. My favorite book was *Wood's Natural History,* in three big green volumes, and I knew every reptile, bird, and beast in those volumes long before I knew my multiplication table. Having no playmates of my own age I had to make up my own games, and one of them was to trace and cut out in paper the animals in the books, and make a zoo of my own. I used to feed and look after them, and it was more fun than playing paper dolls. Later I had pet mice instead. They outran their cages and used to live and bring up their families in the big dollhouse in the playroom.

When I was nine, two years after my father's death, we came to America for the first time. Brownie, best loved of the mouse family, came too, but Dobbin had to be left behind. Dobbin was a skin horse who had belonged to my brother, and he was too big to pack, so he went with other toys to the

Children's Hospital. It was in remembering Dobbin, long after, that I wrote a story called *The Skin Horse.*

That first voyage was most exciting. In New York, where we stayed that summer, there was Central Park almost next door to wander in—a much lovelier Central Park in those far-off days than it is now, for many parts of it were still quite wild, and besides the zoo and the donkeys and the merry-go-round there were all kinds of birds and butterflies and strange insects that I had read of but never seen. I used to bring home huge caterpillars and queer grubs in paper boxes, to see what they would turn into, and my family were very nice about it, though I did notice that most of my specimens managed to escape and disappear mysteriously after a day or two.

From New York we went to live on a farm in Pennsylvania. Except for "lessons" quickly scampered through every morning I was free to spend my time as I chose. There was berry picking, corn husking, coasting in winter—all the country things one had read about in *St. Nicholas*—and a horse and buggy in which we took long drives about the countryside. A year that passed all too quickly, and then Philadelphia and regular day-school at last, with an occasional year or so back in England again (I never seemed to go to school on our long English visits) and finally two very happy years in the convent school at Sharon Hill, Philadelphia, about the longest consecutive schooling I ever had, and the last.

I was seventeen; I had always wanted to write and it seemed about time to begin. In the next few years—they were spent backward and forward between England and America—I managed to accumulate a grand collection of rejection slips and little else; then I did get a story accepted from time to time, and my first novel, a very short one, was published when I was twenty-one.

It was not until much later that I began writing for children. I married; we went to live in Paris and later in Italy. New surroundings, new friends, two small children —all this was far more exciting and interesting than just writing. For though I have always liked thinking and planning stories, I don't so much like sitting down and writing them out, and for some years now I had had a very good excuse to myself for not doing it. Then for four long years the War filled everyone's minds and lives. When it was over we returned to England for a time. My daughter Pamela was already drawing and painting; her first exhibition was in London that year. I wanted to write again, but I disliked everything I had written before. I wanted to do something different, but did not know what it should be. So I wrote *The Velveteen Rabbit*, and by a sort of accident it became the beginning of all the stories written since. For by thinking about toys and remembering toys they became suddenly very much alive—Poor Cecco and Tubby and all the family toys that had been so much a part of our lives. Toys I had loved when I was a little girl: my almost forgotten Fluffy, who was the Rabbit, and old Dobbin the skin horse. And after the toys, animals, which I had always wanted to write about but somehow never had. Enough, anyway, to keep one busy.

Now I live most of the time in the country. I would still rather dig in the garden or talk to the cat or make patchwork quilts than write. But there is one comfort about it; that once you get to the point where your characters begin to become alive, as they must in any real story, they become so engrossing that they crowd out other things. Even a garden. Almost, but not quite, cats.

* * *

In later years Mrs. Bianco made her home on Grove Street in New York City's Greenwich Village section. She died at nearby St. Vincent's Hospital after a brief illness at the age of sixty-three, survived by her husband Captain Francesco Bianco, an authority on rare books and printing, a son, and her daughter Pamela (Mrs. Robert Schlick), a well-known artist and illustrator of children's books.

"For more than twenty years," wrote Anne Carroll Moore in a memorial article in *Horn Book,* "the name of Margery Bianco has been associated with a rare quality of criticism and appreciation as well as creative work of unusual character and distinction. . . .Her influence during the period of a rich flowering of children's books in the United States was a very potent one." Describing Margery Bianco, Louise Seaman Bechtel wrote: "Though I have seen her always in New York, yet I think of her inevitably with birds, flowers, animals, sun and clouds, and country air." Most of Mrs. Bianco's

more than thirty books are still in print and all of them are as beloved of young readers today as when they were written.

Pamela Bianco

See *Bianco, Margery Williams*

Alfred H. Bill

May 5, 1879-

AUTHOR OF

The Clutch of the Corsican, The Red Prior's Legacy, Highroads of Peril, Etc.

Autobiographical sketch of Alfred Hoyt Bill:

I WAS born at Rochester, New York, and was taken to Faribault, Minnesota, when I was five months old. Faribault at that time was a frontier town. I can remember the tepees of the little Indian reservation up the Straight River and the braves and squaws in their blankets clustered in the back of the church on Sunday mornings; and my father, who was an Episcopal clergyman, used to make long drives with sleigh and horses through the bitter winter cold to preach in the country schoolhouses or the town halls where there was no church.

"A delicate child," as they phrased it in those days, small illnesses kept me frequently out of school. But, long before I could read to myself easily, my father read aloud to me of evenings such books as C. C. Coffin's *Boys of '76, Ivanhoe, The Lady of the Lake,* and *The Lays of Ancient Rome.* From my mother I heard *The Courtship of Miles Standish* and *Enoch Arden;* and my grandmother told me stories of my great grandfather Rogers, a sea captain sailing out of Newburyport, who had been three times a prisoner of the British in the War of 1812 and later spent many months in a South American dungeon—I cannot remember why.

This is not a moral tale—unless the moral be that a love of reading must be controlled, like the love of any other of the fine things in this world. If I had controlled it, spent my afternoons at baseball and my evenings on my algebra and Latin prose, I should doubtless have got to college before 1899; and when I was graduated in 1903, there might have been some reason for somebody else beside myself to feel a certain satisfaction that I was the only boy, I believe, who ever got into Yale from the Faribault High School.

On June 30, 1903, I was married to Florence Dorothy Reid of Plainfield, New Jersey. I had once thought that I would like to be a teacher of history; but in my junior year I had decided that I would like to be a novelist. Of course, it was a mistake. Nobody at twenty-four knows enough to be a novelist—or will know enough for years. The exceptions only prove the rule. But my wife and I remodeled my father's old house at Faribault and settled down to produce literary masterpieces. Only we didn't—either the one or the other.

Weeks would pass without my putting pencil to paper. I got interested in the business management of the church schools, with which my father had been connected. Six years' service in the National Guard culminated in a broiling summer of duty as regimental adjutant on the Mexican border. We traveled a good deal, and the Great War caught us on the steamer, returning with our two small children from a year spent in England and France. In 1918 I went overseas with the American Red Cross, was attached to the 91st Division, A.E.F., and managed to be present at the battles of St. Mihiel and the Meuse-Argonne before the "flu" put me to bed.

Meanwhile I had never actually stopped writing. I can remember three full-length novels and half a dozen shorter ones that went to the publishers during these years and came back without so much as a "let us see something else." There were many other brave beginnings that died anywhere between the fiftieth and the hundred-and-fiftieth page; and out of a score or two of short stories only two were published, in obscure magazines. But it was not until I moved to St. Paul in 1922 that I actually got down to business and kept regular working hours.

In 1924 an idea which I had been carrying around in my head for about a year suddenly struck me as available for the Charles Boardman Hawes prize competition for books for boys. I talked it over with my son, who was then about fourteen, and to whom I had read most of the books my parents had read to me. I read him much of the manuscript as I wrote it, and considered carefully his criticisms and suggestions. The result was *The Clutch of the Corsican*, and his initials stand in the dedication. *Highroads of Peril* followed it the next year—a better tale, I think, although the public evidently doesn't. In 1928, while I was living in the Berkshires, I wrote *The Red Prior's Legacy*, which one reviewer pleased me by calling "a book for any age." I hope he meant, like *Westward Ho!* or *Lorna Doone*. But since then, when I submit the manuscript of a book intended for adult readers, the publishers say, "Mmmmm . . . why don't you do another boys' book for us?"

Reginald Birch

May 2, 1856-June 17, 1943

ILLUSTRATOR

WHEN Reginald Bathurst Birch, English illustrator, was a youngster he wanted be a sailor, and then an actor. These ambitions were not realized, but he did become a famous person. Born in London, he was the son of William Alexander Birch, an army officer, and Isabella (Hoggins) Birch. When he was five his father went to India as manager of the Hoogli Navigation Company. Young Reggie was sent to the Island of Jersey in the English Channel to live with his two aunts and his grandfather, a former surgeon general in the British navy —who later served as the prototype for the

ALFRED H. BILL

old earl in *Little Lord Fauntleroy*. Throughout his long life, Reginald Birch always referred to himself as a subject of the Duke of Normandy—the title by which the King of England rules over the Channel Islands.

His parents returned to England when Reggie was fifteen and the family started on a trip around the world. The journey halted in San Francisco, where the Birches remained for a year and a half. Reginald helped his father make theatrical posters, carving the wood blocks with which they were printed. His work attracted the attention of the portrait painter Toby Rosenthal, who took the lad into his studio, encouraging him to follow an art career. At Rosenthal's insistence young Birch, in 1873, went to Munich to study painting at the Royal Academy. There he participated in the gay life of the student corps.

In 1881 Reginald Birch returned to the United States. His first drawings appeared in *St. Nicholas,* starting him on a career in which he was to illustrate several hundred books and make thousands of drawings for newspapers and magazines, among them the *Youth's Companion, Harper's,* the old *Century,* and the old *Life.* His illustrations for Frances Hodgson Burnett's *Little Lord Fauntleroy* made him famous. Birch's style, characterized by "humor, grace, and charm," never altered.

Reginald Birch went to Europe again in the 1890's, working for some years for a Munich journal, the *Fliegende Blatter.* Back in New York once more he continued his prolific career. But in the late twenties there followed a period of inactivity, until he was sought out in 1933 to illustrate Louis Untermeyer's *The Last Pirate,* tales from Gilbert and Sullivan. It is said that Birch refused to sign the contract for the book until he had read the manuscript to make sure no liberties were taken with the original operas. These drawings re-established his vogue. During the next eight years he illustrated twenty books, but failing health and eyesight obliged him to stop working the last two years of his life.

The artist, who was married twice, had a son and a daughter. He was a contemporary of Joaquin Miller, Mark Twain, and Bret Harte, and had been in San Francisco "in the heyday of the Barbary Coast." He had also known the Paris of du Maurier and George Moore, and had lived in Vienna "at the height of its *gemütlichkeit."* He loved New York, and became a distinguished and almost legendary figure in the city, interviewed by the press annually on his birthday. Described as "an extraordinarily handsome, debonair, well-turned out little man, with a magnificent crown of iron gray hair, an amazingly fine pair of eyes," he was "armed with excellent wit and exquisite courtesy and possessed of unfailing charm." He died a little more than a month after his eighty-seventh birthday.

Claire Huchet Bishop

AUTHOR OF
Pancakes-Paris, The Five Chinese Brothers, Augustus, Etc.

Autobiographical sketch of Claire Huchet Bishop:

I AM French born—completely French—more French than the "French," being from Brittany. The Bretons claim to be the oldest European race, with the Basques. Grandfather was the village storyteller. He was the only one who had an education, and every winter people gathered at his house in the evenings around the fire. He told the Chanson de Roland, and the Breton original version of Tristan and Yseult, tales of King Arthur, and the great dramatic episodes of French history.

He could also recite long poems by heart, which my mother learned from him. She also was a very dramatic storyteller, always completely engrossed in her subject. As a child I used to feel chills running up and down my spine while she was reciting, and then, when it was all over, she would look at my white face and give a robust, hearty laugh, shrug her shoulders, and say to me, "You are stupid!"

Father would have thought it very strange to consider himself a storyteller, but as a matter of fact, when he tells the events of his life the slightest one turns out to be a story, alive with shape and color and movement.

As a little girl I was bored in school. It was far less interesting than listening to Mother and Father at home. I managed to prepare myself for the Sorbonne, but, although I was fairly successful, I disliked intellectual life.

Huchet: *hoo SHAY*

Arni

CLAIRE HUCHET BISHOP

Then in "L'Heure Joyeuse," the first French children's library in Paris, which I had opened on behalf of an American committee, I started telling stories and I enjoyed it. One of the stories was *The Five Chinese Brothers.* Several years later, in America (and married to an American) I told that story again at the New York Public Library. Then, for fun, I set it down; that was the beginning of my writing career in the United States. In France I had written poetry.

My avocations are music, cooking, and gardening.

Pancakes-Paris just happened. A ten-year-old American boy who made pancakes for me, the hardships suffered by French children during the seven years or more of war, an immense desire to try desperately to make the well-fed and warmly comfortable Americans realize what it was like in France where I had just spent a bitter winter, all added up to this book, *Pancakes-Paris.*

Arna Bontemps

October 13, 1902-

AUTHOR OF
We Have Tomorrow, Sad-Faced Boy, Etc.

Autobiographical sketch of Arna Bontemps:

ONE of the first things I remember was the trip to California. I was three at the time and my sister was just one, but both of us became so interested in the things we saw from the train window that we gave our mother and the young woman who traveled with us very little trouble. Then quite suddenly we were in Los Angeles, and there was our large, happy father waiting for us at the station.

Three months earlier he had gone West to look around and see if he could find the kind of place in which he had dreamed of bringing up his children. He had bought a ticket to San Francisco, and his plan was to go farther if necessary, perhaps as far as Canada. Before he reached San Francisco, however, he stopped off in Los Angeles to visit some of our cousins. There his journey came to an end, for he liked the people and the place so well he immediately turned in the rest of his ticket and started looking for a house.

Back in Alexandria, Louisiana, where my sister and I had been born, we lived in a small house surrounded by a picket fence and with a tall pecan tree in the yard. Outside the gate there was a square stone and a hitching post. The stone was in a position to accommodate persons like our handsome young aunts who sometimes rode sidesaddle and needed a convenience like that to help them mount their horses, but my mother and I used it as a place to sit while waiting for the letter carrier.

Almost the first thing to happen in California after our arrival was an earthquake. This could have been an extension of the San Francisco disaster, for I remember my mother running out of the front door and telling a neighbor how the mirror in her dresser had suddenly started flapping back and forth, and I seem to recall that on the same day newsboys came down our street selling extras describing the calamity which had fallen upon that great city by the Golden Gate.

Soon afterwards, it seems to me now, I was being vaccinated and hustled off to kindergarten. Which was all well and good till I lost a gold ring in the sandpile and began to think perhaps school wasn't worth the trouble. Of course I soon changed my mind, for going to school in Southern California was quite wonderful in those days, and I enjoyed it. Though we moved occasionally, and I had to change schools several times before I was ready for college, I can't remember disliking more than one of

Bontemps: *BON tomp*

ARNA BONTEMPS

those I attended. Children as well as teachers sometimes acted strange at first, but as soon as they saw you could do problems quickly at the board, that you could get good hits sometimes when the bases were full at recess time, and that your shyness in public didn't necessarily mean you were afraid, everything was all right.

At seventeen I went to a fine little college in the northern part of the state. Summers I attended UCLA in Los Angeles, and in three years I graduated. But those were the years that made a writer of me. From the window of my room in the dormitory of that college among the mountains I listened to the sound of the trees at night, and a feeling of loneliness came over me. Was it because my mother had died? Was it because I was away from home? Was it something about a high school girl? All of these were important, but I think I was suffering mainly from being seventeen and from listening to the trees too long at night.

Next thing I knew I was writing poetry. Then I tried essays, and then fiction. The poetry was published in magazines right away and won a few prizes, but eight years were to pass before my first book of prose appeared. During those years I became a teacher in a private academy in New York City. Also during those years I met and married a girl from Georgia, and two of our children were born. Soon afterwards, per-

haps in self-defense, I began writing stories for youngsters, for the number of our own has now increased to six, and I have tried to see to it that there are enough of my books to go round.

Meanwhile, I have traveled a little, written stories, plays, and essays as I found time, and read constantly. Perhaps it was this old habit of reading for pleasure, this passionate love of books that finally made a librarian of me. For this work I received professional training in the Graduate Library School of the University of Chicago. I am at present the librarian of Fisk University in Nashville, Tennessee.

* * *

"What manner of man is this Arna Bontemps, who writes with such clarity and rhythm? A modest person, of medium height," says Ione Morrison Rider in the *Horn Book*. "In a confused world, and meeting his full share of problems as a human being and as an artist, he seems to preserve a core of serenity that transcends circumstance. He has dignity, reserve, restraint; makes no effort to impress; yet to meet him is to be struck with the certainty, 'Here is a *person*.'"

Jean Bothwell

AUTHOR OF
The Little Boat Boy, River Boy of Kashmir, Etc.

Autobiographical Sketch of Jean Bothwell:

NOVEMBER is the most beautiful month of the year. It's my month. I was born in it. And every seven years my birthday comes on Thanksgiving Day. The year does not matter. One time I missed getting a good job because they thought I looked too young. On the other hand, I occasionally feel a hundred and two when there's a deadline coming. So the year has nothing to do with it.

But when I do feel a hundred and two, I shut my eyes and see again, as I saw them on walking many a summer morning, the lovely shining snows of the Pir Panjal, through the leaves of the willow trees outside my houseboat window in Kashmir. And the hundred and two feeling goes away.

The story of Hafiz, in *Little Boat Boy* and *River Boy of Kashmir,* was written be-

Bothwell: *BAHTH wel*

cause I had two lovely summer holidays on Dal Lake. Although I did not know a little boy named Hafiz then, I knew others, and his story could have happened to almost any Kashmiri child whose father owned a houseboat.

My father was a minister, a Scot who saw fun and drama in everything, and I learned to see it, too, because he took me with him, everywhere, from the time I could walk. He could do a sermon and make a beautiful garden equally well, and we had a garden wherever we lived in a number of Nebraska towns. My mother made my frocks and was a good cook. So their gifts of creative power must have been passed on to me to make stories with.

Guests from all over the world came to those parsonage homes of ours. They made speeches in my father's church and through their telling, strange foreign people became very real. I remember now a bottle of water from the Jordan River, a little god of soft white stone from India, a painted silk fan from Japan, and other things they left with us after those exciting visits. They must have left something else that was only felt, for I am sure that is why a foreign land drew me to itself, almost irresistibly, when I grew up.

My beginnings in writing seem a little misty. I liked doing themes, and a fresh

JEAN BOTHWELL

sheet of paper, with nothing written on it, still gives me a nice feeling. But even better I liked reading, and became the child I was momently reading about, to the extent of feeling terribly sorry for myself if I had to wipe dishes or dust the chairs when that child didn't.

My own little library was started for me in my eighth summer, with three new books all at once. One was *Little Women,* done in a dark green cloth cover. Years later, I was determined if I ever got a story published, it too would be bound in dark green. But when that time came, I was so excited I forgot the binding and *Little Boat Boy* appeared in a pale grey, which immediately seemed the rightest color in the world for a first book.

It wasn't until college (Nebraska Wesleyan University at Lincoln) that active writing began, on the college daily and the annual. The two poems accepted by *Good Housekeeping* after I went to India were the first paid-for publication I'd had. But they were enough. If I could sell a poem I could do a story, though editors didn't think so for quite a while afterward.

The first time I saw New York I felt that here at last was the home town I'd always wanted and that I would come back and live in it some day. Even in the twelve years in India I didn't have a home town. So now, for six years, I've claimed New York for mine. But I think it's because I'm a little homesick to see India again that I write with that background. So many pleasant things happened to me there.

One was a pet, the only one I ever had, anywhere. He was a topaz Persian, with a white vest and his name was Ugly, though he was the most beautiful cat that ever lived. He didn't like traveling even when I got him the biggest cat basket they would weave, so he'd have room to stand up and turn around. He hid once on the flat roof of my bungalow, and almost made us miss the train, because he knew we were going away.

Some day, and before long, the stamps and books and elephants I collect will push me out of my apartment and into a house. Then perhaps I can have another cat.

Boutet de Monvel

1850-1913

ILLUSTRATOR

Joan of Arc, Etc.

"**A**T first I painted pictures like the rest of the painters," said Louis Maurice Boutet de Monvel, "and perhaps I should have been doing that still if I had not been driven to illustration."

He had married at twenty-five and found need to support his family. He went from publisher to publisher in search of orders. Finally, thoroughly discouraged, he happened to dine at the house of a friend who was secretary to the head of a French publishing house. The publishing house was seeking an illustrator for a small history of France. "Well," said the wife of his host, "why not Boutet de Monvel?"

This good word spoken by chance opened to him the doors of the Delagrave publishing house. He was told to do a series of forty little pen drawings about three times the size of his thumb nail, which would illustrate prominent facts in French history. So carefully did he do them that as a result of the new work that came to him he was obliged a few months later to refuse many orders from other Parisian publishing houses.

Before this Boutet de Monvel had never painted children. When he took it up his marvelous memory came to his aid, and his resources were almost endless. He had been brought up in "a houseful" of little brothers and sisters. He was always very observant and used to watch their funny little figures, attitudes, and ways at play. He drew his children from memory. He felt it was a mistake to draw from models, but that the movement and expression in his mind should be put directly on the canvas. He made each child an individual. He painted such sympathetic and charming pictures that it was not long before he was sought out by many parents to paint portraits of their little ones also.

The most prominent characteristic of his work was originality. After the *History of France,* he illustrated a French edition of *St. Nicholas* for several years. Soon he had the idea of collecting in an album with illustrations the songs and dances of French children. It was so successful that the next year he followed it by another book of songs. He also illustrated books for young people by such noted writers as Anatole France, Jean de la Fontaine, and others.

Once the publishers asked for another book and he had nothing in mind. Crossing the Tuileries Gardens, he came across the little statue of Joan of Arc by Frémiet, and in a flash he knew he had found his subject. From his earliest years he had been closely associated with reminders of Joan of Arc. The principal street of his birthplace, Orléans, was named for her, and the place was full of her statues and of reverence for her. So he produced his *Joan of Arc,* which remains his best-known work.

Boutet de Monvel was the pupil of some of the most distinguished artists in France in his day, but he broke away from conventional influences and developed his art in his own way. He exhibited his first picture in the Salon at the age of twenty-four, and while illustrating he continued to exhibit, and received medals and distinctions. His skill in painting groups and artistic scenes may have been an inheritance, several of his ancestors being famous on the French stage. His grandfather fought in the American Revolution as a captain of engineers. He himself made one trip to America, in his fiftieth year, to exhibit his paintings.

Boutet de Monvel lived and worked in one of the old quarters in Paris. He cherished the dream of moving his studio into the country, but the dream was still unrealized when he died at sixty-three.

James Cloyd Bowman

January 18, 1880-

AUTHOR OF

Pecos Bill, Tales From a Finnish Tupa, Winabojo, Etc.

Autobiographical sketch of James Cloyd Bowman:

PERHAPS the most interesting facet of my personality is that the child has ever been father to the man. During my boyhood I crammed my mind chuck-full with secrets of the great out-of-doors. The deep woods haunted me as did the birds and the rabbits and the squirrels, and everything else wild and free. I loved horses and rode a cow horse, trained on the western range. The sight of an American Indian set my heart thumping, not in fear but with awe-

Boutet de Monvel: *boo TAY de mon VEL*   Bowman: *first syllable rhymes with "hoe"*

JAMES CLOYD BOWMAN

struck wonder. Negroes were so uncommon in our town that my mouth fell open whenever I happened to meet one. And when the steam calliope paraded down the street, I trod the clouds. I followed at the heels of this Pied Piper of my dreams in ecstasy. Anything and everything wild and strange carried me out of this world.

Some of my friends tell me I have never really grown up. All I know is my imagination still carries on in the same old way. My daughter and her playmates discovered this when I told them stories out of my childhood with a rapture even they could not experience.

While I was doing graduate work at Harvard, Barrett Wendell awakened my interest in American folklore. During a lucent interval I realized what I had missed as a boy in not knowing these wild tall tales. Then and there I decided to retell many of them for boys and girls everywhere. First thing I knew I was as excited as when a boy at the circus. I am sure no one has ever enjoyed reading *The Adventures of Paul Bunyan* half so much as I enjoyed writing it. Later I turned to the legends of the cowboys, and spent many happy, exciting days researching in the stacks of various libraries and in the memories of men of the cattle country. Thus was born *Pecos Bill: The Greatest Cowboy of All Time.* When I found leisure I searched through the legends of the American Indian

to see if the wild tales I had read as a boy were reliable. I ended up writing *Winabojo: Master of Life.* When I began coming to Florida to spend the winters I became intrigued with the legends of a popular hero of the colored race. Again I spent many happy hours reading books and interviewing colored folks, and many happy days writing *John Henry: The Rambling Black Ulysses.*

One day my daughter and two of her playmates begged me to write them a mystery story. I made a bargain that they were to help me. Together we concocted a plot around a deserted summer hotel in our town, and produced *Mystery Mountain.* When a boy at my mother's knee I heard over and over again the adventures of her family in migrating from "York State" across the Alleghenies to the frontier. Naturally my mind returned to these stories and set me researching concerning the keelboat age, and I started *Mike Fink: The Snapping Turtle of the O-hi-oo and the Snag of the Mas-sas-sip.*

So you see birthdays do not mean a thing to me. Time stands still as far as me and my imagination are concerned. And I hope it will continue to be this way to the end of the journey.

Helen Boylston

1895-

AUTHOR OF
Sue Barton: Student Nurse, Etc.

Autobiographical sketch of Helen Dore Boylston:

I WAS born in Portsmouth, New Hampshire, in 1895, and had, I believe, an exceptionally happy childhood, for though I was an only child my parents had good sense and I was neither overindulged nor overdisciplined. Also, since there were no cars, there were no restrictions on playing hopscotch, or tag in the middle of the street, bicycles were safe, and in winter one could get a free ride anywhere on the runner of a passing sleigh—a delight now lost to children.

I was educated in the Portsmouth public schools and did neither badly nor well. My adolescence was as lively, unstrained, and innocent as my childhood had been. At eighteen I entered the Massachusetts Gen-

HELEN BOYLSTON

eral Hospital nursing school in Boston, where I spent three strenuous, happy, and somewhat startled years. Two days after graduation I enlisted in the Harvard medical unit for duty overseas with the British Expeditionary Force, in the First World War—from which I emerged in 1919 as tired and confused as everybody else. On the strength of this I joined the American Red Cross and had about a year and a half of reconstruction work in Europe. We worked hard, we saw a great deal of Europe, we had adventures, and were frequently caught in minor wars and revolutions—but it is my personal opinion that we did very little general good, and I was glad to return home to the Massachusetts General Hospital, where I taught nose and throat anesthesia for about two years.

It was at the end of this period that a writer friend read my war diary and insisted on sending it to the *Atlantic Monthly*, in which it was published serially—and I discovered, to my surprise, that I was going to be able to earn my living writing.

I have done so ever since, and in the meantime lived two more years in the Balkans—Albania—seven years in Missouri, one in Arizona and California, and the last fifteen in peaceful subsidence in Westport, Connecticut. Fourteen of these last years were spent in quarrelsome slavery to the dour whims and obstinacies of my Scotch

terrier, George, and since his death I have taken to cats. They are far less bossy.

Besides my war diary, I have published eighteen (I think) short stories, and nine career books for girls—the "Sue Barton" series, and the "Carol Page" series. I live alone and like it, and would infinitely rather write for children than for adults. I like children, very much, and have two god-children, aged four and six, who live next door and spend much of their time here. These and my camera are my only hobbies, unless one wants to count Jane Austen's novels.

Esther Brann

AUTHOR AND ILLUSTRATOR
Nanette of the Wooden Shoes, Lupe Goes to School, Bobbie and Donnie Were Twins, Etc.

Autobiographical sketch of Esther Brann:

I ALWAYS wanted to be an artist, but I certainly never expected to be a writer. This is how it happened.

After I finished high school, I went to art school. I went to Cooper Union, the National Academy of Design, the Art Students' League, and the Fontainebleau School of Fine Arts in France.

"Now," I thought, "after all that schooling, I certainly ought to be able to get some advertising or illustrating to do and earn a little money." So I packed up my best drawings and called on practically every advertising agency and publishing house in New York City. Nobody wanted me to advertise their soaps or illustrate their books.

"Well," I thought, "if they don't want me to illustrate other people's books, the only thing to do is to write one of my own and illustrate it myself!" So I did, and the Macmillan Company published it. The name of that book is *Nanette of the Wooden Shoes*, a story of a little French girl. Since then I have written and illustrated *Lupe Goes to School*, a Spanish story; *Nicolina*, and Italian story; and *Yann and His Island*. (This book has also been published in Scandinavia, for Swedish and Norwegian children to read.)

I have also illustrated Edna Albert's *Little Pilgrim to Penn's Woods* and *The Shawl with the Yellow Bells*, and Mary Jane Carr's *Children of the Covered Wagon*.

I have written and illustrated several picture books of my own. *Bobbie and Donnie Were Twins* is about my twin nephews, who really are named Bobbie and Donnie. They look so much alike it is very hard to tell them apart. When anyone asks, "Who are you? *Bobbie* or *Donnie?*" Bobbie will say, "*I'm* Donnie!" and Donnie will say, "*I'm* Bobbie!" and no one can tell the difference. My other picture books are *Around the World, Patrick Was His Name, Patrick Goes A-Hunting* (about our dog), and *Another New Year.*

My greatest achievement is my son, Alan Richard, who is now five years old. My latest book, for the very youngest, is all about Alan Richard. It is *Book for Baby.*

My husband enlisted in the Navy in December 1942 and served for three years as Commander and Lieutenant Commander in the Navy. He was stationed on Guam for thirteen months, and has received two letters of commendation. Alan Richard has been "on the go" ever since he was eighteen months old, as we followed my husband to various posts. We have had houses in Pensacola, Florida; Norfolk, Virginia; Yonkers, New York; and Hayward, Camp Parks, and Long Beach, California.

We are settled now in Los Angeles, where my husband has opened his office. My writing name is Esther Brann, but my "married name" is Mrs. Richard Schorr.

ESTHER BRANN
with her son

Carol Brink

December 28, 1895-

AUTHOR OF

*Caddie Woodlawn, Magical Melons,
Lad With a Whistle, Etc.*

Autobiographical sketch of Carol Ryrie Brink:

I WAS born in Moscow, Idaho. I was given the family name of Caroline, which had been shortened to Kitty, Carrie, and Caddie in other generations. Because my birthday came near Christmas my mother decided to call me Carol.

My mother's family had come from England and New England, moving westward with the frontiers of civilization from Boston to Missouri, to Wisconsin, to Idaho. My father, Alexander Ryrie, came directly from Scotland. He was the first mayor of the little western town where I was born and he helped plan and lay out its streets.

This little town was important to me as I grew up. I loved its blue mountains and yellow fields. I knew the names of its wild flowers and its birds. One of the nice things about a small town is that you get to know everybody who lives there and to value each one for himself, rather than for what he does or has.

By the time I was eight I had lost both my parents. I had no brothers or sisters, and I might have been very lonely if I had not gone to live with a wonderful grandmother and aunt. Aunt was full of fun and ideas for doing interesting things. Gram was a fine storyteller. The stories I liked best were the ones she told about her own childhood in Wisconsin when she was a little girl named Caddie Woodhouse.

Gram's house was large and pleasant. It had a big barn and an orchard, and seemed almost like a little farm in the midst of town. I had pet dogs, cats, chickens, and, best of all, a fat, sorrel pony who carried me all over the blue Idaho hills. On these long rambles with my pony I used to make up stories to tell myself. The pony, the mountains, my own stories made me very happy. I said to myself, "When I grow up I am going to write books."

I attended the Universities of Idaho and California, and after my graduation I married Raymond Brink, a young mathematician whom I had known for a long time. We

CAROL BRINK

of books by Charles Dickens, Jane Austen, and many other famous authors.

Charles Edmund Brock was born in Cambridge and attended the Higher Grade School there. The only art teacher he ever had was Henry Wiles, a friendly sculptor of Cambridge. He was a youthful worshipper of Randolph Caldecott's drawings and was influenced ·by them.

When Brock was twenty he illustrated a few "Nonsense Rhymes" for a friend, who showed them to a member of a publisher's staff, and in this way he obtained his first commission to illustrate a book.

It was four years before he produced his first well-known work, a set of pictures for *Gulliver's Travels.* After that he made illustrations for *Westward Ho!,* the *Essays of Elia,* and an entire edition of Thackeray's prose. Then he illustrated the works of Jane Austen, Mrs. Gaskell, George Eliot, and others.

Brock was thirty-five when he made color illustrations for Charles Dickens' *A Christmas Carol* and *The Cricket on the Hearth,* two of the books for which he remains best known. Years later he illustrated further Dickens volumes. He also drew pictures for Eleanor Farjeon's *Martin Pippin in the Apple Orchard,* Goldsmith's *The Vicar of Wakefield,* and Mrs. Molesworth's *Cuckoo Clock.* His drawings appeared in *Punch, Graphic,* and various other English magazines.

Brock's enthusiasm for the "good old days" he illustrated was reflected in his home and studio. In his home, Cranford, on Grange Road in Cambridge, were found quaint mirrors, "tallboys," old china and silver, and many other antiques — here a spinet, there an ancient bookcase. In the studio a large library including old fashion journals, along with old furniture and a wardrobe of costumes, aided him and his brothers in making their drawings.

Brock was a portrait painter as well as a book illustrator, and belonged to the Royal Institute of Painters in Water-Colours. He was married to Annie Dudley Smith, but they had no children. For recreation he enjoyed music and lawn tennis. He died less than a month after his sixty-eighth birthday.

went to live in Minnesota, where he was, and still is, a teacher at the university. We have two children, and, when they were little, I began to write stories for them. Later the stories grew larger and turned into books. Some of the books, *Anything Can Happen on the River, Mademoiselle Misfortune,* and *Lad with a Whistle,* were inspired by adventures we had when we were living in France and Scotland. Another book, called *All Over Town,* grew out of the days when I rode my pony around our little Idaho town. The book children love best, however, is *Caddie Woodlawn,* and of course you have already guessed how that one came to be written. It is based on the stories I loved so much when I was a little girl, the stories of my grandmother's childhood. In 1935 it was awarded the John Newbery Medal, and Caddie herself was as proud and happy as I was.

C. E. Brock

February 5, 1870-February 28, 1938

ILLUSTRATOR

IN a quiet garden in the old university town of Cambridge, England, stood a large studio where four brothers were accustomed to work together. The name of the eldest brother, C. E. Brock, is known to boys and girls everywhere as a favorite illustrator

C. E. Brock's youngest brother, Henry Matthew ("H. M.") Brock, is also an illustrator of young people's books, and is still living and active at the time of this writing. He was born in Cambridge on July 11, 1875, and attended the Higher Grade School about five years after "C. E." He received his art education at the Cambridge School of Art. His first illustrations were published when he was eighteen. At twenty-six he first exhibited at the Royal Academy and the Royal Institute of Painters in Water-Colours (of which he also is a member).

H. M. Brock is best known for his illustrations for Thackeray's *Ballads* and the *Roger de Coverley Papers,* together with a *Book of Fairy Tales* and *Valentine and Orson* and *Jack the Giant Killer.* The *Book of Fairy Tales,* containing "Puss in Boots," "Jack and the Beanstalk," "Hop-o'-My-Thumb," and "Beauty and the Beast," has large type and several black and white illustrations and eight colored pictures for each story. He is also the illustrator of Whyte Melville's novels, Holmes' "Breakfast Table Series," Leigh Hunt's essays, and Jerrold's essays, among other works. He is a frequent contributor to *Punch* and other magazines. Doris Joan Pegram is his wife, and they have one son and two daughters. Their home is Woodstock, Storey's Way, Cambridge.

EMMA L. BROCK

Emma L. Brock

1886-

AUTHOR AND ILLUSTRATOR
The Runaway Sardine, The Greedy Goat, Drusilla, The Topsy-Turvy Family, Mr. Wren's House, Etc.

Autobiographical sketch of Emma L. Brock:

I CANNOT remember that first military post, for I was only two years old when we traveled away. But I can remember the second one, the long flight of steps that led down the bluff to the steam train by the river and the Indian prisoners shoveling snow and grinning at us through the windows.

I can remember long journeys in trains, many long journeys in sleeping cars, and kind Negro porters. I can remember Pike's Peak and the bears in a zoo in Denver and more long journeys. I can remember arithmetic that I could do and spelling that I could not, and circuses in small tents, and bicycles. I can remember drawing a twisted violet so that it looked like a twisted violet. I can remember the great roar of Chicago and the horses in the market, their noses buried in feed bags, turning their heads to let the bus pass by. I can remember a bridge over the Chicago River that whirled slowly to let a boat glide through. I can remember the blueness of Lake Michigan and thunder storms and blue jays in the pine trees in our yard and the hammock under the oak trees.

I remember journeys to my grandmother's in Michigan and the bees and the hollyhocks and the wintergreen woods and the old flour mill. There were more long journeys and the mountains of Montana and thirty-five degrees below zero. There were Indians in town and wild horses escaping and running along the streets, and gold found under the postoffice. I remember geography and drawing maps on the black board, fairy tales, and the end of grade school.

There was the longest journey of all and the Hudson River and the roar of New York, clanking cable cars, rumbling elevated trains, and plunging truck horses. I remember the Battery and the sea gulls, the red ferry boats to Brooklyn, the picnics at the seashore and the white fog that seemed to rest on your eyelids. There was Latin and algebra and drawing live rabbits and a story about a spider that they said was good.

There was German and physics and "100" in drawing. There was a summer of Sir Walter Scott in a hammock and another of Dickens.

Then came Philadelphia and French and astronomy and the great question between college and art school. What really happened was another long journey and the University of Minnesota. There was much writing and psychology and Chaucer and sociology and boards and committees and commencement day on Campus Knoll. Then there was study at a Minneapolis art school and work in the Minneapolis library and again—New York.

That was in 1921 and I was there for seven years. I remember drawing, drawing, drawing at the Art Students' League and working in the crowded children's rooms of the New York libraries. I remember theatres and plays and concerts and the Bronx zoo and the gulls at the Battery and the departure whistles of European liners. I remember the publishers who were kind and the breathless excitement of the first book they gave me to illustrate, *The London Doll*. I remember studying with Joseph Pennell and the etchings I made of what he called my "funny people" and their push carts from eastside New York.

And best of all I remember my first journey to Europe and the storm at sea and the whales and the porpoises and the first lighthouse of England. I remember the little castles of France and the big cathedrals and the paintings in the caves of prehistoric men, and the hedges and little crooked villages of England.

I remember later trips to Europe. It was fair time in Brittany and there was a circus in town with merry-go-rounds and fortune tellers. I remember the big market in the cathedral square under red canopies and white umbrellas. They sold everything from ducks to bedroom shoes. There was a pig market on the hill with each pig squealing on a different note. The townspeople and the country people wore gay holiday aprons and embroidered jackets and there were sardines everywhere.

I remember sketching ducks in the canals of Holland and women in huge white lace hats riding bicycles. I remember hunting for goats in the Tyrolean Alps and finding just one goat. The others were all up in the mountains to get fat. I remember sitting under a willow tree by a stream that ran between the many-storied pueblos in Taos, New Mexico, and watching the Indian women baking bread in outdoor ovens.

I remember walking and overtaking the leisurely ox carts in the French Basque country. I remember looking for the pancake house in the Black Forest, but the pancake house was always just ahead hidden in the trees. I remember the old stone towns built high in the Italian hills and the yellow stucco towns built low on the shores of the Mediterranean.

And can you imagine what is my favorite pastime? Sailing the seven seas.

* * *

Almost every part of the world where she has lived or visited has gone into Miss Brock's books at one time or another. Few writers for children have achieved such varied backgrounds, and her books have been praised for their authenticity, "amusing and human" quality, and "folk-tale flavor."

H. M. Brock

See *Brock, C. E.*

Wilfrid S. Bronson

October 24, 1894-

AUTHOR AND ILLUSTRATOR
Pollywiggle's Progress, The Chisel-teeth Tribe, Turtles, Paddlewings, Fingerfins, Etc.

Autobiographical sketch of Wilfrid Swancourt Bronson:

IT is not easy to know just what is best to tell about one's self or what, if told, will interest anybody else. Perhaps the wisest way to tell about Bronson will be to mention the things in his life which have mattered most to him.

Well then, I was born near Chicago (Morgan Park), Ill., October 24, 1894—too late for the opening of the first great World's Fair they held there. It had gotten started very well without me. My mother has said that I was all purplish and yellowish when I first arrived (something like a Spanish hogfish, I presume) but that the colors seemed to gradually blend and I became a brownish hue, three shades darker than the rest of the family. I have been mixing colors ever since. For I was born

WILFRID S. BRONSON

wanting to draw and paint — and nearly knowing how. Of course I couldn't make my baby hands do just what I meant them to at first, but I tried from the moment I could put a pencil point to paper. And the things I have always drawn the best are wild people and wild animals. It was fine at seasons like Thanksgiving to be borrowed from my class in public school by teachers from other rooms, to draw decorations with colored chalks on their blackboards. But it didn't make arithmetic any easier next day.

When I was fifteen I went away from home, washing dishes, chopping wood, and waiting table in a north woods camp. Here I met my first Indians, porcupines, loons, and wildcats. Every summer after that I worked on a farm, in a camp, in a mountain hotel, anywhere to get me close to the places where wild things were.

After high school days and two years' study at the Chicago Art Institute I drifted pretty much all over the United States till we entered the World War. During part of my time in the army I was stationed near New York and determined to return there when the War ended, which I did. There I worked in the studios of mural painters for a number of years and whenever animals were needed in the designs I drew them. I heard about Roy Chapman Andrews going to the Gobi Desert and tried to be enlisted as staff artist. Dr. Andrews kindly told me that there were two Chinese artists already

engaged over there for two chen a week and one shirt a season. But I kept hoping to go on some expedition somewhere. One day I met a wealthy gentleman who wanted to create the finest museum of oceanic animals in the world and he chose me to be the staff artist. For five years we worked, making three long winter voyages to tropic seas. I was but recently married and spent nearly a year of those first five years as a sailor husband. At the end of that time the bulk of my paintings were presented to the Peabody Museum at Yale, with the mounted fishes and collected specimens.

When the work ended I sought some other way to use the knowledge I had gained of fishes and such things, and so began the writing of my books. *Fingerfins* was the first. Two years later I was engaged for an expedition to the Galapagos Islands and there learned much about penguins, tortoises, etc., which later became subjects for more writing. *Paddlewings* was one result.

Then a year came with no expedition so I went exploring in a quarry pond on my own little chunk of the Catskills. *Pollywiggle*, the story of a bullfrog, was written almost with pond water for ink.

Shortly after *Pollywiggle* I was invited by Max Reed [see autobiographical sketch in this volume] to collaborate on *The Sea for Sam*, and since then I have written and illustrated *The Wonder World of Ants, The Chisel-toothed Tribe, Horns and Antlers, Children of the Sea, Stooping Hawk and Stranded Whale, The Grasshopper Book, Hooker's Holiday, Turtles,* and *Coyotes.* There have been articles for *Nature Magazine* and there is a monthly nature page for *Story Parade Magazine.*

It has always seemed to me a fine thing to both write and illustrate one's book, each part helping to make clear the other, all the work of one mind and hand. I'm hoping that some day I shall have a chance to go and work in Africa. I think I should do my best work there for it has always been the Mecca to which I turn in my worship of wild things. If opportunity (to go there) taps ever so lightly on my door I shall surely hear her. I'm listening, hard, for that is one of the things which matter most to me.

Some day no doubt I'll die. That may not matter much at all, but the work I'd like to do before that time, the books to write and picture, full of the interest and beauty of creatures which live forever out of doors —that's what makes all the difference.

L. Leslie Brooke

September 24, 1862-May 1, 1940

ILLUSTRATOR AND AUTHOR

Johnny Crow's Garden, The Golden Goose Book, Ring o' Roses, Etc.

Autobiographical sketch of Leonard Leslie Brooke, written for THE JUNIOR BOOK OF AUTHORS a few years before his death:

THERE never was a time when the name of Johnny Crow was not familiar to me. When I was a very small boy indeed, the singing of a song about Johnny Crow's Garden by my father was a regular observance. But the words themselves were never the same. He would begin "And the . . ." —my brother or I would suggest an animal, and it was a point of honor that he should thereon provide an impromptu rhyme telling what that animal did "in Johnny Crow's Garden," its behavior being to us always a matter of glorious uncertainty and inconsequence.

In course of time I myself carried on the tradition with my own sons, and then it was that my wife suggested a picture book of Johnny Crow rhymes. At first I demurred, feeling that there would be no cohesion or sequence in them for a book, but gradually as I began to think more about him, Johnny Crow himself seemed to grow clearer to me as a personality, and his character to spread itself through his whole Garden till at last it became obvious that it would be he himself who made any book about him.

As to my other picture books, they are for the most part built on the classics—the old nursery rhymes and stories—"Ring o' Roses," "The Three Bears," "The Man in the Moon," "The Three Little Pigs," "Tom Thumb," and so on; but two of my authors stand high today in other fields. *The Truth About Old King Cole* was written by Sir George Hill, the present head of the British

L. LESLIE BROOKE

Museum, while Mr. Robert Charles, the author of *A Roundabout Turn* is now the Chief Inspector of Elementaary Schools in England.

For myself, I was born in Birkenhead, England, September 24, 1862, and had my art training in the Royal Academy Schools. Since then I have made a great many drawings—in every one of which the problem of how I should begin it has been only less disconcerting than the problem of how I should finish it off.

In drawing for children there seems to be but one essential rule—draw what you yourself like drawing: the child will not mind a bit if there are things he does not quite understand, but if ever he gets the impression that anything was drawn by you with an eye on his parent first and not wholly on himself—well, you're done for so far as that child is concerned.

* * *

Thousands of worn and tattered volumes of the Johnny Crow books in homes and libraries wherever English is read and spoken bear eloquent testimony to the unique place Leslie Brooke's pictures and rhymes have achieved in the hearts of children. In addition to the details he has given above, here are a few more facts about the life of this gentle and well loved man:

In 1894 he was married to his cousin Sybil Diana, who was the daughter of the clergyman and author, the Reverend Stopford Brooke. They made their home in a small village in the Berkshire region of England and had two sons, Leonard and Henry, to whom *Johnny Crow's Garden* was dedicated in 1903. In fact, most of Brooke's picture books came in the years they were growing up. Saddened by Leonard's death in action in 1918 while serving in the Royal Air Force in the First World War, Brooke did little work of his own in later years, although he continued to illustrate the books of other authors. An exception was *Johnny Crow's New Garden,* which he dedicated to his eldest grandson, Peter, in 1933. Appreciative readers found in it the same freshness and delight as the original Johnny Crow books, created for Peter's father and uncle thirty years before.

In their latter years Mr. and Mrs. Brooke made their home at Hampstead, close by Hampstead Heath, on the outskirts of London. It was there that Leslie Brooke's "singularly beautiful life" (to quote Anne Carroll Moore) came to a close on May Day 1940, in his seventy-eighth year. Although Brooke never came to America he had many American friends with whom he corresponded continually and whom he welcomed to his home whenever they visited England. He had a great devotion to children and took a special delight in encouraging young illustrators. So well loved was Leslie Brooke on both sides of the Atlantic that in May 1941, a year after his death, *Horn Book* magazine devoted a full issue to his memory, with articles and appreciations by Anne Carroll Moore, Reginald Birch, James Daugherty, Bertha Mahony, and many others.

Brooke's inimitable illustrations have been called "joyous," "irresistible," and "timeless," and the simple but humorous rhymes which accompany them have delighted generations of young readers and adults alike. As Bertha Mahony has written: "The unfailing taste and judgment of his work stand as a heartening banner. . . . His books in their gaiety, humor, and sound workmanship should serve to make us realize anew the slow, never-ending power of the beautiful, the true, and the good."

Walter R. Brooks

1886-

AUTHOR OF

To and Again, the "Freddy books," Etc.

Autobiographical sketch of Walter Rollin Brooks:

I WAS born and spent my childhood in Rome, New York. It was a nice childhood. There were no movies or radios in those days, and we had to organize our own entertainment. We wrote and put on plays up in our barn, for one thing. The audience had to shut their eyes while the scenes were being shifted between the acts. The audience was mostly aunts and they got tired of shutting their eyes after a while and made us a curtain. The first writing I did was part of an act in one of these plays.

When I was fifteen our home was broken up and I was sent off to a military school near Peekskill. I spent my vacations with my sister in Rochester, and after two years I went there to live. I went to college there, and after my sophomore year, to New York to study medicine.

I don't suppose I was ever very ambitious. At least I had never decided I wanted to be anything special. I was interested in medicine and my family had somehow taken it for granted I should become a doctor, but I was interested in a lot of other things, too. Maybe I would have kept on with medicine, but I was particularly interested in a girl in Rochester, which was a long way from New York. So I abandoned medicine, and Anne Shepard and I were married the next year.

Although I had always read a good deal more than anybody but my mother had thought was good for me, I had never tried to write. Like everybody else I had often said, "I bet I could write a better story than that!" And one day a friend and I decided to try. He started a story while I thought up a plot. We wrote the story in two hours, sent it off, and got fifteen dollars for it.

Well, it looked pretty easy, but of course it wasn't. It was five years before I sold another, and fifteen before I could make a living out of stories alone. In the meantime I have written publicity, advertising, half a dozen novels (two were published), and have worked on the editorial staffs of several

WALTER R. BROOKS

magazines. I have had about 150 short stories published, and fourteen children's books.

The first children's book was *To and Again.* I wrote it for my own amusement when I was alone in Washington one hot summer doing publicity for the Red Cross. I had always liked stories about animals talking, and my tales about the animals on the Bean farm are, I suppose, echoes of the stories of Lily Wesselhoeft, which were my childhood favorites. In the first book all the animals shared equally in the adventures, but by the third one, Freddy the pig, through his resourcefulness, had assumed the leadership. Pigs in general are not built for the heroic role; I am rather puzzled myself to know why Freddy, rather than a dog or cat, should have become my permanent hero. Maybe because Kurt Wiese, who illustrates the stories, draws such very sympathetic pigs.

D. K. Broster

September 2, 1877-February 7, 1950

AUTHOR OF

The Flight of the Heron, The Gleam in the North, Ships in the Bay!, Dark Mile, Etc.

Autobiographical sketch of Dorothy K. Broster, written for the THE JUNIOR BOOK OF AUTHORS shortly before her death:

Broster: *BRAW ster*

I WAS born outside Liverpool, where the Mersey is wide, as English rivers go. Almost my first recollections therefore are of ships; and to this day the sight, now so sadly infrequent, of a fullrigged ship, even of some coasting schooner, has a power of enchantment which nothing else possesses.

In my childhood I was generally acting some long-continued story or other with a friend; at one early period, I remember, the current drama was concerned with Red Indians, and involved the exchange of a great many letters, which were sometimes written in "invisible ink" (i.e. milk or lemon juice); sometimes burnt in places to simulate survival of a prairie fire which must have raged with surprising regularity.

At ten years old I went to boarding school at a place near the sand dunes of the Lancashire coast, and, when I was sixteen, to the then largest girls' school in England, the Ladies' College, Cheltenham, which I left at nineteen with a scholarship for St. Hilda's College, Oxford. I was at the University for four years, specializing in modern history, in which I took an honors degree.

After passing my final examinations I became secretary to the Regius professor of modern history at Oxford, and was for some years helping him in the literary side of his work. This left me little leisure for writing —which had always been my desire—but finally my friend Miss G. W. Taylor and I contrived to finish *Chantemerle,* a long historical novel dealing with the War of La Vendée, which we had had upon the stocks for some years. This was published in 1911, and followed two years later by a story of the "Oxford Movement" and of the France of Louis Philippe, *The Vision Splendid.*

Then came the War, which uprooted me from Oxford. At the end of 1914 I was in Kent, nursing Belgian soldiers from the Yser; in April 1915 I was sent out to France, under the auspices of the Anglo-French committee of the British Red Cross, and for the rest of that year I was nursing French soldiers at Yvetot, the little Norman town between Le Havre and Rouen whose name will be familiar to readers of Béranger. The hospital was an Anglo-American foundation staffed entirely by English and Americans, and occupied all but one wing of the big disused seminary where, as I afterwards discovered, Guy de Maupassant had been a pupil. A couple of wards were

D. K. BROSTER

run by the American Red Cross, of whose members I retain very pleasant memories. I was however invalided home at the beginning of 1916—though from no more romantic cause than a temporarily stiff knee, due to some obscure trench germ.

Before the outbreak of war I had started my first uncollaborated story, *Sir Isumbras at the Ford,* but it was impossible to give one's mind to fiction in those days. Later I took it up again, and it was published in 1918. Since then I have gone on writing—drawn, I suppose along that none too smooth path of the historical novel by my early training. For it is not easy to make a good blend of history and fiction when one does really care both that the historical part shall be accurate even in small details, and that the story itself shall have a life of its own, and not be overshadowed by the historical background.

One writes, of course, because one wants to, and cannot imagine not doing so. At the bottom I believe one is really telling *oneself* a story. The interest in working it out is a kind of exploration, a finding out "what happened next." Occasionally one goes along a wrong path in this quest, and has to come back again. Yet it still remains a strange phenomenon (Kipling, I think, has somewhere called attention to it) that when one has a pen in one's hand—and sometimes even when one hasn't—situations and ideas

come into the mind quite unsought, as if from an entirely outside agency. I always work my plots out first in outline, and sufficiently far ahead in detail; the main idea of any of them I have almost always found to spring, generally unbidden, from a sort of mental picture of some person or persons, "felt" as to character, and seen more or less distinctly in some incident, not necessarily the central incident of the book. The rest blossoms out of this.

* * *

As reported by the London *Bookseller,* Miss Broster died in her native England on February 7, 1950, in her seventy-third year. Her books were equally popular with young people on both sides of the Atlantic.

Edna A. Brown

March 7, 1875-June 23, 1944

AUTHOR OF

The Four Gordons, The Spanish Chest, The Silver Bear, How Many Miles to Babylon, Etc.

Autobiographical sketch of Edna A. Brown, written for THE JUNIOR BOOK OF AUTHORS a few years before her death:

I WAS born on March 7, 1875, in Providence, Rhode Island, the daughter of Joseph Farnum Brown and Adelaide Victoria Ballou. On my father's side were generations of Quaker ancestors, stretching back to Chad Brown, who came from England to Boston in 1638. As a child, I was often taken to Friends' meeting, and early recollections are of gentle Quaker guests, among them members of the Whittier family. My mother was a direct descendant of Roger Williams and of Mathurin Ballou.

Being the youngest and never strong physically, my early education was at home. I remember being taught to write, but I seem always to have known how to read! Certainly, I read everything in sight, and fortunately, good books abounded. My playmates were chiefly pet animals, a little Italian greyhound, a pony, and a never-failing supply of kittens. Some were the meek kind, that could be dressed in doll-clothes and wheeled about. Perhaps it is due to these many pets that kittens are always eager to prance into my stories. A paw or a fuzzy ear appears, and, unless I harden my heart immediately, the rest of the fur baby follows.

Because I had few child playmates, I created imaginary ones, and entertained myself making stories. When I did go to school, which was not until I was ten, I perfectly adored writing compositions. Indeed, all through my school days, English lessons and written exercises held no terrors, but I never have been able to add a column of figures twice and attain the same result.

My father and mother died in my childhood, and I lived with a married sister. At an early age I became an aunt, and my nieces and nephews furnished many ideas and incidents for stories. "Copy" was all about me, and absorbed for later use.

Study at the Girls' High School, Brown University, and the New York State Library School, occupied some years. My choice of profession, though due to love of books, was amusing because I had never as a child been permitted to use a public library for fear of germs. The first library book I ever borrowed, at the age of thirteen, was *The Life of the Reverend Sydney Smith*! An odd selection. It must have been required for some school assignment.

Pleasant paths of travel have known my feet: much of my own country and a great deal of Europe, including one leisurely trip

which consumed nearly two years and afforded much material for writing.

My health proving unequal to work in a large library, I came to Andover, Massachusetts, in 1906, to take charge of the town library, and have been there ever since. My first book, *The Four Gordons,* was published in 1911. I wrote it because there seemed few wholesome stories for girls in their early teens. I have tried not only to write books which children really like, but which give them standards of happy home life. I hope I have succeeded. At any rate, every one of my books has been approved by the American Library Association *Booklist.*

I have never married and I live in a little Cape Cod cottage with a flagstoned walk and a white picket fence, over which look larkspurs and Madonna lilies. Lilacs stand by the gate and behind the house is a crooked apple tree. The windows look east and west, and there is "a rosy hearth and sunlight on the floor."

* * *

Altogether, Edna A. Brown wrote almost a score of books and plays for young readers. In 1939, after more than thirty years as head of the Andover Hall Memorial Library, she retired from library work. She wished to devote her time to writing and the enjoyment of a quiet life in her much loved home in Andover, the little Cape Cod cottage mentioned above. Never strong physically, death came to her after a short illness on June 23, 1944. Her last book *How Many Miles to Babylon?* was published in 1941, written, she said, at the request of many children "who have asked me to write another story."

There is a universal appeal to all ages in Edna A. Brown's books which makes them her best memorial. As the *Library Journal* put it simply, "She understands children." *The Silver Bear* and its sequel *The Chinese Kitten* are ever popular with little children old enough to read. And, despite the passage of years since they were written, youth still enjoys *The Four Gordons, Uncle David's Boys,* and many others of the teenage group. She also wrote two novels for older people, *Journey's End* and *That Affair at St. Peter's.*

EDNA A. BROWN

Margaret Wise Brown

1910-

AUTHOR OF

Little Fisherman, Little Lost Lamb,
Little Island, Etc.

Autobiographical sketch of Margaret Wise Brown, who writes both under her own name and the pen name "Golden MacDonald":

MARGARET WISE BROWN

THIS is to say that I was born in a brick city on a wide street of cobblestones. The street ran down the hill to the East River where boats came from all over the world and blew their whistles and sailed by. My father made rope and his docks were at the foot of this street and there was a smell of hemp and tar and rope in the air. At the other end of the street was a large brick church rising into the sky. And when the doors were open there was the flash and flicker of gold and candlelight and the mystery of stained glass windows. That is all I can remember except the sound of horses' hoofs. All this was in one of the many parts of New York City.

My mother and father came from Virginia and Kentucky and Missouri and I always heard of those places. Once my great-aunts from Kentucky, who I had been told were giants—they were very tall and beautiful— arrived in our house for dinner and I came down in front of the fire to meet them. They were going across the ocean on a boat next morning.

All this is very dim and before I was four years old.

Then I drove one day in a big open car, with my grandmother's hat tied on her head with a big blowing veil, to Long Island where we moved into a red brick house under some sweetgum trees. From then on I grew up along the beaches and in the woods of Long Island Sound. This was the country. And from then on I was terribly busy, hitching up all the dogs I could find to pull me around on my sled in the snow and picking cherries high up in cherry trees, and chasing butterflies, and burning leaves, and picking up shells on the beach, and watching the new flowers come up in the woods as the seasons passed. I had thirty-six rabbits, two squirrels—one bit me and

dropped dead—a collie dog, two Peruvian guinea pigs, a Belgian hare, and seven fish and a wild robin who came back every spring.

I don't remember many books at that time. Stories of Roland and of the Golden Fleece and Black Beauty and Beautiful Joe and Peter Rabbit and Snow White were all true to me. It didn't seem important that anyone wrote them. And it still doesn't seem important. I wish I didn't have ever to sign my long name on the cover of a book and I wish I could write a story that would seem absolutely true to the child who hears it and to myself. True as Hansel and Gretel, true as Br'er Rabbit, true and wonderful as Aladdin and his Wonderful Lamp.

I have written more than sixty books and I keep writing them because I like to make them up, because I can't stop.

In New York City I now live in a wooden house with a brick floor and fireplaces and a garden. I have a young Kerry blue terrier named Crispin and a black cat with a big fluffy tail named Hyacinth.

In the summer I go off into the woods in Maine near the edge of the ocean and paint pictures.

* * *

Miss Brown's *Little Island,* published under her pen name "Golden MacDonald," was awarded the Caldecott Medal in 1947.

Paul Brown

November 27, 1893-

ILLUSTRATOR, AND AUTHOR OF
Merry Legs, Piper's Pony, Pony Farm, Etc.

Autobiographical sketch of Paul Brown:

EVER since I was born, in Mapleton, Minnesota, I have wanted to draw horses. But before I could do that all the time I had to grow up and get my schooling. Being a poor student I finished only part of the course at the High School of Commerce in New York City because I wanted to draw instead of doing arithmetic and English.

After I left school I had to put off drawing again because the First World War came along and I went to France. In the Second World War I ran preinduction classes all over this part of Long Island. But toward the end of the war it was a sad story. I woke one morning to find I had been appointed head of the men's unit of the Red Cross motor corps for Nassau County. I organized a group of over three hundred men who worked day and night at Mitchel Field unloading the C 54's which came in laden with stretcher cases fresh from the battlefields. It was a very sad business but we had the satisfaction of doing our bit well by handling the stretchers gently and then driving

PAUL BROWN

our ambulances so the bumps in the roads wouldn't be felt by the wounded men.

Now to fill in the gap I skipped over between wars. Several years after the First World War I went back to St. Paul, Minnesota, and married Harriet Smith. We have three children, Geery, Nancy Ann, and Whitney, plus Trouble-Maker, our grand old dog.

Since 1916 we have made our home in Garden City, Long Island, which location has given me fertile fields for the study of horses close to home. Then, too, I have traveled all over this country to see polo, racing, and horse shows. I even went to England every year for ten straight years to gather information about my favorite subject, horses. During all my research I never learned to ride and had no actual contact with horses such as riding, grooming, or training them.

All this travel and study gave me the sort of sound foundation for my work that I needed and the result has been that I'm so happy in my work that I don't work. I play all the time from morning till night.

In this play I've made illustrations for many advertising agencies and for almost every magazine, including some English publications. I've also written articles for several of them and suggested copy and campaigns for advertisers.

Let me tell you fellows it's been a happy pastime and if you want to get into one of the arts, you do it and you too can play all the time. But remember these two things: first, find out all you can about your chosen subject and second—this is awfully important—*Don't copy anybody any time.* Be yourself.

In writing something like this a person is supposed to mention clubs and sports. My best club is the volunteer fire department. I've been chasing fires for twenty-eight years. Of course, I belong to the American Legion and a high school fraternity, of which I am proud to this day. The sports I like best are football, four-wall handball, and, believe it or not, the best of all is croquet outdoors and parcheesi indoors.

Jean de Brunhoff

1899-1937

AUTHOR AND ILLUSTRATOR OF
The Story of Babar, the Little Elephant, Etc.

JEAN DE BRUNHOFF, French artist-author of the Babar books, was one of four children. He had two brothers, Jacques and Michel, and a sister who later became Mme. Lucien Voel and edited *La Journal des Modes.*

Jean studied painting under Othon Friesz, having his first exhibition with a group of artists at the Galérie Champigny, in Paris, of which he was a member. A subtle painter, he got along well with this little group.

He was also completely at home with children. In fact, it was his own three who inspired the stories which brought him such success with children's books.

He had married Cecile Sabouraud, daughter of a well-known French physician. To amuse their sons and their sons' friends, Cecile invented stories about an elephant. One day, attracted by the sight of the attentive children, de Brunhoff stopped to listen, and he wrote the story down, drawing little pictures to illustrate it. He did the same with later stories, and these grew into bedtime tales. Thus was born, in 1932, *The Story of Babar, the Little Elephant.* After fifty thousand copies had been sold in France, it was translated into English.

The story follows Babar from his hammock in the jungle to a solid bourgeois life in Paris, which he finally leaves, driving an automobile, with two elephant cousins; one of them, Celeste, he marries. Back in the jungle he is chosen king because of his aristocratic aplomb and his wardrobe.

Marguerite Mitchell in the *Horn Book,* called Babar "distinguished nonsense." Of the second book, *Travels of Babar,* a reviewer in *Books* said, "The tale has the sweet reasonableness of its predecessor. Granting the existence of a little elephant who walks on his hind legs, wears clothes, and speaks French, this is the way he would act."

Still another critic called de Brunhoff's work "sensitive, and colorful and discreet . . . nothing tricky, nothing 'smart' all as simple and direct as a nursery rhyme. It is the old story of the poet among everyday people, with his nostalgia for the golden age, the longing for escape from his surroundings, from his sick body, twofold escape, dutifully he accepts the pattern, is a part of it, is accepted as such; in his heart he knows he does not belong."

At the time of de Brunhoff's death, Louis Charonnet wrote in *Beaux Arts*: "He was one of those persons whose spell is immediate. In the regiment where I knew him it was impossible not to pick him out under the most ordinary uniform, among all his companions. An intelligent and subtle spirit, . . . an attitude of gentleness, affability, and refinement which was irresistible." Ida Treat described him as "tall, slightly stooped, with a smile that was somehow younger than his age. . . . His face was thin . . . and the eyes were beautiful: the eyes of a man who lives much alone, who looks at the world and is not of it, mountaineer eyes, and a quick boyish smile."

Always delicate, with weak lungs, Jean de Brunhoff developed tuberculosis and moved from Paris to Switzerland, where he lived for several years. There he died on October 16, 1937, at the age of thirty-eight.

Conrad Buff

1886-

ILLUSTRATOR AND CO-AUTHOR OF
Big Tree, Dash and Dart, Etc.

Autobiographical sketch of Conrad Buff:

THE pleasantest memory of my childhood and perhaps the most trying, too, has to do with drawing. I loved to draw but paper was hard to find in the Switzerland of my youth. I saved every scrap of cardboard, wrapping paper, old letters, envelopes, anything, everything to draw upon. Even today I find it difficult to waste materials, and I have a great respect for paper, paint, brushes, canvas, and inks.

I soon found school boring, for I wanted to draw and not to figure out sums, but when I reached high school a vivid and enthusiastic teacher suddenly awakened my interest in knowledge. Few children in Switzerland, however, finish high school and at fourteen I was apprenticed to my uncle Jacob, a pastry cook who had a confectioner's shop. In the half year I was with him I learned to bake rolls, bread, pastries of all kinds, and to understand the tricks of the trade. Today I sometimes practice

Jean de Brunhoff: *ZHAHN de BROON awf*

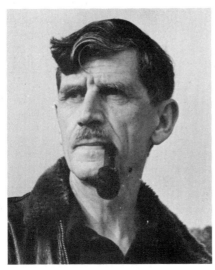

CONRAD BUFF

In 1904 I reached this country by way of the uncomfortable steerage. I bypassed the big Eastern cities, and then found myself in the state of Wyoming. Wyoming in those days was a wild land, but it was not too wild for me. The vast stretches of country, the freedom of the people, the lack of man-made restrictions made Wyoming the heaven I had always dreamed of. I felt this country was more my real home than the land of my birth.

For several years I struggled to earn a living and learn at the same time the difficult English language. I herded sheep. I washed dishes. I cooked in cafes. I dug ditches. I even drove mules and worked on a railroad. I did all the menial jobs the immigrants of that day were forced to do.

Eventually I drifted south to California. The happy climate, the lovely and varied landscapes, the ease of life fascinated me. I loved this state. Now life became rigid and severe. I worked for a time, saving every penny. Then I left the job and painted and drew until every penny was gone, when I went to work again. This kept on for some years. All the time I learned by failure and success. Eventually my work became accepted in local and then national exhibitions. My canvases won some awards of merit.

With my marriage in 1922 to Mary Marsh came encouragement and time to paint in longer periods. Our two sons were born. We began to see life through their eyes. Because of them came the idea of writing books for children. In the past five years, my wife has written five books for children. It has been my pleasure to illustrate them. I have also had ample time to paint large murals in various buildings, to develop color lithography, to travel extensively throughout the Southwest, to exhibit in many galleries. I feel it was a happy day when I turned my face to the United States I have come to love.

I believe the creative artist, if he can earn enough to live simply, has the richest of all lives. He is never bored. Life is never routine. He may not be wealthy in this world's goods, but he is wealthy in appreciation, interest, and a deep enjoyment of the visual world.

the art on my friends, much to their surprise and enjoyment. They think it strange a man should know how to bake a lemon pie, or to create cookies and pastries.

When I was fifteen my love for drawing got the better of me. I implored my parents to send me to drawing school. The course took three years, after which time I was supposed to be skillful enough to be a competent designer of laces and embroideries. This is one of the main crafts of Switzerland.

For three years I drew and painted and was happy. But when I finally graduated from this trade school, I learned that I was both too slow and much too independent ever to be really successful in the commercial field of embroidery design. The old, dull designs, which were repeated again and again, made me very unhappy. I wanted to create new and freer patterns. The industry would not allow this of their designers. I insisted I wanted to be an artist. My disappointed parents were unable to finance me in further study, and tried to persuade me how difficult would be the life of a painter. But I was not to be convinced.

Since I had no money to study in Paris or Munich, I naturally, like so many others, thought of the United States. As a growing boy I had read many stories of life in the wild West of America and had a boy's usual romantic idea of adventure among cowboys and Indians.

Mary Marsh Buff

1890-

AUTHOR OF

Dancing Cloud, the Navajo Boy, Etc.

Autobiographical sketch of Mary Marsh Buff:

ONE of the earliest memories of my childhood in Ohio centers around painting. On rainy days my twin sister and I would lie outstretched on the floor of the living room, painting in watercolor, the black and white illustrations of *Harper's* or *Scribner's*, or *St. Nicholas*, magazines of the day. When not painting or playing over the large grounds of our suburban home, we read. Our parents had acquired a good library for their six children, but I remember mostly the books of poetry. Since I loved poetry, it became natural for me to memorize many poems and I acquired a feeling for the rhythm of words.

These twin loves of drawing and reading followed me throughout my childhood and into college. But when the opportunity came to study painting, first in Oklahoma, then in Cincinnati and Chicago, and finally at Bethany College, Kansas, painting became my exclusive passion.

After graduation from Bethany with a bachelor of painting degree, I ventured into Montana, then sparsely settled, where my mother had taken out a homestead. I loved the wide open country, the crispness of the air, even the intense cold. I spent all my leisure time painting, hiking, or horseback riding.

When a teaching position opened in Lewistown, Montana, I spent three fruitful years teaching children, followed by three at the state normal school in southern Idaho teaching future teachers.

In 1920 I left Idaho for California, becoming assistant art curator at the Los Angeles Museum. The position allowed me to select paintings for exhibitions and to arrange them in the galleries, as well as to write short articles. A year or so later my future husband had a one-man show at the museum and our acquaintance ripened into friendship and then into marriage. I soon left the museum and became a housewife as well as art editor of a weekly column in a local paper. Our two boys were born, and

MARY MARSH BUFF

as they grew out of babyhood I again returned to my great love of teaching art. In a private progressive school in Hollywood I found responsive children. There we remained three years.

After we left the progressive school, the idea occurred to us to write and illustrate a book on Navajo Indians. We visited the northern part of Arizona and became so friendly with a Navajo family that *Dancing Cloud* was born.

The next year we went to Switzerland so my husband might again see the land of his birth, which he had left in 1904. That summer inspired *Kobi: A Boy of Switzerland*. Then the war broke out and travel became impossible, so we decided to stay in California. As we watched the little fawns in Yosemite Park and fed the gentle does, the idea of a picture book on the first year of a fawn occurred to us. So came *Dash and Dart*.

Our books have grown out of our own experiences. My husband has always been most cooperative in our joint work. We are very happy when working on a book together. As the text begins to take color and form in his illustrations, we both get a great thrill. We have come to believe the creative life is the happiest of lives.

Addison Burbank

See *Newcomb, Covelle*

Thornton W. Burgess

January 14, 1874-

AUTHOR OF

*The Mother West Wind Books, Bedtime
Stories, The Burgess Animal Book,
The Burgess Bird Book, Etc.*

Autobiographical sketch of Thornton W.
Burgess:

ON January 14 in the year of our Lord
1874 in the old town of Sandwich,
down on Cape Cod, occurred the most mo-
mentous event in my life—I was born. I
don't remember it. It made no stir outside
the family circle. It was important only to
me and my parents. When I was nine
months old my mother was left a widow.
Whatever of success I may have attained
since I owe in large measure to her; to her
careful training, her courage, her understanding of my love of nature, her loving
sympathy with my boyish pursuits, her ambition for my future, her faith.

I attended the public schools of the village, an average student, working out of
school hours at whatever I could find to do,
for most of the time the home treasury was
dangerously near to being empty and the
nickels and dimes and occasional quarters I
could earn were needed. So I early learned
how to work and the blessedness of it. And
those were happy days. I sometimes wonder

THORNTON W. BURGESS

if the children of today with everything
done for them, doing nothing for themselves, are as happy.

And there was plenty of recreation. Living within sound of the thunder of the surf
in a nor'easter and the smell of the pines
when the wind was from the west I early
heard the call of the out-of-doors and all
my spare time was spent in fields and
woods, on the marshes or the beach. I had
a passion for hunting, fishing, searching for
bird nests, and collecting wild flowers.

In 1891 I was graduated from high
school with college ambitions, but by this
time Mother was a semi-invalid and a year
at a commercial college in Boston was the
best that could be managed toward the
higher education. Then followed two unhappy years as cashier and assistant book-
keeper in a shoestore in Boston. I was like
one of Peter Rabbit's children just starting
out in the Great World—utterly lost. I
hadn't the remotest idea what I wanted to
do, but I did know that it was nothing to
do with commerce or figures. I still hate
them.

Then quite suddenly I knew I wanted to
write. I went to Springfield, Massachusetts,
to take the job of office boy in the editorial
rooms of the Phelps Publishing Company
at five dollars a week, and lived on this.
Shortly I became a reporter on a local weekly
published by the company, and also worked
on the various farm papers of the associated
Orange Judd Company, doing all sorts of
things from verse to children's stories, special articles and advertising copy, all splendid
training. When the Phelps Company took
over *Good Housekeeping Magazine* I became one of the editors. I remained with the
company until the magazine was sold in
1911.

In 1902-03 I did special articles for other
magazines and was a heavy contributor
under the name of W. B. Thornton to
Country Life in America. Most of this work
was on nature subjects. Vacations and such
holidays as I had were spent afield. In 1905
I was married, losing my wife at the birth
of our son the following year. In 1911 I
was married a second time and to the advice,
sustaining faith, and encouragement of my
wife I am deeply indebted for much that
has been accomplished. Her share has been
large.

Burgess: *BUR jess*

In 1910 I wrote my first book, *Old Mother West Wind*. People still buy it. It contained sixteen stories, all the animal stories I knew, or so I thought. Since then I have written over 11,000 stories. The following year *Mother West Wind's Children* was published, and then followed over sixty books, big and little, including twenty in the "Bedtime Story Book" series, the *Bird Book, Flower Book, Animal Book*, and *Seashore Book* for children, and four Boy Scout books. A number have been published in London and four in Paris. One has been translated into Chinese and individual "Bedtime Stories" have been translated into several languages. More than six million copies of my books have been sold.

The lecture platform seemed to be an unavoidable accompaniment of success as a writer. (How I did hate "Declamation Day" at school!) Then came radio and more than six years of weekly talks to an unseen audience.

As a boy I dreamed of being a naturalist and my mother dreamed of my being a preacher. Now at over seventy both dreams appear to have been somewhat realized for they call me a naturalist and certainly I do preach—the gospel of the oneness of all nature and love for and humane treatment of the lesser folk in fur and feathers. I still live in Springfield, still love to fish and to hunt—with a camera—and have learned that the heart of a child knows nothing of the passage of years and is as responsive to the truth at eighty as at eight.

I could not go to college, but in 1938 college came to me, the honorary degree of Litt. D. being conferred by Northeastern University.

Nora Burglon

AUTHOR OF
Children of the Soil, Sticks Across the Chimney, Etc.

Autobiographical sketch of Nora Burglon:

A CRICKET came to the house the same day Nora Burglon was born and the servants nodded their heads and said it was an omen. When Kisa, the seeress, heard of

From a portrait by Muriel Hannah
NORA BURGLON

the child's mascot, she said, "There is meaning to this. For those who would know what the future holds for the child, this is it: Her songs are to be heard in every land where the crickets sing," said she.

Nora Burglon's father said, "There are to be no shrieking sopranos in this family." For that reason he steered the child clear of a musical training, but for those who can hear a melody in prose, perhaps the prognostications of Kisa were not vain words after all.

Her writing is of the people. The simple people, their customs and problems. Because she is interested in them she assumes others may share her interest. Over the heavier woof threads of fact she spins the bright pattern of fancy.

* * *

Having specialized in the field of pedagogy, Nora Burglon came to write especially for children. Her *Children of the Soil*, the Boston *Transcript* said, is "a book about the sort of children one loves to know and remember, written with a freshness of understanding that makes it a joy to read. There is about it nothing forced or strained. It will be as good reading fifty years from now as it is today." And the American Library Association's *Booklist* called *Sticks Across the Chimney*, "an amusing story not un-

Burglon: *BURG lun*

tinged with adventure, of Siri and Erik who live with their mother on a farm in Denmark, where lies an old Viking mound. There is a freshness and spontaneity in the characterization and in the children's efforts to be of help to their mother."

Miss Burglon was born in Minnesota, of Scandinavian parents. Her home is now in Everett, Washington.

Virginia Lee Burton

1909-

AUTHOR AND ILLUSTRATOR OF
Katy and the Big Snow, The Little House, Mike Mulligan and His Steam Shovel, Etc.

VIRGINIA LEE BURTON

VIRGINIA LEE BURTON was born in Newton Centre, Massachusetts, where she lived for seven years while her father was dean of the Massachusetts Institute of Technology. The family then moved to California, where "Jinnee" made her first mark in the art world by winning a scholarship to the California School of Fine Arts. There she studied both art and dancing. She and her sister practiced on a bar in the living room, with the result that her sister got a stage job.

With her father, Miss Burton returned to Massachusetts in 1928. Here she went to art school three nights a week, but also worked so hard at dancing that she got a contract. But, as she was about to set out with a traveling company, her father broke his leg. Jinnee was the logical person to take care of him, so she gave up her part in the ballet and remained at home.

Luckily for children, Miss Burton turned to art almost entirely, although she taught dancing later at the Burroughs Newsboys Foundation and at a YMCA. She continued her art lessons and became a sketcher for the Boston *Transcript*'s famous dramatic critic, H. T. P., in 1929. At this time she was studying at the Boston Museum under the sculptor, George Demetrios, to whom she was married in 1931. They lived for a year in Boston and then moved to Folly Cove, Gloucester, Massachusetts, where they have been ever since.

Miss Burton's first book, the story of a particle of dust, was declined by thirteen publishers. She then read it to their son, Aris, who was four years old and who promptly fell asleep. Since then she has submitted all her stories and illustrations to this most critical audience.

Virginia Lee Burton's *Choo Choo*, her first published book, was written for their son Aris, and *Mike Mulligan and His Steam Shovel* for the second son, Mike. *Calico: The Wonder Horse* was done after a great deal of research into the fascination of the comic books. Mrs. Demetrios saw the intense interest with which her sons and their friends read the comic books, deplored their unelevated qualities, and decided to include the appealing elements of the comics in a book of her own that would be done with real artistry. This she did, getting the reaction of youthful readers to each scene in the book.

The Caldecott Medal for 1942 was awarded to a later book, *The Little House.*

The Demetrios' life at Folly Cove is gay and extremely active. Jinnee started the Folly Cove Designers, whose linoleum block prints on linens, dresses, and curtains are so popular in New York and elsewhere. She and her husband do a great deal of square dancing and Jinnee also paints under the direction of her husband. Their house and the "barn" are the center of constant fun and creative activity, good conversation, and good living.

Rafaello Busoni

1900-

ILLUSTRATOR AND AUTHOR
Stanley's Africa, Somi Builds a Church, Etc.

Autobiographical sketch of Rafaello Busoni:

I WAS born in Berlin, Germany, but that did not make me a German. My father was Italian and my mother is Swedish, and because in Europe, in most countries, people inherit the nationality of their father, I am an Italian.

Our home was very international. My father was a piano-player who had to travel part of the year in many countries; hence his friends and pupils came from all over the world and it happened quite often, when we had a real rally, that five or six languages were spoken in the same room. Indeed I had to grow up to be about twelve before I realized that there are also worthwhile people who speak but one tongue.

I had lots of hobbies, collecting stamps being number one, but drawing being a close second. I remember I was about six to seven when I struggled with the still intricate problem to draw a nose from front. I drew a lot from nature and a lot from memory. Quite naturally I tried to illustrate what I had read and quite soon I realized that an illustration might add something to a story if it is not a mere repetition of what the text already told in so many words.

I attended school in Berlin, New York, Switzerland. But when, turning sixteen, I did the same class for the fourth time and in the third country, I got tired of school and decided to become a painter. My father tested my seriousness in his own peculiar way: he went away and left me really alone, expecting me either to use my time painting or to squander it. I painted, and that decided a great deal.

I never attended an art school and consider myself self-taught. I had my first exhibition in Switzerland when I was seventeen, but my second only when I was twenty-five. My painting did not make me abandon illustrating, however, but as not all the books I liked were for publication, I sometimes lettered the entire book by hand, like a monk, as they say.

My residence was Berlin, is now New York. I traveled a great deal in Switzerland, France, Spain, Sweden, and elsewhere. I

RAFAELLO BUSONI

came to the United States in 1939. Hitler drove me out of Germany and when I came to this country I met a big challenge, for here I was an unknown man. But there is no country for giving breaks and chances as the United States, and I doubt that any American artist coming to Europe under similar conditions could tell of such understanding and warm welcome. I was given assignments and I have illustrated many junior books and it looks as if there are many more to come. A publishing company asked me to write and, although I feared I could not do it because of poor English, they insisted. Out of it came two books, so far, and I hope to add more. As one of my special interests is geography, geographical books have become my favored subjects. In the adult field theater, dance, and the great novels tempt me most.

Randolph Caldecott

March 22, 1846-February 12, 1886

ILLUSTRATOR
Randolph Caldecott's Picture Books, Etc.

RANDOLPH CALDECOTT, English artist in whose honor the Caldecott Medal has been established, was born in the historic walled town of Chester, in western England. Not much is known about his childhood beyond the fact that he was a student at the Henry VIII School in his native city. The boy was fond of birds and

Rafaello Busoni: *raf ay EL óh boo SO nee*   **Caldecott:** *CAWL de cot*

animals and from the age of six used to draw and model them; but his father, an accountant, did not encourage him in this.

When he was fifteen years old, the lad left Chester to work in a bank in Whitchurch, Shropshire, living on a farm two miles from the town. He enjoyed rural life and "used to go fishing and hunting, to the meets of hounds, to markets and cattle fairs," always carrying a sketchbook in which to record his impressions. At twenty young Caldecott went to a bank in Manchester, and there, although he missed the farm and all the kindly country ways, he had the life of an artist, joining the Brasenose Club and studying at the Manchester School of Art. Before long his sketches began to appear in the local magazines and papers.

In 1872 Caldecott removed from Manchester to pursue an art career in London. Soon the young man was supplying the *London Graphic* and *London Society* with his humorous and original sketches of fashionable life, hunting scenes, landscapes, dogs and birds. He also found time to study at the British Museum and the zoological gardens. When Caldecott was twenty-six, he went with his friend Henry Blackburn, editor of *London Society*, to the Harz Mountains in Germany. Selections from his sketchbook served as illustrations for Blackburn's *The Harz Mountains: A Tour in the Toy Country* (1872). Blackburn took some of these drawings to the United States, and

subsequently Caldecott's market enlarged to include American periodicals — *Harper's Monthly Magazine* and the New York *Daily Graphic*.

For the next few years the artist spent his summers in a cottage at Farnham Royal, near Windsor, working on the sketches for Washington Irving's *Old Christmas* (1876) and *Bracebridge Hall* (1877). These two books established him in the field of illustration. Caldecott's two journeys to Brittany with Blackburn produced sketches for the latter's *Breton Folk: An Artistic Tour in Brittany*. Later, the drawings made on a trip to Italy provided the illustrations for Mrs. Comyn Carr's *North Italian Folk: Sketches of Town and Country Life* (1878).

In 1879 the artist settled at "Wybournes," a small house near Seven Oaks, "in order to make some studies of animals—to wit horses, dogs and other human beings— which I wish to use for the work I shall be busy with during the coming winter." Previously he had made two picture books, *The Diverting Story of John Gilpin* (1878) and *The House That Jack Built* (1878), with the engraver Edmund Evans. This partnership produced in all seventeen books, of which perhaps the "most typically Caldecott, the most typically English" is, according to Hilda Van Stockum, *The Three Jovial Huntsmen* (1880). Other books in this series include *A Frog He Would a-Wooing Go* (1883) and *The Fox Jumped over the Parson's Gate* (1883). Caldecott had met Juliana Horatia Ewing in 1879. They had a mutual interest in birds, and the artist illustrated her *Daddy Darwin's Dovecote* (1884). He also did the "masterful" drawings for Mrs. Ewing's *Jackanapes* and *Lob Lie-by-the-Fire*. Caldecott's sketches, which Evans found "so racy and spontaneous," were drawn in pen and ink on smooth-surfaced paper, photographed on wood, and then engraved. There were blocks for six colors. His work is characterized by "vigorous action . . . an ebb and flow of perpetual motion." His observations held a gentle satire, but he had no malice. Throughout his life the artist had modeled in clay. He also worked in oil, and exhibited at the Royal Academy.

A man of great charm, with "genial, overflowing spirits," Randolph Caldecott was tall and handsome, with blue-gray eyes, and light brown hair. In 1880 he was married to Marion H. Brind. They lived in a small

RANDOLPH CALDECOTT

house with an old-fashioned garden about twenty miles southeast of London. Always rather delicate, Caldecott had frequently sought to improve his health by change of climate. Early in 1886 he went to Florida, again seeking the sunshine, and intending to sketch the American scene. He died of tuberculosis in St. Augustine in his fortieth year, "at the height of his powers and reputation."

The one hundredth anniversary of his birth and the sixtieth anniversary of his death were marked in 1946 by the publication of Mary Gould Davis' *Randolph Caldecott*. Many reproductions of his drawings were included in the volume.

Walter Camp

April 7, 1859-March 14, 1925

AUTHOR OF

The Substitute, Jack Hall at Yale,
Football Without a Coach, Etc.

WALTER CAMP, the boy, was tall and gawky, with not as much muscle on his arms and legs as other boys of his age. He was not naturally strong. He said to himself: "If I am to excel in sports, I must build myself up, and cultivate speed and agility." Accordingly, he took exercises each morning in his bedroom at home, went on long runs on the roads around New Haven, Connecticut, and at recess time kicked his black football around the schoolyard. He attended the Hopkins Grammar School in New Haven. Thirty miles away was New Britain, the town where he was born, the son of a schoolmaster.

At seventeen he entered Yale University in New Haven. For six years (the rules were different then) he played football as an outstanding halfback who could run, pass, and kick. He took part in all other outdoor sports of the college—played on the baseball team, ran the dashes and hurdles, won swimming races, represented Yale in intercollegiate tennis, and rowed in his class crew. He also wrote doggerel and was class poet. In conference with representatives from other schools he was responsible for reducing the number of men on a football team from fifteen to eleven, instituting the scrimmage system, and establishing the position of quarterback. From that time he

served continuously on the Football Rules Committee, and was known as the chief "developer" of football in America.

He was six years at Yale—four years as an undergraduate and two years in the medical school. He quit medicine because, as he confided to a friend, he could not bear the sight of blood. In New York he went to work as a salesman for the Manhattan Watch Company and within a year had become associated with the New Haven Clock Company, a connection which he maintained the rest of his life, rising from the position of clerk to president of the company. In his twenty-ninth year, he went to live in New Haven and married Alice Graham Sumner. They had two children, Walter and Janet.

He soon became head football coach and director of athletics at Yale. Because he had to be in his business office during practice hours, most of his work as advisory coach was done in the parlor of his little house on Gill Street, where the other coaches would gather in the evenings. He followed the development of his teams through the eyes of his wife, who went regularly to the practice field. During the twenty-odd years of his football regime, he achieved a winning record unequaled by any college in the country and he established football as the major college sport.

Camp devoted his spare moments out of season to the writing of football stories for boys, which grew out of his intimate knowledge of the game and of the youths who played it at Yale. His hero was usually a lad who goes to Yale full of the desire to excel and makes good on the team, just as Camp himself had done. One series is concerned with Dick Goddard and his friends, and includes *The Substitute, Jack Hall at Yale,* and *Old Ryerson*. Another series, comprising *Danny Fists, Captain Danny,* and *Danny the Freshman*, centers around a red-headed, hot-tempered young athlete named Danny Phipps, first at Manor Hall and then at Yale. He also wrote many nonfiction books about sports, of which the best known are *Football Without a Coach, Athletes All,* and *The Book of Sports and Games*.

During the First World War Camp put the members of the President's Cabinet and

Congress through daily physical exercises to keep them fit, and supervised the athletic program of the United States Navy. From these activities he evolved his famous "Daily Dozen," a set of exercises which achieved nation-wide popularity through the medium of magazine articles, books and phonograph records, making him one of the highest paid non-fiction writers in the country.

In his fifty-first year, Camp resigned all connection with Yale athletics. After that he maintained his position as the nation's foremost football authority by selecting his annual All-America Team, a practice begun as a coach and continued for thirty-five years, until his death in 1925.

Mary Jane Carr

April 23, 1899-

AUTHOR OF
Children of the Covered Wagon, Young Mac of Fort Vancouver, Etc.

Autobiographical sketch of Mary Jane Carr:

WHEN I was a little girl in school, history was the subject in which my grades were lowest—my most difficult study. History seemed to me a tiresome procession of hard, cold facts that never would stay fastened in my mind, until I hit upon the plan of rewriting the lessons, playing up the dramatic highlights against the background of hard, cold facts; in other words, making stories of my history lessons. After that discovery my interest in history grew and my grades in the difficult subject were much, much better. I suppose it was then, in the seventh or eighth grade, that, all unconsciously, I was laying the foundation for my adult writing of historical romance.

I was born in Portland, Oregon, one of a family of nine children. From the time I was able to read I wanted to be a writer. My father, an attorney who had been a teacher in his youth, paying his way through the University of Michigan by tutoring, used to read to us children on winter evenings. He read both poetry and prose, always from the classics, and long before I was able to understand the meaning of the words, I loved the rhythm and music of

MARY JANE CARR

poetry. "Some day," I thought, "I'll write poetry!"

I was about eight when I attempted my first "poem" but, alas, it was so sad that when I had written only eight lines I was overcome by my own emotion and, in tears, laid the unfinished manuscript aside. After my father's death, when I was a young woman, I found those unfinished lines among his papers and I remember my youthful struggle to write a poem.

I attended St. Mary's college for girls, in Portland, now known as Marylhurst, and then started to work at journalism—a wonderful training school for a writer, I believe. My college history teacher gave me my first position on his newspaper, the *Catholic Sentinel*, where I worked in all departments from proofreading to editorial writing. Later, I was on the staff of the Sunday *Oregonian* of Portland, conducting a department for boys and girls.

My first book, *Children of the Covered Wagon*, was published in 1934, and has gone into many printings. Now as I am writing, a contract from Walt Disney has arrived for me to sign, and eventually we shall be seeing that story on the screen. My first three books were transcribed into Braille and excerpts from them are included in anthologies and in many school readers. Also I have had many short stories published, and a book of verse for young children.

Valery Carrick

November 7, 1869-

AUTHOR OF

*Picture Tales From the Russian,
Tales of Wise and Foolish
Animals, Etc.*

VALERY CARRICK as a little boy in Russia could never get enough of the old folk-tales which his mother, his nurses, and the peasants on his father's estate used to tell him. As soon as he was old enough to draw he made amusing pictures of the familiar characters in the tales—the fox and the wolf, the goat and the ram, and the Russian peasant folk.

He was born in St. Petersburg. His father, William Carrick, was a Scotsman who had been brought to Russia as a baby and had taken up permanent residence there. His mother, a Russian lady, was a writer and journalist and one of the first champions of the feminine cause in Russia.

Valery was eight years old when his father died, leaving him almost entirely under the Russian influence of his mother. He used to spend his vacation time among the Russian peasants, studying their way of living, which, he said later, made him "esteem highly the soul of the Russian people."

When he grew up he began his artistic career as a caricaturist. During his first visit to England he made caricatures of well-known British personages for the *Westmin-* *ster Gazette,* the *Manchester Guardian,* and the *Liverpool Post.*

In his fortieth year he decided to retell for young people the tales he had loved as a boy. He began to write down and illustrate some of the best-known popular folktales of his native land. His first book was *Picture Tales From the Russian* and it was followed by *More Russian Picture Tales, Still More Russian Pictures, Animal Picture Tales From Russia, Tales of Wise and Foolish Animals,* and *Picture Folk-Tales.*

Valery Carrick's "picture tales" have won a place in the hearts of thousands of boys and girls. Mary Gould Davis, director of story telling in the New York Public Libraries, says: "The younger children like all of Valery Carrick's stories. They are clearly and simply told and the vigorous black-and-white drawings by the author make the tale dramatic even to children who cannot read it for themselves."

When the Revolution broke out in Russia, Carrick's estate was taken away from him and he migrated with his Russian wife to Norway, where he made his home at Hvalstad and continued to retell and to illustrate folk-tales from various countries, publishing them mostly in Norwegian magazines.

Anne Casserley

AUTHOR OF

*Michael of Ireland, Barney the Donkey,
Whins on Knockattan, Roseen, Brian
of the Mountains, Etc.*

Autobiographical sketch of Anne Casserley, written from Dublin, Eire:

MY Dear Children,
The Editor has very kindly asked me to write something for THE JUNIOR BOOK OF AUTHORS, so I am taking the opportunity to tell you something about the animals, and perhaps the people, who come into my stories.

The Kerry Cow was a real cow. She lived in a field with many other cows, and every day my little sister and I used to go and feed them with cabbage leaves and turnip tops. When they saw us, they always knew that we had something for them, and used to come running to us, headed by the Kerry Cow herself. One day, the farmer who owned the cows went into the field carrying

VALERY CARRICK

Valery: *VAL er ee*

ANNE CASSERLEY

an armful of young cabbages which he meant to plant somewhere, and when the cows saw him, they thought the cabbages were for them, and all came galloping up, helter-skelter, tails in air. The farmer was very much frightened, for he thought the cows had gone mad and were going to attack him.

Marley, the Applewoman's hen, was also a real hen, and quite as intelligent as the hen in the story. Roseen was a real pig—a very real pig—but she did not belong to us. I think, perhaps, she was made of sterner stuff than the Roseen of the storybook, for at times she would look at you out of her small eyes, from under her great flapping ears, in a way that made you feel uncomfortable. She had a rather sad end. It might have been safer, perhaps, if, like the storybook Roseen, she had gone away to live on the hillside with the fairies.

Katty, the turkey-hen, belonged to my sister, and I can assure you her beak was just as strong and as sharp as the Leprechaun found it in the story, for Katty pecked me also, and more than once. Tomcat was our own pussy who went away to live in the woods and hunt rabbits. He used to come back occasionally, but each time he came he was prouder and fiercer and more independent than before. At last, he stayed away altogether. I am not absolutely certain that he set up housekeeping with the Leprechaun, but all things are possible.

There was also a Clogmaker who had a wife, and who used to spend long days in the woods cutting and carving out clogs for the country people to wear; and there was a Peddler who used to come, now and then, from beyond the mountains, carrying a basket of—what seemed to us children—magically wonderful trinkets. You must remember that we were little country children, and had never seen cities full of great shops such as you may have seen.

But I am sorry to say that we never in our lives saw the Fairies themselves. The country people told us that they lived in a green glen not far away, and they showed us the old, gray fairythorn 'round which Fairies danced, and the country children vowed that they had often seen them, all in green and red, among the bracken and the heather. We often heard curlews, which, as everyone knows, are the Fairies' birds, calling to them through the warm, dim, summer nights. But the Fairies themselves we never saw! And then we grew up and went away from the mountains to live in a city, and as Fairies never come near a city, I am afraid there is no hope now that we shall ever see them at all.

We used to play in the larch planting, and make fires in the open, and roast potatoes, just as Paudeen did in the story. But our cooking, sad to say, was not a success, for our potatoes were burnt outside and raw inside, until we begged our maid to give us cold potatoes which had been already boiled. Then our roast potatoes were excellent, and quite as good as those of the Clogmaker's wife in the story.

Often when we wandered on the hillside, or sat on the slippery, red heather, my sister would beg me to tell her stories. I loved to tell, she to listen. When we grew older, however, we went away to school and college and story telling was forgotten, until, long years after, I found myself with small nephews, as eager to hear my stories as ever my sister had been. So story telling began again, and that is how, in course of time, Michael and Paudeen and Brian came into the storybook world, to walk and talk with the Kerry Cow, Roseen, Katty, Marley, Tomcat, and the other animals. I should very much like you to write and say what you think of all of them, and also tell me about your animal friends, and if some day you mean to write stories about yours as I have about mine.

Always your sincere friend,
ANNE CASSERLEY

Arthur Bowie Chrisman

July 16, 1889-

AUTHOR OF

Shen of the Sea, The Wind That Wouldn't Blow, Treasures Long Hidden

Autobiographical sketch of Arthur Bowie Chrisman:

ARTHUR BOWIE CHRISMAN

ARTHUR BOWIE CHRISMAN, hereinafter to be known as I, Me, or Mine, was born upon a sultry summer's day, July 16, 1889, on the farm "West Brook," one mile north of White Post, Virginia. My parents were Issac Arthur and Mary Louise Bryarly Chrisman, both descended from early colonial settlers. I was the sixth child and third son born into our large family.

Now, it is one of my weaknesses always to babble of the old times, which were the good times, and say very little of myself—which, after all, is one way to render a person understandable. So, backward turning, the first of my line to settle in America was Jacob Chrisman, who married Magdalena, daughter of Johannes Joosten Hite. Joosten Hite came to these shores shortly after the turn of 1700, secured a grant of land in the Great Valley, and in 1732 with his sons and sons-in-law completed Virginia's first settlement west of the Blue Ridge. Thus my ancestors had the privilege of participating in one of those remarkable westward surges by which our country was peopled.

At about the time when my Jacob Chrisman was blithely placing his life in hazard amongst the panthers and wolves of our valley wilderness, another Jacob Chrisman was peacefully writing books—safe at home. This Jacob wrote very learnedly in the Latin, on most any subject that drew his fancy. By some strange quirk of coincidence, he actually discussed the Chinese. His books are not widely read today, true it is, but they are still in existence. I am extremely proud of my learned early cousin, but he does make it just so much harder for me. . . . I simply can't let him beat me . . . out-write and out-last me.

Really, there is not much to say about myself. I learned to read (and very rapidly too) soon after I could crawl, and to write after I could walk. Early in life I had for a boon companion Mr. Burke, who in his young manhood had been an Indian fighter. He made for me beautiful leggings, and

bows and arrows, and chinquapin bracelets. But above all, he told me marvelous stories of his adventures in the West.

Later I found still another companion, Mr. Looky, who knew the lore of wild animals, and never tired telling stories.

It is not strange, then, that I too soon became a storyteller . . . making up queer little tales and telling them to some children who lived on our farm. In the beginning my tales dealt with the adventures of a certain "Little Pig." I took much delight in "Little Pig" and always saw to it that he came out of each escapade a tiny bit fatter and a trifle more wise.

But my favorite stories for telling took for their hero a much wilder character, one "Wonderful Peedie the Monkey." They were action stories of the extreme type, always told out of doors, and usually up a tree. Wonderful Peedie (me) thought nothing of dropping ten feet from bough to bough when the Terrible Tiger got after him. Strange to say, there was never so much as a deep scratch received while reciting and chanting and wildly acting the stories of Wonderful Peedie the Monkey. Yet, once while in the favorite storytelling tree, soberly picking cherries and taking no risks whatever, I fell and hurt my ankles pretty badly.

So . . . I landed on my feet. But poor me, my cherries spilled over all creation.

Bowie: *BOO ee*
Chrisman: *KRISS man*

My eighteenth birthday had passed before I wrote any stories with the notion of seeing them in print. Alas . . . I couldn't sell them.

Six years passed before an editor accepted one of my short verses—for which I received no pay.

At last, while working on a story involving an Oriental character, I went to a Chinese shop to inquire about the foods my character should eat. This led to an acquaintanceship with a Chinese gentleman who gave me much aid. I was soon deep in a study of Chinese history, and at last brought out one of the stories appearing in *Shen of the Sea*.

I was also able to secure the aid of a translator to help me along in my work. Nevertheless, I let seven more years pass between the writing of that first story and the completion of my book.

My motto is a favorite Chinese saying: "Walk slowly, perhaps the river will have receded when you come to it."

* * *

Arthur Bowie Chrisman has indeed "walked slowly" in his writing career. He has written only three books; yet is among the best known of modern writers for young people. His first book, *Shen of the Sea*, was awarded the Newbery Medal, given annually for "the most distinguished contribution to American literature for children," in 1926.

Alfred J. Church

January 29, 1829-April 27, 1912

AUTHOR OF

The Aeneid for Boys and Girls, The Iliad for Boys and Girls, The Odyssey for Boys and Girls, Roman Life in the Days of Cicero, Etc.

THE great gift of Alfred J. Church to the world was to make the classics better known. To tens of thousands of youth he brought the grace, wonder, and beauty of the classical age, imparting its atmosphere in simple and faultless English.

Church brought to his literary work the background of a scholar. He was the third son of a solicitor, John T. Church, and received his education at King's College, London, and Lincoln College, Oxford, from which he was graduated at the age of twenty-two. This was followed by a three years'

curacy and thirty-one years of teaching, the last eight of these being as Professor of Latin at the University College, London. He also served for some years as rector of Ashley. The publication of his more notable books commenced about the time he was made headmaster of Henley Grammar School, at the age of forty-one.

Previous to that he had become connected with the *Spectator*, particularly in writing reviews. This connection he maintained for forty-four years to the end of his life. His published works, in addition to school books, consist of over thirty volumes. These include stories, translations, and other writings, and touch upon such classical writers and subjects as Pliny, Ovid, Homer, Virgil, Herodotus, Livy, Cicero, the Greek tragedians, and the fall of Carthage. Several of his books were written expressly for the young. His versions of *The Iliad* and *The Odyssey* have enjoyed a long popularity.

Professor Church had a keen enjoyment of humor. He used to tell with zest of an incident when he was curate at St. Peter's under F. D. Maurice, when he overheard two visitors talking, one saying he had given up coming to hear Maurice as it seemed his fate to hear "only the curate." He would tell anecdotes with a very slight, almost imperceptible stammer that curiously heightened the effect of his words. Odd mistakes of the printer caused him particular delight. At one time when his difficult handwriting caused the printer to set up "the recent decorations of St. Paul's" as "the recent desecrations," he remarked, "No doubt the printer is right, but still I had better have what I wrote."

Church knew the Thames all his life and as a boy and youth spent much time upon it. He had a life-long fondness for fishing as well as for cricket. While teaching at the University College in London he published his *Hours on the River, from Henley to Oxford,* later published under the title *Summer Days on the Thames*. This is full of such commonplace things connected with the region as guide books usually miss.

He was always ready for new pursuits, and when over seventy became a golfer and a fruit grower in a small but proficient way. He was a critic without prejudice, with evenness of temper and a large-minded humanity.

He was a striking example of the value of intellectual concentration in preserving the vigor of mind and body. He wrote to within four days of his death at the age of eighty-three, with the same fineness and distinction he had shown throughout his life.

Ann Nolan Clark

1898-

AUTHOR OF

In My Mother's House, Little Navajo Bluebird, Etc.

ANN NOLAN CLARK is a teacher and a writer. She has taught in various kinds of schools, supervised others, and for the last three years has been in Central and South America as materials specialist for the Institute of Inter-American Affairs.

Being a practical person and a writer, she was impatient with the usual textbooks so ill adapted to the everyday needs of non-English-speaking children—Spanish Americans, Indians, and Latin Americans. So she began writing her own. One of these, a home geography made for Tesuque Indians, was so attractive it won a New York *Herald Tribune* prize. Then as special writer for the United States Indian Service Mrs. Clark produced many bilingual books. These were translated, illustrated, printed, and bound by Indians.

Of *In My Mother's House* the *Library Journal* says, "Written to answer the need for books with the Indian point of view for use in Indian schools, the book has great significance for white children as well. Indian children helped make the book, helped write the sentences that read like free verse."

Born in New Mexico, traveling and living for years in Indian country, and knowing Indians so well, Mrs. Clark has written books like no other Indian books ever seen. They are *for* Indians, not just *about* Indians. Reading them, the white child has a pleasant experience and a true one of Indian ways, an appreciation that red children are quite like any other children.

Of *Little Navajo Bluebird* Virginia Kirkus wrote, "The young heroine of six is a member of a devoted family who live in a hogan of round mud-plastered walls, windowless, and dependent on a hole in the roof for the disposal of fire smoke. They have their flock of sheep, drink goat's milk, lie on sheepskins; the mother weaves lovely blan-

ANN NOLAN CLARK
with two Costa Rican pupils

kets while the father makes beautiful silver jewelry."

Both *In My Mother's House* and *Little Navajo Bluebird* were Junior Literary Guild selections. Mrs. Clark's magazine and school reader series, bilingual and other Indian books, and Braille and radio reproductions published for children, have been written while she was actively dealing with children, but soon she hopes to devote full time to writing at home on her Red Dog Ranch in Tesuque, New Mexico. There are adult manuscripts to be finished and blooded cocker spaniels to be raised and trained for their obedience degrees.

Elizabeth Coatsworth

May 31, 1893-

AUTHOR OF

The Cat Who Went to Heaven, Away Goes Sally, The Sword of the Wilderness, The Wonderful Day, Etc.

Autobiographical sketch of Elizabeth Coatsworth:

BUFFALO in 1893, when I was born, was still a large town where everyone knew everyone else, and people sat on their verandas on summer evenings and waved at their friends driving by under the elms that lined the streets. The varied rhythm of horses' hoofs and the jingle-jingle of sleigh-

ELIZABETH COATSWORTH

bells go in and out of all my memories of childhood.

For eight months of the year I had little time for play, for I went to a school that was modeled on the English system. Its hours were long and its discipline severe—living as I did two miles away I was seldom home before dusk.

But in the summer we were free all day long. Early in June we moved to "the Beach," a group of houses strung comfortably along a low wooded ridge overlooking a very beautiful bay on the Canadian shore of Lake Erie. There the days each seemed as long as a whole week of winter: the trees were all made for climbing; the water shelved shallow and warm from a smooth sand beach inviting even the very young to swim and canoe; the countryside behind us was filled with comfortable farms, from which the Mennonite women in their black bonnets would come to sell the cottagers milk and eggs and chickens; and best of all there were unspoiled woods beyond, at the point of the crescent bay, still marked by the old Indian trails, and mysterious with Indian burying grounds and tales of treasure.

In these two places my sister and I grew to big girlhood, but since we came of a traveling family, we were not always at home. When I was less than a year old we went to California, father, mother, grandmother, nurse, and two babies, and we even stopped off and took the stage to Santa Fe where we visited the pueblos and my un-

winking baby eyes first stared solemnly at Indians and their way of life, and an interest in them began perhaps, which has never since died.

At five I was looking down on clouds from the high Alps, and galloping on donkeys across Egyptian deserts in a little red jacket whose patent leather belt was used to strap me for security to the pommel. When I was twelve we spent two years in Southern California and I had my first glimpse of Mexico and Aztec ruins.

I was fond of books in those days—more fond than I am now—but my memories of Vassar are more of our exploration—particularly in winter—through that lovely Hudson countryside, than of my courses. The next year, in 1916, I took a Master's degree at Columbia, and then came a never-to-be-forgotten year of adventure in the Orient, during which we went on horseback through the Philippine head-hunting country, explored little-known temples in Java, saw the early spring come over beautiful ruinous China, and slept in Buddhist monasteries of the Korean Diamond Mountains, where we were sometimes the first white women the people had ever seen.

There followed years of books and travel. I had always written poetry and began now to publish it more and more. Then one day while talking to Louise Seaman, who was then establishing at Macmillan's the first department of children's books in the country, some point, now forgotten, came up in our discussion, and I wrote *The Cat and the Captain* as part of the argument. Since then writing books for children has become a pleasant habit, and I have written many, including a Japanese tale of *The Cat Who Went to Heaven,* which won the Newbery Medal of its year.

In 1929 I married Henry Beston [see autobiographical sketch in this volume] who has written *The Firelight Fairy Book* for children and *The Outermost House* for grown-ups, an account of the changes of the year on the great Nauset beach of outer Cape Cod, and of his solitary life there on its dunes. We have two daughters, Margaret and Catherine, and divide our time between an old house looking down the harbor at Hingham, just south of Boston, and a farm with nearly a hundred acres of hayfield and wild woodland that lies on a promontory jutting out into Damariscotta Lake in Maine.

There any fine day near noon you might see two tall dark-haired people, the man probably in shorts with a studded belt about his waist, and his wife in a brown gingham dress, strolling towards the trees that fringe the lake, their morning writing done, and picnic baskets covered with red fringed napkins in their hands.

The years have passed and the little girls are big girls now at boarding school in the winter. But they still love the farm and the lake and the Maine way of life. Our own pattern of the months has remained much the same, but with more and more time spent at the farm which we know as well now in winter with frost half an inch thick on the windowpanes and the gallant wood stoves fighting back the cold, as in summer when the summer clouds rise white and tall over the five sunny chimneys.

There have been periods of travel in Mexico or Yucatan. We have ridden the trails that wind among the sahuaros of Arizona, and one summer we spent on the St. Lawrence while Henry was finishing his book for the Rivers of America series. But mostly we have lived our quiet cycle, and the number of our books has grown and grown.

I have written five books about a child named Sally and her adventures in the America after the Revolution, trying to give some of the exciting aspects of a life at once civilized and lived on a frontier near the sea, when our trade was just expanding. There have been three books laid in modern Massachusetts, dealing with the same family of two sisters and a little brother, and a dozen others: *Here I Stay* for older girls, and *Alice-All-by-Herself, Trude and the Tree House,* which the government is translating into Italian, *Thief Island, Houseboat Summer,* and many more.

There have also been books for adults: a novel, and books of poetry and stories of country life. I have repeated the old tales which our neighbors have told us, and Henry has caught the passing of the year about us and through us in his weekly column which is appearing in the *Progressive* as "Country Chronicle." We are grateful for the continuities and steadfastnesses of the country, and to have work before us which we love.

Catherine Cate Coblentz

1897-1951
AUTHOR OF
Beggars' Penny, Martin and Abraham Lincoln, Etc.

Autobiographical sketch of Catherine Cate Coblentz:

I WAS born in a small town in Vermont just before the turn of the century. Save for a short time in western Canada, my younger sister and I spent our childhood largely in this town. We lived next door to the village library on the one hand while a path led to the hills and the woods on the other. I read every book in the library, some of them many times, and I learned where every flower grew on the hills and in the woods.

When I was eight I remember reading a book about children of that age, in which the author did not seem to understand how very old eight was. I decided I would remember just how one felt at that time so I could one day write for eight-year-olds.

My first published writing was at twenty, a poem on September, which the village newspaper printed. My first "sale" came a year or so later. This was a story about Mayflower dolls, and it brought a prize of two dollars from the *Woman's Home Companion.*

When I was in the ninth grade the village librarian eloped. Probably because I had been in the library so much, she had taught me her system, and since I was the only one in town who knew it, I became librarian for the summer.'

About this time too I started teaching the youngest children in Sunday school, and discovered the only way to keep them quiet for a whole hour was to tell them stories after the "lesson" was finished. I learned much about story telling, which I still use.

Then my father, who had been a schoolteacher, died. So while a high school freshman I took on the after-school job of general reporting for the village weekly newspaper. My first task was to write stories of a funeral and a wedding! I thought I should have to resign right away. However, in the drawer of my desk I found a little green-paper booklet on newspaper style, which listed all the questions a newspaper reporter should ask. As long as I stayed on the paper that little book went with me. After my first day the gathering and writing of news items—"local lumps" the newspaper termed them—seemed fairly easy!

At the time of the First World War I came to Washington as a government employee at the Bureau of Standards, attending university classes at night. At the Bureau I met a physicist from Ohio, William Weber Coblentz, and we were married six years later. He too enjoyed the wonders of nature and of books. We spent our honeymoon and several summers at an astronomical observatory in the Southwest. There I wrote my first books.

Our own two children, a daughter, Catherine, and a son, David William, stayed with us only briefly. So we have shared the lives of other children about us.

Our home is in Washington, but since my husband's work has taken him to different places there have been new hills to wander on, new discoveries to make. There have been many children for our friends. And there have been different libraries where I have sometimes discovered stories lost in history, which it seemed to me that children would enjoy.

Becoming acquainted with the people and the problems of yesterday is, I believe, one way of knowing the people of today. Such knowledge and understanding should aid in solving the problems of tomorrow.

CATHERINE CATE COBLENTZ

"C. Collodi"

November 24, 1826-October 26, 1890

AUTHOR OF
The Adventures of Pinocchio

C. Collodi, the Italian author of *The Adventures of Pinocchio,* wrote the following account of his childhood a few years before his death:

SOME years ago when I was a little boy just as you are, my dear little readers, about your very age, that is eleven or twelve years old, as is quite natural I used to go to school. I used to go every day except Thursdays and Sundays. The Thursdays in the course of the year were very few, so few, only one a week, but the Sundays, thank God, the Sundays came every eight days.

So I too went to school but I cannot say whether mine was elementary school or the high school, because in my times, years ago, it was simply called school. And when we boys said school we meant a room, large and almost clean, where we were obliged to pass about six hours a day and where we even learned to read and write and count. The school I went to was a long study. It was lighted by windows, one on each side and one in the back of the room which remained hidden by a big dark curtain. Near the two walls, to the right and the left of the teacher's desk, there were two long lines of desks. The scholars sitting on the right side were called Romans, those on the left were called Carthaginians. Each faction was governed by an emperor, and for the dignity of this emperor, you understood well, two scholars were chosen who in the course of the month had the most points of merit for good conduct and for diligence in daily lessons.

I remember once the title of emperor was given to me, but it was a passing glory. After two hours of ruling, for one of my mischievous actions the teacher had me come down from my throne and instead I was seated in the dunce's chair. But let me tell you the truth. I outlived this disgrace in a few months and I was able to face the class again. You see, even as a boy I was not born to be an emperor.

Now guess if you can who was the most irresponsible, the most disobedient, and impudent boy in the whole school? If you don't know I will whisper it in one of your

Collodi: *col OH dee*

ears, but don't tell your father or mother—it was yours truly.

Not a day passed that I did not hear a boy call, "Teacher, will you make Collodi stop?"

"What did Collodi do?"

"He is eating cherries and putting pits in my pockets."

Then the teacher would come down from his chair and make me feel the sting of his dry and hard hand, and order me to change my seat. An hour later, after I changed my seat, a boy would call, "Teacher, will you make Collodi stop?"

"What is he doing?"

"He is catching flies and putting them into my ears."

Then the teacher would give me another example of the thinness and hardness of his hands and again I would change my seat.

Yes, I was always changing places. There wasn't a Roman who would accept me as a Roman. At last I was sent among the Carthaginians. There I found myself seated next to the best little boy in the school, whose name was Sylvan. He was as nice and fat as a turkey. He was a boy who studied little and slept a great deal. He even slept at school and confessed that he liked it better than sleeping at home.

One day Sylvan came to school with a new pair of trousers. When I saw them my idea was to draw a beautiful picture on them. So when my friend began drowsing, leaning against the desk his head between his hands, without losing any time I put my pen into the inkwell and I began to draw on his trousers as far as I could reach. I drew a lovely soldier on a horse. The horse's mouth was open wide, just about to eat a big fish, so that you could understand that it was Friday, the day on which one usually ate fish. To tell you the truth, I was very much satisfied with myself and liked it more and more each time I looked at my sketch.

Alas, it didn't impress my friend Sylvan that way. Upon waking up and finding the sketch of the soldier and the horse and the fish, he began to cry and shout as loud as he could, making you think someone was pulling his hair.

"What is the matter?" shouted the teacher, getting up and putting his glasses on his nose.

"I-I-he-that bad Collodi painted my trousers," and getting up he held up one of his legs and showed the design which I had made with so much pride and such cleverness. Everybody laughed, but the teacher. He did not. Instead of laughing he came down on me like the fury of a wind storm, without losing any time in discussion, and he proved very handy in curing me of my passion for painting on other people's trousers.

That day proved a black, unforgettable day for me. The next morning when I came to school the teacher, with a very black look, sat me at a very solitary desk in the back of the room.

"Take your books and stay there where you will be alone and where you will be out of reach of the other boys."

Like a wet duck I hung my head and obeyed. The first and second days I accepted my solitude. The third day I could not bear it any more. My companions looked at me and laughed. Behind by back, you remember, was the window with the long dark green curtain. Just when I was very much bored, I noticed a tiny hole in the curtain. My next thought was to make it bigger, a bit each day, so that I could eventually put my head through it. This took me a week to accomplish because the curtain was of strong stuff.

At last the little hole was a large hole and I signed to my companions to pay attention to me and they would see a magnificent spectacle. No sooner said than done. The teacher was engaged in reading compositions to the class and I went back to the curtain and began to work my head into the hole. The hole was large but my head was larger and could not go through. But I forced and forced so much that at last I succeeded.

Imagine the roar of laughter that this occasioned, seeing a head through a hole, appearing as though it had been stuck there with four pins. But the teacher would not laugh. Naturally I tried to get my head out of the curtain but it would not move. I became so frightened that I began to cry like a child.

Then the teacher turned to the pupils and said to them, "Look at Collodi, the good, studious, amiable Collodi, the boy who is so good to his companions. Cannot you see how the little boy is crying? Have pity on him. Come out of your seats and dry his tears."

I leave it to you to imagine how those lads responded. They didn't have to be asked twice. Laughing and scrambling and in line like a procession, two by two, they came in turns close up to me and rubbed their hands over my face.

The lesson was a bitter one. From that day on I persuaded myself that if one is impudent and disobedient in school he loses the good will of the teachers and the friendship of the scholars. I too became a good boy. I began to respect the others and they in turn respected me and after a month of praiseworthy conduct I was again nominated Emperor of the Romans. The Romans in my school, however, could never get to the point of calling me majesty and called me simply Collodi.

* * *

Collodi's real name was Carlo Lorenzini. He took the name Collodi, which he used as an author, from the little village where his mother was born. He was a native of Tuscany, a province of Italy, and lived in the city of Florence. He held high positions in the government for many years, was decorated for valor in the army, and was editor of a leading newspaper.

Upon his retirement from public life he devoted himself to writing stories for young people. He is chiefly known for *Pinocchio*, the story of a little wooden marionette, which has been translated into many languages and is loved by children all over the world. It is available in English in several attractive editions. The best known of these is the one with illustrations by Attilio Mussino, a friend of the author.

Collodi died within a month of his sixty-fourth birthday. Some years afterward his brother, Paolo Lorenzini, wrote a sequel to *Pinocchio*. He called it *The Heart of Pinocchio*, but is was never as popular as Collodi's own book. Another author named Eugenio Cherubini wrote another sequel called *Pinocchio in Africa*.

Padraic Colum

December 8, 1881-

AUTHOR OF

Children of Odin, The Adventures of Odysseus, The Golden Fleece, Etc.

Autobiographical sketch of Padraic Colum:

Padraic Colum: *PAW drig CAWL um*

WHEN I am asked for an autobiographical sketch I am filled with dismay: There is hardly anything to be said about my life—hardly anything that could be of interest to outside readers.

I was born nearly in the middle of Ireland. The town I was born in has nothing to be said for it. However, my father happened to be the master of a workhouse; consequently I was born where waifs, strays, tramps congregated.

In those far-back days the workhouse was an oddly significant institution in Ireland. It was mainly for people who were too poor to support themselves — these were the paupers, mostly old men and women or younger people more or less incapacitated or defective. Having the run of the institution from the kitchens to the dormitories, as a child I saw a lot of these paupers and was often entertained by the gossip and the histories of old men and women who were survivals from an Ireland that had disappeared.

But I wasn't nearly as much interested in the resident-paupers as I was in the "casuals"—people who entered for a night and went away in the morning, coming into the workhouse for a night's shelter and supper and breakfast. This particular workhouse was on the highway between the east and west, between Leinster and Connacht, and the "casuals" whom I watched coming and going through the big gate were men and women who were genuine wayfarers, nomads, the "masterless men" whom English writers noted as being common in Ireland generations before—tramps and their women and children.

There were also itinerant artisans, men who followed decaying trades, and ballad singers with tramp fiddlers and pipers. As I watched them taking the road of a morning, going I knew not into what mysterious region, the romance of the road was brought home to me and I think it has never quite left my mind. It is on account of these early impressions, I think, that so many of my poems and stories are about wandering people.

While I was still a child I left the town I was born in and went to live in the next county. There, in my grandmother's house, I heard stories before I read them and songs and scraps of poetry before I had to learn any at school. I was fortunate, I believe, in

PADRAIC COLUM

getting this sort of oral knowledge which left me with an interest in legends and traditions.

Then I went to live near Dublin. Dunleary, the town I grew up in, has been beautifully described by L. A. G. Strong in *The Sea Wall*. In my twenties I was living in the city, in Dublin. What is called the Irish Renaissance, the Celtic Revival, was a very vital movement then, affecting not only writers but ordinary young men and women, leading them to learning the Irish language and so giving them an interest in the oldest traditions of the country and preparing them to act in a revolution which took place before they reached middle age.

The Irish Theatre was being promoted by William Butler Yeats. George Moore was living in Dublin. Douglas Hyde, the head of the Gaelic movement, was lecturing. Arthur Griffith, the founder of Sinn Fein, was running his weekly journal. All sorts of talents were looked for in the generation which was coming on: amongst them, my contemporary, was James Joyce, then at the university.

It was a good time to come of age in. I was brought into all the activity that was going on: my first poems were published by Arthur Griffith; I entered the group in which were William Butler Yeats, "A. E.," Lady Gregory, J. M. Synge, the Fay brothers, who were instrumental in making the Irish Theatre an actuality and not merely a literary project. I had a play produced while I

was twenty, and my second play, *The Land,* was the first success that the Irish Theatre had. Later with James Stephens and Thomas MacDonagh, one of the leaders of the revolution of 1916, I founded the *Irish Review*.

Then in 1914 I came to America for the first time. It was while in America, in the first year I was here, that I began to write stories for children. My beginning in this field was something of an accident. In order to keep what knowledge I had of Irish I used to translate every day some passages from that language. The only text I had at one time was a long folk story. This I translated. Then one of the editors of the New York *Tribune* who had charge of a children's page asked me if I had anything that could go on that page. I handed in my translation and it was published as a little serial.

The famous illustrator, Willy Pogány, who had just come to America, saw the stories and suggested that I should do a children's book which he would illustrate. I put the translations together, added greatly to them, and wove them into a long narrative, which was *The King of Ireland's Son.* Afterwards the Macmillan Company commissioned me to make the *Iliad* and the *Odyssey* into a children's book. And so I started writing books for children—I have written nearly twenty of them now.

In 1923, on the invitation of the Hawaiian legislature, I went to the Islands to make a survey of their traditional stories and reshape them into stories which could be used to bring the imaginative past of the Polynesian people to the newer groups in the Islands. I published these stories in two volumes, *The Gateways of the Day* and *The Bright Islands.*

And this, I am sorry to say, is all I can think of by way of an autobiographical sketch.

Maribelle Cormack

January 11, 1902-

AUTHOR OF

Road to Down Under, Wind of the Vikings, Swamp Boy, Etc.

MARIBELLE CORMACK was born in Buffalo. She says her ancestry is "straight Scottish," for although her mother came from Crawford County, Pennsylvania, her father was born in the Orkney Islands and Maribelle grew up in a little bit of Scotland transported to the New World and set down in western New York State. Many of the Cormacks' neighbors had come from the Orkneys and they all used to meet twice a year for singing the old songs and repeating the old legends and poems.

Most Scottish of all was Maribelle's home. According to the *Horn Book*, "Each week her family got the *Orcadian*, printed in the Islands, and her father always looked to see the exact time the boat would sail for his land, called Eday, which means in old Norse, the Island of the Isthmus.' "

The summer she was twelve the family went to Scotland and took that boat to Eday. There they found her grandfather's old home, Quoyfaulds, unchanged. Much later she was to draw on recollections of this visit for her *Wind of the Vikings*, the story of a young American girl sent to live with her father's people in the Orkneys.

Back in Buffalo Miss Cormack attended Lafayette High School, and went on to Cornell, where she received an A.B. in English literature. She then did graduate work at the Universities of Vienna and Geneva. In 1928 Brown gave her the degree of Master of Arts in botany. She spent two years at the Buffalo Museum of Science in the education department, and for the past quarter century has been at the Park Museum in Providence, Rhode Island, where she is head of the education department and director of the museum.

MARIBELLE CORMACK

Miss Cormack has published three textbooks (nature readers) and nine storybooks for young people. Several of these latter were honor books or book club selections, and several have been done in Braille.

Miss Cormack takes a deep interest in astronomy. She has gone on three Brown University Skyscrapers eclipse expeditions: to Mt. Katahdin, Maine, in 1932, to Roblin, Manitoba, in 1945, and in 1947 to Araxa, Brazil. She is also a charter member of the Rhode Island Astronomical Society. For other interests she lists travel, and languages both living and dead.

In addition to writing, Miss Cormack lectures on birds, wild flowers, popular astronomy, and on what she calls, "the adventures of a scribbler, the chances and mischances of a writer in selling stories to the hardhearted publishers, the zest of the search, and the humorous obstacles which lie across the writer's path."

Walter Crane

August 15, 1845—March 15, 1915
ILLUSTRATOR

A BOY was sketching an old shaggy pony on the outskirts of London one day, when its owner, a milkman, came to get the pony. The milkman looked at the boy's sketch and said that if he came to his farm he would give him a glass of milk for it. The bargain was accepted and in the farmyard the boy found all sorts of animals, which pleased him even more than the milk, for the milkman said he might come again and sketch them.

The boy was Walter Crane. He was the son of an artist and had "tinkered with a pencil" ever since he could remember. He was born in Liverpool but had spent his early boyhood at Torquay in South Devon on the south seacoast of England, where he and his brothers loved to watch the ocean waves dash on the rocks, and at the age of eleven had come to live in London. In the out-of-doors he found endless subjects for his itching pencil. Indoors he amused himself by making color illustrations of poems he liked. One of these, to Tennyson's *Lady of Shalott*, earned the praise of the famous art critic Ruskin and brought him an apprenticeship with W. J. Linton, who was considered the foremost wood-engraver of his time. Beginning at the age of thirteen, he worked three years under Linton, emerging a full-fledged artist.

At sixteen he exhibited a painting at the Royal Academy. The next year he made his first book illustrations. Then he got a job making the designs for the paper covers of cheap railway novels. His designs were engraved by Edmund Evans, who persuaded him to try his hand at colored picture books for young people and who worked with him during the rest of his career. He was twenty when he began this work. During the next ten years or so, at the rate of about four a year, he produced more than forty picture books of favorite nursery rhymes. Of these picture books, young readers of the present day in America know: *Buckle My Shoe, This Little Pig Went to Market, Little Red Riding Hood, The Sleeping Beauty, Song of Sixpence, Cinderella, Old Mother Hubbard, Beauty and the Beast, The Yellow Dwarf,* and many many others. His picture books are riots of color, with fanciful border decorations, and sometimes the text is done by hand in bold red and black letters. There are entertaining title pages and end papers and somewhere you will always find his amusing signature, which is a long legged bird set within his monogram.

For two years while he was doing this work, Crane lived in Italy, where he went after his marriage at the age of twenty-six to Mary Frances Andrews. His conception of Mother Hubbard's famous dog was taken from a peculiar type of poodle that was popular in Rome while he was living there.

When the picture books were finished, Crane made three little square books of nursery songs, with the music set on one side of the page and illustrations on the other. The songs for the first two books came from Mother Goose and the third from Aesop. The books were: *The Baby's Opera, Baby's Bouquet,* and *The Baby's Own Aesop.* These still remain favorite picture books after considerably more than half a century.

The tunes for both *The Baby's Opera* and *Baby's Bouquet* were arranged by Crane's sister Lucy. She also translated *Grimm's Household Stories* from the German and this book contains some of her brother's best-known drawings. The "Goose Girl" illustration from this book was reproduced in tapestry by his friend William Morris and is now in the South Kensington Museum, London.

In addition to these books prepared by himself, Crane also made illustrations for about sixteen children's stories by Mrs. Molesworth and two books of Robert Louis Stevenson, among others.

His travel took him to Italy, Germany, and Hungary, where his work was greatly admired. With his wife and family of two sons and a daughter, he made a lengthy visit to the United States. Americans found him a simple man with a Van Dyke beard who might pass unnoticed in a crowd and was always enthusiastic and willing to give of his talent.

He died at his home in West Kensington, London, at the age of sixty-nine.

Phyllis Crawford

February 8, 1899-

AUTHOR OF
"Hello, the Boat!" Etc.

Autobiographical sketch of Phyllis Crawford:

I WAS born and brought up in Little Rock, Arkansas, where I went to the public schools. Until I was eleven I played mostly with boys, all older than I. They could do everything better than I could, and so I was just a sturdy little person who tagged along and kept lots of things to herself for fear of being teased.

Then we moved to a new neighborhood, where I made two good friends who were sisters, and we had a great deal of fun.

Sometimes, though, I used to climb over the back fence when I saw them coming and go out into the pine woods by myself to pick wild flowers and find lovely patches of green moss and listen to the mockingbirds and catbirds. I used to fix a lunch and let Poose, the white cat, smell the sandwiches so she would go with me. She chased grasshoppers and butterflies while I sat under a tree and read or made up little songs I never told anybody.

High school was exciting, but I never really got over the feeling of being the one who just tagged along until I went to college. There I liked so many people and took part in so many activities that I lost a great deal of my self-consciousness. I majored in psychology and worked on the weekly paper and the monthly magazine, which I

PHYLLIS CRAWFORD

edited as a senior. After graduation I taught English for a year and then went to library school. After that I did editorial work until I married.

When the *Index of American Design* was started by the Federal Art Project, I joined the staff as head of research in the New York office. In 1937 I left the *Index* to write. During the Second World War I worked in a war plant (*Second Shift* is about that job), picked lima beans on a Farm Bureau project, and gave blood as often as the Red Cross let me. From 1944 to 1947 I worked as an editor, and then I went back to my typewriter.

One of the notions that annoy me is that writers and artists and so-called creative people have a special quality that makes them different from carpenters and teachers. and soda jerkers. If there is any difference, it is in their capacity to keep on working even when people do not appreciate their work. I know that when I was born there was no fairy godmother standing behind my crib to bestow gifts on me. I have always been a very average person, who finds most people, all cats, and all outdoors interesting. I feel strongly about integrity in people and honesty in politics and business, and I like movies, the ballet, music from Louis Armstrong to Brahms, and everything that is funny.

Writing books is hard work for me, and it was not the only thing I wanted to do

when I was a child. I wanted to be a musician, until I found out how much you had to practice. And I wanted to be an artist too, but I gave that up because I could not imagine painting the same picture again and again until it was just right. I decided on writing because it was the only work that seemed worth all the practice and the effort I had to give to it.

When I was younger I wrote poetry, stories, and all kinds of pieces for school papers. But when I was grown and it was time to start writing in earnest, it was not so easy; nothing was good enough. I would start a short story and then put it away because it was so poor. I began to wonder if I should ever finish anything.

In 1926 I made a New Year's resolution to stop thinking about writing unless during that year I could sell one story or finish ten. By September I had a pile, but as usual they were not very good. Then I wrote a story poking fun at Elsie Dinsmore. The *New Yorker* accepted that story and many more, to which I signed the name "Josie Turner" because I did not want anybody to expect me, Phyllis Crawford, to be funny all the time.

Suddenly I had one of those spells that come to many writers: I could not write a story to save my life. This lasted seven years. Although I do not know how I knew when it was over, I left the *Index of American Design* and expected to sit right down to write, but I could not get started.

Then one day I heard that the Julia Ellsworth Ford Foundation was offering a prize for a children's book. I dropped everything and wrote a story. More than two months passed without any word from the contest and I began to run out of money. I knew I ought to get another job, but I could not give up hope of winning that prize though I posted notices all over my apartment to remind myself how slim my chances were.

Finally the day came when I lost hope; I spent a whole evening telling a friend how foolish I had been to count so much on winning. She was very consoling, and said it might not be so bad to go back to a job. What neither of us knew until the next day was that at that very hour the contest judges were deciding to give the prize to *Hello, the Boat!*

I have managed to write several more books and to hold down jobs now and then without feeling I have given up writing forever. Nowadays I always have more books planned in my head than I can find time to write.

Ellis Credle

1902-

AUTHOR OF
Down, Down the Mountain, Little Jeemes Henry, Etc.

ELLIS CREDLE

Autobiographical sketch of Ellis Credle:

WHEN I was a little girl I lived in the somber low country of North Carolina. My home was far from any railroad and cut off from the world by swamps and forests; yet it did not seem to me we were isolated. On the contrary, I felt myself right in the middle of things.

I went away to college. After graduation I took a teaching position in the Blue Ridge Mountains. The country was majestic but I found the work so uncongenial that I was very unhappy.

Then in 1925 I went to New York with the vague idea of becoming an interior decorator. I soon saw that this was a business as well as an art and I did not feel myself cut out for a business career. I quit school in mid-term and began to study commercial art. After six months my money ran out. Hoping always to return to art I took one job after another. I was salesgirl, librarian, guitarist. I distributed soap, painted "imported" Japanese lampshades, ushered in Carnegie Hall. I was governess and made up stories for the unfortunate children of the hard-pressed rich.

After eight such futile years, the W.P.A. art project gave me my chance. I was put to work in the American Museum drawing reptiles, then in the Brooklyn Children's Museum doing murals. Each week I was given a whole day off, which I devoted to making a picture book about the Blue Ridge Mountains. After many rejections *Down, Down the Mountain* was published in 1934.

Life looked bright to me. I blew in all advance royalties on a cruise to South America. On the way I met Charles de Kay Townsend, and we were married the following year. After that came three more books. My husband and I then decided to

collaborate on a photographic picture book. We went to North Carolina, where he made pictures for *The Flop-eared Hound.* When this met with success we traveled into the Blue Ridge country to make a book which we called *Johnny and His Mule.*

This trip brought us financial ruin. The book was "accepted" by a schoolbook publisher, and held for five years without publication. At the same time the publisher of my other books, with the excuse that I had broken an option clause in my contract, withheld all my income for two years.

During this state of affairs our son Richard Townsend was born. I concluded that writing for children was unprofitable, decided to give it up, and turned my time to learning to write adult literature.

In 1941 my husband became photographic technologist with the National Gallery of Art. We moved to Washington. I succeeded in getting *Johnny and His Mule* from the schoolbook firm and it was published. Financial reparations were made by the firm that had withheld my royalties, but oh, for the lost years—who can return them? However, another book for children is under way and it is my hope now to continue with both adult and juvenile writing.

Fleming H. Crew

See *Gall, Alice Crew*

Credle: *pronounced "cradle"*

Helen Coale Crew

December 8, 1866-May 1, 1941

AUTHOR OF

Alanna, Under Two Eagles, The Trojan Boy, Etc.

Autobiographical sketch of Helen Coale Crew, written for THE JUNIOR BOOK OF AUTHORS a few years before her death:

BALTIMORE, Maryland, was the place where my cradle had its first rocking. But most of my childhood was spent some two or three miles out of the city, in a hospitable home set in the midst of twenty rolling acres, and looking as though it were rooted in the green lawn under the great oak trees. For playmates for one small girl there were five brothers, and the six had the most delightful parents in the world.

Being Quaker children we all went to the Friends' Academy in the city to be educated, beginning with McGuffey's *Readers* and ending with Virgil's *Aeneid.* There are vivid recollections of those days of washing mistakes off one's slate with one's tears, of weeping over Latin verbs, of being "kept in," and of being, nevertheless, completely happy. Who indeed, at twelve, could always determine whether it was Caesar or the Aedui (or any other enemy) who won a given battle? The trouble seemed to be that the battleground was always swarming with ambassadors and messengers, and was a place of confusion as great as one's own. At home our old Irish Mammy took up the cudgels for those of the six who had been kept in, denouncing the guilty teacher as being "black-hearted entirely," and hoping that their black hearts would be "scalded with grief." Mammy Bridget was a tyrant, firm and faithful, the last court of appeal. Father was always a very present help in trouble. Mother was our playmate.

On Sundays we went to Friends' Meeting with our parents, and occasionally our nurse took the youngest two on a week-day to the Cathedral. And how the youngest two were fired with the ambition to make over the modest Meeting House into a colorful Cathedral! It was a thing to think of and plan as we sat by our parents on Sunday in that quiet hour when—we knew —Father and Mother were listening to the "still, small voice."

Bryn Mawr College from 1885 to 1889. The biology laboratory was a place of wonder and delight. The chemical laboratory was a place of wonder and puzzlement. The woods, the hills, the fields, the old Gulf Road, the old Lancaster pike, in rain or snow or undiluted sunshine, were places of happy comradeship. Best of all Professor Paul Shorey's classroom, where we came to learn that the Latin people were as real as ourselves, and that Horace and Catullus, Terence and Ovid and Martial, were absolutely human and fascinating.

Marriage with Henry Crew in 1890; a year at the Lick Observatory on Mount Hamilton, California, where we saw the silver linings of the clouds every morning early and experienced earthquakes on several occasions; and then we came to Evanston and the Northwestern University. Here we raised our three childen, before the days of the cluttering up of the streets with automobiles, praise be!

I wasted a heaping baker's dozen of years writing adult stuff, and then came to the thing I love best of all. And now, my mind being full of pictures (by reason of the pleasantest of all miracles, namely, that you don't have to take down old pictures from the walls of your mind in order to hang new ones there) and my pencil having learned to keep a few jumps ahead of my thoughts, I am as happy as a whole skyful of larks, writing stories for boys and girls of thirteen.

Thirteen is a magical age, lying between childhood on one side and high school on the other. New ideas are coming thick and fast at thirteen, but the old ideas are still of value and not yet put on the rubbish heap. While I am too far behind the times to know all the complicated thoughts of to-day's boys and girls of thirteen, I still remember the thoughts of the thirteen-year-old girl I "knew the best of all" long years ago. She was a happy reader. It is for her, after all, that I write. I like to think that maybe she would like my stories because (if for no other reason) I never commit the crime of "writing down" to anyone younger than myself.

*   *   *

Bertha E. Mahony and Elinor Whitney found Helen Coale Crew's books "full of vigor" and praised their "sympathy, humor, and distinctive literary style." Most enjoyed by teen-age readers, in addition to those mentioned at the heading of this sketch, are *Saturday's Children, Laughing Lad, The Shawl With the Silver Bells, The Lost King,* and *The Singing Seamen.* Mrs. Crew died in Evanston in her seventy-fifth year, survived by her husband, a distinguished physicist, and their two daughters and a son.

Gertrude Crownfield

October 26, 1867-June 3, 1945

AUTHOR OF

*The Little Tailor of the Winding Way,
Alison Blair, Jocelyn of the Forts,
Freedom's Daughter, Etc.*

Autobiographical sketch of Gertrude Crownfield, written for THE JUNIOR BOOK OF AUTHORS a few years before her death:

MY Dear Young Readers Everywhere: My books are for you, and because you read them we meet together on the printed page, though we may never see one another face to face. Our love for books and reading is what makes us friends. I don't remember learning, but I could read any English book when I was six years old. Only books that were worthwhile came into my parents' house, so that my taste for good reading was formed unconsciously, and very early.

I was born a good many years ago in Baltimore, Maryland, but my heart is and always will be young. I have never married. Although I went to public school for a few years, most of my education was received at home, under private tutors, and by special work in college classes.

When I was not quite seventeen I began to teach boys and girls in Ohio, and was happy in doing it. I ended my teaching in Marinette, Wisconsin, and came to New York City, graduated as a professional nurse, practiced nursing for several years, and had just entered medical college when a prolonged severe illness put a permanent end to my medical studies.

While I was in my own sickroom I was, without realizing it, drawing nearer and nearer to you, for although I had made occasional attempts to write stories and verse before that, it was then that my mind began to weave one story after another steadily,

and that now and then something was published.

As soon as I was well enough to be busy, during the mornings I became office assistant to a prominent nerve specialist, and gave my afternoons to trying to teach myself how to write stories and verse that you would like to read. A good many years slipped by in that way, but now I give all my time to writing. I shall never forget how I felt when I sold some verse or when a story came out on the front page of *St. Nicholas,* or when *The Little Tailor of the Winding Way* was accepted for book publication. It meant that I was going to be one of your fiction writers, although before the book came out I had close to a hundred articles on child hygiene published in magazines, telling your parents how to take care of your health.

Hoping that I might be able to make you love your country and its stirring history as I have always loved it, hoping with all my heart that I might make that history come alive for you, and be no longer dry facts and tiresome dates, but actual throbbing life, with real people moving through the exciting scenes and dangers of an earlier day, as they did move and feel and suffer and aspire and accomplish, I have written for you a group of novels with a thoroughly accurate background of American history, and life.

Although in every one of these books the hero and heroine are fictitious, they are faithful types of the actual young people of their day, and I have allowed them to do nothing that any young person of their times could not have done.

I have spared no pains in giving you a true picture of these historic times, people, manners, customs, and speech. For every book I have visited the scenes, and on every one I have lavished many months of diligent research. Captain John McBride, one of our United States Army officers, has guided me in military details and possibilities.

Out of a deep love for my country and for you I have given you these books.

* * *

Miss Crownfield died in New York City in her seventy-eighth year, after a long illness. May Lamberton Becker, among others, has praised the "always careful detail" of her historical fiction. Her historical novels are still favorites of girls of teen age.

Irving Crump

December 7, 1887-

AUTHOR OF

*The Boys' Book of Railroads, The Boys'
Book of Cowboys, Our Firemen,
Our Airliners, Etc.*

Autobiographical sketch of Irving Crump:

IRVING CRUMP

PRESIDENT Lincoln's war cabinet was responsible for bringing my grandfather, James Crump, from Manchester, England, to the little town of Saugerties, New York, to superintend the manufacture of cannon iron for the Union Army. He, it seems, was an expert in forging these diabolical tools of Mars. At any rate that is how our branch of the Crump family came to this country. There were other branches of our family in Virginia and the Carolinas, doubtless of the Confederacy, and unhappily being blasted by these selfsame weapons that "Grandpa Jim" was shaping in the glaring blast furnaces at Saugerties. I was born and brought up for a considerable period on the outskirts of that little town in the shadow of the Catskill Mountains, and there I learned to love the field and woods and streams and books that dealt with adventure out of doors.

At the age of ten I had a number of ambitions all closely related. One was to meet and know Dan Beard. And another was to write stories for boys as full of adventure as those written by Kirk Munroe, my favorite author, and Charles G. D. Roberts, who was his very close second in my favor. I wanted to know Charles Livingston Bull, who was coming into prominence then as an animal artist, illustrating Mr. Roberts' books, and last, and the remotest possibility of all it seemed, I had a desire to edit a magazine for boys. This last desire was probably fathered by the knowledge that Kirk Munroe had been editor of *Harper's Round Table,* the boys' magazine of a generation before my time, of which I possessed many thumbed copies.

To be sure during the interval between ten and twenty-one my interests varied occasionally between wanting to enter West Point, being a cowboy or mining engineer, or seeking adventure as an explorer. But always my mind swung back to writing stories for boys and at the age of twelve I attempted one or two with sad results. They were never finished. But I continued to be an avid reader, though never a particularly good student. History and English were pleasant subjects. Everything else was a hardship, and my education by the time I had completed it was—to say the least—very lop-sided. So were my interests, however. Unless everything I did gripped me from a romantic standpoint I was bored.

My father tried to stimulate an enthusiasm in me for stocks and bonds, but they had too much to do with mathematics, which I abhorred, so I persuaded a brother member of my fraternity [at Columbia University] to find me a job as a reporter. Newspaper work was exactly what I wanted. It combined romance and action with writing, and I enjoyed six years of pursuing news over thirty-seven of these United States and parts of Canada, and meanwhile I wrote my first fiction story. Strangely enough it was not a boys' story. It was an adult tale of the Kentucky Mountains and I sold it to *Collier's.* Immediately after that I wrote a second story of true adventure and sold it to an English magazine, *Wide World.*

That flash of success went to my head. "I'm a genius and I never realized it. How long has this been going on?" I asked myself and I promptly resigned my newspaper position and decided to live by my pen, or typewriter, as it happened to be. That was a terrible mistake. I did not sell another story for several years and I gradually realized that I was not as clever as I thought

I was. To make a living I had to write everything from advertising copy to publicity material for Buffalo Bill's Wild West Show to keep the wolf from my door and my small but lusty family from being hungry, for I had married Marguerite Duryea Whitney, a descendant of Eli Whitney, of cotton gin fame, whom I met when we both were students at Erasmus Hall in Brooklyn.

After a time, however, I discovered by reading other men's stories just how a tale should be written, or about how it should be written anyway, and by working hard nights, Saturdays, and any other time I could get, I began to write stories that did sell. They were stories about animals chiefly, because I have always spent all of my spare time in the forests or along the streams and rivers most accessible to me.

Then one day out of a clear sky Walter P. McGuire, then editor of *Boys' Life*, asked me if I would try to write some stories for boys, and I remembered that that was what I wanted to do most anyway. I wrote a series of short stories and then a serial, and before I even suspected it I was known as a boys' author, a distinction I was proud of. Two book publishers became interested in my tales and I began to work for them and when Mr. McGuire was asked to become editor of *American Boy,* I was invited by the Boy Scouts of America to become the editor of *Boys' Life*. There at the age of twenty-nine, I achieved all of my boyhood ambitions. I was writing for boys, I was editing a boys' magazine, and I met Dan Beard, becoming his very good friend. I also collaborated with him in writing one of his few fiction books, *The Black Wolf Pack.* As editor I also came in contact with my boyhood hero Kirk Munroe, then a very old man who lived in Coconut Grove, Florida, and who was no longer contributing to any of the magazines. I also met and learned to love Charles Livingston Bull. I became his neighbor and friend and remained both until he died. I am proud to say he illustrated many of my stories.

My work in the boys' field has always had a strong appeal to me. Though I have contributed to many adult magazines and at one time was managing editor of *Pictorial Review,* my interest was always in writing for boys. Added to my magazine work I have written no less than six radio shows, among them Jack Armstrong, Og, Son of Fire, and a serial dramatization of *Treasure Island.* I have also done several motion pictures directed especially at the boys' field, and of course I have been closely associated with both the Local and National Council of the Boy Scouts of America.

Alice Dalgliesh

October 7, 1893-

AUTHOR OF

Relief's Rocker, America Travels, America Begins, The Blue Teapot, A Book for Jennifer, The Silver Pencil, Etc.

Autobiographical sketch of Alice Dalgliesh:

WHEN I was a little girl I lived in the southern part of the island of Trinidad in the West Indies. My home was a big rambling old house on the side of a hill. From the veranda we looked across the sea to the mountains of South America. There were always boats anchored in the bay and I was never tired of looking at them. Somehow I never can keep the sea and ships out of my stories. Ships have always had a special interest for me because of the sea-faring tradition in my family.

In the dry season I played out of doors most of the time, but in the rainy season there was always plenty of time for reading. Even now when I see *Alice in Wonderland* or *The Swiss Family Robinson* I think of the patter of raindrops on a corrugated iron roof. I liked to read almost everything: children's books and grown-up books. My father was Scotch, my mother English, and my father's Scottish books were my favorites. We had a whole shelf of Sir Walter Scott's novels and I liked to hear my father tell how "Wattie Scott" used to go over from Abbotsford to my great-grandfather's farm to sit in the kitchen with the shepherds and sheep dogs and exchange stories.

Next best to reading I liked to "pretend" and the hill at the back of the house, with its tangled tropical growth, was a fine place for playing "explorer." We did not seem to mind the fact that snakes quite frequently wriggled across our path. It was all a part of the game! We built fires and cooked out of doors, we played "desert island" and built huts of boards that we found.

When I was thirteen years old we went to live in England and there I went to Wimbledon Hill School. It was quite hard for me to get into the ways of a big English

Dalgliesh: *dal GLEESH*

ALICE DALGLIESH

school but I was very proud of my blue serge school uniform and school hatband. I loved summer vacations on the south coast, and the biggest thrill of all was to visit the places that made English history really mean something. I don't think I shall ever forget the first time I went to Canterbury Cathedral. It was almost as thrilling as the first time I saw snow—my first Christmas in England.

I began writing stories when I was six years old and kept on writing them. The second year I was in England I won a prize for a story sent to the children's page of a magazine, a five-pound box of chocolates! Filled with enthusiasm I wrote more stories and won two more prizes. Finally the editor of the magazine suggested that I had written enough stories!

When I was nineteen I decided that I would be a kindergarten teacher. I thought that would be one way to find out more about writing for children. So I came to America and took my kindergarten training at Pratt Institute in Brooklyn. I was too busy to write stories then, but I found out how much I liked to tell them. During the first year of my teaching I had charge of a story hour in a settlement house, a stimulating experience for I had a group of very lively Italian children of all ages.

I took my bachelor's degree in education at Teachers College, Columbia University, and taught in elementary grades for several years. Then I accepted a position in Horace Mann Kindergarten, took my master's degree in English, and began teaching a course in children's literature in Teachers College.

This course I still teach, although I have given up kindergarten work to become children's book editor for Charles Scribner's Sons. I have also been in charge of reviews of children's books in the *Parents' Magazine*. A few years ago I became an American citizen.

My first book was *A Happy School Year*, a little reader telling of the doings of my first grade children. My three books of Sandy Cove stories grew out of summers at Sandy Cove, Nova Scotia. "Roundabout" was the name of my cottage there. *A Book for Jennifer* owes its English background to my family background in that country. *The Silver Pencil* and *Along Janet's Road* are partly autobiographical, and use the backgrounds of four countries. Some of my stories are also set in Connecticut, where, in Brookfield, I have a two-hundred-year-old house the name of which is "Three Fires."

I think that writing books for children is the most rewarding experience that anyone can have, and part of the reward is letters from children.

Hawthorne Daniel

January 20, 1890-

AUTHOR OF

The Gauntlet of Dunmore, The Honor of Dunmore, Ships of the Seven Seas, The Shadow of the Sword, Etc.

Autobiographical sketch of Hawthorne Daniel:

SUCH biographical facts as relate to myself have always seemed highly unimportant to me. Perhaps that is why most of them have become so dim and misty in my memory. Just why anyone should care to know that I was born in Norfolk, Nebraska, on January 20, 1890, is more than I can see, and as a matter of fact, I imagine that very few *do* care. That my father's family has lived in Virginia and North Carolina since very early in the seventeenth century has mildly interested me, for it seemed to put my roots reasonably deep in American history, especially as my mother's family has lived in Pennsylvania, Ohio, and

Nebraska for almost as long a time. But for any but the most obvious of the details of these genealogies I am invariably forced to turn to my sister, who has them all at her finger tips.

My earliest recollection is of being taken by my eldest sister to the railroad station at Norfolk Junction in order to see the troops from Fort Omaha or Fort Crook, or both, go through on a train in order to put down some threatened Indian troubles not so very far from where we lived. That was, I believe, in 1893, but I doubt if the Indians really offered much of a threat. From that time on I recall incidents here and there— all unimportant.

Few towns in the United States are farther from salt water than Norfolk, Nebraska, and I have always imagined that that was the reason for my interest in the sea. It was just about the farthest thing off. None of my family, so far as I have ever heard, had been to sea. But by the time the Spanish-American War had come I had definitely decided that I would be a sailor, and by the time it was over I had as definitely decided that I was going to the Naval Academy at Annapolis.

By that time, however, we were living in Charlottesville, Virginia, where my brother was attending the University of Virginia. My father, who was an M. D. from Baltimore College, had decided when his eldest son was ready for college to return

to his own Alma Mater (by this time become Johns Hopkins) for certain post-graduate work. Hence the family's move to Charlottesville. My father's ambition, however, was not realized for he died within a few months of the time we had made the move.

When I was twelve, we returned to Nebraska—to Omaha, this time—and five years later I was appointed to the Naval Academy. My naval career, however, was destined to be short. Entering the Academy with the class of 1912, I was within two months, sent to the hospital with a bad knee which, two months later, caused the unfeeling authorities to request my resignation. I next tried to study mechanical engineering at Iowa State College, but that lasted only one year. This time my health broke down, and for three years I did little enough. I tried to be a farmer in Canada, with results excellent for my health and bad for the farm. I spent a little time on a Texas ranch. I got an odd job or two, and somehow—to this day I do not know just why or how— I began to think about writing.

The result was that in 1914 I left for New York and Columbia University. That year I sold one or two things to the old *Outlook* and in the summer of 1915 I tried my hand as a reporter on the *Omaha Bee*, returning to New York and Columbia University in the autumn.

This time I also attended New York University, and became a sort of part-time assistant to Edward Mott Woolley, as well. I am inclined to believe, now, that I never regularly completed the second semester, that year, either at Columbia, or at New York University. What I *do* remember is that I met Arthur Page and French Strother, the editor and managing editor, respectively, of *World's Work*, sold them an article, and got a job, through them, in the circulation department of Doubleday, Page & Company.

The next spring the United States entered the World War, and a month before the actual event I enrolled in the Naval Reserve, with the rank of ensign. Having been assigned to the converted yacht "Harvard," I was fortunate to be a part of the first American fighting force to sail for France.

My luck was still bad, however. A few months after we arrived in France, I was ordered to the Brooklyn Naval Hospital and shortly thereafter had to resign from the Navy for the second time.

HAWTHORNE DANIEL

Returning to Doubleday, Page & Company, I found that a position on the editorial staff of *World's Work* had been saved for me, and for four months or so I tried to fill it. The War was on, of course, so I tried to get in the service again, and succeeded—this time as a private in the Tank Corps. I was commissioned a lieutenant, however, and assigned to the 303d Heavy Tank Battalion, the first battalion to be sent overseas.

We trained in England—in Dorset—and while mapping the countryside I became familiar with the region in which three of my children's books have been laid. I did not write them, however, until eight years later.

Our battalion reached France in September 1918 and failed to get into action, and in March 1919 I was again at my desk on *World's Work*.

I now began writing more than I ever had before. Magazine articles were my major writing activity, but during my evenings I began a novel, *In the Favour of the King*, which was published in 1922—with more success, I must admit, than it deserved.

That year, also, I married Nelle M. Ryan, of Omaha, Nebraska, and began (in my spare time) my second book, *Ships of the Seven Seas*, for which Franklin D. Roosevelt wrote the introduction. This has always been my pet book, for I have never overcome my youthful interest in the sea, and though I have passed it by in this sketch, I had, at odd times, knocked about the water to some extent.

And now things began to change. I left *World's Work* in 1923 to become managing editor of *Boys' Life*. In 1925 I resigned from *Boys' Life* in order to "free lance." Then it was that I wrote my first juvenile book, *The Gauntlet of Dunmore*, and, somewhat rapidly, wrote a number of others. I wrote serials, short stories, articles, and books, juveniles and others. My wife and I lived and worked in New York, in Vermont, and in Florida. We traveled here and there, and altogether did what one might have expected.

Then, at the end of 1927, I became editor of *Natural History Magazine* and Curator of Printing and Publishing at the American Museum of Natural History. In 1936 I became managing editor of the *Commentator*, resigning early in 1939, since when I have devoted myself exclusively to writing and lecturing. In 1945, as a war correspondent accredited to both the Navy and the Army, I spent several months among the islands of the Pacific and the islands of the East Indies, visited Australia, Ceylon, India, and China, and went on from there to Iran, Egypt, and Europe, returning to the United States by way of England and Iceland. Two of the books I wrote during the war, incidentally, are *Islands of the Pacific* and *Islands of the East Indies*, and in them I attempted the somewhat ambitious task of giving the major facts about *all* the islands in those two immense areas.

Since returning from overseas I have devoted most of my time to writing books, with an occasional magazine article thrown in for good measure, and have visited every state in the Union in the course of my lectures.

My wife and I, with our daughter Nancy Nelle, live in Westchester County, New York, about half an hour from New York City, and as I write this I am wondering when I shall get around to writing another juvenile novel. Soon, I hope, for I have been writing about the world's problems more than enough of late, and it would be something of a vacation to do another historical adventure. I hope I'll get to it before too long.

James Daugherty

June 1, 1889-

AUTHOR AND ILLUSTRATOR
Daniel Boone, Andy and the Lion, Abraham Lincoln, Poor Richard, Etc.

Autobiographical sketch of James Daugherty:

MY earliest recollections are of an Indiana farm in winter and a grim and terrible one-room school which I bitterly attended.—Of a sleepy little southern Ohio town in the corn belt.—Of red cattle and spotted hogs and big-hearted farm folks.—Of squirrel hunting in the oak groves and bass fishing in the little holes and creeks and forks with my uncles and grandfather—who looked like an old eagle with his Roman nose and beetling brows and one eye. But he had the tender heart of a woman and saved me often from a well-deserved licking. He was full of tall stories of Daniel Boone and his buckskin men, handed down by

Daugherty: *DAWR i tee*

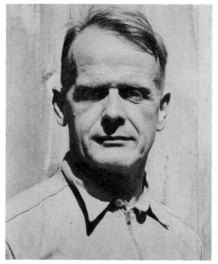

JAMES DAUGHERTY

word of mouth and not out of books. They blended well with the Negro songs and stories of my dear fun-loving Virginian mother.

My remembrance of the people of this world is of a gentle folk loving good books and gay talk and very hospitable, not the brutal and savage types of a certain kind of Midwestern fiction.

When I was about nine a government job brought my father to Washington, D.C., as he had been ruined at farming. I remember the zest of the fiery hot summers spent in the grand old Potomac and sewer-fed Rock Creek and crumbling Alexandria and Georgetown. My formal schooling was of the public school variety including high school, to which first and last I put up unflagging resistance.

Throughout my youth my father and I were inseparable companions. He was instinctively a scholar and had graduated from the University of Michigan. A splendid reader "outloud," he poured the whole stream of English and American literature from Chaucer to Mark Twain into my enraptured childish consciousness, during long hours, even days, while I drew pictures as the splendour rolled by. He also directed me to the Library of Congress and the night class of the Corcoran Art School. At that time this unique school charged no fees whatever. I first encountered painting in the bright and speckled guise of Mr. Hugh

Breckenridge, the fine American impressionist, and I spent my first full-time year away from home at the Philadelphia Art Academy.

After this, two romantic years in London, where my father was an agent for the Department of Agriculture and where I nominally studied under Frank Brangwyn. Of this robust person I stood in such awe that I learned practically nothing of the little it concerned him to impart. But to be eighteen and footloose free in England, France, and Italy, in the carefree pre-war days!

In London I first read Walt Whitman and took fire from his vision of America, and shook the dust of Europe permanently from my feet and returned to the States arrogant and ignorant. I took a studio atop a waterfront factory near Brooklyn Heights with a sweeping view of the harbor, city, and bridge that even Walt never dreamed.

Then came the Armory show and Modern Art, now so mellow; and me going cubist with a new wife and baby to support; weary soliciting of magazine editors for illustration; and drudging at advertising drawings—a waste of precious years too well known to many American artists.

Then the [First World] War and Baltimore and Newport News, camouflaging ships of the seven seas along milling docks or in the deafening roar of ship yards. Life was real again.

Coming back to the dingy studios of Fourteenth Street in New York and the more congenial Washington Square of the old days was another start and the game more interesting with the opportunity of painting murals in the new moving picture palaces of the late Mr. Loew. It was an exciting time. We all were protagonists of an art theory and had the courage of other people's convictions—mostly Mr. Matisse's. Of the vivid friendships of that time, memory of my friend Henry Reuterdahl remains a heroic and combative spirit devoted, and practically a martyr to the American Navy, and one of our genuine illustrators of distinction; a great-hearted giant in spirit and body.

Though loving New York we decided to take to the country, and found a sufficiently ruined cabin on a snug Connecticut hillside. And there I have stuck in comparative peace and perfect quiet. About this time I showed my work to May Massee, then of the Doubleday Page Company, who to my amazement handed me Stewart Edward White's *Daniel Boone,* remarking "Do what you like, have a good time, and God bless you." God did his part and I did my best, and I have illustrated some fifty books since with increasing enjoyment. I have also been happy in working for the *New Yorker, Forum,* and *Golden Book.* I have found the publishers for whom I have worked intelligent, liberal, and genuinely working for the really fine thing. More power to them!

Under the New Deal I had the unique experience of painting some thousands of feet of mural in a large Connecticut high school (Stamford) and the fine privilege of daily contact with some 2,500 students and teachers, not a few of whom I have drawn and painted.

Young America—so gay—so beautiful—very poised, very searching, and very patient with a blundering elder genertaion. In their good sense and good cheer may they find the key to a new world of sanity and peace and beauty.

*   *   *

Already one of the best-known contemporary American illustrators, James Daugherty in 1938 turned author with *Andy and the Lion.* This was followed by his own *Daniel Boone,* which won the Newbery Medal as the outstanding children's book of its year, and such other favorites as his *Poor Richard* and *Abraham Lincoln,* all illustrated, of course, by himself. His wife, Sonia V. Daugherty is also a well-known author for children, and James Daugherty has illustrated most of her books. They have one son and live in the Connecticut hills near Westport, not far out of New York.

A friend has described "Jimmie" Daugherty in these words: "Tall, muscular, straggling, possessed of arms and legs that defy all dancing school theories of grace but that never appear awkward, alive with a vitality and a rhythm that color and shade his personality, he might have stepped from any one of the number of books he has illustrated." And his fellow artist Lynd Ward has written: "In the renaissance in book illustration that has taken place in America in the past dozen years, Daugherty is an outstanding figure. He has grown with those years and now stands in a kind of symbolic relation to our culture, his talent firmly

rooted in American experience, his creative motivation well attuned to the techniques of our age, his voice well able to speak out for the values of democratic life."

Ingri & Edgar Parin d'Aulaire

See *Aulaire, Ingri & Edgar Parin d'*

Julia Davis

July 23, 1900-

AUTHOR OF

Stonewall, Vaino: A Boy of Finland, The Swords of the Vikings, Mountains Are Free, No Other White Men, Etc.

Autobiographical sketch of Julia Davis:

I WAS born in Clarksburg, West Virginia, a town in the foothills of the Alleghenies, and divided my time between that place and a farm in the Shenandoah Valley until I was nineteen.

After two years at Wellesley, I went to England for a year, returned to New York, and graduated at Barnard.

Marriage took me to Denmark for two years, where I gathered the material for my first book, *Swords of the Vikings,* which appeared in 1927. A book on Finland, *Vaino,* is also a result of that Scandinavian visit, and because of the nature of the ma-

JULIA DAVIS

terial I found myself launched as an author for children.

In the course of some rather hectic years I published five other children's books, largely on historical subjects: *Mountains Are Free, Stonewall, Remember and Forget, No Other White Men,* and *Peter Hale.* I also worked for five years as children's agent in an adoption bureau.

The years since 1939 have been largely devoted to bringing up four children who came into my hands in different ways. Two adult books have appeared, *The Sun Climbs Slow,* and *The Shenandoah,* for the Rivers of America series, also a number of short stories and articles.

My husband has had some very interesting war experiences, and since his discharge from the army has been representing the McGraw Hill Publishing Company in England, where I have spent some time with him. We hope before too long to re-establish ourselves in New York, and in a cottage which we have bought at Stonington, Connecticut.

* * *

Prior to the middle 1930's, Miss Davis' books were signed Julia Davis Adams. She is now Mrs. Paul West in private life.

Lavinia R. Davis

December 7, 1909-

AUTHOR OF

Roger and the Fox; Melody, Muttonbone, and Sam; Hobby Horse Hill; Etc.

Autobiographical sketch of Lavinia Riker Davis:

I WAS born in New York City, the daughter of Samuel and Frances Townsend Riker. I don't remember it, possibly because it was quite a while ago and my earliest recollections are concerned with a chipmunk approaching the sand box in Red Bank, New Jersey, where by family owned a farm. The chipmunk was pointed out to me by Minna Wolfe, who was the family nurse and the dearest and most important figure in my childhood. She taught me to save my pennies, to keep relatively clean, and she also listened to my earliest fictional efforts, which sometimes took the form of stories and frequently of quite thumping lies.

I announced to Minna, and I believe to my parents, at a tender age that I intended

LAVINIA R. DAVIS

to become an author. I put it on a nice level and said a poet, "like Shakespeare." I may have heard of the Bard from my older sisters but had most certainly not read him, having confined by attentions to Beatrix Potter and Thornton Burgess, and the "Goop" books, not to mention *Slovenly Peter,* and the tales of Andersen and Grimm. These last were read aloud to me by Minna in German, which language I must have understood at that time.

I attended the Brearley School in New York beginning in the primary and graduating (actually I was home with scarlet fever on the big day) in May 1928. I alternately loved and loathed the Brearley, which emotions I regard as natural toward a school where the teaching was (and still is) the best to be had and the pupils are made to *work.* I still harbored a desire to write though I was no longer vocal about it and outwardly devoted myself to the Horse, riding in Red Bank through the long summer days and during winter afternoons at the old New York Riding Club, now a memory like the dinosaur. Even the Horse paled compared to my interest in the social whirl, between the ages of sixteen and nineteen.

On January 11, 1930, I married Wendell Davis, a New York lawyer. At that point my life really began, not only because I was happier than I had ever imagined possible but also because I began to write. I worked on *Fortune* magazine and attended courses in juvenile writing at Columbia.

After leaving *Fortune* I did magazine articles and short articles for country newspapers on a free-lance basis and then gradually began writing fiction, starting with short stories for various church school publications. Our eldest son, Edward Shippen, was born January 1932 and our second son, Wendell Junior, in June 1933.

A banner year was 1936. My first book was published and our first daughter, Vicky, was born. Another major step of that period was the purchase of a farm in Brookfield, Connecticut, which we first used as a weekend and summer base out of New York but which is now our year-round home.

During the war my husband was in the air corps and we followed him around the country as much as we could. When he was stationed at Wright Field, Dayton, Ohio, I gathered the material for *Stand Fast and Reply,* and when he was transferred to southern New Jersey I found the background for *A Sea Between* and two adult mysteries. The Davis "we" by this time also included another, Gaily, born in 1939, and a son, Campbell, born in 1941, and a much loved Norwegian nurse called Rene. The youngest member of the family, Frederick Townsend Davis, did not appear until we had moved back to Brookfield in 1946.

I now divide my working day between writing, doing the family cooking, and harassing my long-suffering children. For diversion I like swimming, skating, skiing, and riding, and am equally inept at all of them. I also love to go off on bicycle trips with my husband and sons and am not averse to going to the theatre or seeing friends in the Big City any time the opportunity offers.

* * *

Mrs. Davis writes: "I put in [the above biography] the names of my six children as I am proud of them, but decided not to include the names of all my books lest it sound like one of the begat chapters in the Bible." She lists almost twenty books she has written, commenting that she thinks "the list is fairly accurate, but," she adds, "if you want to be sure you had best check with my publishers as the only book I'm ever really interested in is the one on which

I am currently working." She has done several Crime Club books, for adults, and some half dozen of her juvenile stories have been selections of the Junior Literary Guild.

Mary Gould Davis

February 13, 1882-

AUTHOR AND STORYTELLER
The Truce of the Wolf, The Handsome Donkey, The Girls' Book of Verse, Etc.

Autobiographical sketch of Mary Gould Davis:

I WAS born in a square brick house on an elm-shaded street in Bangor, Maine, on February 13, 1882.

There were eight of us children, five boys and three girls. I was the seventh. From as far back as I can remember my highest ambition was to be included in the things that my brothers did, the games that they played, the books that they read, even the lessons that they studied.

We younger children had an Irish nurse who was devoted to us and to my mother and whom we loved and trusted. She had a share of the Celtic humor and imagination and her stories, the games that she invented for us, were among the joys of our childhood.

I have always traced my enthusiasm for good mystery stories back to Mary's invention of a mythical old man who "lived in the strawberry patch." Just back of the house there was a terrace that was planted with strawberries, currant bushes, and raspberry bushes. A low door into the cellar opened onto it. Mary would dress herself in my father's old clothes and appear suddenly in the cellar or out in the garden. Sometimes she left scraps of food on the cellar shelves, or clothes thrown across a chair, as though someone had been living there. Sometimes she made strange noises that drew us fearful, but delighting in our fears, from play. Evidently he was a kindly old man, because little gifts of "goodies" and things that we needed for our playhouse would appear on the cellar shelves for us to find and appropriate. We knew all the time, of course, that the old man was Mary. But I can still feel the thrill of "the old man who lived in the strawberry patch."

When I was seven a very exciting thing happened. My father's work took him to

MARY GOULD DAVIS

the Cumberland Mountains in Kentucky and we all went with him. It was a dramatic change from a New England city, from a New England tradition that went back for many generations, to a little, raw, "boom" town high up in the Southern mountains, where the streets were just beginning to be cut through, the bridges over the narrow river just beginning to be built, and where half of the people lived in tents instead of houses. The house that my father had built for us was something like the house in Bangor—red brick, square, and comfortable looking. But the life that we led there was entirely different. There were no schools in the little new town, so the older children went North to boarding school and, later, to college, and we younger ones had a governess. She led, I am afraid, a rather hard life!

The pine and chestnut woods that stretched away behind the house, the mysterious, narrow roads that led up into the mountains were so tempting, the care of our dogs and cats and chickens and horses so important—lessons seemed trivial in comparison. We were out of doors all day long, winter and summer, exploring the lovely valley, learning to know the strange, remote people to whom the mountains on our horizon line were home.

Many of the things that had been in the Maine house had come South with us—the familiar furniture and china, linen and silver, the bronze statue of Mercury and the marble Ariadne that had been my mother's wedding presents, the pictures, and—best of all—the books. We were all great readers and I "inherited" from the older members of the family all sorts and kinds of books. Perhaps the most precious among them were the old bound volumes of *St. Nicholas* and *Harper's Round Table.* In their pages I first met Rudyard Kipling and Frank Stockton, Howard Pyle and Mary Mapes Dodge. Through them I learned to know the Palmer Cox "Brownies," the "Cheerful Cats and Other Animated Animals," and E. B. Bensell's whimsical drawings for "The Poor Count's Christmas" and "How the Aristocrats Sailed Away." My mother read aloud to us every evening and often in the early morning we younger ones would slip into her room and get into bed beside her to listen to our favorite poems, not read but *said* in her warm, friendly voice that seemed to give new meaning to each word. There are whole volumes of poetry that I cannot read now without hearing her voice.

We went North often for the summer and one year, when we were passing through Boston on our way to Kennebunkport, my mother took me to a bookshop and left me beside a table piled high with children's books.

"You may choose one," she said. "Any one that you want." But before she went off to find books for the other members of the family she took down from a shelf and laid beside me a little, fat, brown book. I was already deep in an English edition of Perrault's fairy tales with lovely colored pictures. I wanted badly to have it for my own, but I knew that mother had put the little brown book there because she liked it herself, so I took it up and looked it over. The pages were closely printed, the type small, the few pictures not very attractive. It was a long time before I could lay the tempting Perrault aside. But I finally went to mother with the little brown book in my hand. "I have decided to take this," I said. It was Louisa Alcott's *Little Women.*

We went North again to live, first in Brooklyn and then in Manhattan, in 1896. And New York has been home to me ever since. With my haphazard education I was far behind most girls of my age, so I was sent to a private school. I had a hard time at first with mathematics and science, but an unusual teacher in literature and history opened new horizons to me. I graduated, took post-graduate work in Latin and literature, and was ready for college in the sophomore year. But, for some reason, the idea of going away to college did not appeal to me. Perhaps because I was reluctant to leave my rather exciting family. There were a few years of travel and idleness, and then I suddenly decided that I wanted "to go out into the world and seek my fortune." My father was not very enthusiastic over the idea, but my mother was too wise to oppose it.

So, one day in the autumn, I went to the Brooklyn Public Library and applied for a position on the staff. The months of training and testing were difficult ones. Yet deep down underneath the problems and perplexities, the mental and physical weariness, there was a strong faith in this work that I had chosen to do. From the first the boys and girls who came and went in the branch libraries interested me keenly. In those early days I got from them far more than I gave. Their reaction to the books that I knew and loved fascinated me. Before many months had passed I knew that I had "found my job."

Later on, when we had settled down on Manhattan and I had become a member of the staff of the New York Public Library, this desire to share good books with boys and girls, to find them the things that they really wanted in the best and the most enduring form, grew and deepened until it became not only my "job" but my greatest interest.

From the days when my mother had read us "Hansel and Grethel" and "Puss in Boots" I had loved the folktales. The desire came to me to really study them, to trace them back to their own country, to see with my own eyes their actual settings. My first journey in search of them, this time seeking the King Arthur legends and "The Song of Roland," was in 1923. Five times since then I have crossed the ocean and each time a group, or sometimes more than one group of the folktales have become living records rather than stories of a dead past.

One year I had six months of freedom and I spent them tracing the Italian folktales. Up in Tuscany and Umbria I came across the stories that make up the volume called *The Truce of the Wolf,* following St. Francis for the title story from Assisi to Gubbio, from Gubbio to lovely, remote La Verna. Up in the High Apennines I first met Nanni the wise donkey, Assunta the cow, and old Benedetto the cobbler. Two years later I went back to Northern Italy with the artist (Emma Brock) who drew the pictures for *The Handsome Donkey.* We lived for a time in a little village above Bologna called Vidiciatico. Guided by a young Italian girl who knew the mountains well, we tramped the roads, wandered through the tiny villages, talked to the peasants and the shepherds, made friends with the children and the dogs and the donkeys, and fixed firmly in my mind and in Miss Brock's notebook the background for the story.

In the summer of 1935 I went to Spain and met Miss Brock in Granada, where we lived in an old drover's inn on the road to the mountains and worked together on a collection of Spanish folktales that had been recorded by Dr. Boggs of the University of North Carolina. We called the book, which was published in the following year, *Three Golden Oranges.* In 1939 I traveled by slow stages to the north end of the Island of Skye, seeking the Gaelic folktales and the legends of very early Christian saints. There the Second World War caught me and I got back to New York on the first American liner to cross the Atlantic while the United States was still neutral. In 1945 I collaborated with Ernest Kalibala in writing a series of his native folktales of the Baganda Tribe in East Africa. The hero of *Wakaima and the Clay Man* is probably the original of Br'er Rabbit in *Uncle Remus.* In 1946 I wrote a short biography of the English artist, Randolph Caldecott, which was published in celebration of his hundredth birthday.

In 1945 I retired from the New York Public Library to go on with my work as editor of Books for Young People, a department of the *Saturday Review of Literature.*

Robert Davis

1881-1949

AUTHOR OF

*Gid Granger, Partners of Powder Hole,
Padre Porko, Etc.*

Autobiographical sketch of Robert Davis, written for THE JUNIOR BOOK OF AUTHORS a few months before he died:

WHEN I was teaching history at Middlebury College, Vermont, I calculated that my parents and four grandparents had all been born and lived within twenty-seven miles of Middlebury; the preceding generations, so far as we could discover, had lived nearer still.

When my cousin, the well-known Bob Davis, was editor and columnist on the New York *Sun*, I contributed a good many yarns to his column, "Bob Davis Reveals." We were both oldest sons of home missionaries, his father having gone to Wisconsin and mine to Michigan. Neither of us ever felt we had lived up to our ancestry.

My life seems to have fallen into two parts—before and after "the accident." In 1929 a train, at a grade crossing, ran into my truck. I was in bed eleven months [at his farm in France—ED.] and the doctors said, "The man will never move again except in a wheel chair." But I have a wonderful wife. We had a houseful of children and for a farmer to be crippled looks like the end of things. I used to lie there and worry about the taxes and what would happen to us. She said, "Why don't you write something for the Paris New York *Herald Tribune?*" She sent two dollars to Larry Hills, the editor of the paper, saying that if he got a piece from me he was to send me the two dollars and a letter of thanks. That's the way it worked out. That first two dollars opened a new door. Before I was able to walk I was writing the daily editorial.

Our children used to sit on my bed after supper and we'd tell stories, particularly about a wise old pig who spoke all the languages. We called him Professor Pig. Before we knew it, the children would knock off in the afternoon, go into a huddle, and contrive new scenarios for the Professor. As we live near the frontier and many words of the patois are Spanish, when my wife pushed us to write down some of

ROBERT DAVIS

the stories, we gave a Spanish slant to his name—Padre Porko. It's funny how, sometimes, what seems to set you back gives you a boost.

At present I am in Andorra—the proudest and most self-conscious little republic on earth—fifteen miles long. I am just finishing a yarn for teen-age boys called *Smuggler's Son.* The two occupations of agriculture (during the growing season) and storytelling (during the winter season) fit nicely together. The one tends to keep a man healthy and the other to prevent him from dying at the top.

The one thing important about my life is the fact that when war broke in France, in 1938, I had 332 pure-bred Holstein females, the biggest herd of the breed, so far as we knew, in Europe.

* * *

Robert Davis was born in Beverly, Massachusetts. Descended from five generations of Congregational ministers, he attended Union Theological Seminary in New York, was assistant to Henry Van Dyke, and then for ten years pastor of a wealthy suburban church. Going to Europe in the First World War he was commissioner for the American Red Cross, chief editorial writer of the Paris edition of the New York *Herald Tribune,* and a correspondent and reporter in thirty-one countries. For nineteen years he did not return to the United States.

In spite of Mr. Davis' multitudinous duties during this period, his real interest lay in his dairy farm and vineyard in France, his wife—a Greek from Constantinople, and his children. His four sons were interested, respectively, in the tapestry business, factory management, skiing instruction, and architecture. His three daughters went to school all over the world, and speak French, German, Greek, and English.

From 1932 to 1936 Mr. Davis was director of the American Library in Paris. "But," he wrote, "it was more a business reorganization. Nevertheless a stack of lovely young librarians spent a decorative six months in Paris. Today they must be topflight administrators somewhere between the Atlantic and the Pacific. We were proud of them. They gave a very nice impression to the Europeans of what a fairly serious-minded American girl can be."

In 1937, 1938, and 1939 Mr. Davis was in Spain writing a series of articles for the *Herald-Tribune*. While there he heard the folk tales that were incorporated into *Padre Porko*. In the spring of 1940 he was on a similar assignment in North Africa, and took several weeks off to visit the Berber tribesmen and collect material for his second children's book, *Pepperfoot of Thursday Market*. The manuscript was sunk in the Mediterranean and had to be rewritten from memory. As an American was then persona non grata in Morocco, Mr. Davis was soon forced to return to the United States.

With the fall of France he lost his farm, his cows, and his cellar of venerable wine so carefully chosen for his old age. Worse, his wife and three daughters were virtually interned, as the farm was in the occupied zone. After months of anxiety, however, they reached the United States, the only passengers on a small freighter.

The work of twenty years lost, Mr. Davis started at sixty as professor of history at Middlebury. There he stayed until he reached the compulsory retirement age. (He was by that time acting president.) He decided to join his family in France, whither they had gone after the war. Over there he discovered that not only was his vineyard still workable, but the Germans had made a pillbox of his house by adding four feet of reinforced concrete to the already thick walls, with the result that it should last another three hundred years!

Robert Davis was very like his own Padre Porko—plump and pink, jolly and sympathetic, a rare storyteller with a great interest in people, animals, and food. With masterly understatement he said of himself, "I have never arrived anywhere, but I've had a wonderful time." He had two rules, one from his Vermont background the other from his continental life: to pay cash; to drop a job the minute it ceased to be fun.

In the summer of 1949, on a visit to Proctor, Vermont, from France, where he still made his home, Robert Davis, working on the revision of his new book, *Smuggler's Son*, died on September 25.

Marguerite de Angeli

March 14, 1889-

AUTHOR AND ILLUSTRATOR OF

Thee, Hannah!, Elin's Amerika, Henner's Lydia, The Door in the Wall, Etc.

MARGUERITE LOFFT was born in Lapeer, Michigan, the daughter of S. G. and Ruby A. (Tuttle) Lofft. She was educated in the public schools of Lapeer and Philadelphia. "As far back as my memory goes," she writes, "there was always an itch to draw, the longing to put things down in words." Her earliest specific memories of Lapeer include "large family gatherings at which there might be as many as forty-five people, excellent food,

MARGUERITE DE ANGELI

de Angeli: *de AN jel ee*

and much laughter." She remembers listening to her grandfather tell about his home in Sheerness, England, where for generations the Loffts made giant ship anchors.

Encouraged by a teacher, Marguerite had dreams of becoming a singer. For a time she sang contralto in a church choir, but she met John de Angeli, who convinced her that no career could be so satisfying as being married and raising a family. They were married in 1910 and had five children, John, Arthur, Nina, H. Edward, and Maurice. While the first three were small she began to study drawing with a neighbor, an illustrator. After a year of work her first commissions came, and they were only a beginning. By 1934 she was illustrating stories she herself had written.

As commissions increased so did the family. Both kept her busy. "One child was never happy unless near me in the studio," she once wrote. "He would stand at the foot of the stairs and call incessantly until he was brought upstairs and put into his pen. Quiet reigned for the few moments it took me to get back to work, then miserable wails began again. When I put the pen around myself and the easel and let the child have the studio in which to roam, all was peace once more."

Mrs. de Angeli has always had an interest in the foreign born and in minorities. Among her books on the subject are *Henner's Lydia*, dealing with a Pennsylvania Dutch family; *Elin's Amerika*, the story of a little girl who came here with the first Swedish people in 1643; *Up the Hill*, set in a Pennsylvania mining town, and telling of a Polish boy who wants to become an artist; *Jared's Island*, in which a Scottish boy, wrecked off New Jersey in 1760 and rescued by a young Quaker, later runs away to live with Indians; and *Bright April*, a Junior Literary Guild selection, treating the later adjustment of a Negro girl who first meets race prejudice at the age of ten, when a young white girl refuses to sit next to her at a Brownie party.

The de Angelis live in Toms River, New Jersey. Marguerite de Angeli has blue eyes and brown hair beginning to gray; she is just above medium height. Their five children have grown up and nearly all are married, so Mrs. de Angeli feels that life is beginning again with the grandchildren.

In 1950 Mrs. de Angeli's *The Door in the Wall* was awarded the American Library Association's Newbery Medal as the most distinguished American contribution to children's literature of the previous year.

Walter De La Mare
April 25, 1873-
AUTHOR OF
Peacock Pie, Songs of Childhood, Down-Adown-Derry, Mr. Bumps and His Monkey, Etc.

WALTER JOHN DE LA MARE was born in England in the little village of Charlton, in Kent. His father, James Edward De La Mare, churchwarden and brother of a clergyman, descended from the famous Huguenot of that name, died when Walter was three. His mother, Lucy Sophia Browning De La Mare, was the daughter of a naval surgeon who helped reform the treatment of passengers on convict ships bound for Australia, and was related to the poet Browning.

The dreamy boy was always somewhat shy and his school days were not very happy. The world of literature first opened to him through a volume of *Gulliver's Travels*. When at St. Paul's Cathedral Choir School at London the fascination of print led him to found, when only sixteen, the *Choristers' Journal*, a small weekly, for the early numbers of which he did much of the writing, running it off by duplicating in some form. After a few months it was found possible to print it and it was made a permanent monthly organ of the school. The following year De La Mare left the school and went into the London office of the Anglo-American Oil Company, in the statistical department. At this monotonous work he spent the next eighteen years, saying of it, "I think that one can find an interest in any task which has *got* to be done." He continued to write stories and poems, however, often at his desk, and at one time he got out two issues of a company magazine bound with brown paper, he being the editor, publisher, and main contributor. At this time he looked the poet, imitating the students of the Latin Quarter with abundant wavy hair, low turndown collar with a flowing black tie, and a broad flat-brim hat.

His first story, "Kismet," was published in a magazine five years after he left school,

De La Mare: *del a MAIR*

WALTER DE LA MARE

and from that time his writings appeared regularly in magazines. Then, and for a number of years, he used the pen name Walter Ramal, an anagram of his own name. At thirty-five, his financial position being improved by a Civil pension of a hundred pounds a year, supplemented by what he earned by reviewing, he retired from business to give all his time to writing.

Songs of Childhood, his first book, was a volume of verse, nursery rhymes, fanciful, gay and tender lyrics and songs, originally written for his own children. It was soon followed by *Henry Brocken*, the story of a boy's adventures in lands peopled by characters from literature, and *Poems*, another book of verse for the young. These three were published before his retirement. His poetry, much of it for young people, has won high praise. Among the dozen or more titles are *Peacock Pie*, *A Child's Day*, *Down-Adown-Derry*, *Come Hither*, *Poems for Children*. Louis Untermeyer has said of *Peacock Pie*, "The first third of it contains more inspired and unforgettable nursery rhymes and nonsense lyrics than were ever collected anywhere except in Mother Goose's own anthology."

Approximately half of De La Mare's published work has been prose. His writings include three fairy books: *Crossings*, a play written for a boy's school at Brighton; *Broomsticks*, a group of short stories; and *The Three Mulla-Mulgars*, a story of three monkeys of royal blood who traveled through the jungle to find their hereditary country, the "Valleys of Tishnar." His *Memoirs of a Midget* is perhaps his most noted book of prose, the story of a dwarf told sympathetically and beautifully. It won the James Tait Black Memorial Prize, the most important literary award in England. Some of his other titles in prose are *Stories from the Bible*, *Old Tales Told Again*, and *The Riddle*, containing stories for the young.

The work of De La Mare has much of fantastic imagination, grace, subtleness, elusiveness; much of "otherworldliness" and unseen influences. He has said that "what we see and hear is only the smallest fraction of what is," and that in the world of childhood the faculty for these things is most awake. He writes of the magical, fanciful, dreamy, enchanted, of fairies, mermaids, elves, of the land of "Tishnar," "that which cannot be thought about in words, or told, or expressed. So all the wonderful, secret, and quiet world beyond the Mulgars' lives is Tishnar—winds and stars, too, the endless sea and the endless unknown."

De La Mare is described as of medium height, square build and dark complexion, with "a smile of exceeding sweetness." A retiring man, "more at home in a garden than in a club," he lives with his wife and four children at Taplow, not far from London, in a red brick house on a beautiful hill, with a bay window giving a superb view of Windsor Castle and the English countryside.

Adèle de Leeuw

1899-

AUTHOR OF
Career for Jennifer, Rika, Nobody's Doll, Etc.

Autobiographical sketch of Adèle Louise de Leeuw:

MY mother taught me to read when I was very young, and books from that time on had a fascination for me. A little later I found some discarded notebooks of my father's, and I thought how wonderful it would be to fill those lovely blank pages with writing—my own writing. So I did.

Adèle de Leeuw: *a DEL de LAY oh*

All through my school days in Ohio, where I was born, and in Plainfield, New Jersey, where I still live, I filled innumerable blank pages with poems and stories. My sister, four years younger than I, liked those blank pages, too—only she decided it would be nice to draw on them. Although at first I was highly displeased at having my writings superimposed on, later I began to think that if she were going to draw on what I wrote we ought to collaborate. I used to say, "When we grow up, I'll write books and you will illustrate them." And that's how it turned out to be.

I did not go to college. My parents gave me the choice of going to college or traveling over the world with them, and I chose the traveling. I've never regretted it. The four of us spent long, happy months in South America, in the West Indies, and North and South and East and West in this country; together we stayed in England and France and Holland (where my father was born) and in the Netherlands East Indies. I made notes sometimes—but chiefly I was busy soaking up impressions with my eyes and ears—and Cateau made sketches.

In between our travels I became assistant librarian at the Plainfield Public Library. There I had story hours for children; I told fairy stories and bird tales and adventure stories, and Cateau illustrated them on a big blackboard. Some of my happiest memories are of seeing those rows and rows of upturned faces, and of watching them storm downstairs afterwards to get books with "stories just like that in them." Then I became the secretary to my father, who had an office in New York as a consulting engineer. He was often away, and I had time to write. Those were happy days, too—going out to lunch with him, exploring all New York's little byways, and learning to honor anew the profession of engineering. When Father gave up his office I went into writing seriously—books and stories and articles, travel and poetry; and I've been at it ever since.

Everything I turned out for several years was for adults. Then one day I got a letter from a publisher asking me to call on her. She had been given my book, *The Flavor of Holland*, as a bon voyage gift, and she had found it so helpful during her stay in Holland that she wondered if I couldn't do the same sort of thing—give a picture of a country but in novel form—for young people. I said I'd try, and three novels for girls, based on travel in foreign countries, followed. When it was time for a new book I happened to see a clipping about a young girl who turned a discarded trolley car into a shop, and since I had always had a secret desire to run a bookstore, I combined the two into *A Place for Herself*. This was the first "career" novel, and was the forerunner of a whole series I did on different professions.

In between I've done books for younger children because somehow in writing for them I can imagine I have back again the old story hours.

It's fun to see the copies of my books translated into some foreign language. It's fun to get letters from readers all over the country telling me what they like in some book of mine and telling me, too, about themselves, their ambitions and plans and pets. And it's great fun going about, as my sister and I do together, talking and drawing in grammar and high schools. There really isn't enough time for all the things I'd like to do—making ceramics, taking photographs in color, trying out special recipes—because first of all comes writing. But I wouldn't have it any other way, for through it I've come to know a

ADÈLE DE LEEUW

great many delightful people and to feel that young people all over the world are my friends. That is surely a rich reward for any author.

Cateau de Leeuw

See *de Leeuw, Adèle*

Raymond L. Ditmars

June 20, 1876-May 12, 1942

AUTHOR OF

Thrills of a Naturalist's Quest, The Reptile Book, Strange Animals I Have Known, The Forest of Adventure, Etc.

Autobiographical sketch of Dr. Raymond L. Ditmars, written for THE JUNIOR BOOK OF AUTHORS a few years before his death:

RAYMOND L. DITMARS

AFTER being invited to write a short autobiographical sketch about myself, comes the thought that, in order to start it properly, I should explain that I was born in Newark, New Jersey, and after elementary schooling, graduated from the Barnard Military School in 1891. Soon after, I obtained a position in the American Museum of Natural History, where my work related to mounting and labeling insect specimens. I remained there for five years, then sought more active work as a reporter for the New York *Times*. While on that paper, I was sent to the Bronx to interview the director of the newly formed Zoological Park. That visit ended in Dr. William T. Hornaday finding that I was intensely interested in animals and declaring that I should be at the Park, not with a newspaper.

It seems, however, that there is more I should say about other events that came with the passing of time, one relating to my marriage with Clara Elizabeth Hurd, in February 1903. I have two daughters, Gladys and Beatrice, both married.

Aside from my work at the Park, my principal interest is in writing books and making motion pictures of different kinds of animals. Both record experiences in exploring tropical countries. Much of the motion picture work has been of detailed, scientific kind, recording strange habits of little-known animals, as, for instance, the ways of the vampire bat, studied in Panama during the summer of 1933. When a scientist has accomplished a great deal along such lines, institutions accord him honors of which he is naturally proud. In recognition of scientific work, I have been ·made a· fellow of the New York Academy of Sciences, a fellow of the New York Zoological Society, a life member of the American Museum of Natural History, a corresponding member of the Zoological Society of London, and in 1930 I was awarded the honorary degree of Doctor of Letters by Lincoln Memorial University.

My interest in natural history was strong during my early days in school, and it ran toward snakes. I had managed to capture a few small harmless ones in the northern part of Central Park, in New York City. That portion of the park was quite wild at the time. My parents considered that snakes were best to be seen out of doors, and I was not allowed to retain my specimens more than overnight, when I had to take them back to the park. Finally, they gave me permission to keep a few—and then the collection grew steadily. It also gained some renown, as it seemed a novel thing for a boy to maintain such a collection. Before I was twenty, naturalists in the tropics, knowing of my interest, made gifts of some of the larger kinds. It was then that my parents gave me the entire upper floor of our home, and soon the series of serpents included some of the poisonous kinds I had longed to study. During my newspaper work the collection was maintained, even though I had to care for the snakes at very late hours of the night. When I joined the staff of the Zoological Park, the collection of snakes was presented to that institution.

A few years after coming to the Park, I was also given charge of the collection of mammals, but the snakes, particularly the poisonous ones, remained a source of special study. I designed a method of extracting venom from these creatures, without in any way injuring them. The poison collected was available for chemical investigation and assisted in the development of snake bite serum, which has been of great value in saving many human lives.

Possibly my most exciting experiences, after years of association with different kinds of animals, have been in capturing poisonous serpents and extracting their venom for laboratory use. I have found cobras the most difficult to handle. New investigations are under way in which it is indicated that serpent poisons, much diluted, may prove to be of great benefit in treating certain types of human ailments. The ways of science, however, are slow and cautious about arriving at conclusions, but my boyhood interest in serpents has thus built up along practical lines, and in cooperation with others may be of broad benefit.

* * *

In January 1942 ill health compelled Dr. Ditmar's retirement from active work, and he was made honorary curator of reptiles at the New York Zoological Park (better known as the Bronx Zoo), with which he had been associated since 1899. His health failed to improve, however, and he died in New York City on May 12, 1942 at the age of sixty-five. He was recognized as the outstanding American authority on reptiles.

Beulah Marie Dix

December 25, 1876-

AUTHOR OF

Merrylips, Hugh Gwyeth, Soldier Rigdale, The Fighting Blade, Alison's Lad, Etc.

Autobiographical sketch of Beulah Marie Dix:

MY mother's people, English, Scots, and Irish, were settled before the Revolution in Machias, Maine. My father's people, all of them English, so far as we can trace, settled just outside Boston, in what is now the Newtons, between 1630 and 1640. But I was born in an old New England village, Kingston, and by happy chance passed my childhood in the nearby town of Plymouth. Yes, the same Plymouth, where the Pilgrim Fathers and their wives and children landed, and had such adventures as you may have read about in my *Soldier Rigdale.*

The Plymouth of my childhood was a quiet town with streets overarched with elms that ran down to the blue waters of the harbor, and old four-square white houses, where retired sea captains lived. There was a courthouse, with a fair green lawn before it, where we played when we recessed from the dame school which I first attended. And there was Pilgrim Hall, a museum filled with chairs and tables and pots and kettles, said to have come over in the *Mayflower,* and Indian relics, which included Indian skulls at which I used to shudder. Indians were real and terrific, in the remote days of my childhood, for Arizona was still a frontier territory, and the Custer Massacre fell in the year of my birth.

In Plymouth I went to the public schools and learned what every child is expected to learn in the grades. I liked to read,

BEULAH MARIE DIX

especially Scott's poems, in an old fat calf-bound volume, and the tales of Abby Morton Diaz, and Juliana Ewing. Later I read Dickens and a good deal of Henty. From the very beginning I meant to be a writer, and when I wasn't filling a copy book with cripple-gaited poems and realistic tales of bad little boys—I found them more exciting than little girls!—I was playing long imaginative plays with my dolls. I liked paper dolls better than the big china ones, because you could have whole families of them, and their descendants to the third and fourth generation, like the royal Saxon families in Hume's *History of England.*

When I was twelve years old, my father and mother and my older sister and our cat, Oscar, and I all moved to Chelsea, near Boston, where I entered the high school. I studied hard and had no time to write anything but school essays. I graduated at sixteen, valedictorian of the class, and then I went to Radcliffe College in Cambridge, where I studied chiefly history and English. The first story I sold was one of my sophomore themes. It dealt with an incident in the Thirty Years' War, which I was studying in a history course. *Lippincott's Magazine* paid me ten dollars for the story, and with it I bought myself a winter coat. In the gay 'nineties coats were cheaper than they are today.

My first play was written in my junior year at college, for our dramatic and social club, the Idler. We were forbidden to wear men's clothes upon our stage, though only girls made up our audience. We were compelled to give costume plays, so *Cicely's Cavalier,* my first effort, was laid in England in the seventeenth century. As the roistering hero I was allowed to wear velvet plus-fours unchallenged. The little play was sold at once to Walter Baker Company for fifteen dollars, and I sold my junior themes, all of them historical stories, to various small magazines. Financially that was a good year!

At the age of twenty I took my A.B. degree, *summa cum laude,* Phi Beta Kappa, with highest honors in English, and the George B. Sohier Prize, given to the Harvard or Radcliffe student who presents the best thesis as a candidate for English honors. I was the first girl student ever to take that prize. I returned to college and a

year later took my A.M. degree. During that year I wrote my first book, *Hugh Gwyeth: A Roundhead Cavalier.* Through the great kindness of Dr. Edward Channing, with whom I had studied history, I was introduced to the Macmillan Company, which not only took *Hugh Gwyeth* but commissioned me to write *Soldier Rigdale.*

The rest of my life is very quickly told. I wrote novels, and books for children. For several years I collaborated in writing plays with my dear friend, Evelyn Greenleaf Sutherland. After her death I wrote several plays alone. In 1916 I came out to the Pacific Coast, and since then most of my work has been done for the screen.

I've been abroad several times and have spent a year or more in England, among the scenes in which I laid my historical plays and novels. I have also traveled west as far as Honolulu. In 1910 I married a German-born, naturalized citizen, George Flebbe. Our one child, Evelyn Greenleaf, was born in 1911. She is now Mrs. David Scott, all grown up and married, with a daughter of her own, named Ursula Christiana, born in 1945. Since before Pearl Harbor, we have all lived together right on the ocean in Pacific Palisades, a remote section of the huge city of Los Angeles. We are happy in the companionship of a dignified German shepherd, Hildebrand, and an opinionated black dachshund, Waldi, who are the loyal guardians of the little Ursula.

William Pène du Bois

May 9, 1916-

AUTHOR AND ILLUSTRATOR OF
The Twenty-one Balloons, Great Geppy, Etc.

WILLIAM PÈNE DU BOIS was born in Nutley, New Jersey to the well known American painter and art critic, Guy Pène du Bois, and his wife, Florence Sherman du Bois, a designer of children's clothes. His sister Yvonne is a painter also. The family has turned out several other distinguished artists, stage designers, and architects. Between the ages of eight and fourteen Billy was educated in France.

Two years after returning to America, Billy du Bois, already prepared for Harvard, learned there was no money for college. He stated calmly that he had already planned

Pène: *PANE*
du Bois: *due BWAH*

Arni

WILLIAM PÈNE DU BOIS

to write and illustrate books for children. He never swerved from that decision. At nineteen he saw his first book, *Giant Otto,* published, and the next year, *Otto at Sea.* In 1938 came *The Three Policemen,* and in 1940, *Great Geppy.* The day he went into the army he gave his publisher a book, and on the day he left it five years later he turned over *The Twenty-one Balloons,* which won the Newbery prize for 1947.

On his last leave, du Bois married Jane, daughter of the painter Louis Bouché; she had always been the little girl next door.

Du Bois once called the Lycée Hoche, a boarding school in Versailles, one of the most important influences in his life. He said of it, according to the *Horn Book*:

"Everything was done smartly to the sound of bells and whistles. . . . In the morning when the bell rang six o'clock we all got up together and dressed, up to the point of having put on underwear, socks, shoes, and shirt without collar (we wore separate starched collars). Then the master, who slept modestly in a bed on a raised dais surrounded with pink curtains, would blow a whistle and we all washed together. (There were forty boys in each dormitory.) Then at another whistle, we all dumped the water together out of the great line of sinks in one fell swush. Then we finished dressing and lined up in a column of two's and marched to breakfast, a breakfast consisting of a large bowl of coffee and a big piece of dry bread. Of course we all sat down together to the tune of a whistle toot. . . .

"All our food at lunch and dinner was served on one big deep plate, including soup and dessert. We were issued one huge napkin every Monday which had to last us the whole week. The soup was already served when we entered the refectory so that if it was a soup we didn't like, it seemed quite proper to mop it all up with the napkin."

Mr. du Bois learned most about drawing from his father, next most from a teacher of arithmetic at the lycée. "Every morning he would stack our homework papers in a neat pile in the middle of his desk and then proceed to look at them one by one, not as correct or incorrect papers, but as neat or sloppy examples of orderly procedure. He would hold them up as if he were studying etchings, look at the name of the student, and express his critical opinion of the work. He would either say, 'Ah, c'est beau!' and stack it in a pile to his right, or make a sad, dejected grimace, and tear it in four equal parts which he stacked to his left. I remember doing a magnificent page of arithmetic, my favorite subject, in which I neglected to rule one short line under a subtraction of two one-digit figures. 'What have we here?' he said. 'An artist? Monsieur du Bois is drawing free hand.' He neatly tore my work in four pieces.

"We were able to do these over during recess."

Meticulousness learned at that school has stayed with du Bois all his life. His brushes and pens must all be laid out just so and everything must be in perfect order before he starts work. Water in which he rinses his brushes cannot be in any ordinary jug; it stands in a blue and white colonial glass antique.

He allows himself to do no more than one picture a day; that one must be perfect. He has his own standard of judgment.

"I have never dared to test a book of mine on children before publishing," he once said, "for fear that they would be completely bored, a situation which could only prove to be most distressing and perplexing.

"As a child I hardly read at all, though I loved to look at books. I was the sort of fellow who just looks at pictures. I try to keep such impatient children in mind in making my books.

"The only extensive reading I did other than required reading, was in copies of two ferocious and forbidden magazines . . . called *Les Aventures de Nick Carter* (pronounced Neek Cartaire), and *Les Aventures de Buffalo Bill*. I also did some scattered reading of a peculiar type in other adventure books. If, for instance, I read a caption under a thrilling frontispiece which said, 'Bill Ballantine slipped from his trapeze and fell into the lion cage below (see page 178),' I would quickly turn to page 178 to find out whether or not he was chewed up. The rest of the book never seemed to me to be worth reading.

"This lack of interest in reading was probably due to the fact that I was never too familiar with the language of the country in which I was living. I was just barely starting to read English when, at the age of eight, I left for France, and just fairly proficient in reading French when, at fourteen, I returned to America. Back in America, I had forgotten most of my English."

Since his childhood William du Bois has had three continuing enthusiasms: France, circuses, and Jules Verne. The last has led to an interest in all mechanized methods of transportation, especially balloons. He aims to have a real one some day. Meanwhile he has models.

Besides his own books, he illustrates books of other authors, often very different in character from his own, sometimes more sophisticated. (In 1950 he designed the Book Week poster.) He does a conscientious job, and enjoys these different pictures, but his own books always deal with good people. He is continually founding utopias, real democracies, full of noble people. Even his villains are not really vicious underneath.

Edmund Dulac

October 22, 1882-
ILLUSTRATOR

Autobiographical sketch of Edmund Dulac:

I WAS born in France in the old city of Toulouse. I was educated at the college and university of that town and ended my studies with the usual Ll.Ph.B. degree. It was at first intended that I should enter the

EDMUND DULAC

legal profession or a diplomatic career, and I read law, or pretended to, for two years. But I also attended some of the classes at the local art school. I won a prize; the idea of my becoming a barrister or a diplomat was given up, and I was allowed to become a full-time art student. In 1903 I went to Paris and spent a few weeks at the Julian Academy. I settled in London in 1905, and was naturalized a British subject in 1912.

I painted my first picture at the age of eight on the lid of a wooden box, with colors that my father, who dabbled in painting, let me use as a great favor. It represented a landscape with a cottage and a willow by a stream, in the foreground a cow with a soldier holding a letter with five red seals.

In Paris I exhibited at the Salon. My first exhibition in London was held at the Leicester Galleries in 1907 and consisted of the drawings I had done for the *Arabian Nights*. It was followed by yearly shows of illustrations for a number of books.

In 1919-20 I drew weekly caricatures of prominent people for the *Outlook*, and the next year began to contribute an annual series of drawings to the *American Weekly* of New York. I painted a number of portraits, amongst others that of Madam Wellington Koo, wife of the Chinese ambassador. In addition, I designed stage settings, masks, and dresses. I also composed music.

Dulac: *due LAK*

When the liner *Empress of Britain* was built I was commissioned to decorate the smoking room. She is now at the bottom of the sea, with little fishes darting in and out of the carvings in Chinese style and knocking their noses against the mirrors.

Shortly before his death, King George V instituted an annual poetry prize for which I modeled the medal, and when King George VI came to the throne, I was responsible for the Coronation stamp, the King's cameo head on the lower denominations, and all the rest of the current stamps now in use. I designed more stamps for the colonies that rallied to the Free French during the last war as well as their banknotes and the first stamp, "Marianne," to be used in France after the Liberation.

My other occupations are various. I am much interested in music, mainly the folk music of Europe and the Orient, and used at one time to make bamboo flutes, especially those that are played with the nose, as in the Polynesian islands. It is natural that aesthetic questions should interest me deeply. I have written and lectured on art and its relation to psychology in history, and if I add to all this that I often indulge in a little carpentering as a rest, you will have a fairly complete picture of the artist at work and at play.

* * *

While much of his work is for adults Mr. Dulac has beautifully illustrated several children's books. Especially notable among these, besides the *Arabian Nights*, are *The Sleeping Beauty, Stories from Hans Andersen, The Dulac Fairy Book*, and *Treasure Island*.

Norman Duncan

July 2, 1871-October 18, 1916

AUTHOR OF

Battles Royal Down North, The Adventures of Billy Topsail, Doctor Luke of the Labrador, Etc.

AT the age of twenty-nine Norman Duncan went to visit the bleak, rugged, inhospitable shores of Newfoundland. He had never before had close contact with the sea; in his boyhood he had feared it and dreamed of its horrors. Now he came to gather material for writing, and for three summers lived among the simple, quaint fisher folk on the tempest-battered coasts of

that region. With the deep sympathy, understanding and tact of his nature, he won their confidence, studied the tragedy of their lives, the hardihood, heroism, the grim struggle for food and shelter, and the simple faith, and with the talent that was his he wove the sea stories of the North that were to make his name known as one of the foremost writers of the sea.

It was Duncan who first developed the literary possibilities of that region. He had already published his first important contribution to literature, *The Soul of the Street*, a book containing a series of sympathetic sketches of Syrian life in the lower section of New York City. He had also done important newspaper work, and had shown special ability in descriptive writing and character portrayal. It was not, however, until he was sent to Newfoundland and to Labrador that he found his real work in a background woven into his sympathies and productive of some of his best books and stories. *The Way of the Sea, Doctor Luke of the Labrador, Dr. Grenfell's Parish*, and other books soon followed. A Canadian by birth and education, Duncan belonged to the States during his manhood and working period, although he never claimed citizenship here. Born in Brantford, Western Ontario, and spending his boyhood in various Canadian towns, he attended the University of Toronto, where he took part in all forms of social and literary activity, but left before taking a degree. He made his start in reportorial work in Auburn, New York, soon afterward establishing himself with the New York *Evening Post,* where he filled various positions. His first stories were contributed to magazines, his *Soul of the Street* having appeared originally in that form.

His stories, which he took from life, were the result of his intimate study and observation. Yet he cared more for general vividness and moral force than for accuracy of details. As he said of one of his books, *Billy Topsail, M.D.*, "it is decently founded on fact." His Doctor Luke in *Doctor Luke of the Labrador* was taken by many to be a delineation of Dr. Grenfell, the medical missionary of the North, on whose boat he cruised for several weeks. This, however, when it was brought to his attention, he took pains to deny. It is probable that Dr. Grenfell was the original of Dr. Rolfe in the short story "Doctor of Afternoon Arm," as well as suggestive of other incidents he records.

His adventurous, active life was cast in other fields also, but in none other did he find the same strong impressions as in his visits to the North. *Harper's Magazine* sent him on two trips which included the countries of Palestine, Arabia, Egypt, and Australia. He was also engaged for many years in teaching English and rhetoric at Washington and Jefferson University and the University of Kansas, in the former enjoying the companionship of his brother, who was professor of chemistry.

Always generous to those in need, Duncan died a relatively poor man, although he earned large sums of money by his pen. He passed away suddenly at the age of forty-five from heart disease while playing a golf match at Fredonia, New York, and was buried at his birthplace, Brantford.

ROGER DUVOISIN

Roger Duvoisin

1904-

ILLUSTRATOR, AND AUTHOR OF
Three Sneezes, They Put Out to Sea, Etc.

Autobiographical sketch of Roger Antoine Duvoisin:

I WAS born in Geneva, Switzerland. My father was an architect and kept busy building houses while my mother kept even more busy dressing me in long robes with polka dots and tying blue ribbons in my hair.

Like most children, I loved to draw. Galloping horses were my favorite subject. But I labored in vain trying to draw the hoofs; they always looked like oversized shoes. Fortunately an uncle of mine had a special talent for drawing horses and I looked forward to his visit with great expectation as I always made him fill sheets of paper with magnificent horses, prancing on their elegant hoofs.

Trees also were my despair. They have so many leaves that I lost hope of drawing them all. I was sad when I looked at my trees whose leaves hung from the branches like Christmas tree ornaments. But I got help there too. My godmother, who was a well-known painter of enamels, said she knew a trick that would help me and she showed it to me. After that my trees were really bad.

Thus I scribbled so many strange things and used up so much white paper that my godmother declared she could see my future very clearly. I would be a painter of enamels. My mother concurred. But my father shook his head. He thought I would make a better chemist. He was alone against two—so he compromised. I would be an artist but not a painter of enamels; a mural painter and a stage designer. That was closer to his own profession. So, when I became of age, I entered art school.

Out of school, I began to paint murals and stage scenery and also posters and illustrations. I did much with ceramics too and I even became manager of an old French pottery plant. I soon left this, however, to design textiles in Lyons and Paris. I did well, for, as I learned later, the former manager of the pottery plant had sworn he would shoot me one dark night for having taken his job. It was this idea of designing textiles that led to my becoming an American citizen, for in Paris an American textile firm offered to bring me to America if I would promise to stay there four years at least.

A trip to America was an exciting adventure, so I came over looking forward to some interesting experiences.

After four or five years the textile firm went bankrupt—through no fault of my own—and I found myself jobless. This happened during the depression. But as I was very happy here, I had no desire to sail back to Europe. Instead, I published a book

Duvoisin: *DUE vwah zan*

I had written for my young son, and ever since, I have been illustrating and writing books for children and drawing illustrations for magazines.

In 1938 I became a citizen.

* * *

Mr. Duvoisin now lives in Gladstone, New Jersey.

Charles A. Eastman

1858-1939

AUTHOR OF

Indian Boyhood, Wigwam Evenings, Indian Scout Talks, Etc.

AS a small motherless boy, Charles A. Eastman listened to the legends of his native Indian tribe, the Santee Sioux. His mother, a half-blood Sioux named Nancy Eastman, had died soon after he was born at Redwood Falls, Minnesota. When he was about four he was given the name Ohiyesa (Winner) in honor of a Sioux victory in athletic games.

He was still four when the "Sioux massacre" took place in Minnesota. His father and his two elder brothers were imprisoned by the United States as participants in the massacre, and the boy was adopted into the family of his uncle. He learned to hunt, to go without food, to run for a day and a night without rest. There was time for fun, too. With his playmates he wrestled, swam, coasted on sleds made of buffalo ribs, and irreverently imitated the dances of the medicine men.

When he was fifteen his father, after long imprisonment, was pardoned. Now Ohiyesa must leave the tribe and learn the way of the white man as his father and brothers had learned it from the missionaries in prison. Reluctantly he put on the white man's clothes and journeyed to Flandreau, South Dakota. He cut his long hair and became Charles Alexander Eastman, the son of Jacob Eastman (as his father now called himself). During the next seventeen years he went to several schools, finishing at Dartmouth College and Boston University.

Graduated as a doctor of medicine at thirty-two, he went to Pine Ridge Agency in South Dakota as government physician. Here he met and married Elaine Goodale, a Massachusetts girl who had been teaching the Sioux. After three years they left Pine Ridge for St. Paul, Minnesota, where he practiced medicine and in his leisure hours put on paper some of his earliest recollections for their small son, Ohiyesa the second. *Indian Boyhood*, the story of his first fifteen years, appeared when he was forty-four. Its success encouraged him and from stories he had heard in his youth he made another book, *Wigwam Evenings*, written with the help of his wife, after they had repeated the tales at their own fireside for their six children.

While writing these books Eastman was working on behalf of his people. He spent three years among them as Indian Secretary for the Y.M.C.A., and then three years in Washington, urging their rights. Another three-year period as government physician at Crow Creek, South Dakota, was followed by six years occupied in revising family names of the Sioux Indians for the government. During the administration of Calvin Coolidge he was United States Indian Inspector.

The success of his first book made him so much in demand in the East as a lecturer and writer on Indian life and history that he removed his family to Massachusetts, where they made their home at Northampton.

For eleven years Eastman and his wife conducted a girls' camp at Munsonville, New Hampshire. He was a national councilman of the Boy Scouts of America. He died January 8, 1939, in his eighty-first year.

Jeanette Eaton

AUTHOR OF

Young Lafayette, Betsy's Napoleon, Leader by Destiny, Narcissa Whitman, Lone Journey, Etc.

Autobiographical sketch of Jeanette Eaton:

NOT a day goes by, as I wend my way through the dramatic streets of New York, that I do not thank my lucky stars for two blessings. First, that I was born in the Middle West, and second, that I live most of the time on a farm near the Delaware River in New Jersey. For, fascinating as the great city is, it offers a limited knowledge of our vast country.

Yes, in Columbus, Ohio, my infant eyes first opened. Because they were blue-gray and because my fuzz was almost black, my

JEANETTE EATON

mother thought I had a typical French coloring to go with my name. But I perversely became a towhead almost at once and only grew more brunette with time. Nor was there anything of Gallic demureness in my aptitude for climbing trees, walking the tops of board fences, playing football with my brother and cousin, and romping with our adored mongrel in our small garden.

Only because I was always scribbling verse and writing stories did I hold out to my parents any hope of becoming something besides a tomboy. Recently I came across notebooks full of foolishness in a hideous scrawl which I was obliged to recognize was once mine. My dear mother must have cherished the outpourings as a sort of insurance against a future devoted to physical prowess. And I certainly have no prowess at all. What I am pleased to term my swimming, riding, and playing outdoor games never fail to draw from experts a look of pitying tolerance. But a gypsy streak is stubborn to cure and I still love to wear slacks, to sleep out-of-doors, and to do unpremeditated things.

Since he was a book-worm himself, my father always defended my omnivorous reading. Whenever useful work threatened, I was sure to be out of reach—flat on my stomach under a snowball bush, lost to the world in a book. I loved fairy tales and Lewis Carroll's peerless creations. Novels of Dickens, Thackeray, George Eliot, and (be-

lieve it or not) Henry James fascinated me at an early age. Now that I have little time to read for pleasure alone, I look back enviously at that print-greedy child.

It was not until I went to college, however, that I captured something of the scholar's delight in learning. First in getting an A.B. degree at Vassar and later in taking an A.M. degree at Ohio State University, I was taught how to organize research material. Yet it was some time before I used that knowledge. Thirst for activity and experience led me in and out of many occupations. Many of them, fortunately, gave me contact with school problems. Thus my personal acquaintance with children was supplemented by a vivid sense of the millions of children who must learn that reading is not a chore but a joy.

At last, after a year in Europe, I began writing for a living. You can hardly think of any type of article which I haven't composed for magazines and newspapers of high and low degree. Every kind of writing was exciting to me. But when I had an opportunity to write a little book for children, I knew I had my vocation for life.

Many are the vital challenges offered by the audience of young people. It is peculiarly honest. It demands that a book be interesting first of all, but also that it offer real nourishment. For the young a biography must be presented in dramatic form and both the character and the period must come true. To meet this demand I have had the rare joy of poking about in far places both here and abroad.

Such travel is far more rewarding than the average kind of sightseeing. What with meeting scholars keen to help a serious project and what with working in libraries, universities, and museums, the student has rich opportunities to savor the atmosphere of a region. To make the past arise behind the present-day aspect of a city, with its motor cars and busy life, is like straining to see something through a fog. Travel must be followed up by enormous reading and the study of old maps. Then one can discover old Paris, Fourteenth Century Siena, Medieval Rome, Revolutionary Philadelphia, primitive Rhode Island, the untamed West, and even Darkest Africa.

No wonder that in my farm studio books, maps, and encyclopedias are piled around me in heaps! Such fortifications do not protect me from the interruptions which are bound to occur in the country. If it isn't the plumber, it's the man with a load of manure for the garden! Perhaps this is just as well. No writer should be cut off from everyday living. Certainly the person concerned with biography must ever keep in mind the stern demands of the present.

Now more than ever in its history the integrity of this country is being tested by world events. Life in an Atomic Age offers profound problems which young people must be prepared to meet. I believe that a vital source of help comes from acquaintance with great persons who have trod this earth. The noble courage with which they have overcome obstacles, the inspired wisdom of their decisions and their deeds, prove to the youthful heart that the spirit is the realest thing about an individual. It rises above cheap temptations. And no bomb can destroy it.

Irmengarde Eberle

November 11, 1898-

AUTHOR OF

A Good House for a Mouse, Phoebe Belle, The Very Good Neighbors, Right Dog for Joe, Etc.

Autobiographical sketch of Irmengarde Eberle:

FOR many years now I have lived in New York, and this city and state have become my home. Yet I still have a feeling of belonging, too, to the broad sunny land of the Southwest where I grew up.

I was born in beautiful, historically interesting, old San Antonio, Texas. Both my parents died when I was a small baby, and I came to live with my aunt and grandmother in the suburbs of the city. There was much outdoor play for me, with my two sisters and the neighborhood children. The climate of that region is subtropical, and we were out in the wild-flower-covered empty lots, or the open pasture to the north of our house, much of the time all the year around. Here I came to know some of the small wild animals about which I later wrote several books. In the suburb, too, I came to know persons of several different races and to develop a strong sense of the brotherhood of all people.

My interest in story telling began at an early age. At six I invented story games

IRMENGARDE EBERLE

which we played with the other children of the neighborhood. At eight I submitted a little story to a shoe company contest and won a prize of one dollar—a great amount in my life then!

The public schools of San Antonio gave me the first part of my education; and later I attended the Texas State Women's College at Denton, taking an art course. Upon graduation I came to Connecticut to visit friends. Before the summer was over I had a job designing drapery fabrics in New York City, and stayed on. My work was displayed in an exhibition at the Metropolitan Museum of Art; but my interest in writing had always been strongest, and came forward more vigorously now. I gave up designing and went into editorial work.

I held several assistant editorships on magazines in the next few years, and then advanced to editorships. During all these years I also wrote stories and articles, and was a contributor of short short stories to Franklin P. Adams' "Conning Tower." I had a home of my own to run now, too, and a young son to look after. For some years I held only occasional jobs that entailed going to an office, and spent most of my time doing free-lance writing.

Since 1937 I have given my time almost entirely to writing books for children. Several have been factual, but more are fiction. Some, as *The Very Good Neighbors*, were Junior Literary Guild selections; *A Good*

Irmengarde Eberle: *ERM en gard EB er lee*

House for a Mouse won a *Herald Tribune* honor award. There are also *Big Family of Peoples, The Right Dog for Joe, Lorie,* and over twenty others. Because children have such a fine genuineness, it is a pleasure to write for them.

Paul Eipper

July 10, 1891-

AUTHOR OF

Animals Looking at You, In My Zoo, Circus, Etc.

Autobiographical sketch of Paul Eipper:

MY mother often told me that the baby carriage in which I was wheeled about during the first year of my life was almost always in the Zoo, next to the cages of the big beasts of prey. My father was no lion tamer but only a shareholder of the Stuttgart Zoo, but anyway the air I breathed as a baby seems to have been indicative of my life to follow. For even today I cannot imagine anything finer or more thrilling than to be right in amongst a lot of tigers and lions or other large specimens of the cat family.

But perhaps I should introduce myself now in a more regular way. I was born on July 10, 1891, at Stuttgart, capital of Württemberg, in Germany, where I went to school for ten years. Since I was very fond of books and read a great lot of them—especially on the subjects of animals and explorations—my grandfather decided that I should become a book dealer. Being obedient like the good boy that I was, I let myself become apprenticed to a book merchant, but after three years I ran away to Munich to study animal portraiture.

Unfortunately I did not make a living out of my pictures and so I had to go back to the book business in which I remained for twenty years, working in Leipzig, Hanover, Munich, Westphalia, and Berlin. During that time I married and have a fine big boy now who wants to be an aviator. He is also very good at photography and can therefore be of use to me when I make trips for the purpose of discovering more about the lives of wild animals.

In 1929 I wrote my first book, *Animals Looking at You,* which has been translated into eleven languages. Eight other books

followed that one. I frequently talk over the radio, too, and give lantern slide lectures. I hope, together with my wife and son, to live to be 400 years old. For the first 300 years I should like to travel and see every corner of this world and then for the last 100 years I would like to tell everybody all about my adventures.

The most important task of my life is to make people understand animals and to take care of them and I want to profit by this opportunity to impress upon my readers in the U.S.A. and elsewhere that animals are just as much God's children as we humans are.

*   *   *

Herr Eipper wrote the above sketch some years ago. His American publishers report that they have been unable to learn his whereabouts since before the outbreak of the Second World War.

Commander Edward Ellsberg

November 21, 1891-

AUTHOR OF

On the Bottom, I Have Just Begun to Fight, Thirty Fathoms Deep, Ocean Gold, Etc.

Autobiographical sketch of Commander Edward Ellsberg:

WHILE born in New Haven, Connecticut, November 21, 1891, my earliest recollections are of Colorado, where my family went a few years after. We lived in Denver with the Rocky Mountains practically in our backyard; one of my most vivid memories still is of a ride up Clear Creek Canyon when at the age of five I was scared stiff watching the outer wheels of our wagon threaten every second to go sliding over the edge of a narrow mountain road and down the precipice.

Growing up, my brothers and I had the plains around Denver as a hunting ground; our main game was only prairie dogs, which, however, for boys with .22 rifles was quite ideal. The principal drawback to any hunting trip in summer was the inability ever to find a place afterwards to cool off, for in either the Platte River or Cherry Creek (the two nearby streams) you could wet only half yourself at once, and as for swimming in them, an alfalfa field was just as practicable.

Eipper: *EYE per*

Ellsberg: *ELZ berg*

It may have been this lack of water which gave me an interest in the sea, and I read avidly all the boys' books I could find with a nautical background.

Meanwhile I went through grammar school and into high school in Denver, the idea of becoming a mining engineer being my ambition, chiefly I think because the nearby Colorado School of Mines had the best football team in the Rocky Mountain region. My father was strongly opposed to any such notion and wanted me to study law; this was a source of some friction in our household but it resolved itself without dispute my last year in high school when the Mines football team took a trouncing from every college in the conference. Next year, without objection, I entered Colorado University at Boulder, all prepared to study law.

Hardly was I firmly settled as a freshman at Boulder, with the Rockies now literally within a stone's throw, when my boyhood dreams suddenly became real—an opportunity to enter Annapolis came my way. While my parents disapproved of sailors as much as they had of mining engineers, this time I had by way and the summer of 1910 saw me as a plebe tugging away at what felt like a young tree in a ten-oared cutter on Chesapeake Bay under a hot sun, and half-wishing myself back in the mountains.

Four vivid years at the Naval Academy, interspersed with summer cruises in battle-

ships on both sides of the Atlantic, marked by three thrilling football victories over the Army and one heart-breaking defeat, and in June 1914 I was graduated, commissioned an ensign in the Navy, and sent to join the *U.S.S. Texas,* on which during the next two years I served, taking part in the occupation of Vera Cruz, and serving in various capacities from assistant navigator, junior torpedo officer, junior officer in one of the fourteen-inch turrets, to reach finally, as broadside division officer, the command of the ship's batteries of five-inch guns.

In 1916, I was detached from the *Texas* and sent to the Postgraduate School at Annapolis and later to Massachusetts Insitute of Technology for a special course in Naval Architecture, which was interrupted in 1917 by our entrance into the First World War.

The Navy's part here was mainly to provide the ships and get the Army to France. I was sent to the New York Navy Yard, shortly promoted to lieutenant in the Construction Corps, and for the next year struggled mainly to refit German merchantmen (badly damaged by their former crews) and make them into transports. The ex-*Kaiser Wilhelm II* was my major assignment in this task and frankly the Navy Yard forces performed miracles in rebuilding the wrecked engines of this ship and utilizing every inch of space (cargo or otherwise) in packing in the troops. I still pity the seasick dough-boys whom we shipped, stowed four and five high in bunks down in the bowels of that ship, renamed the *Agamemnon,* but we got them there safely and in time in spite of German sabotage in New York harbor and German U-boats on the high seas.

A few odds and ends of jobs, such as rebuilding the smashed bottoms of the cruisers *Olympia* and *Huntington,* injured in convoy service, and fitting out mine sweepers, and I was sent as outside superintendent on the dreadnaught *Tennessee,* on which battleship I supervised the construction from double bottoms to launching, and then with the war over, went back to Tech in Boston to finish my course.

During my first stay at Tech, I became engaged (Wellesley was close by); during the war I was married to Lucy Knowlton Buck (Wellesley 1916) and now with an M.S. from Tech we settled down in 1920 in Boston, where I was attached to the Bos-

EDWARD ELLSBERG

ton Navy Yard. Here between building more ships for the Navy and refitting old ones, I spent the next four years, of which the high lights were the birth of a daughter Mary Phillips (1921) and the development and installation, mainly on cruisers, of an improved system of vacuum evaporators for distilling fresh water from sea water, which topic was so much discussed at home that when I came home, the standard greeting from my then three-year-old daughter always was: "Daddy, how are your evaporators?"

In 1924, as a lieutenant commander I went back to the New York Navy Yard and spent most of the ensuing year, loaned to the Shipping Board, in refitting the ventilation and forced draft system of the *Leviathan.*

And then, in September 1925, the submarine *S-51* was rammed and sunk in the open Atlantic, twenty-two fathoms deep. I was sent by the Navy Department as Salvage Officer; there off Block Island for the next nine months we struggled with the sea on the surface and on the bottom for the *S-51*; finally in July of 1926 we won and brought in the submarine, a success outstanding in the history of deep-sea diving, for which I was awarded by the President the Navy's Distinguished Service Medal.

A few months later, after sixteen years' service in the Navy, I resigned and went back to civil life as Chief Engineer for the Tide Water Oil Co., to work in a field where I found engineering as difficult, as interesting, and as exacting as in the Navy, and with less prospect of monotony than in a Navy sharply curtailed by various limitations of armaments treaties, but I soon found that my ties to the Navy still held.

In December 1927, the submarine *S-4*, in collision with the destroyer *Paulding*, went to the bottom off Provincetown with her entire crew. I volunteered for rescue work, was hastily recommissioned as a lieutenant commander in the Naval Reserve, and sent, unfortunately too late for saving life, to Provincetown, where with my old shipmates of the salvage squadron, the raising of the *S-4* was started in a manner similar to the method used on the *S-51*; I stayed two weeks for the initial operations—the job was completed in the spring about four months later.

Shortly after, by special act of Congress I was promoted to Commander in the Naval

Reserve for services on both *S-51* and *S-4*, and I have since then fortunately had nothing further to do with submarines.

When World War II came and Pearl Harbor thrust us into it, I returned to active duty in the Navy and was immediately sent to the Middle East, where at Massawa on the Red Sea, I was placed in command salvaging the wrecks scuttled in that port by the Italians—there were over three dozen wrecks of large vessels sunk all over the place. Massawa is the hottest place on earth. My men and I had a rough time of it in the Red Sea, but during the desperate days of 1942, we managed to make Massawa function again, for which the Navy awarded me the Legion of Merit and I received the thanks of the British Admiralty. Furthermore, I was promoted from Commander to Captain. [However, he still signs his books as Commander Ellsberg.—Editor.]

When General Eisenhower's forces invaded North Africa toward the end of 1942, I was hurriedly detached from the Red Sea and sent to North Africa as Principal Salvage Officer under General Eisenhower. During this period, commanding the combined salvage forces of the British, the Americans, and the French, I had charge of clearing the Mediterranean ports of wrecks and of keeping afloat and getting into port the Allied transports and warships torpedoed by the Nazi U-boats or bombed by Axis planes. For the success achieved in these task, I was awarded a second Legion of Merit.

On the conclusion of the North African salvage work, I was sent home to America as a hospital case, but some months before the Normandy invasion, I was back on the European front, this time in England helping prepare for D-Day. My task, before and during the invasion, lay in getting over to the Omaha Beach the artificial harbor, an almost unimaginable seaport—breakwaters, pierheads, and piers—built complete in England and towed across the Channel to the Normandy Coast, commencing on D-Day, where much of the installation was placed under fire from the Germans still holding the bluffs overlooking Omaha Beach.

Writing has always been a hobby of mine. At Annapolis I twice received the Navy League Medal for articles on naval subjects; the *Youth's Companion* back in 1916 published my first short story. But that ended my literary efforts until the *S-51* salvage, which resulted in my writing *On the Bottom*. This was followed by *Thirty Fathoms Deep*, a story for boys first published in *Boys' Life*; by *Pigboats*, a story of submarines in wartime; and by *S-54,* a collection of short stories published in the *Saturday Evening Post* and *Adventure*. After this, I wrote three more books for boys: *Ocean Gold, Spanish Ingots,* and *Treasure Below,* all dealing with diving after sunken treasure. These came out some years apart, during which time were also published *Hell on Ice, Men Under the Sea, Captain Paul, I Have Just Begun to Fight* (a juvenile version of *Captain Paul*), and, in 1946, after the close of World War II, *Under the Red Sea Sun.*

Elizabeth Enright

1909-

AUTHOR AND ILLUSTRATOR OF
*Thimble Summer, Then There Were Five,
The Four-Story Mistake, Etc.*

Autobiographical sketch of Elizabeth Enright:

I WAS born in Chicago, but did not live there long. After a year and a half my parents brought me to New York. Both were artists. My father, W. J. Enright, was, and is, a political cartoonist. My mother, then Maginel Wright Enright, was an illustrator. She now makes another kind of picture, very beautiful, too, of wool.

Naturally with so much drawing and painting going on in the house, I felt I had to draw, too. From the age of three I drew hundreds and hundreds of pictures, adopting and abandoning many different styles, but the subject matter was always the same: fairies, mermaids, princesses, kings, ogres, giants, and wicked witches. I believed in, or pretended to believe in fairies for a long time, and knew the stories of Hans Christian Andersen and the brothers Grimm practically by heart.

When I was six my mother took me to see Anna Pavlova. I decided at once to be a dancer and spent hours thumping and banging around the living room to the music of the victrola, even learning to walk on my toes while wearing sneakers. Nothing much came of all this but discouragement and sore toes. I went on drawing.

ELIZABETH ENRIGHT

After finishing high school I studied at the Art Students League in New York for two years, and then spent part of another year in Paris.

I got my first real job at twenty, illustrating a fairy tale, and in the same year was commissioned to draw the pictures for *Kees,* by Marian King. I was very happy about this and finished the preliminary drawings the night before my marriage.

I illustrated quite a few books after *Kees,* but by and by thought it would be fun to illustrate the kind of book I wanted in exactly the way I wished; so I wrote the book myself. I did not go about it quite as one is supposed to—I made most of the pictures first and then wrote the story around them—but I enjoyed myself a lot. The book, *Kintu: A Congo Adventure,* was published in 1935. During the process I discovered I really liked writing much better than drawing, so after a while I started another book, this time about a little Wisconsin farm girl. The book was called *Thimble Summer,* and to my great joy was awarded the Newbery Medal in 1939.

Since then I've written four other children's book and one for adults. I gave up illustrating, except for my own books, some time ago. I still like to draw, though, and am always scribbling faces on everything.

My husband is Robert Gillham, and we have two sons, Nicky and Robin.

Eleanor Estes

May 9, 1906-
AUTHOR OF
*The Moffats, The Hundred Dresses,
Rufus M., Etc.*

Autobiographical sketch of Eleanor Estes:

Arni
ELEANOR ESTES

THE town of West Haven, Connecticut, where I was born, is in a hollow with hills behind it, the New Haven harbor and Long Island Sound lapping against two sides, and a small river meandering along its eastern margin. It was a perfect town to grow up in. It had everything a child could want, great vacant fields with daisies and buttercups, an occasional peaceful cow, and even a team of oxen with whose help cellars for new houses were dug.

There were marvelous trees to climb, woods where there were brooks, and springs, and wild flowers growing. There were swimming and building in the sand and fishing and clamming in the summertime, and ice and snow and sliding down hill in the wintertime, with rowboat exploration of the small river for eels and killies in the betweentime. It had all the joys of a small New England town and yet it was near enough to New Haven for special excursions and occasions, such as the circus, or Santa Claus in Shartenberg's.

In this town I was born, and went to school, and learned to spell, and add two to two. When I graduated from the high school there, I went to work in the children's department of the New Haven Free Public Library. In 1928 I was made head of it. The Caroline M. Hewins scholarship for children's librarians was awarded to me in 1931 and I came to New York to study at the Pratt Institute library school. In 1932 I married Rice Estes, then a student and now a professor of library science.

As a children's librarian I worked in various children's rooms of the New York Public Library until 1940 when my first book, *The Moffats,* was accepted. I scarcely remember when I did not have the idea I wished to be a writer.

Due to my mother's and father's fondness for and interest in them, books have always been an important part of my life. My mother could quote profusely from all the great poets. She had an especial love for Tennyson, Shakespeare, and Heine. And

for the old folk tales. She was very dramatic in her presentation of these and I still shudder when I recall the way she told "Great Claus and Little Claus," which I have never since heard told so well. She had an inexhaustible supply of songs, stories, and anecdotes, fictitious and remembered ones, with which she entertained us as she went about her housework. She took a great joy in painting and drawing, and wrote quantities of light verse, to fit any special occasion, having had herself a wish to become a writer.

Of my father it was said he could add a column a mile long and a mile wide in his head. His name was Louis Rosenfeld and he was born in Bridgeport, Connecticut, of Austrian and Scotch-Irish parents.

My mother was born Caroline Gewecke, in New York City. Her father was of French descent and her mother German, and there were many musicians in the family. "Little old New York," because of our mother's stories, seemed like our second home. Washington Square and University Place, Greenwich Village, the East River and the North River, the Palisades, masquerades in old Madison Square Garden, the Metropolitan Opera House, the dreadful *Slocum* disaster, these, because of her vivid re-creation of them, were extremely real to me, my two brothers, and my sister.

Consequently when, in 1931, I came to live in New York the sensation was rather like that of coming to my other home, my childhood and early days in West Haven seeming like a long holiday in the country.

I like drawing and painting and also I like to sit and look at the ocean and the sky and do nothing. But of course, best of all, I like to write. Since *The Moffats* I have had four books published. The pictures in all these were drawn by the noted sculptor, Louis Slobodkin. The Moffat books are being translated into Dutch, French, Italian, and Norwegian, and another book, *The Hundred Dresses,* into Turkish. At present I am writing a novel for adults.

It is difficult for me, once I have written of an incident or an impression, to differentiate between fiction and fact. However, I am certain that all the above facts *are* facts, not fiction.

Marie Hall Ets

December 16, 1895-

AUTHOR AND ILLUSTRATOR OF
In the Forest, Mr. Oley: The Sea Monster, Etc.

Autobiographical sketch of Marie Hall Ets:

I WAS born in Wisconsin in a town that isn't there any more—it got lost in the city of Milwaukee.

There were already two older girls and a boy. Two more brothers came later. My father was first a doctor, then a minister, and we younger children loved all the moving.

My earliest memory is of my older brother telling me that my parents had wanted a boy to play with him instead of me. I was more sorry than he that I was not a boy—and nearer his age—but I knew of no magic to change me. Summers in the north woods when he took a forked stick and started out to hunt snakes I had to, too. We strung our trophies on a fence. I never had as many, nor any of his huge old pine snakes, but I sometimes had copperheads. Once in town when he said I was afraid to jump from the barn roof I did that, too. Later, I'm ashamed to admit, I got the detestable habit of yelling when I saw my brother coming and I fear he was often punished when he didn't deserve it. (Now we are friends, though.)

Summers at the lakes in the North Woods I loved to run off by myself into the dark forest. I would sit for hours listening to the pine trees and waiting for the timid young creatures of the woods to come from their hiding.

In town there were always crowds of children in our yard. I must have gone to school some time, for I remember the games at recess, and the art supervisor who made such a fuss over my drawings. She took me into her private class of adults and taught me to copy beautiful pictures in watercolor—the Grand Canal of Venice and ships on the sea. After that I didn't know how to do anything but copy.

After one year in college I rebelled, studied interior decorating in New York. and got a job making sketches, first in San Francisco, then in Los Angeles. A few weeks after I married Milton Rodig from Stanford University, he died in an army camp and I left art for social work. While training and getting a degree from the University of Chicago I lived at Chicago Commons settlement house. My social work was mostly with or for children, including a year in Czechoslovakia.

Because of ill health I left social work to try children's books. I took work at the Art Institute of Chicago and under Frederick Poole and at Columbia University. After marrying Harold Ets, a faculty member at Loyola University School of Medicine, I started the pictures for *Mister Penny.* I first tried to do the drawings and tale as children would do them, but neither Mr.

Arni

MARIE HALL ETS

Poole nor May Massee would let me. So after that I didn't try to be anyone but myself. During the next years, illness—my own and later my husband's—gave little time for books. Harold Ets died in 1943. The following spring I came to New York, found a single room, and am still here trying to write.

Jean-Henri Fabre

December 22, 1823-October 11, 1915

AUTHOR OF

The Book of Insects, The Life of the Spider, Etc.

HENRI'S parents were poor, so poor that one day they decided to raise ducks to eke out their scanty means. Henri would mind them and take them to the brook some distance away.

While the ducks splashed about, Henri explored and collected wonder after wonder —beetles, shells, stones, snails. He came home with his pockets bulging until the cloth broke.

"You rascal," cried his father. "I send you to mind the ducks and you amuse yourself picking up stones, as though there weren't enough of them all around the house! Make haste and throw them away!"

Henri had inherited from none of his ancestors the great love of natural things that was to fill a life nearly a century long. He was born at Saint-Léons, a small market village of southern France, of parents obscure and all but illiterate. While still almost a baby his inquiring little mind began to observe the life around him. On the lean farm of his grandfather, a herdsman, at Malaval, where he was sent that there might be one mouth less to feed, he discovered the singing of the grasshopper and explored the farmyard and the wild solitude of nature.

In his seventh year Henri returned to his father's house to attend a school kept by his godfather. A very queer school it was: "at once a school, a kitchen, a bedroom, a dining-room, and, at times, a chicken-house and a piggery." School teaching was only a small part of the master's duties, and at times lessons were altogether forgotten. The boy was ten when his father removed to Rodez, trying unsuccessfully to run a restaurant. Somehow amidst all the difficulties and poverty Henri managed to obtain an education, to win a scholarship, to become a teacher, and later a professor at the universities at Corsica and at Avignon. He was always studying in his spare time to advance the improve himself. He learned many sciences. He married, too, and had a growing family which he must support, a family that adored him.

He made his classes so interesting that they were crowded. He was worshipped by the students. But he aroused the jealousy of others. The teachers couldn't understand his interest in science, his enthusiasm, his independent ways. He was unpopular, too, because of his shabby clothes. At last, after twenty years at Avignon he moved his family to Orange where he wrote textbooks. All his life he had kept up his love of natural things. He never wanted to dissect things as other scientists did, but to study the living things as they are in their own tiny existences.

After a while he bought a place of his own at Serignan, a little house with much wasteland around it. Soon the landscape blossomed and became loud with the hum of insects, which were attracted by the strange and beautiful plants raised. Fabre never cared to leave this outdoor laboratory of his. It was said "he traveled to the ends of the universe, in his garden at Serignan."

He was married twice and had eight children, who joined in many of his observations. He toiled incessantly in obscurity and poverty and cared nothing for fame. He would spend hours lying or sitting on the ground, oblivious of his discomfort, a wrinkled old man with a lovable personality, "a face almost as strange as that of an insect, and the same microscopic, brilliant eyes." No wonder the ignorant people who saw him sometimes thought he was eccentric and peculiar and not altogether sane.

But at last his charming, poetically written stories of insect lives, and his accurate observations, attracted the attention of other great men, and he came to be widely known. Honors came to him. He was given the cross of the Legion of Honor and was presented at court. So reluctant was he to go to Paris for it that the Minister of Education threatened to send his gendarmes after him. At the earliest possible moment he hurried back to the plain comfort of his home.

Jean-Henri Fabre: *ZHAHN ahn ree FAH bruh*

His main writings were published in ten great volumes, *The Recollections of an Entomologist.* In 1910 he received a pension from the French government, but was not to enjoy it long. Five years later he died at the age of ninety-two, and the house where he lived and worked for the last thirty-five years of his life was bought by the French nation to be kept as a lasting memorial to the "Homer of insects."

C. B. Falls

December 10, 1874-

ILLUSTRATOR OF
A B C Book, Mother Goose, When Jesus Was Born, Etc.

THAT his small daughter, Bedelia Jane Falls, might learn her letters and her nursery rhymes from books of her very own, C. B. Falls designed and illustrated for her the two decorative volumes by which he is best known to young people.

In his studio high above Madison Square in New York, he made the books in spare moments when he was not busy teaching classes at the Art Students League or the school for disabled soldiers, or producing posters, murals, or etchings on commission.

First came the *A B C Book.* He cut on wood its animals and letters—"A is for Antelope, B is for Bear," and so forth—twenty-six woodcuts in all. The book, brightly-colored, was published in his forty-ninth year. Then he illustrated a gaily decorated volume of the old nursery rhymes of *Mother Goose.*

The reputation gained through these volumes brought Falls the requests to illustrate Rachel Field's *An Alphabet Book* and also *When Jesus Was Born,* the Christmas story retold by Walter Russell Bowie.

Seven years after the *A B C Book,* Falls fashioned *The Modern A B C Book,* in which the pictures belong to the machine age, from Airplane to Zeppelin. Bedelia Jane was by this time a big girl of twelve or so, and not much interested in alphabets, but Falls knew there were hundreds of other boys and girls born after her who wanted the book.

Charles Buckles Falls was born in Fort Wayne, Indiana. It was his ambition to be a lawyer, but he drifted by chance into architecture instead. He began his career in an architect's office in Chicago, in the neighboring state of Illinois. Soon he chose art for a career because he liked it better than anything else in the world. He joined the art staff of the Chicago *Tribune,* but did not remain long. When his petition for an increase in salary from twelve to fifteen dollars a week was refused, he recklessly quit the job and went to New York to seek his fortune.

There followed several years of hardship and poverty. He slept in parks or lived in cheap boarding houses while working endlessly at his art. Only occasionally did he sell a drawing. Finally success came to him. He became a poster artist of recognized rank and won the praise of Joseph Pennell as the best color artist in America. He also became widely known as a mural painter and etcher.

His first attempt at book illustrating was for Jessie Braham White's *Snow White and the Seven Dwarfs,* in his thirty-ninth year. When he was forty-two he married Bedelia Mary Croly of New York. Their only daughter, Bedelia Jane, was about five years old when he made her first book. According to Alice Page Cooper, "It is rumored in literary circles that the royalties of these sprightly books are bequeathed in perpetuity to the lady of their inspiration."

Falls lives with his family at Falls Village, Connecticut, about a hundred miles from New York. He is described as "a small, plump man with quick eyes and hands, a gentle manner and a quiet voice." When he works he wears "a black coat splashed with twice as many colors as there are in the rainbow."

Eleanor Farjeon

1881-

AUTHOR OF
Martin Pippin, Mighty Men, Ten Saints, Come Christmas, Cherrystones, Etc.

Autobiographical sketch of Eleanor Farjeon:

I WAS born in the Strand, in London, in 1881, and was the third child of my parents: B. L. Farjeon, the novelist, who trod in Dickens' footsteps, and Margaret Jefferson, the eldest daughter of Joseph Jefferson, the American actor.

I had two elder brothers, Harry and Charlie, and two younger, Joseph Jefferson

Farjeon: *FAR zhun*

and Herbert. Charlie died when I was a few months old, and our nursery consisted of four. We had an unusual up-bringing for children in those Victorian days; my mother was gay and gentle, my father impulsive and whimsical. Ordinary education counted for little with him, and I never went to school, and such nursery governesses as came to the house were told not to bother me.

But my parents knew everybody in the Bohemian literary and dramatic world, and we grew up in an atmosphere rich with imaginative suggestion. From the age of four I, with my brothers, was taken to the theatre and opera freely; as soon as I could read I was immersed in my father's enormous and very varied library; and at seven I was writing my own works on the typewriter.

Indeed, we all four wrote: tales, plays, magazines, and poems; and our nursery-life was run by my brother Harry, with fantastic imagination and the most rigid justice. Codes had to be adhered to, but the games and "treats" were prodigal. My generous, excitable father had a way of turning such occasions as Christmas, birthdays, holidays, and parties into fairy tales; and as I was naturally shy and sensitive, it is not surprising that I was happier at home than anywhere else.

At an early age Harry showed brilliant musical gifts. When he was sent to the Royal Academy of Music, where he swept the board with scholarships and prizes, I shared his life there by supplying him with "books" for operas. The Academy, for the first time in its history, hired a public hall and performed an opera by one of its students—our work was called "Floretta," its theme a love-adventure of Henry of Navarre which I had turned into very naive verse and Harry had set to very tuneful melodies; and I made my public bow (in pigtails) at the age of 16. This was followed by two operettas, base imitations of W. S. Gilbert, who, instead of bearing rancor, sent me kind letters about them. But, except for a rather remarkable blank-verse poem on "Chaos," none of my early work will bear inspection.

I was still living a sort of dreamy home-life which I hated being broken into by the outside world, when my father died in 1903. Then my grandfather sent for us all

to come over to America; many of our American relatives had visited us from time to time, but he had never seen us. That trip to Buzzard's Bay, in 1904, was a revelation—a new country, a new life, a colony of lively and delightful uncles and cousins and aunts, and above all, my adorable grandfather.

I think we might have settled in America for good, if Harry had not just received his appointment as a professor of harmony and composition at the Academy. This took us back, and when my grandfather died in 1905 there was no question of a further change. I continued to write at home, slowly discovering what I most wanted to write, and how.

I never really "found" myself till during the [First World] War. My first successes were with the two series of *Nursery Rhymes of London Town*, which I set later to simple tunes of my own, that are now sung in most of the junior schools in England. Then, to avoid the effect of the London air-raids on my mother, I took a tiny laborer's cottage in the liveliest part of Sussex, where I worked in my garden, cooked, and gathered my firewood all day, ran on the downs all night, and wrote—the rest of the time! Here *Martin Pippin in the Apple Orchard* was written, and posted, tale by tale, to "V. K. H.," a Sussex-loving friend in the trenches; and when *Martin* had been published I felt I had found my feet.

After the War I had to leave my cottage, as the village cowman came back to it; my mother's health failed, and I settled near her in London. I was lucky again in finding a fairy-tale of a cottage, with a tiny walled Queen Anne garden, in the old part of Hampstead, and for twelve years I divided my time between that and my mother's house, till she died in November 1933. During those years I wrote innumerable things—fantastic fiction, poems, music, children's tales and games, and one novel. Quite recently I have taken to writing plays.

I still own my Hampstead cottage; but my thoughts are drawing me Sussex-ward again, and I am almost sure I shall find myself there again one day.

* * *

One of her American editors describes Eleanor Farjeon as "rosy, dark-haired, bright-eyed, and on the day that I saw her

[she] wore a crisp print frock with a white ruffled petticoat—as crisp and dainty as if she were the 'Spring-green Lady' herself. Indeed, she seems to belong to Sussex and the Downs and Gilman's apple orchard. She is 'hearty' in the most delightful sense of the word and in her company you share her genuine, childlike zest for all things— from the book she found on a bookstall that day to the taste of the strawberries and the memory of picking them, warm with sun, under the leaves.

"She is a person whose eyes and mind and heart are always wide open, though one cannot read her poems without knowing that she has mightily won her joy. But she *has* won it and has it to give away. Joy, I think, is the keynote of all her stories, her poems, and her people and music."

Walter Farley

1915-

AUTHOR OF

The Black Stallion, Son of the Black Stallion, Etc.

Autobiographical sketch of Walter Farley:

FROM the room where I write my Stallion stories I can watch my broodmares and colts grazing and running about the pasture. I want to tell you how I got them, in the hopes that you, too, may be able to get your horses the same way.

Like most of you, I, too, was born and raised in a city. So I know what it is to want a horse very much and not be able to have one. My birthplace was Syracuse, New York. For a good many of the next twelve years I made life pretty miserable· for my parents because I couldn't understand why we couldn't keep a horse in the garage and have him use our lawn for grazing. To pacify me a little, my parents bought me every book on horses, fiction as well as technical books on breeding, training, and horse anatomy. By then I had made up my mind to be either a jockey, a veterinarian, or a breeder of horses.

My big break came at the age of twelve, when my uncle moved to Syracuse from the west coast, bringing a stable of jumpers and show horses. I lived at the stable, and all I wanted was being fulfilled with the excep-

tion of one thing: I still didn't have a horse all my own. Nor was I to have one, for less than two years later, my parents took me to a still larger city, New York.

Fortunately, we lived in the suburbs, and Long Island riding trails were within easy reach—and so was Belmont racetrack where I could go early mornings to watch the thoroughbreds work. All this time, ever since I learned to write, I had kept notes of experiences with horses which I'd either dreamed, shared, or witnessed. And I've never stopped this practice.

I left New York City to go to school in Pennsylvania, and then returned to Columbia University. But, always, on vacations or week ends I rode horses or visited training tracks and stock farms. Still I had no horse of my own, and now I knew I wasn't going to be a jockey, for I was much too tall, or a veterinarian, for my very good friend and professor at Columbia, Mabel Robinson, had encouraged me to write. And what was I writing? Horse stories, and every note I'd made from the age of twelve was coming in mighty handy. I wrote my first book in Dr. Robinson's class, it was the story of *The Black Stallion.*

When the book was published in 1941 I was working in an advertising agency in New York, writing radio and newspaper copy. And when I learned that boys and girls liked the story of the Black, I quit the

WALTER FARLEY

agency and traveled, planning to pick up more material for my books to come. I visited just about every stock farm in the country and, working my way along, went to Mexico, Central America, South America, Hawaii, and the South Pacific islands. And, always, there were horses to see and ride, experiences to put down on paper for more stories.

But then came the war. I was assigned to *Yank*, the army weekly, from 1942 to 1946. And during those years I was able to write one more book, *The Black Stallion Returns*. After being discharged from the army, I wrote *Son of the Black Stallion*, and then was in a financial position to achieve one goal of the three that I had set for myself so many years ago. I bought a farm in Pennsylvania, where I could breed and raise my own horses. And that is exactly what I'm doing now.

If you're sincere in your love for horses, you'll manage to have your own some day . . . just as I have. And I envy you the early morning you see your first foal, stilt-legged and wavering, looking at you with large, wondrous eyes while he tries to decide whether you or the mare beside him is his mother. If you write about him, we may some day be reading your story of a stallion of another color.

I'm married, and my wife, Rosemary, and I have a young daughter, Pamela, who will have a horse of her own.

Gregor Felsen

1916-

AUTHOR OF
Bertie Comes Through, Some Follow the Sea, Etc.

Autobiographical sketch of Henry Gregor Felsen:

I WAS born in Brooklyn, New York, but left there in time to attend a one-room school in Wawarsing, New York. As I was the only one in my grade, my standing in the class was always a doubtful matter, since I claimed I was at the top, and the teacher indicated I was at the bottom. I passed everything and followed that up by high school in Kerhonkson, New York, and then Erasmus Hall, in Brooklyn.

GREGOR FELSEN

I interrupted my junior year at Erasmus to run away from home, and I still have the telegram from the chief of police in the Florida city stating that I was without funds and wished to return home, and would my parents please oblige with the fare.

I spent two rather aimless years at the State University of Iowa, working as much as forty-eight hours a week to keep body, soul, and books in the same room. In my junior year I lasted three weeks, and as I couldn't pay my tuition, I was not allowed to stay in class. I went back to New York and shipped out to South America.

I returned to Iowa with a good tan and no hat on a day when it was about thirty below zero. I stayed around Iowa City and finally found work on the Iowa writer's project, doing articles for the Iowa Guidebook.

By this time I was eighteen, and thought it was high time to settle down. I knew a very nice girl named Penny Vincent, and asked her to marry me as soon as she finished college. I kept coming around to see her so much she couldn't study, so a month after I lost my job, we were married and set off to seek our fortunes with everything we owned in two small suitcases, twenty dollars in cash (wedding presents), and a bouquet of faded flowers, also a wedding present.

We were twenty, it was the midst of the depression. We got along in a way, sometimes sleeping in a room of our own, and sometimes on a friendly floor. We often ate as many as two meals a day. I bounced on and off WPA, tried to sell books, and even opened a fencing studio, where I had one student. Finally my wife got a job with *Look* magazine, and we bought a typewriter. She told me to forget about trying to get a job in the laundry, and write until I sold. I did.

I started out writing fact detective stories with Darrell Huff, an editor of *Look*. When he became the big wheel at a large publishing house, in charge of their weekly Sunday school papers, he took me on as staff writer, after a trial run. I stayed several months and wrote my first book, *Jungle Highway*. It was accepted, I quit the job, and we moved to New York in an ancient Dodge we had acquired. In the next eighteen months I sold five more books and a couple of hundred stories, became a daddy—his name is Dan—and then Uncle Sam beckoned.

I spent two and a half years in the Marine Corps, and my last job there was as a roving editor overseas. I flew around the Pacific for nine months doing this and that for the *Leatherneck* magazine, and came home in one piece. We bought a stone house built in 1780, and lived there until this week, when we are again moving, to Iowa.

Helen Ferris

November 19, 1890-

AUTHOR OF

Girls Who Did, Girls' Clubs, This Happened to Me, Tommy and His Dog, Hurry, Etc.

Autobiographical sketch of Helen Ferris:

ALL my life, many things have interested me. But of it all, two have always come first—people and books. And I am happy that I have always had so many of both.

I was born in Nebraska in 1890, in the town of Hastings, but I did not stay there long. Before I was six, my mother and father and brother and I moved to Lincoln in the same state. There it was that my father decided to enter the ministry and from then on for a number of years, we moved every now and then.

Kesslere

HELEN FERRIS

First, our home was in Ashland, Nebraska, where the members of my father's church were townspeople and farmers—and how I loved going out for visits to those farms! Then we moved to the state of Wisconsin, to La Crosse where the Mississippi River promptly captured my imagination. To me, it will always be *my* river. Milwaukee next—and my first large city for a home with the busy life of a student in a large high school.

I can remember our moving days so clearly—and what a problem all our books always were. There was never any question, however, but that they must be taken along, only I was never permitted to pack them. For I couldn't help sitting down in the midst of the confusion to re-read a favorite, and that wasn't so good for the packing.

Our next departure was for the eastern part of the United States, to East Orange, New Jersey, a move which helped materially in making my secret dream come true—going to Vassar.

By the time we reached Wisconsin, I had already started writing. No one ever suggested the idea to me—I just did it, with my first publication in the *Wisconsin Audubon Magazine* when I was "eleven years, three months."

My four years at Vassar offered me many opportunities for enjoyment of my favorite interests. I specialized quite naturally in English, enrolling in every writing course that was offered. But I specialized, too, in history and economics—history, the story of people and what they have done through the ages; economics, which was to me the story of the struggle to bring a richer living to all men and women and their families.

The campus activities enticed me with their variety, but athletics especially claimed me in the hockey team. At the beginning of my sophomore year, the College Press board was established and from that time until my graduation, I acted as Vassar correspondent for a local Poughkeepsie newspaper and for a New Jersey one, as well, sending them Vassar news every week and thus earning my spending money for the three years.

After college, what? I knew that somehow, some way, I should always be writing but I did not think of entering the work of publishing, nor yet that of library work, either of which would have combined people and books in my days. In fact, I was not sure just what I did wish to do. And so for the summer, I decided to act as counselor in a camp for working girls. At this camp, I met the women who gave me my first position—executive secretary of the women's and girls' social organization in a large department store in New York City.

I entered upon this work the following fall, and for six years my days were multitudinously filled with people, people, people. My first book grew directly from these years' experience—*Girls' Clubs*. The idea for it occurred to me because I myself had had such difficulty finding practical, concrete suggestions for our club organizing and program planning there in the store. For several years before I started upon the writing of the book, I kept notes and chapter plans and when I did write the book, I indeed put it all in! *Girls' Clubs* is the *thickest* book I have ever written.

When the [First World] War came, I resigned from the store to be with the Commission on Training Camp Activities. After the Armistice, again I faced the question of what to do and this time I decided upon writing. For three years, next, I wrote and wrote and wrote. My second book, *Producing Amateur Entertainments*, was then completed. I wrote articles for magazines and newspapers—and I often wonder what

I would be doing today had not an unexpected turn of events led me to the work that, along with my writing, has since absorbed me—editing.

Prolonged appendicitis at the close of my three years' writing deluged me with bills that ate ·up the money I had saved. So I looked about for a part-time position which would give me a regular income and at the same time leave me with some time free to continue my writing. This position I found with the Camp Fire Girls, as editor of their magazine for leaders, the *Guardian*. Editing combined for me people and writing and I quickly discovered that here was something new to me which was very much to my liking.

From the Camp Fire Girls, I went to the Girl Scout organization to edit their magazine for the girls themselves, the *American Girl*. There, despite the fact that my days were filled with girls and authors and illustrators and getting a magazine to press, I wrote my next book with the help of a collaborator, Virginia Moore, *Girls Who Did*, again one directly related to the work I myself was doing. The various chapters in the book were first published in the *American Girl* and so Miss Moore and I had the benefit of the actual suggestions of the girls themselves for our final revision.

From the *American Girl* I went to the *Youth's Companion* as associate editor, again for a part-time position so that I might return to more writing. So it was that the next few years enabled me to write *This Happened to Me*, and to edit *Adventure Waits* and *Love Comes Riding*, collections of stories I thought girls would enjoy, all written by masters of the short story; as well as *When I Was a Girl* and *Five Girls Who Dared*, collections of the girlhood stories of interesting and significant women as told by themselves in their own autobiographies.

But something else happened to me during these *American Girl* and writing years. I married Albert B. Tibbets. Summertimes ever since we have lived in a little white house on Hardscrabble Road near the village of Croton Falls, New York. As I write, I look out upon stone fences and our gardens of old-fashioned flowers beside them. I see our favorite goldfinch swooping toward his nest in the red raspberry hedge we planted two years ago. And if the cloud that is hiding the sun should bring a cold rain, I can move my typewriter in by the fireplace with its old Dutch oven, and touch a match to the logs that are waiting.

My book *Here Comes Barnum* had its beginning right here at this little old white house, for the land which is now ours once belonged to one of the first circus men of the United States. All the countryside is full of circus tradition. A neighbor lent me his old copy of Barnum's autobiography. And that is how, after books for girls and about girls, I did a book about Mr. Barnum.

It was in 1929, when I was at work on my Barnum book, that the opportunity came to join the staff of The Junior Literary Guild, the book club for boys and girls which was then being organized. I am still with them, as editor-in-chief, work that is stimulating and inspiring. To my editorial activities have been added my speaking trips which have taken me to many parts of the country. And in between, I have written *Tommy and His Dog, Hurry* and *Watch Me, Said the Jeep,* as well as collecting further stories for teen-age girl readers in *Challenge, Stories of Courage and Love,* and ballads in *Love's Enchantment.*

At our country home, it has been my pleasure to serve as trustee of our North Salem Free Library, and as chairman of the juvenile committee. In the latter capacity, our committee has cooperated with the Board of Education in opening library rooms in our two rural elementary schools. Whenever I can, I visit those rooms and the boys and girls there.

Rachel Field

September 19, 1894-March 15, 1942

AUTHOR OF

Hitty, Calico Bush, Hepatica Hawks, Taxis and Toadstools, Patchwork Plays, Etc.

Autobiographical sketch of Rachel Field, written for THE JUNIOR BOOK OF AU-THORS a few years before her death:

IT is humiliating to confess that I wasn't one of those children who are remembered by their old school teachers as clever and promising. I was notably lazy and behind others of my own age in everything except drawing pictures, acting in plays, and committing pieces of poetry to memory. I was more than ten years old before I could read, though for some strange reason (that is perhaps significant now) I could write, after a fashion.

The first ten years of my life were uneventful, though pleasant, and I spent them in the little town of Stockbridge in Massachusetts, where I learned to like below-zero weather and to find all sorts of growing wild things, such as arbutus in spring, wild strawberries in summer, and fringed gentians in the early fall. I didn't have many playmates my own age, but I managed to pick up a lot about trees and flowers and animals and outdoor things without the help of organized nature-walks and Girl Scout activities.

The little country school I went to, with about a dozen other pupils, was kept by two dear old ladies. I was a trial to the one who taught arithmetic, reading, spelling, and geography, but a favorite of the one who taught us poetry and planned plays for us to act. These were often quite ambitious, and the peak of my dramatic career was the year I was nine and played Shylock in *The Merchant of Venice* at Christmas and the leading role in *Rebecca of Sunnybrook Farm* (dramatized by the same teacher) in June. I couldn't read then but the parts were read aloud to me and I knew all the other children's lines as well as my own long before the dress rehearsals. Of course I decided then and there to become a great actress.

The next year my mother felt that something really had to be done about my education, for it certainly looked as if I were going to grow up illiterate. So we moved to Springfield, in another part of Massachusetts, and I was plunged into public school life. It was a good deal of a comedown after playing leading parts in theatricals, to discover that I was way behind my age in the more important branches of learning.

I never did catch up with my age in school work, and I never liked studying again till I got to college. I was still able to hold my own in drawing and in writing compositions, and I'm afraid I made use of this to get other scholars to trade arithmetic answers and grammatical parsings for compositions. It was always easy for me to write half a dozen papers, or poems when we began to have them for homework assignments later on. Sometimes it was a little trying when the teacher liked one I had written for some other pupil better than the one I had handed in for myself.

Somehow or other I was promoted to high school, but algebra and geometry and Latin grammar were so much worse than anything that had gone before that I despaired of ever being able to get out of the place. I used to see myself as an old lady in spectacles and gray hair still going to school because I couldn't pass the tests that would let me graduate. It never occurred to me that teachers might pass me on in sheer desperation. Report card day was a terror to me every time.

But I still loved poetry and I began to experiment in the different forms of verse. I would try writing something in the meter of "Thanatopsis" or "The Wreck of the Hesperus" and see why mine didn't sound as smooth and easy to read. I used to steal time from homework for this and I always felt guilty when I did it, though now I think it was probably harder, more concentrated work than anything I could have done. Once in a while a teacher of English would be interested in something I wrote and I occasionally got them printed in the school paper and in *St. Nicholas* League. That League was good training and it also taught me to learn to wait for literary verdicts. It took three months to learn whether a contribution had been accepted. Later when I began sending things to publishers I found I could stand the waiting better than some of my friends who hadn't had League training.

RACHEL FIELD

Well, I got through high school somehow. Perhaps my winning an essay prize helped. Three schools competed for it, so when I won first for mine, those in power helped me graduate with my class. Then I decided that I wanted to write. It seemed about the only thing I could do and I had won twenty dollars from the essay.

So I began hunting for a place where I could go on studying English without having to struggle with mathematics and Latin. I finally was let in to Radcliffe as a special student. Nowadays it isn't allowed, but I am always grateful that it happened to me. I loved those four years in Cambridge. I took all the English courses I could, in literature and composition, and I was lucky in having several professors who were interested enough in me to be very strict in their criticisms.

My last two years there I was in Professor George P. Baker's "English 47," the well-known playwriting course where the students wrote and produced plays under his keen eye. A short play of mine called "Three Pills in a Bottle" was given at that time and people were encouraging about it. Later it was published with others and from that time, 1918, it has been played, year in, year out, by groups all over the country on the average of once a week.

When I left college I came to New York to do several editorial jobs. One of them was writing synopses of books and plays for a motion picture company. It was hard work but it helped me to write in a more condensed way and incidentally improved my typewriting. In odd moments I continued to write verse and short plays and, yes, the usual thing—a novel. It went the rounds and was turned down as it should have been. But some of the editors wrote me letters about it and they all said the first part dealing with the heroine's childhood was the best. They suggested I do more in that vein; write some stories for children. So I sat down and tried to. Of course they all came back at first with rejections. The verdict was that though the ideas were young, I wrote with too long words and in a manner that children would find too difficult. I couldn't seem to feel that this was so. When I was younger I had never minded the longer words in *Alice in Wonderland* and the Hans Andersen stories. Anyway I had to go on writing the way things came to me.

At this time I used to cut out pictures from black paper and paste them on white cards, and I fitted some of these to the verses I had done. At last, after being returned from five publishers, my first book of verses and silhouettes, *The Pointed People,* was accepted by the Yale University Press. I had the misfortune to have it come out the year A. A. Milne's *When We Were Very Young* was sweeping the country. I was sure mine would be lost. But though it didn't have much publicity it sold enough to be kept in print and I began to have letters from children and teachers about it.

Then Scribner's brought out my first little group of one-act plays, and Louise Seaman of the Macmillan Company took me in hand. She accepted *Eliza and the Elves* (with its fascinating pictures by my friend Elizabeth MacKinstry to help sell it) and through her interest and help I began to develop other ideas for juveniles. May Massee, who was then at Doubleday, Doran, encouraged me with the smaller books (*An Alphabet for Boys and Girls, Polly Patchwork,* and others) and these I illustrated with my own rather crude pictures. I enjoy writing better than drawing, but still some people like the little pictures I make for the younger books.

In London in 1926 I saw a little dog in a shabby Punch and Judy show, and he was responsible for *Little Dog Toby,* and then two years after, with Dorothy P. Lathrop, the wooden doll "Hitty" was discovered in an antique shop on West Eighth Street. Together we planned her adventures, and I found an outlet for a lot of the material I had looked up on early American life and whaling. I wrote it with many interruptions and sent it on chapter by chapter to Miss Lathrop in Albany, where her enchanting pictures were made. People warned me that young readers would not care for a book written in the first person and full of so much about whaling. But I remembered that anything about ships had fascinated me. I believed that shipwrecks and desert islands and adventures by land and sea would always appeal to children, and if I could make it exciting enough they would not mind that a doll told the story or that she had to explain things now and then.

It was a great joy to Miss Lathrop and to me and to Miss Seaman of Macmillan's, who took such a special interest in the book, when *Hitty* was awarded the Newbery Medal for 1929. The award was presented in Los Angeles that year and "Hitty" and I flew part of the way out to receive it. Which only goes to show that books sometimes take one much further than anyone could have guessed — especially in those hours when one is struggling to put the words on paper!

From the year that I was fifteen I have been going each summer to a small, beautiful, wooded island off the coast of Maine and I suppose that it, more than any one other thing in my life, has helped me with my writing. For it means roots and background to me. It creeps into nearly everything I write and I never want to be anywhere else when summer comes round. Many of my verses in *The Pointed People* and *Taxis and Toadstools* were written there; and much of *Hitty,* and all of *Calico Bush,* has that coast of Maine setting.

* * *

Few modern writers for young people have been so well loved as Rachel Field. Her stories, verse, and plays, are read from the primary grades through high school, and *Hitty* has been called the "only true juvenile classic written in America in a generation."

In 1935 Miss Field turned to adult fiction and best-sellerdom with *Time Out of Mind,* a novel of her beloved Maine coast. Two later adult novels, *All This, and Heaven Too* and *And Now Tomorrow,* were also outstanding critical and popular successes and attracted the attention of the moving pictures. In 1935 also Miss Field married Arthur Pederson, literary agent; they moved to California in 1938, and had one daughter, Hannah. For Hannah she wrote several of her loveliest verses, almost her only writing for children in her later years.

Rachel Field was described as always gracious, unassuming, informed and informative, open-minded in discussion but determined, even stubborn, once she reached a conclusion and was certain she was right.

A delightful conversationalist, she had also "the gift of silence." Of medium height, she had curly auburn hair, blue eyes, a generous mouth, a low-pitched voice, and an infectious laugh. She enjoyed housework and growing things and was an enthusiastic cook. Her greatest talent, next to her literary ability, was for friendship. No effort was too great to provide pleasure for a friend, and her hand-made gifts, letters, and Christmas cards are still treasured by those who knew her best, and even by many who never met her face-to-face.

The wealth and acclaim of her last years failed to change her simple and warm-hearted tastes, and she lived quietly and modestly with her husband and infant daughter on a sunny California street in Beverly Hills. Failing to rally after an operation complicated by pneumonia, she died on March 15, 1942, after an illness of only ten days, in her forty-eighth year. Burial was in the old family plot at Stockbridge, Massachusetts. In July 1942 *Horn Book Magazine* devoted an entire memorial issue to her life and writings.

Parker Fillmore

September 21, 1878-June 5, 1944

AUTHOR OF

Czechoslovak Fairy Tales, Mighty Mikko, Wizard of the North, Etc.

Autobiographical sketch of Parker Hoysted Fillmore, written for THE JUNIOR BOOK OF AUTHORS a few years before his death:

AS a young man just after college I went to the Philippines as a teacher. I was sent to a small town in southern Luzon with instructions to establish public schools on the American model. Those were my only instructions and, odd as it may seem, I was furnished with no school equipment whatever—no paper, no pencils, no books, no desks.

The city fathers were friendly and did what they could for me. They assigned me a house with two big rooms for a school and two native assistants, a man and a woman, who had been village school teachers in Spanish days. With the help of the man teacher I made two big blackboards by nailing together some boards and painting them black. For chalk we collected lumps of lime. I realize now that with a lump of lime and a homemade blackboard I began writing what was to become my first book for children—a Philippine reader.

When we were ready to open school I had the town policeman round up all the children of school age. From the start I used only English in the schoolroom and as a result I had the youngsters speaking English in no time. I developed a vocabulary by teaching them first the English words for the objects about us—house, chair, dog, cat, boy, girl, and by actual demonstration such everyday verbs as eat, drink, sit down, stand up, sleep, speak, sing. The blackboard lessons gradually took the form of little stories about Philippine boys and girls at home, on the street, in school, in church, in the market place. I used the same characters day after day until their personalities became established and at last we always knew beforehand what each would do and say in any new situation.

It was six months or more before some American readers arrived. They were a bitter disappointment. They were full of apples and snowballs and, alas, neither apples nor snowballs were indigenous to the Philippines. My pupils much preferred the little stories of Philippine life which I developed for them day by day.

Bachrach

PARKER FILLMORE

After three years I returned to America and when a textbook publisher asked me to write the stories for a Philippine reader which his company was planning to bring out, I was able to do them out of my own experience.

My stories dealing with American children are usually spoken of as stories about children rather than stories for children. I suppose this is because they are merely stories instead of "moral" stories. Twenty years ago it was felt that any story for a child should have a plain moral and not treat of life too realistically. So the stories in *The Hickory Limb*, *The Young Idea*, and *The Rosie World* were read and laughed over by adults but neither parents nor librarians thought them quite proper for children. Today they would pass muster easily.

The third class of writing I have done for children is a series of folk tale and fairy tale books. During the First World War I lived on the upper East Side of New York in the midst of the Czech settlement. Propaganda for the cause of Czech liberty passed through the Czech department of the neighborhood library, which had what is probably the finest collection of Czech literature and prints outside of Prague. It was while working among these people that I became interested in their folklore. This interest bore fruit finally in two books drawn from Czechoslovak sources and one from Jugoslav sources: *Czechoslovak Fairy Tales and Folk Tales*, *The Shoemaker's Apron*, and *The Laughing Prince*.

Later, with a Finnish friend, I began delving into Finnish folklore and renewed what had been a boyhood enthusiasm for the Finnish epic, *The Kalevala*. I wrote one book of Finnish folk tales entitled *Mighty Mikko*, and one book drawn from some of the stories in *The Kalevala*, entitled *The Wizard of the North*. I think my own favorite among my children's book is *The Stuffed Parrot*, a story I made from part of an endless bedtime saga I used to tell my small daughter night after night for months.

* * *

Parker Fillmore was born in Cincinnati, Ohio, of old American stock on his father's side and Scotch-Irish on his mother's. His childhood and youth were spent in Cincinnati and he received his A.B. degree from the University of Cincinnati. After three years in the Philippines as a governmental teacher he returned to Cincinnati and for several years was associated with the banking house of W. H. Fillmore and Company. Later he moved to New York City, where his home was at the time of his death. This occurred, however, in Amherst, Virginia, while he was visiting friends.

Marjorie Flack

October 23, 1897-

AUTHOR AND ILLUSTRATOR

Angus and the Ducks, Angus and the Cat, Angus Lost, Ask Mr. Bear, Walter, the Lazy Mouse, Etc.

Autobiographical sketch of Marjorie Flack:

I WAS born at Greenport, Long Island. Greenport was a beautiful place for a little girl to grow up in. There were beaches of white sand on the Bay, and beaches with rocky cliffs on the Sound, and there was a stretch of woods to walk to.

As far back as I can remember, pictures and stories were always an important part of my life. I can remember drawing pictures in the sand, pictures on the walls (and being punished for it) and pictures on every piece of paper I could find. For every picture there would be a story, even before I could write.

When I was eighteen I came to New York to study art at the Art Students League. There I met Karl Larsson, the artist, and we were married in 1919. The next year our daughter, Hilma, was born.

My first book was written with my friend, Helen Lomen, who had lived almost all her life in Nome, Alaska. When I heard her tell about the Eskimo children and their life among the reindeer, I thought of how little the average child knew of Alaska, so we decided to make a book of the present-day Eskimo child. My second book was about a boy in New York, and I tried to put into it all the things which Hilma and I liked most about the city. The next year I wrote *Angus and the Ducks*. This is a true story about a real dog and some real ducks. The other Angus books are also built around real incidents. The cat was Hilma's cat, and she really did hide on the roof. Wag-Tail Bess was our own Airedale.

While I was writing *Angus and the Ducks*, I became so interested in the ducks that I found out all I could about them. When I found out that their ancestors had lived in China on the Yangtze River, I read all the books I could find of the life on the Yangtze River, and wrote *The Story About Ping*. I asked Kurt Wiese to make the pictures for it, because he had lived in China.

Ask Mr. Bear is a story which I used to tell to Hilma when she was very young. She would ask for it over and over, and often would add to it herself so that years later, when I came to put it in a book, I was not sure exactly whether I had told it to Hilma or Hilma had told it to me.

Tim Tadpole and the Great Bullfrog I particularly enjoyed working on, because it gave me a fine excuse to wander in the spring woods and to loiter by the edge of frog ponds, and to spend hours at the Museum of Natural History.

I feel that children should always be very happy that Anna Roosevelt Dall has written for them *Scamper—the Bunny Who Went to the White House*. While I was at the White House, drawing the pictures for the book, I tried to draw them in such

Mina Turner

MARJORIE FLACK

a way that children would feel that they were there too.

Many of my books have developed from observation of the place in which I was living at the time. Rockport, on Cape Ann, Massachusetts, inspired *Wait for William*, *William and His Kitten*, and *What To Do About Molly*.

I was fortunate enough to be at the MacDowell Colony, in Peterborough, New Hampshire, for four summers. A pet mouse in my studio there helped me to write one of the books I like best, *Walter, the Lazy Mouse*. *The Restless Robin* also grew from an experience I had there, while watching over a young robin fallen from the nest. I met Du Bose Heyward at the Colony, and this led to my illustrating his delightful story called, *The Country Bunny and the Little Gold Shoes*.

I was married to William Rose Benét, the poet, in 1941. This same year my daughter, Hilma, married Jay Hyde Barnum, the artist. I made the illustrations for my husband's book, *Adolphus the Adopted Dolphin*, at Marineland at St. Augustine, Florida; and enjoyed drawing the fascinating bottle-nosed dolphins from life.

My daughter's son, Timothy, is now giving me ideas for books for the very young. As he grows older perhaps I shall be writing for children a little older each year. So far, there has been *The New Pet*, written while he was still a baby; then *I See a Kitty* and *Away Goes Jonathan Wheeler*, illustrated by Hilma.

The Boats on the River developed from listening to Timmy chant, very much as *Ask Mr. Bear* grew from his mother's conversations at his age. His father has made beautiful drawings for this book.

My husband and I own a summer home at Pigeon Cove, Cape Ann, Massachusetts. *The Happy Birthday Letter* grew from this locality and, of course, more books will evolve from it.

Some of my books are translated into Swedish, Portuguese, and Spanish. Nearly all of them are published in England. It gives me great pleasure to know that children in so many countries enjoy my books. But I must always give credit to the places where I have lived, and to the children who have helped me. I enjoy writing and illustrating in the hope of giving the children as much pleasure as they have given me.

JOHN J. FLOHERTY

John J. Floherty

1882-

<small>AUTHOR OF</small>
*The Courage and the Glory, Men Without Fear,
Inside the F.B.I., Etc.*

Autobiographical sketch of John Joseph Floherty:

WHEN I was a very small boy I showed reportorial symptoms: I was forever asking questions or prying into things to see what made them work. Once I probed with a pin a valuable watch my father prized highly. I did not try *that* again.

In school I was not a very industrious student although I always managed to get good marks. A tireless reader, I merely winnowed the pages of books in the hope that from the chaff would fall an occasional kernel of interesting information. These I stored squirrel fashion. Strangely enough, those morsels of fact, collected without purpose, have proved useful many, many times in my writing.

A healthy lad, I did rather well at outdoor sports. Indoors my love of investigation predominated. Besides a strange collection of mechanical odds and ends with which I loved to tinker, I was proud owner of a chemical laboratory. Unfortunately it came to an untimely end; a sizable flask of hydrogen exploded with a report that shocked my family. Thereafter the realm of chemical experimentation was out of bounds.

More to compensate for the loss of my laboratory than because of an abiding love of art, I became interested in drawing and received much encouragement from a family friend, an artist of some repute.

After college I decided to take a fling at the sea as a kind of postgraduate course in human relations. It was a hard but invaluable experience. During that semester at sea I learned that under the work-stained dungarees of my shipmates were stored often stories and drama that the gold braid on the bridge considered not worth mentioning, since they were all merely a part of the day's work.

A sailor home from the sea, I began serious study at the Art Students League in New York and spent long hours between classes in the drudgery of practice.

I entered journalism as an artist reporter. Happy in my job, I progressed rapidly. In a few years I became a member of the executive staff of one of the country's largest publishing concerns. Some thirty artists, photographers, and writers were under my direction.

It was during this period I discovered that our teen-age son and daughter and their young friends showed sharp interest in factual stories. Occasionally I told them of interesting experiences I had had and illustrated my talks with rapid sketches. I also learned that many of the current children's books were not popular with them because of oversimplification.

A member of a volunteer fire company, I had observed the strange fascination that fire and fire-fighting apparatus have for young folk, and indeed for their elders. These and many other observations suggested that perhaps there was a need for factual books in which illustrations and accurate reporting told a straightforward story.

Fire Fighters was my initial effort in the juvenile field. Its success prompted me to report other American activities in which there was a colorful story.

Floherty: *FLO er tee*

In the twenty books I have had published, I have followed the same formula: inside facts, human interest, and accuracy.

While securing material and pictures, I have traveled the equivalent of twice around the world by ship, plane, train, motorcar, and other conveyances. I have interviewed thousands of people from cabinet officers to cab drivers. I went to sea aboard the Coast Guard cutter *Pontchartrain* to observe the great hurricane of 1938.

I have lived in lighthouses and on lightships and have taken potluck with the mud-covered men at the oil wells. I have fraternized with G-men and Secret Service men and have spent many a damp hour with the sand-hogs in one of New York's underwater tunnels. I have questioned scientists and sailors, policemen and test pilots, and men in a score of other callings. In short I have seen America at work and the wheels of industry, commerce, and government go round. In each of them I have found stories well worth the telling.

* * *

When not engaged in traveling in quest of material for a book, Mr. Floherty lives in Port Washington, New York.

Genevieve Foster

1893-

AUTHOR OF

George Washington's World, Abraham Lincoln's World, Etc.

Autobiographical sketch of Genevieve Stump Foster:

NEW YORK STATE was my birthplace, but Whitewater, a little town in southern Wisconsin, in the childhood home I remember. My father, who was a teacher of sciences, died in 1894, when I was a year old, and my mother went back to her father's home to live.

It was an old brick house, the house of my grandfather, four stories high. It stood in the center of a large lawn, surrounded by a picket fence. Grandfather died when I was three, and that left only four of us in the big house—my grandmother, my aunt, who was also a widow, but much older than my mother, Mother, and me. Though I was the only child, I never remember being lonely.

Grandma was a lively little old lady, full of fun, and always ready to play games. She taught me to sew and embroider when I was very small. I loved the beautiful colored silks, and she shared my enthusiasm, but always quietly insisted that I finish the piece I ·had begun before starting another. That was a hard lesson for me to learn, but one for which I have been grateful.

"Auntie," as I called her, was an invalid, and spent much time in her room, with a fascinating green bottle of smelling salts beside her. The winter I was five she was ill for weeks, and I wrote letters to her every day and pushed them under the closed door. Somehow or other, although no one had made any effort to teach me, I had learned to read and write.

I always liked to draw. That was taken quite as a matter of course by my mother, for there had always been someone painting, drawing, or modeling in our family.

When I was six I started school. From then on the house and yard were always full of children. One summer three of us who liked to draw had a studio in the top floor. There, also, in an old haircloth armchair, at the age of ten, I started to write the one and only novel I have ever attempted, and of which Chapter One was both the end and the beginning.

I liked school, probably because I was interested in everything and nothing was ever hard for me to learn or to remember —except history! History confused me. And the more I learned, in high school and college, the more confused I became.

I was graduated from the University of Wisconsin. By that time I was eager to go to an art school, for I had had no time to draw during college. I came to Chicago and studied for a year. The director seemed pleased with my work. Encouraged by him, I ventured to start out as a commercial artist, and for several years I did all kinds of drawings for newspapers, booklets, and magazines. The name I signed then was Genevieve Stump. It was interesting work, but I was never entirely satisfied, and gave it up when I was married in 1922 to Orrington Foster.

For the next few years my interest was centered in our home and our two small children, a boy, named for his father but called by the nickname Tony, and a girl, Joanna, four years younger.

Glidden

GENEVIEVE FOSTER

When they were both out of the baby stage, I dusted off my drawing board again, and began making illustrations for children's stories. This was fun, but still I was not entirely satisfied. And one day it finally came to me how I might combine all the things I liked best to do. I would try to find out what I myself had always wanted to know about history, and write a book about it, that children, and perhaps their fathers and mothers too, might like to read.

In 1941, when *George Washington's World* was published, Joanna was in the seventh grade, and Tony in high school. He was graduated from Cornell University in 1945, the year after *Abraham Lincoln's World* came out. And when Joanna was a freshman at Vassar I was finishing the illustrations for my third book, *Augustus Caesar's World*.

Claud Lovat Fraser

May 15, 1890-June 18, 1921

ILLUSTRATOR

Nursery Rhymes, Etc.

CLAUD LOVAT FRASER was born in London on May 15, 1890, the son of Claud Fraser, a solicitor, and Florence Margaret (Walsh) Fraser, an artist. The boy was educated at the historic Charter-

house School in London, leaving at the age of seventeen to be articled as a clerk in his father's firm. He read law for several years, but spent part of his time "sketching the picturesque square outside his father's office, or the folk that hurried past . . . the city's streets." Eventually his talents were recognized and in 1911 he was allowed to study under Walter Sickert at the Westminster School of Art.

At the age of eleven, young Fraser had begun to illustrate his letters with drawings, which even at that early date showed dramatic quality. His first published work —six caricatures—appeared in a privately printed volume in 1910. His drawings were reproduced in the *Art Journal* in 1911 and his decorations for Haldane Macfall's *The Splendid Wayfaring* in the *Art Chronicle* in 1912. An ardent theater-goer, Fraser became more and more interested in stage design. He met Gordon Craig and Sir Herbert Beerbohm Tree, both of whom influenced his career. Another influence was Léon Bakst, whose costume plates for the Russian ballet inspired Fraser's décor for Macfall's play, *The Three Students*. A prolific worker, Fraser turned out a flood of designs for book and music covers, bookplates, posters, book illustrations, and commercial advertising. His work was based on "an observation and understanding of the world in which he lived." But his inspiration came from the eighteenth century. He was "above all things a stylist," using the reed pen, often supplemented with color washes.

A man "of fine general culture," Fraser also wrote poems and essays under the pseudonym "Richard Honeywood." In 1913 he joined Ralph Hodgson and Holbrook Jackson in a short-lived project for publishing broadsheets and chapbooks under the imprint of The Sign of Flying Fame. Each publication was embellished with Fraser's "quaint and delightful" decorations.

When the First World War broke out, he was commissioned a lieutenant in the 14th Service Battalion of the Durham Light Infantry, going to Flanders in 1915. Early in 1916 he was invalided home, and for the remainder of the war held a government post. After his marriage, in 1917, to Grace Crawford, an American singer, and the birth of their daughter, he designed toys and also illustrated a number of children's books, of which the most notable are the gay and imaginative *Nursery Rhymes,* two fairy tales from the French of Charles Nodier—*The Luck of the Bean-Rows* and *The Woodcutter's Dog*—and Walter De La Mare's *Peacock Pie.* The decorations for another volume, *Pirates,* displayed Fraser's "love of the fantastic and romantic."

In 1919 Fraser designed the costumes and scenery for Nigel Playfair's production of *As You Like It.* The next year his work for *The Beggar's Opera* was completed and the day after the first performance in June 1920, Claud Lovat Fraser found himself famous. According to Robert Edmond Jones, "his many costume plates and his sketch for the permanent setting . . . exhibit a powerful, mordant humor completely in accord with the spirit of the opera." In 1921 he created "sumptuous" designs for Lord Dunsany's *If,* and for several ballets for Mme. Karsavina.

His health undermined by the war, Fraser now began to show signs of increasing fatigue. Taken suddenly ill while on a holiday in Kent with his family, he was removed to a nursing home at Sandgate, where he died on June 18, 1921, at the age of thirty-one.

Claud Lovat Fraser has been described as a "genial giant" with "a witty kindness, a gallant and boyish gaiety." Greatly interested in music, he had also a "deep fondness for literature," and once wrote, "I can't do without beauty and beautiful things." His friend John Drinkwater called him "a man all chivalry and light . . . with qualities of passion and sensitiveness of imagination and understanding."

Allen French

November 28, 1870-October 6, 1946

AUTHOR OF

The Story of Grettir the Strong, The Story of Rolf and the Viking's Bow, Heroes of Iceland, Red Keep, Etc.

Autobiographical sketch of Allen French, written for THE JUNIOR BOOK OF AUTHORS a few years before his death:

I SUPPOSE I am a "typical New Englander" because I was born and brought up in Boston, and have lived for many years in Concord, Massachusetts. New England ways of thought are native to me, and I am still strong for the better aspects of Puritanism. I must look like a professional man, for at filling-stations, or such places, I am often addressed as Doctor or Professor, though I am neither. But I have been a teacher, and have always been a student, and if these facts appear in my face or in my books, I suppose it is natural.

I was born November 28, 1870, and was educated in the Boston public schools. Put into the Latin school too early, I struggled with the classics for three years, then transferred to the high school, and so went to the Massachusetts Institute of Technology. It was not until I graduated from its general course and had had a year of study in Europe that I finally went to Harvard, where I worked chiefly in English. This subject I taught later in both my colleges. Teaching helped me to control my imagination, which I had excited since boyhood by wide reading. Meanwhile however, by overwork, I had plunged myself into six years of illness. Yet in spite of ill health a man can cultivate knowledge of life in general, which is needed to guide imagination.

Thus though my "History of Hull, Massachusetts," written at the age of eight, was purely imaginary, it was not until I had some knowledge of writing and of life that editors thought my writings worth printing. I began with short stories written for the *Youth's Companion,* but went on to serials for *St. Nicholas.* It was in this field of juvenile books that I worked for some years.

It was my ill health which produced the first of them, in 1901. My doctor took me to his camp for boys, and out of my experience grew my serial, *The Junior Cup.* As this was too short for a book, I had to write more, placing the scene at a boys' school. No American boy needs to be told where I got the material for the final baseball episode. At the same time I had been working in historical fiction, on a subject that I have been pursuing (or which has been pursuing me) from that time to this: the siege of Boston in 1775-76. A romance, founded on it, was printed in 1902 as *The Colonials.* In 1911 I published a short book on the siege. And even today the subject is still occupying me.

As my health grew better, I married and settled in Concord. Out of my gardening notes grew some of my books. Out of my sailing, one summer, grew *The Golden Eagle*. This was one of a series whose characters interested me, the other two books being *The Runaway* and *Pelham and His Friend Tim*. These are all New England stories.

A curious chance took me to an entirely different field. In the Old Corner Book-store, at a counter of secondhand books, I picked up one with the curious title of *The Story of Burnt Njal*. The first two pages were enough to fascinate me with a glimpse of life in Iceland a thousand years ago. I bought the book for twenty-five cents, recast it as *Heroes of Iceland*, and after much reading of other sagas, wrote what I suppose is my best Icelandic book, *The Story of Rolf and the Viking's Bow*.

This is a story of pure imagination, growing out of a love of romantic times. Another, founded on the stories of King Arthur, is *Sir Marrok*, first published in *St. Nicholas*. Books of this sort are difficult writing, unless steadied by common sense, which I tried to exercise in both cases.

I do not write of these books in their exact order, nor have I listed all that I wrote, particularly my novels which are out of print. Since 1925 I have taken to writing history, where I still keep to the New England field. Some of my books treat of the Concord and Lexington story, as I discover more and more about it.

* * *

It was at Concord that Allen French died on October 6, 1946, in his seventy-sixth year. He was president of the Concord Antiquarian Society and a former vice president of the National Thoreau Society.

Rose Fyleman

1877-

AUTHOR OF

Fairies and Chimneys, The Fairy Flute, The Fairy Green, Pipe and Drum, Etc.

Autobiographical sketch of Rose Fyleman:

I WAS born in Nottingham, in the middle of England, so long ago that I shall soon be an old lady.

I wrote stories and verses when I was quite a little girl and even had one printed in a local paper when I was about ten, a much less usual thing then than now.

Then I went to college, meaning to be a teacher, and did teach for a year or two. Then it was found out that I had a voice, so I went abroad and studied singing in Germany and Paris and London.

I sang in public, gave lessons, helped in my sister's school, and still wrote verses; so I had a busy life. And then one day a friend suggested that I might write for *Punch*. Now, in England we think a good deal of *Punch*, and the idea seemed ridiculous, but I thought I might as well try, and they accepted the verses, "Fairies at the Bottom of Our Garden." Of course I was very much elated.

Since then I have gone on writing verses and stories. Before long I gave up my other work and only wrote and sometimes lectured. It has all been great fun.

I am very fond of traveling and have been to nearly all the European countries and have enjoyed it all immensely. I've been twice to the States. And I hope you won't think I'm just flattering when I say that I have never seen anything more impressive than the first sight of New York from the steamer. Another thing that very much impressed me was the efficiency of your children's libraries wherever I went.

ALLEN FRENCH

Fyleman: *FILE man*

Howard & Joan Coster

ROSE FYLEMAN

I've been to Canada, too, and I had a glorious time on each trip to the American continent. Everyone was charming to me.

I can hardly remember the names of all the books I have written and I can never remember more than three of my poems. Once when speaking in a big American city I tried to recite one of my poems, which they had asked me for (it was from a book I had not brought with me) and when I suddenly stopped and said I could remember no more, a tiny girl put up her hand. "I can remember it," she said. So I asked if she would say it, which she did, perfectly. I was told afterwards that she was considered one of the shyest children in the school.

I'm hoping to do another book of poems soon and I hope to come to the States again before long.

*　*　*

Rose Fyleman's first book of verse was called *Fairies and Chimneys*, and it appeared in the year the First World War came to an end. Since then she has published *The Fairy Flute, The Fairy Green, Fairies and Friends*, and other books of fanciful poems full of elfin humor. Her stories include *Forty Good-Morning Tales, A Princess Comes to Our Town*, and *The Rainbow Cat*, and she is the author of *Eight Little Plays for Children*.

Her writing is done at all sorts of odd times and in odd places. She believes that her knowledge of music has been exceedingly helpful to her in the writing of verse.

She had a country cottage when her apartment in London was burnt to the ground in 1941, but is now back in London again.

"R.F.," as her friends call her, sees fairies not only in the bottom of her own garden, but everywhere she goes. Lady Adams says that "R.F. has her own particular brand of fairies; fairies who hop in and out of pumpkin coaches, who flit through the air like butterflies. Take a walk down Fleet Street with her and she sees them sitting daintily on the window-sills of the solemnest London daily newspapers; more surprising, she makes you see them too. R.F. is a second Tinker Bell. She will never grow up."

As Miss Fyleman herself put it in an article in *Horn Book Magazine*: "To be a successful writer of poems for children you have to be a *certain type of person*." Rose Fyleman *is* that type of person.

Wanda Gág

March 11, 1893-June 27, 1946

AUTHOR AND ILLUSTRATOR

Millions of Cats, Nothing at All, Gone Is Gone, The A B C Bunny, Etc.

Autobiographical sketch of Wanda Gág, written for THE JUNIOR BOOK OF AUTHORS a few years before her death:

I WAS born March 11, 1893, in New Ulm, Minnesota. This neat little German town gave me a background so European that I often forget I have never been outside of America. My father, the son of a woodcarver, was born in the Böhmerwald and my mother's family came from what is now Czechoslovakia. I spoke no English until I went to school.

In our home drawing and painting were taken for granted. My father decorated houses and churches on weekdays, and painted in his attic studio on Sundays. In my mother's family the creative urge, though undeveloped, was irrepressible. We children all drew as soon as we could hold pencils. In the evening all seven of us sat around the kitchen table, and after lessons (sometimes before!) we drew and wrote until bedtime. It never occurred to me that life might go on without these

WANDA GÁG

superfluous. In the end I was glad to paint lamp shades at twenty-five cents an hour. Upon trying commercial art again I gradually began to find my place in it. This taught me how to draw so my work would reproduce properly—in all other ways it was a setback. I continued my fine arts studies by reading and thinking and attending exhibitions, but my long hours of work left no energy to practice my theories.

For a while I lived with a family in which there were two children. They often begged for stories and I would invent some on the spur of the moment. They asked for them again and again, and with each repetition the stories became more compact. Finally I wrote them down, illustrated them, and tried the juvenile field again. Nothing came of it. I was used to rebuffs and quietly deposited the stories in my well-filled "Rejection Box." These stories were *Millions of Cats, The Funny Thing,* and *Snippy and Snappy.*

My commercial work by this time had become lucrative and promised a bright future. I did not care for that future. The strain of expressing other people's ideas, when my own were clamoring for attention, became too great. I broke my connections, took my small savings and rented a house in the country, telling myself fiercely that now I would draw what I pleased, even if *nobody* liked it.

To my surprise this rather selfish move had gratifying results. A New York gallery accepted my drawings and gave me a one-man show. I was happy in this work. Besides drawing and painting, I made woodcuts, etchings, and lithographs. I thought no more about my stories. One day a woman who had been following my other work heard I had some juvenile material tucked away. She was connected with a new publishing firm and asked to see what I had. As a result the stories grew into books and have seen more of the world than I have. (The first, *Millions of Cats,* was published in 1928.)

things, and when I discovered that to many people drawing was not as important as eating and sleeping, I was puzzled and disillusioned.

This was a simple life and a happy one. It did not last. Our parents died before we were grown up. I, the oldest (fourteen), was dazed by the problem which confronted us. Advice was offered but although I was shy and dreamy, I proved difficult to handle—I had my own ideas as to what was best for us. I felt convinced for instance that we must not be separated, that we must all go through high school, and that it was not only unfair but impracticable to ask me to give up my artistic ambitions. I made my plans accordingly and clung to them with an obstinacy which no one, myself included, had suspected me capable of. There was very little with which to carry out these plans, but we all worked together and after many difficult years it was accomplished.

In the meantime, by means of scholarships and help from friends in St. Paul and Minneapolis, I had been able to attend art school in these cities—later I went to the Art Students League in New York. After that I moved the children to Minneapolis and faced New York on my own. I tried magazine covers and failed—one cannot be too thankful for such things. Next I tried juvenile illustration — no one seemed impressed. Then commercial art—I was clearly

In time all the younger Gágs joined me in New York. Some of them are with me now on our New Jersey farm. We draw and write and build things. We sow seeds and help them grow. Most of the old problems are solved now, but new ones are constantly springing up. Life is still complicated, sometimes joyous, always interesting.

* * *

The Gágs called the New Jersey farm "All Creation." "Because," said Wanda, "ever since we've been here whoever comes seems to want to draw, to write poetry, to paint, even to sew—but to do something." And busiest of all were the Gágs. Flavia and Wanda, the youngest and the oldest and at that time the only unmarried sisters, spent the first winter making the place habitable and the second making it attractive. In these efforts they were greatly helped by Howard, who came to live with them. All three worked like beavers, carpentering, plastering, painting, and papering. Rose Dobbs describes the gay lilac, orange, and blue mural over the bathtub painted by Wanda as "a delectable swimming hole scene, with a few of the millions of cats in the water, the Funny Thing grinning wickedly at them from behind a clump of characteristic Gág bushes, and Snippy and Snappy off in a corner happily occupied with their big blue knitting ball." There were seven Gágs, Wanda, Stella, Nelda, Asta, Dehli, Howard, Flavia—all girls except Howard.

Later Wanda married Earl Humphreys and lived in an apartment in New York City. She died there at the Doctors Hospital.

A critic once wrote of Wanda Gág: "Today she stands unique among artists for her insight that can see beauty even in sordidness and for her sure craftsmanship that can reveal that beauty to others." During her life she won several prizes and now many of her drawings and paintings have places in museums, both large and small, in the United States and abroad.

Alice Crew Gall * & Fleming H. Crew

Authors of

Bushy Tail, Ringtail, Wagtail, Etc.

Autobiographical sketch of Alice Crew Gall and Fleming H. Crew:

WE are brother and sister, as perhaps you know, and we were born in McConnelsville, Ohio, where we spent our childhood together. This is a quiet, friendly little town at the edge of a lovely river, and is surrounded by tree-covered hills and rolling meadows.

* Died 1949.

Like most boys and girls, we loved the out-of-doors and were fond of taking hikes into the near-by woods and fields or along the banks of the small streams that flow down to the river. In the summer there were berries on these hillsides, and nuts in the fall. And there were always exciting excursions to be made to some shady pond where frogs and turtles lived, or through some secluded ravine where the more timid birds found shelter.

It was on these hikes that we learned to know the small wild creatures that we were to write about when we grew older. We learned to love them, too, though we never realized quite how much until years later when we had left our home and gone out into the busy world. Then we thought of these creatures we had left behind and decided it would be fun to write about them.

And it has been fun, even more fun than we thought. For each book we have written has carried us back in memory to the time when, as children, we saw these creatures making their nests and burrows and living their lives, just as they always have back there on the hillsides and along the river banks we knew so well.

When the time came for us to go out into the world and live grown-up lives, the paths we followed took us far apart; for one of these paths led to New York, the other to Cleveland. But though we were no longer together we were still eager to write about the small creatures we had known and loved in our childhood, in the hope that we might help other children know and love them too.

And so one day we began a story about Wagtail, a little tadpole. For weeks and weeks we sent the things we wanted to tell, back and forth to each other until at last our story was finished and ready to be made into a book. We had enjoyed doing this so much that soon we were writing another story, and another and another, each one more fun to do than the one that went before.

Even today we are still writing books for children. But we no longer have to send our chapters back and forth to each other as we did at first, for now, after many years, we have both come back to our old home town to live.

Here are the same tree-covered hills, the same rolling meadows and lovely river. And best of all, we think, the small creatures still play about the hillsides and meadows, where we can see them living their lives while we do the other books that we are looking forward to doing in the years to come.

Shannon Garst

July 24, 1899-

AUTHOR OF

Kit Carson, Cowboy Boots, Etc.

Autobiographical sketch of Doris Shannon Garst:

I WAS born in the small mining town of Ironwood, Michigan. When I was four we moved to Denver, where we remained until my last year of high school. We then moved to Hood River, Oregon, where my parents bought a fruit orchard.

After four years of country school teaching in Oregon, I found a civil service position in Wyoming, the land of the cowboys, where I have made my home ever since. Living as I do in the heart of the cattle country, it was inevitable I should write stories of cattle ranching.

I've often wished I had been born a boy because boys have more fun and more adventures than girls do. Perhaps it is my hankering for adventure that led me to write biographies of persons whose lives were brimful of excitement. I have always thought the real life stories of such characters much more exciting and dramatic than made-up stories; nevertheless, I plan to write more fiction because it's such fun to let one's imagination take over. I think it's even more fun than writing biographies.

It's my opinion that writing for children is the most satisfying sort of work there is. Young people appreciate books more than adults do. You seldom hear of a grown person's reading a book more than once, whereas a child will read a book he likes over and over again.

So far I have fourteen books to my credit, but I consider my greatest achievements to be my three children—two boys and a girl. They are really fine people.

I sent several of the stories I made up for my children to juvenile magazines. The editors accepted them—so I found myself a

SHANNON GARST

writer. Perhaps I never should have had time to write a book if Babs hadn't come down with a light case of scarlet fever. She wasn't sick and I had so much time while we were quarantined that I got my first book written. That activity turned out to be habit-forming, for I've been writing books ever since.

Doris Gates

1901-

AUTHOR OF

Blue Willow, Sensible Kate, Etc.

Autobiographical sketch of Doris Gates:

I WAS born in the Santa Clara Valley near San Jose, California. It is reported of me that on the eve of my third Christmas, when asked what I wanted Santa Claus to bring me, I replied, "A baseball and a bat and a train of cars." This will prove I was a tomboy. A few years later, the dearest wish of my heart was to own a burro. By this time we had moved onto a prune ranch; there was an empty stall in the big red barn, and one day a little gray burro named Jinny came to live in that empty stall. She was the greatest friend of my childhood, and my first book, *Sarah's Idea*, is largely about her.

It is said that all the books an author writes are written out of the things that

DORIS GATES

Attilio Gatti

1896-

AUTHOR OF
*Mediterranean Spotlights, Wrath of Moto,
Here Is Africa, Etc.*

Autobiographical sketch of Attilio Gatti:

"WHAT started you in your career of expeditions and explorations?"

That's the question I'm asked almost every time I meet somebody. In most cases, another one follows at once. "How did you come to make writing your profession?"

To be truthful, here is what I should answer on each occasion. "I became an explorer because of an unexpected kick I got in my pants. I started writing books in English because I didn't know even twenty words of this language. And the giant gorilla of the mountains had a lot to do with both these decisions.

Am I crazy? Yes—I mean, no!

But let me explain.

I was born in northern Italy in 1896. This will make me seem to you a sort of historical monument. But, at the time, I thought nothing of it.

My father was an officer in the Italian cavalry. One of his colleagues had been loaned by Humbert I, then King of Italy, to Leopold II, King of the Belgians, who was then opening what today is the Belgian Congo.

This captain was a rough and tough type of man—as he well had to be, because he was dispatched to the high jungles of the Kivu, in the dead center of Africa, and, singlehanded, he had to establish over them the authority of the King of the Belgians, win the friendship of tribes of savages, see to the building of terribly difficult roads, and so on.

When he returned he paid a visit to my family and spent some hours giving them a brief story of his extraordinary adventures. These included his dealings with the Pygmies, who to him looked more like apes than men and grew to only four feet and six to nine inches high; and with the giant gorillas of the mountains, which grew up to six feet six inches of stature and six hundred pounds of weight, and had more the appearance of men than apes.

have been a part of his life. I think that is true; at least it has been true in my own case. *Blue Willow*, my second book, and the best liked, came as a result of experiences as a children's librarian in the San Joaquin valley. There I saw hundreds and hundreds of boys and girls whose only home was a badly battered old automobile in which they followed the crops from place to place. We called these people "migrants" and their lives were very hard and often heartbreaking. I told stories to these children in migrant camps. And gradually the story of *Blue Willow* and Janey Larkin began to take shape in my mind. I was sure as I wrote it, and I am sure today, that boys and girls want more than anything else to have a home to which they go day after day and week after week. More than trains of cars or burros, they want a permanent home; and so I made that the great desire of Janey.

All my books so far have been laid in California, the only spot of earth I know really well.

My home is in southern California, where my husband, William Herbert Hall, is a practicing attorney. The only other member of our household is a Doberman pinscher by the name of Hilda. My favorite sport is swimming, and my only hobby is cooking. My favorite occupation is (you've probably guessed it) writing books for boys and girls.

Attilio Gatti: *a TEEL ee oh GAT ee*

Well, I was only seven or eight years old, but already chock full of curiosity. Unobserved, I slipped into the room. Quietly I absorbed every single word of the captain. But when he tried to imitate the terrific cry of an enraged giant gorilla I wasn't impressed. On the contrary, forgetting all caution, I started laughing like a fool— thereby revealing my presence.

Mildly annoyed, the captain turned around and gave me a kick in the pants. Of course, the gesture was meant purely as a joke. But it wasn't the kind of joke I liked. And the captain's boots were heavier than he realized. At any rate I never forgot that kick. Nor all the talk about the giant gorillas it had concluded, as if by a slightly too energetic exclamation mark. Nor the words that my deeply offended dignity prompted me to say as the only possible retort. "I shall find out. One day I shall find out for myself that the giant gorilla doesn't make any such funny noise!"

And I did. It took me years, plenty of them. First, I had to go through every possible kind of school. Then, what now is called World War I came, and I had four years of it, on horseback and in trenches, in the first tanks, and in the ancestors of today's planes.

Finally at the end of the war I was sent to Egypt in the hope that I should recover from a bad flu made worse by a wound in the lungs. Before I knew it I was well and resigning my commission and starting on a big game hunting expedition. A new life had begun for me—one that was never to lose its fascination.

In a while I realized that, much thrill as there was in stalking and hunting great beasts, there were a thousand more interesting things still to be done in Africa: strange tribes whose customs were still a secret; animals still undiscovered or practically unknown; secluded regions still unexplored; human and animal races hidden in the most distant past, proofs of whose history were still to be guessed, unearthed, pieced together.

And so it was that, in the following years, I organized and led ten long scientific expeditions, which kept me a total of fourteen years on African soil. And so it is that even today, while I'm writing these lines, I'm busy preparing my eleventh venture, the Gatti-Hallicrafters Expedition to the "Mountains of the Moon," the Ruwenzori Range which, almost spank on the African equator, soars up to nearly seventeen thousand feet.

As for the giant gorilla of the mountains, it took me six expeditions before I got around to it. But then I spent years in studying its life and habits and behavior. And I found out that—captain's kick or not—its yell of rage was a spine-chilling, unforgettable cry, quite different from that poor rendition of it I heard in my youth.

As a matter of fact, it was the telling of this story to an American junior book editor which prompted this lady to ask me to write a book about the gorilla. This was during my first visit to the United States. I had never written a book. I had talked to this editor in French because I didn't know even twenty words in English. Yet, to my protest, she answered: "Oh, come on! If you put your mind to it, you can write it."

The challenge was too much, I guess, for me and for my wife, Ellen Morgan Gatti, who is American born and whom I had just met in those days. I never could have done it without her marvelously patient and understanding assistance. But, truly enough, the book came out, *The King of the Gorillas.*

ATTILIO GATTI

And that is what I have been doing ever since. Some more books. Another expedition. Some more books. So came out six books for young people and four adult books, all about Africa.

In the meantime I became an American citizen, and while I almost forgot my native Italian, and French, Spanish, Portuguese, and Arabic, English became my own language, and my wife had learned to speak also Kiswahili, Kingwana, and other African languages as fluently as I do.

Now, for some years we have been living in a quiet place on the Vermont-Canadian border. And when I say "on," that's what I mean. The International Boundary goes through the whole length of our house. For instance, it cuts my office in two. On the American side is the desk where I am finishing a new book. On the Canadian side are the large maps on which I work to put the last touches to the organization of our new venture to the "Mountains of the Moon."

Quite some years have passed since I got that kick in my pants. But, as you can see, its effects are far from spent, as yet!

KATHARINE GIBSON

Katharine Gibson

1893-

AUTHOR OF

The Golden Bird, Pictures to Grow Up With, The Goldsmith of Florence, Etc.

Autobiographical sketch of Katharine Gibson:

I AM wondering, if I were you, what I would want to know about me. I can't quite see why you should be much interested, but as grown-ups are always grateful for attention from young people, I shall try to tell you, as best I can, what I suppose you would like to know. Mostly boys and girls ask, "How did you happen to write stories?" Well, I have wondered, too. I can't spell or punctuate and I got very bad marks on compositions and themes and was thoroughly discouraged.

I think writing came largely by not writing, though I would be the last to recommend that. I had too much time on my hands because of an eye difficulty that kept me out of school a great deal. To amuse myself I made up hundreds of stories with myself as heroine and everyone else mostly shadows or villains. This would have been sheer waste except that I did get interested in words, their sound and weight and color. But the grinding discipline of writing came much too late.

What writing I did was the result of knowing so many boys and girls, hundreds and hundreds of them, during the many years I was working with them as a member of the staff of the Cleveland Museum of Art. My first books were written with and for those children. Now the writing has become the main job and I am working with the Artists and Writers Guild of New York City.

In order to answer other questions you may have, I suppose I ought to say I got born. That was in Indianapolis. If you want to know what growing up there was like, read *Penrod* and *Seventeen*, by Booth Tarkington. I had a brilliant older brother and sister and used to wonder how all the family brains got used up before I came along. Before it was all over, there were five architects in the household. My father started that. I used to wish they'd talk about something interesting! It was tiresome hearing nothing but floor plans and where to put stairs and why did everybody build everything as if this were Europe and not America and as if America had no ideas of its own.

Finally I got married. My husband is a Unitarian minister, but don't let that frighten you; it never did me. He can spell! With him I have traveled a good deal, especially in England. These trips have come into the books as have my Irish terrier and my black cat, Congo. "How did you happen to write stories?" With all this around me, they wrote themselves. I just typed them and not very well either.

*   *   *

When Katharine Gibson — Mrs. Frank Wicks—and her husband are not traveling, they live in Indianapolis.

Joseph Gollomb

November 15, 1881-May 23, 1950

AUTHOR OF

The Lincoln High Books, Up at City High, Window on the World, Etc.

Autobiographical sketch of Joseph Gollomb, written for THE JUNIOR BOOK OF AUTHORS shortly before his death:

I WAS born in the glittering capital of Czarist Russia, then known as St. Petersburg, and till I was ten life seemed to me as full of glamor as of terror. Daily I was thrilled by the processions that passed my father's engraving shop, regiments of infantry and cavalry, flags flying, bands playing, swords and bayonets flashing, brilliantly uniformed officers on prancing horses. I knew they were on the way to the Czar's Winter Palace for review and what youngster could resist following them? I know I was swept along. Then on church feast days there would be religious processions, gorgeously clad priests, banners, images, chants. The fact that as a Jew I was supposed to be aloof from it all made me put up a feeble resistance to the show, until night. Then the whole city would light the wicks of paraffin-filled little glasses that lined the curbs, green, blue, red, yellow, and I simply had to revel in the sight.

The city is full of canals. In the summer gaily colored little steamboats gave you rides on them for the cost of a streetcar fare. In the winter the canals were transformed into skating rinks rimmed with evergreens and lit up with festoons of colored electric bulbs, with brass bands playing and skaters gliding to the music. Then there were street fairs and picturesque public ceremonies and many another feast for a youngster's senses. And of course there were ice skating, bobsledding and sleigh riding.

So much for glamor. What I remember as often is a thunderous knocking on our apartment door, in the dead of night, and the heavy voices outside. "Open. Police inspection." It would happen once a week or more. The point is that you never became accustomed to the shock of being awakened in the night by these "domiciliary visits" carried out in the spirit of raids on criminal nests. The most law-abiding citizens had to submit to them; that's the way of it in a police state. What made these visits all the more terrifying for me was that some of the elders in my family were not law abiding. They were plotting the overthrow of Czarist tyranny. I guess that most Americans, were there a tyrant over us, would be in the ranks of revolutionists. At any rate some of my nearest kin were.

In addition as a Jew I could expect anything from a beating from my non-Jewish schoolmates, to hearing of pogroms, mass lynchings of Jews by mobs. Finally my father had enough of it and brought the family to New York.

We settled in the greatest slum in the world, the lower East Side. We were poor but I did not know it. All my neighbors lived as we did, so a youngster took it for granted that it had to be so. Besides I was a healthily nosy kid and there were more colors, sights, sounds, and interesting hu-

JOSEPH GOLLOMB

mans and activities to intrigue me than St. Petersburg ever afforded.

For one thing my gang—I joined one as soon as I could speak a little English, which didn't take long—had boys in it who years later became famous as painters, writers, teachers of philosophy, professional athletes, lawyers, doctors, gunmen, teachers, business leaders, racketeers, war heroes, settlement workers, and what not.

In addition there was the colorful traveling we kids did on our roller skates. Within easy reach of our homes were Chinatown, Little Italy, the Syrian Quarter, the gay white ways of Fourteenth Street and Broadway, and the Gold Coast of Fifth Avenue.

There were no public playgrounds on the lower East Side then, but that did not keep us from holding athletic meets in the gutters, playing baseball and soccer in the streets and in the backyards, basketball in settlement house gyms, and swimming in the floating free baths in the East River, rich with sewage.

At the age of twelve I calmly decided I would be a writer. I wrote for my elementary school paper, later for the periodicals in the City College. My father died when I graduated and with his family to support I had to grab a steady job, teaching public school, day and evenings. I took my Master of Arts degree at Columbia, and after ten years at teaching I plunged into the most uncertain of careers, newspaper work and free-lance writing.

It was then that I really saw the world. Wars and revolutions; the inside of Scotland Yard—by a bit of reporter's luck I was the only American newspaperman to be allowed in, and not under arrest; the insides of palaces of royalty and the hiding places of revolutionists; capitals of luxury and plague spots where epidemics were raging; Monte Carlo and Moscow, and what have you.

I wrote about what I saw. But the books that have lived longest are the three I wrote about life in the De Witt Clinton High School, where I taught for several years. *That Year at Lincoln High*, for instance, has been selling now over twenty-seven years. They were the first books I wrote. After that came novels, books on politics, espionage and crime.

Then came the Second World War and I saw even professors of philosophy at a loss what to think about our upset world. One day I happened to be talking to a group of high school boys. As confused as their elders, they had to make life-and-death decisions. Some of them were killed in action soon after, some wounded. I was so affected by their necessity of having to make grim choices· in a confused and changing world that I wished with all my heart I could help, say something, write something that might contain the gist of what ·I had learned in my years of observing and reporting. That is why I have come back to writing for a high-school-age public in *Up at City High, Tiger at City High,* and *Window on the World,* a newspaper story. If these books have any reason for survival it is because they are a plea for friendliness, tolerance, teamwork, international cooperation and eventually a United States of the World.

*   *   *

Joseph Gollomb lived for many years on East 17th Street in New York City. It was in his apartment there that he died of a heart attack on May 23, 1950, in his sixty-ninth year.

Hardie Gramatky

1907-

AUTHOR AND ILLUSTRATOR OF
Little Toot, Hercules, Loopy, Etc.

Autobiographical sketch of Hardie Gramatky:

LIKE most people bent on a creative life I started out at an early age thrashing about for an anchor. I tried any number of jobs on which to get a start. I was cashier in a bank. I did a stretch in a logging camp. I was a deck hand on a freighter. I even tried two years of university. Then I ghosted a well-known comic strip and ended up in Hollywood as an animator for Walt Disney. There I got married and actually settled down for six years.

When the ol' urge got me again my wife and I packed up and came East. I got a free-lance assignment from *Fortune* magazine to do "pictorial reporting." Standing in water up to my hips, I painted on-the-spot pictures of the Mississippi flood. From there *Fortune* sent me up to Hudson Bay to do pictures at thirty below zero. Then they were kind and sent me to the Bahamas.

Hardie Gramatky: *HARD ee gra MAT kee*

HARDIE GRAMATKY

It was between those trips that I wrote *Little Toot*. At the time I had a studio in an old loft building off Wall Street overlooking the East River. As I worked on some hack job I looked out the window and made color notes of the wonderful parade of boats forever going by. I must have made several hundred of these sketches; and al ways it seemed that one tiny boat stood out among all the rest. It had so much personality that a story developed out of it, and that was *Little Toot*.

Although I had difficulty at first in selling the idea (several big publishers turned it down on the grounds that "children weren't thinking that way"), once the book was published it was an immediate success. Then as the sales began to mount we had several offers from Hollywood on the story. I finally sold it to my good friend Walt Disney, who featured it in his *Melody Time*. It has also been on radio, television, and has even been a float in the Tournament of Roses parade in Pasadena.

My next book was *Hercules*, the story of an old-fashioned fire engine. Then came *Loopy*, the airplane that wanted to fly by itself. It was not due to *Loopy* that during the war I got an assignment with the Army Air Force. On the contrary a colonel once told me he had it on his shelf of "nontechnical" books.

My most recent book at this writing is *Creeper's Jeep*, the story of how a jeep on

a farm makes a hero out of the farmer's easygoing, good-natured offspring.

Meanwhile, I keep up my illustrations for magazines. I have taken my share of watercolor prizes, twenty in all; and consider it a rare honor to be represented in such permanent collections as those of the Chicago Art Institute, the Toledo Museum of Fine Art, and the Brooklyn Museum. I am a member of Salmagundi Club, the Society of Illustrators, and the American Water Color Society. I have recently been elected an Associate of the National Academy.

Last but not least, I should like to mention my small daughter, Linda. Being a very level-headed and practical person, she is the proving ground for all my work. She is my severest critic.

Elizabeth Janet Gray

October 6, 1902-

AUTHOR OF
Meggy MacIntosh, Adam of the Road, Penn, Sandy, Young Walter Scott, Jane Hope, Etc.

Autobiographical sketch of Elizabeth Janet Gray:

I WAS born on October 6, 1902, a very belated addition to a family that had long since considered itself complete. My mother started life as a New Jersey Quakeress, tracing her descent from Thomas French who left Northamptonshire, England, just in time to precede William Penn up the Delaware.

My father was an Aberdonian born, with all the love of the Scotsman in America for the traditions and romance of the country he had left behind. The great interest of his later life was the drawing together in friendship of the English-speaking peoples, and the beautiful Scottish-American war memorial in Prince's Street Gardens, Edinburgh, rose out of his vision and his impulse. He died shortly before it was unveiled.

I was sent to the Germantown Friends School, that four-square old school under the shadow of big walnut trees on the edge of the Meeting House grounds, that gives so much to its children and wins in return from them such deep and lasting affection and loyalty. At thirteen I played Titania in the Shakespeare festival (being then very

Bradford Bachrach
ELIZABETH JANET GRAY

small for my age) and started on what I was pleased to call my literary career. I was no Daisy Ashford. I was severely practical and kept well within the bounds of my experience.

I wrote a moral story for children which I sent to the *Young Churchman* and for which the *Young Churchman* paid me all of two dollars. The real thrill in the affair —aside from seeing the story in print, which came later—lay in the fact that the *Young Churchman* never for a moment suspected that I was not entirely grown up. In fact, the editor's inspired letter of acceptance began, "My dear *Mrs.* Gray."

Before I was quite seventeen I entered Bryn Mawr College, perhaps the most naive and ingenuous freshman that ever strayed through Pembroke Arch. And that in those days after the First World War when sophistication and disillusionment were the first requirements of a young girl and to be caught in a naivete was the ultimate disgrace. I was very mortifying to myself most of my freshman and sophomore years.

Out of college at twenty—a gratifyingly old and world-weary twenty—I began at once to look about for a job, but decided, after being told till I was raw with irritation that I was too young and inexperienced, to be a "daughter at home." There was a year of odd jobs of tutoring and grading papers, of writing short stories and cynically papering part of the wall of my bedroom with

the rejection slips. The Sunday School magazines stood by me nobly, and I broke into the Contributors Club of the *Atlantic Monthly* with an essay on the Scotch. It was unsigned and I later had the fun of hearing an outlying member of my family appropriate parts of it, without acknowledgment, to decorate an after-dinner speech.

Weary of leading what we then called a parasitic existence I suddenly, on an impulse, signed up with a teachers' agency and found myself within a week teaching English, ancient history, and community civics (I was never sure just what they were) in a high school in a New Jersey seashore resort. Winter on the deserted coast was delightful. Every afternoon when school was out I ran off to the lonely boardwalk where, wrapped up in a steamer rug, I sat in the lee of a boarded up pavilion, facing the tumbling, steel-gray winter sea, and writing.

The following year I went to Drexel Institute to acquire a degree in library science, but it was the book that had come out of the winter at the seashore and a previous spring in the New Hampshire mountains that set my feet on the path that best suited them. It was this first book for girls that won me the friendship of May Massee. Her letter came, after three months in which hope flowered, drooped, faded, dried up, and was swept out—only to blossom afresh at the enigmatic note which suggested my going to New York to talk it over. And what a day that was! Being young herself, Miss Massee forgave me for being young, and I found then, as I do now, her zest and discrimination an invaluable stimulus and help.

A year of library work, and another year of teaching followed. Then I married Morgan Vining of the faculty of the University of North Carolina. We built a little house in an acre of oaks, elms, and cedars, and I combined housekeeping with writing and teaching Library Science in the U.N.C. Summer School. *Meggy MacIntosh* and *Jane Hope* came out of those brief years.

After my husband's death in an automobile accident in 1933, I returned to Philadelphia to live with my mother and sister, to travel and to write. *Young Walter Scott, Beppy Marlowe, Penn, The Fair Adventure, Adam of the Road* (Newbery Award, 1943) and *Sandy* (Herald Tribune Spring Festival

Prize, 1945) were the products of the next eleven years. The *Contributions of the Quakers* and *Anthology with Comments*, also written during that time, have been published by Pendle Hill, Wallingford, Pa.

Why do I write for children? I rather think because they enjoy their books so much, read and re-read them instead of tossing them aside after a cursory skimming —which is satisfying to a hard-working author. Or perhaps I might ask myself why I write at all—and that is easier to answer. I write because I can't help it.

In 1934 I returned to the faith of my mother's family and became a member of the Society of Friends. In the silence of the Friends meeting for worship, I found new strength and meaning for my life at the time when I desperately needed both. When the Second World War overwhelmed the world, I wanted to make a contribution in the way of Friends, not to the fighting of the war, but to the great task of reconstruction and reconciliation. When the opportunity came, I joined the staff of the American Friends Service Committee in Philadelphia, and spent a year and a half writing reports, appeals, and articles about the work of the Committee in America, Europe, and Asia.

In May 1946, I decided to hand over my desk at the Service Committee to someone else and return to creative writing. The Education Commission which had visited Japan earlier that spring had been asked by the Emperor to find an American Christian woman to teach the Crown Prince English. To my amazement the Service Committee asked me if I would be willing to have my name suggested for this appointment. It was, obviously, a great opportunity, and a great responsibility. After thinking it over carefully, I replied that if certain "weighty Friends" thought that I could be useful, I could not refuse to consider it. In June Dr. George D. Stoddard, head of the committee, sent two names, mine and one other, to the Imperial Household, and in August, I was chosen for this unprecedented post.

In her new constitution Japan has renounced war as an instrument of national policy. It is my hope, in this fabulous and yet very human job which I have entered upon, that I can make some contribution to the great cause of peace and cooperation among the nations of the world.

Kate Greenaway

March 17, 1846-November 6, 1901

ILLUSTRATOR AND AUTHOR

A Apple Pie, Kate Greenaway's Mother Goose, Under the Window, Etc.

KATE GREENAWAY was born in London on March 17, 1846, the daughter of John Greenaway, an engraver, and Elizabeth Jones Greenaway. When she was a year old she was taken to the country near Rolleston, in Nottinghamshire, and there spent several years on a farm. The influence of this early environment where she learned to love flowers and colors remained with her for the rest of her life. After her return to London, she and her brother and sisters used to roam the streets, and became "connoisseurs" of shop windows and Punch and Judy shows. Fascinated by the royal family, the young Greenaways followed their activities in the *Illustrated London News*, naming their dolls for the royal children. Thirty years later Kate Greenaway, grown famous, was to visit the royal palace as a guest.

At school little Kate was always drawing pictures. She was also fond of reading poetry, a taste which was encouraged by her Aunt Mary, a wood engraver. When the child was twelve years old she was sent to an art school. Later Kate Greenaway studied at Heatherley's life classes in South Kensington, and then went to the Slade School of Art, where she took many prizes. Her

KATE GREENAWAY

first work was the designing of Christmas and birthday cards and valentines, which had "an extraordinary vogue." She painted in water color, using for her subjects children and young girls, flowers and landscapes. About 1873 her sketches began to appear in *Little Folks* and by 1877 she was a contributor to the *Illustrated London News*.

She had been writing verses for children for some time, when in 1879 she went to Whitley to visit Edmund Evans, a friend of her father's, taking with her a collection of fifty of her poems and drawings. Evans, a master craftsman of color printing who engraved the work of Randolph Caldecott, a friend and contemporary of Kate Greenaway's, was charmed with her material, which he printed as a book, *Under the Window*. It sold quickly and soon made the artist famous. French and German editions were brought out, and parents began to clothe their children in the quaint costumes of the early 1800's, which Kate Greenaway had used for her illustrations because she disliked the fashions of her own day. It was said that she "dressed the children of two continents."

For the next twenty years Kate Greenaway continued to produce books for children, but she never deviated from her style, which was characterized by "an air of artless simplicity . . . freshness, humor, and purity." Her works include *The Birthday Book, Mother Goose, The Language of Flowers, Marigold Garden,* and *A Apple Pie.* She also did a series of *Almanacs,* 1883 to 1897 (1896 excepted). She liked to provide her own text, saying, "Children like something that excites their imagination — a very real thing mixed up with a great unreality like Bluebird," but she did illustrate Browning's *Pied Piper of Hamelin* and Bret Harte's *The Queen of the Pirate Isles.* Her pictures, according to Anne Carroll Moore, "have in them elements of security in family relationships and of beauty and wonder in the natural world." She portrayed children's "graces, their little foibles, their thousand little prettinesses, their little characteristics and psychology of their tender age. . . ."

Although "K.G." (as she was called by her intimates) was shy and modest, she had many friends among the famous. Ruskin, who wrote and lectured about her work, calling some of her drawings "ineffable,"

corresponded with her for years. She was frequently a guest in his home, and also in that of the poet Frederick Locker-Lampson, whose children she sometimes used as models.

Kate Greenaway was short and plump, dressed plainly, was fond of gardening and of taking long walks with her dog. To friends she wrote "endless loving letters" illustrated with drawings, and often gave her paintings away. In her later years Kate Greenaway suffered with acute muscular rheumatism; she died at her home in Hampstead, London, in her fifty-sixth year.

In 1946 the centenary of her birth was commemorated by a full-length biography, Covelle Newcomb's *The Secret Door: The Story of Kate Greenaway*; by an anniversary issue of the *Horn Book*; and by numerous articles and appreciations in England and America.

Elizabeth W. Grierson

AUTHOR OF
Tales From Scottish Ballads, The Scottish Fairy Book, Etc.

Autobiographical sketch of Elizabeth W. Grierson, written for THE JUNIOR BOOK OF AUTHORS a few years before her death in 1943:

I WAS born on a Scottish sheep farm called Whitchesters, more than fifty years ago, and I still live there during the summer. Whitchesters is near a town called Hawick, and it is in Teviotdale, on the fringes of the Cheviot Hills. So it is Sir Walter Scott's country, quite close to Brauxholme Tower, the scene of "The Lay of the Last Minstrel."

I was brought up a regular country child and knew all about lambs and calves and chickens and other young things. I had a governess and did not go to school till I was twelve years old. Then I went to school in Edinburgh, which is a very beautiful and historical city.

I spent three years there and after that I studied in Germany, in the town of Hanover. I shall always have very pleasant memories of that time. Especially of the lovely skating which we had in the winter on the flooded and frozen meadows which lie around the town.

Grierson: *GREER son*

When I left school I lived at home for a long time and I sometimes found the country rather dull. I must have said this to a friend of mine who lived in London, for one day I got a letter from her in which she remarked, "Why don't you try to write a story, since you have so much time on your hands?"

I had never thought of doing such a thing, but I determined to try. So I wrote a very short story and sent it to a children's magazine called *Sunday*. To my great surprise it was accepted. Then I thought I would write something else. I knew a lot about old Scottish ballads, so I made stories out of these and showed them to a publisher, who said if I would write enough to make a book he would publish it. It was called *Tales From Scottish Ballads*.

After that he asked me to write a book about Edinburgh for children, as he wanted a companion volume for a book about London. I had always loved Edinburgh, so I accepted the proposal at once.

So this was how I became an author. Do you not think that some of you young people who read this might begin the same way? So many people think writing is a matter of genius. I think it is often a matter of perseverance.

Since my book about Edinburgh I have written over twenty books. I shall go on writing, but I do other things as well. In Edinburgh there are a great many poor people all living crowded together in old narrow streets, and there are lots of children who, because of the circumstances of their lives, have not much chance of growing up good citizens. So for many years when winter comes around I have gone to Edinburgh for six months to work along with other women at what is called settlement work, trying to help poor mothers and the little children who live in the poorest part of our beautiful city.

I expect some of you will say, "How awfully dull!" But it isn't. It is about the most interesting work in the world. One makes such friends and one learns so much about other people's lives. So if any girl who reads this feels bored with existence, I advise her to get a job as a Girl Scout leader or a club worker or even as a Sunday school teacher. And she will see how interested in her work she will become.

At one time I spent a year in the East. I went to visit a friend who lives on a tea estate and I saw how tea and rubber are grown. I traveled all over Ceylon and India, staying with missionaries and learning about their work. It may interest you to know that I stayed with some American missionaries at a town called Madura in South India. I learned all I could about missionary work and now can tell people in Scotland about it.

George Bird Grinnell

September 20, 1849-April 11, 1938

AUTHOR OF

The Story of the Indian, Beyond the Old Frontier, Etc.

AT the age of twenty, after graduation from Yale, George Bird Grinnell went to the Far West where for six months he collected vertebrate fossils for the Peabody Museum in New Haven. The expedition was escorted by a troop of cavalry because the country was full of hostile Indians. This was Grinnell's first contact with the Indians, who later became his friends and peopled his stories for boys.

He was born in Brooklyn, New York. Among his ancestors he counts five colonial governors and Betty Alden, who was the first white girl born in New England. When he was a small boy his parents moved to Audubon Park, New York City, formerly the estate of John James Audubon, the famous bird lover. Madame Audubon, widow of the naturalist, lived on the estate and conducted a school, which the boy attended. Surrounded by mementoes of Audubon, he acquired an early interest in natural history. His father encouraged him to collect bird skins and other specimens.

After studying at preparatory schools and traveling extensively in Europe, he went to Yale, of which one of his ancestors had been president more than a hundred years before. For three years following the trip to the Far West, he was in business in New York. One summer he took part in a buffalo hunt with the Pawnee Indians.

At twenty-four he went to New Haven as assistant in the Peabody Museum. That summer he accompanied General George A. Custer, as naturalist, to the Black Hills of South Dakota, and the next year he served

Grinnell: *GRIN ul*

in the same capacity for Colonel William Ludlow, Chief Engineer of the Division of Dakota, on his reconnaissance to Yellowstone Park.

The confining work in the Museum caused his health to break down and he was obliged to leave after six years. He had served for four years as natural history editor of the magazine *Forest and Stream,* and now he went to New York as president of the Forest and Stream Publishing Company, a connection which he retained for thirty-one years.

Through the medium of the magazine he had an opportunity to crusade for the conservation of wild life. He brought about the enactment of the first law protecting Yellowstone Park game. He fought the practice of killing small birds of bright plumage for women's hats and dresses, and to help curb it, founded the Audubon Society, named after the man whose work had been so familiar to him from boyhood. He made successive hunting trips to the territory now known as Glacier National Park, discovered the glaciers there, and finally succeeded in having the area established as a national park.

At the age of forty Grinnell began to write stories for boys, based on his long association with the Indians, his exploring expeditions, and his observation of the Western scenery. The best known of his books is *The Story of the Indian,* an account of the life of the North American red man.

Grinnell was a close friend of Theodore Roosevelt and was co-editor with him of several books on game hunting. In his busy career he acted as commissioner named by President Cleveland to deal with the Blackfeet and Belknap Indians, visited the Indians at the Standing Rock Reservation at the request of President Roosevelt to straighten out certain difficulties, and went to Alaska as a member of the Harriman expedition.

For more than fifty years he lived in the same house in Audubon Park. In 1925 he was awarded the Roosevelt Medal for service in the promotion of outdoor life. He died at his home in New York City, after several years of failing health.

Berta & Elmer Hader

AUTHORS AND ILLUSTRATORS
Jamaica Johnny, Spunky, The Big Snow, Etc.

BERTA and Elmer Hader are a husband and wife who write and illustrate books for young readers together.

Here is the story of Berta Hader's life in her own words:

I was born in a small town in Mexico, so long ago that I do not even like to think of the date. My parents were both citizens of the United States and they left Mexico when I was about two years old, so I do not remember the land of my birth.

Like most children I went to kindergarten, grammar school, and high school, and then for two years to a university.

I always liked to draw and when I was about nine or ten years old my mother sent me to an artist's studio to study drawing during the summer vacation. A friend of my mother's used to encourage me by ordering art work from me. I remember making a book of *Sunbonnet Babies* for her. The money she gave me for it went into my savings bank for Christmas presents. In school I always took the art courses and enjoyed drawing more than any other school work.

When I was in the third grade, I won an essay contest which was participated in by all the school children in the city where I lived. As a prize I was given a very fine copy of *Tom Sawyer,* a book I loved. Perhaps because of my success in this essay contest, I used to think I wanted to write, too, and so when I entered the University of Washington, I enrolled in the School of Journalism. After two years in the University, I decided I would concentrate on a career as an artist.

I began as a fashion artist and in my spare time I studied drawing, painting, and especially portraits in miniature. I studied in several classes in the California School of Design, and then I came to New York, where I was married in 1919 to Elmer Hader, a fellow artist from San Francisco. We worked together making feature pages for children for *Good Housekeeping, McCall's, Pictorial Review,* and the *Christian Science Monitor.* Then we began to illustrate children's books and to write them too.

We lived in a tangled woodland on the west bank of the Hudson River, at a point

Hader: *HAY der*

BERTA HADER
ELMER HADER

place. It takes a long time to build a house when you do it all yourself, and we expect to be working on this one the rest of our lives—for we plan to make all our own furniture too.

And now let Elmer Hader tell *his* story:

To look at grown-ups, it is sometimes difficult to realize that once upon a time they were children like yourselves, and that once too they were wee babies. Yet such is the case. On September 7, 1889, in the little town of Pajaro, California, I first opened round blue eyes and gazed in wonder at the world about me. And I still gaze in wonder as I follow my guiding star along the path of life.

Just like most of you I went to kindergarten, to grammar school, and to high school, and then—poof! Everything went up in smoke. For my family had moved to San Francisco and the earthquake and fire destroyed the whole city. I was a bugler with the Coast Artillery of the National Guard and joined my company the morning of the quake. The first few days of the fire our company was in the heart of the city, saving supplies. We dashed in and out of the burning buildings carrying armfuls of groceries as the firemen played the water hose above our heads. The heavy smoke so filled the air that we couldn't tell whether it was night or day.

After the fire had grown cold, and what was once the gay city of San Francisco was now only a pile of broken brick and ashes, I worked for a few months with a surveying party in the American River region. Then while San Francisco was rebuilding, I got a job firing a locomotive. And I might still have been working for the railroad, but for the fact that the art school had been rebuilt, high up on the crest of Nob Hill. I had always liked to draw, and I decided to quit railroading and go to school again. I was just seventeen.

I was fortunate enough to win scholarships during my first three years of study. Then I wanted to continue my studies in Paris, but that took money. Like most people I thought that all actors made a great deal of money and I tried my luck for three years in vaudeville. Well, to make a long story short I got to Paris where I stayed for three happy years (two years and six months, to be exact). I painted out-

called the Tappan Zee by the early Dutch settlers. We have wild rabbits, pheasants, many kinds of songbirds, squirrels, chipmunks, and even a family of skunks living in our woods. In the winter, the deer from Palisades Park often come to drink in our pool. It seems amazing to us to have so many wild creatures in our woods, when we live just twenty-five miles from New York City.

In our free time we work in our garden or on our house. We have built a house of red sandstone from an old quarry on our doors in the summer and studied in the Academy during the fall, winter, and early spring. I was delighted when I had a large winter landscape accepted for the spring Salon of 1914. Then I returned to America, just before the outbreak of the world war. I had to put aside my brushes when the United States entered the war, and I was very glad when peace was declared and I could return home again.

Then it was that I married Berta Hoerner, a fellow artist, and came to live in Nyack, a charming old village on the Hudson River. There we started making pictures for children together. Sometimes Berta starts the picture and I finish it, or I start the drawing and Berta does the finishing work. And we write our stories together, too. Sometimes the idea is Berta's, sometimes mine. We write and make pictures about things and places we liked when we were children, and we hope that today's children will like them too.

While most our time is taken up by book making, we have managed to build a stone house for ourselves and our friends on the banks of the wide Tappan Zee (the second widest part of the Hudson). The house snuggles into the steep hillside just above a little waterfall that tumbles and splashes its way over the moss covered rocks to the pool at the foot of great willows. Here we work in our studio, day in, day out, and often until late at night, getting pictures and stories ready for our books. Our first books were seven of the "Happy Hour Series," after which we wrote, or illustrated, many more books.

* * *

In 1949 the Haders' *The Big Snow* was awarded the American Library Association's Caldecott Medal.

Thomas Handforth

1897-1948

AUTHOR AND ILLUSTRATOR OF
Mei Li, Etc.

Autobiographical sketch of Thomas Schofield Handforth, written for THE JUNIOR BOOK OF AUTHORS a few months before he died:

WHEN I was a small boy I used to peer into a tunnel in a cliff near the shore of Puget Sound in the state of Washington. The tunnel was said to have been used by Chinese smugglers, who had been driven from Tacoma about the time I was born there. I. used to wonder if I could go through the tunnel all the way to China to visit its celestial people.

In the woods near our home I used to play with all sorts of people, giant and pigmy, whom nobody else could see. Little folk who were visible, such as frogs, pollywogs, and beetles, I used to bring to kindergarten, and let them out on the floor, until the teacher requested me not to come any more.

Ever since I can remember I have been drawing. My first sketches are of familiar subjects such as dogs, Mount Rainier, and my pet tree toad, Lallapaloosa; but more numerous are pictures of ancient times: Egyptian sphinxes, Druid stones, Babylonian kings and princesses. Intermittently from the age of seven to nine, I worked at a series of drawings called "A Marvelous Circus of Men, Birds, and Animals from a Far-Off Planet."

Fairy tales of the Orient interested me more than others, because of the illustrations. In their backgrounds of jagged mountains, inland seas, and islands, I found a highly imaginative version of the scenery around me.

The Keep-a-Going Bicycle Club of neighborhood boys was organized when I was about twelve. We used to sleep out wherever we might be at the end of a day's bicycling—under a tree or in a barn—and I managed to return from these expeditions with a sketch of a woodsman or a chipmunk or a queerly twisted root that had pleased me, or a sailing schooner passing by in the bay. In juvenile art competitions, national and local, I won numerous awards including the coveted *St. Nicholas* League medals.

I decided I was going to be either a clown or a sailor or an artist. Before I finished high school I had eliminated the first two professions. I went one year to college, then to art school in New York, and later Paris. After that came grasshopper leaps all over the world.

Most of my pictures through the years have been done directly from life. One of the first books I illustrated was a true story

From a self-portrait

THOMAS HANDFORTH

about a woman in the French Alps. I stayed in the farmhouse of the heroine, who posed for me at the very spots where the incidents had taken place. The drawings for Elizabeth Coatsworth's Moroccan story, *Toutou in Bondage*, were done in Morocco. In *Tranquilina's Paradise,* the path to Paradise was a trail out of Taxco, Mexico, to a little pond in the hills where I liked to go swimming. The characters in *Mei Li* were all neighbors of mine who came to sit for me in my house in Peking, China; the little dog, Igo, and the thrush were my own pets. While camping one summer on a mountain meadow in Kashmir, India, I wrote and illustrated *Faraway Meadow*, in which the buffaloes are caricatures of my friends who were camping with me.

When I have written the stories for books I have usually first considered what I wanted to make pictures of, and then evolved a story out of this subject matter.

I have done etchings and lithographs, and painted in many odd places. In Mongolia, at the court of Prince Teh, life was as it had been in the days of Kublai Khan. In India I traveled with a troupe of temple dancers. Even when I returned to the state of Washington one time, I stayed with the Quillayute Indians, who adopted me into their tribe. But during the two world wars when most soldiers were being sent hither and yon, the army kept me at home in stateside barracks!

In recent years I have resided in California, but the urge of the Keep-a-Going Club often returns: to keep on going to distant and more colorful lands.

* * *

Mr. Handforth died October 20, 1948, in Pasadena. Two years later *Horn Book* magazine published a special memorial issue in his honor. His works hang in the Metropolitan Museum of Art in New York; the Library of Congress; the Chicago Art Institute; the Fogg Art Museum, in Cambridge, Massachusetts; and in the Bibliothèque Nationale in Paris. In 1939 he received the Caldecott Medal for *Mei Li,* which he both wrote and illustrated.

Gertrude Hartman

1876-

AUTHOR OF
*The World We Live In, The Making
of a Democracy, Medieval Days
and Ways, Etc.*

Autobiographical sketch of Gertrude Hartman:

AS I look back over the years of my life I do not find that anything unusual happened in my childhood. I was born and brought up in Philadelphia and made my way uneventfully through the public schools of that city.

Schools in those days were very different from the schools of today. We learned "by heart" the lessons assigned by the teacher from the textbooks. The next day we recited as much as we could remember. So it went on month after month, year after year. I remember I sometimes made my teachers miserable by asking questions about some historical event which had aroused my interest. Always the reply was the same: "Yes, that is very interesting, but we haven't time to go into it or we shall not cover the ground." Many years later, when I began writing histories for young people, I decided to put into them all the interesting things I had not been able to read in my histories when I was growing up.

After graduating from the Philadelphia Normal School I taught in public schools for several years. Then I decided to go to Bryn Mawr College. This was followed by several years of teaching and executive

GERTRUDE HARTMAN

posts in schools. During that time my interest in the newer type of school steadily mounted. In 1923 I became the first editor of *Progressive Education*, a magazine which aimed to spread knowledge of the newer methods of teaching.

I had always been interested in writing but my busy professional career left little time for anything except some professional books for teachers. In 1930 I decided to give up editorial work and devote all my time to writing. There followed a series of histories for boys and girls. In the last few years I have written two history textbooks.

In all these books I have tried to make the people of the past live again, to tell what they did day by day, what they thought, what they believed, and how they improved their way of living. From this kind of history we learn that each generation has its work to do in making the world a better place in which to live. One generation creates something upon which the next generation builds. In this way the world we live in today has been gradually built up through the ages.

History explains to us that today a new age is struggling to be born. Through the work of the people of the last century and a half—particularly that of scientists and inventors—nations and people formerly far away from one another have been brought into close communication. Today there is indeed One World, every part of which is in close relationship with every other part. It is the work of the people of today to learn how to live in peace in the One World which the forces of history have produced.

Helen Eggleston Haskell

AUTHOR OF

Katrinka, Katrinka Grows Up, Peggy Keeps House, Nadya Makes Her Bow, Etc.

Autobiographical sketch of Helen Eggleston Haskell:

DEAR Friends of My Book Children: Because I am the mother of Katrinka, Peggy, Nadya, and some others, the editors have asked me to write a short sketch of my life. I find it difficult because I do not seem to know myself as well as I know the people I created for my books.

I was born on the first day of spring, in the village of Fairwater, Wisconsin, in the long Connecticut Colonial homestead on my grandfather's farm. I was the second in a family of six girls and a boy, the children of Julian and Helen Eggleston.

The exact number of the good many years that have passed since my birth I shall not set down because, although one may have been feeling but twelve or fourteen and planning to skate on a pond that has frozen over or, if it happens to be summer, to swim or play golf, the moment one speaks of the years one has lived, in an exact number, one grows conscious of them and feels one will appear ridiculous engaging in young activities, loaded down with all the good many years that, until a moment ago, had been forgotten. However, I do not regret having lived these years because years are like the stories of a building from which one looks over a city, each added story widening the view.

When I was four years old Father bought a square green-shuttered white house with a square green-shuttered ell in Ripon, Wisconsin, a small town built around a college whose tree-studded campus runs down a hill. Here my brother and three younger sisters were born.

Ours was a roomy house and comfortable. Like all small town houses in those days it had a barn in its back yard. This usually sheltered a team of horses, three ponies, a duck-shaped sleigh, a high piano-box buggy, a two-wheeled bright oak pony cart, cross and side saddles, and a shining black three-seated democrat wagon in which the entire family and three dearest friends could ride, when going on picnics to Green Lake or on visits to grandfather's farm, six miles away.

In the small paddock adjoining our barn we, with neighbor children, tried often, but unsuccessfully, to ride a horse, bareback and standing up; and, in the barn loft, worked on a trapeze, preparatory to circus careers, and held dress rehearsals for plays before formal productions in the double parlors of our house, where sliding doors separated stage from audience. In spring, when most of the hay had been eaten and a large floor space in our barn loft cleared, there was practicing for fancy roller skating careers that would require high boots with fur-edged tops, for the purchase of which money was saved in a small bank that looked like the town hall and stood on the marble-topped bureau in my bedroom.

We dreamed of other careers. A champion walker raced through the town and for weeks afterwards we were champion walkers in the making. Later, ambition turned to ice figure skating and trick bicycle riding.

HELEN EGGLESTON HASKELL

One summer I longed to establish an independent home in a two-room cottage that stood on the edge of town, set in a garden surrounded by cherry trees. Here, after adopting a baby sister, I would live with my dearest friend who would also adopt a small sister. We would dress our children beautifully and sensibly in pink and pale blue paper cambric slips with overdresses of white tarlatan, the garden, cherry trees, and a cow furnishing us with food.

In that long-ago time, days were full of activity but, in the evenings, we settled down quietly and happily with our mother, who would sing to us or read from *St. Nicholas* and *Youth's Companion*, or tell us "Once upon a Time" and "When I Was a Little Girl" stories of her own. These we never tired of hearing and now, looking back over the high buildings of the years, I realize that whatever small gift I have for story telling, comes to me from my mother.

At eighteen I entered Ripon College. Up to that time I had given no thought to writing as a profession although to entertain younger members of the family, I invented long continued fairy stories in which my people came and went through a door in the sky at the horizon line, until a small sister ran away to find the door, after which my fairy folk made entrances and exits through a knothole in the sweet apple tree.

Upon finishing my college course I was advised by an English professor to take up journalism. Soon afterwards I began to write regularly, getting out a weekly fashion letter and some stories for juveniles for a Western newspaper.

In 1903 I married William E. Haskell and for ten years did almost no writing. In 1914 I went to work seriously on mystery stories and romances. As a change from these stories for grown-ups, I wrote *Katrinka*. Children liked her. It made me happy.

For me the writing path has not been an easy one. It is a lonely way. However, I learned when I first set out on it, that it is only when one is lonely that one writes one's best and, paradoxically, that one is never lonely when one is writing one's best.

May all good mornings and good nights be yours.

Hildegarde Hawthorne

AUTHOR OF

Romantic Rebel—the Story of Nathaniel Hawthorne, Wheels Toward the West, The Lone Rider, Etc.

HILDEGARDE HAWTHORNE

Autobiographical sketch of Hildegarde Hawthorne:

I WAS born on September 25, never mind when, in the city of New York, but, with excellent judgment, left it at the age of six weeks, taking my parents with me on my way, first to Germany, then to England. There, in a pleasant house and garden in Twickenham, well known for the song of "Twickenham Ferry," we remained for some eight years, brothers and sisters adding themselves as time passed. As far back as I can remember we lived in a world of make-believe, much of it on the sea, a sea consisting of our little front lawn, with a rug on it that stood for a ship. Perhaps it was because many of our ancestors had been sea-faring men, perhaps because an old retired sea captain lived in a house on our lane. This man was our *beau idéal,* the more so because we were forbidden to spend any time with him, which gave us the pleasing notion he must be very wicked. Our nurse asserted, in fact, that he drank and swore. We naturally hastened toward him whenever we could manage it, and were always cheerfully welcomed. Once he gave us each a pinch of snuff, almost succeeding in strangling us to death, but we appreciated the humor of the situation and forgave him.

Another year or two was spent in France, on the seashore at Hastings, and in a house in St. John's Wood, close to Regent's Park, London, and the Zoo. The Zoo captivated us, and we used to save all our pennies in order to ride the elephant.

I was always inventing stories to tell the rest, always the one to make up the adventures that were the stuff of our life. I mixed the dreams of night with the events of the day, especially one dream, where I used to fly down the stairs, take demi-turn in mid-air, and sail happily out of the open front door to the lawn. For years I believed I actually did this, and even today I'm not absolutely sure I didn't.

We were brought up on fairy lore. Our German nurses were full of it, and I learned to read on Grimm and Hans Christian Andersen. As we grew old enough my father used to read aloud almost every evening *Gulliver's Travels,* Lamb's *Tales from Shakespeare, Robinson Crusoe, Tanglewood Tales,* and *Wonder Book,* the rousing poems of Scott and Macaulay, Edmund Spenser's *Faerie Queene,* Tennyson's *Idylls of the King.* He varied his voice for the various characters, and I shall never forget the marvelous sounds he produced to fit the strange creatures of *Alice in Wonderland* and *Through the Looking Glass,* or the tiny treble he used for Alice herself. It was on stuff like this that we were reared, and none of us ever went to school. Life always seemed lived on the edge of miracle, and the visitors who came were the painters, the writers, the explorers of the time, men who make the best of companions for children. They told us yarns from the wide world over, brought us tiny diamonds from Kimberley, monkeys from Asia, toys from Japan, parrots from the forests of South America, and lovely shells from the South Seas.

At last we were brought home to America and were bitterly disappointed to find no Indians waiting for us. But we loved the farm where we went to live. We swam, we rowed, we paddled, we rode and drove horses, milked cows, and raised chickens. I began to write verse, and even to publish it. In Jamaica, West Indies, our next haven, I continued to write, and when my aunt, Rose Hawthorne Lathrop, came and took me to Europe, where I spent two years study-ing French and Italian, I continued to send stories, poems, and essays to the magazines. I came back and was given a regular com-mission to write for *St. Nicholas* and pres-ently began to review books for the New York *Times.* I also wrote a travel book or two. Then came the war and I went over-seas, and when the war was over got mar-ried to John M. Oskison, also a writer. We went to live (after a short time in New York) in France and Corsica, where I began to write books for children—which has be-come my chief work. I have written other stories, too, biographies of my grandfather [Nathaniel Hawthorne], Thoreau, Emerson, Longfellow, and others. It seems natural to me to write for young people and I hope to go on doing so till the drop of the hat. I am now living in Ridgefield, Connecticut, and really believe I've settled down for keeps, with a little house, a little garden, and a small fat kitten.

* * *

Hildegarde Hawthorne is (as has been indicated above) a granddaughter of Na-thaniel Hawthorne, the great American writ-er. Her father, Julian Hawthorne, son of Nathaniel, was also an author. His works were best known around the end of the nineteenth century. He lived to be eighty-eight, dying in 1934.

Carolyn Haywood

1898-

AUTHOR AND ILLUSTRATOR OF
*Here's a Penny, the "Betsy" books,
Primrose Day, Etc.*

Autobiographical sketch of Carolyn Hay-wood:

I WAS born in Philadelphia and educated in the Philadelphia public schools. As long as I can remember I wanted to be an artist. As a little girl I was always drawing and painting and I thought the most won-derful thing in the world, next to posing for a magazine cover, would be to illustrate a story book. It never occurred to me in my school days that I should some day illustrate my own books.

After graduating from the Philadelphia Normal School, I won a scholarship to the Pennsylvania Academy of the Fine Arts.

There I studied drawing and painting and won a Cresson European scholarship and a prize for work showing the most poetic and idealistic point of view. I received private instruction in illustration from Elizabeth Shippen Green Elliott, whose illustrations appeared in *Harper's* and *Scribner's* maga-zines in the early part of the twentieth cen-tury, and from Jessie Willcox Smith, who for over fifteen years painted the covers for *Good Housekeeping.* After returning from Europe I painted a number of murals and worked as an assistant in the studio of Violet Oakley. At that time Miss Oakley was work-ing on a series of murals for the Pennsyl-vania State Capitol at Harrisburg.

From these three gifted pupils of Howard Pyle I heard much of the advantages of writing and illustrating one's own books, as he did. Finally I decided to try it, but in a very small way. I planned a picture book with a very brief text. In trying to find a publisher I met an editor of junior books who suggested that I write about American children doing the kind of things American boys and girls like to do. So the picture book never appeared, but I wrote *"B" Is for Betsy,* which was published in 1939. And that is how I became an author.

I still paint, although my time for it is limited because writing one book a year and making forty illustrations for it takes a great deal of time, but I do find some time in which to paint children's portraits. We have

CAROLYN HAYWOOD

fun, too. I tell them stories and they tell me all about their pets and their school and their friends. Oh, yes—my little-girl dream to pose for a magazine cover came true many times for I was the mother in some of Jessie Willcox Smith's *Good Housekeeping* covers.

Le Grand Henderson

See *"Le Grand"*

Marguerite Henry

April 13, 1902-

AUTHOR OF

King of the Wind, Misty of Chincoteague, Justin Morgan Had a Horse, Etc.

Autobiographical sketch of Marguerite Henry:

MARGUERITE HENRY

A CURIOUS thing happened one spring to a small flock of ducks owned by a neighbor of ours. Driving rains washed all the duck eggs down the creek—all but one. The lone egg hatched out, and instead of the usual spring sight of several mother ducks each with a trail of little ducklings, there was one yellow duckling with a whole formation of mammas waddling along in wedge shape behind him.

The lone duckling seemed especially favored. He had so many mammas to teach him how to swim and hunt and fish.

In many ways my childhood was similar to the lucky duckling's. I was born into a family of three sisters (two full grown) and a grown brother, so instead of having only one mother to hover over me it seemed as if I had a whole flock of mammas and two papas! If I called out the window to a playmate, "Mamma says I can't go with you today," the answer usually was, "Ask one of your other mammas."

We lived in a modest little home in Milwaukee and no youngster had a happier period of growing up. Marie, my oldest sister, made my dresses, embroidered and sashed in blue, and gave me music lessons. Elsie, a young nurse, taught me the doorknob method of pulling teeth and provided an allowance which was all the more exciting because of its irregularity. Fred, my big brother, used to take my hand and run with me, so that I flew through space in the most

astounding manner, like a creature who could glide without wings. And Gertrude, who was nearest in age, became my mother confessor. When I reached through the fence and took a sprig of parsley out of Alderman Smith's garden I came to her, my conscience pricking so sharply I couldn't go to sleep at night. She told me I'd sleep fine if I went back and told the alderman how sorry I was. She was right!

I still go to her, hopefully, with each story I write. Editors *could* be wrong, but not Gertrude.

Papa was a printer and his shop a wondrous place. Presses whirred. Long sheets of paper streamed out of them. They went in clean and came out covered with words. Papa's desk was more exciting than Pandora's box. It yielded big fat tablets in pink, green, yellow and blue, and bundles of pencils that wrote in a big black swathe. No thin, gray inconspicuous lines came out of papa's pencils. Everyone noticed when Papa wrote. And everyone listened when he yodeled or sang folk songs or recited a whole passage of Shakespeare.

Mamma wore starched white shirtwaists and carried her head like a thoroughbred. When she went to a party, we all danced attendance. One found her handbag, another brought her hat, her coat. In snowtime we brought out her boots and put them on for her. We were proud of Mamma!

The only horse we had was Bonnie by name but not disposition. She was flighty and had a habit of biting my brother in the breeches. She was sold without my ever really knowing her. In fact, I had to wait until I grew up to learn about horses. Now my husband and I have a tiny plot of land near Wayne, Illinois. Here we keep Misty, a Chincoteague pony, and Friday, a Morgan horse. And usually there is a pleasant coming and going of neighboring children.

* * *

Soon after Marguerite Breithaupt graduated from Milwaukee State Teachers College she met and married Sidney Crocker Henry and they settled in Chicago, where she started writing, having articles printed in periodicals as diverse as *The Nation's Business* and *The Saturday Evening Post*. In 1939 the Henrys moved to the weathered cottage on a two-acre plot they call Mole Meadows.

To date Mrs. Henry has written twenty-nine children's books. These include two series of pictured geographies for third and fourth grades: eight about Latin American countries and eight about neighboring countries and island groups; also many stories for the very young. Lately she has tried books for children somewhat older, with great success. *The Little Fellow* was a Junior Literary Guild selection as was *Justin Morgan Had a Horse*. The latter also won the Junior Scholastic Gold Seal Award and the Award of the Friends of Literature. The manuscript of this book is preserved in the archives of the University of Vermont.

In 1949 *King of the Wind* was awarded the American Library Association's Newbery Medal as the most distinguished American contribution to children's literature of the previous year.

Fjeril Hess

1893-

AUTHOR OF
*Buckaroo, The Mounted Falcon,
Sandra's Cellar, Etc.*

Autobiographical sketch of Fjeril Hess:

"NAME, please."
The tall figure in a blue smock looked up from her sticky work of pasting up a "dummy" for the printer when the question was popped at her suddenly. She glared a trifle indignantly through her horn-rimmed spectacles and jerked her green eye-shade over her left eye impatiently.

"Fjeril Hess. F-J-E-R-I-L."

"What a funny name! How is it pronounced?"

"The j is due to a Scandinavian forebear in the dim distance and is pronounced like the j in fjord, at least by Scandinavians and Slavs, who aren't paralyzed by the appearance of the letter j. Others call me 'Farrel'— 'Furrel'—'Fajarrel'—I answer to almost anything beginning with F."

"Any middle name?"

"No, but my family all call me Hep, college idiom for Fjeril."

"Born?"

"I think so, but when I applied for my first passport we couldn't find a record of the fact." The blue smock pulled her left ear gently, a habit during moments of abstraction, and settled her glasses more comfortably on her nose, also a habit.

"When and where?" the question came impatiently.

"I'm old enough to vote, won't that do?"

"No, indeed!"

The blue smock sighed. "1893. It looks like such a long time ago when it is written down, but it seems only yesterday that I opened my eyes to Omaha, Nebraska, bawling lustily to be taken to California."

"And were you?"

"Before I was two years old. We lived in Temecula in southern California, a tiny spot near—heavens, I don't know what it's near and I can't spell it. Then we moved to Salt Lake City, Utah."

"So you settled down in the land of the Mormons?"

"Not exactly. My father was an official of the Union Pacific Railroad Company and we moved oftener than a Methodist minister's family—Ogden, Utah; back to Omaha; Portland, Oregon; New York City; back to Ogden; Los Angeles; San Jose, California. I have lived in so many different places that I don't know whether I say pail or bucket, hedge apples or mock oranges, yesterday or yisterdy, Chicago or Chicaga. But I never say 'Frisco!'"

"College?"

"MacMurray College, B.A., L.H.D., Jacksonville, Illinois—Stephen Douglas' old town."

"First job?"

Fjeril: *FYAIR il*

Paul Parker

F JERIL HESS

"Teaching a ranch school in Nevada's Big Smoky Valley. Read *Buckaroo*; it's based on fact. Will James says—"

"And next?"

"Foreign community work in Passaic, New Jersey, see *Handkerchief Holiday* for that story. I went through the great influenza epidemic of 1918 in Pittsburgh as my initiation into social service."

"Then what?"

"Czechoslovakia for three years right after the Armistice of 1918. Read *The Mounted Falcon, The House of Many Tongues*, and *Castle Camp,* and save my breath—it's all true—"

"Based on fact, let's say."

"You see I do a full-time job, I don't just write books, so I have to squeeze them in as I can. I am Director of the Publications Department of the national Girl Scout organization right now—have been for many years and my work keeps me busy from nine till five. I write only in the evenings."

"Why not holidays and week ends?"

"Because I'm a landowner. I have a tiny house called Chalupka—which means 'little cottage' in Slovak—up in Rockland County, New York, near New City. I have three and a half acres of woods and meadow, a perfectly wonderful garden—"

"Hold on! We're talking about books, not real estate. And after Czechoslovakia?"

"I was managing editor of the *Woman's Press Magazine* for several years and learned

to subdue commas and how to use a paste jar."

"And—"

"Spent several months on the northern coast of Newfoundland. There will be a book for you!"

"We are talking about the past, not the future."

"Then I went home to California to my mother, father, sister, two brothers, my nevvies and niece."

"Quite a family."

"I dedicated *The Magic Switch* to my four-year-old niece and when she saw a stack of copies in our bookstore she couldn't understand why there were so many of them and said, 'Why Heppy, that's *my* book!' "

"Did you say your bookstore?"

"My brother's—my sister's husband—in San Jose, California. But you can read all about it in *Sandra's Cellar.*"

"Is that another of these in-the-future books?"

"No, indeed. It is laid in a bookstore and it tells about my printing press and my Book Keller and—"

"Wait a minute. Don't you ever write about anything but yourself?"

"Myself? Why, I don't write about me, but about places I've been, jobs I've had, people I've known."

"And the heroines of these stories?"

"Certainly aren't me! I give a character a few of my faults and borrow all her virtues from other folks and she does the rest. Anything else you'd like to know?"

"Sure. What do you do in your spare time besides garden at Chalupka and write books?"

"Well, I don't knit or crochet or play cards—except two-handers like cribbage and pinochle. I'm a pretty good carpenter and an A-1 painter. I helped paint a whole hospital in Newfoundland."

"What are these funny clothes you have on in these photographs?"

"They are from my costume collection. I give folk-song programs in costume when I have time for them. I know several hundred songs, I guess, and folk tales."

"Do you play the piano?"

"Well, I'm pretty good at "Chopsticks." No, I like a stringed instrument for my kind of songs — guitar, taropatch, balalaika — I have quite a collection. I have an accordion too but no one will let me play it."

"I should hope not. Well, thank you very much. I guess I have more than 750 words."

"Don't you want any details? I didn't tell you about my books on girl scouting or some of the other ranch books! We have just skimmed the surface."

"Nope. I'll try reading some of those books you've mentioned, and draw my own conclusions!"

"Impertinent, I call it." Blue Smock glared out of the window of her New York office and wondered as usual why such a very tall chimney as the big one over by the East River was needed to send such a very small, very white wisp of smoke up into the sky.

Agnes Danforth Hewes

AUTHOR OF
*A Boy of the Lost Crusade, Spice Ho!,
Glory of the Seas, Etc.*

Autobiographical sketch of Agnes Danforth Hewes:

MY fairy godmother's priceless gift to me was to let me live my first twelve years in Syria.

That, in a nutshell, is my feeling about Syria! That is why I wrote my first book, because I loved Syria so much—its magnificent brilliant scenery, its dear warm-hearted people, its customs come down from Bible times, its beautiful dignified speech, its rich historical background—that I wanted American children to love it, to see it with my eyes. I felt as if no one could afford to miss knowing my Syria. I feel so still.

So *A Boy of the Lost Crusade* came to be written. When I heard that my little niece looked up from reading my *Boy* and sighed, "I wish *I* could have lived in Syria!" I was happy, I'd succeeded in doing exactly what I wanted to do. My Syrian friends say, when they read this book, "How could you remember everything so exactly all these years?"—for *A Boy* was written long after I left Syria to live in America, when, in fact, I had four boys and a little girl of my own!

How do you suppose I answered these dear Syrians? Somewhat in Queen Mary of England's words when she said that if after her death her heart were examined, the word "Calais" would be found written in it. So I say "Syria" is written in my heart!

Strictly speaking, Syria's language, Arabic, is my mother tongue. It came about in this way: My father, a medical missionary, died when I was just beginning to talk. My mother was very ill at that time and for long afterward, and my grandmother, also a missionary, was in America on furlough, so I was left entirely to the care of my dear good nurse and to the other house servants, all of them the kindliest, most generous, gentlest-mannered souls I have ever known. So, naturally, I grew up speaking Arabic. When my grandmother returned to live with my mother she found a little granddaughter who couldn't answer her English—or shall I say American—greeting! By the time I was five I was speaking the two languages side by side, though I always preferred Arabic.

Up to twelve years I was taught at home, and when I entered American schools I ranked with children of my own age.

It was those first twelve years of mine that are responsible for my writing. There I was, living on the Lebanon Mountains, always in sight of the Mediterranean. The very air I breathed teemed with history.

It was cedars from *my* Lebanon that had been floated down that blue sea in front of me to build the great temple at Jerusalem. There, in plain view, was the site of ancient Sidon, and just around a headland,

AGNES DANFORTH HEWES

that of Tyre, those queen cities of ancient Phoenicia whose rich merchandise the daring Phoenician sailors peddled all around the Mediterranean, and carried past the pillars of Hercules to the shores of England and the Baltic Sea! Then there were the ruins of the Crusaders' castles up and down Syria—I was born almost in the shadow of one of them! Alexander the Great marched through this Syria of mine—have you read of his siege of Tyre?

But of all the varied streams of history that have poured through Syria, the one that has most attracted me is that of trade, especially the trade that brought the Occident and the Orient together. From the first time I saw a string of camels come in from Damascus, the romance of trade laid hold of me. My *Swords on the Sea* tells you just how I feel on that subject.

Some years ago, when I revisited Syria, I drove along the shore of the Bay of Acre. Do you think I didn't see the Corn Fleet riding there at anchor? Maybe you think I didn't see the Bedouin *Sitt*, and the *Afrit*, too!

Spice and the Devil's Cave goes on with my theme, the web of trade that inevitably and inextricably drew together East and West.

At first it may seem to you that *Glory of the Seas* strikes a strange trail. No! It's my same old trail, the trail of trade, the quest of the Occident for the Orient's treasure, only carried a step farther west: Venice and Genoa; then Portugal; then America. For, you see, those clipper ships, the Yankee glories of the sea, were really on their way to the Orient, to China. I chose to make San Francisco the highlight in my story—as in fact it was to Boston of the fifties. But after all, the Boston-San Francisco clippership trade was only one episode in the age-old quest of the Occident—this time America—for the treasure of the magic East!

Perhaps you'd like to know that some years ago, I visited the site—as nearly as it can now be located—of Donald McKay's shipyard in East Boston, and his house on White Street; I studied models of his matchless clippers; and last of all, one enchanted autumn day I spent at his grave at Newburyport. I don't need to tell you how I feel about him—you'll know when you read *Glory of the Seas.* You'll know, too, that

I couldn't have written about Boston as I did without knowing and loving it.

I wrote *Glory of the Seas* looking down on the Golden Gate in San Francisco, through which had dashed the *Flying Cloud,* the *Sovereign of the Seas,* the rebuilt *Great Republic.* I live, you see, on one of San Francisco's hills, "next door"—as my favorite Benny Paradiso says—"to the sky," where I can see the blue bay sparkling and feel the breeze frisking in off the water. From one edge of the Orient, Syria, almost around to the other edge, Cipangu and Cathay—they're just across the water from me, you know, here in San Francisco!

In the years since *Glory of the Seas* was published, the boys and girls who read it are no longer boys and girls. Meanwhile I have written seven or more books—and meanwhile, too, a new audience has taken the place of the first one. I think, don't you, that it's high time we said Hello?

Perhaps you'd like to know which of my books I like best. Without a moment's hesitation, it is *The Codfish Musket.* I worked on this book for three solid years—and you know we love best that to which we have given our best. Some words of Christopher Morley's are my writing motto—"May truth be with me as I write!"

* * *

Agnes Danforth Hewes was educated at Elmira College and Radcliffe. In 1901 she was married to Laurence Ilsley Hewes, who has since become a famous engineer and writer of technical books and articles.

William Heyliger

March 22, 1884-

AUTHOR OF

S.O.S. Radio Patrol, Son of the Apple Valley, Etc.

Autobiographical sketch of William Heyliger:

I BELIEVE a man who can earn his bread doing the one job in the world he most enjoys doing sits in the lap of fortune. I count myself a fortunate man. I get a tremendous amount of pleasure out of writing for boys. I am doubly fortunate because this seems to be the type of writing I am best qualified to do.

Heyliger: *HY lig er*

WILLIAM HEYLIGER

I was fourteen years old, I think, when I became captivated by the newspaper stories of Richard Harding Davis and Jesse Lynch Williams. These men directed the course of my life. A year later I began to write. Prophetically, my first story was what has come to be known as the school-athletic story. Entirely ignorant of the mechanics of authorship I wrote on both sides of sheets of foolscap, punched a hole in the top, tied the sheets together with a blue ribbon, and mailed the masterpiece to *The Saturday Evening Post*. I have always had a suspicion that the day my ribbon-tied story was received the *Post* staff was unable to compose itself for the rest of the day.

A regiment of suns have crossed the sky since I sold my .first boys' story years ago. They have been crowded years, busy and happy, and during that space I have camped with boys, met them face to face in high school auditoriums in ten states, and written for them continuously. The volume of my work that has gone between cloth covers may seem unduly large; and yet it represents but little more than one book a year. Some of those books I should like to forget; some of them are good. All represent the best I could do at the time they were written. I have never come down to writing pot-boilers.

If I have a philosophy of writing it is this: there is no such thing as writing down to the boy; a man is fortunate indeed if he can write up to him. For he represents an audience more emotionally responsive than any other audience in the world. I try to reach the boy's emotions. Sometimes I like to think I succeed. At any rate boys who began to write to me twenty years ago still drop in on me with an occasional letter.

If at times my books seem to strike too deep a note of idealism I can plead only that I know of no other way to write. I began as an idealist. I am still an idealist. For that I offer no apology. This world of ours, often glorious, often sordid and stupid, can do with a few ideals.

V. M. Hillyer

September 2, 1875-December 21, 1931

AUTHOR OF

A Child's History of the World, A Child's Geography of the World, Etc.

IN his Introduction to *A Child's Geography of the World*, V. M. Hillyer wrote:

"To me as a child geography was a bugbear of repellent names—Climate and Commerce, Manufactures and Industries, and products, *products*, PRODUCTS. It seemed that the chief products of every place in the world were corn, wheat, barley, rye; or rye, barley, wheat, corn; or barley, corn, rye, wheat. In my geography modern Greece had but a paragraph—because, I suppose, it did not produce wheat, corn, barley, rye. Geography was a stomach geography; the head and the heart were left out.

"I loved the geography pictures and maps but hated the text. Except for an occasional descriptive or narrative paragraph the text was wholly unreadable—a confused jumble of headings and sub-headings and sub-headings. . . .

"When my turn came to teach geography to beginners nine years of age, I found the available textbooks either too commercial and industrial on the one hand, or too puerile and inconsequential on the other. Statistics and abstractions were entirely beyond the ken of the child of nine, and random stories of children in other countries had little value as geography.

"As I had been a traveler for many years, had visited most of the countries of the globe, and in actual mileage had been five times the distance around the world, I thought I would write a geography myself. Vain conceit! A class would listen with considerable attention to my extemporaneous travel talks, so I had a stenographer take down these talks verbatim. But when I read these notes of the same talk to another class, then it was that I discovered a book may be good—until it is written. So I've had to try, try again and again, for children's reactions can never be forecast. Neither can anyone tell without a trial what children will or will not understand."

With the background of his own travel, his sympathy for children, and instinct for the story and vivid phrase, Hillyer taught geography in his own unique way. He told of his own childhood, of running away when a little boy with the intention of running straight around the world back to his own home; of starting to dig a hole through the center of the earth to the other side; of putting on a cap and playing conductor, shouting "All aboard for Baltimore, Philadelphia, New York, and points north and east!" over and over again. When he taught school he again played conductor, this time conducting his young charges around the world in imaginary travel as fascinating as a real trip. The manuscripts of this and other books, notably *A Child's History of the World* and *A Child's History of Art*, were tried out on different classes for several years and altered each time according

to the children's reactions before they were finally published.

Virgil Mores Hillyer was born in Weymouth, near Boston, the son of Virgil and Amy Adlington Hillyer. His childhood was spent on Capitol Hill, Washington, D.C. He was educated at Kent School and Harvard, graduating at twenty-two, and two years later became headmaster of the Calvert School, Baltimore, which was then only two years old, remaining there until his death. He was one of the most successful teachers of children, and his educational methods gained an international reputation. They were in use in countries as far away as China, Persia, and South Africa. He established a correspondence school with people enrolled in every part of the world.

Hillyer wrote a number of textbooks which were in use in his school and elsewhere. The most popular were those on history, geography, and art.

Like most school children of his time, Hillyer had been taught for the first eight years or more only American history. "So far as I knew," he said, "1492 was the beginning of the world." He felt the narrowness and injury of such a limited view. So, taking existing textbooks of world history, condensing them as much as possible, adding explanations suited to the age of those he taught, and drawing on his fund of interesting comments, he produced *A Child's History of the World* in 1924.

In *A Child's History of Art* he was assisted by E. G. Huey. It was unfinished at his death, but completed as nearly as possible in his style by the vice principal of his school, Miss Helen Knight.

Dorothy & Nils Hogner

AUTHOR AND ILLUSTRATOR

The Animal Book, Our American Horse, Barnyard Family, Etc.

Autobiographical sketch of the Hogners, by Dorothy Childs Hogner:

WE are writing this in our studio apartment in New York City. There are goldfish in an aquarium on the mantel over the fireplace, our only pets at the moment.

While I sit at the typewriter which I taught myself to use (not hunt and peck, though!) Nils sits at his large easel, painting a sketch he is planning to exhibit in a

V. M. HILLYER

Nils: *rhymes with "pills"*
Hogner: *HOHG ner*

DOROTHY HOGNER
NILS HOGNER

even more, we enjoy our camp in Connecticut, where we go in summer.

In winter we drive up there quite often to feed the birds. We have about eleven acres of woodland, in a remote spot, and when the snows are heavy we have to walk through drifts to get there. The birds are always glad to see us, the chickadees, the nuthatches, the juncos, and even the wild shy grouse, which will come out and eat corn when we are there, if we sit very quietly inside, looking out of the window.

Of course, these birds, and all the wild animals which live there, the chipmunks, squirrels, rabbits, and others, make wonderful characters for our books. We have put up a salt lick too, so the deer come near our back porch, and sometimes we catch a glimpse of a fox, or of the handsome shy lynx cat which lives in the near-by forest.

There is only one animal we do not find amusing. That is the woodchuck. We liked him at first, but he is such a glutton. He enjoys filling himself on greens we plant in our garden, and we are both very fond of gardening. So we and the woodchucks do not get on!

We raise both vegetables and flowers. We plant most of the common vegetables such as tomatoes, carrots, and cabbage, and the common flowers such as roses and zinnias, but we also like to raise uncommon plants such as the native American root artichokes which blossom like sunflowers. We have an herb garden well started. We dry mint, basil, marjoram, and others, and also make our own herb vinegars. We are particularly fond of herbs because we both like to cook. We believe cooking is an art just like writing or painting, and home-grown herbs are so much better than those bought in the store. I specialize in salads, and Nils makes remarkable sauces.

Although we were both born in the East, and now live in New York and Connecticut, we have visited a great many other places in America because we are fond of camping. We like nothing better than to take a tent and camping outfit and an old car and start out without too much of a set plan. We have camped from here to Mexico and up into Canada. Besides doing books for children, we have written and illustrated three travel books for grown-ups, from material gathered on these expeditions.

But right now we are not planning a trip because we had a bulldozer scoop out a

one-man show of murals. He is treasurer of the National Society of Mural Painters. Nils used paintbrushes and oil paint before he began to make black and white drawings for books. He likes to illustrate very much, but he also likes to paint big spaces, such as the walls of the officers' club at Halloran General Hospital, Staten Island, where he designed a gay Persian hunting scene. Right now he is working on a picture of potato diggers on a farm, and so you can see where our thoughts are! We enjoy the city and like living here in winter, but, perhaps pool in our little brook, and there is a great deal of work yet to be done before it will be ready for the native trout which come up our little brooklet from the main stream. Yes, we both love to fish, but we do not catch the fish in our own pool because we make pets of these trout! You should see them jump for grasshoppers. Incidentally, the pool is now deep enough for diving and we expect to go swimming every day.

Richard A. & Ruth Holberg

ILLUSTRATOR AND AUTHOR
Oh, Susannah, Wee Brigit O'Toole, Etc.

Autobiographical sketch of the Holbergs by Ruth Langland Holberg:

I WAS born in 1891 in Milwaukee, Wisconsin, and I lived there until a few years after I married Richard Holberg, born 1889, who also was a Milwaukeean. I had an older brother and a younger sister. Between being a tomboy and reading as many books as possible, I had a good time. From early childhood I liked to draw, so it was natural that I went to art school. I specialized in painting children out of doors.

When I married Richard Holberg, an advertising artist, we moved to New York City. There we met many writers as well as artists. It was then I began writing poetry. It fitted in with my painting landscapes. We both painted in Europe and Provincetown.

Because artists have made Rockport, Massachusetts, a painters' colony, we spent many happy summers within sight and sound of the sea. Finally we decided to stay all the year. Mr. Holberg had been illustrating young people's magazines so it was possible for us to live away from a city. In 1930 we became citizens of Rockport.

I suppose it was because there were so many interesting children in the village that I began to write books for children. Mr. Holberg drew the illustrations. This work made us very happy because we had no children of our own.

When Mr. Holberg died in 1942 other illustrators made the pictures for my books. Remembering my childhood in Milwaukee started me writing about Mr. Syrup, our milkman, and his teasing ways. He would take our dolls to the neighbors and we had

RUTH HOLBERG

to hunt for them. He invited children to his farm for picnics and sleigh rides. I wrote three little books about him.

I was interested in how Milwaukee grew and that is told in *Hester and Timothy*. When older people heard how much I liked to have them tell me about their childhood, I used their stories for other books.

Living on Cape Ann (Massachusetts) has deepened my interest in the history of our country. People around here are descended from the first settlers. Captain John Smith who founded Jamestown, Virginia, visited this Cape and called it Cape Tragabigzanda for a Turkish princess who saved him from slavery. That stirred me to write the story of his exciting and adventurous life. It was so packed with his incredible experiences that I made a separate book, *Michael and the Captain*, about the time when he was fighting the Turks in Europe. Michael, a boy living in Serbia, longed to meet his hero, Captain John Smith, and he did, in an amazing way.

History always bored me when I went to school. It was nothing more than too many dates and names to remember. The books I write with historical backgrounds are meant to make history come alive. There were children who lived in those days of 1812 who must have thought it exciting to have the British come into Lobster Cove on Cape Ann, to burn the fishermen's boats and the sloops that defied the Embargo Act.

Holberg: *HOHL berg*

I know that place well and the true stories about it. This is told in *At the Sign of the Golden Anchor.*

Writing for children is great fun and it is an education for me too.

Rupert Sargent Holland

October 15, 1878-

AUTHOR OF

Freedom's Flag, Plays of the American Colonies, Etc.

Autobiographical sketch of Rupert Sargent Holland:

MY father's family came originally from Virginia and my mother's from Pennsylvania and Massachusetts, and I was born in Louisville, Kentucky, October 15, 1878. There I played in a garden as large as a city block until I was six years old, when the family moved to Philadelphia, where my father, who was a physician, was to be Dean and Professor of Chemistry at the Jefferson Medical College.

Here my sister, brother, and I found a new playground in Rittenhouse Square and here I went to the William Penn Charter School. We boys had to go to Quaker Meeting every Wednesday and sit in more or less silence for an hour or two, which probably did us no harm, though I doubt that it inclined our minds to religious meditation.

After seven years I went to Harvard, where my chief interests were theatricals and writing for the magazines. I told my adviser I wanted to write and asked him what English courses to take. He said, "The only way to learn to write is to go ahead and write." So I did, and wrote so copiously that I became an editor of the *Crimson*, the *Lampoon*, and the *Advocate*. I knew writing was to be my chief business—I had started to write a history of English literature when I was ten—but the law appeared to be a more profitable occupation when I graduated from Harvard in 1900, and so I went to the University of Pennsylvania Law School and learned enough to get my LL.B. degree in 1903.

I practiced law in Philadelphia for a number of years, part of the time as attorney for the Legal Aid Society; and whenever I could I wrote. My first book was a collection of college stories, *The Count at Har-*

vard; my second—the result of a visit to Europe—was a book about modern history entitled *Builders of United Italy*; the third was *The Man in the Tower*, a story on the type of *The Prisoner of Zenda.*

The boyhood adventures of famous men had always interested me, and I wrote a series of stories about them for *St. Nicholas*, which was later published as *Historic Boyhoods*. This was followed by six other books in the "Historic Series." For *St. Nicholas* I also wrote *The Knights of the Golden Spur* and *Drake's Lad*, both tales of historic adventure. Then I was asked to write *The Boy Scouts of Birch-Bark Island*, and this was the first of a number of books about Scouts.

I had always liked mystery stories, and so I set to work to invent some puzzles for detective heroes to solve. Among these the most popular has been a sea yarn, *The Mystery of the "Opal."* This was partly written by the sea, for my wife and I and our three children, two boys and a girl, spend our summers on the Maine coast at Prouts Neck. The rest of the year our home is at Wayne, in the country west of Philadelphia, and not far from Valley Forge.

Here I wrote *Mad Anthony*, the story of General Wayne, and many other books of our country's history. My most recent is *Freedom's Flag*, a biography of Francis Scott Key.

RUPERT SARGENT HOLLAND

A love of adventure, of stirring deeds— whether in past days or modern times—is the reason I like to write for boys and girls. With them the story is the main thing; once get the hero started on his course they will follow over hill and dale as joyously and loyally as the children trooped at the heels of the Pied Piper of Hamelin.

H. C. Holling

August 2, 1900-

AUTHOR AND ILLUSTRATOR OF
*Paddle-to-the-Sea, Tree in the Trail,
Seabird, Etc.*

BORN in Henriette, Jackson County, Michigan, Holling Clancy Holling graduated from high school at Leslie, Michigan, in 1917, and from the Art Institute of Chicago in 1923. While connected with the Field Museum of Natural History in Chicago, he took a private course and did work in anthropology under Dr. Ralph Linton, who is now with Columbia University.

Mr. Holling's occupations and activities, past and present, include work on a Michigan farm and carpentry. He has also served as grocery clerk, factory worker, and for two seasons as a sailor on Great Lakes ore boats. Three years were spent in the taxidermy department of the Field Museum and several years as idea man, artist, and copy

H. C. HOLLING

writer in a national advertising firm. He is now living in Altadena, California, where he has his studio and is a writer and illustrator of books for children. He has also designed and constructed several restaurants and one dude ranch.

Much of the material in Mr. Holling's *Paddle-to-the-Sea, Tree in the Trail*, and *Seabird* is known to him at first hand, for his amusements and hobbies include the use of primitive artifacts, implements, weapons, and "lost art" processes, the study of wild animal behavior, music (with emphasis on primitive and ancient instruments and scores), canoeing, archery, hunting, fishing, all types of camping and woodcraft, and field trips by foot, horse, and canoe. He has traveled a great deal in the wilderness. In addition, he does much historical research.

Mr. Holling's wife, Lucille Webster Holling, is an artist, too; she has worked with her husband on illustrations for several of his books.

Lucille W. Holling

See *Holling, H. C.*

Clara Whitehill Hunt

1871-

AUTHOR OF
*About Harriet, The House in Green Valley,
Peggy's Playhouses, Etc.*

Autobiographical sketch of Clara Whitehill Hunt:

I WAS born in the pleasant city of Utica, New York, in 1871. My father was a teacher of the natural sciences in the Utica Free Academy. Both my parents came from Sudbury, Massachusetts, where Mother grew up on the land granted to her forebears in 1637. Father's first American ancestor was a "freeman" of Concord in 1641 and Father prepared for Amherst in the Concord High School in the days when Emerson's gracious presence on the streets of the old town was a benediction upon young and old.

I had a very happy childhood in Utica, but the long blissful summers on the New England farm were so utterly perfect that life in town between September and June seemed drab by contrast.

CLARA WHITEHILL HUNT

I went to the public schools of Utica in days when classes were small and teachers had time to be friends of the family as well as of their pupils. In spite of the marvelous advantages of today's New York school children I would not change places with them. I have always hated crowds and loved individuals. I am sorry for children who must continually get in line and be managed by traffic cops!

As soon as I was graduated from the Academy I began to teach. Before long I was principal of a small primary and kindergarten school. Here I became so much interested in the reading of my boys and girls and in the new "trained" librarian of the public library, who lent me such generous lots of books for my children, that I decided to learn to be a librarian myself. And when, as a student in the New York State Library School at Albany, I found that public libraries were beginning to make a special place for children in their plans, I knew instantly that was the place for me. I have never changed my mind. Do you remember Leonard's motto in *The Story of a Short Life? Laetus sorte mea*—"happy is my lot" —that is the way I feel about being a children's librarian.

After library school, a short experience organizing a children's room in the Apprentices' Library, Philadelphia, and four years as children's librarian in Newark, I went to Brooklyn to take charge of the work with children in the young Brooklyn Public Library. I watched the library grow from small beginnings to its place as one of the largest public libraries in the United States. Special rooms, books, and children's librarians are provided in branches in all parts of Brooklyn, and for one district I had the fun of helping plan a whole building just for boys and girls. This children's library is quite famous in the library world.

My first book, *What Shall We Read to the Children?* grew out of questions asked me by mothers when I spoke at kindergarten mothers' club meetings. I had lectured at library schools and written articles for magazines before I dreamed of such a thing as making my talks into chapters of a book.

About Harriet is the story of a little friend of mine. I used to think how amazingly different was Harriet's life in this enormous city from that of country and small-town children. "Why, Harriet's days would be almost as strange to country children as the ways of people of foreign countries," I thought one day. And out of that thought came the little book.

Something else than descriptions of city ways went into the story, I hope you notice, some things I cannot leave out of any story I write for children: good fathers and mothers, delightful books, and the country! After *About Harriet* I took my story-book children to the country—to the coast of Maine in *The Little House in the Woods*, to the mountains and other places in *Peggy's Playhouses*, and to a beautiful little Vermont village in *The Little House in Green Valley*.

One of the nicest things about being a children's librarian is the chance to discover fine books to give to boys and girls. *Memoirs of a London Doll* and *Lady Green Satin and Her Maid Rosette* were two charming, neglected books about children of other lands which I persuaded a publisher to reprint. *Children of the Moor*, a story of some brave Swedish children, is another for which I wrote an introduction. I take particular satisfaction in my introductions for other authors' books. I have a strong feeling that if all our boys and girls will make friends, in their story books, with boys and girls of other lands, then when these young readers grow up they will not be half so likely to be fooled into going out and killing those friends when political leaders try to stir up that imbecile thing—war between the nations.

We are told everybody should have a hobby outside his daily work. I haven't any. "The world is so full of a number of things" I could never concentrate on one to the exclusion of other interests. I am glad I have learned of life that if one has health, imagination, and love of beauty, a person with very little money can have a mighty good time.

Mabel Leigh Hunt

1892-

AUTHOR OF

Benjie's Hat, Have You Seen Tom Thumb? Etc.

Autobiographical sketch of Mabel Leigh Hunt:

I INVENTED my first short story when I was about three. It had an impressive beginning, swift action, and a happy ending. I related how I left Heaven, at God's own suggestion, to brighten the home of the Doctor Hunts, in Coatesville, Indiana. Right joyously I made a beeline for their kitchen window. My mother chanced to be within, making a cherry pie (in November!). She admitted me, exclaiming, "Why, Mabel, are you here?" "Yes. How would you like me for your little girl?" I asked. "Very much," she responded. I said I would stay. We had cherry pie for supper.

Greencastle, a college town, was my next home. My memories of this fifteen-acre play-paradise, with its huge house and magnificent trees, are bright with the happiness and "dreamery" of my early childhood. However, that first airy journey of mine must have left me a bit delicate (in chilly weather, you see, wearing nothing but a little gown, and practically no hair). During occasional illnesses I conversed with my own private fairy. Or I played with paper dolls, pretending they were story-book characters. However, reading was always my supreme delight. Our house was littered with loved books; new magazines were eagerly welcomed; periods of family reading aloud and word games were frequent. My scholarly father exacted accuracy from us in speech by revealing ancient and fascinating word origins. Our mother lightened her household tasks and held us entranced with

MABEL LEIGH HUNT

singing words—nursery rhymes, poetry, legends, ballads, and hymns. She was a *giving* mother, sharing with us the accumulating treasures of her heart and mind. If there is good in me, or in my writing, it is because I was blessed with such intelligent and generous parents.

When I was ten we moved to Plainfield, remaining there until my father's death, when we settled in Indianapolis, my present home. Add to elementary and high school two years of college—my formal education. Add extensive travel here and abroad. Training in work with children at Western Reserve's Library School (1923-24). Association with the Indianapolis Public Library until 1938. Add, finally and always, a rich garniture of good friends and good times.

I was a long time discovering "something to write about." Around 1934 I was suddenly inspired to try my wings. How thrilling to find I could fly! Since then I have written many books. The knowledge of children and their literature gained in library experience has helped immeasurably. There will never be time enough to transfer to paper the stories that keep crowding my mind. Any favorites I might have among those already published would be my Quaker stories, since Quakerdom is so much a part of me and my double Quaker ancestry.

In writing, I am doing, with great enjoyment, what I always most wanted to do.

Not only that, I write for the most delightful people—*children*. The thought of them as my friends, far and near, never fails to render me rather breathless. They deserve my very best.

"M. Ilin"

1895-

AUTHOR OF
What Time Is It? Black on White, 100,000 Whys, Etc.

Autobiographical sketch of I. A. Marshak, who writes his books under the pen-name of "M. Ilin":

BEFORE I tell you how I started to write, I'll first tell how I began to read.

My first book was one by Dickens. It began like this: "Marley was dead, like a stone." I did not understand the words or the lettters. I spent more time on one line than I do now on several pages. But I decided not to give up. On the first page I did not understand a thing. On the second I understood a few words, and when I came to the end of the book I knew very well who "Marley" was and what happened to him and some more things I had never known before. After Dickens I read Mark Twain; after Mark Twain—Pushkin; after Pushkin—*Hiawatha*; after *Hiawatha*—*The Iliad*; after *The Iliad*—*King Lear*.

I did not like children's books. The idea that these authors looked down upon their little readers and considered them little "idiots" did not appeal to me. (When I myself write children's stories, I try not to forget for a moment that a person of ten years of age is not less wise than one at thirty years, and probably has more curiosity.)

My older brother, who is now a famous writer, used to provide other books for me. His first stories were not written but told to me by heart. It happened like this. My brother used to take me on an outing. We wandered through the streets for hours and on the way he told me long stories about travelers, hunters, and knights.

After I'd read a great number of books and heard a great many stories I decided to try my own hand at writing. My first book was published only in a single copy, with a drawing of a tiger on the title page and some verses inside. I also once edited a newspaper. I was the editor, the printer, and the only subscriber. Ordinarily, an editor of a newspaper wants to have a large public, but in my case it was different. I did not want anybody to read my paper. Being afraid of teasing, I hid my newspaper under my pillow and afterwards hid it underground. So no one has ever seen my paper.

After a great many years, when I was a student, I tried to write again, and this time I was in earnest. I was finally asked to write a chemical page for a children's magazine. A painter made the drawings and it was my task to add three lines under every drawing. To differentiate myself from my brother, the writer, I used the pen-name of "Ilin."

This way chemistry brought me to writing. Chemistry and writing went a long time together.

To my great sorrow a sickness of my lungs took me away from my chemical activities. Now my main work is writing. By the way, I don't only write, but study as well. I am glad there are so many things in this world worth knowing and which I don't know. In my opinion all studies are interesting. When I was a child I used to sit for hours in the evening and study the stars and sky on the map. During the day I used to spend a lot of time near the ant hives trying to learn the work of ants. Now I am more interested in the work of the human being.

Will James

June 6, 1892-September 3, 1942

AUTHOR OF
Smoky, My First Horse, Etc.

Autobiographical sketch of William Roderick James, written for THE JUNIOR BOOK OF AUTHORS a few years before his death:

I KNOW a lot of things I'd rather do than write or talk about myself: I'd a heap rather be roping or branding, or just mix in a corralful of good horses. But now it seems like I'll have to climb to the top pole of my corral, squint along the zigzaggy back-trail of my life, and tell you something of the turns in it. I'd like to live the most of it over again and specially when I was at the peak of my riding. That was over twenty years ago.

I was born in Montana. When I let out my first squawk there was only a few inches of quilting between me and the prairie sod, my first squint at sunlight was under a canvas flap and the first sounds that come to my ears was the jingling of my dad's spurs, the nickering of horses, and the bellering of cattle.

My dad was a cowman, born and raised in West Texas. He'd trailed many long herds of longhorns from the south to the north. He liked the north on account of plenty of good grass and water there, and when he'd saved enough money he married and started north, figuring on settling down and going into the cow business there. I don't know how far north my folks would of went but I was told they was still planning to go on when my coming stopped the outfit in Montana. That seemed far enough north for me anyhow. And now, even though I have a good outfit within a couple of hundred miles from where I was born, plenty of cattle and horses, in a country of good grass and water and timber, I often hanker for the south and I drift that way often. For you see, both my dad and mother was from the south.

My mother died when I was a year old. My dad followed her three years later. He was killed while handling cattle. I don't remember my dad but very little, mostly at

WILL JAMES

the time when he brought me a little saddle and a horse all for my own self. That was just a little while before he *went*. At my dad's last wish I was then adopted by a French Canadian trapper and prospector, who, for some reason I never got to know, had been a mighty great friend of my dad's, and he 'turned out to be as mighty fine a foster father to me as any real father could ever been. I know I must of been a daggone nuisance plenty of times but he sure never showed that I was. Like when on his prospecting trips, I didn't care to go with him unless I was riding my horse and sometimes I'd ride too far out of his sight to suit him.

When I got older and trapping seasons come he began taking me north, away up into Canada, and far enough up so there was mighty few hours of daylight during winters and the nights was near as light as day. I didn't like the far north because a horse was of no use up there, and I'd have to leave mine behind till spring come and we'd be drifting south again.

I was thirteen years old when drifting south one spring the trapper was drowned while reaching into a river for a bucket of water. I can't describe how I felt at losing him, but I was now in the heart of the cow country and my hurt sort of healed in time by the interest I took to try and be the cowboy my dad had been. I already had a mighty good and early start.

I've rode for most of the biggest cow and horse outfits between the Canadian and Mexican borders, and on all kinds of horses that was never gentle. I've run and caught many wild horses and was on horseback most everywhere I went, even during the world war. Horses and cattle and range country was all I knew and cared to know. And I'm still the same, even if I've broke in to writing and drawing, for in that work I'm only living my life over again as I put it down on paper, and on my ranch. I live pretty well as I used to, only I don't have to be out riding in no bad storm unless I want to.

It was a horse I was breaking that finally broke me into a chance to make use of my natural talent for drawing. I've drawed every chance I got and ever since I can remember, and while I was in town and recuperating from my latest accident I was told how I could make big money drawing for magazines. I'd never thought of that before, and after many tries I finally succeeded in selling a magazine a few drawings. That was my start at drawing for a living instead of riding. But I had no idea of ever writing for magazines till I was told I should try. But I thought I'd have to go to school and study English for that.

The trapper had teached me how to read and write a little and I'd picked up some more on that through some old magazines I'd found at different cow camps. I finally decided to try writing on a bet that my story wouldn't sell. I wrote a short article, sent it East, and lost my bet, for I sold it to one of the biggest magazines going. That was not so long ago and now I have many books out all illustrated with my own drawings and paintings. I've never had no school education and I've never sketched nor painted from life; maybe I should but I don't seem to have time and I only draw and write from memory and what I've seen and experienced myself. If my readers keep on being as satisfied as they've proved to be, I'll be very happy to try and please them some more.

As far as writing for young people I find that they're only a little more interested in my books than the older people, and that might be because they have more time to read and their minds are more open to adventure, but I write for everybody in general, like I would talk to friends who are interested in what I have to say. I only tell of the true life and happenings with the cowboy and his work. That don't need no flowering and I don't know of any jaw-twisting words to make my writing hard for anybody to read. Parents have bought my books for their children and then read the books themselves before the children could get a squint at 'em. Like with my book *Smoky* or my life's story *Lone Cowboy* and my others, grandpa or grandma, or big brother or sister are mighty apt to have first bolt on 'em. But, Junior and Little Sister, I hope I have a chance to talk to you sometimes through them books of mine and that you enjoy riding along with me.

* * *

Time magazine once said of Will James, "He was a cowboy until a bucking horse threw him into writing." In 1927 the Newbery Medal was awarded to him for *Smoky*. He died in Hollywood at the age of fifty.

Margaret Sweet Johnson

1893-

AUTHOR AND ILLUSTRATOR
(WITH HELEN LOSSING JOHNSON) OF
The Smallest Puppy, Joey and Patches, Dixie Dobie, Etc.

Autobiographical sketch of Margaret Sweet Johnson:

IN writing an autobiographical sketch, however brief, it is important to give the influences and heredity which have led one to become a writer or illustrator, or both.

My mother, Helen Lossing Johnson, who collaborated with me in producing our dog and horse stories for children and who passed away in 1946, in her eighty-first year, was the daughter of Benson J. Lossing, author of the *Field Book of the (American) Revolution*, and many other historical works. He illustrated many of his own books, making the original drawings, and engraving them on wood. My mother illustrated some of his later books. She studied at the Academy of Design, was especially interested in painting landscapes and horses, and exhibited in the National Academy, New York, and elsewhere.

My father, Frank Edgar Johnson, was much interested in natural history, specializing in ornithology. A member of the Audubon Society and the Linnaean Society of New York, he gave lectures on his chosen subject.

With this background it is not surprising I grew up with a love of nature and a talent for drawing and painting the animals I loved. I learned natural history from my father almost as soon as I could talk. My mother encouraged me in drawing, and gave me able criticism. Several years at art school and years of drawing and painting animals and landscapes from life have been my only education along that line. I had some years of experience in free-lance illustrating before my mother and I started our series of books for young people.

In school English was my favorite subject, and in this study my marks were usually excellent. My parents gave me good books, often beautifully illustrated editions of stand-

MARGARET SWEET JOHNSON

ard works, and I have always read a great deal.

Expressing myself in writing was never difficult, and the first bit of work I sold to a magazine was not a drawing (which I was trying to sell) but an article on silver foxes.

Dogs have always been important members of our household—and cats have run a close second!

I learned to ride, during summers spent on farms, by getting astride horses which were being taken to and from pasture. Later I had my own good saddle horse and, with a dog or two to run beside me, I was perfectly happy.

The history of dogs' long association with man, and the many breeds produced, has been most interesting to me for years. Recently I have concentrated on drawing dogs, and painting dog portraits professionally, attending most of the near-by dog shows. My mother accompanied me to many of these shows; and while she did not draw dogs, she became quite an expert on the characteristics of the different breeds.

Then, in the middle 1930's, an editor of children's books looking over my drawings of dogs suggested I try writing a book for my illustrations. Mother and I discussed plots, breeds of dogs to write about, and finally decided upon a Dalmatian. So we wrote and illustrated our first book, *Tally Ho*.

In making our illustrations, Mother drew most of the horses, all the human figures, and such details as houses and wagons, while I drew the dogs and wild animals. I have done most of the actual writing, but Mother contributed much in the way of interesting incidents, and expert editing. Together we produced seventeen books, and I am continuing our work.

When I married, it was to a man of my own name—Johnson—so I have remained Margaret S. Johnson.

Siddie Joe Johnson

1905-

AUTHOR OF

Debby, Texas: The Land of the Tejas, Susan's Year, Etc.

Autobiographical sketch of Siddie Joe Johnson:

I WAS born in Dallas, Texas, but when I was seven my family moved to Corpus Christi, a small town on the Gulf coast. My younger brother and sister and I were really country-bred children, for our place was at the edge of town and we were free to roam the South Texas countryside, on foot or on horseback, as we pleased. I soon grew to love the water—the sound and the sight and the smell of it. And it has always seemed to me I was lucky to have been young in that particular place.

As soon as I started to school I started writing rhymes. My mother and teachers thought they were wonderful, but I know now they were very bad even for a child. At twelve I wrote a whole composition book full of "poems" as a present for my mother. Some of them were not so bad.

I went to high school after a while and went to football games and parties and wrote marvelous stories for the other girls and boys to read. Thank goodness, none of those stories still exist! In my senior year I left the public high school and went to Incarnate Word Academy, a Catholic school for girls. There I met many girls from the ranches surrounding Corpus Christi, some of them Mexicans from old Southwest families —girls I might not have known at the public school.

Then for a while I stayed home and worked and dreamed and wrote. My poetry

SIDDIE JOE JOHNSON

began to be published. The magazine *Poetry* took some. I won a Poetry Society of Texas prize or two. And then, when my little sister finished high school, we went off to college together.

In 1933, a year after I had received my B.A. from Texas Christian University in Fort Worth, my first book of poems was published. I was teaching school at the time, in the old oil-boom town of Refugio. After a year I returned to Corpus Christi to work in the public library, though at that time I had no library training. I wrote a few short stories during that period and quite a bit of poetry, some of which appeared in national magazines.

Gradually I took over the children's work in the library. I began to hold story hours. But up to that time, aside from a poem or two, I had not thought about writing for children, though my whole interest was work with them. I particularly liked to work with little Mexican boys and girls.

In 1937 I went to Louisiana State University for a library degree, and that next summer started writing my first children's book, *Debby*. I became head of the children's department of the Dallas Public Library in 1938. In 1940 *Debby* was published. I still like it best of all my children's books. Debby, of course, is myself as a child.

My next book was the story of a family of pioneer children in Denison, Texas, in 1872. The family is really my father's family, though I had to make them all about fifteen years older than they really are to put them back in Denison's birth-year, 1872.

The next year a publisher asked me to write the text for a picture-book history of Texas. This book, *Texas: The Land of the Tejas*, appeared in 1943.

In late 1945 another book of poems was published by the Kaleidograph Press of Dallas. It was co-winner of their annual manuscript award. But it is the children's books that really please me.

I love being the Dallas children's librarian. I love hearing those who like my books call me by my whole name, "Hello, Miss Siddie Joe Johnson." I love telling stories to them. And sooner or later I intend to write other stories for them.

Elizabeth Orton Jones

June 25, 1910-

AUTHOR AND ILLUSTRATOR OF
Twig, Maminka's Children, Big Susan, Etc.

Autobiographical sketch of Elizabeth Orton Jones:

I WAS born on June twenty-fifth, which happens to be exactly half-past Christmas —a very fair arrangement, I've always thought. The year was 1910 and the town was Highland Park, Illinois. Here I lived and went to school; here I roller-skated and rode my bike, took music lessons, bought penny candy at Larson's store, and was a girl scout. I had long red braids and freckles. The "kids" called me *Jonesy*. My family, of course, did not.

I was the first child, for a number of years the only child, for my brother and sister arrived much later. In our house there was always music, reading aloud, fun and laughter. There were people who liked to come and be with us—people from various walks of life—people of various nationalities and races. There was always much to talk about and to share with others. But, too, in our house, time was carefully set aside for silence in which to think and to imagine.

I liked to think and to imagine, to read and to write, to look at pictures and to draw, to make things. I liked the out-of-doors, animals, birds, insects—and everything that grew. I liked outdoor sports, too, especially swimming.

When grammar school was over I went East to preparatory school. Then I came back to the Middle West to the University of Chicago, where I majored in art. After receiving my degree, I went to France to study painting, first at Fontainebleau—then in Paris. When I returned I found I missed Paris very much. I made some pictures of certain little shops I remembered—little street scenes I had loved. In every picture were children. I found I missed the children of Paris even more than Paris itself. I "made up" two little French boys and named them Mich and Tobie. Out of each picture I had drawn I "made up" an adventure for Mich and Tobie. I wrote their adventures down. And that was my first book for children: *Ragman of Paris*. Even before it was finished I knew that making books for children was what I wanted most to do.

I made another book: *Maminka's Children*. From the time I was born until I was twelve, two Bohemian girls lived at our house and worked for us. Out of my love for them—out of the fun we all had had together, this book grew.

Many were the Sunday afternoons I used to spend in our front yard, alone, before my brother and sister were born, or while they were still very little. Sometimes I was Robin Hood or Will Scarlett. Sometimes I was a grand lady with a season ticket to the opera. The season ticket was a locust leaf. The front yard was the opera house, "packed" with people. I sat in a box. The box was a mulberry bush. The stage was a high, flat place on the lawn. Many an opera by Wagner was "given" here, and many an opera by myself! Out of my firm belief in the magic of this sort of thing grew another book: *Twig*.

I have made pictures for a number of books by other people. One of these was Rachel Field's *Prayer for a Child*, for which I was awarded the Caldecott Medal. The Caldecott Medal makes one feel very humble.

My mother (Jessie Mae Jones) and I have made three books together. Making books with one's mother is a very rare experience.

I have a studio in Highland Park, Illinois, which is a part of our family house. I also have a house in Mason, New Hampshire. I spend part of the time here—and part of the time there. My cat, Piley, travels back and forth with me. Right now, I am here—in Highland Park—looking out through my studio window at boys and girls doing the same things I used to do—going along the same street to the same school.

Did you ever watch an awkward young cicada without any wings crawl up a tree and fasten his feet to the bark? Did you ever watch to see his skin split—to see him emerge from it a full-grown adult with wings? He sits for a while near the transparent shell of his old self until his wings are strong enough to carry him. Then—away he goes, leaving his old self fastened to the tree.

I see my old self out there among those boys and girls. I see *Jonesy* with her long red braids. The boys and girls cannot see her, for she is just a shell, transparent and empty. But she helps me remember how I used to feel. She helps me see how boys and girls today are the same as the "kids" I used to know so well—as the "kid" I used to be. That helps me understand how boys and girls all over the world are the same, no matter what their language or their color. And *that* helps me realize how much there is to talk about—how much fun there is, and laughter, and silence, too, to share; how many books there are to make; and how many friends—everywhere.

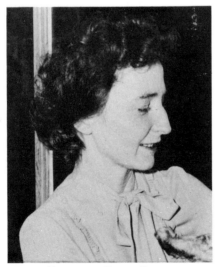

ELIZABETH ORTON JONES

Clara Ingram Judson

1879-

AUTHOR OF

*Soldier Doctor, Abraham Lincoln, The Green
Ginger Jar, Petar's Treasure, Etc.*

Autobiographical sketch of Clara Ingram
Judson:

A RECORD of my life can begin near the
middle for that is when I started to
write professionally. One day while our
daughters Alice and Mary Jane were in
school I had the idea that newspapers should
carry a daily feature for children. I wrote
some short stories which were accepted by
the editor of my home town paper, the Richmond (Indiana) *Item.* In six weeks the
Indianapolis *Star* took the feature and soon
my "Bedtime Tales" were published by a
national syndicate.

Beginning in 1915, more than fifty books
of mine have been published. These include nineteen in the "Mary Jane" series,
animal stories, books on how to do useful
things at home, four books for grown-ups
on budgets and the use of money, "Play
Days," the "People Who Work" books,
biographies, and the "They Came from . . ."
books. Three of my books have been choices
of the Junior Literary Guild.

I was born in Logansport, Indiana, and
moved to Indianapolis when I was six. My
three younger brothers and I went to public
schools. Later I graduated from the Girls'
Classical School. I taught in public school
and from the year I was sixteen taught
regularly in Sunday schools. After I was
married to James M. Judson we lived for
ten years in Richmond, Indiana, then moved
to Chicago and later to Evanston, Illinois.

During the First World War the United
States Treasury Department asked me to
speak on thrift at high schools of Illinois.
After the war I was asked to travel again,
speaking for the Department of Justice at
large community meetings, and later I addressed the P.T.A.'s women's clubs, farm
and home bureaus, 4-H clubs, schools, universities, and national conventions. With
the coming of radio I broadcast in Chicago
and elsewhere and for some years had a
weekly radio program. All my lectures related to home life. The most popular topics
were the use of time and money.

CLARA INGRAM JUDSON

During this period I was keeping house
and writing books and magazine and newspaper articles. (More than two thousand
stories, plays, and articles for children and
grown-ups have been published.) I did
copy-writing for advertisers and publicity
writing and speaking for banks and other
businesses.

My lecturing and thousands of letters
from radio listeners brought me in contact
with many people. I came to resent the
expression, "melting pot" and to realize
that America is "the beautiful" because she
is like a tapestry, woven of varied threads,
sturdy, gay, creative, combined to make a
whole. I planned work designed to interpret this thought to young readers. Some
years ago I began to carry out my idea by
writing biographies and "They Came from
. . ." books, which are historical novels
about the foreign-born in America.

May Justus

1898-

AUTHOR OF

*Honey Jane, Mr. Songcatcher and Company,
The House in No-End Hollow, Etc.*

Autobiographical letter from May Justus:

FIRST, let me say I consider it a very
great honor to meet you in this beautiful
book. But perhaps we have met before.
Some of you have read my books about folk

MAY JUSTUS

in the Tennessee mountains. If so, you know a good deal about me. I am a Smoky Mountaineer. My childhood home was a cabin very much like Matt's and Glory's in *The Cabin on Kettle Creek*. My father taught school in a big log house which was also used as a church.

One of my happiest memories is of the fun we had there. Many of the games and songs I learned from my schoolmates you may find in my stories of boys and girls at school. The fiddle tunes are mostly those I learned from my father's fiddle. The old ballads are those which tripped from my mother's tongue. The glad and sad adventures of my book children are rooted in my experiences as a little girl—experiences. shared by my brother Hal and my sister Helen.

But come, take a brief glimpse of the little world I inhabit now—the tip-top of the Cumberland plateau in middle Tennessee. Summerfield is the name of our community, though mail comes to Tracy City several miles away.

The Little Brown House where I live and write is next door to the schoolhouse where I taught for so many happy years. There is a gate in the fence between my front yard and the playground. My best friends are the school children. Friday is my visiting day over at school. On my visits there I read my newest stories and poems. Sometimes I teach new songs and games.

The Little Brown House has an attic room which serves as a children's library. Against one wall is a bookcase one of my schoolboys made years ago. In it are books for the older boys and girls. The books for the younger children are on low shelves which they can easily reach. The rough boards of the walls are covered with gay book posters and original illustrations from many of my books. Some of these were made right here on the spot by artists from New York and Chicago who came South to get true local color for their work.

Most of my twenty-five books I wrote during twenty-five years of teaching. If you have any more fun reading these books than I have writing them, I'd like to hear about it! And I have plans in my head right now for three more books.

James O. Kaler

See *"Otis, James"*

Eric P. Kelly

March 16, 1884-
AUTHOR OF
The Trumpeter of Krakow, Land of the Polish People, From Star to Star, Etc.

Autobiographical sketch of Eric P. Kelly:

THAT a fast moving world has swept me through scenes of indescribable change is something I rejoice at. I often wonder what it would seem like to have lived in the Middle Ages with its unchanging vistas or to have been rooted deeply in the Victorian era with its peaceful attitudes toward life and thought.

One of my first recollections as a child was that of being lifted up in a parent's arms to behold the destruction by fire of the old carriage district in Amesbury, Massachusetts; with that fire went the last vestiges of handicraft in American carriage-making. My father had made carriages before the coming in of the machines had driven him into the ranks of the merchant class.

The sudden new realization of adventure in the West led my people to pull up stakes and start for Colorado. My mother was a confirmed adventurer—she had been born in Australia and had crossed the ocean many times as a girl, journeys that took long weeks and months in a sailing vessel. My father was bookish—he had started one of the first circulating libraries in his home town.

This break was indeed a break; the Kellys had always made their home in Massachusetts, New Hampshire, and Maine, since the earliest Kelly came in with a crowd of settlers in the early days of Newbury. But on my way west as a boy of five I felt the spirit of adventure, the mountain peaks filled me with that intense longing and ambition that they seem to affect so many people with, and the sight of troops returning from the last Indian campaign was another thrill to the pulses.

Those happy years in the 'nineties in Denver: the children excited over the World's Fair, the silver movement, and the rise of Bryan with most of us selling *16 to 1* buttons in the streets. With bicycles we toured every inch of the country about Denver and in the summers explored mountain parks and winding canyons.

But the Denver life came to an end and we went back to New York, where, minus a backyard, I suffered terribly, and attended the De Witt Clinton High School. Later we returned to Amesbury and I entered Dartmouth College in New Hampshire with the class of 1906. My summers were spent working at the Isles of Shoals off the brief New Hampshire coast with that Leighton family, one of whom, Celia Thaxter, has immortalized the islands.

Eric P. Kelly

College finished, I went to work. It was the Rooseveltian (T.R.) era, and newspaper work was at once a thrill and an opportunity. I began on a little paper in Westfield, Massachusetts, went up to the *Springfield Union*, edited a small paper in New Jersey, worked for a news agency in New York and in Boston, was on the staff of the *Boston Herald*, and worked later for the *Boston Transcript*. All this time I was trying out my style in stories; Mr. Arthur Stanwood Pier of the *Youth's Companion* took my first after I had worked at story writing for ten years, and also took my second and third stories a few years later.

With some responsibilities at the time the First World War broke out I found I could be of some service in teaching French to men going overseas, and was later sent to France to cooperate with the French organization, the Foyer du Soldat, which was doing for French soldiers what our welfare organizations were doing for our own. In these foyers I met Polish exiles whose admiration of Americans was very great, and actually urged us to go with them to Poland and help in the new work of educating their people. Some of us went to see Mr. Paderewski in Paris and he was quite enthusiastic about some type of organized welfare in Poland, and with material furnished by American societies we went into Poland with food and supplies a few months after the Armistice.

Here I learned the language, became acquainted with the people and traveled about so constantly with welfare material and food that I became somewhat familiar with the country. I also learned something of the Polish spirit, its depth and its sincerity, its enthusiasm, its intenseness, and its vast reverence for the creative spirit and art and music and the beauty which they imply. It was a new experience to me, for the very flexibility of their personalities and their life and thought released expression in myself; expression which New England and Anglo-Saxon environment had tended to chill. I found my style, I found myself, I found an expression other people seemed to like. Along with my Polish studies, I took up Russian and Czech and found much of similarity among them.

After three years of this, I returned to America, taught at Mercersburg Academy, wrote stories for Mr. William Fayal Clark of *St. Nicholas*, whose praise did much to keep me writing, went to my alma mater to teach English, and kept on writing. In 1925 and 1926 I taught and studied at the University of Krakow in Poland and wrote *The Trumpeter of Krakow*, while roaming near the old church day and night.

The Second World War brought me new responsibilities. I was sent by the Office of Foreign Relief of the Department of State to Mexico to build homes and to assist Polish refugees. My village at Santa Rosa, León, was quite fortunate, and needless to say, I was happy to be of service to a people I love.

After the war I returned to take up my work at Dartmouth after a four-year absence.

Louise Andrews Kent

May 25, 1886-

AUTHOR OF

*He Went with Christopher Columbus,
He Went with Marco Polo, Etc.*

LOUISE ANDREWS KENT

LOUISE ANDREWS was born in Brookline, Massachusetts. Her parents were Walter Edward Andrews and Mary Sophronia (Edgerly) Andrews. She was born at the time, she says, "when people still wore bustles and velvet basques. Summers on an island in Frenchman's Bay only made the winters at home seem more fun. I did much the same things that children do now —coasted, skated, climbed trees, played with whatever dogs were on hand, rode horseback, paddled canoes, rowed boats, fished, and played baseball. I went to different schools, public and private, in Brookline and Boston. Afterwards I spent four years in the library school of Simmons College."

She graduated in 1909. "Then luckily for the profession of librarian—as well as for me—I got married." She married Ira Rich Kent, later a prominent editor and publisher, on May 23, 1912. They had two daughters, Elizabeth Hollister Kent and Rosamond Mary Kent, and made their home in Brookline, Massachusetts.

Author of eleven books, joint author of two more, Louise Andrews Kent has also contributed short stories to magazines. In 1911 she wrote a column under the name of Teresa Tempest for the Boston *Traveler*, and she contributed editorials to the Boston *Herald* from 1928 to 1931.

In addition to writing and raising a family, Mrs. Kent has served as trustee for the Park School in Brookline and on the governing board of the Women's Industrial Union. She was once a trustee of Simmons College but says she had to give up being on committees when she took on writing. As their titles suggest, many of Mrs. Kent's books have historical backgrounds, which have been highly praised for their authenticity.

Jim Kjelgaard

December 5, 1910-

AUTHOR OF

Big Red, Rebel Siege, Forest Patrol, Etc.

Autobiographical sketch of James Arthur Kjelgaard:

I WAS born in New York City. My position in the family was somewhat disadvantageous since there were three older brothers, any one of whom could boss me around and all of whom did. This unbearable condition was partially relieved since I had a younger brother whom I could "tell off" until he grew to be six feet four in his stocking feet. There is a sister, too. Betty, by the way, is also a writer.

I was not yet out of three-cornered pants when the family moved to a farm in the Pennsylvania mountains—Tioga County, to be exact. The farm was a marvelous place.

Kjelgaard: *KEL gard*

My father owned, or acquired, about seven hundred and fifty acres of land, which was stocked with a herd of dairy cattle, horses, sheep, dogs, chickens, and everything else in the way of farm animals.

The biggest job of us younger brothers used to be keeping the cattle out of places they should not go. Cattle, incidentally, have a marvelous penchant for making themselves sick eating too many apples. Since there were extensive apple orchards and few fenced pastures, we had our hands full most of the time.

Eventually our father sold the farm, we moved to the town of Galeton, Pennsylvania, and Father resumed the practice of medicine. Nobody in Galeton has to walk more than half a mile to find: (1) good fishing, (2) good hunting, (3) good trapping.

Rest assured we speedily discovered all three. Between intervals of attending school we ran trap lines, shot deer, and fished for trout. As we grew up and graduated from school we continued our outdoor activities. Of course we also expanded them. I think I never shall forget that tarpaper-covered shack on top of the mountain where, though we had intended to sleep separately, three of us had to climb into one bunk whereon were piled all the blankets while the fourth kept the stove red hot. Even so, water pails inside the shack had nothing but ice inside when morning finally came. There was

JIM KJELGAARD

another shack to which I departed alone for the purpose of trapping beaver. Despite a roaring fire and a mattress on top of my blankets I shivered all night.

Eventually all of us drifted away to one job or another. My older brother, Johnnie, became a forest ranger. I myself held a dozen jobs, and at one time or another have been laborer, teamster, factory worker, plumber's apprentice, surveyor's assistant.

I started writing because things seemed just naturally to be heading in that direction anyhow. Aside from some published stories and articles I've written four books for boys. I hope, of course, to write more.

As for the rest I am married to a beautiful young lady and have an equally lovely daughter, Karen.

Emilie Benson Knipe
Alden Arthur Knipe

AUTHORS OF
*The Lucky Sixpence, Diantha's Quest,
A Maid of '76, Etc.*

The following story of the lives of Emilie Benson Knipe and Alden Arthur Knipe, husband and wife who collaborated, was written by Mrs. Knipe:

I WAS born at my grandmother's in Philadelphia, at midnight of June 12, 1870. My father, who confessed to various superstitions, always fixed this date. My mother hinted that I was a later comer and did not actually make my advent until a few minutes after the clock had sounded the hour.

Alden Arthur Knipe arrived, also in Philadelphia, on June 26 of the same year, so we began early in life to do the same things in much the same way. For instance, we both remember Sunday breakfasts which invariably included stewed kidneys, and suppers (for on Sunday Philadelphians ate dinner at two) with lobster salad; and in each house the mistress, who did no other housework, prided herself on her skill in making mince pies, fruit cake, and salad dressing.

We were both educated at private schools. Dr. Knipe then attended Haverford College and later went to the University of Pennsylvania for his professional training.

Knipe: *NIPE*

He was athletic and some of his records still stand at Haverford, while at Pennsylvania he was always placed in the intercollegiates and was captain of the '94 football team, which, with only eleven men and no substitutes worthy of the name, played two forty-five minute halves and defeated all comers, including Cornell, Harvard, and Princeton.

While interested in theory and experiment, Dr. Knipe never cared for the practice of medicine and his evolution into a writer was a natural one, since his grandfather was Timothy Shea Arthur, who founded *Arthur's Home Magazine*, the forerunner of all the popular women's magazines, but who is best known as the author of *Ten Nights in a Bar-Room*.

My youth was quite different. I have an older sister whom I do not remember except as a grown-up and very beautiful young lady. I admired her excessively and respectfully, but I never had any desire to emulate her career at Newport and elsewhere. I was sandwiched between four brothers, and I harbored no doubt that if I did exactly what they did, was afraid of nothing and learned to shoot, swim, and manage a boat (accomplishments not then usual for a girl) I should, when I grew up, be as good a man as any of them.

I was somewhat weaned from this ambition when it was discovered that I had an aptitude for drawing. I studied art, then took a position on a newspaper and began timidly to venture into the field of magazine illustration. Finally I rented a studio in Philadelphia.

Meanwhile Dr. Knipe had become a professor at the University of Iowa but disliked the work, so we decided to marry and move to New York. His first writing, for *Scribner's Magazine,* was at once successful and I continued my illustration.

It was during an illness that I began to write. Dr. Knipe and I were discussing vitality in books, and I said I thought I knew what contributed to the continued sale of *Little Women*, for instance. It was a winter of deep snows and I was unable to do anything save sit before the fire with a French bull puppy in my lap; so, more to amuse myself than with any thought of practicality, I wrote our first juvenile *John Fales —Gentleman,* a title later changed to *Little Miss Fales.* The puppy refusing to be dis-

placed, this was done on a lap-board over his head. Dr. Knipe did considerable rewriting and reconstruction on this and sent it to *Harper's.* It was at once accepted, this news reaching me in the hospital. *The Lucky Sixpence* was a direct outgrowth of this book. After that, sometimes one of us wrote the first draft, sometimes the other, and when a book was finished neither could tell where the other individual's work began or ended. We even collaborated on two novels, but there we found the Knipe name a disadvantage as a trade mark denoting juveniles, so we have both written books for grown-ups under pseudonyms.

* * *

On May 23, 1950, after a brief illness, Dr. Knipe died at his home on Sutton Place, New York City, shortly before his eightieth birthday. He was survived by Mrs. Knipe.

Rose B. Knox

1879-

AUTHOR OF

The Boys and Sally, Marty and Company, Etc.

Autobiographical sketch of Rose B. Knox:

I BELONG to the Deep South—Alabama. My people from away back are Southern planters and professional folk, save one grandfather, a Connecticut Yankee. Times were pretty hard throughout my childhood but we children—over fifty first cousins of us and no telling how many second and third ones—minded not at all. Our home was in a small town, but I spent much time with an aunt on a cotton plantation, where I was the only girl of my age in a crowd of boys. Outdoors was literally the only place big enough to hold us. The first bumble bee sighted was our high sign for bare feet, and thenceforth till winter we refused shoes save for state occasions. We hunted, fished, climbed, and rode horseback, or roamed about the plantation, with a thumb in every pie, be it syrup making, cotton picking, ginning, or hog killing.

School was long an unknown quantity, for my lessons were at home until I was a big girl. I devoured Dickens, Scott, Shakespeare, Cooper's Indian tales and whatnot. Many of these I retold to the boys, or, on occasion, I made up stories for them. Except, however, for a few poems, I didn't

ROSE B. KNOX

write anything, my spelling being exceedingly frail; and, anyway, telling was so much easier.

Thus it went till a sad blow fell—the edict that I was too old to go barefooted another *single* time; that skirts must come down and hair go up. But all was not lost. Work and play at boarding school proved interesting and the vacation mostly a gay pilgrimage of visits, to University commencement, with beaux galore, for buggy-rides, dances, and un-listened-to addresses; to house-parties, where barbecues, watermelon-cuttings, coaching, and dancing were the order of the day. Then presently, a proud graduate of Agnes Scott College and the Atlanta Kindergarten Normal, behold, I was a full-fledged teacher in a cottonmill village. Later, after studying in Chicago, I taught in Mississippi State College for Women.

My bursting into print was entirely accidental. During a long illness I found myself doing a long needed book for teachers, *School Activities and Equipment.* Next I decided to try my hand on a school reader about cotton. My manuscript, however, simply refused to stay in the cotton patch and presently *The Boys and Sally* were having a grand time down on a plantation, with a finger in every pie. And to the tune of some ninety thousand words.

All innocently, I mailed copies to three publishers simultaneously. Two editors sur-

vived the reading, and were interested if lavish cutting could be done. My resistance was stout, but further trials won the same verdict. So cut I finally did, and thus, greatly shorn, and greatly improved thereby, my *Boys and Sally* made their bow in 1930.

By this time realization had come that I belonged to the Old South, and the Old South was gone. Also that many enchanting pictures of the South were fading from view. I wanted tremendously to hold a few of these for present-day children, so I wrote *Miss Jimmy Deane, Marty and Company, Footlights Afloat, Patsy's Progress,* and many others. A new story about Patsy was just getting under way when Pearl Harbor changed the world for all of us. Forthwith Patsy was gone, back to her own happier times, where, try as I might, I could not follow her. So I came to Washington as a free-lance writer for press and other organizations—with a ring-side seat at that great and tragic show—the war in Washington! Out of these experiences, perhaps, may come another book some day.

Anne D. Kyle

October 18, 1896-

AUTHOR OF

*The Apprentice of Florence, Red Sky
Over Rome, Etc.*

Autobiographical sketch of Anne D. Kyle:

MY father was minister of the United Presbyterian church in Frankford, a suburb of Philadelphia, and there I grew up, played, went to school, and sampled every book I could lay my hands upon.

I can remember lying at full length on the floor of my father's study on long hot Sunday afternoons, absorbed in the marvels of Ridpath's *History of the World.* I remember too that this pastime was regarded with some disapproval by my religious father, who was particular about "Sunday reading." But after all history was different from fiction, though often stranger, and so I was left undisturbed to revel in the practices of the ancient Druids, in the careers of Attila the Scourge of God, of Messalina, Lorenzo de' Medici, and Martin Luther. And presently when the bare facts of history proved inadequate for my curiosity I began myself to improve upon them. One of the first stories I wrote was about that unknown peasant boy who was chosen to break the news to some hot-tempered King of England that his favorite son had been accidentally drowned. I don't remember what happened in it, but I'm sure it had a happy ending!

The Bible was another "history book" which provided me with inspiration. I remember writing about a Hebrew woman named Malah who was one of the Children of Israel that followed Moses across the Red Sea. I know I was quite proud of her name because I made it up—my father, I think, was a bit skeptical about it!

This interest in history, begun on the floor of my father's study, was increased by three trips abroad during school vacations. Then, two years after I graduated from Smith in 1918, we set out westward, which was easier in 1920 than going to a still war-wrecked Europe. We had a wonderful trip through Japan and China and India and the result was a "travel" book over which I labored mightily and which I considered a masterpiece, though I couldn't get any publisher to agree with me!

After nearly a year of journeying in the East, both Far and Near, we settled down to eight delightful months in Rome. I had been to Italy before, but only briefly, on the way to and from Egypt. In 1926 I was again in Italy and in 1929 I returned once more. The four succeeding winters were spent in Florence because I wanted to find out as

Bachrach

ANNE D. KYLE

much as I could about that amazing city which, barring electric lights and tramcars and automobiles and traffic policemen, is so little different from what it was in old Cosimo de' Medici's day. Out of this study grew *The Apprentice of Florence*. I could pick out for you his counterpart any day from among the youngsters that play in the narrow Florentine streets or learn their trade in the tiny shops or "botteghe" that are so little changed since the days when Giotto and Ghiberti and Botticelli and Michelangelo learned their trade in them.

Red Sky Over Rome came out in 1938. Then the war and its attendant complications interrupted my writing. However I am now at work on another juvenile.

Édouard Laboulaye

January 18, 1811-May 24, 1883

AUTHOR OF

The Laboulaye Fairy Books, Etc.

ÉDOUARD RENÉ LEFEBVRE LABOULAYE was born in Paris under the First Empire, his family being undistinguished but intelligent and progressive. After a college education he became an advocate in the Royal Court of Paris, and at thirty-eight a professor of comparative legislation at the College of France. He was a great success as a lecturer. He had the advantages of fluent speech, captivating humor, and a handsome personal presence, and it was said many would sit through the lecture hour before his to make sure of a place when he spoke.

Édouard Laboulaye was an example of the eminent company who have found relaxation from weighty affairs in byways. A brilliant lawyer, a member of learned academies, and of the French Parliament, a professor and director of the College of France, and an outstanding author, lecturer, and scholar of his time, he yet found time to write three delectable books of fairy tales that have for decades charmed young and old alike.

When he died he received tributes from the foremost scholars and statesmen. But to him his greatest reward was the thought of remembrance by his young readers. "In repeating my tales to the young folks whom I shall never see," he wrote in his dedication, "you will remember him who loved

Laboulaye: *lah boo LAY*

you when you were little; and perhaps you will find pleasure in talking to them of the old man who delighted in trying to amuse children, while they will listen with sparkling eyes, and be proud of their great-grandfather. I desire no other fame; this immortality suffices for me."

Walter De La Mare

See *De La Mare, Walter*

Harold Lamb

1892-

AUTHOR OF

The Boy's Genghis Khan, Durandal, Etc.

Autobiographical sketch of Harold Lamb:

I WAS born in New York and went to school in Friends Seminary. I think I did not learn as much in school or in college later—Columbia College and the Pulitzer School of Journalism—as in reading for myself outside the classrooms. This reading of everything that interested me began in my grandfather's library, and has kept on steadily.

My studies, therefore, have been individual, and in fields that interested me, such as the exploration of Asia in the early times before European powers appeared on the scene. This interest in central Asia led to the languages and people not just of today but as they had been in the past. Later on it was possible to reconstruct some rather ancient periods in Asia.

I have written since I was about ten years old; in school we set up a hand press and published our own writings. At college I contributed stories to the *Columbia Monthly*. Received the H. C. Bunner medal in American Literature.

After that, still in New York, I took a job in an editorial office, and contributed individual columns to the newspapers, doing stories for the pulp magazines like *Adventure*. The editor of that magazine, Arthur Hoffman, allowed writers to follow their own imagination to any length on any subject, and that helped us all more than I can say. Today, twenty-five years later, I am writing for the *Saturday Evening Post* and *Collier's*, but the stories are not very different from those in the early *Adventure*.

HAROLD LAMB

In the first war, I served as a private in the 107th Infantry, and in this last war was in confidential service for the War Department abroad, in Asia.

All in all, I have spent nearly seven years inside Asia or near it, and have traveled over most of its western portions. At times I have tried to follow the routes taken by explorers like Marco Polo, or Rubruquis, and military leaders like Genghis Khan or Alexander of Macedon.

It was more interesting to do this as I had followed very closely, before then, all available narratives of the early explorers, as well as the history and geography of the different regions in the original narratives of the men who lived during the periods of the past. To form a clear idea of such a period, you have to know the folk tales, the customs, the literature, and all the habits of life in the different parts of Asia. You have to be able to read the languages. Persian is most important, because the mass of the medieval chronicles of Asia were written in that language, or in Arabic, as they were written in Latin within Europe.

Most of my books have to do with the past in western Asia and Russia. Many of them have been translated and published in the Asiatic countries for the people there to read. In fact, it is not easy to go into a country without finding something of mine in print there. Several Russian stories were translated into Ukrainian. Other works turned up in Urdu in northern India, in Turkish, and Finnish.

So these books are perhaps better known through Asia than here in the United States, and I have as many friends there as here.

During the work on the two volumes of the Crusades, I was helped by a Guggenheim Fellowship, to pay the expenses of study and travel. The Iranian government awarded a decoration, more, I think, to the books than to myself.

I am married and have two children, a boy and a girl. As to hobbies, I play tennis still and like to work in the garden and play chess. As to appearance, I am six feet and one inch in height, and weigh a bit more than 160 pounds.

Louise Lamprey

April 17, 1869-January 15, 1951

AUTHOR OF

All the Ways of Building, The Story of Weaving, The Story of Cookery, Etc.

Autobiographical sketch of Louise Lamprey, written for THE JUNIOR BOOK OF AUTHORS shortly before her death:

BORN in my grandmother's house in Alexandria, New Hampshire, a story-'n'-a-half cottage in the middle of a lumber tract, I spent my childhood as a country minister's daughter in New Hampshire, Maine, and Vermont.

I never went to grade school until I was thirteen, but was taught at home. My real education in those years was through miscellaneous reading, the old *St. Nicholas* and other magazines, and one village library that had the old Mühlbach novels, Scott, and Dickens. We read Shakespeare together at home, and other classics, and I learned to read French by myself at the age of ten. My favorite amusement used to be telling myself stories when alone, and I always tried to make them sound like the stories I read, which probably was of some value to my vocabulary.

I was one of the first Mount Holyoke graduates after it became a college, taught a short time, went to Washington and was for eight years an editorial writer on two papers. My first job in New York was in the Republican campaign headquarters in 1904, and after that I held various writing

LOUISE LAMPREY

and office jobs, including one that took me to London in 1912-14. For five summers I was storyteller, craft teacher, and dramatic counselor in a children's camp.

I'd always told stories to children when the chance offered, but that experience confirmed the belief left over from my own childhood, that children like a story with real literary value better than trash. I think they naturally like history, Bible stories, folklore, and the great plays and novels, when put in a form they understand. Included in the material I have used in story form with children between seven and twelve are *Ivanhoe, The Talisman, The Merchant of Venice, The Tempest,* and *The Mysterious Island,* which I told to the junior group of five-and-six-year-olds one year. I think little children always like desert-island stories. One year I had a "dictionary class" to satisfy the youngsters who asked where words came from, and another year we made a Punch and Judy show.

I think children like best a story or employment a little ahead of their ability; anything is better than talking down to them. In teaching woodcarving I have found they delight in taking designs from an old heraldry book, carving and painting them in the proper colors, and hearing their history, as in such ballads as "The Heart of the Bruce."

I started writing books during the First World War, when I wrote *In the Days of the Guild*, the idea of the book being that we had had so many stories of medieval life dealing with kings, queens, and castles that it was time to tell about the common people and their children—weavers, smiths, glass-makers, builders, and so on. This was followed by *Masters of the Guild*, and then by half a dozen books of stories about events in American history and five books dealing with children in ancient or prehistoric ages in England, Rome, Greece, Egypt, and pre-Roman Gaul.

In writing historical fiction it has always been my aim not to put in anything that could not have happened, or that will have to be unlearned in later student life. It is amazing how much interesting historical material there is which has been overlooked in writing for children.

* * *

Miss Lamprey made her home for many years at Limerick, Maine, and wrote most of her later books there. She had moved to nearby Shapleigh, in the same state, only a few weeks before her death, in her eighty-second year.

Marion Florence Lansing

June 10, 1883-

AUTHOR OF

Liberators and Heroes of South America,
Liberators and Heroes of Mexico
and Central America, Etc.

Autobiographical sketch of Marion Florence Lansing:

ONCE upon a time a little girl watched her mother take in big envelopes in the morning mail and was told she must not disturb her until she had read her proof. She sat down with her playthings and prepared to keep very still. But soon her mother, without looking up, tossed in her direction a long piece of paper. The little girl picked it up. She would play at "reading proof." She found she could do more than play at it. There were big letters on those pages the names of which she knew. Then she saw a word she thought she knew. She tiptoed over to the bookcase and pulled out her favorite picture book. Under the picture of a dog was a word of three letters. She put her finger on it and carried it back to her chair. Then she hunted down the long page of proof till she found—yes!— those very same letters. That was the name of the picture. It must be the word "dog."

When the proof was read, she showed her mother what she had found. "Yes," said her mother, "that is the word 'dog.'" After that her mother, who was Jenny Stickney Lansing, always threw the second set of proofs of the Primer and First Reader she was making on the floor, and the little girl picked them up and hunted for words she knew by sight in her picture book. Before the books were done she had learned to read.

Then one day the little girl, who was Marion Lansing, went with her mother into Boston to see Mr. Ginn, who was publishing these Stickney readers. He took her on his knee and said to her, "Will you make books for me when you grow up?" And she answered, as any five-year-old would, "Yes." But the best part of that story for the girl, who was myself, was that she did.

Probably most people, from very long ago to this twentieth century, have been sure they were born at just the right time and were living in the most interesting period of the world's history. But surely we who stand at the beginning of the new age when all the world has become one world are very fortunate.

My family story goes back to the first century of the American colonies. My mother, Jenny Stickney, was descended from

MARION FLORENCE LANSING

William Stickney of England, who came to Massachusetts before 1638. My father, John Arnold Lansing, was of Dutch descent, his first American ancestor having come to the Mohawk Valley in New York about 1650. I was born in Waverley, Massachusetts, and moved soon to the nearby town of Cambridge, where I have lived ever since. From the Cambridge Latin School I went to Mount Holyoke College, founded by Mary Lyon in 1837. On its hundreth anniversary, in 1937, I had the satisfaction of honoring this pioneer in women's education by a book, *Mary Lyon Through Her Letters*. A year at Radcliffe followed, during which I studied under the historian Edward Channing of Harvard who started me in the writing of American history.

During that year I also discovered in the Harvard College Library one of the finest collections of fairy and folk stories in the world. From this collection I edited and wrote the seven volumes of "The Open Road Library." Another editing experience was for "Our Wonder World," a library for reference and reading in ten and later eleven volumes.

History has always interested me. I spent a year between high school and college traveling abroad, going as far as Istanbul, then Constantinople. Within the last few years I have been greatly interested in South America and have matched up our history with that of these neighboring Americas in several books, including *Liberators and Heroes of South America* and *Liberators and Heroes of Mexico and Central America*.

While Cambridge is my winter home, no record would be complete without a word about my summer home on Cape Cod, where I have a cabin among the pines near our family cottage, from which I can drive to all the beaches and history-filled places and find out how history was really lived instead of getting it only in libraries and out of books.

Dorothy P. Lathrop

April 16, 1891-

ILLUSTRATOR AND AUTHOR

Who Goes There? The Fairy Circus, Colt From Moon Mountain, Skittle Skattle Monkey, Etc.

Autobiographical sketch of Dorothy Pulis Lathrop:

I WAS born in Albany, New York. My father, Cyrus Clark Lathrop, was a businessman during many years of his life, but his chief interest was in work with young people. He founded the Boys' Club in Albany, and was instrumental in establishing the Juvenile Court in the same city, and in various reforms relating to the young. My mother, I. Pulis Lathrop, is a painter. It undoubtedly was seeing her at work, being in her studio, and there encouraged to use her brushes and paints that gave me my interest in art. From her came much of my training in painting, and talk of art and artists was from a very early age part of my daily life. My sister, Gertrude K. Lathrop, is a sculptor.

Perhaps it was from my paternal grandfather, who had a bookstore in Bridgeport, Connecticut, that I inherited most strongly my interest in books, which turned my drawing and painting in that direction. In fact during all those early years, I wrote far more than I drew. And it was with the desire to write and to illustrate my own books that I went to Teachers College, Columbia University, where I could study both writing and art, getting at the same time a diploma in teaching, which my father thought a more practical profession than either writing or illustration.

Although I taught only two years, I was always grateful for having gone to Teachers College and so to have come under the influence of Arthur W. Dow, whose radical theories of teaching art gave every encouragement to, and opportunity for, creative work. I then studied illustration for a year at the Pennsylvania Academy of Fine Arts under Henry McCarter and, for a short time, painted at the Art Students League under F. Luis Mora. I am a member of the National Association of Women Painters and Sculptors.

I began to illustrate in 1918 while I was teaching and have been illustrating pretty steadily from that time on. For years I did little writing except occasional articles and lectures on illustration, and a few book reviews. It was in 1931 that, encouraged by Louise Seaman of the Macmillan Company, I wrote and illustrated my first book, *The Fairy Circus*.

How I came to write and draw for children I do not know. Perhaps it is simply that I am interested most of all in the

DOROTHY P. LATHROP

things many of them like best—creatures of all kinds, whether they run, fly, hop, or crawl, and in fairies and all their kin, and in all the adventures that might happily befall one in a world which is so constantly surprising and wonderful.

I still live in Albany and share with my sister a two-roomed studio building back of the house. This we built when we began to work seriously, since it was increasingly evident that my mother's studio could hardly hold comfortably three working artists at once. Our studio is set back among the apple trees, and there we can have all the animal models, permanent or transient, that we need. It is far enough from the heart of the city to be noisier with birds than with traffic, and many wild animal, bird, and flower models walk conveniently up to our windows.

* * *

In addition to the drawings for her own many books, Dorothy Lathrop has illustrated about thirty books by other authors, including those of such well-known writers as Walter De La Mare, W. H. Hudson, Sara Teasdale, and Rachel Field. In 1938 she won the first Caldecott medal ever awarded. It went to her *Animals of the Bible.*

Bertha Mahony describes an exhibition of work by Mrs. Lathrop and her two daugh-

ters at which she was "impressed not only by the rare and distinguished talent displayed by the three, but also by its strong positive quality, a quality inherent in the Lathrop character."

Eleanor Frances Lattimore

June 30, 1904-

AUTHOR OF
*Little Pear, Little Pear and His Friends,
Peachblossom, Etc.*

Autobiographical sketch of Eleanor Frances Lattimore:

I WAS born in Shanghai, China, the fourth in a family of five children. My father and mother came from Washington, D.C. For a number of years Father taught in a college at Paotingfu, North China. I was about a year old when we went to Paotingfu, so that is the first place I remember.

We lived in a house that had once been a temple. If any of you have read *Jerry and the Pusa,* you will know something about what Paotingfu was like. Many of the happenings in that story were true. I described the temple and the college and the city as well as I could remember them, and made Jerry's family a little like ours.

When I was eight Mother took all five of us children to Switzerland to put the older ones in school there. We lived in Lausanne for a year, and then in the summer Mother took three of us to Germany. That was the summer the First World War broke out. We were quite scattered. Father was in China, one of my sisters was in school in Switzerland, one brother in England, and Mother with the rest of us in Germany!

As soon as we could we left Germany for Switzerland, where we stopped for my sister. Then we went on to England to join my brother. After a few months at Oxford we all went back to China, with the exception of my older brother, who was left in school in England.

The last years we were in China we lived at Peiyang University, near Tientsin. When I decided to write a book about China I thought first of the country around Peiyang and of the villages near by and the Chinese children we used to see. So I wrote *Little*

Moffett Studio

ELEANOR FRANCES LATTIMORE

Agnes C. Laut

February 11, 1871-November 15, 1936

AUTHOR OF

*Pathfinders of the West, The Overland Trail,
Lords of the North, Etc.*

Autobiographical sketch of Agnes C. Laut, written for THE JUNIOR BOOK OF AUTHORS a short time before her death:

I WAS born on the Ontario side of Lake Huron, and soon our family moved to Winnipeg. Little old Fort Gary Gate still stood. The Hudson's Bay Store was still really a fur store and to it came in winter the long dog sleighs of Indians with furs. The jingle of the bells, the Indians and traders in either red, white, or green blankets with fur caps and gauntlets and beaded moccasins were all very wonderful to me against the dazzling white snow.

Later when I was about fourteen, crossing these same flats between Assiniboine and Red River, I began peeping into the half-breed shanties. In them I would pick up for one or two dollars books on the old Western life. Was I surprised to find such books in the shanties? No, for I knew many of the half-breeds traced their white blood back to great fur traders, who in the early days had married chief's daughters to keep their houses clean and to get the protection of great Indian tribes. Such marriages were legalized in Canada—the Indian wife was heir to the husband's property and could not be cut off. The white trader in such a marriage was never known as a "squaw man."

And so began my great interest in Western life, and naturally when I reached my twenties my first novel, *Lords of the North*, took its title from the great fur traders.

Later, when I came East, I visited Quebec and Montreal, whence the Scotch traders came as contrasted with the Hudson's Bay Company men, who came by sea to the shores of that vast inland ocean. All this history was so much more romantic than any romance that could be fancied that I began writing the history of the trails from East to West—from Lewis and Clark in the northern states to Coronado in the south.

I am single, but have always kept my family about me. I came to live in the Berkshire Hills, on the New York State

Pear, and it was the easiest book I've written, even though it was the first one.

We came to America in 1920 and lived in Berkeley, California, for two years. While we were there one of my sisters and I went to the California School of Arts and Crafts. We had both always loved to draw and planned to be artists when we grew up.

All the time we lived in China we children were taught at home by our father. I've never been to any school except art schools. I lived in New York off and on for a number of years. I studied for a year at the Art Students League and at the Grand Central School of Art.

It was after visiting a friend in Denmark that I had the idea for the story *The Seven Crowns*.

It was rather by accident I became a writer. Drawing is what I've always liked to do best. But it is hard for a beginner to get stories to illustrate, so I started writing in order to have something to illustrate. Most of the members of my family either write or draw. I have drawn children all my life, and writing about them seems natural too. I've never forgotten what it felt like to be a child.

In 1934 I married Robert Armstrong Andrews, free-lance writer and designer. We have two children of our own now, Peter and Michael. We live on Edisto Island, South Carolina, about forty miles below Charleston.

Laut: *rhymes with "shout"*

side [at Wassaic, New York] about twenty-five years ago. These lovely hills and valleys are not so majestic as the Rockies, where I have a camp at Jasper Pass, Canada, but one grows very fond of them, with their flowing springs, never hot summers, and golden autumn frosts.

I have had a very happy life and rejoice in friends from New York City to San Francisco and from Athabasca to New Orleans.

* * *

Author, journalist, and social worker, Agnes Christina Laut died at her home in Wassaic at the age of sixty-five after an illness of several weeks. Of her work the *American Historical Review* said, "Miss Laut's historical writing was in somewhat popular vein, but much of it has substantial merit."

Marie Abrams Lawson

See *Lawson, Robert*

Robert Lawson

October 4, 1892-
AUTHOR AND ILLUSTRATOR OF
Rabbit Hill, They Were Strong and Good,
Ben and Me, Etc.

Autobiographical sketch of Robert Lawson:

I WAS born in New York City. Shortly thereafter my family moved to Montclair, New Jersey, where I was brought up. Finishing high school there in 1911, I entered the New York School of Fine and Applied Art, studying illustration under Howard Giles.

In the fall of 1914 my first published drawing, a full page decoration for a poem on the invasion of Belgium, appeared in *Harper's Weekly*. For the next three years I did illustrations for various magazines and designed scenery for the Washington Square Players, the then new and struggling organization which later was to develop into the Theatre Guild.

In 1917 I enlisted in the Fortieth Engineers, Camouflage Section, and spent a year in France doing camouflage work at the front and teaching it in the artillery schools.

After the war I received my first commission from W. Martin Johnson, then art editor of *Delineator* and *Designer*. For

three or four years I worked almost entirely for those two magazines. Those few years of association with this often harsh but always understanding taskmaster did a great deal to form and develop my work. At that time I illustrated for him a long fairy story by George Randolph Chester and Carl Sandburg's *Rootabaga Stories*, as well as doing several covers and many full page color drawings illustrating ideas of my own.

In 1922 I married Marie Abrams, also an illustrator and author, and for several years we both did magazine and commercial illustration as well as huge numbers of greeting cards. In 1930 the depression put a stop to most of this work and I took up etching, completing in the next two or three years twenty-odd plates. One of these was awarded the John Taylor Arms Prize by the Society of American Etchers.

In 1930 also I was given my first book to illustrate—*The Wee Men of Ballywooden* by Arthur Mason, followed the next year by his *From the Horn of the Moon*. From that time on the number of book commissions gradually increased until by 1936 my time was about evenly divided between books and other illustration.

In that year I illustrated Munro Leaf's *Ferdinand*. After that the demand for book illustrations left little opportunity for other work and I devoted most of my time to them, in 1937 illustrating ten books. The following year, 1938, I wrote my first book,

ROBERT LAWSON

Ben and Me. It went well enough to encourage more writing and at present I am writing most of the books I illustrate.

To date I have illustrated fifty-odd books, twelve of which are my own. In 1940 *They Were Strong and Good* was awarded the Caldecott Medal and in 1944 *Rabbit Hill* was given the Newbery Medal, by the American Library Association.

Shortly after our marriage we settled in Westport, Connecticut, where, in 1936, we built our present home "Rabbit Hill." We are still married, have no children and few hobbies except reading, writing, illustrating, and gardening.

Munro Leaf

December 4, 1905-

AUTHOR OF

The Story of Ferdinand, Wee Gillis, The Watchbirds, Manners Can Be Fun, Etc.

Autobiographical sketch of Munro Leaf:

MUNRO LEAF

PROBABLY my chief qualification for writing books for American children is that I have led such an average typical American child's life. Ever since I can remember I have been interested in people, what they do and why they do it. Put that together with something I decided at about the age of six, that is that children are people, and sooner or later I was bound to write about and for them.

I was born in a little place called Hamilton that is now part of the city of Baltimore. Early in my life my family moved to Washington, and there I went to public school until I entered the University of Maryland.

As a boy I led a life that was half city and half country, thanks to the lucky fact that my home was near the wonderful woods, fields, brooks, and ponds of the National Soldiers' Home. I played games, studied some, got into trouble and out again in the normal ways. I was a boy scout and had the good fortune to have a scoutmaster who was everything a boy could hope for.

When I went to Maryland, I studied some more, played all the games I could, joined a fraternity, made a lot of friends, and had a wonderful time for four years, graduating in 1927 with a bachelor of arts degree.

During my summer vacations from Maryland I tried a little of everything: worked in a lawyer's office, pick-and-shoveled on a Virginia road building gang, ranch-handed in Montana, went to Army Reserve Officers camp, and shipped out on a British tramp steamer carrying coal from Baltimore to Dublin, Ireland.

After Maryland I went up to Harvard and took a master of arts degree in English literature and then taught and coached in preparatory schools in Massachusetts and Pennsylvania for three years.

Then I went to New York and sneaked into the book publishing business, first as a manuscript reader and later as a director in a publishing company.

In 1934 I wrote my first children's book, *Grammar Can Be Fun.* When I made scratchy little drawings to show what I thought an artist should do, people laughed at them and it was decided I might as well go ahead and illustrate the book. I've been doing the same kind of scratches ever since and they don't seem to get any better or worse.

The year 1936 was a pleasant one for me and my wife Margaret. That fall both *Ferdinand* and *Manners Can Be Fun* came out and today, many years later, she and I and our two sons, Andy and Gil, eat some of our meals with thanks to those two books.

The better part of the four war years were spent in the army, but even there I could squeeze in time to keep writing for children.

It's a pleasant way to spend your time and if you believe as I do that the children of today will shape the world of tomorrow, it's one way to try to help us all get along together better than we ever have before. I can honestly testify that "Writing Can Be Fun."

* * *

The Story of Ferdinand, Munro Leaf's best known book, has been called one of the few juvenile classics of recent years. In its original form, with Robert Lawson's delightful illustrations, and in moving pictures and on the radio it has pleased adults almost as much as the younger readers for whom it was written "in forty minutes one rainy Sunday afternoon."

Joseph Leeming

1897-

AUTHOR OF

Fun With Magic, The Costume Book, Fun With Puzzles, Etc.

Autobiographical sketch of Joseph Leeming:

MOST of my books are about how to make things, though every now and then there is time to write one about ships and the sea. I mention this because it was through my love of the sea that my first book came to be written.

One day, a good long time ago, I met the children's editor of one of the big publishing companies. When she heard I had written some articles for children's magazines, she said, "Now you must write me a book." Nothing was farther from my mind. But she insisted, saying, "Everyone without exception has at least one book he or she can write." "All right," I said, "I'll write you a book about ocean shipping."

The upshot was that after a good many months of horrible toil I sent her the manuscript of my first book, called *Ships and Cargoes*. It practically wrote itself, for I had been at sea in merchant steamers and in the navy, and simply wrote about all the things that had interested me most. The rewriting, however, took months. That is how I started to write books, and I found I liked it. For me it became the one hobby I liked most.

JOSEPH LEEMING

A short while after *Ships and Cargoes* was published, my sister came for a visit from California. "You've written a book," she said. "Now write another one to keep my two small boys, who incidentally are your nephews, happily occupied when we have a rainy day.

"But you don't have rainy days in California," I protested.

"Don't try to be funny," said my sister. "And don't try to get out of it. There's your desk. So just sit down and get going."

That was how the long series of *Things Any Boy Can Do* and *Fun With Paper* and other things had its start. Sometimes it took more time to make the things I was describing than it took to write the book about them. But I can honestly say it has all been fun.

All the time I have been writing I have worked at a job. Writing has really been a hobby, even during the last fifteen years when I have been in editorial and publicity work, frequently writing almost all day long. To change to another subject in the evening is a mental refresher—except every now and then when publishers are in a terrible hurry.

The geographics of my life and times, in more or less chronological order, have been Brooklyn, Colorado Springs, Buffalo, Pawling School, Williams College, the ocean, Montreal, Washington, New York. But the mental voyaging through books, like that

Leeming: *rhymes with "seeming"*

of many other people, has been the source of happiness far more than the places. I imagine I have talked with more authors, through their books, than I have with people in the flesh.

Since I seem to be known chiefly because of my "Fun" books, I am going to close by stating that it was fun writing them. Yes, even work is fun if it is the kind you like. What I always hope is that other people will like reading my books as much as I have liked writing them.

Adèle De Leeuw

See *De Leeuw, Adèle*

"Le Grand"

1901-

AUTHOR AND ILLUSTRATOR OF
*Augustus and the River, Augustus
and the Mountains, Etc.*

Autobiographical sketch of Le Grand Henderson, who signs his books with the pen-name "Le Grand":

BEFORE I started to write, I was born, in Connecticut.

Sometime after that I studied painting at Yale.

Once, for no special reason, I went to St. Paul, Minnesota, built a small houseboat, and started down the Mississippi River in it. It took me nearly a year to drift down the two thousand miles of winding river to the Gulf of Mexico. On the way my boat was frozen in, stuck on mud banks and sand-bars, lost in the woods during a flood, and shot at by some persons who thought I was someone else. So many things happened on this trip that I decided to write a book about them. And that was how the first Augustus book came to be.

It was so much fun getting the material for that book that I decided to get some more. This time I went to the Louisiana bayous and hunted ghosts and the treasure the pirate La Fitte is supposed to have buried somewhere in the swamps. I didn't find the treasure but so many other things happened that I wrote the second Augustus book.

By this time it was a habit. I went on a trip, things happened, and I wrote another book. Sometimes so many things happened

that it was necessary to write two books. This was the case when I went to Maine. There I learned about the Maine sea captain who invented the hole in the doughnut. I felt that surely such an invention needed to be written about and so I wrote *Cap'n Dow and the Hole in the Doughnut.*

Also, while we were cruising off the Maine coast in a schooner, the ship's cook decided to leave, and as I had once been known to boil an egg I found myself established as seacook for a crew of fourteen persons. This was hard on me but probably harder on the others. However, we all lived through it—and I found I had another Augustus book to write.

After the ocean, I decided the Arizona desert would be a nice place and went there. Naturally *Augustus Rides the Border* and *Augustus Tackles the Desert* needed to be written after I had camped beside the Rio Grande and stayed for a time with some Papago Indians beside the only water hole in a big expanse of desert.

Oh yes, I mustn't forget how I came to write my first book. I was sitting on a bench one night near the Central Park Zoo, in New York City. It was snowing and it was late so there were no other people.

A policeman came by and decided that anyone who would sit on a park bench in a snowstorm must be a suspicious character. He asked me what I was doing.

I wasn't doing anything. I was just sitting watching the snow. That didn't seem like

"LE GRAND"

a very good answer to give a policeman and as I had to tell him something, I said I was writing a book.

He didn't seem to believe me. He asked me what kind of book. I happened to be sitting near the yak's cage. I had often wondered about a yak so I said I was writing a book called, "Why Is a Yak?"

That puzzled the policeman so much he went away. After he went I began to think about what I had told him. I decided maybe I *should* write a book called "Why Is a Yak?"

So I did. And that is why I wrote my first book.

* * *

When he is not traveling around collecting experiences for Augustus, Le Grand Henderson lives in Thomaston, Georgia. He has written and illustrated six other books, in addition to his dozen about Augustus.

LOIS LENSKI

Lois Lenski

October 14, 1893-

ILLUSTRATOR AND AUTHOR

Judy's Journey, Little Fire Engine, Indian Captive, Strawberry Girl, The Little Train, The Little Airplane, Etc.

Autobiographical sketch of Lois Lenski:

I WAS born in Springfield, Ohio, the daughter of a Lutheran minister. When I was six my parents moved with their five children to a small village called Anna, where I spent my childhood. One of our family jokes was that we had increased the population of the town from 200 to 207!

I am sure our arrival caused a great sensation; one of the wagon loads which was hauled down the main street was topped by a large wire bird cage, with a tin toy dog, belonging to my small sister, standing upright inside! Here we lived until I finished high school at Sidney, eight miles away, and here it was I learned to know and love small town and country life.

In 1911 we moved to Columbus, where my father became professor at Capital University, and later dean of the Theological Seminary. I graduated from Ohio State University College of Education, in 1915, expecting to teach. But one of my teachers in the art department suggested my going to New York to study art for a year; and after the first year I felt I must have more.

For four years I worked at the Art Students League for half the day and did all sorts of odd jobs in the other half to pay my expenses. I went to London for a year, where I studied with Walter Bayes at the Westminster School. There I did my first illustrating—three books. With this experience behind me, on my return, and with the improvement of publishing conditions after the war, I soon found openings with American publishers. In 1927 I had my first one-man exhibition of oils and water colors in New York. My second, an exhibition of water colors, was held in 1932.

In 1921 I married Arthur Covey, the well-known mural painter. We are now living in an old colonial farmhouse in Harwinton, Connecticut, near Torrington, where we have separate studies.

For a number of years I illustrated books by other authors, trying always to adhere strictly to the period, mood, and atmosphere of each book and to give it an original character of its own.

The writing of my own books has been a gradual development. It began with two stories of my Ohio childhood, *Skipping Village* and *A Little Girl of 1900*, and developed through a group of simple nonsense books. My picture books were inspired by the interests and needs of our son, Stephen, when he was at the picture-book age. They were the beginning of the ever-increasingly popular "Mr. Small" series. All my picture

Lenski: *LEN skee*

books are tried out on various groups of children before publication, to get their reactions, both critical and appreciative.

My books for older boys and girls may be classified as various interpretations of the American scene, which is the focus of my fundamental interest. The two Ohio books were later followed by seven historical books based on careful research and an attempt to interpret American child life of the past, and bring to life for modern child readers various early periods in our country's history.

More recently I have embarked on a series of regional American books for "middle-aged" children. *Bayou Suzette,* a story of the French-speaking bayou people of Louisiana, was the first, and won the Ohioana Medal in 1944. The second, *Strawberry Girl,* story of a Florida Cracker family, won the Newbery Medal in 1946. The third, *Blue Ridge Billy,* is a story of the mountain people of North Carolina. The fourth, *Judy's Journey,* about sharecroppers, won the 1947 award of the Children's Book Committee of the Child Study Association, as a book for young people "which faces with honesty and courage real problems in today's world."

Material for these regional books was gathered first hand in the localities described. I went to stay in the region, listened to stories of their experiences told by people living there, and made numerous sketches of them, their houses, and details of their surroundings, which I later incorporated in my illustrations. It is my hope to introduce in this series other fascinating and little-known regions of our country to American child readers.

Henry B. Lent

November 1, 1901-

AUTHOR OF

Clear Track Ahead, Aviation Cadet, Air Patrol, Etc.

Autobiographical sketch of Henry B. Lent:

I HAVE two boys. As soon as they were old enough to talk, they started to ask questions, and they have never stopped! I soon discovered that an average father, in order to answer his sons' questions, should be a combined locomotive engineer, fireman, policeman, captain of an ocean liner, avia-

tor, steam shovel operator, brakeman, riveter, broadcaster, movie director, and even "the man on the flying trapeze"!

I could not be all these things, but as a boy, I too was a question-asking urchin. More than that, I always wanted to "try" things to see what made them go. Sometimes my curiosity got me into trouble. There was the steam roller, for example, that workmen had left near our home with the fire banked for the night. By pushing and pulling all the levers I suddenly discovered there was still enough steam in the boiler to move the contraption. The only way to stop it seemed to be to run it into a convenient tree—which I did.

As I grew older I tried my hand at various jobs. One summer, home from college, I spent on a fishing schooner in the Bay of Fundy and driving a team of oxen on a Nova Scotian construction job. Several summers I worked with construction crews in New York State, driving a truck, running a cement mixer, pushing a wheelbarrow, and with a gang of building wreckers.

All this work was very helpful when I started to write *Diggers and Builders.* The real reason for this book, as well as those that have followed—was to answer the questions Henry and David asked me. Although we live on a farm fifty miles from New York, I work in a skyscraper office building off Fifth Avenue. Sometimes the boys went to the city with me. They saw rivet gangs at work and derricks lifting steel beams and girders. They wanted to know more about how skyscrapers are built. The facts I did not already know I found out by talking to riveters, derrick foremen, steel workers, and contractors.

The next year an electric train was left under our Christmas tree. I learned then that it is one thing to ride a hundred miles a day on a train, as I did, and quite another to answer a hundred questions about the jobs of the engineer, brakeman, conductor, signal tower man, train dispatcher, wrecking-train crew, and the other men who run a railroad. I found the answers and put them into *Clear Track Ahead.*

Soon after that book was published, the boys went with me to New York to meet their grandfather, who was returning from Europe. The excitement of seeing a great ocean liner come up the channel started a long train of questions that finally resulted in *Full Steam Ahead.* In order to write this

HENRY B. LENT

book I went to Europe and back on one of the largest liners afloat. For most people an ocean voyage is a time for rest. For me it meant dodging down companionways, exploring kitchens and engine rooms, peeping into boilers, and standing in the wheelhouse on the bridge.

My boys are grown up now, but I find the world is still full of youngsters who want to know what makes engines run and airplanes fly. In fact, my books have been slanted more and more toward the Air Age, starting with those I wrote during the Second World War.

One year I spent some time at the factory where a famous airplane was designed and built. The high point of my visit was a flight in a new plane with the chief test pilot. My experiences are recorded in *Fly It Away!* Since then, I have learned to fly myself and have written a book in which I describe what happens when a sixteen-year-old boy signs up for flight instruction in a Piper Cub. The book is called *Eight Hours to Solo.* My younger son, David, learned to fly at the same time. I found it very helpful to check my experiences against his as I wrote the book. Learning to fly was fun. I hope to keep at it and log up enough hours to get my private license.

* * *

Henry B. Lent was born in New Bedford, Massachusetts, and as a boy lived in New Haven, Connecticut. He went to Yale and to Hamilton College. He is associated with a New York advertising agency and makes his home in Redding, Connecticut.

Elizabeth Foreman Lewis

1892-

AUTHOR OF

Ho-ming, Girl of New China, Young Fu of the Upper Yangtze, Etc.

Autobiographical sketch of Elizabeth Foreman Lewis:

YOU who are studying the history of England may recall that an English queen once said, "After I am dead you will find 'Calais' written on my heart."

Sometimes, I think that the word "China" may be as deeply engraved on mine, for that country and her people have for years claimed the most of my thought, time, and energy.

The Chinese, through forty or fifty centuries of national existence, were noted for absorbing their enemies. This was accomplished not by great effort apparently, but by the quiet influence of China's civilization on the minds of all who came to know her. Since this has been the case with enemies, you can see for yourselves how easy it is for that nation to make friends ever more friendly. Ask anyone who has lived among the Chinese, "Do you like them?" You will very likely receive an enthusiastic answer six or seven paragraphs long.

Indeed, when China's admirers cannot find a sufficient number of people to listen to them, they write books on the subject, just as I have. Nothing could have persuaded me to write a book, until someone suggested, "Do one on China!"

And when that happened, what did I do? I sat right down and wrote a short story about a Chinese girl in a typhoon, and a kindhearted editor recklessly accepted it for publication. That was the beginning of the end, for I kept on doing short stories for six years. To my own great surprise, I then found myself the author of a whole book, *Young Fu.* Following that came *Ho-ming, China Quest, When the Typhoon Blows,* two books for adults, and more short stories. Now I am working on two other books. You see how it is?

Certainly, except for having done an enormous amount of reading in my time, I

ELIZABETH FOREMAN LEWIS

had no slightest preparation for a life spent with pencils and typewriters. As a girl I wanted to study medicine; instead I went to art school. I did architectural plans for doll houses, statistics for a railroad, institutional church work—these in America. In China I taught English literature, physical education, commercial law—on the mission field you learn to do whatever is needed most. After a number of years illness forced me to come home. Since then every minute I have been able to spare from family and household duties, I have either talked or written about China.

Seriously, there is good reason for all this. The Chinese are the oldest of living nations, and within their boundaries lives one fifth of the world's total population. They have, accordingly, had more time than most countries in which to shape a wise way of life and more people to try it out.

These opportunities have taught them that it pays to do the best possible under all circumstances and to expect some bitter to be mixed with the sweet in life. Through many centuries their sages have told them that five qualities — benevolence, self-respect, courtesy, knowledge, and integrity—make a man valuable to his family, his community, and his nation. If he can cultivate, also, a respect for learning, an appreciation of beauty, and a sense of humor, these will help him face trouble more calmly when it appears.

China's leaders were too wise to expect many men to have all these good traits, but they realized that when people are challenged by high standards, they usually try to reach them. A surprising number of Chinese have succeeded in doing this; even those who fail seem to possess a real appreciation of beauty, learning, and humor. These attractive characteristics make this great and ancient people generally well liked.

* * *

Elizabeth Foreman Lewis was born in Baltimore, Maryland, and was educated there and in New York. In 1917 she went to China under the auspices of the Methodist Church and worked in Shanghai, Nanking, and Chungking. She was married in 1921 to John Abraham Lewis, son of the late Bishop Wilson Seeley Lewis, of Iowa and China. Her only son, John Fulton Lewis, is a newspaper editor. Their home is at Briar Cliff on Severn, Arnold, Maryland.

Her first book, *Young Fu of the Upper Yangtse*, was awarded the Newbery Medal for 1932. This and her other books have been published also in England, translated into many languages, and transcribed into Braille. Most of her short stories are to be found in various anthologies, prize collections, and school readers.

Frank B. Linderman

September 25, 1869-May 12, 1938

AUTHOR OF
*Indian Why Stories, American, Indian
Old-Man Stories, Etc.*

Autobiographical sketch of Frank Bird Linderman, written for THE JUNIOR BOOK OF AUTHORS a few years before his death:

I WAS born in Ohio. Perhaps the blood of earlier Lindermans who pioneered in New York, Pennsylvania, and Ohio, was somewhat responsible for by boyhood desire to go West. Anyhow it came to me early, and never left me. And how I feared the West of my dreams would fade, and become a settled country before I could reach it! But at last, and perhaps just in time to save me from having to run away, I won my parents' reluctant consent to leave home.

I had long ago decided where I wished to go; but tonight, because my dream was coming true, I spread a large map of the great Northwest upon the floor of my own room to study it for the hundredth time. Maps of the new Northwest were not very accurate then; and yet I must make no mistake tonight. I had to have unspoiled wilderness wherever I went, because I secretly intended to become a trapper there. I shall never forget the deep satisfaction I felt when I again, and for the last time, decided that of all the sections of the Northwest shown upon my map the country around Flathead Lake in northwestern Montana Territory was farthest from railroads or other civilization. I could scarcely wait for morning.

This was fifty years ago, and it was March, early springtime. I was a little more than sixteen years old. However, another boy of my own age, accompanied by his father's Negro coachman, came with me to the Flathead country; but he did not stay. This was then Indian country, and heavily timbered. It was wild, a hunter's paradise with great rivers and lakes, and thousands of game trails through the dark forests. Timber wolves howled about our campfire every night, so neither my white boy companion nor the Negro slept a wink during their four or five nights in Montana. The wilderness was too much for them. They left me here, and went back to "the States."

Alone, I became a trapper. During roundups I rode the range for small cow outfits on the Indian reservation, and spent the winters trapping in the mountains, so I nearly always had plenty to do. Sometimes I was alone for months; but nearly always I had a partner, sometimes an Indian. However most of my partners were white men, old plainsmen, and mountaineers who taught me the ways of the wilderness; and they were strange ways, now all but forgotten.

The Indians were my friends from the beginning. I hunted with them, trapped with them, and lived with them when they were real, and unspoiled by civilization.

Perhaps the oldtime Indian was right in his belief that the white man is the natural enemy of all natural things. Anyhow the wilderness, my wilderness, did not last long. The railroad came to it; and then the country began to settle rapidly. The old days were forever ended for both the Indian

and me, so I turned to mining, becoming an assayer and chemist. I followed this business for many years after I married.

* * *

Mr. Linderman died after a heart attack, in Santa Barbara, California. He had been secretary of the Montana State Mining Association, and a member of the Legislature. A newspaper man, he was an honorary member of the Montana State Press Association and also of the American Indian Defense Association.

Maj Lindman

AUTHOR OF
Snipp, Snapp, Snurr; Flicka, Ricka, Dicka; Etc.

Autobiographical sketch of Maj Jan Lindman:

IT is a long time since I was a child. I suppose you understand that when you think of all the books I have had published. And the very first thing I must tell you is that my real Christian name is Mary, not Maj, which name I was called for the sake of brevity.

My father was a college teacher and civil engineer, and we lived in a town in Sweden called Örebro. My mother was a very clever and charming lady, and I loved my parents dearly. I also had a little sister. She was six years my junior and died when she was twelve. That was my first great grief.

I had a very happy childhood but not so many amusements as young people have nowadays. On sunny winter days, when not in school, we were skiing or skating. Sometimes we were joining a dancing party or going to the theatre. In the summer holidays we traveled with our parents to the seaside, and Christmas we always spent with our grandfather on Mother's side. He was chief secretary to the provincial government in Upsala, and lived at the Castle. I can tell you that Upsala Castle is very old— from the sixteenth century—and we girls were fascinated by its thick walls and dark corners; and we earnestly believed that old kings' ghosts were about.

When I was fifteen I completed my nine-year course, and at nineteen I began painting in earnest. I entered the Royal Academy of Arts as a pupil. I had a good time and my teachers thought a good deal of my gifts. But soon I left off my work to be

Maj: *MY*

married. In a few years I had three children, one boy and two girls.

There was not much time left for painting after the children's arrival. Later on, though, it became necessary to earn money, so I set off to work again. Now I made book covers, illustrations, Christmas cards. I also painted some portraits in oil.

One day I got the idea for a picture book which was to deal with three little boys who wanted to buy a pair of red slippers as a birthday present for their mother. And so the three little brothers—Snipp, Snapp, and Snurr — were born. It was in 1922. Many years later came the Flicka, Ricka, and Dicka books. I have also made several books that are not published in America, and I have written a couple for girls in the twelve-year age.

Now my children are grown up and have children of their own. Naturally I am more free, and just before the war I went twice to Paris for studies. You always have more left to learn, you know. In these days we have moved into a nice villa with a garden in a place quite near Stockholm, by name Djursholm. In the house are only my husband and I and our little dog, a long-haired, black-and-tan dachshund whose name is Black Baron.

Sometimes our children are visiting us; sometimes we take the car and make a trip to our farm; and—mostly—I am writing or painting. I have had many kind letters

MAJ LINDMAN

which tell me that American children like my books, and I hope you understand that it makes me very, very happy!

Hugh Lofting

January 14, 1886-September 26, 1947

AUTHOR OF
The Story of Dr. Dolittle, Etc.

Autobiographical sketch of Hugh Lofting, written for THE JUNIOR BOOK OF AUTHORS several years before his death:

IT was during the First World War, and my children at home wanted letters from me—and they wanted them with illustrations rather than without. There seemed very little to write to youngsters from the front; the news was either too horrible or too dull. And it was all censored. One thing, however, that kept forcing itself more and more on my attention was the very considerable part the animals were playing in the war and that as time went on they, too, seemed to become Fatalists.

Oftentimes you would see a cat stalking along the ruins throughout a heavy bombardment, in a town that had been shelled more than once before in that same cat's recollection. She was taking her chances with the rest of us. And the horses, too, learned to accept resignedly and unperturbed the falling of high explosives in their immediate neighborhood. But their fate was different from the men's. However seriously a soldier was wounded, his life was not despaired of; all the resources of a surgery highly developed by the war were brought to his aid. A seriously wounded horse was put out by a timely bullet.

This did not seem quite fair. If we made the animals take the same chances we did why could we not give them similar attention when they were wounded? But obviously to develop a horse-surgery as good as that of our Casualty Clearing Stations would necessitate a knowledge of horse language.

That was the beginning of an idea: an eccentric country physician with a bent for natural history and a great love of pets, who finally decides to give up his human practice for the more difficult, more sincere and, for him, more attractive therapy of the

HUGH LOFTING

animal kingdom. He is challenged by the difficulty of the work—for obviously it requires a much cleverer brain to become a good animal doctor (who must first acquire all animal languages and physiologies) than it does to take care of the mere human hypochondriac.

This was a new plot for my narrative letter for the children. It delighted them and at my wife's suggestion, I put the letters into book form for other boys and girls.

There are points of primary importance in writing for children.

First, the writing must be entertaining and nothing may interfere with that entertainment. There is never any excuse for putting over a preachment under the guise of entertainment. The main trouble with children's books is that many writers and publishers feel that because they are catering to young minds pretty much anything will do.

Another trouble with the average writing for children is that authors always seem to think they must "write down" to them. I have found that the intelligent children (and I'm afraid the intelligent children are the only kind I am interested in) resent nothing so much as being written down to or talked down to. Which, of course, is very natural. We adults resent it also, if we think a superior intellect is patronizing us. What the intelligent child likes is being "written up" to. He wants promotion; he wants to

get into the adult world; he wants progress; and I have always maintained that no idea is too subtle, no picture too difficult to be conveyed to a child's mind, if the author will but find the proper language to put it in.

Another thing: there should be just as many kinds of stories and books for children as there are kinds of stories and books for grown-ups. I have often quoted my daughter's interest when at the age of five, she learned her mother had just returned from an employment bureau, where she had gone to hire a cook. Elizabeth wanted to know all about it. She was looking forward, no doubt, to the time when she would hire a cook. The poor child did not realize, of course, that by the time she would be grown up, there would not be any more cooks. Well, I have never seen a story for children about an employment agency, but after all, why not? It is really pathetic that the majority of writers for children feel that the only material children are interested in is pussy-cats and puppy-dogs, when really there is nothing in the whole wide world that they are not interested in.

This is proved by the fact that, whenever a book is a real success for children, it is also a success and an enjoyment for grown-ups.

There has always been a tendency to classify children almost as a distinct species. For many years it was a constant source of shock for me to find my writings amongst "Latest Juveniles" or "Leading Juveniles." It does not bother me any more, but I still do feel there should be a category of "Seniles" to offset the epithet. If writers would only get away from this classifying of children as a separate species we should get very much better books for the younger generation. For who shall say where the dividing line lies, that separates the child from the adult? Practically all children want to be grown up and practically all grown-ups want to be children, and God help us, the adults, when we have no vestige of childhood in our hearts.

* * *

Hugh Lofting, born in Maidenhead, England, was as much Irish as he was English. His early childhood was spent at home with his parents and brothers and sister. To the latter he liked to tell stories, but they were not always appreciated, he said. Of these days he also recalled a combination zoo and museum of natural history kept, until discovery, in his mother's linen closet. He went away to school when he was eight and from that time spent only short periods at home.

If, as a boy, he determined on any career for his future, it was not that of author-artist. Journeys to unexplored lands, and adventurous travels held out the greatest lure for him. He came to America and attended the Massachusetts Institute of Technology in 1904-05 and returned to England to complete his technical training at the London Polytechnic in 1906-07.

In 1912 Mr. Lofting married and settled in the United States. Then came the war and in 1916 he enlisted in the British Army. When he was separated from his children, he began sending illustrated letters and little stories to them from the trenches in France, as he has related above. Hugh Lofting wrote nine books about his famous character, Dr. Dolittle, and they have been translated into twelve languages. He was working on another Dr. Dolittle book when he died at his home in Santa Monica, California, after an illness of two years.

Carlo Lorenzini

See "Collodi, C."

Maud Hart Lovelace

1892-

AUTHOR OF
Betsy-Tacy, Heaven to Betsy, Etc.

Autobiographical sketch of Maud Hart Lovelace:

R EADERS of the Betsy-Tacy books already know quite a bit about me, for Maud Hart Lovelace as a little girl was very much like Betsy. I was born in Mankato, Minnesota, which certainly resembles the Deep Valley of my stories. I lived with my father, mother, and two sisters in a small yellow cottage at the end of a street which, like Betsy's Hill Street, ran straight up into a green hill and stopped. There I had innumerable happy adventures with two friends whom I have named Tacy and Tib.

After grade school and high school in Mankato, I went to the University of Min-

nesota. I traveled in this country and in Europe, and I was in London when World War I broke out. I can still hear the bands playing "Tipperary." In 1917 I married Delos Lovelace, then a lieutenant in a machine gun battalion but later a writer and newspaper man. I began writing historical novels, both alone and in collaboration with my husband.

Merian was born in 1931, and as soon as she had reached an age to listen, I started telling her stories of my childhood. These grew into the Betsy-Tacy books. I thought the series would end when Betsy reached her teens, but about that time I chanced upon my own high school diaries. Merian, a freshman herself, was delighted with them, and I was impressed with how similar high school in 1905 was to high school in 1945—fudge, dates, ouija boards, singing around the piano. So Merian and Betsy have been going through high school with a book for each year.

Children keep asking how much of these stories is true—a question difficult to answer. The background is true, many of the incidents are true—but twisted about, of course, to make the plots. Almost all the characters are true, but sometimes two or three people have been combined to make one.

Tacy and Tib are absolutely true, and on a recent joyous trip to the Middle West I visited both of them—Tacy in Buffalo where I played with her grandchildren,

MAUD HART LOVELACE

Tib in Chicago where she introduced me to a niece as yellow haired and daring as Tib was at her age. A character out of *Heaven to Betsy* drove me from Minneapolis to Mankato where we visited the Big Hill, the Secret Lane, and Little Syria. Another character gave a dinner party which brought together many members of the old high school crowd. (Yes, we stood around the piano and sang!)

My home now is a white blue-shuttered house in Garden City, Long Island, near New York, where my husband is on the staff of one of the big newspapers. As a family we like reading and writing (but not arithmetic), music and plays, traveling anywhere, the beach, ping-pong, meals out-of-doors, company, and—of course—each other.

ELOISE LOWNSBERY

Eloise Lownsbery

1888-

AUTHOR OF
The Boy Knight of Reims, Marta the Doll, Etc.

Autobiographical sketch of Eloise Lownsbery:

AS a child in Cedar Rapids, Iowa, I talked to three oak trees framed in my bedroom window. They grew in the woods opposite our home. At night their great masses were outlined against the starry sky. I told them how I longed to travel, to see mountains and the sea, to visit all the countries on earth. Often after an early supper I went alone to sit on the high bank of a pond and watch the sunset. Where did the sun go? If only he would take me with him to show me all the beauty and wonder he saw!

Like every child I had only to wait and to grow. For with college at Wellesley came the first sight of flaming scarlet and rose and golden maple trees, and during spring vacations at Rockport, the great wide blue pounding sea.

And when, after college, for Father's health we moved to California, what a joy to catch a glimpse of the first high remote white peaks! Friends soon took me up to them. A swift electric car left us at the foot of Mt. Wilson, up which we toiled all night, arriving at the six-thousand-foot

summit at dawn, exultant in the glory, in spite of feet that shrieked at every step. And soon I was camping out in the mountains, leading groups of Camp Fire youngsters up to the top of Old Baldy, ten thousand feet and more.

Then came World War I and the impelling need to go over and help with the Quakers. And now intimately I knew France and loved it with its people. And I knew her cathedrals: Chartres, Notre Dame, and especially Reims.

So that was how I came to visit far lands. And later after I had married Carl Stearns Clancy he promised to show me the beauty of far places. So we motored through Europe and later, because he must film Egypt's new king and queen, we visited Egypt and Palestine.

There remain India and China and South America, Russia, and the rest of the world to see. But reading the autobiography of Selma Lagerlöf taught me that one can live one's whole life in one spot, one village, or even in one house, and still be free to journey in one's mind to Patagonia or to Land's End, to the Isles of Spice or to Lhassa, by the magic of reading other people's books. Or one can imagine stories that never happened on any land or sea, but just in the country of one's mind. Still I would rather go to India than read about it in all the books ever printed.

Until recently, being so concerned with other lands, I had paid scant attention to our own. Only since coming to live in Washington have I begun to delve into the history of our country and to find it fascinating. Our home is ten miles from the Capitol in a corner of the Virginia jungle. A jungle is enchanting in any land, if you can omit the mosquitoes, chiggers, ticks, fleas, and flies. For honeysuckle vines festoon the trees and cover all the earth. Small streams wander in the gulleys, and wild flowers, azaleas, and dogwood make of it a lovely garden.

So we have pushed back the jungle a bit for our home, which looks down on the Potomac River, so that sunrises and moonrises are always ours for the taking. The land once belonged to the Indians, then to the King of England, then to George Washington. Now it is ours, at least it is so written down in the big book at Fairfax County Courthouse. But actually the birds and the gray squirrels own it. Scarlet tanagers and blue jays, bluebirds and woodpeckers, white-throated song sparrows and juncos; and above all, spring and fall the thrushes own us and fill the air with heavenly song.

So now that we are putting down roots, tending a garden here so near to Mount Vernon, I tell our great oak trees I would like to write of Washington, Jefferson, and Franklin, or of the beginnings of our country. Because it is a very great and good country, destined perhaps, to spell freedom, opportunity, happiness to the whole wide world.

Like every other person who has written for children, I imagine, I long to write that little book which will be deathless, so that there will be no more greed or arrogance but such a union of heart with mind as shall make all the world a happy place for children to grow, so wars will be against evil and ignorance, and no more against human beings. But perhaps not I but you will write this mighty book.

As a preparation for it, I suggest you study languages that you may know the best thoughts of the greatest writers, that you may know and love the other peoples of the world as well as your own.

Jannette May Lucas

1885-

AUTHOR OF

The Earth Changes; First the Flower, Then the Fruit; Man's First Million Years; Etc.

Autobiographical sketch of Jannette May Lucas:

I WAS born in Washington, D. C., quite a few years ago, when it was a much less populated city. We might not call on every neighbor in the block but we said "Good Morning" and knew where each lived. I went to public school there. First to a grammar school only a little way from home and later to Western High School, which then seemed at the very edge of the city. That was really in Georgetown and every day I passed the house where Francis Scott Key once lived.

When I was almost through high school my father went to take charge of the Brooklyn Museum and the family went too. None of us liked Brooklyn as well as Washington, though it was cooler. But my sister and I liked the Packer Collegiate Institute where we went to school much better than we had liked our schools in Washington.

Then I went to Teachers College, Columbia University, because I thought I wanted to teach history. But I never did. Instead I was offered a chance to take charge of the Osborn Library of Vertebrate Paleontology

JANNETTE MAY LUCAS

Jannette: *ja NET*

(fossils with backbones) in the American Museum of Natural History. I had never studied science, but my father, before he became a museum director, had been a pretty good vertebrate paleontologist and I found I knew more than I thought. Besides, all the men on the department staff were kind and always answered any questions I needed to ask. I could always manage to find the books they wanted, keep them in order, and file the necessary cards as well as make them. I stayed there for over twenty years.

I met a lot of people there, and Max Reed came to finish his first book, with which I had a chance to help. Then Helene Carter came to make illustrations for a book of Dr. Ditmars. This meant finding out a great deal about the continents of the past, most of which is in foreign languages. I had done a lot with that and she suggested we do one together. That was the way I wrote *The Earth Changes*. Then I began to write about some of the questions I used to ask and to which I had managed to find answers either because people were kind enough to tell me things which were in terribly "stiff" books or because some one had already said it simply enough for me to understand. That is the way I have written my other books.

Now I have moved to Plymouth, Massachusetts, which was my father's old home. I had already spent many summers there and I find winter very pleasant too. Plymouth has interesting Revolutionary history as well as history of the Pilgrims' time. It is fun to find out about it.

Robert McCloskey

September 15, 1914-

ILLUSTRATOR, AND AUTHOR OF
*Make Way for Ducklings, Homer Price,
Blueberries for Sal, Etc.*

Autobiographical sketch of Robert Mc-Closkey:

I WAS born in Hamilton, Ohio. I attended public school, and from the time my fingers were long enough to play the scale I took piano lessons. I started next to play the harmonica, the drums, and then the oboe. The musician's life was the life for me, that is, until I became interested in things electrical and things mechanical. I

ROBERT MCCLOSKEY

collected old electric motors and bits of wire, old clocks and meccano sets. I built trains and cranes with remote control, my family's Christmas trees revolved, lights flashed, and buzzers buzzed, fuses blew, and sparks flew! The inventor's life was the life for me, that is, until I started making drawings for the high school paper and the high school annual. I was presented with a scholarship to an art school in Boston, and from Boston I went to New York to attend the National Academy of Design. I painted during the summers on Cape Cod, and received a scholarship to study in Rome. The artist's life became the life for me.

It is just sort of an accident that I write books. I really think up stories in pictures and just fill in between the pictures with a sentence or a paragraph or a few pages of words.

Besides being an artist, I am the husband of my wife, Margaret, and the father of my daughter, Sarah.

During the war we lived in Alabama. I was a sergeant and drew training pictures for the army. Now at last we have a home on an island off the coast of Maine.

When I was young I surrounded myself with musical instruments and tried the musician's life. Then I worked for hours with motors and wires and tried the inventor's life. With paints and brushes and such I have lived the artist's life. But you know, living on the sea I have been spending a lot of time with sea gulls and fish lately.

Just this morning while I was shaving, I noticed a very slight difference in my whiskers. I examined them carefully but it is too early to tell whether they are changing into scales or feathers.

* * *

Robert McCloskey's *Make Way for Ducklings* was awarded the Caldecott Medal for the year 1941.

Harold McCracken

August 31, 1894-

AUTHOR OF

The Biggest Bear on Earth, The Great White Buffalo, Etc.

Autobiographical sketch of Harold McCracken:

HAROLD McCRACKEN

THAT I was born in Colorado Springs is not particularly important because I left there before I was two. My father had been a pioneer western newspaper publisher, whose personal specialty was collecting and writing the stories of the notorious characters of the Old West. He became interested in a gold mine in the famous Cripple Creek district, in which he invested and lost everything he had except a ranch in Idaho, which he had purchased without ever seeing and had been unable to sell.

It was on that undeveloped ranch I spent my boyhod. My earliest recollections are of seeing my dad chase a black bear on horseback, watching the coyotes which were an almost daily sight from the ranch house, and of wandering off and getting lost in the sagebrush. My earliest ambition was to become a "professional grizzly bear hunter."

The only schooling I had, until I was nine, was what my mother gave me. When we moved to Des Moines I had my first experience in a schoolroom.

My parents had always wanted me to become a minister, and after finishing my high school work in summer school, I entered Drake University. But my interest was considerably stronger in prehistoric Indians and natural history than it was in the ministry. Instead of studying I hunted for arrowheads and collected birds and their nests for the Iowa State Museum. And in the early spring of 1912 I left school and went to live with a relative on a mountain ranch far up in the Canadian Rockies of British Columbia.

The Canadian National Railroad was just being built and during the summer I drove a four-horse stage, transporting construction workers farther up the river toward the pass through the Rockies. In the fall I hunted bear and deer with the Cree Indians; and in the winter I alone ran a little log trading post, buying and bartering for furs from the Indians.

After a year in British Columbia I entered Ohio State University with the intention of becoming an archeologist. But the taste of high adventure in the Canadian Rockies had gotten deep into my blood, and in 1915 I organized my first expedition to Alaska and the Yukon. I left in the early spring of 1916 to spend two years collecting big game specimens for the Ohio State Museum. Although I used all my funds in the first three months, I did stay for two years—having a hundred times as many adventures as I would have had with all the money I needed. In order to get out to the end of the Alaska peninsula, home of the giant Alaska grizzlies, I worked my way as a galley slave on a notorious tramp steamer, the *S.S. Dirty Dora*—but I got five of those big bears, including one of the largest ever shot by any person at any time.

I returned from Alaska to volunteer as a fighting pilot in the aviation section of World War I, but failed to qualify because of "poor eyesight" and wound up in aviation research work in the Department of Physics, Columbia University, where I helped develop one of the forerunners of radar.

After the war I returned to Ohio State University and entered the school of journalism—but was not permitted to continue the course after the first semester. They decided I was too dumb! So I returned to Alaska for a season of gold mining in the Mount McKinley country. After that I organized a photo-scientific expedition to make motion pictures and to study the Alaska brown bear and other big game. On this trip I went in winter by dog team into the bear country along the coast of the Bering Sea and followed the bears until snow came again at the beginning of the next winter.

Then I came to New York City, to try to become a writer, but I found easier success as a lecturer, pioneer radio commentator, and maker of airplane stunt films for the movies. I was probably the first person ever to fly with a movie camera on the end of the wing of an airplane.

In 1928 I made my fourth trip to the Far North, as leader of the Stoll-McCracken Siberian Arctic Expedition of the American Museum of Natural History. Our ship was the schooner *Morrissey* and her skipper the famous Captain Bob Bartlett, who in 1909 had taken Admiral Peary to within walking distance of the North Pole.

Since that expedition I have spent most of my time writing, and have done twelve books.

"Golden MacDonald"

See *Brown, Margaret Wise*

Phyllis McGinley

1905-

AUTHOR OF

The Plain Princess, The Horse Who Lived Upstairs, All Around the Town, Etc.

Autobiographical sketch of Phyllis McGinley:

I WAS born in Ontario, Oregon, but since I left there at the tender age of three months I can scarcely lay claim to being a Native Daughter. I lived on a ranch in eastern Colorado through my childhood, where the vanishing West had not quite vanished. I remember watching bronco-busting instead of baseball games on Sundays, for instance; and riding a buckskin pony three miles to school, where my brother and I were the only pupils. And I remember blizzards and antelopes and coyotes and cattle being branded, although we shortly started raising wheat and sugar beets on our own place.

After my father's death when I was twelve or thirteen we went "back home" to Ogden, Utah, where my mother had been born and brought up and where her family had been pioneers (but never Mormons). Her name was Julia Kiesel, and her father and numerous brothers came from Germany —part of the exodus of Germans who left the country after Prussianism first enveloped it. In fact, I like to boast to my husband, whose Connecticut Yankee ancestors have been hanging around these parts since the 1600's, that I am pure third-generation immigrant—German on one side and Irish on the other.

After being graduated from college at the University of Utah, I taught a year at home and then reversed Horace Greeley by coming to New York. Found I wasn't suited to doing much of anything except teaching school or writing poetry, so I did both, one full time and the latter whenever I could. I'd always written verse, by the way, since at the age of six I went introspective and turned out this little stunner:

Sometimes in the evening
When the sky is red and pink
I love to lie in a hammock
And think and think and think.

Which must be the beginning of my life-long preference for composing my stuff in a horizontal position.

I quit teaching after four or five years of it, to free-lance for a short time and then (in a fit of free-lance jitters) to write copy in an advertising agency for five months and to help edit *Town and Country* for two. I was married then to Charles Hayden (1937) and have been pretty busy ever since with buying and furnishing and remodeling a house here in Larchmont Manor, New York (an elderly house rather than an old one, since it was built around Civil War time); having two babies, Julie and

Lotte Jacoby

PHYLLIS MCGINLEY

Patricia; and writing more verse than I ever had time for before.

My eccentricities are few—putting sugar in my soup is the only one I can think of at the moment—and I'm what is known in the trade as a "good, reliable worker." That is, I always make a deadline. I am not very prolific and labor painstakingly over every piece I do. My burning ambition is to write a musical comedy in the Gilbert and Sullivan tradition, but until some producer gets around to asking me directly to get to work, I'll probably be too busy to start it.

Constance D'Arcy Mackay

AUTHOR OF

Costumes and Scenery for Amateurs, Patriotic Plays and Pageants for Young People, Etc.

Autobiographical sketch of Constance D'Arcy Mackay:

TO begin with, although I was born in St. Paul, Minnesota, daughter of Robert G. and Anne D'Arcy Mackay, I have lived most of my life and done all of my writing in New England and New York City, my permanent home.

I was an only but not a lonely child, for I early had two worlds to roam in—

D'Arcy: *DAR see*
Mackay: *mac KAY*

the world of fact, peopled by grown-ups and playmates; and the world of make-believe filled with characters that sprang from the books my devoted mother read aloud to me until I was old enough to read them myself—fairy tales of Grimm and Andersen; particularly Andersen's "Snow Queen" and "The Little Mermaid" which were (and are) my favorite fairy tales.

When I was old enough to read, another thrilling adventure was in store for me: I was taken to the theatre to see a play for the first time—a beautiful ballet, *The Arabian Nights*. Not long after this I saw *Cinderella*. As all children know, it is only a step from seeing a play to trying to act a play. Soon I discovered this entrancing new experience of play-acting could be enjoyed in two ways: the first of these was with a little theatre of my own which I constructed from cardboard boxes, with characters cut out of gaily illustrated paper books, and scenery from the same source. Yet even more exciting and varied was the play-acting undertaken with my circle of youthful friends. This was mostly out of doors, and never before an audience. We made up the plays to suit ourselves, gradually passing from fairy plays to those dealing with Prince Hal or Robin Hood.

Soon costumes were in demand. From attic findings we improvised cloaks and trains and swords. My parents had a large and rangy library which included Guizot's *Illustrated History of France and England*, which proved a mine for costume pictures. Many years later I was to write a book *Costumes and Scenery for Amateurs*; but nothing could have been further from my thoughts at that time. Many children begin very early to dream of authorship. I never did. I scribbled a bit as all children do; yet nothing I wrote showed any promise. After I was eleven the play fever abated. It certainly never showed itself in high school; but it blazed up again when I entered Boston University, 1903-04, where I wrote not only plays for the college but a three-act play *The Queen of Hearts*, which was accepted by a professional children's theatre company then resident in Copley Square. However, writing in earnest did not begin until 1905, in New York.

Marian Hurd McNeely

July 26, 1877-December 18, 1930

AUTHOR OF

The Jumping-Off Place, Winning Out, Etc.

CONSTANCE D'ARCY MACKAY

Here again it was a children's theatre that attracted me—the Educational Theater for Children, on the East Side, in which Mark Twain and William Dean Howells took such an interest. For this I wrote *The House of the Heart*, a one-act play with its scene laid in the heart of a child. After its production it became the first play in a volume of one-act plays accepted by Henry Holt & Co., through Roland Holt, the vice president, whose wife I became in 1923.

Together, sharing an intense interest in the theatre about which he wrote most vividly and delightfully, my husband and I traveled in Europe, hunting out the newest and the sites of the oldest theatres—from ancient amphitheatres in Italy through the English and some of the French cathedrals where miracle and morality plays first began, down to the very latest children's theatres in London and Paris.

Literary work and the friendships it brings are an enduring satisfaction. Interested as I was in writing for juveniles, I was also interested in writing for adults, and in writing articles on the theatre for the magazines.

During the recent war I was a consultant on what plays to use for work with young people, and, in spite of radio and movies, found the interest in the stage play just as keen as ever.

ON March 4, 1929, the day President Hoover was inaugurated, Marian Hurd McNeely's youngest daughter, Sylvia, wrote in her "diry":

"Oh, Mother nearly won a prize. She sent a story to a contest. The name of it was The jumping-of place."

The contest was for the best book for young people. Dorothy Canfield Fisher, who was one of the judges, was deeply impressed by Mrs. McNeely's story and wrote her a letter congratulating her upon its excellence.

The story tells of four sturdy young orphans, ranging in age from eight to seventeen, who establish a home on the lonely, wind-swept prairies of South Dakota. They endure heat, drought, snakes, blizzards, and other hardships to win the claim left by their uncle who died. Mrs. McNeely dedicated this book "to the two who were there with me," meaning her husband and her sister, with whom she once homesteaded on the South Dakota prairies and had the experiences which gave her the material for this, her best-known book.

Mrs. McNeely was born in Dubuque, Iowa. Her father was a prominent lawyer and citizen of the town, being president of the bar association, a member of the board of education, a trustee of the library, and president of the humane society. Marian Hurd, as she was then called, attended the local schools. She worked on a newspaper for several years and collaborated in the writing of two books.

At thirty-three she married Lee McNeely and she devoted the next fifteen years or more to raising her family of four children. She and her husband homesteaded on the Rosebud Indian Reservation in South Dakota for two years, then settled in her native city of Dubuque.

As soon as the last of her children had reached school age, she resumed her writing. She was fifty-one when the first book of which she was sole author appeared. A year later Mrs. McNeely published *The Jumping-Off Place*, and then went to work on a third book, *Winning Out*, but she did not live to see the publication of this book. She was tragically killed by a reckless driver in front of her home in Dubuque one week before Christmas of her fifty-third year.

Winning Out appeared posthumously, followed by a collection of her short stories. Most of these had appeared in *St. Nicholas* or the *Youth's Companion*. One was left half-finished in her typewriter, cut short by death.

Mrs. McNeely was well known for her poetry, in addition to her stories and novels. She was a frequent contributor of children's verse to such magazines as *St. Nicholas*, the *Youth's Companion*, and *John Martin's Book*, and selections by her were frequently included in annuals published by the magazines.

In 1931 Sylvia McNeely made her debut as an author, at the age of eleven, with the publication of the *Diry* which she had kept during the year 1929. Her mother had secretly typed it out and sent it to a publisher. Tempted by the offer of one dollar to clinch the agreement, Sylvia finally consented to the publication of her book.

Mrs. McNeely once wrote the following characteristically amusing synopsis of her life:

"Born in Dubuque, Iowa, after the (Civil) War. Was sent to high school for an education which I never got. Spent four years reading poetry, back of geometry and physics textbooks.

"Worked as columnist on Iowa newspapers. Spent one spring in the hill towns of Italy, married one man, and homesteaded for two years. Banked our all on a railroad which never came, so homesteading was a financial failure. Husband a decided success, being self-effacing, sunny of temperament, and handy with tools.

"Have never had a Muse. I write whenever the house is empty and I remember that the children are yet to be educated. Have written three books, two of them co-operative stories and one of them my own. Am writing another. Have written much magazine verse, some short stories, and a million obituaries.

"Have no claim to notability except the fact that I am raising four children on a government salary. When I add that they are the expensive variety of children, addicted to appendicitis and triple A shoes, the reason for at least a modest pride can be understood."

In a preface to *The Way of Glory*, Dorothy Canfield Fisher described Mrs. McNeely as "humorous, gentle, clearsighted, pungent, modest, indomitable—*charming*!"

May McNeer

AUTHOR OF

The Story of the Southern Highlands, The Story of California, The Story of Florida, Etc.

Autobiographical sketch of May McNeer:

FLORIDA is a state as varied in the background of the groups of people who live there as it is in wild life and scenery. I was born in Tampa, of a Southern family, and grew up in a world quite different from that of the tourist centers and play resorts.

I worked for the Tampa *Times* and the Tampa *Tribune*, and then left to study journalism at the University of Georgia, later transferring to the Pulitzer School of Journalism of Columbia University. I graduated there in 1926, and married Lynd Ward. We spent the following year in Europe, most of it in Leipzig, Germany, where my husband studied graphic arts at the Academy.

We were both more interested in books than in anything else. And so on our return Lynd Ward went into book illustration, and I began to write for children. Our first book together was *Prince Bantam*. Col-

MARIAN HURD MCNEELY

MAY McNEER

laboration for us has been a lot of fun, and of some benefit too, since we both go in for a thoroughgoing criticism of each other's work. The books I have enjoyed doing most are those we have worked on together. They include *Stop Tim*, *Waif Maid*, and *Golden Flash*. I have worked with other artists on such books as *The Story of the Great Plains* and *The Story of the Southern Highlands*. I have also had short stories published in *Story Parade*, *Calling All Girls*, and *Polly Pigtails*, as well as in several anthologies.

All my writing is for children, and all of it is historical. Why that is I do not know, except that I get so much pleasure out of working with the past and trying to make it interesting to young people of today.

We have two daughters, Nanda and Robin. Our home is in Leonia, New Jersey, where we are close enough to be a part of New York City, and yet far enough away to have an old barn which we have remodeled as a studio.

Alida Sims Malkus

September 19, 1895-

AUTHOR OF
The Dragon Fly of Zuni, Along the Inca Highway, The Stone Knife Boy, Etc.

Autobiographical sketch of Alida Sims Malkus:

Alida: *al EE da*
Malkus: *first syllable rhymes with "pal"*

I AM the eleventh of thirteen children. I was born in New York State, in the beautiful fox-hunting Genesee Valley. My first memory is of grandmother's place there and of being perched before the saddle on my aunt's hunter as it soared over the gate. My next memory is of Michigan; my father and mother took their brood of eight up to the Great Lakes country to grow up. We all learned to swim and watched the great lumber rafts come down from Superior. Since that time I have swum in everything from a cattle tank on the desert to the onyx-black waters of a sacred Maya well in Yucatan.

When I was seven I first went West with my parents, and on a trip to Colorado's Garden of the Gods I rode a donkey. It went forward only when belabored from behind, but when, in despair, we turned back toward the stable, it flew. My love of riding became a fixed passion then and there. My schooling was always thus cheerfully interrupted whenever my parents decided to travel, but I had a passion for information, and, it must be admitted, for much that had no relation whatever to the truth, but that seemed beautiful and so utterly desirable that I could easily believe it, or tell it. My father was a judge, a wit, a scholar, and a linguist; my mother a beautiful lady, with a lovely voice and abundant grace of soul. To be with them was an education, though I cannot remember that my father ever stooped to our mental level to teach us anything, but rather we gathered the crumbs that fell from the grown-ups' banquet.

I loved to draw; in school I filled my double slate inside with pictures, and I was often permitted to spend days putting huge drawings on the board, copying such appropriate paintings as "The First Thanksgiving." I was incessantly busy and very confident. I would be an artist, everyone felt. I was very happy in creating anything, especially dolls and toy theatres. I was a tomboy too, climbing every fence and barn gable, wriggling through pipes, climbing walls with bare hands and feet.

At thirteen I entered high school and contributed to the high school paper with ribald verse. I drew covers and illustrations and wrote articles and plays. Later, and this was a pity, I became timid about either

ALIDA SIMS MALKUS

drawing or writing, and so any work I was to do was delayed for years. Also, those whom I most admired were highly educated, but *not* creative, and in the atmosphere of such informed critics, and with my own taste thus so sharpened, I was afraid to produce anything myself. My confidence vanished. I could not believe how wonderfully we can improve with just doing, or that the childish writing and drawing over which I struggled and wept could ever grow into anything.

When I was fifteen my mother had again to go West for her health. It was decided I might go to art school in San Francisco. The art school was a glamorous, castle-like hall, crowning a hill, up steep streets overgrown with grass. In New Mexico on the way home I saw for the first time Indians living as they had lived for many hundreds of years; red *men*, not degraded beggars. The dazzling, shining air of the land, the bigness, the brilliant colors, made so deep an impression that I was forever drawn within the enchantment of the West.

Two years later I went back. At the Valley Ranch I lived in a little log house under the shadow of the Rockies. There were horses to ride, mountains to ride them over, snow-capped peaks to ascend in summer, high mountain meadows carpeted with flowers and wild strawberries, and such mysteries as rivers that sank into the living rock, to disappear completely. In those

years I learned the West by eye and by heart. I hunted lion and wild turkey, I slept on the deserts with my eyes and mouth full of sand storms as bad as any Arabian sirocco, and escaped devastating cloudbursts by a margin of ten feet. I prayed with the "Whipping Brotherhood" in their tiny chapels, danced old Mexican dances on hard-stamped adobe floors, rode on the roundup of Southern ranches, sometimes fifty and seventy-five miles in a day, three to four fresh mounts being furnished me, with the feudal splendour of a domain that covers a "pasture" of sixty fenced miles.

The summer that Villa was to raid Columbus I went down into Sonora to a silver mine in which I owned shares. Revolutionists surrounded us; drought came and there was nothing but beans and cactus buds to eat. Bandits came. We hid in the mine, then finally escaped by a terrific ride and a lucky chance—an engine running out from the mines at Nacozari.

After that experience I went to Puerto Rico, got a job in the censor's office during the First World War. At the end of the year I returned to New Mexico where I got a job on an Albuquerque paper. Afraid or not, I had now to begin at last to write. I felt that with news I would be violating no rules of writing. But the editor thought differently. My copy knew no laws of typesetting. I was fired for "incompetence," and immediately hired by the opposition paper, where I wrote features while a kindly editor elucidated for me the mystery of "up" and "down" in copy writing.

On that paper I met Mr. Malkus, and a year later we were married, in New York, both of us being by then on the staff of *McClure's Magazine*. Newspaper and magazine articles, short stories for young people, kept me busy until small Willem was two. Then Mrs. Harcourt asked me to write a book of the West. Little Hubert was six months old when that book, *Raquel of the Ranch Country*, was written. It was, of course, a story of much of my own life in the Southwest, and of the grand people whose hospitality I knew in Doña Ana County, New Mexico, the scene of those famous cattle feuds, of Billy the Kid, and Pat Garret.

A few years later I went down to Yucatan, lured by the fabulous ruins of the Maya.

From the shelter of the Carnegie rest house I explored the ancient city, from ball court to astronomical tower. The wonderful architecture seemed to come alive with the people who had raised its walls, and there among the gleaming temples *The Dark Star of Itza* took shape. Published some sixteen years ago, it was broadcast in both Spanish and English to open the Good Neighbor radio program over CBS in 1942.

We lived around: Connecticut, Brooklyn —the Flatbush where quaint Dutch tombstones still testify to the early settlers (our forebears through a Van Rensselaer grandmother)—New York, Michigan. As one grows older a film of memory seems to unroll, and other scenes that one has lived among through almost forgotten years, appear, vividly painted. I see that everything we see, hear, experience, what we read and do in those years, will have its bearing on what we are to do later.

At the present writing the writer lives each winter in the heart of Manhattan, trying to link together the heritage of the past with the astronomical, extravagant present, being guided and gently corrected by two young veterans who insist that their parent keep abreast of their times, and live within them. Their belief that man is looking forever upward, and will advance in Godhead with knowledge, sweeps their elders along with them into magic realms of the future. And if the questing spirit which drove Polynesian navigator and Viking alike over strange and unknown seas which superstition peopled with monsters and mermaids, should bear man also to the limits of our solar system, it will drive him as well to conquests of a realm still greater, and as little known—man himself, his mind and spirit.

With humility and trepidation then we face the challenge of writing to a new generation; but suspect secretly that while looking into the dazzling heart of the atom and glowing in its released power, that generation is still the child of man's past, the dwarf on the giant's shoulder. Less of fantasy than Paul Bunyan, nearer reality, and equally satisfying, were the Buck Rogerses and the Supermen on which that generation shaped its concepts.

Corinne Malvern

See *Malvern, Gladys*

Gladys Malvern

AUTHOR OF
Jonica's Island, Dancing Star, Good Troupers All, Valiant Minstrel, Etc.

Autobiographical sketch of Gladys Malvern:

I LEFT home at an early age. To be exact, I think I was about four or five. Home was in Newark, New Jersey; but it really wasn't home at all, because I wasn't old enough to know what a home meant.

From then until I was twenty-one, home to me was anywhere—hotels, trains, boarding houses; for my sister, Corinne Malvern, and I were "stage children." When I stopped being a "stage child," I became what they called an ingenue, and then a leading lady. But by this time I had decided I didn't like wandering about, and I began to think how nice it would be to have a home like other people.

I could visualize a lamp on a table and a nice easy chair—and books. I thought that would be just about the pleasantest kind of life anyone would want—just to *light* somewhere, and have your own things about you, things you'd bought for yourself because

GLADYS MALVERN

Malvern: *first syllable rhymes with "pal"*

you happened to like them. And when you coupled all this with *writing* books as well as *having* them—well, that was pretty close to heaven!

By this time my sister had given up acting and gone in for art. So I finally gave up the stage, too, and thought I'd write for a living. That shows how optimistic I was.

To write doesn't cost anything, but buying stamps to send out what I wrote had a way of adding up to money, because it hardly seemed I'd dropped the stories into the mailbox before there they were again!

So I went into the advertising business. We were in Los Angeles by this time, and we had the kind of house we wanted, plus the lamp and the easy chairs and the beautiful, beautiful books. Advertising is a very good business. I liked it immensely and stuck with it for about twelve years. But after work, being very stubborn in this matter, I continued to write. And I wrote. And I wrote. Finally—oh, after I'd torn up any number of manuscripts—I sold a book. And the next year I sold another. And the next year—*another*!

And somehow or other I began to feel encouraged. In fact, after I'd sold three novels, I felt so brave I gave up my advertising job. We sold the lamps and the easy chairs and most of the books, and came blithely to New York.

Then I started writing for radio, and after I'd done it for about two years, I decided that wasn't very much fun. It was about this time that I wrote *Dancing Star*, my first book for the "young adult" crowd. I've been happily writing for this group ever since, and I want to go on writing for them as long as they'll let me.

My sister and I share an apartment which practically overhangs the Hudson River. Here she has her studio—with a perfectly stunning indoor garden—and here I do my work—with a typewriter and a flock of pencils. We're each doing the work we love, and we're happy that people seem to like what we do.

* * *

Gladys Malvern's sister, Corinne is a well-known illustrator of children's books. She often makes pictures for her sister's stories. One of these, *Valiant Minstrel*, was awarded the Julia Ellsworth Ford Prize in 1943.

Walter De La Mare
See *De La Mare, Walter*

I. Marshak
See *"Ilin, M."*

Stephen W. Meader
May 2, 1892-
AUTHOR OF
*Red Horse Hill, Boy With a Pack,
Long Trains Roll, Trap-Lines
North, Etc.*

Autobiographical sketch of Stephen W. Meader:

I WAS born in Providence, Rhode Island, and spent the first twelve years of my life there. Our home was in the grounds of the Providence Friends' School — now Moses Brown School — where my father taught mathematics. Founded 150 years earlier, the school still had its own farm in the midst of the growing city. An old apple orchard surrounded our house. I remember that on my birthdays the trees were always in bloom and the robins singing.

I had few playmates, but amused myself by tunneling in the tall orchard grass and exploring the chestnut groves. Whenever I could, I visited the old stone barn and admired the horses and cows. The rest of the time I read and drew pictures—usually of animals.

At seven, I started going to Montague Street School. At that age I was shy and afraid of games. Only in my imagination did I perform heroic deeds. Father's library was a large one and I devoured every book in it that looked interesting. When I wasn't reading myself I listened to mother as she read aloud. In this unorthodox way I acquired a "fund of useful information" that has stood me in good stead.

When I was twelve we moved to New Hampshire, where my Meader ancestors had settled in 1627. We lived near Rochester, N. H., and I attended Rochester High School. It was a great change for me. For the first time I lived an active outdoor boy's life—swimming, fishing, hunting, skating, coasting. Father was in the lumber business and was away most of the time. As the oldest of five children, I was the man of

Meader: *MEED er*

STEPHEN W. MEADER

Bachrach

In the spring I got a job with a Chicago publisher, and after three months an opening with the Curtis Publishing Company, of Philadelphia, brought me East again. I was married on December 16, 1916, to Elizabeth Hoyt, of Montclair, New Jersey.

It was not until three years later that I dug up the dusty manuscript of the pirate story, and finished it. Through the good offices of my friend "Kit" Morley it was sent to the new publishing firm of Harcourt, Brace and Company, and accepted.

Since then, writing boys' books for Harcourt has been my principal hobby, though I have others—among them drawing and canoeing. Such stories as *The Black Buccaneer, Longshanks,* and *Away to Sea* grew out of historical periods that interested me. *Red Horse Hill, King of the Hills,* and *Lumberjack* are reminiscent of my own boyhood experiences in New England. The total list now includes twenty books.

Bread and butter for the family is earned by writing advertising for N. W. Ayer & Son, in Philadelphia. We have four children, two boys and two girls. All are now grown up, and the two eldest are married. Our home is in the pleasant old Quaker suburb of Moorestown, New Jersey.

the house. I had a horse to take care of, wood to split, fires to tend. Occasionally I went with father to his lumber camp in the woods. Our summers were spent at Grandfather Hawkes' farm on the shore of Lake Cobbossee, in Maine. There was hay to make and corn to hoe, but there was also time for camping and paddling a canoe.

I was graduated from Rochester High School in 1908, and spent a year in Providence, at Moses Brown School. In the fall of 1909 I went to Haverford, the Quaker college near Philadelphia. There I was fortunate in coming into intimate contact with such great teachers as Francis B. Gummere and Rufus Jones. I went out for football and made the track team, but my real interest was in writing. That was a literary era at Haverford. Christopher Morley and his fellow Olympians of the class of 1910 set a pace which we strove vainly to follow.

When I received my A.B., in 1913, I went into social work in Newark, New Jersey. For two and a half years I was with the Children's Aid Society and the Big Brother Movement. Then the funds of the latter organization ran low. That winter, while I was looking for a new job, I started writing a book. Pirate stories had always fascinated me. In the Newark Library I chanced across a dry historical treatise on the Carolina pirates, which gave me a background for *The Black Buccaneer.*

Enid Meadowcroft

1898-

AUTHOR OF

The Gift of the River, On Indian Trails With Daniel Boone, By Secret Railway, Etc.

Autobiographical sketch of Enid La Monte Meadowcroft:

IN a backyard shed in Cranford, New Jersey, four little girls once looked proudly at a smudgy hectographed sheet which bore the heading "Junior Pickwick Papers." It was the first issue of a new weekly newspaper, written and produced by their own hands and offered to the public at five cents a copy. Though that little newspaper never made a fortune for its publishers, it taught one of those little girls what fun it is to put ideas into written words.

My family had moved to Cranford from New York City where I was born, and back to New York we moved again, shortly after the death of my father the year I celebrated my eleventh birthday. There, although my

Bachrach

ENID MEADOWCROFT

mother taught singing and lectured on folk music the wolf was never far from the door, and for several years my two younger sisters and I did all sorts of after-school jobs to help fill the family pocketbook. We were poor as church mice, but happy. And I was especially so when a family friend offered to help me through normal school so I might achieve an ambition I had cherished since my first day of school, when I had dashed home to announce to my family that I was going to become a teacher.

It was in the four-room school of Harrington Park, New Jersey, that at last I faced my first class—a roomful of wriggling first and second graders. And it was here that my experience as the editor of "Junior Pickwick Papers" first stood me in good stead. The little school had no library to speak of, but it had a hectograph, and I soon began to spend my free time writing and hectographing stories for my wrigglers to read. Not until several years later, however, did I have the courage to attempt a full-length book. That was *The Gift of the River*—a history of ancient Egypt, and I wrote it because I had found, in reading some Egyptian history, stories I thought would fascinate older children if only they could be told in such a way that those children could understand them.

History had always seemed pretty dull stuff to me when I was in school, consisting chiefly of wars, politics, and dates. Now that I was reading history just for fun, I found it was a story of *people* and because I like people I could not get enough of it. Later when I was teaching in a boys' school in New York City and my second graders were more restless than usual I told them stories of the people who had made their country. And when they wanted a story of the Pilgrims which they could read all by themselves I wrote one for them—*The First Year*—let them read each chapter as it was finished, and listened to their suggestions as to how it might be improved. That was the beginning. Since then I have written a number of books for second graders through junior high schoolers, all with an historical background, and shall, I hope, write many more.

In Lakeville, Connecticut, where my husband, Donald M. Wright, and I now live there are all sorts of things to lure me away from the typewriter—the beautiful lake to swim in and skate on, the beautiful roads that lead over the Berkshire foothills, the wistful eyes of a shiny black cocker pleading for a romp. But as the days pass there is nothing quite so rewarding as the growing pile of typed pages which will in time become another book.

Florence Crannell Means

May 15, 1891-

AUTHOR OF

*Candle in the Mist, Shuttered Windows,
The Moved-Outers, Great Day
in the Morning, Etc.*

Autobiographical sketch of Florence Crannell Means:

I WAS born in an elm-shaded white parsonage in Baldwinsville, New York, and my father's next pastorate was in Corning, in the same state.

Entrancing vignettes of New York state remain in my memory: carriage rides along "the back road to Painted Post," in the scarlet and gold of autumn; trailing arbutus under last year's leaves; bracken-shaded mossy hollows set with fairy goblets. After we had moved to Topeka, Kansas, when I was eight, I wrote passionately of it:

Oh, I long for the home of my childhood!
Oh, I long for the sweet woodland dells,—

Crannell: *rhymes with "panel"*

My childhood seems to have been spent under Father's study table—I the only person permitted in that room when he was writing essays, poems, sermons. I was allowed an occasional square white sheet of sermon paper for my "poems" and drawings and paper dolls; and at intervals he took me on his knee and made blot pictures or wrote gay little rhymes. Always his study was a far better place than my playroom, for ministering to my huge families of dolls and for lying on my stomach to read the *Youth's Companion, Little Women, Oliver Twist,* and *The Mill on the Floss!*

Our favorite family evenings were spent with Father reading aloud while Mother mended, Sister embroidered, and I drew. We were all bookworms; but Mother disciplined herself more sternly than the rest (Fannie Eleanor Grout came of hardy, conscientious pioneer stock) when she early found that she was blind and deaf from the moment she gave herself to a book. With us all, though, books came before clothes and such things. Sometimes they were in ugly cheap editions, but what of that? I shall never love fine copies of Dickens as I did our old set, dimly printed on yellow paper and bound in faded red.

Since there were no boys in the family, I was Father's "Son Tommy," and he my comrade, as Mother was my adored confidante. I have not known another mind so deep, high, clear, and richly stocked as

FLORENCE CRANNELL MEANS

Father's; though now I think I see its like in my daughter.

Both Father and Mother encouraged my dreams of being missionary, writer, artist, or teacher in the Crannell Free Kindergarten in Albany, memorial to my aunt Euretta. Is it significant that all these dreams have had some realization in spirit? For I have written many missionary stories and many tales for small children; and some of them I have illustrated—though not too artistically.

Summers in Minnesota "at Grandpa's" I count among the formative influences of childhood and adolescence. My brilliant, imperious, lovable Grandfather Grout and my exquisite and gentle grandmother are sketched in my pioneer tales.

When I was thirteen, the illness of my beautiful elder sister, Effie, brought us to Denver. My sister improved, and that tomboy year was a rare one for me. There were few girls in our suburb, so I played with boys, rode half-broken horses, caught "horny-toads" and lizards, and raced the unfenced prairie with the big, lovable, whiskery dog which I inevitably named Dougal.

After this came three years in Kansas City, where Father spent altogether a quarter of a century as president of the Kansas City Baptist Theological Seminary. Then my sister's relapse brought us back to Denver, where she had three tranquil years before her passing, and where I have lived most of the time since.

High school; art school; Greek and philosophy under Father; other subjects in college extension courses up to the present time; such has been my sketchy education.

In 1912 I married Carleton Bell Means, a young Kansas City man who had just completed his law course. His intense delight in literature and all the arts has made him enjoy my writing as keenly as I, and he has always helped "make time" for my work, invariably voting for a poem in place of a pie. Honestly! Still, I like to make pies, too; and omelets and waffles and chicken fricassee and things like that.

Our only child, Eleanor Crannell Means —now Eleanor Hull—started to school at seven and romped gaily through to a B.A. at eighteen and a B.F.A. two years later. Her writing, painting, cooking, hiking, swimming, riding years with boy and girl friends were a constant inspiration to my writing for children and young people. Now, with four small stair-steps of her own, she continues to stimulate her mother's writing, and to squeeze in a little herself.

As a family we have spent our summers in that part of our Rockies I first knew at thirteen. We love them, birds and flowers, trees and streams.

We are all interested in persons of other races, also, and increasingly so as the world proves the need of our understanding and appreciating each other. For years I have spent as much time as possible among the Hopi and Navajo Indians in the Southwest, visiting a great many other tribes besides. I have gained a Hopi name, Tawahonsi, and a Hopi "granddaughter," Florence Means Lahpo, about to be graduated from high school and contemplating nurse's training. We have an adopted Chinese daughter and grandchildren in Shanghai, a Spanish-American "grandson," Japanese-American "nieces" and "nephews," and "nieces" in Burma.

Altogether, we continue to find life absorbing, and writing the most fun of anything we can imagine. And the thing I most want my books to say is just this: Whether they are red or white or yellow or black, folks are folks.

* * *

All Mrs. Means' books have sprung from this conviction. It came to her early, perhaps because her father, Dr. Crannell, was not only a scholar, a poet, and a wit, but also a man with absolutely no racial consciousness.

In 1945 Mrs. Means won the Award of the Child Study Association of America for *The Moved-Outers*, her stirring story of the evacuation and relocation of Americans of Japanese ancestry during the Second World War.

Mrs. Means, herself, Siri Andrews describes as "a slender woman with soft yet sparkling dark brown eyes and graying black hair, a sweet smile, and a gentle manner which at the same time has force and character behind it, a sense of humor and a faculty of being able to laugh at herself. . . . One has memories of a gracious home. Perhaps not enough has been said about her deep religious faith, which is the force behind all her actions nor about her liberal views, her tolerance, her objectivity, her keen sense of humor."

Marjorie Medary

July 24, 1890-

AUTHOR OF

Topgallant, Buckeye Boy, Edra of the Islands, Etc.

Autobiographical sketch of Marjorie Medary:

I WAS born and grew up in Waukon, Iowa, eighteen miles west of the Mississippi. My grandparents, all four of them, had come to Iowa as pioneers in the 1850's. My father was editor and publisher of a weekly newspaper; so, very early in life I became familiar with the smell of printer's ink. On press days my sisters and I often helped fold the papers, but we were never encouraged to learn to set type. Probably Father thought girls would only make pie out of a font of type!

My earliest appearance in print occurred when I was eight. A hardware merchant had offered prizes for the best stories about things displayed in his window, and my story about a tin dipper was among those chosen to be printed in the paper.

My third year of high school was pleasantly interrupted by a trip to Florida with my older sister to visit relatives who had planted orange groves back in the 1870's when Mother was a girl. Her stories about her visits to that land of lakes and palmettos and pine woods had made the place glamorous, to use a favorite word of today. It exceeded even my expectations. I promptly wrote a poem about the sunset over Lake Beauclaire. We helped pack oranges, gathered strange leaves and flowers to press, rode in a buckboard behind the mules, and visited some of the "cracker" families. Those adventures found their way into my first book, *Orange Winter*, twenty-five years later.

After graduation from high school I followed my sister to Cornell. There a truly great teacher opened to me the riches of English poetry. As my horizons expanded, my desire to write grew, especially after some commendation of themes and other papers. I dreamed dreams and filled a notebook with sophomoric poetry. In my junior year I was chosen associate editor of the college magazine, but ill health kept me at

MARJORIE MEDARY

home and when I returned the magazine was defunct.

A fellowship plus the generosity of my grandfather gave me a year of graduate study at Northwestern University. I enjoyed courses in Old and Middle English because of my native delight in words. I explored the Celtic sources of the King Arthur legends for my thesis and, with equal zest, the current plays in Chicago theatres. It was my first opportunity to see great acting.

Equipped with an M.A. degree I started teaching just at the outbreak of the First World War. My first job took me to New England. After two years I returned to teach in Indianapolis. I learned to enjoy teaching as I found boys and girls with talent for writing who could be guided toward their goal. During those war years there was much to distract me from my own efforts, but I continued at intervals to send out manuscripts and to collect rejection slips.

Finally one summer I summoned courage to attend the Bread Loaf Writers' Conference. The comments I received on my manuscripts were almost all discouraging. They must have been the spur I needed. They roused a kind of fierce determination in me to prove I could write and—be published. I asked for a year's leave of absence from teaching and set to work. But I also worked part time at a course in editing and part time in the lending library of the Bookshop for Boys and Girls

in Boston. The surroundings, plus the fact that two of my stories accepted that winter happened to be about children, served to open my eyes. Why not write for children?

The next year I found a position in a publishing house in New York as an editor of textbooks, and I attended a seminar on writing at Columbia. There around a table with a dozen others, I learned to accept and give criticism. I had begun a story of pioneer days in Florida, based partly on my mother's girlhood experiences and partly on my own. When it was finished after nearly two years I entered it in a contest. It won no prize but it was accepted for publication. My joy was clouded by the fact that Mother did not live to see it published.

In 1941 I discovered in eastern Connecticut a house which has almost all the charms I think a house should have—a wide view, a sheltering elm, a fireplace, and plenty of room for guests and books. There I now live seven months of the year. The winter months I spend in Boston or New York, still editing and writing.

Cornelia Meigs

December 6, 1884-

AUTHOR OF

Invincible Louisa, The Willow Whistle,
The Wonderful Locomotive, Etc.

Autobiographical sketch of Cornelia Lynde Meigs:

TO be a member of a large family is excellent training for many things, among them story telling. One of my older sisters told me many tales when I was small; I, in my turn, adopted her technique and told many others to the only member of the family who was younger. My father was an excellent teller of tales, as had been his father, so a particularly large number of family legends went, without loss of vividness, from generation to generation.

Since my father's kindred had been, in long succession, officers in the army and navy, and my mother's father and mother had been pioneers from Vermont to Illinois, stories current in our house made the settlement of the Middle West, the War of 1812, the brush with the Barbary pirates, and the Civil War as familiar as any events

Meigs: *rhymes with "eggs"*

within this century. It was, for the most part, stories of naval adventure which fired my imagination the most.

From the time I was born in Rock Island, Illinois, until my removal to Bryn Mawr, Pennsylvania, I have lived all my life in the Middle West, at Keokuk, Iowa, where my father was government engineer in charge of improvements on the Mississippi River. A great many summers, and some winters also, were spent in New England, where both sides of my family originated.

Thus the thirst for seafaring stories could be assuaged by first-hand marine records in Plymouth, Salem, and Marblehead, and a taste for New England history could well be satisfied in Massachusetts and Vermont. It was study at Bryn Mawr, where I was a member of the class of 1907, which first showed me how deeply interesting history could be, and what were the possibilities in such a field of writing.

Like a great many other people I wanted to write, but for a long time let my life be filled so full of responsibilities and miscellaneous occupations that there was no real time for it. I was a teacher of English at St. Katharine's School at Davenport, Iowa, when I wrote my first book. There were young children in this school to whom I used to tell my stories, and from their unconscious criticism I learned much of great value as to what does, and does not, interest their active and easily diverted minds. Even so, my book had some vicissitudes in finding a publisher, but it finally appeared in 1915, a collection of stories of fantasy, *The Kingdom of the Winding Road*.

I learned two things from this experience—two very important things which have to do with authorship: one, that you must have sufficient confidence in your project to make time for it no matter what are the demands and distractions; the other, that inspiration has to be attended by intensively hard work, sometimes even replaced by it—apparently—to bring a writing enterprise to its proper end.

A succession of books has followed *The Kingdom of the Winding Road*. During the years of writing them I kept house for my father and repeated my early New England summers by having large numbers of my sisters' children stay with me at Marble-

CORNELIA MEIGS

head, Massachusetts, and Brandon, Vermont. Since 1932 I have been a member of the English department at Bryn Mawr.

* * *

Miss Meigs teaches English composition and creative writing; she has been contributing hosts of short stories to children's magazines. One of these, "Fox and Geese," won the *Child Life* prize story contest in 1938. She has written twenty-four full-length books, not one of which is out of print. Moreover at the annual conference of the American Library Association in 1934 she was awarded the Newbery Medal for *Invincible Louisa*, her biography of Louisa Alcott. In her graceful speech of acceptance she gave credit for the book to Miss Alcott, saying: "If I could stretch my voice across the years, I should say, Louisa, this medal is yours. And I do assure you that Louisa and I both thank you." But although the medal is awarded annually "for the most significant contribution to American literature for children" there is little doubt that it was intended as a recognition of her previous work as well as of the book specifically mentioned, for few writers for young people have had all their books received with equal praise. It was not, however, her first prize. In 1927 she won the $2,000 Beacon Hill Bookshelf Prize with *The Trade Wind*.

"No story of Cornelia Meigs can be told without some word of her nieces and nephews appearing constantly," writes Doris Patee, "for they have been part of her life ever since they were born. . . . There are twelve of them and some have lived with her since they were children. (She says they used to sit by the typewriter and watch the story come out, and tell her very frankly what they thought of it.) They are all grown up now, but their devotion to their aunt is as strong as when they listened to her stories."

Her farm in Vermont is called "Green Pastures." On it is a "stately white house large enough for all her friends and relatives, and full of an atmosphere whch extends all the way from the beauty and quietness of a mountain view at the front and a lovely garden at the back, to that gay, rollicking, holiday spirit that comes to a house where young people rush in to change from tennis or dash off for a swim. Here Cornelia Meigs has a beautiful study and it is here she can do most of her writing, secure in a separate wing where there will be no interruptions, but near enough to share the happiness she has always found in having her family about her."

Leja Gorska

KATHERINE MILHOUS

Katherine Milhous

1894-

ILLUSTRATOR, AND AUTHOR OF

The Egg Tree, Lovina: A Story of the Pennsylvania Country, Snow Over Bethlehem, Etc.

Autobiographical sketch of Katherine Milhous:

AS I sit writing in my studio I hear the rumbling of the press in the adjoining printing plant. It is a sound that has followed me all my life. My first studio was in my father's printing shop, when, as a very small child, I would sit dangerously near the presses and draw on scrap paper. My father, Oscar Thomas Milhous, had several different shops in Philadelphia in the district between Old Christ Church and Independence Hall. It was in 1729, the year plans were drawn up for the building of the State House, that his people came to this country.

Above my drawing table in a little oval frame is the picture of a Quaker gentleman —Samuel Milhous—in Colonial costume, but with a sword. Quaker records tell me that the Milhouses came from Ireland and settled in Chester County, Pennsylvania. But to that strain, as the years passed, have been added the Methodist shipbuilding Champions, the Catholic Dalys, and a flavoring of Pennsylvania Dutch.

My schooldays were spent with my small sister Dorothy in a New Jersey camp-meeting town. There were no art classes, so that, if I wanted a picture, I simply took up my paintbox and made one. There were no libraries, either, but my mother managed to assemble one by buying up bargain sets of books on her rare trips to Philadelphia. I read all the books of all the sets.

My father's business did not thrive in the small community, so, when I begged to go to art school, my mother pawned her wedding ring to send me. That put me on my mettle. I commuted daily to Philadelphia, made newspaper drawings at night, and worked for a scholarship, which I won. I had to.

Suddenly we moved back to Philadelphia. There I shared a studio—the first of three— with an artist friend. We work now in adjoining studios, each on her own books. But we did not always stay in those studios. Sometimes we found ourselves jogging along the country roads in a caravan pulled by a plough horse. It was on these trips that I got the background for *Lovina* and *Herodia: The Lovely Puppet.*

Milhous: *MILL* house

We traveled abroad, too, and painted in England, Belgium, France, and Italy. In St. Francis' country I made sketches that I used later for *The First Christmas Crib*. My second Christmas book, *Snow Over Bethlehem*, stems from my Pennsylvania background.

During the depression when there was no work to be had, I studied sculpture at the Pennsylvania Academy of the Fine Arts, and again went abroad, this time the winner of a Cresson traveling scholarship. Home again, and with the depression still on, I became a supervisor on the Federal Art Project. A series of Pennsylvania Dutch posters I designed were on exhibit when a publishers' convention met in Philadelphia.

An editor who saw my posters wrote asking me to do a book. I did the book and have been making books ever since, both my own and also illustrations for others'.

On my studio wall opposite the Quaker gentleman hangs a rug woven by the Indians of the Bolivian mountains, its colors barbaric and beautiful. Both these things are a part of me and therefore a part of my books. I have always designed and dummied my own books, with the result that, during the war years, my publishers asked me to design other people's books. My work sent me down to lower New York to judge the color printing on the great offset presses. So I end where I began, with the printing press, which is still thudding away in the next room.

* * *

In 1951 Katherine Milhous' *The Egg Tree*, a charming Easter story about a Pennsylvania Dutch family who painted eggs and hung them on a tree for all to enjoy, received the American Library Association's Caldecott Medal as "the most distinguished American picture book for children" published in the previous year.

Elizabeth Cleveland Miller

July 13, 1889-November 1936

AUTHOR OF
Children of the Mountain Eagle, Pran of Albania, Young Trajan, Etc.

Autobiographical sketch of Elizabeth Cleveland Miller, written for THE JUNIOR BOOK OF AUTHORS shortly before her death:

I WAS born in Seymour, Connecticut, and I lived as a baby and child in New York City, in Harlem, mostly—for Harlem was country then, and my parents wanted their children to be able to play in the fields and woods!

My father was a clergyman and when I was five we moved to Ridgewood, New Jersey, where he was rector of Christ Church and where we stayed for ten years.

I had two older sisters and a younger brother and sister so I was right in the middle of a big family and we used to have great fun together. I used to draw odd-looking people and animals for my younger brother and sister to play with. I had a lot of time for drawing and painting as I was considered a "delicate" child and spent nearly three years out of school. I was author, editor, and publisher of at least a dozen doll-size magazines for which I induced my brother and sister to subscribe through the payment of paper money, which was a family medium of exchange and which we children made by the thousands of dollars.

I was a great miser too, and had boxes and boxes of paper money and bureau drawers filled with my treasures, which I kept for years and years, never giving my used things away with the generosity of my next oldest sister, who told me there was no use in keeping them since you could not take them to Heaven with you!

I had my office in the nursery, which was often rigged up with strings and little

ELIZABETH CLEVELAND MILLER

baskets that traveled here and there delivering magazines and paper dolls. I often took payment for my work in blank pieces of paper so I would not run short of paper for my various ventures.

We moved to New Bedford, Massachusetts, when I was fifteen and there at the high school I had some encouragement from my English teacher. It was so easy to write that I always felt a little guilty at the commendation I received. I won the Bourne Prize for an essay in my senior year—a piece of fiction it really was—and of course I was editor of the high school paper, but took little interest in it, as it was very much supervised by the teachers.

In 1909 I went to New York to study kindergartening at the Ethical Culture School. I chose this career as I had always felt a great interest in children and had always some very little friends to whom I told stories and for whom I drew pictures and devised magical games. I trained for two years and later took a primary course and taught first in a settlement kindergarten and later in private schools. However, my lack of ability to play the piano pushed me very early out of the kindergarten field. For seven years I taught in New York City, also doing work with clubs of young people at the settlement houses, and at the Lighthouse with blind children. I took courses at Columbia in geology and related subjects as a sort of antidote to all my teaching and pedagogical work. I was planning to complete my studies at Teachers College and get my degree when the war came along and I enlisted with the Y.M.C.A. as a canteen worker.

After the Armistice I was sent to Germany and worked until the men entrained for America, when I unexpectedly had a chance to go to the Balkans with the Red Cross. I was sent to Scutari, or Skodra, Albania, and told to do Child Welfare work. There I started and ran for two years a big place I called the "Children's House," where we fed, clothed, cured, and schooled the children of the mountain people who because of war, hunger, feud, or other troubles had been forced into Skodra as refugees.

While working there I took a trip into the mountain country I have described in my books *Children of the Mountain Eagle* and *Pran of Albania*. Both books grew out of my experience in Albania and my great love for this hardy mountain race.

After this I worked with young people and children in Breaza, Rumania, and it is this section of the world which I used as a setting for *Young Trajan.*

Later I worked with children again in the devastated regions of Northern France continuing with the Red Cross until 1922 when after a brief trip to North Africa I returned to America.

After my return I did some work with the Consumers' Cooperative Cafeteria while I got adjusted to life in my native land after an absence of more than four years.

In 1923 I took a position in a progressive school in New York City, and the year after that I sold my first story to the old *Century Magazine*, married, and sold a second story to the *Atlantic Monthly*.

In 1925 my son was born and before he was a year and a half old I had written my first book.

I now live in a white farmhouse outside of Darien, Connecticut, with my husband and son. I spend mornings writing and the rest of my time in the enjoyment of our home.

*   *   *

At the untimely death of Elizabeth Cleveland Miller, "a star went out and a joyousness departed from the lives of her friends." Her effect upon them is well described in the *Horn Book* by Florence Guy Seabury, who says that after one of Miss Miller's visits, "The world appeared to be full of a number of exciting things, so much to do, so many places to see, books to read, fascinating people to meet. Carried along by her zest I was aware again of the fun of being alive in such a universe as ours."

A. A. Milne

January 18, 1882-

AUTHOR OF

When We Were Very Young, Winnie-the-Pooh, Now We Are Six, Etc.

A. A. MILNE liked the name Christopher and his wife thought Robin was nice, so they named the baby boy Christopher Robin. But they always called him "Billy," or, as he preferred it, "Billy Moon."

Milne: *MILN*

A. A. MILNE

Christopher Robin, however, was too nice sounding a name not to use in poetry, and Milne found himself writing verses like this:

Hush! Hush! Whisper who dares!
Christopher Robin is saying his prayers.

or this:

They're changing guard at Buckingham
    Palace—
Christopher Robin went down with Alice.

And so Christopher Robin became the central figure in four books for boys and girls, two of poetry—*When We Were Very Young* and *Now We Are Six*—and two stories—*Winnie-the-Pooh* and *The House at Pooh Corner.*

Winnie-the-Pooh was a teddy bear. He joined the Milne family on Christopher Robin's first birthday (they were just the same size then) and from that day they were inseparable companions. They played together on the nursery floor, hunting wild animals among the chairs that were the jungles of Africa, or had lengthy conversations over the tea table, Christopher Robin supplying the bear's growls.

Milne put Pooh into the stories, along with Piglet, Eeyore the old gray donkey, Kanga Roo, and the other nursery animals. And Ernest Shepard, the artist, came to see them before he drew their pictures for the books. But the little boy in the poems and stories named Christopher Robin, Milne insists, was not the real Christopher Robin,

but a child of his own imagination. He admits that Billy was much in his mind when he wrote the books, but says he was also thinking of himself as a boy and of all other children.

You can imagine how he felt, then, when dozens of admiring letters came to Billy Moon as the hero of the books and when American tourists came to see him in his nursery and tickled him under the chin. Deciding that the boy had had more publicity than he ought to have, he stopped writing Christopher Robin books and announced that he was through writing for young people—at least until he becomes a grandfather.

Milne tells this story of his own career up to the time he began to publish books:

"I was born in London, on January 18, 1882, but nobody believes it. At the age of eleven I went to Westminster School with a scholarship and for a year worked very hard, but at twelve I began to feel I knew enough and thereafter took life more easily. Perhaps the most important thing that happened there was that I began to write verses and parodies for the school paper. One evening when another boy and I were looking at a copy of a Cambridge undergraduate paper, the *Granta,* which had come to the school, he said solemnly: 'You ought to edit that some day.' So I said, equally solemnly: 'I will.' This sounds like the story of the model boy who became a millionaire; I apologize, but it really did happen. I went to Cambridge, in spite of the fact that everybody meant me to go to Oxford, and edited the *Granta.*

"I left Cambridge in 1903 with a very moderate degree and a feeling in the family that I had belied the brilliant promise of my youth, and it was about time I got to work and did something. Schoolmastering and the Indian civil service were two of the professions suggested. The first was not very exciting; the second meant more examinations to pass; so I said I was going to London to write. I had enough money left over from my Cambridge allowance to keep me for a year, and by the end of the year I saw myself the most popular writer in London—editor of the *Times, Punch,* and the *Spectator,* member of all the important literary clubs, and intimate friend of Meredith and Hardy. My family was not so optimistic. They saw me at the end of the year deciding to be a schoolmaster. However, they gave me their blessing; and I went to London, took expensive rooms and settled down to write.

"By the end of the year I had spent my money that I had earned by writing—twenty pounds. So I moved to two cheap and dirty rooms in a policeman's house in Chelsea and went on writing. The second year I made about one hundred and twenty pounds and lived on it. In the third year I was making two hundred pounds, for several papers were now getting used to me, but in February 1906 a surprising thing happened. The editor of *Punch* retired, the assistant editor became editor, and I was offered the assistant editorship. I accepted and was assistant editor until the end of 1914."

While he was working on *Punch* he married Dorothy de Sélincourt and began to publish his essays in book form. During the First World War he served in France until he had a breakdown and then, after a period in a hospital, he was signaling instructor at a fort on Portsdown Hill. When he was demobilized his old post on *Punch* was waiting for him, but he decided to devote all his time to his own writing. It was not long before Christopher Robin, at the age of three, inspired him to write verses for young people. After he stopped writing Christopher Robin books he made a play from Kenneth Grahame's famous animal story, *The Wind in the Willows*, calling it *Toad of Toad Hall*.

Some of Milne's poems have been set to music by H. Fraser-Simson and published as *Fourteen Songs From "When We Were Very Young"* and *Songs From "Now We Are Six."* He is the author of many well-known plays for grown-ups, notably *Mr. Pim Passes By, The Dover Road,* and *The Perfect Alibi.* He has also written a detective story called *The Red House Mystery.*

Milne is tall, tanned, and athletic, with light receding hair. His clean-shaven face is alert, and he has blue eyes and a wide sudden smile. Golf is his one recreation and he is good at it. He says his work comes easy to him. He lives in a red house in a green square in Chelsea, London.

Carl Moon

1878-1948
AUTHOR AND ILLUSTRATOR
The Flaming Arrow, Painted Moccasin, Etc.

Autobiographical sketch of Carl Moon, written for THE JUNIOR BOOK OF AUTHORS a few years before his death:

I WAS a little boy living in a little town in southern Ohio when I first thought of going out West to hunt Indians. I loved Indian stories. The kind my mother read to us told mostly of how bad the Indians were and how brave the white heroes were who fought the redskins.

I was still very young when I made up my mind to go West into the Indian country as soon as I could grow up. When I was twenty-three I did just as I had said I would do, but instead of hunting Indians with a gun and bowie knife, as the story book heroes always did, I was to hunt my Indians with a camera, paint brushes, and a writing pad. It was a lot more fun than the gun and bowie knife way, and a lot safer.

When I arrived in Albuquerque, where I was to have a studio of my own, I found I was very near several Indian villages and that Indians from as many as four or five villages came into town to sell their buckskins, beads, and pottery, for that was some fifty years ago when buckskins and good bead work were still plentiful.

So it was in New Mexico I at last found my first redskins. Here among the Indians that came to my studio to see me, and the many Indian tribes I visited later, I found I did not need a gun or a knife. I was fond of these friendly people and they seemed fond of me. I sometimes visited their villages for weeks at a time, and they told me many things about themselves.

When I first began to write about them I wrote for magazines and newspapers. These first writings were not for children and they told mostly about the many Indian rites and ceremonies I had witnessed. I drew and painted many pictures of the Indians, but the illustrations for my magazine work were from my photographs.

When I had lived about four years in Albuquerque I moved to Grand Canyon, Arizona, to begin a large collection of Indian pictures for a business firm engaged in selling almost everything that pertained to

CARL MOON

Indians. It was while I was making this collection, that took seven years to complete, that I married Grace Purdie, who later wrote the many Indian books most American children know so well. During the time I was making this collection, which was followed by a still larger one for the Huntington Library, Mrs. Moon and I often traveled together through the big Indian country and it seemed natural and easy to write stories about our Indian friends.

We wanted to give white boys and girls a better idea of the red man, and especially the Indian children, than most of the earlier writers had given.

We both helped in writing our first two books, but after that we decided to write our stories alone as we were to write for children of different ages. It was then I wrote the first of my own books—*The Flaming Arrow*—and Mrs. Moon wrote *Chi-Wee* and the long list, longer than mine, that followed it.

We moved to Pasadena, California, where we continued our writing and art work, and our two children, Francis and Caryl, to whom we told bed-time stories when they were little, grew up and now have homes of their own.

It seemed logical for me to make the pictures for our books and I love most to make the colored paintings for the jackets and the drawings for the end papers. Although we wrote some twenty-one books we never could write all the stories we wanted

to tell. The charm of the wide free Indian country with its silent desert, its tall mountains and fascinating canyons, and the simple and happy life of most of the Indian people, these are things not easy to squeeze into little books, but we had fun trying.

Grace Moon

AUTHOR OF
*Chi-Wee, Nadita, The Runaway Papoose,
Far-Away Desert, Etc.*

Autobiographical sketch of Grace Purdie Moon, written for THE JUNIOR BOOK OF AUTHORS a few years before her death:

AT last I am in a really true adventure! I am on the *in*side of a book peeking out! It's such a queer feeling! I've been on the outside peeking *in* for so long that now I feel so outside-in, or inside-out—anyway, its different!

First, I think I'll have to come alive—! A long time ago—more years than I like to think—a little girl was born in the Middle West. That was me. Black hair and round eyes and a curiosity about everything so big it hasn't been really satisfied to this day.

We had just the right-sized family: mother and father and little brother and me, and we were very happy together. We traveled a great deal, my father's business taking us to many countries and cities, "but," my brother said to me while he was yet very small, "we must be *Indians*, 'cause we were born in *Indian*apolis, *Indiana*!"

So the Indian feeling was born in me and had to come out some way. I met someone else, after awhile, who had that same feeling. The very day I was marrying him a newspaper man called over the phone— "What *tribe* does Mr. Moon belong to? Isn't he an *Indian* artist?"

He *is* an Indian artist but the Indian part is in his pictures, not in him—and they are certainly true to life—but, after we had traveled together through Arizona and Oklahoma and New Mexico and had lived with the Indians of many tribes and had written many books about them, we almost began to feel, inside of us, that we were part Indian, after all.

Indians are so interesting and real. They are so much a part of the glorious country

GRACE MOON

they live in. I love to write about them—especially the children. I used to paint them too, but days seem so much shorter now than they used to be, there isn't time to do *half* the things I'd like to, and, anyway, one picture-maker in the family is enough—especially when that one is Carl Moon. Don't tell him I said it!

We have had adventures in the Indian country, many of them, and back of almost all the things that happen in my books are real life things that happened to us. One time we were traveling in the Canyon de Chelly, in one of the first automobiles that ever went into the Canyon, and just at the place where the rock walls begin to come together we sank into quicksand up to the bed of the car. It was only a very small car, a Ford, but it was too heavy for us to lift and if we stood near it, trying to push, we ourselves sank in the soft, wet sand. Indians, on their ponies, began to arrive on the scene offering much advice which did not help. They sat around on rocks and higher ground and talked and laughed and one even ran a pole through the spokes of a wheel and pried at it for a while.

But then someone finally had an idea. With ropes they tied the ponies, about ten of them, to the car. For a while the ponies stood there not knowing what to do; then my husband told us to all take newspapers and crash them together at the ponies' heads —which we did with a surprising result:

they ran away! Taking the car with them safely up onto the dry sand of the upper canyon. It was the same trip that gave me the idea for my book, *The Runaway Papoose.*

Homesickness for the desert made me write *Faraway Desert,* which I finished in record time to get my little girl back to the "smell of the sage and the stew in the pot," where I wanted to be myself.

Mr. Moon and I both think Heaven must be very much like the Indian country, with wide, open spaces of sunlight and sage and the smell of a faraway campfire burning.

We now live in California and our children are grown, but we still love the Indians and hope to write about them for many years yet.

* * *

Grace Moon died in Pasadena September 6, 1947.

Anne Carroll Moore

July 12, 1871-
AUTHOR OF
Nicholas, Nicholas and the Golden Goose, The Three Owls, Etc.

Autobiographical sketch of Anne Carroll Moore:

I WAS born in Limerick, York County, Maine. Limerick was and still is ten miles from a railroad in the heart of the Ossipee Valley. The White Mountains can be clearly seen from the bare hilltop from which I first looked out over the world. The Atlantic Ocean lies out of sight twenty-five miles away.

My father, Luther S. Moore, was a lawyer and a pioneer among agricultural leaders of his native state. He was one of the first trustees of the State Agricultural College, which later became the University of Maine.

Within three miles of the farm on which he grew up my father bought a vast alder swamp and proceeded to reclaim it. He then built a spacious house and barns and miles of stone walls; he planted trees and orchards and created a beautiful old world garden protected by a wind-break of tall pine trees. There was everything and more on the place to enlarge the vision and impress the mind of a growing boy or girl, and my seven brothers and I derived no small part of our education for life in any community from our spacious home environment, freedom to go and come, and early participation in the varied social life of a self-contained village in which lived every kind of character. I cannot remember ever feeling bored or at a loss for things to do, places to go, or interesting people to know.

From the age of ten until I graduated at seventeen I attended Limerick Academy. School was always an intensely social experience to me. I did my real study at home and spent school hours "listening in" on recitations, reading French, Latin, or English with one or more congenial spirits, exchanging political views, or planning dramatic entertainments.

After graduating from Limerick Academy I spent two years at Bradford (Massachusetts) Academy. It was a puzzle to know what to do on leaving Bradford in the 'nineties if one did not want to teach or become a missionary. I finally determined to "read law" with my father as two of my brothers had done. My father's sudden death put an end to a plan we had already entered upon with mutual pleasure and anticipation. For four years I was completely absorbed by family obligations. When these responsibilities were lifted I felt the need of constructive training of some kind and I entered the Library School of Pratt Institute, from which I was graduated in 1896.

During that year I discovered and fell in love with the city of New York although I confidently hoped to be a pioneer in travel-ing library work in the State of Maine. I corresponded with the State Librarian and the State Superintendent of Education and accepted without hesitation a proposal of the latter to give a course of daily lectures on library methods of study to teachers of elementary schools at a summer school held at Saco, Maine. In conjunction with these lectures I opened the library of Thornton Academy and invited the teachers to come and discuss their problems with me. This was an innovation and prophetic of future experience in demonstrating that essential library and school problems concerned with books are the same in Maine, New York, Iowa, Utah, and other states where I have lectured.

I have held only two library positions, that of Children's Librarian of the Pratt Institute Free Library from 1896 to 1906 and that of Supervisor of Work with Children in the New York Public Library from 1906 to 1941. In neither position have I had a predecessor. Both have involved shaping policies, training assistants, and wide comparative reading of children's books with books in general.

I still thrill to the season's output of new books when called upon to make a selection for the *Horn Book*. I have crossed the seas to visit children's libraries in Sweden, Norway, Denmark, England, France, Belgium, and Holland, but I always come back to New York as my own place. It is a romantic and a never-ending adventure to share the reading of boys and girls of many races in a great cosmopolitan city.

*   *   *

Anne Carroll Moore is in many ways the best-known person in the field of children's literature in America. To young readers she is known as the author of the "Nicholas" books and as the editor of Irving's *Knickerbocker's History of New York* and *The Bold Dragoon*. Among adults she is recognized for her leadership in children's library work and as an authority on young people's reading. Her *My Roads to Childhood* and *Three Owls* books are considered foremost critical sources on contemporary literature for children. She is also known widely as a lecturer and as the author of numerous magazine and newspaper articles. In 1932 she was awarded the Diploma of Honor by Pratt Institute, and in 1940, the degree of Doctor of Humane Letters by the University of Maine.

ANNE CARROLL MOORE

Clare Newberry

1903-

AUTHOR AND ILLUSTRATOR OF
Mittens, April's Kittens, Smudge, Etc.

Autobiographical sketch of Clare Turlay
Newberry:

I WAS born in Enterprise, Oregon, but
spent most of my childhood in Vancouver, Washington. My grandparents were
all pioneers, and I am a mixture of English,
Scotch, Irish, French, and German.

According to my mother I began drawing
shortly before my second birthday, and
from then on pencils, crayons, and later
watercolors were favorite playthings. I always adored kittens, and drew them from
the very beginning. At six or seven I began
to want to be an illustrator of fairy tales,
and in my teens I spent a good deal of time
making careful watercolor pictures for my
favorite stories. At sixteen I sold my first
drawings—a series of paper dolls for *John
Martin's Book.*

After graduating from Vancouver High
School I spent a year at the University of
Oregon, where I began to draw from life.
After that came a year at the art school of
the Portland Art Museum, and a term at
the San Francisco School of Fine Arts. Then
I quit school to be married, but continued to
study by myself in my spare time for several years.

In 1930 I went to Paris, where I worked
mornings on my first book, *Herbert the
Lion,* and sketched afternoons at the
Grande Chaumiere croquis class. *Herbert
the Lion* was published in 1931, and the
same year I returned to the United States
and continued studying by myself. By this
time I had decided to be a portrait painter,
and it was not until 1934 that I began to
draw cats from life (although I had always
been interested in them and had put them
into nearly all my stories and illustrations).
Now, however, I began to study them with
the same intensity with which I had formerly studied human beings, and the more
I worked the more fascinated I became.

In 1936 my first kitten book, *Mittens,*
was published, and became a best seller.
Mittens was my own tabby kitten, and the
little boy in the book was my son Stephen.
The next year *Babette,* the story of a Siamese

CLARE NEWBERRY

kitten, was published. Then came nine more
books.

All my illustrations, with the exception
of those in *Herbert the Lion,* are done
from life or from life studies. I use pencil,
conté crayon, pen-and-ink, watercolors, and
pastels.

At present I divide my time between
New York City, and Taos, New Mexico,
where there are not only plenty of cats and
dogs to draw, but many other animals as
well.

Covelle Newcomb

1908-

AUTHOR OF
Vagabond in Velvet, The Secret Door, Etc.

Autobiographical sketch of Covelle Newcomb:

COVELLE NEWCOMB was born in San
Antonio, Texas. Her first literary try
was an essay on the newspaper career of her
grandfather, the late Honorable James Pear-
son Newcomb, fiery journalist and secretary
of state under Governor Davis. For this she
won a scholarship to the University of Texas
and a twenty-five dollar check. She spent
the money and saved the scholarship as a
souvenir, attending instead Incarnate Word
College in San Antonio, and then making
her way to Washington University in St.
Louis, and to Hunter College, New York

Covelle Newcomb: *koh VELL NEW kum*

COVELLE NEWCOMB

University, and Columbia University, in New York.

Before she made writing her profession Miss Newcomb took a fling at a pre-med course, then child delinquency, then criminology, but these interests, she came to realize, were impulses rather than the solid and lasting urge that launches one upon a life-time career. Even so, writing seemed the last resort. She tried teaching first.

She is four feet eleven inches small. Advised she would never make the grade at teaching English to youngsters who towered over her and who, because of her size, would never take her seriously, she listened to these warnings until she came to believe them herself. Tired of making the effort, useless at best, to appear tall in authority if short in length, she decided it would be easier to hold the attention of young people by means of the printed page. Also reading, she figured, performed the magic of creating mental pictures of the author which could be quite gratifying, whether true or not. This has happened in her case. Most of her readers, she says, imagine her to be tall, dark, and glamorous, and a great number of her fans still address her, when writing, as "Dear Sir"!

This illusion was pleasing until she went out lecturing. Teachers and students were amazed to see a small, slender, blue-eyed blonde standing at the door. On several occasions she was met by a portress who mistook her for a student and shunted her

around to the back door. In fact, this has happened so often that she has acquired the title, Back Door Author.

She doesn't know how she became a writer. "It just happened."

"Writing," she says, "has a charm and fascination and madness all its own. It is a perpetual challenge and a perpetual gamble, one's success depending entirely on the public taste, on reaction to subject matter and to the manner in which it is presented. You stand ready to win or to lose, but in either case the plaguing urge to try again remains."

Covelle Newcomb is married to artist-author Addison Burbank (*The Cedar Deer,* etc.), who illustrates most of her books. They live in Port Jefferson, Long Island, New York.

Miss Newcomb's first book, *Black Fire,* was published in 1940. In 1942 she received the Downey Medal for "the finest American children's book of 1941 written in the Catholic tradition," for her story-biography of Cardinal Newman, *The Red Hat.*

She is a member of the Gallery of Living Catholic Authors, the Authors' League of America, the American Writers' Association, and the New York Pen and Brush Club.

Miss Newcomb's vigorous interest in story-biography stems from the conviction that its value in giving young people a sense of kinship with the world's great men and women cannot be overemphasized.

Helen Nicolay

March 9, 1866-

AUTHOR OF

The Boys' Life of Abraham Lincoln, The Boys' Life of Alexander Hamilton, Etc.

Autobiographical sketch of Helen Nicolay:

WHILE it is hardly true to say I began writing biographies for young people "by accident," it was certainly not premeditated. As a child I was much interested in drawing, and there was a foregone conclusion that I should become an artist, drawing being an engrossing and suitable occupation for an only child who was not over-strong, and whose parents seemed to like to have her in their immediate neighborhood. My first literary venture, a novel begun at the age of seven, was so manifestly common-

Nicolay: *nik oh LAY*

place and lacking in imagination that even its author recognized the fact.

But from the time of my birth on March 9, 1866, in Paris, where my father was acting as American Consul General, I lived in a literary atmosphere. My father had been an editor before he became President Lincoln's private secretary; and soon after my parents returned to America when I was three years old, my father began active work upon the literary task that occupied him for the next twenty-five years—writing in collaboration with John Hay their ten-volume life of Abraham Lincoln.

That great task became the central fact around which our lives revolved; and as my father was almost an invalid, handicapped by very serious eye trouble, this necessitated much reading aloud and writing from dictation on the part of members of the family. I believe I was twelve when I was allowed to copy a footnote just as it was to go into the great book. If I live a hundred years I shall never again feel so happy and important. As I grew older I was given a more serious part in the work, including that of reading proof. In fact, this sort of training became my equivalent of a college course, for I never went regularly to school.

My father dictated rather slowly, and being the kindest and most patient of men, he did not object to my having two sheets of paper on the desk before me; one for the task in hand, the other upon which I might scribble at my own sweet will during the intervals of waiting. (I am happy to say I never got the papers mixed!) Almost automatically my sheet of paper began to show attempts at poems and plays and short sketches—most of which shared the fate of their elder sister, the novel begun so long ago; but my parents were always wise and sympathetic, never laughing at my attempts, or unduly praising them. In time this sort of thing gave me confidence in the use of words, and I look back upon it as an important part of my training.

After my father's death I was called upon to write the concluding pages of a one-volume life of Lincoln that he had almost completed. Then the publishers asked me to write *The Boys' Life of Lincoln*—a condensation of the work already done by my father—and after that the other biographies came along in succession, each, in a way, being the outgrowth of the last.

When asked why I call my books "Boys' Lives" of this or that great American, I can only answer that so far nobody I have consulted has been able to suggest a better title. What is really meant is a biography written from a young person's point of view. "Young folks" is a clumsy phrase; no boy worth his salt would be caught reading a book for girls—while girls do not object to reading books written for boys, and are often astonished to find the viewpoint so like their own. Clearness of statement, enough historical "background" to give an idea of the state of society in which the subject of the biography lived and worked, and a sympathetic outlook have been my aim.

That covers the "why" and the "how" of my writing. There is little to add, except that I have lived most of my life in Washington, beautiful as a city and most interesting as a place of residence, where history and historical people flow by in a never ending stream. My summers are usually spent on the shores of a beautiful lake in New Hampshire, where I have a cottage and a studio. I am still interested in making pictures, though that has taken second place now, and is used chiefly to make watercolor notes of places and things seen on trips abroad or in our Western national parks.

I am unmarried, but, I hope, not an old maid. At any rate, many young people honor me with their friendship, and seem to consider me about their own age.

Jeannette Covert Nolan

1896-

AUTHOR OF

The Story of Clara Barton of the Red Cross, Florence Nightingale, Etc.

Autobiographical sketch of Jeannette Covert Nolan:

LOOKING back through the years, I am unable to fix upon the exact date at which I decided to become an author, but I know I must have been rather young because I was only nine when my first "work" appeared in print. This was a poem published in *St. Nicholas* in a contest conducted by the League. Though my memory of the poem is vague—it was an ode to spring—I still cherish the silver badge I was awarded. As I recall, my happiness at receiving the badge was somewhat marred by a realization

Covert: *KOH vert*

that many other successful contestants were very much younger than I, and a fear that perhaps I had postponed too long the launching of a literary career.

I was born and reared in Evansville, Indiana, attended the public schools there, and was graduated from the high school, where I had served as editor of the weekly paper and the senior yearbook. I did not go to college, a fact I have never ceased to regret; but at seventeen I was fortunate enough to get a job as reporter and feature writer on the staff of the Evansville *Courier*, a job I thoroughly enjoyed and in which I continued for nearly three years, until my marriage.

Later, as our three children were growing up and I turned again to the business of writing, I had reason to be grateful for my newspaper experience and training. There is nothing, I think, more valuable to an author than the discipline imposed by a newspaper office's routine and I heartily recommend it to any young person whose ambition is to write.

In 1931 I sold to *St. Nicholas* my first piece of fiction, a short story, "The Prisoner." The next year my first book, *Barry Barton's Mystery*, was published and this was soon followed by a second juvenile novel, *The Young Douglas*. Since then I have contributed short stories and serials to several young people's magazines and have written twelve books for boys and girls. I take great pride in being listed as a Junior Author; though I have written a number of adult novels, I feel more at home and at ease with young people. I like their responsiveness and appreciation; also I have learned a lot from them and have implicit faith in both their intelligence and their basic integrity.

Most of my books have been biographies or stories with a historical setting. Reading is one of my two hobbies; the other is being outdoors—walking and exercising if I must, but preferably just sitting either in sunshine or moonlight. Despite these predilections, and the fact that I have no regular schedule for writing, I somehow manage to spend a good many hours each day at my desk.

For several years I have lectured on creative writing at the Indiana University writers' conferences and am an instructor for the Indiana University Extension. I taught one year at the James Whitcomb Riley Hospital for Crippled Children; and, spacing these activities, have written articles, editorials, and a column for Indiana newspapers. Many of my books have had English editions, syndicated publication in newspapers, and have been translated into Braille. A number of my short stories are included in anthologies and in textbooks used in literature courses in schools. My present home is in Indianapolis.

Frances Jenkins Olcott

AUTHOR AND COMPILER
Bible Stories to Read and Tell, Bridge of Caravans, In the Bright Syrian Land, Etc.

Autobiographical sketch of Frances Jenkins Olcott:

IN the city of Paris, near the Garden of the Batignolles, was my birthplace. My elder sister, born in the aristocratic quarter of the Madeleine with exiled royalty across the way, used to hurt my young feelings by saying, "You are bourgeoise. You were born in the Batignolles." But nowadays the election officer says, "Put her down born in the United States."

This confusion, due to my having been born in the Consular Service, does not obscure many delightful childhood memories of Nantes-on-the-Loire, to which ancient city of the Dukes of Brittany my father, Franklin Olcott, was transferred. The musical French of that Loire district was my first

JEANNETTE COVERT NOLAN

speech, forming the vocal organs, though the speech itself faded like an echo, later in America.

There followed some years in Albany, New York, where I had two homes, my parents' and my Grandmother Olcott's. Followed after, a few years in the country suburbs of Albany, years of delight in nature, of study, of research, of kindling thoughts; for my father and mother were my tutors. My mother, with her remarkable, eager mind, fine critical powers, and delicate feelings for words, exercised a strong influence on my writings. She herself, Julia Olcott, translated children's stories from the French.

My father, American born, was university bred in Germany—at Goettingen and Wuerzburg—and had a research mind. He delighted in poetry and in the exact use of strong or beautiful words. Because for many years he had served in the consular service in different lands, he was cosmopolitan, and his conversation was an education in itself. He tutored me in German and the classics much as German students in his day were trained, letting me outline my own lessons for the large part, and making me trace even slight details to their sources. That was no drudgery to me, for my mind was naturally formed that way.

Not to be overlooked are the religious influences of my two homes: the dignified, more formal influence of my grandmother's; and the Bible-reading atmosphere of my parents'; for the latter held family Bible reading and prayers night and morning. Both influences have wrought deeply upon my writings.

From early days, it was my ambition to become a librarian. Because I had been privately tutored I had to acquire a high school certificate before entering the New York State Library School. So I took regents' examinations for the certificate. Then came the entrance examinations to the Library School. I entered and graduated. Who can describe the radiant happiness of those library school days?

One may ask: What are the American products of an education so largely European in character? One of the products was the development of the first educational system of children's libraries for a whole community, by the Carnegie Library of Pittsburgh when I was head of its children's department. The system became a pipe line, pouring streams of good reading for children into the homes, schools, and other institutions of Pittsburgh. The deparment became a laboratory to test methods of guiding reading, to evolve standards for selecting juvenile books, to work out practical problems of discipline and organization.

Since leaving Pittsburgh and devoting myself to writing, another product of this accumulation of influences and experiences has been about twenty-four volumes, carrying into homes, schools, and libraries the inspiring messages handed on to me by many others.

One thread of my own has woven itself through this my life's fabric, an understanding love for children, forming a purposeful and distinct design—the literary education of youth—which in return seems to bring me the love and confidence of the children.

One strong influence on my mind, from babyhood, gave me a fascination for all things Oriental. My father, United States Consul in Jerusalem, brought home large photographs of the Holy City. The domed, minareted city, displayed on our walls in panorama and detail, was ever before my eyes. My imagination fired, I have edited two volumes of the *Arabian Nights*, a volume of Persian tales, and after a recent stay of more than a year in the Holy Lands studying Biblical geography and history, I have written two books for young folk and Bible readers.

During the rest of my life, the Lord willing, I plan to make better known, to our young people, Bible things in the Holy Lands.

Virginia Olcott

AUTHOR OF
Holiday Plays for Home, School and Settlement; World Children's Series; Etc.

Biographical sketch of Virginia Olcott by her sister, Frances Jenkins Olcott:

VIRGINIA OLCOTT, social worker and author, was born in Albany, New York, youngest of a family of ten brothers and sisters. Before she could speak, she was dramatizing with the older ones long stories that continued from day to day. The little girl, with blue eyes and copper-colored curls, lived in this drama land of play. Her dramatic instinct developed and bore practical fruit.

Virginia was privately tutored; but because her parents believed in letting their children follow natural tastes, she unconsciously absorbed riches from great literature. But being practical as well as esthetic, on coming to live in New York when she was seventeen, she entered a kindergarten training school, graduated, and taught in kindergarten and on playground. Here again her dramatic instinct had exercise. A year's service as children's librarian at the Carnegie Library of Pittsburgh stimulated her gift of dramatic story telling.

There followed nine years during which she was associate head worker of the Schools Settlement, Brooklyn, New York, and also director of dramatics. She wrote plays for her groups of young people, trained the actors, and staged the plays. These one-and two-act dramas were later published in book form.

Social settlement work among foreign-Americans creates a sympathetic international understanding. So what more natural than that Virginia Olcott should visit some of the homelands from which came the foreigners among whom she had lived and worked in America? She began to travel. She spent a year in France working with French war orphans. She collected up-to-date data for plays and stories.

Twenty foreign countries Virginia Olcott has visited, living among the people, watching the children. She has found a friendly welcome, whether among Dutch, Swedes, Norwegians, Danes, or Italians, as well as among Syrians and other folk of Bible lands. She has gone into a Lapp tent in Lapland, and let the Lapp woman finger her American clothes with delight. But meanwhile Virginia Olcott, the trained observer, was noting the details of Lapp housekeeping; while outside the tent she noted and inquired about the details of the reindeer industry.

After having returned from a long journey and from months of study and collecting facts, seated in her studio in New York, she has clothed in flesh and blood the children of the lands she has visited.

It has been said of Virginia Olcott, she "dreams of an international friendship among children," and "she knows children in . many lands. She visits them in their strange homes—now sitting with children in a mud hut in Syria, drinking thick coffee;

now peeping at them keeping house in a Moorish courtyard in Algeria; now smiling at Jerusalem babies; now helping little French war orphans. Perhaps yesterday she was watching children drink lemonade in Egypt, or go to school in Switzerland. And, tomorrow, who knows where American Virginia Olcott will be?"

Helen Fuller Orton

November 1, 1872-

<small>AUTHOR OF</small>

*The Cloverfield Farm stories, The Treasure
in the Little Trunk, Etc.*

Autobiographical sketch of Helen Fuller Orton:

I WAS born and grew up on a farm in western New York, twelve miles east of Niagara Falls. Our rambling farmhouse stood at the end of a long lane. In the village of Sanborn, a mile south, the family got the mail and the groceries, had the horses shod, and took the train for the city. In Pekin, a mile north, we went to church· and to school. That village stands on the crest of the mountain ridge, which extends from the Niagara River to Rochester. From the main street we could see Lake Ontario twelve miles to the north, and on clear days could even see the Canadian shore, forty miles away.

My first schooling was in a little red schoolhouse that stood a mile away from our home if we went cross-lots. When the weather was good the walk through orchards and meadows was very interesting and pleasant. But it was so far that I was not sent to school till I was seven and a half. I was taught reading and arithmetic by my mother and father; and I early browsed among the books in the old-fashioned parlor.

In those days my father, Merritt B. Fuller, farmed in summer and taught school in winter. Twice he was called in to take over a school when the large boys "put the teacher out." My mother, Lucy Ann Taylor Fuller, besides looking after four children and attending to household duties and teaching a class in Sunday school, managed to take the Chautauqua course, do the forty minutes of required reading each day for four years, and go to Chautauqua on Commencement Day to get her diploma. So I

HELEN FULLER ORTON

grew up in an atmosphere of country life and of books.

I had a sister named Amanda, older than myself, and two brothers younger, Clarence and Merritt. Our ancestors all came from England in the early 1600's and settled in Massachusetts and Connecticut. One signed the Mayflower Compact. His name was William Brewster.

The Fuller family lived in what the city relatives referred to as "a lonely place," but we children never found it lonely or dull. There were endless things of interest—birds, small animals, and wild flowers in the woods and meadows, brooks where we could sail little boats, an old orchard where we could climb and make playhouses among the branches of the big trees. There was fun in the snow in winter.

Always books and magazines were lying about. We children would race to the gate to get the *Youth's Companion* or *St. Nicholas* when someone came from the village with the mail.

After a year at the little red schoolhouse, there came a few years in the village school; then high school in Lockport, the city ten miles away, where I liked best English literature, history, and Latin, and least writing compositions. I always greatly loved music and stayed out of high school a whole year to practice at the piano four hours a day.

In 1895, after teaching two years, I married Jesse F. Orton and we went to live in Ann Arbor, Michigan, where he taught eco-nomics and studied law in the University of Michigan. Without formal registration, I attended classes and did the first year's work, taking economics, history, and psychology.

We moved to New York in 1908 from Grand Rapids and now live in Jackson Heights. Our three older sons were born in Michigan. Our youngest is a native of New York City.

For years I told stories to our own boys and the neighborhood children, often making them up as I went along. Early in 1920 I wrote my first story, "How Rover Got the Cows out of the Corn." For the next three months I kept on writing stories, one each week, drawing largely on my own happy memories. I took the fifteen stories to a publisher, who brought them out in 1921 under the title, *Prince and Rover of Clover-field Farm*.

In the next five years three more Clover-field Farm books came out, as well as *The Little Lost Pigs*. These were followed by more books, one each year.

By this time I was finding it fun to write for boys and girls and was eager to try my hand at a historical story. I was greatly interested in the migration of New England people to western New York in the early part of the nineteenth century when the Genesee country was opened for settlement, and I began to study the period intensively. The result was *The Treasure in the Little Trunk*.

This book met with such a kind reception that I was encouraged to attempt another historical story. I was asked by a prominent educator of western New York to study the history of the Niagara frontier. From that study came *The Gold-Laced Coat*, in 1934. Writing historical stories is fascinating, re-quiring an author to read old records, manu-scripts, letters and diaries, to study old maps, and to visit historic places.

The stories that have given me the most fun in writing are mystery stories for boys and girls of the in-between age. How they love a mystery tucked away in a story! I find I can make it exciting without bringing in crime or violence or anything horrible or offensive.

For many years I have lived in New York City, not on the island of Manhattan, which the Indians sold to the white men for twenty-four dollars, but across the East River on Long Island. From my study windows I can look five miles toward the west to the skyline of the great city, a beautiful sight. I love that sight, but I also love the place where I grew up, within sound of the roar of Niagara Falls. There I roamed the fields with my brothers, picked wild flowers in the woods, climbed the big old apple trees, rushed into the house to give Mother the first violets of spring, gathered nuts in the fall, and trudged through deep snow to school in winter. It was a happy life and it was the foundation of my books for children.

* * *

Mrs. Orton has had more than twenty-five books published. Some years ago, when she brought out her twentieth, E. L. Buell wrote that it had "the same simplicity of style and easy flow which have made many of its predecessors so helpful to children who are just beginning to experience the delight of reading to themselves."

"James Otis"

March 19, 1848-December 11, 1912

AUTHOR OF

Toby Tyler, Mr. Stubbs' Brother, Etc.

ONE morning in the early 'eighties an unkempt, shabbily clad stranger appeared at the door of the editor of *Harper's Young People.*

"Are you the editor?" he inquired.

"Yes."

"Buy all the stories?"

"By no means," the editor replied, "I do not accept more than one in a—"

"Of course that is understood," the stranger interrupted. "But what I want to get at is, do you pay for a story when you accept it, or must the author wait until it is published?"

"Our custom is to pay for a manuscript upon acceptance, but—"

"That is what I was told, and that is why I came here first. I am desperately in need of a little ready money. Two weeks ago I was the editor of a bankrupt American paper in London. At the final smash I had barely enough to pay for a steerage passage home. I have here a story I wrote on the way over, working at it night and day; and it is a bang-up yarn, if I do say so. Now, if you will just let me read it to you—"

To his great disappointment he was told that it would take three days for a decision. When the editor, noting his hungry look, took him to lunch and they were seated in a private room in the old Astor House he produced his manuscript without apology and began to read aloud. Ignoring both food and the suggestion that he postpone his reading until he had eaten, he read on until the editor knew he had to have the story.

"And you'll pay for it at once?"

"Oh, no," replied the editor. "It is too late to get the money today, but if you will leave the manuscript with me and call at the office—say, day after tomorrow, I will—"

"Great Scott, man! Don't you understand? I must raise the money on that story today—now! Why, my wife is still on that horrible ship, held—oh, well, no matter! I simply must raise money somehow on this story today or—"

Breaking the usual procedure in paying for manuscripts, the editor borrowed enough to make a first payment on it. *Toby Tyler* was published in one of the earliest volumes of *Harper's Young People,* and James Otis, neatly dressed and so changed when he called again a few days later that the editor at first failed to recognize him, from that time was a frequent writer for that magazine.

James Otis, or James Otis Kaler, as he was known outside his books, had made his living with his pen for years before he wrote *Toby Tyler.* Born in Maine at Winterport, then called Frankfort, he had no inclination to follow the occupation of his father, who was a leading hotel man, and left home when barely seventeen after a public school education, determined to make his own way. He had a natural gift for writing, and soon became associated with the Boston *Journal.* Later he went to New York, working on the staff of several papers there and in many odd bypaths of literature. At one time he wrote beautiful sermons that were syndicated by a house in Philadelphia and no doubt preached to congregations in many parts of the country. In his spare time he wrote stories and finally secured an editorial position with Frank Leslie's *Boys and Girls* and also contributed to *St. Nicholas* and other periodicals. His most distinctive early work was *The Perkins Letters.*

Money meant very little to Otis except when he had none. At one time he invested nearly all he received for a story in an unseaworthy steam yacht and was perfectly happy so long as he had enough to pay wages for its necessary repair.

Toby Tyler, his most popular work, was published in 1880. Otis has told us that Toby was a "really" boy and not an imaginary one, that he lived in that sleepy little village which Otis called Guilford, and grew up and had children of his own. He has also told us that Uncle Daniel, Aunt Olive, Abner, Bob, Leander, and others were real. Like Toby, Otis had a restless disposition, and for a while he traveled with a circus as a publicity man, wandered about the country with the show, and made the acquaintance of the fat woman, Mr. Stubbs, Old Ben, and all the rest of its fascinating life. Job Lord was a character he created himself. *Mr. Stubbs' Brother*, a second volume, soon followed, and thirty-two years after *Toby Tyler* he published the third volume of the series, *Old Ben*. As time went on the number of his books rapidly increased. He won popularity with other stories, also. He published nearly a hundred and fifty books, mostly stories for young people.

At about fifty Otis returned to Maine, where he became superintendent of schools at South Portland. Here he enjoyed association with young people, for whom all his life he had a deep sympathy. He had an ideal home life, and two sons, Stephen and Otis. He was a jovial, sociable man, with a great fondness for outdoor life. In vacations he wrote, read, and enjoyed the sea breezes in a modest summer home at the end of a long point of land stretching out into the sea beyond South Portland, or camped and fished among the forests and lakes. He died in Portland at the age of sixty-four.

Maxfield Parrish

July 25, 1870-

ILLUSTRATOR OF
Arabian Nights, Wonder Book and Tanglewood Tales, Etc.

"**F**RED is more of an artisan than an artist," once remarked the distinguished etcher and landscape painter, Stephen Parrish, of his son, Frederick Maxfield Parrish. Maxfield inherited leanings toward both art and mechanics, the former from his father, several members of whose family, Quaker folk of Philadelphia, where Maxfield was born, were artists. From the side of his mother, Elizabeth Bancroft Parrish, whose people were mechanics, he inherited a love of machinery.

The earliest ambition of the little curly-headed boy was to be a carpenter, but at the age of five he commenced to draw, and all through high school and college he drew and manifested his decorative talent. When he had finished college he applied for a job in an architect's office, but being advised to get an art education first he entered the Pennsylvania Academy of Fine Arts, and later studied under Howard Pyle at Drexel Institute. His first picture, a drawing of clowns, was sold while he was still a student to the distinguished architect Walter Cape.

At twenty-five Parrish married Lydia Austin, a woman of unusual artistic talent. A location of rare beauty was acquired for a home in the New Hampshire hills, and a little cottage built upon it. Then illness came and under the doctor's orders he traveled for some time with his wife. At Saranac he tried to work out-of-doors in a temperature so low he had to sit on one hand to warm it while he worked with the other, and the ink froze. From the Adirondacks he went to Arizona, where he absorbed the vivid colors of canyon, mountain, and painted desert, leading to many pictures reproduced in the *Century Magazine*. A trip to Italy followed, in the course of which he became familiar with the particular landscape beauty of that country, later to be used in illustrating Edith Wharton's *Italian Villas and Their Gardens*.

A deep-toned picture, "The Sandman," won his admission to the Society of American Artists, the first of a number of art societies to which he later belonged, and a poster competition of the *Century Magazine* in which he won second prize, being debarred from the first because his picture required five instead of three printings, brought him to the notice of the public and gave him the opportunity to make a number of posters and pictures for the *Century Magazine, St. Nicholas, Harper's Magazine, Scribner's,* and others. At one time he contributed exclusively to *Collier's* for a period of two years. Soon he began to be sought as an illustrator of books.

Parrish has been called "one of those rare illustrators who never disappoint." His illustrations for Kenneth Grahame's *Golden Age* and Irving's *Knickerbocker's History of New York* won for him high praise and recognized position. Grahame's *Dream Days* and Eugene Field's *Poems of Childhood* gave him further opportunity to express the poetic beauty and simplicity of the child world, and the *Arabian Nights' Entertainments* the world of imaginative romance. One of his most beautiful pictures for Field's poems was for "The Dinkey Bird," showing a child swinging through space from a limb of the Amfulala-tree.

The work of Parrish is strongly individual, and is marked by a richness of color, his "Parrish blue" being distinctive. His pictures are often elaborate, and sometimes show great attention to detail; his humor is without ugliness. In his strivings for original effects he liked sometimes to paint on very heavy parchment, obtaining sumptuous and luminous effects in color by repeated glazes over a design laid in and lightly modeled. He was also fond from childhood of making paper cut-outs, and could often contrive with the scissors figures that he would otherwise find it difficult to draw.

Someone once said he used to regret that Parrish landscapes could not be duplicated in nature, and later, in motoring up the hills on the New Hampshire-Vermont border, he discovered the whole countryside might have been laid out by this artist. Parrish spends most of the year in his home in the Cornish hills of New Hampshire—finding in its remoteness the necessary solitude for his work. The cottage which he moved into before the roof was on, and, with the aid of the local carpenter, added to at his leisure from time to time until it became a beautiful, rambling story-and-a-half structure of fifteen rooms and five baths, thoroughly expresses his individuality and workmanship within and without. One of his proudest achievements is to have built a home to which his three grown sons and his daughter love to return.

In the back of his home is his studio, and on the floor below a fully equipped machine shop, with lathes, drills, saws, presses, and other machines electrically run, which have the same attraction for him as artistic work. "A mechanic who paints pictures," he once called himself. Here he makes with his own hands columns and vases to throw the shadows and other objects for his artistic work, as well as ornamental metal work, paneling, choice furniture, and things for the improvement of his home.

Ethel Parton

December 1, 1862-February 27, 1944

AUTHOR OF

Runaway Prentice, Vinny Applegay, Tabitha Mary, Melissa Ann, Etc.

Autobiographical sketch of Ethel Parton, written for THE JUNIOR BOOK OF AUTHORS a few years before her death:

I WAS born in New York City. Parents: Mortimer Thomson, American humorist, pen name Philander Doesticks, and Grace Eldredge, daughter of Sarah Willis Eldredge, pen name Fanny Fern, whose father, Nathaniel Willis, was the founder of the *Youth's Companion*, first periodical for children, which had a century of independent existence before merging with the *American Boy*. Still further back in the days of the Revolution, another Nathaniel Willis edited a patriotic newspaper in Boston.

Belonging on my mother's side to Massachusetts, in the northeastern corner of which, in the small, ancient city of Newburyport on the Merrimac River, I have spent most of my life; on my father's I belong to New York, where I spent the first few years of my childhood.

My mother died when I was a month old, my father while I still was very young. I was brought up in the home first of my grandmother, "Fanny Fern," and later of her daughter, my Aunt Ellen, and of my uncle by marriage, James Parton, biographer, lecturer, and essayist. Never for a moment was I allowed to feel myself an orphan, and when I came of age I legally changed my name to Parton, at their wish and my own.

I had a most happy childhood, fortunate in my home, my friends, and my teachers. I did not attend school until nearly eleven, being taught at home by Mr. Parton, who was a wonderful teacher, and having from the time I could handle books the free run of his library. In Newburyport I went to the remarkable school of Jane Andrews, writer of books for children; then to the Newburyport High School (or more precisely to the Putnam Free School, practically an endowed division of it).

Before I graduated in 1880, my first articles had appeared in the *Youth's Companion*, to which, as a member of the editorial staff, I later contributed miscellany for over forty years. After graduation I declined the opportunity of college to remain at home as secretary and literary assistant and occasional collaborator for James Parton; a choice which was, I am sure, though made for other reasons, of more than equal educative value.

Not until after leaving the *Youth's Companion* did I turn to the writing of books. I had already written some few ballads and stories for children, with historical themes and settings, most of which appeared in *St. Nicholas*; and I found it was for children I most wished to write.

For *The Mule of the Parthenon*, my first book, though the second published, I spent months of delightful preparation, steeped in the literature and history of ancient Greece. *Melissa Ann* came next, and with Melissa and its successor, *Tabitha Mary*, I turned to the city where I live, whose history and traditions I have absorbed not from printed chronicles alone, but from living lips, as they are passed down, even today, in fine old deeply rooted families. I have been able to weave into a fictional narrative also many true incidents told me by my aunt and grandmother, in the days when I used to beg for a "when-you-were-a-little-girl" story. And I have found much enjoyment in trying to bring alive for American children of our own time a group of old-fashioned New England girls and boys.

Another pleasure is that I find thinking so much of the ways and feelings of children brings my own childhood back to me. This gives me a warm comradely feeling with my own book-children so that when they have fun, I have fun too. It is like getting away from grown-ups and being all of an age together.

I might perhaps think this the best pleasure of all, except that, of course, the very best is when flesh-and-blood children of today (with their imaginations in good working order) are nice enough to find my children of the past as real as I do.

* * *

Ethel Parton was an early suffragist. Although she had been on the editorial staff and writing for the *Youth's Companion* (started by her great-grandfather, Nathaniel Willis) for more than forty years, her first and her most famous book, *Melissa Ann,* was not published until she was sixty-nine years old. She died in Newburyport in her eighty-second year.

Edith M. Patch

July 27, 1876-

AUTHOR OF
Holiday Pond, Holiday Meadow, First Lessons in Nature Study, Etc.

Autobiographical sketch of Edith M. Patch:

UNTIL I was eight, I lived at the edge of Worcester, Massachusetts, where I could play in a pine grove, on a checkerberry hill, beside a brook where tadpoles and minnows swam among the watercress stems, and in a meadow bright with daisies.

In 1884 I said good-by to the much-loved New England home and went to Minnesota. My father bought a farm north of Minneapolis. There I took delight in roaming across a prairie in which grew flowers with such strange names as gosling,

EDITH M. PATCH

painted cup, puccoon. I met western meadowlarks that wove dome-shaped roofs over their nests of dry grass; and I called quietly at their homes to see when their eggs hatched and how their nestlings' feathers were growing. It was interesting, too, to watch the pocket gophers—those industrious little tunneling engineers with fur-lined pockets in their cheeks.

One of my favorite trails led about a mile from our home to the Mississippi River. When the logs in the river were close enough together, I ran on them— jumping from one moving log to another near it. The floating logs served as a drifting bridge of the most exciting sort. By running and jumping rapidly, I often crossed this bridge to reach an island so beautiful I think of it every spring. The boughs of the tall trees formed a leafy roof high overhead; and the island carpet was sometimes white with the flowers of bloodroot, and at other times colored with blue phlox or yellow violets.

Since I spent much time out-of-doors, it was natural for me to think about what I saw in the woods and fields. When my teachers asked their classes to write essays, I would often write about some bird or butterfly or blossom. During my senior year at high school, I wrote about the life of the monarch butterfly, which was one of my favorite insects. A grade teacher to whom my teacher showed this essay asked me to read it to the children in her room. When I had finished, the teacher said to me, before all the boys and girls in the room, "Promise me that, whatever else you do during your life, you will save some time to do nature writing for young people." Her voice was very earnest and I was surprised, but I promised I would do as she wished.

I have kept that promise I made in 1896 by writing more than fifty nature stories which have been published in magazines for children and I have written eighteen books for junior readers.

Perhaps you think fifty magazine articles and eighteen books is not very much writing to do in so many years. You are right, and I must explain that I have been busier in other ways. In 1903 I came to the Maine Agricultural Experiment Station to organize and to take charge of the Department of Entomology. (*Entomology* comes from a Greek word meaning *insect.*) I was occupied there for thirty-four years studying insects and writing bulletins about them for farmers and scientists. In 1914 I bought my present home at Orono, Maine, with river ledge, meadow, and woodland, and gave it the Scotch name, Braeside, in honor of the bluebells.

I retired from the experiment station in 1937 as entomologist emeritus and was given the honorary degree of D.Sc. by the University of Maine. In 1938 I spent several months with eighteen American entomologists traveling in Europe. In August of that year we attended the international congress of entomologists in Berlin.

Grace A. Paull

1898-

ILLUSTRATOR, AND AUTHOR OF
*Squash for the Fair, Pancakes
for Breakfast, Etc.*

Autobiographical sketch of Grace A. Paull:

I WAS born in upstate New York, received my schooling in Utica, Glens Falls, and Montreal, Canada, my art training at Pratt Institute and with Alexander Archipenko, George Bridgman, and Allen Lewis. I have worked at lithography with George C. Miller. I am fond of the medium and have found it very adaptable to book illustration. The black and white drawings are made on stones, after which they are transferred from the original proofs to the large press plates. Three of my books have been done by this method. I do, however, use other media and enjoy them also

Summers I usually spend at my brother's farm near Utica. There I have a small studio for working, also two nieces and four nephews who keep me supplied with ideas for stories as well as models for illustrations. Unfortunately for me some of them are outgrowing their usefulness in these respects.

Winters I am in New York. This arrangement enables me to keep in touch with publishers, bookstores, and art galleries.

Hobbies are my small flower garden in the country and doing lithographs and water colors.

Paull: *PAWL*

GRACE A. PAULL

This about covers the subject, except that for several years after art school and before breaking into illustration I designed greeting cards.

Howard Pease

September 6, 1894-

AUTHOR OF

Secret Cargo, Thunderbolt House,
The Tattooed Man, Etc.

Autobiographical sketch of Howard Pease:

ONE day my sixth grade teacher said, "This is Friday afternoon, our free period. How would you like to write short stories? All those in favor?"

Hands swung aloft. One girl pupil remarked, "That might be fun, Mrs. Gaines; but how in the world do you do it?"

Our teacher had come prepared; she had forty pictures clipped from magazines, many of them advertisements. She held up a picture of a camel caravan crossing the desert. "Who would like to write a story about this?" she asked. A boy held up his hand and received the picture. My hand did not go up until I saw a picture of a steamer heading into a storm at sea. . . . At the end of the term we printed a little magazine filled with our work, and that is how I still happen to have a copy of my first short story—"Turn Back, Never!"

That little story was written when I was twelve years old in Stockton, California, where I was born and went to school. From that same teacher I acquired a conviction that has never left me: Writing is a craft to be studied and practiced and learned. Stories of mine later appeared in our high school magazine, and later still in my college magazine. Once started, I couldn't stop. I'm still at it, and still learning (I hope).

At the end of my freshman year at Stanford University I went to France for a year as a sergeant during World War I. While there I wrote a long letter to my two young nephews telling them of a visit to Bluebeard's Castle. Upon my return I was told that their teacher had said, "Your uncle's letter was read aloud in every room in our school. Tell him he ought to be writing for children."

That was an idea I carried about with me while I worked in a gasoline service station every day and tapped out stories on my typewriter at night. Once a month I went to San Francisco for a lesson in fiction writing with an elderly novelist who took a few pupils. Some time later, at his suggestion, I wrote a short story in collaboration with one of his other pupils. This was an adventure story for boys and it promptly sold to the *American Boy* magazine. At once I decided this was to be my chosen field of writing. In need of fiction material, I shipped out of San Francisco one summer, first as a wiper in the engine room of a freighter, then as a fireman.

During my first eighteen months of teaching in a country grammar school I wrote my first book, *The Tattooed Man*, which was the result of two voyages together with a walking trip taken alone from Marseilles along the coast to Italy. *The Jinx Ship*, my second book, was started while I was a member of the black gang on a ship in the Caribbean; it was worked on during a winter in New York, and finished during the following summer in California. *Secret Cargo* was written after a tropical winter on the South Sea island of Tahiti, and *Highroad to Adventure* after a motor trip down the Pan-American highway to Mexico City. With the publication of *The Ship Without a Crew* I gave up

HOWARD PEASE

teaching to devote all my working time to writing.

Being a Native Son whose grandparents were California pioneers who crossed the plains in a covered wagon, I have always been interested in my California background. From this interest has come *Long Wharf*, a tale of the San Francisco waterfront in 1850, and *Thunderbolt House*, a story of the great earthquake and fire which leveled San Francisco in 1906.

Most of the time my home has been in Palo Alto, California; but in the spring of 1946 the call of the open road struck not only me but my wife and son as well. When the fourth member of our family, our dachshund pup, made no objection, we pulled up stakes and circled the United States with a house trailer dragging behind our car. In exploring the Connecticut shore we were so charmed with small Bell Island that we said good-by to our trailer and moved into a house facing Long Island Sound. Here our son of high school age sails and races his Snipe off our front porch. But since all four of us are Californians, I suspect that within a few years we shall return to our former home on the West Coast.

* * *

Mr. Pease received the 1946 Award of the Child Study Association for *Heart of Danger*.

Anne Merriman Peck

July 21, 1884-

AUTHOR AND ILLUSTRATOR
*Roundabout South America, Pageant of
South American History, Etc.*

Autobiographical sketch of Anne Merriman Peck:

IT is no wonder I have always wanted to go places and see the world, for my mother and father started my adventurous career by taking me sailing on the choppy Hudson River when I was a small baby. My father was then a young clergyman with his first parish in the old town of Piermont-on-Hudson, and it was there I was born.

Brothers and sisters came along later, and we children had rather a roving childhood. My father, wanting to help the people who most needed him, moved from one small place to another in the country regions of Connecticut. It was hard on my mother, but we were always delighted when the packing cases came out. It meant we were once more to have a new place and new people to get acquainted with.

Our growing up demonstrates how children live in a world of imagination if they have a chance. We had few companions, but there were meadows, trees, or the seashore to form a setting for our games and stories. I was always happy with the world of books, or with paper, pencils, and colors to make pictures of my fancies and the things which pleased me.

There was never any doubt about what I wanted to do. Immediately after high school I began to study in art school. Two years were spent in Hartford, Connecticut, and then came the adventure of New York! I am sure any one of you who plans to make a profession of one of the arts considers New York the goal of your dreams, even as we did in my generation.

What a stimulating, vivid place for an art student! There was not only the fun of painting in the school (New York School of Fine and Applied Art) and of its jolly life, but the city itself. With my sketchbook I wandered through the colorful East Side and other foreign quarters, the waterfront, and other fascinating sections, drawing people and street scenes.

After two years of study I set out to make a place for myself, trudging from one art

ANNE MERRIMAN PECK

editor to another with a big bundle of draw-ings under my arm. What a proud day it was when I received an order to illustrate a series of children's books! On the proceeds of that job I, with an artist girl friend, set sail for France.

That was a summer of romance and ad-venture. We explored Paris and traveled about the country, going third class and staying in cheap little inns. We made friends with the charming people, limbering up our school French into a conversational medium, painting everywhere we went. That trip made me a confirmed vagabond who would escape any time she could to wander about the Old World.

The years that followed brought much work, marriage, and a baby boy who be-came a delightful new model, sometimes much against his will! There were more trips to Europe when I could manage it. Then, when an author failed to keep her contract to write a travel book for boys and girls which I was to illustrate, came my chance to write about the places I loved. Perhaps the success of that first book, *Story-book Europe*, was due to the fact that in it I renewed my first enchanted wanderings about Italy, France, and England, my won-der and delight in the places and people of Europe.

So it was really by accident I became a writer. But it was a happy accident which brought me the work I like best to do—de-scribing for boys and girls in both text and pictures the people and places of the world.

Since I have followed my own boy through childhood to college years I have a special interest in youth. With my book *Young Germany* I began to study the young people of other countries, how they live, what they think about, and what they want. I have written a story of *Young Mexico*, and of *Young Canada*. Recently I have been writing historical books about people in Latin American countries. I hope to go on writing and drawing for boys and girls of America about youth in other countries, so that through understanding you may be friends, even at long distance.

Lucy Fitch Perkins

1865-1937

AUTHOR AND ILLUSTRATOR

The Dutch Twins, The Japanese Twins, The Norwegian Twins, Etc.

Autobiographical sketch of Lucy Fitch Per-kins, written for THE JUNIOR BOOK OF AUTHORS shortly before her death:

THOUGH all my ancestors were New Englanders from the date of the land-ing of the *Mayflower* on, I was born in the backwoods of Indiana. My father, upon leaving college (Amherst), took up teach-ing and eventually became principal of a Chicago school. In 1865, however, he gave up his profession to engage in the lumber business in what was then a wooded area of Indiana, and there, soon after, I was born—and there my family lived until I was fourteen.

During this period my parents taught us at home, and we also made long visits to the ancestral home in Massachusetts in order that my sister and I might have some school experience and contact with other children. My father eventually removed permanently to the old home in Massachusetts, about twenty-five miles from Boston.

At eighteen, immediately after graduation from high school, I went to the art school at the Museum of Fine Arts in Boston, and there studied for three years. For a year after my graduation, I illustrated for the Prang Educational Company of Boston, and then went to Brooklyn to teach in the newly established art school at Pratt Institute.

Here I spent four happy winters teaching and studying with my students, and at the end of that period married Dwight Heald Perkins, a young Chicago architect whom I had met when we were both students in Boston. Since that time, our home has been in Chicago (Evanston) and here our daughter Eleanor Ellis and our son Lawrence Bradford were born.

The life in Chicago was intensely interesting from the first, and we lived fully in the events and thought currents of the time. During several years I did a good deal of illustrating, which was the line of work for which I had prepared myself.

It was not until later that I thought of writing for publication, though expression in words as well as in drawing was native to me. Then a friend who was also a publisher one day took me seriously to task. "You should write," he said, and urged this idea so persuasively upon me that the next day an idea for a book for children suddenly came to me.

I made a dozen little sketches, presenting the idea, and it happened that this publisher came to dine with us the next evening, and I showed them to him. "There is your book," he said. "Go ahead and write it, and I want it." So I wrote *The Dutch Twins*.

Though this was not literally my first book (I had previously published two), still it was the real beginning of my writing. The former books had been written relative

LUCY FITCH PERKINS

to the illustrations. Now the illustrations became secondary to the text.

At this time I became deeply impressed with two ideas. . . . One was the necessity for mutual respect and understanding between people of different nationalities if we are ever to live in peace. In particular I felt the necessity for this in this country where all nations are represented in the population. It was at about this time that the expression "the melting pot" became familiar as descriptive of America's function in the world's progress. The other idea was that a really big theme can be comprehended by children if it is presented in a way that holds their interest and engages their sympathies.

To do this, the theme must be personalized—made vivid through its effect upon the lives of individuals. A visit to Ellis Island also impressed me deeply at this time—I saw the oppressed and depressed of all nations flocking to our shores. How could a homogeneous nation be made out of such heterogeneous material? I visited a school in Chicago where children of twenty-seven different nationalities were herded into one building, and marveled at what the teachers were able to accomplish. It seemed to me it might help in the fusing process if these children could be interested in the best qualities they bring to our shores.

So I wrote books giving pictures of child life in other countries, and then, for the benefit of American and foreign-born children alike, I wrote books which gave some idea of what had been done for this country by those who had founded and developed it.

Several of the series portray the tremendous importance of land ownership in shaping destinies. The abuses of absentee landlordism as a cause for the Irish immigration to this country were personalized in *The Irish Twins*; in the Scotch story the effect on the family of a Scotch shepherd of taking land from productive use for game preserves; and in *The Mexican Twins* the peonage resulting from the ownership of vast estates.

Such themes as these have interested me vitally and in my books I have tried to contribute something to the making of Americans by an appreciation of what has been done in the past to make America what it is today, and of the constructive qualities in the material at hand with which we must build the nation of the future.

* * *

When Mrs. Perkins died in Pasadena, California, at the age of seventy-two, she had had published twenty-four "Twins" books, and was at work on a sequel to *The Dutch Twins.* In 1935 when the two millionth copy of a book from her pen came from the press, Carl B. Roden, of the Chicago Public Library, publicly presented her with a specially bound copy.

Maud & Miska Petersham

AUTHORS AND ILLUSTRATORS
*The Christ Child, The Rooster Crows,
America's Stamps, The Box
With Red Wheels, Etc.*

MAUD & MISKA PETERSHAM

Autobiographical sketch of Maud and Miska Petersham, by Maud Petersham:

FOR the boys and girls for whom we make our books:

Does it seem strange that it takes two people to make the same book? Well it does, with us. Miska is right-handed and I am left. Perhaps that is the reason.

It is not easy to make a book that *you* like, that the grown-ups like, and that we ourselves like. Then the Printer! We have to plan and cut down on the number of colors and pictures so the printing does not cost too much. It is hard work but we love it.

Miska came from Hungary. He is a true Magyar and was born in 1889 in a little town with an unpronounceable name, near Budapest. He always wanted to paint and walked miles each day to the art school in Budapest.

When he was about twenty he left Hungary and went to England. Even his name was different in those days. It was Petrezselyem Mihaly. But when he was in London and found no one could pronounce his name he called himself Miska Petersham.

At night Miska went to an art school in London. In the daytime he tried to earn money enough to pay for his studio and paints. "Fish and chips," which cost but a few pennies at the corner shop, seemed to be sufficient food.

From London Miska came to New York and found he could make a living. He would work very hard for a few months and save some money. Then he would leave his job and paint until his money was gone and he was hungry again.

I first knew him when he came to work in the advertising agency where I was struggling with my first job.

I was born in Kingston, New York, in 1890. Father was a minister and each Sunday we four girls, my sisters and myself, were scrubbed and starched and put onto a hard church pew for hours and hours. I guess we made up for this at home by making life rather hectic for the missionaries and ministers who were frequent visitors at the parsonage.

After I graduated from Vassar I went to the New York School of Fine and Applied Arts and then took my first position with the International Art Service.

From there Miska and I have worked on together. Every time we can manage, between books, we buy a ticket to some place. A steamship whistle always gives us a restless feeling.

Willy Pogány was a friend of Miska's. Once he turned over to us a children's book he was too busy to do. From that time on we have made books for children.

In June 1946 our book of American rhymes and jingles, *The Rooster Crows,* received the Caldecott award for the most distinguished work of its year for children.

Petersham: *PEET er sham*

Our home and studio is in Woodstock, New York, and here our greatest pleasure comes from the time we spend working on books for America's children.

* * *

Besides many stories by other authors, the Petershams have illustrated dozens of books they themselves have written.

Ethel Calvert Phillips

AUTHOR OF
The Story of Nancy Hanks,
Peter Peppercorn, Etc.

Autobiographical sketch of Ethel Calvert Phillips, revised for THE JUNIOR BOOK OF AUTHORS a few months before her death:

ETHEL CALVERT PHILLIPS

I WAS born in Jersey City, the younger of two daughters of George Calvert Phillips and Olive Hanks (Hitchcock) Phillips. My father came from Kentucky and was descended from George Calvert, Lord Baltimore, who obtained the grant of Maryland. That is how I come by the Calvert in my name. My mother's family was from New England. Her grandfather built the first silk mill in America at Mansfield, Connecticut. One of her ancestors was Nancy Hanks, Abraham Lincoln's mother, about whom I have written a story.

My home in Jersey City was in the lower part of the town near the Hudson River. One of the first things I remember is being held up at the window at night to have pointed out to me the gleaming light of the Statue of Liberty. I liked, too, riding on the ferryboat from Jersey City to New York when I was shown Lower New York Bay and told of Henry Hudson anchoring the "Half Moon" there on his first visit to the island of Manhattan.

As a little girl I dearly loved dolls. I still have two of them, my old rag dolls Flip and Polly. There is something human and real to me about dolls. Perhaps that is why I have written so many books about them. I was a great reader, too. But in case you may think I always sat still with a book in one hand and a doll in the other I shall tell you that I was better at playing fence-tag than any boy or girl in our neighborhood. And one of my nicknames was Tom, short for tomboy.

I was educated at Hasbrouck Institute, the School for Ethical Culture, and Teachers College, Columbia University, where I studied to be a kindergarten teacher.

I taught first in a settlement house kindergarten on the lower East Side of New York City. The tenements all about us swarmed with the little Russian Jewish children who came to our kindergarten. They were bright and eager to learn. They were affectionate, too. "I love you and you love me, ain't it?" was Izzy's way of telling me we were friends.

My next kindergarten was among the Italian children. They were lively, warmhearted, and gay. They played games and acted stories with zest. They loved music and color. I shall never forget Concetta, whose mother was a ragpicker. Concetta's dresses were made of bits of rag sewed together. One day Concetta and I went shopping and bought at a real store, not from a pushcart, the first whole dress she had ever owned. She picked it out herself. It was a bright pink and blue and yellow plaid.

My last teaching was among the Spanish children who live along the western waterfront of New York. Many of their fathers and mothers had come from the seaports of Spain and so felt more at home within sight of ships and moving water. These Spanish children were proud and reserved. But, oh, to see Carmen and Manuel, castanets in hand, dance the Spanish fandango! And their confidence won, they proved the warmest and most faithful of friends.

While I was teaching and trying to help these small foreigners to become good American citizens, I was writing stories for children. I did not write about these little foreign people. But there is something of all of them in the boys and girls of my books. For I have learned that children are very much alike in spite of difference in nationality and ways of living.

I live now in Nutley, New Jersey, where a flower garden and the writing of stories occupy most of my time. My house is not far from the Passaic River. And I like to think that, years ago, the little Indian boy in my book *Ride-the-Wind* lived in his wigwam upon the very site where my house now stands. How surprised he would be could he come back now and look across the river, as I do, at the shining towers of the city of New York.

*   *   *

On February 8, 1947, after a year's illness, Ethel Calvert Phillips died at her home in Nutley, of a heart ailment.

Arthur Stanwood Pier

April 21, 1874-

AUTHOR OF

The St. Timothy books, Etc.

Autobiographical sketch of Arthur Stanwood Pier:

I WAS born in Pittsburgh, the son of William S. and Alcie M. Pier. At the age of thirteen I was sent to St. Paul's School at Concord, New Hampshire, and there prepared for Harvard College, which I entered in 1891. After graduating in 1895, I took up the study of law in Pittsburgh, but soon abandoned it in order to accept an editorial position on the staff of the *Youth's Companion,* published in Boston. My connection with the *Youth's Companion* lasted nearly thirty years, during which time besides doing routine editorial work I wrote many short and serial stories.

My writing was not wholly of a juvenile character, as I contributed stories to various adult magazines, and published a volume of essays, a short history of Harvard University, and several novels. From 1916 to 1921 I conducted a course in English composition

at Harvard; from 1918 to 1930 I was editor of the *Harvard Graduates' Magazine*; and in 1930 I returned as a master to St. Paul's School where I taught English until 1944 when I reached the retirement age.

In 1909 I married Elise Hall in Boston; she died in 1922. My son Arthur prepared for college at St. Paul's, graduated from Harvard College in 1935, from Harvard Medical School in 1939, served as a major in the Medical Corps of the Army during the war, and is now a practicing physician in Boston. My daughter, Rosamond, is Mrs. William Morris Hunt.

I have written a great number of stories about baseball, football, hockey, golf, rowing, and track, but the only game or sport in which I ever attained even a moderate degree of proficiency is tennis.

During the greater part of my married life and until 1930 when I moved to Concord, New Hampshire, I lived in Milton, Massachusetts, which is now my home. In most of my juvenile stories, boarding school or college has been the scene of action; but four of the more recent tales have been concerned with characters and activities in the high school of a small town in New England.

Although there has never been any conscious purpose to enforce a moral in my stories for boys, I suppose the moral in them has usually been apparent enough. They have generally had as their themes sports-

Kimball Studio

ARTHUR STANWOOD PIER

manship, self-sacrifice, or unselfish helpfulness. I have found that the manifestations of those traits and impulses are the most representative occurrences in the relations of boys with one another.

My effort has been to give a truthful picture of life among boys who on account of education, environment, and inheritance might be expected to possess the better qualities of human nature, yet who are not without normal human weaknesses.

Willy Pogány

August 24, 1882-
ILLUSTRATOR

Autobiographical sketch of Willy Pogány:

I WAS born many years ago in a town called Szeged, in Hungary, where I spent my early childhood with my brothers and sisters in a big farmhouse with a huge backyard full of chickens, ducks, geese, dogs, pigs, and horses. The cows were taken away every morning very early to the pastures and driven home in the late afternoon for milking.

When I was only six my parents took us children to Budapest, where we settled down and went to school. I studied very hard, because we were ever so poor and I wanted to become an engineer and to look after my mother, because meanwhile my father had died.

I went to school for many years and was a good student, but I liked best to play soccer and football and row on the Danube. Also I drew pictures and painted in my spare time.

So instead of becoming an engineer when I grew up I tried to be an artist. I went to Paris, where I studied and painted, but nobody wanted my pictures so I was still awfully poor and went without food lots of times. Later when I had more luck and received some money for my works I left Paris and went to London, where I became quite well known as an artist and illustrator.

I married in London an English girl and my oldest son, John, was born in London. After ten years in England we came over to America, where we settled down in New York. Another son was born here, whom we called Peter. I worked very hard in America, and have done, besides illustrating books, all sorts of pictures, mural paintings,

WILLY POGÁNY

etchings, sculpture, and have built hotels and swimming pools. I also became very much interested in the theatre and designed stage settings and costumes for different shows and for the Metropolitan Opera House.

Later I went to Hollywood where I designed sets for movies, which I found very interesting indeed. I also married again in Hollywood and I live there in a house with a beautiful garden, full of sunshine and flowers.

I am always working hard, because it is great fun and hard work to be an artist.

* * *

Willy Pogány's full name is William Andrew Pogány. He attended the University of Budapest for a year and was a pupil at art school in Budapest before going away to study in Munich and Paris.

His success as a book illustrator began in England, with *The Welsh Fairy Book,* by Jenkyn Thomas, and *The Hungarian Fairy Book,* compiled by his brother, Nándor Pogány. Since then he has illustrated more than a hundred and fifty volumes, of which Padraic Colum's series of classic tales retold is well known to junior readers.

Among other popular books illustrated by Pogány are *Bible Stories to Read and Tell,* by Frances Jenkins Olcott, and *The Home Book of Verse for Young Folks.*

Some of his most famous mural paintings are found in the Children's Theatre in the Heckscher Foundation, the Rand School,

Pogány: *poh GAH nee*

and Wanamaker's department store, all of New York. Also famous are his murals for the Niagara Power Company and for the Bavarian Fairy Tale Village of Wyntoon, in northern California.

The New York Society of Architects has given Pogány a silver medal, and he was awarded gold medals at Budapest, Leipzig, and the Panama Pacific International Exposition.

Leo Politi

November 21, 1908-

AUTHOR AND ILLUSTRATOR

The Song of the Swallows; Little Pancho; Pedro, the Angel of Olvera Street; Etc.

Autobiographical sketch of Leo Politi:

I WAS born in Fresno, California. At the age of seven I went to Italy with my family.

When I was fifteen I was given a scholarship for the Institute of Monza (near Milan). This art school had at our disposal the gardens, the zoo, everything beautiful and convenient for outdoor sketching.

We arranged sketches from life into compositions for murals, book decoration and so forth. I remember our good teacher, Ugo Lovetti, and how he took pride in showing us the great wealth of nature. He would take a small flower and gently open it to show us its beautiful lines, shapes and colors. When we were drawing birds and animals he taught us not to see them as static objects but to seek the inner life, which projected movement and rhythm.

At the age of twenty-three I came back to California and settled down on Olvera Street in Los Angeles where I drew and sold pictures. In 1938 I married Helen Fontes. We have two children, Paul and Susanne.

More than anything else I love drawing children. In all my books I try to embody certain universal things—the warmth and happiness of family life; my love for people, animals, birds and flowers, and for the simple warm and earthy things.

My first work in the children's book field was a small book, *Little Pancho*. Then followed the illustration of several books about the Latin American countries. I undertook these assignments with enthusiasm because of my love for the people of Latin America

Erich Hartmann

LEO POLITI

and my admiration for their arts and their great civilizations of the past.

Then the children's book editor of Scribner's suggested my California series beginning with *Pedro, the Angel of Olvera Street* and asked me to write as well as illustrate the books. These I was able to do with even greater enthusiasm because of my love for California, its rich folklore and traditions, and because I live close to the subject.

It was a great honor when the American Library Association awarded me the 1949 Caldecott Medal for *Song of the Swallows*.

It is important in all parts of the United States to bring forth and keep alive the vast wealth of tradition and folklore for our children, especially in this age of rapid technical achievement which fills our life with an overabundance of material things. Unless we can temper and shape our machine age with finer ideals I agree with William Pène du Bois, who says "the machine age is a decadent path indeed."

Beatrix Potter

1866-1943

AUTHOR OF

The Peter Rabbit books, Etc.

THE creator of the beloved "Peter Rabbit," Beatrix Potter, was a determined little lady with a passion for privacy. Biographical details have been so scanty that

Politi: *po LEE tee*

something of an atmosphere of mystery has grown up about her. Actually, there is no mystery. Her story is a simple, tranquil one. Her life, except for the flowering of her extraordinary talent, was a life that must have been duplicated all over England in that late Victorian era.

Beatrix Potter was born in 1866, the only daughter of Mr. and Mrs. Rupert Potter. She grew up in London with three-month family holidays every year in Scotland. The Potters, inheriting wealth from a cotton-spinning grandfather, were no longer "in trade." Mr. Potter was a barrister, although he did not practice. It was a stuffy, conventional household, with the children left almost entirely to nurses and governesses. Beatrix's only brother, Bertram, was sent away to school, but the little girl was educated at home. Her world was the nursery floor of the tall old house; her only amusements those she could devise for herself. Very early she began to draw the squirrels she saw in the square, and the mice that sometimes crept out at night. On the Scottish holidays she learned to know and love the small wild creatures, and to draw them with tender care.

She grew up a shy, retiring girl, ill at ease among adults. To little cousins and other child friends she gave her deepest affection. She wrote them long story-letters, delightfully illustrated. Five-year-old Noel Moore received "The Tale of Peter Rab-

From a portrait by Delmar Banner
BEATRIX POTTER

bit," a whimsical letter written to solace his illness. He passed it around to other children, who liked it too. When they began asking for copies, Miss Potter timidly decided to make it into a book, and thus one of the true classics of children's literature was born.

The first *Peter Rabbit,* published by the author, had a modest private sale and came to the attention of the publishing house of Frederick Warne and Company, who printed it in a commercial edition. It was so popular that the Warne firm soon brought out *The Tailor of Gloucester.* In the ten years that followed, Warne published *Squirrel Nutkin, Mrs. Tiggle-Winkle, Jemima Puddle-Duck* and all the famous others, as dear to children today as they were to their first readers.

With her very substantial earnings, Miss Potter bought Hill Top Farm at Sawrey, near Lake Windermere. As a dutiful spinster daughter she still made her home with her parents, but as often as possible she retreated to Hill Top for the country life she loved.

It was in the Hill Top neighborhood that she met William Heelis, a country lawyer, who proposed marriage after a four-year courtship. Beatrix was then forty-seven years old, but her parents refused their consent as though she had been a giddy seventeen. For once she took a respectful but determined stand against them, and married Mr. Heelis in 1913. It was an exceptionally happy match.

As Mrs. Heelis she settled down to a full-time farmer's life, something she had always desired. She acquired new acreage and a larger house, and began the breeding of Herdwick sheep. In this field she became locally famous, being elected president of the Herdwick Breeders' Association. She was also active in the National Trust, a movement to preserve unspoiled the natural beauties of the lake district, buying up more than 4,000 acres of land with her own money and presenting them to the Trust. Her own home, Hill Top Farm, also went to the Trust by the terms of her will. A serious, hardworking member of her community, she found no time for writing. She did, at the insistence of some American friends, turn out half a dozen books in her later years, but they were only moderately successful. Her fame rests on the long series done between 1902 and 1913, beginning with *Peter Rabbit* and ending with *Pig-ling Bland*.

The later years were brightened by letters and visits from Anne Carroll Moore, Bertha Mahony, Helen Dean Fish, and others qualified to appreciate her great contribution to children's reading. Visitors found her a rosy-cheeked old lady with bright blue eyes, short and plump, modest about her books but very positive on the subject of sheep-breeding.

Beatrix Potter Heelis died at her farm home on December 22, 1943, aged seventy-seven. Her biographer Margaret Lane wrote in *The Tale of Beatrix Potter* (1946): "She died as she had lived, as simply as possible, conscious of what she was doing, without fuss or regret." Preserved by the National Trust exactly as it was while she lived, Hill Top Farm is visited annually by thousands of Beatrix Potter devotees, young and old.

Emilie Poulsson

September 8, 1853-March 18, 1939

AUTHOR AND ILLUSTRATOR

*Finger Plays, In the Child's World,
The Runaway Donkey, Through
the Farmyard Gate, Etc.*

Autobiographical sketch of Anne Emilie Poulsson, written for THE JUNIOR BOOK OF AUTHORS a few years before her death:

I WAS born in the small village of Cedar Grove, New Jersey. My father was a Norwegian, my mother of English parentage, but of American birth.

Life has been extremely interesting to me and full of enjoyment ever since I was seven years old. Up to that time I was an invalid child suffering from a serious eye trouble which began when I was six months old, greatly impaired my sight, and has returned at intervals throughout my life.

However, after I was seven, brighter days came. My eyes and general health improved rapidly and I did not now have to stay in the dark for long periods.

At eight I went to a Newark, New Jersey, public school and was ready for high school in about four years. In the entrance examinations for the high school, another little girl and I proved to be equally matched in spelling. Therefore, we must be examined again to determine which of us should have the city's prize, four charming volumes, in blue and gold—two of Longfellow's poems and two of Tennyson's.

After five successive examinations our records were still equal and we were smilingly dismissed. We had become great friends during the contest and had agreed that we would be satisfied to have the prize divided. When "Prize Day" came, the superintendent told of the five extra examinations and said that the committee had decided to give each of us the four volumes.

This incident is recorded here because of what resulted from the friendship thus begun.

My eyes had grown worse and as I could not use them, kind little Marcella offered to study aloud to me that I might stay in school. The teacher let us go into the dressing room for the study periods. All went so well that at the end of the year, we two ranked highest in the class and my eyes were better. They gave out again, however, in my senior year, so my further education was rather haphazard.

An important truth was gradually dawning upon me—the truth that handicapped persons must not make "a pillow of the handicap," but rather let such disability be a spur to greater effort in the use of whatever powers they possess.

To earn something was not only necessary but was my great desire. My special asset was a love and understanding of young children, gained from close companionship with them when I was not strong enough to play with children my own age; so when health and eyes permitted, I was "mother's helper" or taught in private families.

This happy work was interrupted by another threatening attack of eye trouble which necessitated spending nine months in a hospital, mostly in the dark.

Being told that my sight though saved at this time was too precarious to be used for reading, I went to Perkins Institution for the Blind in Boston, Massachusetts, to learn to make my fingers serve instead, as best they might.

Besides receiving invaluable help of many kinds from this school, I was allowed to attend the Kindergarten Normal School of Miss Garland and Miss Weston, a Perkins teacher reading my lessons to me. Without my kindergarten training I should doubtless never have written my *Finger Plays*. After graduating from this normal school I taught for two years at Perkins Institution.

Perhaps the happiest ten years of my happy life were those which followed, for I spent them as "trotting tutoress" to the five children of a Boston family. We began with kindergarten and later I had the same readers in raised print as the children had in ink print. For arithmetic we used the blackboard chiefly and for writing and drawing there were other teachers.

The children had many animal pets, which furnished material for some of the rhymes and stories in *Through the Farmyard Gate* and *The Runaway Donkey*.

After the children had successively passed into schools, I taught in other families, in Miss Garland's Kindergarten Normal School, gave lectures, conducted classes for mothers, and for seven years (with my sister, Laura E. Poulsson) edited the *Kindergarten Review*.

Finger Plays was my first book. The plays had been published in *Babyland*— 1887 and 1888. As is not uncommon with young writers, I did not know enough to retain book rights to *Finger Plays* so I received no royalties on the book until 1921. Fortunately, it has proved to be a "hardy perennial" and still sells, although naturally not in the numbers which sold during its first thirty-two years.

My other "hardy perennial" is the book *In the Child's World*. Its talks, stories, and other matter have been largely used not only by kindergartners but by teachers and mothers. After forty years the book is still selling.

From the fact that my father was a Norwegian and that my sister and I made many trips to that country to see relatives there, I became greatly interested in the Norwegian books for children. Those I have translated have received a pleasant welcome from American children.

"But how did you get to be an author?" asked a young friend.

The influences were many, the process gradual. A genius may leap to authorship but not so do folk of less ability attain it. I was always an avid reader (whenever eyes permitted); there was much talk in our home of books and authors; and I liked to experiment with writing. Much intimacy with children supplied me with material and

incentive. Moreover, my mother and older sister, Laura, had faith in my small talent and nourished it from my early years by their encouragement.

* * *

Emilie Poulsson died at a Brookline, Massachusetts, nursing home at the age of eighty-five after an illness of several years.

Edith Ballinger Price

April 26, 1897-

AUTHOR AND ILLUSTRATOR
Silver Shoal Light, The Fortune of the Indies, Blue Magic, Etc.

Autobiographical sketch of Edith Ballinger Price:

MY Price ancestors came to Maryland in the "Ark and Dove" expedition in 1634, with a long line of Welsh chieftains behind them. On the other side of the family, my grandfather, William T. Richards, was a famous painter of the sea—and from him, of course, I got my desire to draw. Very early I began to ply my pencil in earnest. From that time on I filled a large stack of sketchbooks with vigorous pictures "out of my head," portraying all sorts of people, and scenes from imaginary stories or from the book I happened to be reading.

At fourteen I began studying at the School of the Museum of Fine Arts in Boston, and academic education went on fitfully around the edges of art school—and by the time I was eighteen, I decided to try to make my way in the world as a full-fledged illustrator.

Thinking editors might be impressed if I sent a story to demonstrate how well my pictures fitted, I wrote one. Then came the surprise that more or less altered my entire existence! The story was *Blue Magic*, and when *St. Nicholas* calmed down a bit from its enthusiasm over the text it remembered vaguely that—yes, there *had* been some sort of pictures sent with the manuscript. So my doom was sealed. From that time on, I had to write books—one after the other.

I kept vainly protesting that I was an artist, not a writer—and just to keep me quiet they used my pictures as illustrations for my books.

So, I keep on writing books; but at heart I yearn to draw, too, and burst out in paint

Katharine Pyle

AUTHOR AND ILLUSTRATOR
Careless Jane, Lazy Matilda, Etc.

Autobiographical sketch of Katharine Pyle, written for THE JUNIOR BOOK OF AUTHORS a few years before her death:

I WAS the youngest of a family of four. I had three brothers.

My earliest years were spent in the country, but I was still a child when we moved to town. We were brought up in a literary atmosphere. Mother read aloud to us evenings—books such as *Lorna Doone*, Scott's novels, and other classics of the time. She wrote book reviews, verses, and serial stories for women's magazines.

Always we had pets: dogs, cats, canaries, rabbits, squirrels, fish; once a tame crow; once a raccoon.

Even after we moved to the city much time was still spent in the country. My next older brother and I were great chums. Accompanied by the dogs we went on long butterfly hunts and soon had good collections.

Later it was my mother and I who went on these tramps, as my brother had tired of my companionship and wanted to be with boys instead.

I was still a child when my brother Howard [see sketch in AMERICAN AUTHORS: 1600-1900] went to New York to carry on his artistic and literary work, and it was he who "placed" my first verse for me. Always I had been "making up" stories and verses—even when I was such a small child that my mother had to write them down for me.

My first book was *The Counterpane Fairy*. After that each year for some dozen years a book or so came out. I have written some twenty-four books in all, as well as a number of fugitive verses. I have illustrated a number of stories by other writers and I have painted a number of portraits.

*   *   *

Katharine Pyle illustrated all her own books. Though her drawings lack some of the dramatic strength of those by her famous brother, they reveal an equal ability to express the romantic and colorful. She also had Howard Pyle's knack of story telling. Many of her stories, like his, were retellings

EDITH BALLINGER PRICE

now and then, to maintain the balance. To illustrate one's own books is great fun, because of course the author has a truer idea of the characters than any outside illustrator can possibly have.

I live in Newport, Rhode Island, and I suppose that is why the sea gets into so many of my tales. Apart from writing yarns, I am interested in Girl Scouting, and for a number of years was "Great Brown Owl," or national head of the Brownies, the younger branch of Girl Scouts, which I helped start in this country. I like English folk dancing, and gardening, and I play very badly on a number of instruments. My greatest excitement and interest is centered about my adopted daughter, who is blind, and who has lived with me since she was a baby of two.

I am pleased with little things, and I approve of people cultivating resources within themselves which will forever prevent their being lonely or bored. I think that in the midst of this complicated new world, some of us ought to try to hold on to quiet things and simple delights. In our towns nowadays we are having to set apart parking places for automobiles, so the streets will not be hopelessly crowded. I believe that more and more we need spiritual parking places in our own lives—quiet occupations or recreations or even little thinking-times alone with ourselves—where we can "park" for a time while the tiresome traffic of life surges about us.

of old favorites. In fact the brother and sister frequently helped in each other's work, and Katharine sometimes wrote verses to accompany Howard's drawings. She died in 1938.

Arthur Rackham

September 19, 1867-September 6, 1939

ILLUSTRATOR

Autobiographical sketch of Arthur Rackham, written for THE JUNIOR BOOK OF AUTHORS a few years before his death:

THOUGH I am not a writer I am allowed a place in this book as the illustrator of a number of fairy tales and other books.

I have very little to say about myself. I was born in London, went to school there, and have lived there all my life. I was married there and my daughter was born there. I have only the one child of my own, though my father and mother had twelve boys and girls, so my own boyhood was spent in a noisy, merry, busy little community of work and play almost large enough to be independent of outside engagements.

I cannot remember the time when I hadn't a pencil in my hand and from the very first my bent was toward the fantastic and imaginative. It has since been my great good fortune to have the chance of illustrating many of the greatest works of imagination, such as Shakespeare's fairy plays; of traditional wisdom and humor such as Grimm's and other old fairy and folk tales; of inventive fantasy, such as *Alice in Wonderland* and *Peter Pan*; and of kindly satire, such as *Rip Van Winkle*.

For the rest, I can only say I firmly believe in the greatest stimulating and educative power of the imaginative, fantastic, and playful pictures and writings for children in their most impressionable years—a view that most unfortunately, I consider, has its serious opponents in these matter-of-fact days.

Children will make no mistakes in the way of confusing the imaginative and symbolic with the actual. Nor are they at all blind to decorative or arbitrarily designed treatment in art, any more than they are to poetic or rhythmic form in literature. And it must be insisted that nothing less than the best that can be had, cost what it may

ARTHUR RACKHAM

(and it can hardly be cheap), is good enough for those early impressionable years when standards are formed for life.

Any accepting, or even choosing, art, or literature of a lower standard, as good enough for children, is a disastrous and costly mistake.

* * *

Arthur Rackham's father, a marshal to the British Admiralty, put him in an insurance office with the idea of his following a business career. But he wanted to be an artist and went to art school at night until he was able to support himself as a freelance artist.

His first book illustrations were for *The Dolly Dialogues*, by Anthony Hope, in his twenty-seventh year. Following that he illustrated more than fifty books. According to Emelyn E. Gardner and Eloise Ramsey, he "wonderfully caught and expressed the magic of fairyland" by transmitting "the spirit and essence of the tales of enchantment which he delighted in helping children visualize. He always kept the heart of a child."

In his thirty-sixth year Mr. Rackham married Edyth Starkie, herself a portrait painter of considerable distinction, whose paintings were bought by the National Museum of Barcelona, Spain, and the Luxembourg Museum in Paris.

Rackham received a gold medal at Milan, another at Barcelona (along with his wife),

Rackham: *RACK am*

and a third medal from the Société Nationale des Beaux Arts in Paris, which elected him an associate. He was also a master of the Art Workers' Guild and a member of the Royal Society of Painters in Water Colors, and his drawings are in the great galleries of Europe.

In his London studio there was a trapeze which he used for many years. His country home was at Houghton in the heart of the South Downs of Sussex, and in his garden stood an old, knotty beech tree, with twisted roots, which often served him as a model.

P. G. Konody described him as follows: "Keen-eyed, clean-shaven, ascetic-looking, with high, round, smooth forehead bulging over his large, round, glittering spectacles, he bears a strange resemblance to one of the unearthly gnomes of his own creation, or to a very wise old owl, with just a spark of innocent mischief."

Arthur Rackham died at his home, Limpsfield, Surrey, two weeks before his seventy-second birthday. About him the New York *Times* said: "One of his books is called *The Land of Enchantment*. He made it and lived in it. It was part of that world that never was and always is. . . . The enchanter is gone but the enchantment remains."

Arthur Ransome

1884-

AUTHOR OF

Swallows and Amazons, Swallowdale, We Didn't Mean to Go to Sea, Etc.

Autobiographical sketch of Arthur Ransome:

MY father was a fisherman who was a professor of history in his spare time, and one of the earliest things I can remember is watching the river and racing up to the farmhouse where we were staying for the Long Vacation to let him know that the trout were rising. History, thereupon, stood still while my father left books and papers scattered as they were on the table, took up his rod, waiting ready by the porch, and hurried to the waterside.

That was over fifty years ago, and my father died when I was still a small boy, but heredity counts for a good deal, and I always find it easier to write books when

the descendants of the trout that used to disturb my father are lying dully at the bottom of the river and not dimpling the water with rises to tempt fishermen from their desks.

Those Long Vacations of years ago were spent in an old farmhouse not far from where I am writing now. A rocky hill named from the badgers who lived in the woods on its lower slopes, climbed up behind it. There were grouse up there in the heather. Below, across a field, was a lake, and boats, and, flowing out of the lake, a little river full of trout. There could not be a better place, and if anybody had asked me then where I was going to spend my old age, I could have told him when I was only five or six. I never had any doubts about that.

But a lot of things had to come first. I went to school at Rugby, right in the middle of England, where (I suppose because some little idiot got himself drowned some time or other) we were not allowed to swim in the Avon, or even to fish in it. After Rugby, I went for a very short time to a university to study science, but badly wanted to write books instead, and so went off to London, where I kept alive and continued my education by running errands and packing up parcels in an office, often working late at night without being paid for overtime, getting to and from the office in an old horse-drawn omnibus painted

ARTHUR RANSOME

Ransome: *RAN sum*

green, and writing the most terrible rubbish when I got home.

Then, when I had earned my first grown-up holiday, I went, of course, straight back to that lake in the North, and spent my two free weeks in writing rubbish all day instead of only half the night. A year later I was selling my rubbish and making some sort of living by it. And then for many years I used to go there every summer to stay with a delightful family of writers and artists who lived in a house close above the water, at the other end of the lake from the old farmhouse of my first memories. The eldest of their children was about my own age, and there we painted and wrote and sailed and camped on an island, and used, when indoors, to be waked in the mornings by hearing my aunt (she was not my aunt but called herself so) playing Beethoven on the piano.

They are dead now, the two old people, and all we young ones have scattered hither and thither and grown old ourselves. But still the lake is there, and the river, and even those of us who have gone farthest keep on coming back. The first of the "Swallows and Amazons" books was written for some of the grandchildren of that family. Their mother was my old friend's eldest daughter.

But before those books were written, all sorts of things had happened to me. I had collected fairy tales in Russia, and been a newspaper correspondent during the First World War and the Russian revolution. I had sailed about the Baltic in a little ship of my own, and later had gone off now and again on journeys to foreign countries, China, Egypt, and the Sudan, coming back to write about them in the *Manchester Guardian*.

That is all over now, and I live in a cottage more than three hundred years old high up on a hillside. I can see forty miles from my cottage door. The lakes I knew best as a boy are close at hand, and, on the nearest of them, a little boat, *Swallow*, lies at her moorings and sails as well as ever she did. There is a long row of fishing rods hanging in the cottage, like the pipes of an organ, people say.

When there is news that the rivers are in good trim, I usually manage to take a rod and go down the hill to one or another of them. This very day, the moment I have put this paper into its envelope, I shall be off to fish a river that was fished by my father long before I was born, and by my grandfather before him. In such a place, what with sailing and fishing (and a pair of spotted flycatchers nesting just under my window) it is perhaps surprising I ever get anything written at all. But writing is the one profession in which one can have one's cake and eat it, and it seems to me that in writing children's books, I have the best of childhood over again and the best of being old as well, which is a very great deal more than I deserve.

* * *

In 1936 Arthur Ransome's *Pigeon Post* received the Library Association Carnegie Medal—English equivalent of the Newbery Medal in the United States. Sir Hugh Walpole called him "the best writer for boys and girls in England alive today."

W. Maxwell Reed

1871-

AUTHOR OF

*The Earth for Sam, The Stars for Sam,
The Sea for Sam, Etc.*

Autobiographical sketch of William Maxwell Reed:

I SUPPOSE an autobiography should start with one's birth. So I will say I was born in Bath, Maine. In those days a large number of full-rigged ships were built there, and launched into the wide Kennebec River. It was a beautiful sight to see these boats slide into the water. I have stood on the banks and watched them slide down the ways and I have stood on the deck of one of them when she behaved like a huge sled. The boat coasts down the slightly sloping hill made by the ways and plunges into the river. It is hard now for me to say which of these two experiences I enjoyed more.

The statement that all things are interesting is nearly true. So when my parents

H. A. Rey

September 16, 1898-

AUTHOR AND ILLUSTRATOR OF
*Curious George Takes a Job, Cecily G.
and the 9 Monkeys, Etc.*

W. MAXWELL REED

Autobiographical sketch of Hans Augusto Rey:

BORN: September 16, 1898, in Hamburg, Germany; third of four children.

Early Activities, 1898 to 1900: Eating, drinking, sleeping, learning to talk and walk. In between, doodling with crayons.

1900, December: First recognizable drawing: man on horseback. Both man and horse had distinctly human faces.

Childhood: Drawing most of the time. Since I lived near a zoo I soon was more familiar with elephants and kangaroos than with cows or sheep. I am still fond of animals and often go to the zoo. Sometimes I dream of having a small zoo of my own, somewhere in the countryside.

School Years: Drawing most of the time, in and out of school. During lessons I hid sketchbooks in Latin or Greek grammars. I thought I fooled my teachers but they later told me they had always noticed, just let me go on doing it.

1916: World War I was going full blast, so after leaving school I was right away drafted into the army. But I did better with my pencil than with my rifle.

Postwar Years: Contrasted sharply with happy times of my youth. Inflation, no money, and no chance of going to an art school. I eked out a living by designing and lithographing posters for a circus. The rest of the time I spent with assorted studies at Hamburg University: philosophy, anatomy, natural sciences, languages.

1924: Matters having gone from bad to worse I accepted a job offered me by relatives in Brazil in their import firm. Thus I found myself composing commercial letters (which I was not allowed to adorn with illustrations) and selling bathtubs up and down the Amazon River. Obviously it was not the right road but it took me twelve years to find that out.

1935: Turning point: a girl from my home town, disliking things in Nazi Germany, showed up under Rio de Janeiro's palm trees. Before three months had passed I was not only married to her but had said

moved to Cambridge and I had to work hard at Brown and Nichols School in order to enter Harvard, I found life still interesting even if I did not have ships to launch upon, because we had plenty of football, tobogganing, canoeing, and horseback riding.

I became research assistant at the Harvard Observatory and finally taught astronomy at Harvard and at Princeton. In those days, and I think it is still true, a man must have an income if he wishes to be a professional astronomer. I soon found that a large steel mill paid a better salary and also provided interesting work. Therefore, I find it true that research, teaching, and millwork are all interesting.

In 1930 I published *The Earth for Sam*. Sam is my nephew and it was the result of a series of letters I sent him to satisfy his curiosity. Naturally I had to follow this book up with a *Stars for Sam* and a *Sea for Sam*. Later I wrote *Animals on the March*. This contains the history of the horse. Perhaps you think the horse was discovered by the Indians. He really came from Asia and then went back to his native land. Afterwards he was brought here by the Spaniards. To satisfy your curiosity about lightning, electric lamps, and the color of the sky I wrote two small books called *And That's Why* and *The Sky Is Blue*.

I am still trying to satisfy the curiosity of my young friends.

Rey: *RAY*

good-by to commerce. Together, Margret and I (she is an artist too) embarked on an artistic career: magazine work, advertising, book illustrations.

1936: Belated honeymoon trip, to Europe. A visit to Paris, planned to last four weeks, lasted four years. Here I did my first picture books for children, and much to my surprise I was not shown the door when I submitted them to publishers. Half a dozen childrens' books, published in France and England, were the crop of that period.

1940, June: Thirty-six hours before the Nazi armies entered, we fled from Paris on bicycles, taking along only a few victuals and some of my manuscripts. After four days of cycling we caught a southbound train and eventually reached Lisbon. From there we went to Rio, and from there to New York.

On October 14, 1940, the Statue of Liberty greeted us through the morning mist. We were prepared for a difficult start but fate was kind: within a month, four of the manuscripts we had brought along were accepted for publication. The autumn sky looked twice as blue to us the day we got this news.

Since then some twenty picture books of ours have been published in this country, and more are to come, I hope. I say "ours" because even those that do not show Margret's name on the title owe much to her help: she usually does the text and criticizes my drawings while they are in progress.

Ever since we came here we have been living in Greenwich Village. We are three: Margret, myself, and Charcoal—our black cocker spaniel. In 1946 Margret and I became American citizens.

Concluding, may I say that making picture books for children is the most wonderful profession I can think of? Not only do you have fun doing it but your fellowmen even pay you for it. Try it some day!

Mabel Louise Robinson

AUTHOR OF
*Bright Island, Runner of the
Mountain Tops, Etc.*

Autobiographical sketch of Mabel Louise Robinson:

I WAS born and brought up in Waltham, Massachusetts. My ancestors have lived in this locality since 1630 so I suppose I am what is known as a New Englander, which seems to imply certain character traits. Though why the people in that section should be all alike when they are privileged to differ elsewhere, I never could see.

We were a family of four children, and we found New England a pleasant place for growing up. We all went to public school, and really believed that private schools were institutions for those who could not make the public school grade. We were so near Boston that we shared whatever it had to offer in the way of the arts. In high school it was the proper thing to attend the symphony rehearsals, rush seat. For this we paid a quarter, stood outside in a mob until the doors opened, and then ran up flights of stairs to the top of Symphony Hall. The best runners got seats. Most of us were bored by the music, but we looked forward to the race the whole week, especially after the day one of the teachers lost her skirt in the course of it.

As soon as school closed we went to Point Allerton for the summer. It was a narrow sandy strip with Boston Harbor on one side and the broad ocean on the other. There we were in and on the salt water all the time; and there it became so much a part of my life that I have never been quite

H. A. REY

MABEL LOUISE ROBINSON

content without it since. Usually it finds a place in my books. Perhaps the thing I enjoy most in Maine now is my sailboat.

Then I went to normal school, taught a while, went to Radcliffe College, and finally took my master's and doctor's degrees at Columbia University, where I now teach creative writing. During the process of getting degrees I taught at Wellesley and at Constantinople College, where I taught many nationalities a great variety of subjects. On the side I had a good deal of fun.

What else? For a few years after I got my Ph.D., I did research work at Carnegie Foundation. And then came Columbia University, where I have a workshop which has so far published over two hundred books.

Naturally I have to publish, too. I have written books for young people of all ages from the "Little Lucia" series to *Bright Island,* and *Runner of the Mountain Tops,* which is for any age that likes biography. My first novel was *Island Noon.* A recent novel, *Bitter Forfeit,* was also published as a serial in the *Saturday Evening Post.* I have written many short stories. And of all the things I have found to do, I still think writing is as stimulating and satisfactory an experience as one could hope to achieve.

I live in New York, spending my week ends at our house in Montrose, a place which the birds have taken over, accepting

me because I am a good provider. The four summer months are for Maine where I have leisure to write, to sail, and to do as I please. It sounds very pleasant. And it is!

Tom Robinson

June 18, 1878-

AUTHOR OF

Trigger John's Son, Buttons, Pete, Etc.

Autobiographical sketch of Thomas Pendleton Robinson:

I WAS born in Calais, Maine, on the St. Croix. My father, Elbridge Robinson, was born on the American side of this river. My mother, Carolyn Hannah, on the Canadian side, where her Hannah ancestor received a grant of land from the King of England after the Revolution. Both my parents were descended from Elder Brewster of Mayflower fame.

When still a baby, I was taken to Driftwood, Pennsylvania. I spent my young years in this then bustling lumber town and in the lumber camps up in the Alleghany Mountains. Like Trigger, I delighted in lassoing rattlesnakes, but we boys were wary of black snakes and copperheads. The thing that really terrified me was the cry of a wildcat when I was alone in the woods after dark.

At twelve I was sent to Boston because it was the Hub of the Universe and its schools the center of the Hub. At Chauncey Hall, I met Ethel Fay, daughter of a professor at Tufts College. When we were sixteen she went with me to our officers' dance, for which she says her first party dress was made and where she carried the first of many bunches of violets.

When I was finishing an architectural course at M. I. T. the gemini of my horoscope became evident, for I started to write. First it was verses to Ethel. Then the Chauncey influence cropped out (our headmasters were Shakespeare enthusiasts) and I wrote a blank verse tragedy, which Ethel still believes will some day be recognized as a masterpiece. Though holding to the idea of being a writer, I took a job as architectural draftsman and we were married. Shortly after, my Tech friend Richard Derby and I formed the firm of Derby and Robinson on Beacon Hill and were elected to the

American Institute of Architects. "Buttons" was an alley cat who lived off and on in our offices.

Our first home was a tiny, old, rose-covered house set in a backyard in Jamaica Plain. One of its chief attractions was a fireplace. Here our son Donald was born. Next we moved to an old house in Newton Centre, whose fireplace had disappeared, so we had to put one in. Here Lincoln was born. Our next was an old house on a farm in Wilmington—still Massachusetts—with three fireplaces. And it was here that Jack was born. Finally we bought the oldest house of all, in Hingham, where fireplaces total five and where we still live. After getting settled we adopted our airedale, Pete, whose story later won me a *Herald Tribune* prize.

Our boys grew up on the farm, combining outdoors with writing, drawing, play-acting, and an interest in world affairs. Among their treasures were *St. Nicholas* gold and silver awards, and certificates of membership in the League of Nations Association signed by Woodrow Wilson. All this time I was spending regular hours in the office, working with Professor Baker at Harvard, where he made me scenic director of the 47 Workshop, and using spare Sundays, evenings, holidays, and vacations to write plays, one of which won the Morosco prize and another, the Drama League-Longmans Green prize. Four others were produced on Broadway.

TOM ROBINSON

Someone suggested my writing children's books, and, later, using my Workshop and Broadway experience to do an acting set of Shakespeare for high school students and other amateurs. Six of these are already published. Donald did glossaries, language and music notes, and is full collaborator on *Macbeth.*

The boys are all married, so we have three daughters and already three grandchildren—Lincoln's. The eldest is Elizabeth Ann, to whom *In and Out* is dedicated. Our Margaret's verses are accumulating. Jim's book will probably be done soon by his father, who has already written two. Donald's publications number five. Jack, following in the footsteps of Elder Brewster and his great-grandfather Fay, is a minister. His many activities—civic, state, and pastoral—call for much use of the pen. Since our household is now reduced to Greylock and his pal, Harry, Ethel acts as research worker, typist, and editor for Robinson books, also often collaborator. We have a grand time.

W. W. and Irene B. Robinson

AUTHOR AND ILLUSTRATOR OF
Ancient Animals, At the Seashore, Etc.

Autobiographical sketch of William Wilcox Robinson:

IN 1898 I was seven and living in Trinidad, a mountain and mining town in Colorado, when my parents decided to take their four children and move to California, where some of their friends had gone and "where roses grew along the streets." I liked that idea, too, and soon all six of us were in California in a small house overlooking the Pacific Ocean. The seashore was exciting—and still is. Ever since those few months spent at Long Beach about 1900 I have liked the ocean, the shore, and swimming better than anything else. Most of my vacations I spend at the beach and most of my driving trips are along the coast.

By the time I was in high school I knew I wanted to be a writer. We were living then in Riverside, where my father owned an orange grove. In fact where we lived the town was made up of orange groves sprinkled with houses. The boys of the neighborhood used to divide into teams and have running fights with oranges that took us

W. W. ROBINSON
IRENE B. ROBINSON

park—Pershing Square—and she illustrated it. I had always been interested in prehistoric animals and when a certain eight-year-old nephew got excited about them, too, the idea of doing a book for children came to us. *Beasts of the Tar Pits* was the result. This book was about the creatures, big and small, that got trapped thousands of years ago in the oil-covered pits that bubble near our home. It was the first of the series of children's books about animals that we have done together. The only trouble with the tar pits was that no dinosaurs ever fell into them. Such beasts lived long, long before there were any tar pits. So, our next book was *Ancient Animals*—about the prehistoric animals, including dinosaurs, of the rest of America.

At the San Diego zoo we saw some exciting snakes, giant tortoises, lizards, and crocodiles and did a book about these reptiles. Elephants were favorites of ours, and we saw lots of them in circuses and zoos. So we put them into a book. There was a lion farm only twenty miles from where we lived, with two hundred and thirty of the magnificent beasts behind the huge stockade. We had to write *Lions*. So the list of books grew and they came to include animals of the Bible, the farm, the zoo, and the seashore. When we watched the army training dogs for war we wrote the story of one of them.

Beside children's books I have written about early California days, when there were great ranchos, few people, and thousands of cattle. Some day I shall turn this material into stories for young readers.

* * *

Autobiographical sketch of Irene Robinson:

I HAVE always liked to draw and I have always liked animals. As far back as I can remember I have loved putting animals down on paper. Those long vacations I had on the Indiana farm near Indianapolis, when I was a little girl, intensified this interest. My aunts let me curry the old buggy horse, taught me how to milk a cow, to pick a setting hen off her nest, and, after a storm, to bring in the half-drowned little chicks and warm them before the fire. How bitterly I wished that I, a city girl, had been born a boy who could live and work on a farm!

Until my husband and I began doing books together—that was in 1931—I painted

over a stretch of six blocks of plowed ground—clear to the wide, lazy canal that was as good for swimming on summer days as it was for irrigating groves.

I wrote a story for the high school paper and became its editor. Everything around me—people, animals, landscape, weather—now was something to write about. In college at Berkeley (University of California) I kept on writing.

It was several years after I married Irene Bowen in Los Angeles that we did our first book together. I wrote the story of a city landscapes, fruit, and flowers. I had gone to Drury College in Missouri and afterward studied painting in Chicago, in Colorado Springs, and finally in Los Angeles—at various schools and with different painters. Today I continue to mix painting and illustrating. The hills, valleys, fruits, and flowers of California are my pleasure, as are the horses, cows, burros, dogs, and other animals I see about me.

I like to draw animals from life, but since our first children's book was about prehistoric animals I had to spend weeks in museums looking at reconstructed skeletons. There I made pencil sketches, then at home did the final illustrations with a greasy, lithographic crayon.

When we began doing books about living animals I sometimes was able to have pets to draw from—like a desert tortoise or a big bullfrog. That has been fun. People always are saying to me, "Where do you get your models?" I answer, "In many places. Sometimes the animals belong to me, sometimes to friends—like the beautiful German shepherd I used as a model for Big Boy." A neighbor's cat may have kittens just when I need to draw kittens. Often I go out into the country to draw horses plowing. Of course if it is an elephant, a giraffe, or a lion, I can't have that pet. Since we live in the heart of a city it's hard to find the right animal at the right moment. I wanted a donkey to be the model for Balaam's ass in a story for *The Book of Bible Animals*. I happened to cross a grassy, vacant lot one morning and there staked out was a small gray burro with a stripe down his back. On several mornings I went to draw him. Then one day he wasn't there and I never knew who owned him.

Once I got into a zoo just before nine A.M. when visitors are allowed. As I walked across the lawn I saw not too far away a lion strolling toward me. I stood still. The lion didn't seem to notice me. Just then a trainer appeared and said, "Jackie, come in. It's nine o'clock." And Jackie, the movie-actor lion, turned around and followed his trainer.

Zoos, circuses, parades, driving trips through the west, lots of time at the seashore, art exhibits, gardening, and cooking— these are what I like.

Feodor Rojankovsky

1891-

ILLUSTRATOR

Autobiographical sketch of Feodor Rojankovsky:

I AM born in Russia on the shore of the Baltic Sea, from the wonderful parents (sometime I will tell about them). Dad was the headmaster of the Mitava High School. We were three brothers and two sisters. Two elder brothers were my first art teachers. Imitating them, with my best friend, my little sister Tania, we made my first illustrated book (never printed)— "Robinson Crusoe." I was nine years old by that time. Later in our school magazine I was the most outstanding illustrator. I believe my reputation was a little exaggerated.

I never liked our drawing lessons nor my art teacher in school. He made us copy boring plaster ornaments. But we had another teacher, one of natural history. He often took us hiking in parks, forests, and on the seashore. He taught us to observe and to love Nature. In written reports we had to give account on our observations. Mine were always illustrated—I could not do otherwise, and this put my teacher in ecstasy.

My serious studies in art started when in 1912 I became student at the Moscow Fine Arts Academy. What a wonderful school it was, what a wonderful city! Such theaters, circus, and all that.

In 1914 the First World War broke out. I was drafted in the army, being infantry reserve officer. My first published drawings and pictures appeared in art magazines when I was wounded and evacuated to the rear.

In 1920 after the revolution I found myself abroad first in Poland, where I worked as stage decorator, art director of a fashion magazine, and finally art director of a big book publishing house in Posnan.

From Poland I moved to Paris. I had at first hard times in this beautiful city, where I lived and worked for fourteen years. When the second war came and the Germans invaded France, I had to leave Paris, my house, and all my books. Before this sad event I worked there for myself, for an advertising agency, moving pictures, and finally as book illustrator for adult and junior people.

Feodor Rojankovsky: *FEE oh dawr roh jan KOFF skee*

From a self-portrait

FEODOR ROJANKOVSKY

In 1941 in Seville a small cargo *Navemar* was brought with 1400 refugees from Europe repeating the experience of Christopher Columbus, and disembarked on September twelfth in New York Harbor.

In my dreams America was far from what it is in reality. I loved in my school times Fenimore Cooper, Mark Twain, Edgar Poe. I loved buffaloes and Redskins.

Here I am working exclusively as book illustrator for young readers. As soon as my work allows me I try to escape from New York on the search for the America of my dreams. I find only its fragments. But I try also to understand the other, the new America for whose sons and daughters I make my books.

Pardon me for closing the page by a quotation. The Russian poet Mayakovsky concludes his poem on Christopher Columbus by these lines which I shall like to repeat on my own part:

> But I would close America, clean it
> a bit and then
> Discover it again!

Francis Rolt-Wheeler

December 16, 1876-

AUTHOR OF
True Stories of Great Americans, Etc.

Autobiographical sketch of Francis Rolt-Wheeler:

THE biographical information I propose to give will be scant. I was born in London, both parents being from County Cork, Ireland, of several generations of writers and university scholars.

I spent several years on sailing ships, and some years in pioneer work in Canada. When still a young fellow, I took up newspaper work, editing. Having taken Holy Orders in the Protestant Episcopal Church, I held several parishes and then the chaplaincy of St. Luke's Hospital, New York, for some ten years. During this period I wrote a dozen or so books—and, just before the First World War, decided to spend my whole time writing. Always an occultist, I gave more and more time to this study, and launched two big astrological reviews, one in English and one in French.

I started to write boys' books because I thought there was a need. I still think so. I deem the radio and the cinema destructive and harmful, laying stress on cheap superficiality and sapping the power to read. Therefore, it is my hope and prayer that America will produce a new crop of writers of boys' books. May they all live long and prosper!

In all I have written some seventy books, I think—but I have never counted. My purpose was always the same—to show that honor and worth, in real adventure, make a man. I have *never* written a line in praise of getting money easily and quickly. Probably, I never shall.

I have one crime on my head, I have made the American Eagle scream, but that is true to life—the bird isn't dumb. And, with a long life behind me, I can't remember a line I am ashamed to have written.

Glen Rounds

1906-

AUTHOR AND ILLUSTRATOR OF
*Blind Colt, Lumber Camp,
Ol' Paul, Rodeo, Etc.*

Autobiographical sketch of Glen H. Rounds:

I GREW up on Montana and South Dakota ranches. After that I sort of prowled the country, covering practically the whole of the United States. When I hit a strange town broke, as I usually did, the only avail-

GLEN ROUNDS

able job was nearly always something I'd never done before. Not being one to let such a small matter stop me, I became in time a pretty good baker, cook, sign painter, lightning artist, sawmill hand, railroad section hand, carnival talker, and a number of other things. Spent short periods in the Kansas City Art Institute and the New York Art Students League. Drifted into writing and illustrating books in much the same accidental fashion I'd gotten into the other jobs. Spent three and a half years in the army, but that wasn't exactly accidental.

* * *

Mr. Rounds now lives in Southern Pines, North Carolina.

Subtitle for *Lumber Camp* is "the life and good times of the new Whistle Punk at Camp Fifteen up Horse Crick way, with many drawings made on the scene by the author." *Pay Dirt* is "the story of how Uncle Torwal and Whitey were chawed off their ranch by grasshoppers and went up in the Black Hills to sluice gold a spell." The same humorous exaggeration found in his subtitles sparkles through the pages of Mr. Rounds' stories, but with it we find a sound base of factual information and an authentic atmosphere. Anne Thaxter Eaton called *Blind Colt* his "finest piece of writing . . . an unforgettable animal portrait, drawn with understanding and a moving simplicity."

Dorothy Rowe

June 20, 1898-

AUTHOR OF
The Rabbit Lantern, The Moon's Birthday, Etc.

Autobiographical sketch of Dorothy Rowe:

ONCE in a city in China an American girl lived with her father and mother and her sisters and brothers. She was called Da Mei Mei which means eldest sister. Her home was a square, gray brick house which stood in a wide garden. A brick wall seven feet high surrounded that garden. Inside it was an American home where the little girl studied her lessons and practiced on the piano. Christmas and Thanksgiving, those American holidays, were very exciting. There was the beloved *St. Nicholas Magazine* coming every month, and *Little Women* and *David Copperfield* to read.

But outside the compound wall there were no American people, no American neighbor children for Da Mei Mei to play with, and not a sound or a smell or a sight like any in cities of America. Da Mei Mei spoke only Chinese outside the great gray gate that led from her garden to the yellow street, and spoke only to her Chinese friends. Sometimes they walked together up to the low hills at the end of Yellow-Mud Alley and flew great paper kites in the March wind; sometimes they went to the sweetmeat shop and spent Chinese copper pennies for candy.

The Chinese children came inside the wall with Da Mei Mei sometimes to romp in the grass under the apricot trees, or sniff the purple wisteria when April brought it blossoming on the trellis by the front door. Sometimes Da Mei Mei went to the homes of her Chinese friends and smiled when their mothers said "Goodness, your hair is nice and black but ,I never heard of blue eyes. See all my children have good brown eyes. But your straight dark hair is very fine."

One of Da Mei Mei's dearest friends was Kwei Shan, a girl just the same age who lived two turns away on the Big Horse Street. Kwei Shan's mother was the nurse who had been with Da Mei Mei's family ever since they came to China, before any of the brothers and sisters were born. Da Mei Mei could hardly tell any difference in her love for her mother and this Chinese

Rowe: *rhymes with "cow"*

nurse, so tender and gentle and fair was Djang Ma. She was never too busy to help Da Mei Mei and Kwei Shan build a cave from the dining room chairs and two steamer rugs, or to fix them special Chinese food for supper if father and mother were to be out for the evening. And always Djang Ma told stories at bedtime, sometimes fairy stories of old China, sometimes songs her mother had taught her, about the Rabbit in the Moon or the fairies who guard the flowers, and always, for the last of all, a song that ended softly, when the children were almost asleep, "Mother of Dreams, send them the rest dreams now."

So, sweetly and swiftly, with adventures and joy, the years went by and Da Mei Mei had grown up and must come to America to college. It seemed very strange and lonely in the far country, but strangest of all was that no one knew anything, really, about China. When Da Mei Mei told them a little they laughed and said, "How funny," until she quite stopped talking of the China she loved so well.

One day a woman who understood the beauty of unshared Chinese stories in Da Mei Mei's heart said, "You should write them for children, young and gay and kind, my dear." And Da Mei Mei began to write. She wrote of stories Djang Ma had told her, and of many of her Chinese friends so the children of America who had

DOROTHY ROWE

never lived in China might read of it at least.

And now Da Mei Mei has a daughter of her own who has never been outside of America. To her she tells over and over again the stories of when she was a little girl herself.

* * *

Dorothy Rowe was born in Rome, New York, and went to China at the age of nine weeks. She lived in Wuhu, Nanchang, Kuling, and Nanking. Her elementary education came from her father and mother at home and Miss Jewell's School in Shanghai. She was graduated from Goucher College in 1919; returned to Nanking; and was married there in 1925 to Benjamin March, who was lecturer on Far Eastern Art at the University of Michigan. One daughter was born in Detroit January 2, 1929. Since her husband's death in 1934, Dorothy Rowe has worked at the University of Michigan, where she is a member of the Department of Fine Arts.

Edwin L. Sabin

December 23, 1870-

AUTHOR OF

*Buffalo Bill and the Overland Trail,
On the Plains With Custer, Etc.*

Autobiographical sketch of Edwin L. Sabin:

BORN, of course. We all have to start that way. I was born in Rockford, Illinois. I did not choose the date. It was so near Christmas that my birthday presents served as Christmas presents too, or else my Christmas presents served as birthday presents. I could not advise anybody to be born at Christmas time.

I did not stay in Rockford long, but before I was a year old went to Clinton, Iowa, where my father had been appointed superintendent of schools. My father was Henry Sabin, my mother, Esther Frances Hotchkiss Sabin; they were from Connecticut, and I am of Colonial and Yankee stock, although the Sabins were originally French Huguenots.

Clinton was an ideal place in which to live. It was an old-time river town. There were steamboats, sawmills, log rafts, fishing, hunting, swimming, camping, and I was brought up with Tom Sawyers and Huckleberry Finns.

Sabin: *SAY bin*

EDWIN L. SABIN

Learned to love the out-of-doors and the ways of the river and the woods, but graduated, for all that, from the Clinton High School, 1888, and then spent four years at the University of Iowa. Then came newspaper work in Iowa and Illinois: that of reporter, city editor, telegraph editor, special correspondent. In 1896 Mary Caroline Nash, of Chicago, and I were married.

In 1900 or thereabouts I turned from newspaper work to writing verse and prose for the magazines. Work on the city staff of a daily paper is good training for a writer. It teaches one to organize one's thoughts and to write under all conditions. In a short time I was writing books. A great many of them have been books for boys.

As it seemed to me, boys would like to know more about the pioneers, explorers, soldiers, and so on who served in the making of these United States, what they did and how they did it; therefore I have written American history stories, the adventure kind. This has been great sport for me and the boy heroes who adventure with me in the stories, and some sport for the readers whom we take along with us.

After having seen considerable of Colorado, New Mexico, Arizona, Wyoming, Utah, I landed in southern California. First it was the coast; at this writing it is the border of the interior desert overlooked by the desert mountains. And if anyone wishes to

know what I like, I will say it is fresh air and big spaces, writing clean stories of honest, real adventure, and adventuring, myself, with my setter dog.

Tony Sarg

April 24, 1882-March 7, 1942
AUTHOR AND ILLUSTRATOR
The Tony Sarg Marionette Book, Etc.

Autobiographical sketch of Anthony Frederick Sarg, written for THE JUNIOR BOOK OF AUTHORS a few years before his death:

TONY SARG was born in Guatemala, of German parentage. His father owned sugar and coffee plantations. Tony's father believed in discipline. At the age of six, young Tony was to start the stern training that fits a man to cope with life. As a suitable beginning, it was decided he should feed the large flock of chickens on the Sarg farm. He was given an alarm clock set for six A.M. and admonished to tumble out of bed the minute it went off, and get busy with the chores. In no time at all little Tony decided that feeding chickens at six o'clock in the morning was very, very far from his notion of fun. But he also knew there just wasn't any use trying to get out of it, as long as there were such things as chickens and military men like his papa.

Now if he could only make a wish or rub a lamp like that lucky fellow, Aladdin, and have those chickens forthwith fed, as if by magic! Right here he began a career that was to make him famous! An idea came into his small brain. He was busy for a time with a vast amount of tinkering. Result: when the alarm clock rang, he simply turned over and went to sleep again! But the chickens were fed. Beside his bed was a string. It led out the window and by a complicated system of pulleys finally reached the chicken yard. Here it was fastened to a little door. When he pulled the string, between yawns, the door opened noisily and invited the chickens into a space where breakfast had been thoughtfully spread for them the night before! Thus, young Tony displayed at a very early age a definitely mechanical mind, which in later years proved invaluable to him as the creator of Tony Sarg's Marionettes.

He has been thinking up and creating clever curiosities. He is a humorous illustrator; mural painter; author of many children's books; creator of huge balloon parades; designer of large mechanical window displays, toys, textiles. He is an illustrator, lecturer, actor, and jack-of-all-trades. Tony Sarg is a most prolific worker. For one of his children's books, which he wrote and illustrated himself with approximately 700 illustrations, he went to the trouble of hand-lettering the entire text, which in itself was a herculean job.

One of the most interesting murals Tony Sarg ever painted is now in the Sherman Hotel in Chicago. It represents a bird's-eye view of old Chicago before the Fire. It is ninety by sixty feet and has thousands of figures, boats, and vehicles of every description. At the Waldorf-Astoria Hotel in New York is an entire room decorated with his animal characters in rollicking fun.

Tony Sarg's studio in West Ninth Street, New York, is a veritable little museum, housing a large and interesting toy collection. Fantastic-looking marionettes clad in armor hang on the walls, and miniature models of interiors, wagons, etc. enliven his interesting studio.

Mr. Sarg has written over a dozen children's books; he has designed toys for children and several wall papers he designed are specially suitable for children's rooms. He has written considerably about marionettes. He collaborated with Anne Stoddard on a little book of marionette plays. In his earlier books, Mr. Sarg introduced two favorite characters; one of them was Mary, his daughter, and the other was her little cocker spaniel named Freckles.

In one or two instances, Mr. Sarg has introduced some trick devices in his books. Mr. Sarg is now at work on a baby book which promises to be most unusual.

* * *

When Tony Sarg was young, his father wanted him to follow a military career and by the time he was seventeen he had acquired a lieutenant's commission in the horse artillery, but he did not like the army and at twenty-three left it and Germany never to return. When the First World War broke out he had become a British citizen and

was living in London, but he was asked to resign from his clubs because of his German origin. So he left Britain in 1915 for the United States, where he became a citizen in 1921.

He died in the Manhattan General Hospital, of peritonitis, about three weeks after an emergency appendectomy and shortly before his sixtieth birthday.

Constance Savery

October 31, 1897-

AUTHOR OF

Enemy Brothers, Emeralds for the King, Etc.

Autobiographical sketch of Constance Savery:

THANK you, Mr. Edward Burn.

You were my father's old friend, a lifelong invalid. We never met, you and I, but you often sent a story book to the eldest of the five little sisters in All Saints Vicarage, Froxfield, Wiltshire.

Thank you, Mrs. Stubbington.

You were one of the Twenty Clergy and Thirty Lay Widows who lived in the Hospital "founded and endowed by the late Most Noble Sarah, Duchess of Somerset," in 1694. Nobody but the late Most Noble Sarah ever called your home a hospital, though the word was written big and plain on the marble shield above the entrance gateway. Froxfield people always spoke of it as the College. Your tiny house, Mrs. Stubbington, was at the far end of the west side of the great quadrangle, under the shadow of the tall chapel. The Vicar of Froxfield was also Chaplain of the College. From the little parlour where you sat invisible, came books for his book-hungry child.

Thank you, Bishop Russell Wakefield of Birmingham.

You sent books at Christmas to the children of the clergy in your diocese, nice fat books that they could not have afforded to buy for themselves.

Kind souls, I thank you again.

I was born on Hallowe'en, when the witches and goblins are about. "Please tell

Savery: *SAY ver ee*

CONSTANCE SAVERY

Ruth Sawyer

1880-

AUTHOR OF

*Roller Skates, Picture Tales from Spain,
The Way of the Storyteller, This
Way to Christmas, Etc.*

Autobiographical sketch of Ruth Sawyer:

I WAS born in Boston, Massachusetts, on a very hot day in August. That is the only fact in my life with which I had nothing to do. From the time when I was very small I was straining nerve and muscle trying to accomplish something that seemed to me important and that I wanted above all things to do. I wanted to skate—and did before I was four. I wanted to swim—and did before I was five. I wanted to dance like the fairies in the Drury Lane pantomime that came to New York City from London when I was six. But dance I never did. When I was seven I heard *The Mikado* and wanted to sing as sweetly as the Three Little Maids from School. Singing I finally gave up as not for me. So what I remember about my early years was being a failure.

What I finally did accomplish—writing books—I never dreamed of doing when I was young. And I am sure my teachers never dreamed of it, either. I never passed English grammar; and to this day I have very queer ideas about spelling and punctuation.

My father was an importer. My mother was very small, very lovely; she went often with my father abroad. That was how it happened that a book called *Roller Skates* came to be written. It is about my tenth year and all the skating I did around New York City. That was a true year. Trinket was true, so was Tony, Mr. Gilligan, Mr. Night-Owl and Uncle Earle. Lucinda was very proud indeed when her book won the Newbery Award in 1937.

I was the last of five children—all the rest were boys. As Duncan, David and Carter, three of them come into my *Year of Jubilo,* and that, too, is a true story. The other books had true people in them, and many true happenings, but they are part imagination. I have always felt that a little girl was lucky to have older brothers. Mine teased me, they knocked good sense into me, they allowed me to go camping, sailing, hunting with them, until the whole coun-

me a story" are almost the first words I can remember saying. As nobody told me enough stories I was obliged to make them up for myself. Sometimes the stories were acted with the help of paper dolls cut out of my mother's pattern books, sometimes told in my head, sometimes written, sometimes recited while I walked about house or garden pretending to play a solitary game of bat and ball. I liked the last way best.

When I was nine we left Froxfield to spend the next sixteen years in Birmingham. My book, *Danny and the Alabaster Box,* gives a picture of the home life among black factory chimneys in the parish of St. Mark. From King Edward the Sixth's High School for Girls, I went to Somerville College, Oxford.

I have never loved any place as I love Oxford, my "dear city of the violet crown."

Two years after I had taken my degree, my father became rector of Holy Trinity, Middleton-cum-Fordley, a small East Anglian village among water-meadows within sound of the gray North Sea.

For a time I taught—I hated teaching!—but when my dear mother died, I went home to help my father in his parish and to care for him in his old age. Now I live with a sister near the seaside town of Southwold, writing, always writing, in a bomb-scarred house over which the air-raid sirens have wailed more than two thousand times.

RUTH SAWYER

tryside called me "Sawyers' Tag." And they helped me to a happy growing up.

The other lucky thing in my childhood was having an Irish nurse, Johanna. She was a wonderful storyteller. From her I got my love of listening and telling stories—and finally of writing them down. Had it not been for Johanna I think I should have never gone into so many foreign countries collecting old tales; and had I never gone then I should never have found Toño Antonio in Spain, or Paco and his Least One in Mexico, or half the stories that have gone into making the Christmas books.

Finally, in case you are interested, I have a husband who is a physician, and two grown-up children, David and Margaret. Best of all—I have a small granddaughter, Sarah McCloskey. It was her father who made that lovely picture book called *Make Way for Ducklings*. We are all living now in Maine—and very contentedly.

Frances Clarke Sayers

September 4, 1897-

AUTHOR OF

Bluebonnets for Lucinda. Tag-Along Tooloo. Etc.

Autobiographical sketch of Frances Clarke Sayers:

WHENEVER I am asked where I am from I draw a long breath and begin to recite as many American place names as a railroad timetable, an action highly appropriate to the daughter of a railroad official who as a young man began his career with the Sante Fe Railroad, and spent his life in its service. It was due to the Santa Fe that Kansas was the state of my birth, and it was due to the Sante Fe that Galveston, Texas, was the place in which I spent my childhood, and which I still count as home. I am, therefore, a Texan born in Topeka, Kansas.

It was the Sante Fe which made it possible for my mother, my sister, and myself to abandon the tropical heat of Texas every summer and go to Ludington, Michigan, where we lived on the top of a sand dune, in a little board cottage, and where we met and grew up with people from Illinois, Indiana, Kansas, Missouri, Ohio, Wisconsin, Pennsylvania, Michigan, and Iowa.

That was in the days before everyone owned an automobile, and the life of the summer resort was simple, carefree, and constant in its friendships. We had wide woods in which to roam, filled with pine, birch, sassafras, closed gentians, wintergreen, wild strawberries, Indian pipes, and bittersweet. We had blue Lake Michigan in which to swim (I never learned to swim) and the whole outdoors in which to play, with no restrictions, except to be home in time for dinner in the middle of the day, and home in time to share the sunset with the family, from the wide gallery of the cottage.

Life in the winter, at Galveston, was more formal. There was school, for one thing, which was always an interrupted process for me because I was that unbearable and awful thing, a "sickly" child. There was Christmas with firecrackers, the Mardi gras celebrations, and the Ball High School picnics on the mainland every May. In Galveston, there was always the boom or the murmur of the great gray Gulf of Mexico; hot moonlight nights, in which the mockingbirds sang rapturously (hearing them was as mystic and beautiful an experience as I have ever encountered); tropical plants and flowers; palms, banana trees; bougainvillea, oleanders, poinsettias, and great tangles of yellow roses everywhere. There was the fascination of foreign ships docked at the wharves, come to load cotton; these my father and I explored Sunday afternoons in the winter.

This yearly shifting of scene, and the fact that my mother's people had been pioneers out of Lord Baltimore's Maryland into Ohio, my father's people pioneers out of New England into Pennsylvania, gave my sister and me an innate awareness of the stretch of the continent, of the variety of people it produced, and of the different attitudes toward ways of living and thinking. This awareness, heightened by my mother's straightforward love for people of all types and conditions, gave us a breadth of view which was to enrich our whole lives.

Two years at the University of Texas were followed by a year at the Carnegie Library School in Pittsburgh, for I had made up my mind as to what my work was to be when I was still a devotee of the *St. Nicholas* magazine. There was an article in that magazine about library work with children, with reference to the central children's room of the New York Public Library. It seemed to me, therefore, that Fate had half an eye upon me when I found myself, in my first position, an assistant in that children's room.

After five years there I joined my family in the experience of living in California. This was followed by my marriage to an old friend from the New York days, Alfred Sayers of St. Louis and Chicago. Seven gay and spirited years were spent in Chicago, then seven more in California. Here I began to write in earnest, between watching the harbor, walking miles through Muir Woods, sitting for long periods of time on the little gallery of the lighthouse which

stood just above the rushing tides of the great Golden Gate, teaching in the library school at Berkeley, "barnstorming" on behalf of books for children in the remote, inland towns of the state, and discovering that I had, as my mother said, "a flair for cooking." The manuscript for my third book, *Tag-Along Tooloo*, was completed in California before my husband and I made the great decision that I was to accept the opportunity to become superintendent of work with children at the New York Public Library.

That was in 1941. Since that time, whatever energy was left for writing has gone into annual reports, and a few scattered articles for magazines and professional periodicals. There is one more story about my childhood in Texas, however, which has simmered up into my mind. At least two thirds of it is down on paper. May it see the light of printer's ink, for there is no more satisfactory way of expressing one's gratitude for the experience of life than to set it down in a form which can be shared with those who have the greater part of the journey before them.

James Willard Schultz

August 26, 1859-June 11, 1947

AUTHOR OF
*With the Indians in the Rockies,
Sinopah, the Indian Boy, Etc.*

Autobiographical sketch of James Willard Schultz, written for THE JUNIOR BOOK OF AUTHORS a few years before his death:

I WAS born in Boonville, New York. Was sent to Peekskill Military Academy to prepare to enter West Point. In 1877, got permission from my mother and my guardian to go to Montana to hunt buffaloes, I promising to return for fall term of the Academy. Never went back to live. Married Mutsi Ahwotan Ahki—Beautiful Shield Woman—of the Pikuni tribe of the Blackfeet. Our son, Hart Merriam Schultz (Lone Wolf), well-known artist, born in 1884.

Roamed the Montana plains with the Pikuni until the buffaloes were exterminated in 1883. Then lived with them on the Blackfeet Indian Reservation until 1904, and since then have annually visited them and our brother tribes, the Blackfeet and the

FRANCES CLARKE SAYERS

Bloods, in Alberta. The now Glacier National Park was my favorite hunting country. Doctor George Bird Grinnell, J. B. Moore, and I were the first white men to explore it and discover its glaciers, beginning in 1885. I myself named several of its mountains and lakes.

My first writings were contributions to *Forest and Stream*, beginning in 1882. Since then I have written more than thirty books.

My greatest desire: in my writings to give a true picture of the Indians; of Indian life as I have actually experienced it.

* * *

The story of how James Willard Schultz happened to write Indian books for boys and girls goes back to the time when he first went West. He tells it himself in the preface to his first adventure story, *With the Indians in the Rockies.*

Schultz gathered the material for his own stories on his annual visits to his old tribe. "Every summer, in Berries Ripe moon, June," he wrote, "eight or ten lodges of us old people get together for the purpose of recording the history and the folklore of the tribe, I, the amanuensis, and my son Lone Wolf the artist of the session of many weeks." The procedure is attended by much ceremony, which includes the painting of his face by the medicine man, the invocation to the sun to help him in recording the tales, and the passing of the sacred pipe from hand to hand.

His Blackfeet Indian name, Apikuni, means Far-off White Robe.

Samuel Scoville, Jr.

June 9, 1872-December 4, 1950

AUTHOR OF

Wild Folk, Boy Scouts in the Wilderness, Lords of the Wild, Etc.

Autobiographical sketch of Samuel Scoville, Jr., written for THE JUNIOR BOOK OF AUTHORS a few years before his death:

SAMUEL SCOVILLE, Jr., was born in Norwich, New York, son of Samuel Scoville, a Congregational minister, and Harriet E. Beecher, a daughter of Henry Ward Beecher and a niece of Harriet Beecher

Stowe. He spent his boyhood at Stamford, Connecticut, and graduated from Yale in 1893. While at that institution he attained no special scholastic distinction but managed to win the quarter, the half, and the mile championship in different years, and the lightweight championship in boxing. He was a member of Chi Delta Theta, the literary society of Yale and did a considerable amount of writing for the *Yale Literary Magazine* and the *Yale Record*, besides newspaper and magazine work, while an undergraduate.

After graduation he was the sporting editor of the *University Magazine* and at the same time studied law and obtained an LL.B. from the University of the State of New York and was admitted to the New York Bar. He married Katharine Gallaudet Trumbull, a daughter of H. Clay Trumbull, a well-known writer and editor. They have had five children.

In 1900 he moved to Philadelphia and has maintained his law office in that city ever since, retaining his New York office also.

Mr. Scoville has published almost a score of books, has had articles and stories in most of the leading magazines in this country, and has appeared in a number of British magazines. His books have been translated into German, Norwegian, Finnish, and Hungarian. His especial hobby is nature study. His other hobbies include tennis and contract bridge. He has also lectured extensively on nature subjects.

Mr. Scoville lives at Haverford, Pennsylvania, a suburb of Philadelphia, and he has a summer home, Treetop, at North Cornwall, Connecticut, a cabin in the pine barrens of southern New Jersey, and a house and woodland and shore property at Falls Point, West Sullivan, Maine.

* * *

All his life Samuel Scoville was an outdoor enthusiast, although he had been told by a doctor to "take it easy" as early as 1900—fifty years before his death at seventy-eight in the Bryn Mawr Hospital, near his Haverford home. For many years up to the time of his death his legal column entitled "The Philadelphia Lawyer" was a popular feature in several Philadelphia newspapers.

Augusta Huiell Seaman

April 3, 1879-June 4, 1950

AUTHOR OF

The Boarded Up House, The Sapphire Signet, Jacqueline of the Carrier Pigeons, Etc.

Autobiographical sketch of Augusta Huiell Seaman, written for THE JUNIOR BOOK OF AUTHORS shortly before her death:

WRITERS of "mystery stories" must, I think, be born with a peculiar type of imagination and curiosity. They must love the unraveling of problems, the solving of riddles, the keeping of others in suspense till the revelation at the end!

I must have early possessed this type of mind. Having been brought up on Poe and Sherlock Holmes (there weren't the hundreds turning out that type of fiction in my young days, as there are now!) my earliest writing for publication, adult short stories, showed a decided tendency toward this form. A little later I turned to producing children's fiction, contributing frequently to *St. Nicholas.*

But I had another strong bent also—for history and historical fiction. And my first three books were pure historical fiction, into the plots of which, however, I could not resist weaving considerable mystery and suspense.

At this period (1910-1913) so far as I know, there were no actual *per se* mystery stories for young folks. It occurred to me there was no reason it couldn't be done and be popular. Why shouldn't there be mystery stories for *young folks*, omitting the crime element, but incorporating all the conjectures, thrills, and suspense which made adult fiction of that type so fascinating?

I resolved to try it, and in 1914, produced *The Boarded Up House*, which ran serially in *St. Nicholas*, and was afterward published in book form. Its success was so immediate that demands for "more" began to come from editors, publishers, and children themselves, and I soon found I had time to write nothing else. For fifteen consecutive years I had mystery-serials in *St. Nicholas* and also in the *Youth's Companion*, the *American Girl*, and other publications. These were always published later in book form.

Almost from the beginning of launching this type of story, however, I had a persistent hankering to get back to historical fiction, but so great had the demand then become for mysteries, that I never found the opportunity to do so. Also I discovered that stories laid in the present were always more popular.

Therefore I saw a way to compromise by writing present-day mysteries, which depended upon an historical period for their backgrounds. This, too, made them more worth while and lasting in character. Children wrote that the books were a help to them in picturing and remembering certain periods of history, and the books began to be adopted by school libraries as supplementary reading to history studies. And the joy I myself experience in digging out obscure and intriguing historical data and situations to weave into the books quite compensates for the lack of opportunity to get back to my other pet form of writing!

Writing for young people is a very great pleasure, because their response and appreciation are always so spontaneous and sincere. It makes life worth while.

* * *

Augusta Huiell Seaman (in private life Mrs. Francis P. Freeman) wrote and published more than forty books for young people. She died at seventy-one at her home at Seaside Park, New Jersey.

Kate Seredy

AUTHOR AND ILLUSTRATOR OF

The White Stag, The Good Master, The Singing Tree, Etc.

Autobiographical sketch of Kate Seredy:

I HATE to talk about myself. Not because I am modest, but because no matter how drastically I try to telescope all the things that have happened to me and all the ventures I've gotten into, the abridged story still sounds like a Baron Munchausen tale.

I was born in Budapest, Hungary. There I had most of my art training, in a catch-as-catch-can way, because World War I was in full swing. Almost two of those years I spent as a war nurse, sandwiching academic studies of anatomy between bouts of patching up anatomy in the raw, in front-line hospitals. It proved too much for my own and it took long months in a hospital to put me back into working order.

Huiell: *HEW el*

Seredy: *SHAIR a dee*

In 1922 the opportunity to visit America presented itself. I came, like the Man Who Came to Dinner, and here I stayed. My chosen line, illustrating, had to be shelved, of course, since it's advisable to understand the story one is to illustrate and first I had to learn English. In the meantime I did some factory work, painting lampshades, and stenciling greeting cards, learning some English in the process that I had to unlearn later. From that I graduated to sheet music covers and, suddenly in 1928, to illustrating first-grade textbooks. That, in turn and in time, led to other illustrating jobs. I should now be an illustrator and not an author had it not been for the depression in the 1930's, when there were no jobs for a still unknown artist. In search of work I haunted editors' offices and met one who, probably because she felt sorry for me, sent me on my way without a book to illustrate but with these words: "I like the way you tell a story. Go home and write a book about your childhood in Hungary."

That was February 1935—as cold as only February of a depression year can be—and home was a decrepit barn of a house in New Jersey. Home I went and, because I had nothing else to do, started to write. I wrote until I was sure I had proven that I couldn't, then sent the crate full of longhand pages to the editor. That was *The Good Master.* Since it became a success I have lost all reverence for people who write books.

KATE SEREDY

Why—there's nothing to it! One just talks on paper. I've been doing it ever since.

In my spare time I've had several near-fatal accidents; bought a farm in Orange County, tried to run it and *that* proved one of the near-fatal accidents. Now I merely live in the old house and let the grass grow wild. One could call my farm a game preserve, because the fields are teeming with creatures—mostly mice, woodchucks, and skunks, though, so perhaps I'd better not call it anything. The house also has a tendency to teem with things—wasps and, as I discovered five years ago, termites. They have all but eaten the house from under me; now I think I've won the five-year war, but one never can tell. I do a lot of woodcarving myself; it's fascinating, so I can't blame the termites.

The house is furnished with lovely old pieces I've rescued from auction sales, attics, and cellars, and refinished myself. Right now I am trying to branch out into pottery and portrait sculpture. Perhaps one of these days I'll trap myself inside my own kiln—but, come what may, so far, it's been fun!

* * *

In 1938, Miss Seredy's *White Stag* won the Newbery Medal.

Helen Sewell

1896-

ILLUSTRATOR

Autobiographical sketch of Helen Moore Sewell:

WHEN I was small my father, who was in the Navy, went to Guam as governor and he took me and my two sisters with him. We sailed from the Brooklyn Navy Yard one gray November day and later returned by way of Honolulu and San Francisco so I had circled the globe before I was eight.

That trip made such a strong impression on me that I can still remember it well—Gibraltar through the mist and the domes and minarets of Algiers white above the blue Mediterranean, Arabs on camels silhouetted against the sky beside the Suez Canal, and the Red Sea (which to our surprise was also blue) and Mount Sinai pink beyond, the albatross which flew aboard during a storm in the Indian Ocean, and a fairy tale Christmas at sea. At Colombo a snake

Sewell: *SOO el*

HELEN SEWELL

charmer performed for us on the deck and somewhere in the Philippines we passed an active volcano glowing in the night.

There were sunny beaches at Guam, covered with shells and morning-glories, and the sea streaked green and cobalt, amethyst and turquoise to the reefs. I also remember well the earthquakes and tropical storms, the lizards and the bats.

After our return to the States we went to school in Brooklyn but spent long and lovely summers at Lake George and on a farm near Schenectady with numerous cousins, aunts, and uncles, and grandmother and grandfather.

I went to art school first when I was twelve and continued to study at intervals for some years.

My only travels since then have been a trip to Brittany and England just before the last war, with my small niece, and one to Jamaica. I had all my life a longing to see a tropical island again.

I have been making books for nearly twenty years with the help of all the children in the family.

Monica Shannon

AUTHOR OF
Dobry, California Fairy Tales, Etc.

Autobiographical sketch of Monica Shannon:

I WAS born up in Canada, where my father and mother were born. Being born in March made me on time for the first spring robin. But when the robins left for the South that autumn, my family left also, settling down for a while in Seattle.

We moved to the Bitter Root Valley in the Rocky Mountains, where peaks are snowy even in July and mountains very green with pines. There we lived on a big, thoroughbred stock farm: miles of grain, thousands of red Hereford cattle with faces as snowy as the peaks.

Bulgarian immigrants worked on the ranch and used to come singing across the fields at sunset time, bringing us buttermilk made the Bulgarian way.

As a child I got around more than some children do, due to Dad, who imported the first Dutch belted cattle into our United States and got me a St. Bernard from Switzerland. With a St. Bernard called Lenore for a nursemaid any child could roam far and wide, "sit in" with Flathead Indians who camped at the foot of our hill to dance when Indian summer set the valley aglow. Lenore and I visited old bee men sitting in apple orchards among their blue hives, called on cowpunchers to watch them cook hot cakes and proudly toss a few out the window to their pet robins.

In elementary school we had to write about our favorite Bible character. I wrote about Joseph because of the sheep herder on the ranch who would walk miles bringing an orphan lamb under his coat and smile when he laid the lamb in the arms of a child. It was such a pleasure for me to know that a sheep herder's little boy had a warm coat of many colors and triumphed over everything, that the teachers not only exhibited the story but on Commencement Day I received a medal.

In grammar school we had to write a short story about the American Revolution. I wrote about children during the Revolution and the teacher bought a white kid book, called it an Honor Book, and asked me to copy my story in it instead of going ice-skating that afternoon. Writing has its downs as well as its ups.

The principal of our public high school insisted that I make two years in one and

MONICA SHANNON

as I was also on the debating team I didn't do much writing, but we won the state debate and the town presented each of us with a gold watch.

During summer vacations my brothers, sisters, and I spent much of our time on horseback; we fished and played tennis.

We moved to California, where I studied library science, and after getting a B.L.S. worked in the Los Angeles Public Library.

Since my two little nieces lived at our house, I made a habit of taking them and their friends out to the woods in my spare time. As they asked for a story and at the same time wished to know about the trees, birds, and wild flowers around us, I began writing down tales of these things for them.

One rainy afternoon a wise and delightful professor of library science dropped into my office. She picked up one of the typed stories lying on my desk and said:

"*California Fairy Tales?* Oh, my! Nobody could write them! But I'd like something to read. Could I take this?"

As someone from the newspaper had called to say the music critic was ill and the public library could have the space if I would make the three-o'clock deadline, I laughed and said: "Just take anything! Your umbrella for instance!"

The professor, formerly a reader for a publishing company, later telephoned: "I was never more pleasantly surprised in my life!"

Neither was I.

* * *

In 1935 Monica Shannon's *Dobry* was awarded the Newbery Medal.

Irwin Shapiro

1911-

AUTHOR OF
*John Henry and the Double Jointed
Steamdrill, Casey Jones and
Locomotive No. 638, Etc.*

Autobiographical sketch of Irwin Shapiro:

I WAS born in Pittsburgh and studied painting at the Art Students League of New York. I soon turned to writing, however, and my interest in American folklore led me to do books for young people. Several of my stories have been published in England as well as in the United States, and a number have been broadcast on the Columbia School of the Air and other radio programs.

I have also written a motion picture story for MGM, and motion picture and drama criticism. I was on the staff of a theater and film magazine and was national affairs editor of *Scholastic* magazine and of *Facts on File*, a news digest.

IRWIN SHAPIRO

Shapiro: *sha PEE roh*

I have worked for varying periods as a typist, a shoe salesman, a clerk in a bookstore, a group worker in a country school, a manuscript reader for motion picture companies, a lathe hand in a machine shop, and as a seaman.

* * *

Mr. Shapiro lives in Flushing, New York, and is author of some eight books, illustrated by James Daugherty or Donald McKay, which are very popular with younger boys and girls. Critics have praised the vigor, humor, and terseness of his story telling. His *Joe Magarac and His U.S.A. Citizen Papers* received the Julia Ellsworth Ford Foundation award for 1947.

Henry Beston Sheahan

See *Beston, Henry*

Charlie May Simon

1897-

AUTHOR OF

Faraway Trail, Art in the New Land, Etc.

Autobiographical sketch of Charlie May Hogue Simon:

CHARLIE MAY is a strange name to give a girl. But it is my own, and a real one. It is the combination of the first names of my parents, Charles Wayman Hogue and Mary Jackson Hogue.

The first clear picture of my life is of the day we moved to Memphis, Tennessee, when I stood before the window and saw a face looking back at me from another window of the house next door. Carriages and wagons were passing up and down the street and I could hear the songs of the street vendors, songs I did not learn until later, of the rag man, the coal man, and the man with "good old turnip greens" to sell. The world was suddenly very big and exciting to me then, for I had been born on my grandfather's farm, in a house built long before by my great-grandfather, in Drew County, far in the backwoods of Arkansas. I didn't realize it at the time, but Memphis and I were not as big as I thought we were, and we grew up together.

I still kept in touch with life on the farm when every summer my mother took us back, my two sisters, my brother, and my-

CHARLIE MAY SIMON

self. There were uncles and aunts our own age to play with, and a baby uncle, younger than any of us. We waded in forbidden creeks, raided watermelon patches to eat only the sweet hearts of them, rode the saplings and pretended they were bucking broncos, and we made mud pies with real cream and eggs. At night, when we were safe in bed, we could hear in the distance the howl of wolves and once in a while the scream of a panther or the shrill bark of a fox passing by.

I learned to read early, for every day when my older sister came home from school I gave her no peace until she told me about everything she had done. I learned to read and write along with her, and soon I was ready to go into the same class with her.

The day I was given my first library card still stands in my memory as one of the most wonderful of my life. To be told I could have any two books I wanted in a room full of books was too good to be true. It was hard to choose on that first day, but I believe eventually I managed to read them all.

Later, when I became librarian of a small branch library in Memphis, I saw that same experience come to many others, a first library card and a room full of books to choose from.

There are many things that formed the background of the books I have written. In a large family with great-grandparents and great-uncles and aunts and cousins many times removed, there were numerous tales of romance and adventure that had happened to some remote relative, or ghost stories and tales of strange happenings. And my father often read aloud to us, stories by Hawthorne and Poe, which made us shiver with fright, but we loved them.

I have lived in many places since that day in 1901 when I first moved to Memphis. At last, memories of the summers spent on my grandfather's farm drew me back to my native state, to live in a stone house in a pine forest overlooking the Arkansas River. The wolves and the panthers and the foxes are gone, but the land is the same.

Louis Slobodkin

February 19, 1903-

ILLUSTRATOR, AND AUTHOR OF
Adventures of Arab, Clear the Track,
Friendly Animals, Etc.

Autobiographical sketch of Louis Slobodkin:

MY father and mother came from the Ukraine to this country in the 1890's. They settled in Albany, New York, and raised four children—three boys and one girl. Since the law for compulsory education was already in effect, in spite of my protests, after kindergarten (which I loved) I was sent to Grammar School Number 14, and later to the Albany High School. It grieves me now but I must confess in neither school was I a very remarkable scholar. And the only explanation I can make is that I was already very much concerned with my career. I wanted to be an artist.

Since I can remember anything at all, I've always been making drawings. When I was ten or eleven my little brother, who liked to play baseball, gave me a large lump of red modeling clay. I never knew where he got it. Promptly I modeled an Indian head (naturally since it was red clay), then a head of George Washington, who became Benjamin Franklin when I squeezed some clay spectacles over G.W.'s difficult eyes. Now I knew the kind of artist I was going to be. I would be a sculptor.

Slobodkin: *sloh BODD kin*

The grammar school days I remember best were the holidays—Christmas and Decoration Day—not only because they meant no school but because I was allowed to decorate the blackboards of our classroom with colored chalks. Aside from the good school library we had and the fact that I did make some pen and ink drawings for our high school magazine, *The Garnet and Grey* (I was chief cartoonist for a few months), I took no pleasure in high school. I was anxious to be off and begin my studies in sculpture.

In November 1918 I came down to New York and entered the Beaux Arts Institute of Design. For six years I studied sculpture, composition, and drawing, supporting myself by working as an elevator runner, dishwasher, factory hand, or at whatever job I could get.

Those days were very full with art school studies, working for a living, and yet it seems we students had plenty of time to listen to good music and to read profound books—of course, elevator service suffered. I enjoyed the art school and I did pretty well—why be modest? All right then, during those six years I was awarded twenty-two medals for life study, composition, and drawing, and I won the Louis Tiffany Foundation Fellowship.

Out of art school I worked for a number of years as an assistant sculptor in the studios of older sculptors—both here and

LOUIS SLOBODKIN

abroad. In the summer of '22 I locked my studio door and shipped down to South America as deck sailor. I made a lot of drawings and watercolors of real sailors at work and when I returned to New York I made small statues from these drawings.

Now for many years I've worked in my own studio here in New York and have made quite a bit of sculpture for public and private buildings and for exhibition.

In 1941 I began my first work for children's books when I illustrated *The Moffats*. Since then I've illustrated and designed more stories by Mrs. Estes and I also designed and illustrated *Many Moons*, by James Thurber. (I got the 1943 Caldecott Medal for my pictures in that one.) There were also other books by other authors.

During this period I continued doing sculpture, and since 1944 I have written and illustrated five books of my own, for children.

Florence Gersh, a Brooklyn girl, and I were married some twenty years ago and we have two fine sons, Larry, now grown up, and Michael, still young, and we all hope to live happily ever after.

Jessie Willcox Smith

ILLUSTRATOR

1863-1935

IT was not until she was seventeen that Jessie Willcox Smith discovered she had any artistic ability. Pictures always had a fascination for her and she spent hours at the galleries wondering and worshiping, but how they were made was a mystery to her. They seemed far from her life.

Her love of children induced her to be a kindergarten teacher, and at sixteen she went to Cincinnati to study. One day her cousin, an advanced art student, was asked by a young teacher in a boys' school to give him some lessons in drawing so he could illustrate his school talks on the blackboard. The cousin's mother consented, but suggested that Jessie join the class also as a chaperon. The first object they were given to draw was a student's lamp. To her own great surprise Miss Smith's drawing was a brilliant success, and she was persuaded to give up the kindergarten work, which was uphill for her, and enter art school. When she finished she began to make drawings

for *St. Nicholas* and other magazines. Then she was fortunate in continuing her studies under Howard Pyle of Drexel Institute. He made many things clear to her.

In order to give his students some real practice, Pyle had an arrangement with some publishers by which he was given books for his classes to illustrate, he being responsible for the quality of the drawings. The class competed for these, the one handing in the best picture receiving the book to illustrate. The first book given to Miss Smith was about Indians. She knew very little about Indians, but by hard work and with the aid of a wonderful collection of Indian curios owned by a friend she turned out work that pleased the publishers. She was dismayed to receive a second book about Indians, but managed to do that also. When it was promptly followed by a third she felt she must speak then or forever be condemned to paint Indians. So she wrote the publishers that she did not know much about Indians, but if they had just an everyday book about children she could do better. She was immediately rewarded with one of Louisa May Alcott's stories and a letter saying they were glad to know she did other things, as they had supposed Indians were her specialty.

Jessie Willcox Smith, daughter of Charles Henry and Katherine De Witt Smith, was born and educated in Philadelphia, and spent her life in or near that city. In her early days she and some friends shared an old building, once an inn, outside of Philadelphia. There they had roomy studios and attractive surroundings. Later Miss Smith acquired a spacious home in Philadelphia, in one wing of which she had her studio.

In her student days Miss Smith never drew a child but always wanted to, and as soon as she was free to do so she turned naturally to them. Only once she tried a model, secured from a family that supplied models of all ages from babies to grandmothers. The little girl was to pose for one of the illustrations for *The Princess and the Goblin*. When the child was put into the position desired and told the story to arouse her interest, she remained without moving a muscle, lifeless and spiritless, all interest gone. At last in despair Miss Smith opened the studio door and told the youngster to go into the garden and play and forget she had come to pose. After that her only models were children she borrowed from her friends, who played around her in all the natural, unselfconscious poses of childhood.

In addition to illustration, Miss Smith did successful portrait painting of children. She did not necessarily favor beautiful children, but liked to catch the spirit within, to bring out some individuality or quaintness of manner. It was often a problem to keep little ones sufficiently interested for a natural and attractive pose, and yet quiet enough for studied work. Often she told stories while she worked, although she found that in the double concentration either the story or the work might unconsciously stop. Once, in painting, on his kiddy car, a boy who was too restless to remain on it unless in motion, she cleared a large space and let him ride round and round in her studio, after chalking a mark on the floor and telling him that, in playing the game, each time he came to the mark he should look at her and smile. The entire portrait was painted in that manner.

Jessie Willcox Smith won many awards and medals. She died at her home, Cogs Hill, in Chestnut Hill, Philadelphia, at the age of seventy-two.

Caroline Dale Snedeker

March 23, 1871-

AUTHOR OF

Downright Dencey, Theras and His Town, The Spartan, The Forgotten Daughter, Etc.

Autobiographical sketch of Caroline Dale Snedeker:

I WAS born in New Harmony, Indiana. This beautiful little town had a great effect on my imagination. It has become the background of three of my books.

For this I must thank my grandmother who throughout my childhood told me stories of early Harmony. I realize now that she told them extremely well. She was a small, slender person, always wearing a cap that was like white fluffy soapsuds. So delicate was its fluted material that it could not be washed, but when soiled was thrown away and another pure cap took its place. She had been in New Harmony when my grandfather, Robert Owen, brought his gen-

CAROLINE DALE SNEDEKER

iusy friends to found a Perfect State and when it was surrounded by impenetrable forests. In short she was an ideal grandmother for story telling.

In New Harmony were preserved nine Italian paintings from the olden time. They represented Grecian gods and goddesses. As a tiny girl I hung over these entranced. Perhaps this is why anything relating to Greece instantly arrests my attention. I cannot remember when I did not love Ancient Greece. When I wrote *The Spartan* (my first book) it seemed to me that no one had ever had so interesting a subject.

My very happy childhood was spent in Mount Vernon, Indiana. Here at the age of nine I began to write. My girlhood was in Cincinnati. Here I studied piano and composition with great ardor and expected to be a musician. Here also I married in 1903 Charles H. Snedeker, then dean of the Cathedral there. My name before marriage was Cara Dale Parke. We moved to Hempstead, Long Island, where we had a busy and happy married life.

My husband took great pains to train me in writing. My parents had never criticized but only encouraged and admired me. But my husband criticized me wisely and sharply, often making me work months on a single chapter. He also directed my historical studies so I became accurate and sure.

Snedeker: *SNED e ker*

It was from Hempstead I went to Nantucket for a summer visit. As I walked up Fair Street I had a strange feeling: "There is a story in Fair Street." It was not at all definite. I did not know that it would be Dencey and Jetsam, and the old whaling captains and the Quakers, but I could feel it there as one senses a perfume one cannot see.

I am often asked how I came to write for children. I reply that I do not. I write for myself. I write the story in the best words I know to express that story. If it is simple the words are simple; if it is a complicated subject—and I do write these—I use complicated accurate words. I am never afraid children and young people will not understand me.

My beloved husband died in 1927. After that I lived in St. James, Long Island, and Cincinnati. I am at present a wanderer; but winter usually finds me in Bay St. Louis, Mississippi, on the Gulf of Mexico, and summer in Nantucket.

"Cornelia Spencer"

May 12, 1899-

AUTHOR OF

Three Sisters, The Land of the Chinese People, Etc.

Autobiographical sketch of Grace Sydenstricker Yaukey, who writes most of her books under the pen-name of "Cornelia Spencer":

IT has taken me a long time to get used to motor cars and radios and movies, even to things like drugstores and ice cream parlors, because I never had them near until I came to live in America. I was born on a Chinese hill, in a big square house that was unlike all the Chinese houses in the great city lying not far away. When I looked out over our garden wall, it was to see Chinese vegetable gardens near by, and in the distance the city of Chinkiang and then the Yangtze River. On that river were some steamboats but more Chinese junks and sampans and there were no racing yachts or canoes. Many people lived along the shores in houseboats but they were not pleasure boats. They were homes because the people had no others.

Until I was ready to go to Shanghai to high school my mother taught me at home. It was not school like yours here. The dining-room table was my desk and Mother heard my lessons when she had time.

In Shanghai I saw people from all over the world. My schoolmates were American and British and Scandinavian and we had courses of study like those in the United States. These prepared me for college work in this country. I entered Maryville College in Maryville, Tennessee, in 1918, and took an A.B. degree in 1921. I liked America but still not as much as I did China so I went back at once to what was my home.

For two years I taught in a Chinese girls' school in the beautiful city of Soochow. This was nice except that I had to learn a new Chinese dialect and since my teaching had also to be in Chinese, it was not easy.

In 1924 I was married and went much farther into China to live. This was the city of Yoyang, about a thousand miles from the coast. It was an exciting place because the railway from Canton goes to Peiping through this city and so did all the war lords and bandit groups and even the Chinese Communists. This meant we always had to be ready to get away in a hurry if there was likely to be any fighting. When my two sons, who were born there, grew old enough to know what these excitements were about they thought it a great lark to dress quickly without lights, pack

"CORNELIA SPENCER"

food in bags, and slip out the great gate of the compound or garden where we lived to waiting boats at the lakeshore and move away from the town.

I came to know the Chinese people in Yoyang well and to love them very much. When I had trouble they were my most sympathetic friends, and when everything was all right, we laughed at the same things.

In 1935 we came to America and have been here since. I have come to love my own country, but I do not forget China. One way of remembering it and of making people know it better is to write and speak of that country. During these years since I have lived here I have been doing both of these things.

ARMSTRONG SPERRY

Armstrong Sperry

November 7, 1897-

AUTHOR AND ILLUSTRATOR OF
Call It Courage, Hull Down for Action, Storm Canvas, Etc.

Autobiographical sketch of Armstrong Sperry:

I WAS born in New Haven, Connecticut. As far back as I can remember, I scribbled and drew pictures. But my real interest in story telling comes from my great-grandfather, who had followed the sea all his life, and who used to tell me hair-raising yarns about his adventures in the remotest parts of the world.

In particular, he told about being wrecked on the island of Bora Bora, most outlying of the Society group, where he spent some months among the savages who lived there. He used to say: "That was the purtiest little island I ever did see. I hope you'll see it for yourself someday, young 'un!"

My first academic training was at the Yale Art School. This was interrupted by World War I, when I enlisted in the navy. After the war I went to New York and put in three years at the Art Students League, in the days of George Bellows and Luis Mora, following up with a year in Paris.

A couple of years in an advertising agency seemed to be the logical progression; but always in the back of my mind was that island my great-grandfather had talked about when I was a kid. That's how, one

day, I found myself in Tahiti looking for a schooner to take me there. I found the schooner, and I found the island. And that fact explains why I have used the South Pacific and the Polynesians in so many of my books for young people.

At present I divide my time between New Hampshire and Vermont. In the latter I have a small farm where I put in a good many hours, between writing and illustrating, in trying to grow good crops out of rocky soil. But every once in a while the ghost of my great-grandfather jogs my elbow and says: "A farm's all right for a landsman, but the sea's the place for *you*!"

It doesn't take too much persuasion! And whenever I feel that jog of the elbow, I pack my belongings and take to the sea and usually come back with a new book— or the material for one. It's an honest way of earning a hard living, but I wouldn't exchange it for any other.

* * *

In 1925, after one of those jogs of the elbow, Armstrong Sperry joined the Kaimiloa expedition as an assistant ethnologist for the Bishop Museum of Honolulu. He sailed among the least known islands of the South Pacific, and learned the languages, the legends, and the music. He drew pictures and stored up memories that have found their way into many of his published books. Between trips he lives on the farm with his wife and two children.

Armstrong Sperry is an artist and a craftsman who labors over each tiny detail, in both his pictures and his writings. The results certainly justify his efforts, for every one of his books is an artistic achievement.

In 1941 his *Call It Courage* was awarded the Newbery Medal.

Johanna Spyri

July 12, 1827-July 7, 1901

AUTHOR OF

Heidi, Etc.

IT was the time of the Franco-Prussian War. Into Switzerland, the country of refuge, came many wounded, and they must be helped. But means were none too plentiful. So the modest, unassuming wife of Bernhard Spyri, town clerk of Zurich, decided to write a story and earn something to help them.

The first short stories were so well liked that after a while she turned to a longer one. She spent several years writing *Heidi*, but it was so popular it ran into several editions, and was translated and became known in many countries.

Johanna spent her entire life within a few miles of Zurich. She was born seven miles from there, at Hirzel, in the simple white country house of Dr. Johann Jacob Heusser, her father. It was a home of culture. Her mother was a gifted woman who wrote some poetry and songs. Johanna was the fourth of six children, but the busy home harbored also the grandmother, aunt, and others, including sometimes also some of the doctor's patients.

The home life of the children was happy. There were homemade playthings, a doll's house, a doll's theatre that awakened delight in plays, a white lamb with a ribbon around its neck. Some evening during Christmas week the Christmas tree would be lighted for one blissful hour. They never knew when beforehand, for the doctor was a busy person and they must await his convenience. On Old Year's Eve they had the privilege of not being sent to bed, and on New Year's Day they heard the impressive bells of Hirzel toll out every hour. There was a harp, too, that Johanna and a friend bought with their joint resources. For two weeks it would be at one house, and for the next two at the other.

Johanna Spyri: *yoh HAH na SPEE ree*

Johanna studied at the village school and with the pastor. But the sunny-faced girl was active and lively and had not much love for school. She was a very clever mimic, and bright and witty. But in drawing she had no talent; once when she had erased so much that a hole appeared in her paper, she was so amused over the picture resulting that her teacher wrote, "Hanneli, you will be a dunce!"

The sparkling-eyed Johanna was most of all an outdoor child. Hirzel was in a wonderfully beautiful neighborhood, situated on a chain of green hills. On one side were the large picturesque Lake Zurich and dark fir forests. On the other the shimmering Bernese Oberland rose in the blue distance. For Johanna the voices of nature held a never-ending fascination. She would stop in the midst of the wildest play to listen to the roaring in the fir trees, just as Heidi did later in her book.

Into this quiet, happy life her brother Theodore brought a tall, slender law student from the gymnasium to spend Saturday nights and Sundays. An attachment developed, and Johanna married at twenty-five and went to live in Zurich. There was one child, a boy, who died while a student. Her husband passed away four years after *Heidi* was published, and she was left alone to write the many more stories of child life laid among the Swiss scenes she loved.

JOHANNA SPYRI

Johanna was so modest she shrank from having her private life made known to others, for she said it was not herself that mattered but only the influence of her books. Her friends respected her wishes, so we know very little of her grown-up life. We can only, for the most part, gather such impressions as are reflected in her stories. But we know she was a somewhat typical Swiss housewife, and we are told that her quiet, uneventful life was singularly pure and beautiful.

Evaleen Stein

October 12, 1863-December 11, 1923

AUTHOR OF

Gabriel and the Hour Book, The Christmas Porringer, Etc.

EVALEEN STEIN probably drew some of her inspiration to write from the fact that her whole family had literary leanings. Her father, John Andrew Stein, although an attorney at Lafayette, Indiana, where Evaleen was born, also did some writing and contributed to magazines. Her mother, Virginia Tomlinson Stein, wrote stories for the young, and her brother, Orth H. Stein, was a writer all his life, a newspaper man and a contributor of both prose and verse to magazines.

After graduating from Lafayette High School, Miss Stein went to Chicago where she studied at the Art Institute. She specialized in illumination and decorative design of manuscripts and mottoes, and her illuminations drew much attention. Her art work was exhibited in various places, including Chicago, Indianapolis, New York, and at the Panama-Pacific Exposition at San Francisco in 1915 she won honorable mention.

Her father died when Miss Stein was twenty-three and her mother then became librarian of the Lafayette Public Library, a position she held for thirty-two years. Here Miss Stein became absorbed in books, and also commenced to write, contributing for some fourteen years to the *Indianapolis Journal, St. Nicholas,* and other publications. Her first book, *One Way to the Woods,* a small volume of nature poems and lyrics, was published when she was thirty-four. Five years later a second volume of verse followed. Many of her poems and much

of her prose she engrossed on parchment with border designs and illumination that reflected the care of the monks of old.

It was as a writer of stories for young people that Miss Stein became best known. Her first two juvenile books gave her recognized standing as a writer. Other interesting work done by Miss Stein was the rendering into English verse of translated poems. She put into her own verse forms Japanese poems translated from anthologies of the ninth and tenth centuries, the little volume being beautifully illustrated by Japanese artists.

In May 1907 several Indiana authors showed their admiration for Miss Stein by arranging an interesting program in her honor at Purdue University. In an authors' reading James Whitcomb Riley, George Ade, Meredith Nicholson, and Charles Major gave selections from their works, after which a dinner party was held at the home of Miss Stein and she was presented by them with a check for a thousand dollars. It was used for a trip abroad, which was a great inspiration to her.

Miss Stein was a lover of flowers, birds, and outdoor life, and spent many hours in the well-planned, beautiful garden that surrounded her home. She was gentle and retiring, and greatly interested in her work, seldom finding time to appear in public. She died at her home in Lafayette at the age of sixty.

Noel Streatfeild

AUTHOR OF

Circus Shoes, Theater Shoes, Etc.

Autobiographical sketch of Noel Streatfeild:

I AM English. Most English people are partly English and partly Scotch, Irish, or Welsh, but I am entirely English. My ancestors settled in England soon after the Norman Conquest in the county of Kent at a placed called Chiddingstone. Chiddingstone Church is full of memorials to my ancestors; the earliest was an ironmaster and he was buried there in the fifteenth century. I have had no very interesting male ancestors but one interesting great-great-grandmother. She was Elizabeth Fry. I think perhaps you may not have heard of Elizabeth Fry in America, but she was a very

Noel: *rhymes with "pole"*
Streatfeild: *STRETT feeld*

NOEL STREATFEILD

well-known English Quaker who reformed our prisons.

Writing was not my first career. I started by being an actress. I did not begin to write until 1930, and then it was novels for grown-up readers. I wrote my first book for children in 1936. I like writing books for children because most of them tell about training or careers. When I write a book to do with the stage or dancing I know quite a lot about it and do not have to study especially; but when it is the circus, broadcasting, or film studios, then I have to go and find out, and very interesting finding out is.

One reason I particularly enjoy writing for children about such things as stage, circuses, and ballet, is that I always wanted to know about these things when I was a child and never did. My father and mother were not interested in the arts and I never met anybody who could answer the questions I was always asking. I never remember a time when I did not want to know how you became a child actor or dancer, or how animals were trained. There were lots of other things I wanted to know too about children living very different lives from my own. I have not found all the answers yet, but when I do I expect I shall write a children's book passing on what I have learned.

We were a big family, five of us. If you are going to write books for children when you grow up there is nothing like having been one of a big family yourself. In a big family something is always going on. You may not always be having exciting things happening to you but something is sure to be happening to one of the others. We were four girls and one boy. As is the custom in England, the boy was sent away to a boarding school when he was eight, so we saw him only in the holidays. In many families in England the girls are sent to boarding schools too, but we were what is called day-boarders, which means we went to school at nine in the morning and had all our meals there and came home at night about seven o'clock. I loathed being a day-boarder. I thought then, and I think still, it is the most miserable thing to be because you get only the work side of school and none of the fun. Everything that was exciting at school seemed to happen after we had gone home in the evening. I never write books about schools because I hated mine so much.

My books are published in England and the United States, and translated into almost every language. I think this is nice because children ought to be able to read true accounts of how children live in other countries. I hope you get plenty of books written about England because then, when you come to see us, as I hope very much you will, you will not feel strangers.

C. M. Sublette

1887-1939

AUTHOR OF
The Scarlet Cockerel, The Bright Face of Danger, Etc.

Autobiographical sketch of Clifford McClellan Sublette, written for THE JUNIOR BOOK OF AUTHORS a few years before his death:

THE decade of the eighties was beyond all doubt a romantic period, when parents forsook the good old names of Tom, Dick and Harry for those they considered more glamorous. Hence my given name, for which I have never been able to pin the responsibility on either parent. However, I have ascertained that at the time of my birth they were reading the dashing Bulwer-Lytton romance, *Paul Clifford*.

The birth occurred in Charleston, Illinois. The paternal stock was French Huguenot,

Sublette: *sub LET*

which settled on the James River in Virginia about 1700 and after the Revolution emigrated westward to Kentucky and thence to Illinois. On the distaff side the descent is North Carolina English, mingled with Scotch and German.

When I was three the family reversed the procedure and moved eastward—to Indianapolis. During my education in the public schools of that fair city—and it was a fair city then—I was forced to prove my given name a misnomer with my fists upon a large number of Johns, Bills, and Henrys. I was not always successful, but I have no regrets.

After high school, my family decided I was to study law, but even then legal ethics appeared to me fearfully and wonderfully fashioned. I went instead to Chicago, studying at the Art Institute and the old Academy of Fine Arts. One day while watching the famous Alphonse Mucha draw freehand, I suddenly realized I might make a fine bricklayer. That afternoon ended my studies.

I wrote a bit of art criticism for Chicago dailies and then began bounding gaily from job to job. I went to work for the New York Central lines, then bounced to electric traction, trade journal writing, and newspaper work. Usually I found I had too many corners for the nice round holes prepared for me in the business world. I drifted West, but came back to the corn country long enough to marry an Indianapolis girl, Mary Shuler, in 1913.

Our daughter, Mary Catherine, was born about a year later. Shortly afterward we began moving about the West. It was perhaps a grasshoppery life, which I regretted for some time, but we had a bit of fun. Eventually we settled in Denver.

There I acquired a taste for fishing and hunting and explored by car, horse, and foot many out-of-the-way places in mountain and desert country. Also a taste for illuminating the obscure incidents of history grew upon me, and all my novels deal with such episodes. I wrote and sold a few short stories. Meanwhile I took a flyer at the oil business; and then went into the commission business, and was early in the field of promoting the growing of green vegetables in commercial quantities in the high mountain areas.

By 1923, my daughter's reading had reached the *Treasure Island* stage. When the Atlantic Monthly Press announced a contest in memory of Charles Boardman

Hawes, their promising young writer who had lately died, Mary Catherine urged me to enter. Somewhat reluctantly, I did so. While *The Scarlet Cockerel* was in the writing Mary Catherine died. I finished the book, more as a memorial to her than for any other reason. It won the competition, and in 1931, I published my first adult novel, *The Golden Chimney*.

I am proud of one fact in my writing life —the accuracy of my historical backgrounds has never been questioned either by critics or by my correspondents. And one book is concerned with Virginia, where everyone knows everyone else's first name back to the beginning. Otherwise I have never been satisfied with a single book.

Hildegarde Hoyt Swift

AUTHOR OF
Railroad to Freedom, North Star Shining, Little Blacknose, Etc.

Autobiographical sketch of Hildegarde Hoyt Swift:

I WAS born in Clinton, New York, where my father, Arthur S. Hoyt, was professor of English literature on the faculty of Hamilton College. I always felt my first tooth was cut on the left hind shoe of Pegasus, since my father's favorite subject was poetry and my mother was a graduate of the Dresden Conservatory of Music.

After a highly irregular education from private tutors and European boarding school, I graduated from Auburn High School and from Smith College, where I was an editor of the *Monthly*, president of "Manuscript," and a member of Phi Kappa Psi.

After graduation I studied at the New York School of Social Work and lived at Union Settlement where I did club work with children. These were difficult months, but I have always felt grateful for them. They gave me my first real knowledge of children—children of all sorts, of varying temperaments, colors, nationalities—"good" children and "little toughies."

I married Arthur L. Swift, Jr., of New York, who was then associate pastor of Center Church in New Haven. It was in New Haven that our first son was born. When my husband was called to the faculty of Union Theological Seminary, we moved to New York. Soon our number was aug-

Altman-Pach Studio
HILDEGARDE HOYT SWIFT

Sir John Tenniel
February 28, 1820-February 25, 1914
ILLUSTRATOR

LEWIS CARROLL, in writing *Alice's Adventures in Wonderland* for his child friend, Alice Liddell, had made little pen-and-ink sketches to go with the story, but when he agreed to publish the story for other boys and girls to read, he felt his drawings were not good enough. So he procured the services of John Tenniel, who at forty-four was at the height of his fame as cartoonist for *Punch*.

Tenniel, out of the fertility of his imagination, pictured the dozens of strange creatures met by Alice in her underground adventures. He drew a Rabbit who actually took a watch out of his waistcoat pocket! He made a wise old Caterpillar sitting on a toadstool with a hookah in his mouth. He fashioned a Duchess ugly enough to give you bad dreams. He created a Mad Hatter, as well as the King and Queen of Hearts, and a Mock Turtle in tears. To illustrate Alice's continued adventures in *Through the Looking-Glass*, he brought to life the White Queen, the Red Queen, the White Knight, and other chessmen, and even drew oysters with shoes!

But when, in the thirteenth and last chapter of the second book, Lewis Carroll wanted him to draw a wasp wearing a wig, he balked. "A wasp in a wig," he said firmly, "is altogether beyond the appliances of art." Besides, he didn't think the last chapter as interesting as the rest of the book. So the author left it out.

Tenniel, working in London, sent his sketches to Charles Lutwidge Dodgson in Oxford. (Dodgson was Lewis Carroll's real name.) No detail was too small for the Oxford professor's criticism and he was constantly making suggestions. "Don't give Alice so much crinoline," he wrote; or, "The White Knight must not have whiskers; he must not be made to look old." It worried him, too, that Tenniel never used a model and he said the artist declared he "no more needed one than I should need a multiplication table to work a mathematical problem!"

Tenniel's drawings for *Alice in Wonderland* became almost as famous as the story itself, giving boys and girls an intimate acquaintance with the story's fantastic characters.

mented by the arrival of a second son. Here in New York we have lived for the most part, except for an occasional lectureship and stay on the Pacific coast, or time out for a trip to Europe.

In the summer our family lived in a log cabin, deep in the Adirondack woods or in an old house far out on Long Island. There was time then for long stories told by firelight or on the moonlit beach. In 1929 I first began to write children's books.

Recently I have been teaching children's literature at the New School for Social Research, New York City, and helping young writers find their wings in a writers' workshop.

It has all been fun; let me say *that*, first, last and foremost! The outline of a life seems too formal, too cut and dried, though experience itself is fluid, varied, exciting. Things that stand out in my memory are the first glimpse of Mount Rainier; the first sight of a redwood forest; climbing the mountains of the English lake country with my father in the early years; long canoe trips through the Canadian wilds during college days; exploring the primitive beauty of Ireland; seeing the matter-of-fact calm of England under the first onslaught of the last war.

Perhaps the most interesting thing of all has been trying to write books for children.

Tenniel: *TEN yel*

For all the success of the "Alice" books, Tenniel was firm in refusing to illustrate any further books for young people. "It is a curious fact," he wrote to Dodgson some years afterward, when he was being urged to work for him again, "that with *Through the Looking-Glass* the faculty of drawing for book illustration departed from me, and, notwithstanding all sorts of tempting inducement, I have done nothing in that direction since."

Tenniel was born in the Kensington section of London and educated there. "I never learned drawing," he said, "except insofar as attending a school and being allowed to teach myself. I attended the Royal Academy School after becoming a probationer, but soon left in disgust of there being no teaching." He then spent a great deal of time in the British Museum, studying the Elgin marbles and also costumes and armor.

At sixteen he exhibited his first painting in London and sold it. For a time he studied fresco in Munich. Later he painted a mural for the House of Lords in Westminster Palace. In his twenty-sixth year he began to do book illustrating.

His illustrations for *Aesop's Fables* resulted in his being given a position on the staff of *Punch* as joint cartoonist with John Leech. When Leech died he reigned supreme. In a fencing bout with his father one time, he had lost the sight of one eye, but this did not bother him in his work. "It's a curious thing, is it not," he said, "that two of the principal men on *Punch*, du Maurier and I, have only two eyes between them?"

About twenty years after the second of the Alice books appeared, he was knighted and thereafter he was known as "Sir John." Tenniel worked for *Punch* regularly for thirty years, missing only two or three issues on account of illness. "In all that time," he said, "I have hardly left London for more than a week; yet I enjoy wonderful health, doubtless to be attributed to regular riding. I carry out my work thus: I never use models or nature for the figure, drapery, or anything else. But I have a wonderful memory of *observation*—not for dates, but anything I see I remember."

In his eighty-first year he retired permanently from *Punch*, after fifty years' connection with the magazine.

Gudrun Thorne-Thomsen

1873-

EDITOR OF

East o' the Sun and West o' the Moon, The Birch and the Star, In Norway, Etc.

Autobiographical sketch of Gudrun Thorne-Thomsen:

LONG ago and far away I was born, as long ago as 1873 and as far away as Trondhjem, Norway. I went to kindergarten there. This is what I remember:

Bundled up from head to foot, so that only a little nose and two red cheeks could be seen, I was placed on my lovely blue sled, and my big brother pulled it. All the snow from the sidewalks was shoveled into a huge wall along the road, so I couldn't see the horses and sleighs over it, but hear the bells —yes, that I could; and the moon and stars were shining brightly and showing us our way to school those midwinter mornings. I liked best marching and skipping and stories, but best of all the going and coming on my sled.

When I was four years old, we moved to Bergen, and while most of the things I remember from Trondhjem have to do with snow—coasting, jingling sleighbells, snowmen, and snowballs—Bergen means harbors full of ships coming and going, and sailboats, small rowboats, fishermen's schooners, hundreds and hundreds of them. From our

GUDRUN THORNE-THOMSEN

Gudrun   Thorne-Thomsen: *GOO drun THORN TOM sen*

attic bedroom window I could look far out to sea. Out there the big ships went until the last sail or line of smoke disappeared. Where were they bound? Should I ever go so far that one standing at the window could not see my ship any more?

Then there was school. I liked to read and recite poetry, but arithmetic, knitting, and sewing—not at all. At recess and after school we sang and danced, old folk songs and folk dances. That was more fun than anything else. We always spent summer vacations in Hardanger among fjords, mountains, waterfalls, and glaciers—and goats. I had my own pet goat, Blaamann by name. He was very proud and wanted his own way, but he could romp and play and walk on his hind legs.

From the age of nine to fifteen I lived in Oslo. School was very important then. Pages and pages and pages of history, geography, science, mathematics, English, German, and French, church history and catechism, marks and examinations which ended in "middelskole examen," which admits you to college!

Then a very great change came into my life. A very large steamer carried me out beyond where I had seen so many ships disappear to America, and Chicago became my home. A new world indeed! Good fortune landed me in the school of which Colonel Francis Parker was the principal, in Englewood, Chicago, and I began to study, to love to learn, for the first time. Though I had always had excellent marks, now I worked not to compete but for the joy of working.

It was there I began to tell stories to children and to grown-ups, too: the old Norse folk tales I had heard as a child. And I translated and adapted them, so children might read them and tell them. I have told stories to children from Canada to southern California, to children in Cuba and in the Hawaiian Islands. There is something very wonderful about all really fine stories. Everybody loves them, old and young. Since I retired, in 1936, I have made a number of records of mine.

I began to teach when I was twenty, at Colonel Parker's Normal School, and I taught for forty-three years. I was principal of the Ojai Valley School in California from its beginning in 1923. Here, too, I told stories, but best of all I had a chance to

help build a school where children are happy, working for the love of work and the joy of accomplishment.

It has been a very busy life, for I had to take time to marry and have children of my own, and there are grandchildren, too. Now I am growing old in the lovely Ojai Valley, among sunshine and blue skies, among mountains, flowers, and fruits. And thoughts fly back easily and often to that first home eight thousand miles away, and I love and am grateful for both my countries—Norway and America. If life may be compared to a tree, my roots are in Norway, but trunk, branches, and leaves belong to America.

Sanford Tousey

AUTHOR AND ILLUSTRATOR OF
*Cowboy Tommy, Jerry and the
Pony Express, Etc.*

SANFORD TOUSEY was born in Clay Center, Kansas, when that part of the Middle West was Far West in its wild-and-woolliness. His family loved thoroughbreds and owned several, so his early youth was lived against a horsey background, but before he was eight the Touseys moved East and Sanford attended high school in Anderson, Indiana, far from the rodeos and round-ups he loved. Indeed, from now on his Western experiences came to him chiefly on his great-grandfather's ranch.

From a portrait by George Brehm
SANFORD TOUSEY

Tousey: *rhymes with "drowsy"*

In Holton, Kansas, not far from the Potawatami Indian Reservation, Mr. Adamson, his great-grandfather, had a general store serving the Reservation Indians. On pay days he used to take the boy to the reservation when he went to collect his bills. Here young Tousey found much to thrill him; most exciting of all, perhaps, were the war dances, complete with paint, war whoops, and tomahawks.

Sanford Tousey started drawing very early. In high school he did a daily cartoon for the Anderson *Morning Herald*. Most of his $7.50 a week pay for this he saved and later used for art school in Chicago.

For some time now Mr. Tousey has had a studio in New York City. There he not only illustrates his own and other authors' stories, but also makes pictures for many leading magazines.. Most of his books, which now number over thirty, are for the very youngest readers.

Pamela Travers

1906-

AUTHOR OF
Mary Poppins, Etc.

Autobiographical sketch of Pamela L. Travers:

I WAS born well into this century in Queensland, Australia, just where the coast faces the Great Barrier Reef; and my childhood, in a house overlooking sweeping fields of sugar cane, was full of the reef's tokens—shells, palm fans, sprays of coral. My earliest memory is of walking through the green forests of the cane, as if through a jungle, and of making nests—which I hoped a bird would inhabit—between the juicy stalks. I chewed cane, when it was ripe, as modern children chew gum.

It was here that I began to write poems and stories, at an early age and always in secret, for such activities were neither welcomed nor encouraged by my busy extroverted family. And this, I think, is the most sensible way to treat the budding artist. Praise him, show his efforts to the world, and you have taken something from him that he will never get again, his secret, his unselfconsciousness.

Later, my habit of writing, producing, and acting in the school play each term was considered useful though not particularly

PAMELA TRAVERS

interesting. And when, at sixteen, my first poems were published it was thought that, though harmlessly, I was wasting valuable time. I believe it was this attitude on the part of my nearest and dearest that enabled me to go on writing instead of having whatever talent I may have possessed doused into nothingness by friendly praise.

From the age of sixteen I was for some years concurrently a journalist, a dancer, and an actress—mostly in Shakespearean plays—and a writer of stories and poems. Later on that last activity swamped all the others. I had been living in England for some years writing for AE's literary weekly, *The Irish Statesman*, and for English magazines when, recovering from an illness, I began to write *Mary Poppins*. The house was a small old thatched manor, mentioned in Doomsday Book and the Sussex countryside that spread out round it was full of history and legend. But I did not need these to excite in me the atmosphere of fairly tale for I had soaked myself in that all through my childhood and had, as it were, borne it along with me till my grown-up years. I have always thought Mary Poppins came then solely to amuse me and that it was not till a friend saw some of her adventures written down and thought them interesting that she decided to stay long enough for me to put her into a book. I never for one moment believed that I invented her. Perhaps she invented me, and that is why I find it so difficult to write autobiographical notes! It is not the facts of

Pamela Travers: *PAM e la TRAV ers*

anyone's life that tell you about him. It is the feelings, the inner events, and to find out the truth about any author you must look for him in his books. They alone are his true biography.

So—I was born and am glad of it. I shall die and when I do you can—if it matters, which I don't believe—add the date. The thing I like doing best is bringing up children and making gardens. I had almost rather have a flower or a tree or a fruit—even a vegetable!—named after me than to see my name on a book. Nevertheless, I hope to live long enough to write several more. And in the meantime, if you are looking for autobiographical facts, *Mary Poppins* is the story of my life.

* * *

When Miss Travers' first Mary Poppins book appeared, even staid and conservative critics were captivated by its "delightful nonsense that defies an age boundary of appreciation," as *Booklist* put it in a review which also said: "Here are related the remarkable things that transpired during the time Mary Poppins served as nursemaid for the Banks family. This astounding person blew in with an east wind and stayed, as she had agreed, until it changed; and after that life was never the same for Jane and Michael."

Tasha Tudor

1915-

ILLUSTRATOR, AND AUTHOR OF
The White Goose, Thistly B, Etc.

Autobiographical sketch of Tasha Tudor:

THERE is not a time within my memory when I haven't drawn pictures and made little books.

I was born in Boston, though I have lived there seldom since, spending most of my life in the country, in Connecticut.

My love of books and pictures began early with the inimitable illustrations by Beatrix Potter, Randolph Caldecott, Arthur Rackham, Edmund Dulac, Edwin Abbey, Hugh Thomson, and others.

My schooling did not start until I was nine, when I was sent to Connecticut to live with old friends of the family and to be taught, with four older girls, by the Uncle Adam of my book *Snow before Christmas*.

Tasha Tudor: *TAH sha TOO dawr*

TASHA TUDOR

He had previously taught our elder brothers. To this period of my life I owe much that appears in my illustrations—the memories of long winter evenings and being read to until scandalously late hours, of the world of being people from books, of the changing seasons, of the woods and fields and doings of the country.

When I was twelve my family bought a place in Connecticut, an old New England farmhouse. There began my love of all that was old fashioned. We spent long hours at country auctions at which I found many of the old dresses my little girl and I dress up in now. There also began my love for gardens and farming, and a strong desire to live on a real farm when I grew up. At this time my winters were spent at Spring Hill School in Litchfield, Connecticut, and in Boston. I drew pictures more than ever in wintertime to bring back the days of summer and the house I dearly loved. Pictures of Alexander the Gander, the Fair, the garden, the dairy, and my cow Delilah. At about this time I attended the Boston Museum School for a year but learned more from being with my mother, who is the portrait painter Rosamond Tudor.

When I was twenty I met Thomas Leighton McCready, Jr., who married me two years later. He it was who seriously started me on my career as an illustrator. He suggested I make up a folio of pictures and call on the various publishers of New York and Boston, which we did but without encouragement. Then by chance I made a little book for a Christmas present for my husband's small English niece, Sylvie Ann. When it was done we showed it to a publisher and it was accepted. So Sylvie Ann did not receive her gift that Christmas, but only a later one, when the book came out as *Pumpkin Moonshine.* I wrote and illustrated seven more books and then made pictures for *Mother Goose Rhymes* and for *Fairy Tales* by Hans Christian Andersen.

I now live with my husband and three children in an old red house in New Hampshire. Alexander and Araminta the geese live here with us with assorted numbers of pets including Mocha and Buttercup, the two Jersey cows, Lassie the collie, and Simpkin and Tabitha Twitchit, the cats.

Our oldest child is Bethany; then come the two boys, Seth and baby Tom.

When Christmas comes all the cousins come, too, and we have such gay times, with a doll's Christmas party, stringing popcorn, making presents, and giving a Christmas marionette show.

Spring brings the sap boiling and sugar on snow; summer, the hot days with picnics by the river, gardening, haying, chasing Alexander and Minta out of the vegetable patch; winter, the quiet of deep snow and the singing of the kettle on the wood stove. Then is the time of long evenings and dressing up, and reading and making things.

The pictures for the books are made somehow between the goings on of full days, mostly due to the patience and help of a very understanding and delightful husband.

Hilda van Stockum

February 9, 1908-

AUTHOR AND ILLUSTRATOR OF
*The Cottage at Bantry Bay, Pegeen,
Canadian Summer, Etc.*

Autobiographical sketch of Hilda van Stockum:

I WAS born in Rotterdam. The house I was born in was often pointed out to me by my father, but bombs have since destroyed it. I had a lovely father. I have described him as Gerrit's grandfather in *Gerrit and the Organ.* I had, and still have, a wonderful mother and two dear brothers, Willem and Jan. Willem was a pilot in the

HILDA VAN STOCKUM
with her six children

last war and was killed. I have described him as Uncle Jim in *The Mitchells.*

Because my father was a naval officer we did a lot of traveling. I had visited the East Indies, Paris, Switzerland, and Ireland before I was seventeen. We went to live in Ireland then, in Dublin, where my grandmother had been born. There I attended the school of art. I'd always been drawing and telling stories. I still have a book I made for my brother Willem when I was five, so I decided to take up art seriously.

After three years of study in Dublin, where I met the family I described in *The Cottage at Bantry Bay,* I completed my art education by attending a four-year course in the Amsterdam Academy of Art. In Dublin I had been left very free and had been allowed to dabble in oils but the Dutch professors were more strict—for two years I could draw only antiques: large plaster casts of Greek sculpture.

I loved painting so much that I took my paint box with me all the same and painted portraits of fellow students during lunch hour. Usually there was a big racket going on then, students got to wrestling and jumping about, throwing empty salmon cans at one another. They used to ask me how I could work in such a din and then I'd answer, "Well, I intend to have ten children and I had better get used to it." I haven't actually ten children yet, only six so far, four girls and two boys, but still I'm rather glad I can work while there is a racket.

In 1931 I returned to Dublin, where I met E. R. Marlin, a student at Trinity College and a friend of Willem's. We were married in 1932. We moved to New York in 1934 and to Washington in ·1935, after Olga was born. Our other children were all born in Washington, D.C. Then we moved to Canada, where my husband is now an official of the Provisional International Civil Aviation Organization. Its headquarters are in Montreal. So as I love children and like writing about them and for them, I have recently written a story about children in Canada.

Jules Verne

February 8, 1828-March 24, 1905

AUTHOR OF

Twenty Thousand Leagues Under the Sea, Michael Strogoff, From the Earth to the Moon, Etc.

THIRTEEN-YEAR-OLD Jules used to voyage on the River Loire around Nantes, France, down to the sea, with his brother Paul. At fifteen there was no corner he had not explored. The boat was only a leaky old sailboat, but to Jules it was a palatial yacht, and the cruises, voyages of discovery and adventure.

The boyhood of Jules Verne was a most happy one. His father, a lawyer from Paris with a taste for literature, had taken a Breton wife and settled at Nantes, where Jules was born and received his early education. He was a normal boy with a love for adventure and water, machinery and writing. At twelve he worked on poetry, spending long periods correcting, never satisfied with what he had done.

Jules was marked out to follow his father, his grandfather, and his great-grandfather in the law, and went to Paris to study. There, however, he took more interest in literature and produced poetical, dramatic, and other work. With the younger Alexandre Dumas he wrote a comedy which was produced. He became a stock exchange clerk. Finally when he was over thirty he wrote *Five Weeks in a Balloon*. This was so successful, going through several editions, that he was encouraged to do more writing along the same line, combining scientific ideas with fiction.

Soon he settled down to two books a year. Although he never studied science, he collected an immense number of facts reading fifteen papers a day, and bulletins of scientific societies, and entering in his notebook things likely to be of value to him. It was said he· had ten or more novels in his head in advance and always one or more finished books in reserve for publication. He was very conscientious. Up before five every morning, he worked until noon, writing and rewriting his sentences as many as ten or fifteen times, and correcting as many as seven or eight proofs.

At thirty Verne married Madame de Vianne, a widow with two little daughters, and settled down in Amiens. He had one child of his own, Michel, who, when he was grown, wrote on scientific subjects. They lived in a spacious three-story house, at the top of which Verne had a plain little study and bedroom combined, with a large map of the world marked with the routes taken by his heroes. He made one trip to America, which suggested his *Floating City*. The imaginary palatial yacht of his boyhood had become a reality, and in his earlier years his principal diversion was to cruise in it.

Verne anticipated much scientific progress. It was said that he "saw the future age as clearly as Walter Scott saw a past one." He saw airplanes, submarines, and accelerated world travel, as well as long-range cannon, melinite shells, and aerial torpedoes. He wrote over a hundred books, and they have been translated into practically every language.

Elizabeth Gray Vining

See *Gray, Elizabeth Janet*

Jo Besse McElveen Waldeck

AUTHOR OF

Little Lost Monkey, Jungle Journey, Etc.

Autobiographical sketch of Jo Besse McElveen Waldeck:

I WAS born and brought up in the small town of Kingstree, South Carolina. Its name was derived from a large pine tree which the early Huguenot settlers claimed as

Jules Verne: *ZHOOL VERN (in French, VAIRN)*

Jo Besse McElveen Waldeck: *JO bess MACK el veen WALL deck*

their king's tree. I attended the local school through the elementary grades and then went on to a finishing school for girls near Asheville, North Carolina. There I fear my interest was focused not so much on my studies as on sports, especially tennis, on mountain climbing, and on editing a school paper of my own origin. However, I managed to graduate in the given four-year period, and then I went to Winthrop College, South Carolina, for a special course.

After college, I worked on the Kingstree weekly newspaper, doing a little of everything. I answered the telephone, wrote news, did proofreading, secured subscriptions, and made layouts for advertisements, which I also sold. This valuable experience led me to choose newspaper work as a profession. Within a few months I became manager for two more weeklies which the editor purchased.

Five years later I left to cover news for the Associated Press and traveled a great deal over South Carolina. After one more experience on a newspaper, *The Morning News*, Florence, South Carolina, I longed for a change of scenery. So I packed bag and baggage and started out in my new car. Finally I landed in Pasadena, California, and spent some time there, writing advertisements, feature stories, and my own newspaper column.

On one of my annual visits to New York, I met Theodore J. Waldeck. We were

Bachrach

JO BESSE MCELVEEN WALDECK

married some months later and started immediately preparing for an expedition. My husband had spent eighteen years in Africa and wanted to explore some new territory. I had become interested in South America, particularily in the little known territory inhabited by uncivilized Indian tribes. Today, as in my childhood, any story of Indian history, customs, and religion holds my interest.

So exploring we did go, to the far interior of British Guiana in South America, touching the borders of Brazil and Venezuela. There we lived among the Carib, Arawak, and Akawai Indian tribes, making friends with them, learning their languages and habits, finding them to be just what I had pictured, and hoped them to be, lovable, loyal, trustworthy, and most efficient. There in the jungle I was initiated as a "white sister" into the Arawak tribe, and my left arm still bears "cuts" of the tribal marks.

Theodore J. Waldeck

1894-

AUTHOR OF

On Safari, Lions on the Hunt, The White Panther, Etc.

Autobiographical sketch of Theodore J. Waldeck:

I WAS born in Brooklyn, New York. When I was quite young my parents died, and my sister and I were sent to live with our grandfather in Vienna. There I attended school. My grandfather was anxious that I become a doctor but I preferred adventure. At eighteen I accompanied the Duke of Mecklenburg, a friend of my grandfather's, on an African expedition. The purpose of the expedition was to determine the borderline between what were then known as British East Africa and German East Africa.

We had no sooner disembarked at an African seaport than I fell ill with tropical fever. My recovery was so slow that the duke decided the expedition could not wait for me, so he left with orders that I must return home when fully recovered. However, when I was well, instead of using the money for my trip home, I equipped a safari of my own and set out to follow his expedition into the interior—something only an

THEODORE J. WALDECK

unexperienced youngster would dare undertake.

This foolhardy adventure luckily was the turning point in my life, for I became convinced I wanted to be an explorer.

In later years I was afforded the opportunity to gain knowledge under the efficient guidance of some of the world's most famous explorers and scientists. I led four expeditions to Africa which took me to Uganda, Tanganyika, and Abyssinia. My most recent expedition was to British Guiana, South America, where my wife, Jo Besse McElveen, and I lived for many months among the primitive Indian tribes in the far interior.

Dillon Wallace

June 24, 1863-September 29, 1939

AUTHOR OF

The Story of Grenfell, The Lure of the Labrador Wild, Etc.

Autobiographical sketch of Dillon Wallace, written for THE JUNIOR BOOK OF AUTHORS a few years before his death:

I WAS born in Craigville, New York. When I was four, my father moved to a small farm and here I lived the happy days of my childhood and young boyhood. I learned to ride as soon as I could sit on a horse. I loved the woods and the fields, and was ever curious about the wild things.

My father was in business, and away from home a great deal. This threw upon my shoulders many duties. At eight I milked cows and helped the hired man about the barn and in the fields.

My brother died in infancy, but I had three sisters. Annie, the oldest, was one year and six months my senior. She was a fine pal and the source of much of my inspiration. At the district school, which we attended, I was a poor student. I spent too much time in dreamings and imaginings. Annie was an excellent reader, and she read aloud to me. We often told each other stories, inventing them as we went along.

In 1876, as a result of the financial panic of the early seventies, my father lost nearly everything he had, and became a semi-invalid. This was the beginning of years of trouble and struggle. When I was fourteen my mother died suddenly. Two years later one sister died and that same year the mortgage was foreclosed on our farm. I had been doing all the work there without the assistance of hired help. Now, at seventeen I found a job in a gristmill. Then my father died and our home was broken up. My two sisters went to live with relatives.

In the gristmill between bags I studied, every spare moment. Annie's letters inspired me; she corrected lessons I sent her. Working hours in the mill were from five in the morning until nine in the evening. In 1883 I left the mill for the telegraph office, where I devoted spare moments to study: reading history and also Dickens, Thackeray, Scott, Cooper, Irving, and much of the poets.

In 1888 I went to New York, to law school, and became a lawyer. In 1903 Leonidas Hubbard, Jr., associate editor of *Outing* magazine, who was planning an expedition to Labrador, invited me to join him, and that spring we sailed for the North. The story of our tragic experiences, and how Hubbard died in the wilderness, I have told in *The Lure of the Labrador Wild,* my first attempt at authorship. Upon invitation from Caspar Whitney, editor of *Outing,* I joined the magazine staff, and headed a second expedition into Labrador in 1905. Returning, I published the record of this expedition.

My publishers urged at this time that I write a book of adventure for boys. That was the first of my boys' books.

In 1910 I did some exploratory work in Mexico and following this I was detailed to make a survey of big game conditions in the Far West. In 1913 I made a third expedition into Labrador. In 1904 I had become a member of the Arctic Club of America, and later, when it was organized, a member of the Explorers Club. In 1911 I organized a troop of Boy Scouts, and have been continuously active in Scouting since. In 1917 Leila Greenwood Hinman, of Cleveland, Ohio, and I were married. Our daughter, Leila Ann, was born in 1919, and our son, Dillon 3d, in 1924.

I have tried to make all of my books interesting, educational, and inspirational. The customs and life of the people will be found correct, and the geography so accurate that the books could serve as guides. Where historical incidents appear, they are recorded from sources of authority.

For several years I have edited the Camping and Living Outdoors Departments in *Hunting and Fishing* magazine, and contribute regularly to this magazine and to the *National Sportsman.*

* * *

Dillon Wallace wrote twenty-six books between 1905 and 1932, when he retired. He was seventy-six at the time of his death.

Lynd Ward

See *McNeer, May*

Leonard Weisgard

December 13, 1916-

ILLUSTRATOR, AND AUTHOR OF
Pelican Here, Pelican There; Down Huckleberry Hill; Etc.

Autobiographical sketch of Leonard Joseph Weisgard:

I WAS born in New Haven, Connecticut, and spent the early part of my childhood committing the usual juvenile misdemeanors. Then it was decided we were to visit my father's English relations.

Going and coming was full of calamity and excitement: train wrecks and fire, boat accidents and crashes. London, Liverpool, and Manchester were to a child dreary, wet, and full of fogs and prunes. But there were

Lucas & Monroe Studio
LEONARD WEISGARD

street fairs and pantomimes which were unforgettable.

We returned to America and I have yet to recover from the nightmare dreams of school in New York. Here was where the battle of books began. Strange school readers with black and blue pictures, and stranger stories of Dicky Dare and Turkey Lurkey.

At Pratt Institute I studied illustrating and left after two years. I spent a good deal of time listening and looking and sketching Manhattan and all the incredible things that go on about New York.

Working for the *New Yorker*, Conde Nast Publications, Crowell-Collier magazines, *Good Housekeeping*, the *Ladies' Home Journal, Woman's Home Companion, Harper's Bazaar* was the best training of all. I have written some and illustrated over fifty books for children. Some of these have been selected by the Graphic Arts Society as outstanding books of the year.

Working for and with children is to me a most exciting challenge. They are original realists with true perception.

I am single, have two dogs and one cat, and we all live in an early American house of Greek revival vintage, in Danbury, Connecticut.

* * *

Little Island, written by Margaret Wise Brown and illustrated by Mr. Weisgard, was awarded the Caldecott Medal in 1947.

Weisgard: *WISE gard*

Rhea Wells

September 24, 1891-

AUTHOR AND ILLUSTRATOR

*Peppi the Duck, Beppo the Donkey,
Zeke the Raccoon, Etc.*

Autobiographical sketch of Rhea Wells:

I WAS born in Jonesboro, the oldest town in Tennessee, of Scotch, Irish, and English ancestry. My family lived on a small farm just outside the town until I was ten. Because of my experiences during this part of my childhood I wrote *An American Farm.*

Naturally, on a farm there were a great many pets. There were dogs, two cats, a parrot, an alligator, lizards, rabbits, and a family of ducks. It is probably because of those ducks that I wrote *Peppi,* so many years later, while I was spending a summer in Austria. All the ducks I had had as a child just naturally turned into Peppi.

When I began to go to school most of my writing paper was used for drawing. These drawings, as I remember them, had little, if any, merit. A few years later I began to paint. My mother still preserves some of those efforts of my early adolescence. They are deplorably bad. It was not the quality of my work that interested me, it was the work itself. My mother and my guardian (my father having died) decided I could go to Chicago to study at the Art Institute.

There were three years of study at the Institute. During this time it was necessary to supplement my very limited allowance by taking all sorts of odd jobs. I worked at nearly everything students do to pay their way through art school. The one thing I can remember distinctly *not* doing is coloring gift cards.

While I was at the Institute, Sorolla came and taught a class in painting. I was tremendously impressed by that jovial little man with his brilliant technique. Years later, my respect for this facile painter was increased when I visited his house—now a museum—in Madrid.

After the Art Institute there was a year of work on a Southern newspaper, where I got a lot of practical experience and learned the process of photo-engraving. It has proved of great value to me since. About a year of newspaper work was enough. I heeded the urge and moved on to New York.

New York has been my address for many years although I did not live there all the time. For one thing there have been two wars. In the first I spent fifteen months wearing olive drab and bursting with patriotism. That finished, I went back to civil life and did advertising art. After a year and a half I went to Europe for a year of study and travel with my wife.

Europe was an entirely new experience for me. Just after the First World War it was really an adventure no matter where you were. Something was always about to happen, and sometimes it happened. Food in Berlin was very scarce that winter. We had to have food cards for nearly everything we ate. Even when we had the cards we could not get the things we wanted. That Christmas in Berlin was the happiest I have ever known. Perhaps that was because I was able to celebrate it with people, who, in spite of adversity, had not forgotten the Christmas spirit.

The following spring I visited several other countries and then spent the summer in the Tyrol. The mountains and valleys around Innsbruck have lured me back many times since. It was quite natural for me to choose that mountainous country as the setting for one of my stories.

It has been a great pleasure to collect material for stories and illustrations from the people who knew all this as a part of their everyday lives. The peasants of Austria, Spain, and Sicily, and the Bedouin of Tunisia have been helpful and hospitable. They have sung and danced for me. They have invited me into their houses and tents, built fires, cooked strange and wonderful foods, displayed rare old costumes, and all this for a foreigner who came to them with a sincere interest in them and their way of living. Language is not a barrier if you gain the confidence of simple people.

It has been entirely due to the encouragement and help of a few friends that I have been able to do the stories for children. I should never have had the confidence to do them without their support. I hope to do more books for children as long as children continue to like my books.

Wheeler, Francis Rolt-

See *Rolt-Wheeler, Francis*

Rhea: *RAY*

Eliza Orne White

August 2, 1856-January 23, 1947

AUTHOR OF

*A Little Girl of Long Ago, When Molly
Was Six, Where Is Adelaide? Etc.*

Autobiographical sketch of Eliza Orne
White, written for THE JUNIOR BOOK
OF AUTHORS a few years before her
death:

I WAS born in Keene, New Hampshire,
where my father had a parish and where
we lived until I was twenty-two. We had a
good deal of land about our house, with a
garden full of flowers, and berries and fruit
trees, and a swing and a croquet ground, so
we had all sorts of out-of-door games. We
kept chickens and pigeons, and kittens always had a happy home and never seemed to
disturb the many song birds that made their
nests in the small orchard. I was fortunate
in having intimate friends, for there was
always some little girl from whom I was
inseparable during my play hours. In winter,
my father would take us coasting on a big
black sled, down a snowy hill and across
an icy pond, and we had sleigh rides to the
accompaniment of jingling sleigh bells.

I was not quite five when the Civil War
began, and for the next few years it made
the great excitement of our lives, for my
mother had two brothers on one side and
two on the other. My small part in it was to
make two comfort bags for soldiers. With
one of them I sent these lines:

> I think your name begins with J,
> Mamma thinks it begins with A,
> When you write please tell it me,
> Who is right we then shall see.

To my delight I had a letter from the
soldier saying, "The little girl was right,
my name is John." I was not quite nine
when the war ended, but I can remember
vividly the evening when we joyfully lighted
our windows in celebration of the end of the
war, so soon to be followed by the gloomy
day when we learned of the assassination of
President Lincoln. When I heard the news
I felt as sad as if I had lost a personal friend.

Shortly afterwards I went with my mother
to make a visit in Springfield, where her
father, Chester Harding, the portrait painter,
lived. I remember seeing him put the finishing touches to a picture of General Sherman.

When I was eleven my father took me to
Boston to hear Charles Dickens read. I am
sure I was as thrilled in hearing him read
"The Trial" from *Pickwick* as if I had been
a grown person. As we sat in the front row
and I was directly opposite him, Dickens
glanced at me from time to time, and I was
sure he was admiring my new gray cape
trimmed with a border of white plush. I
thought it very pretty, myself.

I was always making up stories and I
began to write them as soon as I could hold
a pencil. When I was eleven, an intimate
friend and I decided we would write historical romances modeled on the novels of
Sir Walter Scott. I still have the slender
volume written in my scrawling hand for, to
our delight, my mother was kind enough to
have our stories bound like real books, in
red, with the titles in gilt letters.

I went to the excellent public schools in
Keene, but never graduated from high
school because of a severe case of typhoid
fever, which came at the beginning of my
senior year and nearly ended my life. When
I was seventeen I had a delightful year at a
small school in Roxbury, Massachusetts.

The year I spent abroad with my father
and mother and younger sister, three years
later, did more to make me interested in art
and history than my school life had done.
England and Scotland were full of history
and romance, while France and Italy were
lands of enchantment, and Switzerland in
the early spring a vision of beauty.

ELIZA ORNE WHITE

In 1881 we moved to Brookline, Massachusetts, into the house where I am still living. There is as much land around this house as we had in Keene, so we have been fortunate in having plenty of room for both cats and song birds.

As I am unmarried I have never had much to do with children, but I remember vividly how I felt when I was a child. It is a long time since my first book for children, *When Molly Was Six,* was published, but I took just as much pleasure in writing *Where Is Adelaide?* although half a lifetime had come in between.

The good thing about an imagination is that it defies time and bridges the gap between childhood and what to the uninitiated seems like age.

Robb White

1909-

AUTHOR OF

The Lion's Paw, The Secret Sea, Etc.

Autobiographical sketch of Robb White:

I WAS born in the Philippine Islands because my father was a missionary there. My childhood friends were the children of Igorots because there were no other children around. When Dad went into the army in 1917 I went with him, although they would not let me stay in the army. Since he kept moving from camp to camp I missed a lot of school, so I had a fairly hard time getting through the Naval Academy in 1931.

I had started sailing boats when I was a kid and as soon as I could I went down to the West Indies, where boats were cheaper and the water not so rough as around the east coast.

In 1937 I married a girl from Thomasville, Georgia, and took her down to the West Indies where we bought a little island for sixty dollars and built a house on it. We lived on Marina Cay for three years, then I had to go back into the navy when the war started.

I served four years in the navy, most of them in the Pacific, and came out in 1945 with eight medals.

I have written seven books for children, starting with *The Nub* in 1934. *The Smuggler's Sloop* in 1937 won the *Herald Tribune* prize for the best book for boys. Before the

ROBB WHITE

war I wrote three books. After getting out of the navy I wrote *The Lion's Paw* and *Secret Sea;* both of these were selected by the Junior Literary Guild.

Now I'm back in the navy but, with nobody shooting at me, I am writing another book for children.

* * *

Robb White is a lieutenant commander in the United States Naval Reserve.

Elinor Whitney

December 27, 1889-

AUTHOR OF

Tyke-y, Tod of the Fens, Etc.

Autobiographical sketch of Elinor Whitney:

I WAS born in Dorchester, Massachusetts, but when I was very small my family moved to Milton a few miles away and took up residence in the family mansion which had been built in 1819 on Milton Hill overlooking the Neponset River.

My grandmother, Mrs. A. D. T. Whitney, built a little house on the same property. She was a well-known author and I can remember how funny it seemed to us grandchildren next door when carriages stopped on the hill in front and the occupants were informed in words that we could easily distinguish, "This is the home of Mrs. A. D. T. Whitney who wrote *Faith Gartney's Girl-*

hood, *A Summer in Leslie Goldthwaite's Life, Hitherto,* and many other stories of New England life. Giddap!"

To us she was just "Gannie" and a visit to her meant thin sugar cookies and a bout with a funny old Irish maid whose stories and quaint sayings interested us more than all the mellow wisdom of our distinguished grandmother.

I graduated from Milton Academy and then from the Library School of Simmons College, Boston. My first job was assistant to the librarian at the Boston Museum of Fine Arts, where I stayed for two years. I then had an opportunity to teach at Milton Academy and for four years I taught English to boys and girls from seven to twelve years.

It was not until 1919 that I discovered the Bookshop for Boys and Girls in Boston. It had been in existence about three years in a little room hidden away on the second floor of a rambling building on Boylston Street. I began work in it that very Christmas season, first as selling assistant, and later when it grew into a general bookshop and moved to a street floor location, as assistant director and joint director with Bertha Mahony.

In 1924 we started the *Horn Book* magazine, devoted to books and reading for boys and girls. In 1929 we compiled *Realms of Gold in Children's Books,* followed in 1936 by *Five Years of Children's Books.*

I began my own writing with a slim little book about a beloved family dog, *Tyke-y—*

ELINOR WHITNEY

His Book and His Mark, in 1925, and I illustrated it with scissor cuts. My next book, *Tod of the Fens,* was a story of Boston, England, in the days of the merchant-adventurers. There were other books, too. Then in 1936 I married William L. W. Field, headmaster of Milton Academy, and for six years was very much interested and involved in school activities. Now with my husband's retirement and war work at an end, I hope to continue wth my writing. I am still an associate editor of the *Horn Book.*

Phyllis A. Whitney

September 9, 1903-

AUTHOR OF

Willow Hill, A Place for Ann. Etc.

Autobiographical sketch of Phyllis Ayame Whitney:

MY earliest recollections are of my home in Japan, of the beautiful flowers in our garden and of the salty Japanese cookies I was so fond of as a child. I was born in Yokohama of American parents, who later took me to the Philippines and to China. When I was fifteen I had my first glimpse of the America I had always wanted to see, when my mother brought me to the United States.

High school in Chicago was an adventure for me after living so long in faraway places. However, my schoolmates seemed to think my stories of the Orient were much more exciting. Perhaps it was their interest which led me into an attempt to write such stories for our school paper.

When I was out of school I began to send these stories to magazines and for four long years I wrote without success. Finally my efforts were rewarded and I did sell a story. Eventually I sold many more—well over a hundred in all before I turned to writing books for young people.

My first full length book was suggested to me by the ruins of a fine old colonial house I stumbled on during a vacation jaunt. My imagination led me to picture the house as a background for a story of modern young people and their problems. The book, *A Place for Ann,* was the result. My next, *A Star for Ginny,* was based on my own sometimes hilarious and sometimes hectic experiences when I tried selling books in a

PHYLLIS A. WHITNEY

big department store. Other books followed and then *Willow Hill.*

This was the hardest book to write, but it is the one I cared most about writing. I believe that when you really understand people you thought were different from yourself you cannot help liking them. I wanted to use that theme in a book. So I wrote about Val, who is a high school girl like many I have known, and about Mary Evans, a Negro girl in the same school. One of my happiest moments came when this book won the $3,500 prize in the *Youth Today* contest in 1946.

Oddly enough, I am just as much interested in reading books for young people as I am in writing them. As a result I served quite happily as children's book editor of the Chicago *Sun* for over four years, until recently when I moved to New York and began to do the same sort of work for the Philadelphia *Inquirer.*

I have never wanted to be anything but a writer, and there is no job which could be more exciting, or more fun. Nevertheless, it has its bumps, too, and I think I've experienced them all. Some of this experience I've tried to pass on to others in courses on writing at Northwestern University in Chicago, to writers' conferences, and to my own class of aspiring writers here in New York. My one book of non-fiction, *Writing Juvenile Fiction,* gives my methods and philosophy of writing for young people.

Most writers have at least one very special critic in their lives. My own is my young daughter, Georgia.

* * *

Phyllis Whitney now lives at Port Richmond, Staten Island, and it is in the Staten Island· Institute that she conducts her class in general fiction writing. Besides her book on writing for young people, Miss Whitney is author of *Red Is for Murder,* a mystery story for adults.

Kurt Wiese

April 22, 1887-

AUTHOR AND ILLUSTRATOR
You Can Write Chinese, The Chinese Ink Stick, Liang and Lo, Etc.

Autobiographical sketch of Kurt Wiese:

I WAS born in Minden, a small town of northern Germany, and grew up under a remarkable collection of paintings of the Düsseldorf School. A puppet show and books about foreign countries were two other factors of influence, although I never dared hope that one day I should see the countries I read about, with my own eyes.

However, seven years after having left school, I found myself in the center of China, after an unforgettable trip through Russia, through the snow-covered vastness of Siberia, along the edge of the Gobi desert, and last through fertile Manchuria.

Six years of traveling in China and selling merchandise brought me in contact with its people, and the study of the Chinese language helped me to a better knowledge of this country and its population than foreigners usually have.

When the war broke out in 1914 I went to the German colony of Tsingtao, which was attacked and taken by Japanese troops after a siege of three months. I was taken prisoner but handed over to British authorities and there began a captivity of five years. One year was spent at Hongkong and the remaining four in Australia. Unforgettable again was the trip on board a small steamer through the islands of the South Sea and along the Great Barrier of Australia, till after three weeks our ship passed through the rock gates of Sydney harbor.

Deeply impressed by the landscape and the animal world of Australia, I began to take up drawing and writing and when I

Kurt Wiese: *KOORT VEE zuh*

returned to Germany in 1919 I was so successful with the material I brought home that I found I could do better with my drawings and stories than by going back to China and selling merchandise again.

I stayed in Germany for three years, illustrating and writing my first children's books. I also designed exotic backgrounds for a film company, and as this company was formed by the well-known animal dealers, Hagenbeck of Hamburg, I was constantly in touch with all kinds of animals, studies of which helped enrich my sketchbooks and my knowledge of animals.

When the film company closed its door I followed an urge for a warmer country again and I left Germany for Brazil. There I found the most beautiful tropical country and the intended short trip lengthened into a stay of three years. The first year was filled with travels through the mountainous coastal region back of Rio de Janeiro, with others to the south of Brazil, one of which carried me into the deep jungles of Paraná and a meeting there with a tribe of Indians that still roam these forests in the very same state they did before the country was discovered by white people.

After the first year in Brazil I met a prominent writer of children's books and he asked me to join the firm for which he wrote and illustrate his books. I accepted and spent two happy years in a house that one dreams of, white against a background of flowers and palm trees, drawing for the

Brazilian children. Besides the book illustrations I did work for a newspaper, cartoons and a weekly children's page.

About this time there came a call from the United States, and after a quick decision, I boarded an American steamer and waved good-by to the row of palm trees along the beach of the harbor of Santos. When I arrived in New York snow flurries swept along the gray skyline of Manhattan.

I found all the encouragement needed to communicate my experiences to the younger generation of this country. In fact the response was so gratifying that soon the wish to stay and settle down for good became so strong that I married and bought a little farmhouse at the edge of the woods which cover the rocky banks of the Delaware River about twenty-five miles above Trenton. It seems hard for me to believe I have not lived here all my life. The older generation shared with me the experiences of their lives and that of their fathers; the younger generation goes to a school, which is the house next to ours. They are daily visitors at my studio. They come to see my work and to bring me the things they have found and that they think might be of interest to me.

Pictures of the past have become crystal clear, and past and present seem to unite in a happy background.

KURT WIESE

Laura Ingalls Wilder

February 7, 1867-

AUTHOR OF
The Little House in the Big Woods, Farmer Boy, The Long Winter, These Happy Golden Years, Etc.

Autobiographical sketch of Laura Ingalls Wilder:

I WAS born in the Little House in the Big Woods of Wisconsin.

From there, with my parents and sisters, I traveled in a prairie schooner across Minnesota, Iowa, Missouri, and Kansas, and into Indian Territory, where we lived in the Little House on the Prairie. Then traveling back to western Minnesota we lived for several years on the banks of Plum Creek. From there we went West again, to the shores of Silver Lake in Dakota Territory. We lived in De Smet, the Little Town on the Prairie, and I married Almanzo of *Farmer Boy,* just as I told in *These Happy Golden Years.*

After our marriage Almanzo and I lived for a while in the little gray house on the tree claim. Then with our little daughter, Rose (now Rose Wilder Lane, the author), we went to live in the piney woods of Florida, where the trees always murmur, where the butterflies are enormous, where plants that eat insects grow in moist places, and alligators inhabit the slowly moving waters of the rivers. But at that time and in that place, a Yankee woman was more of a curiosity than any of these.

At last, in 1894, we came to the Ozarks. There is no other country like the Ozarks in the world. This land is the very oldest land on this continent. It rose long ago from the sea and was a lonely island while all the rest of North America was still under the ocean. The island then was an almost flat slope of drying mud and of sea sand pressed into flat sandstone, and nothing lived on it but little sea-slugs and snails that died when the mud dried. Almanzo still finds their shapes molded in the rocks, and sometimes their small curled shells.

For millions of years the streams have been cutting deeper into the flat slope of the island, while all the rest of North America came up from the sea, until now the Ozark streams have cut such deep valleys that the land between them is steep, high mountains. But the Ozarks are really not mountains, they are valleys. So the skyline is always level and blue like the sea, and nearly always there is a lovely blue haze over all the hillsides cut so deeply in this old, old land.

On one low hill that in the springtime is covered with a blue carpet of wild violets, there is a white farmhouse; a U.S. Highway curves at the foot of the hill. Behind the house is a gulch where a little stream wanders, and behind the gulch rises a steep, high hill where tall oaks grow, and dogwoods and redbuds that bloom in the spring.

Almanzo and I live in this white farmhouse with our pet bulldog, and in the barns and pastures are our milk goats and our Rocky Mountain burro. All summer we gather fresh vegetables and berries from our garden and in the fall we gather walnuts and pecans from our own trees.

Almanzo used to have horses and drive through town faster than the first automobiles, until the marshal once warned him that he was exceeding the speed limit. Before there were automobiles there were no speed limits. But now that Almanzo is past ninety years old he has given up horses and drives a car instead.

Pa and Ma and my sisters all are gone; of the family I alone am left. But Pa's fiddle is in the museum of the South Dakota Historical Society, where every year someone will play on it the songs he used to play.

It has been many years since I beat eggs with a fork, or cleaned a kerosene lamp. Many things have changed since then, but the truths we learned from our parents and the principles they taught us are always true; they can never change. Great improvements in living have been made because every American has been free to pursue his happiness, and so long as Americans are free they will continue to make our country ever more wonderful.

Esther Wood

1905-

AUTHOR OF
*Silk and Satin Lane, Great
Sweeping Day, Etc.*

LAURA INGALLS WILDER

ESTHER WOOD (Mrs George W. Brady), now living in Upper Montclair, New Jersey, was born in Akron, New York, the daughter of a minister. She attended many schools before entering the University of Rochester, and later Boston University. She spent several years in New

ESTHER WOOD

York, then went to the Orient upon an invitation from friends.

Miss Wood's favorite hobby was writing children's stories; she collected a suitcase full of notes and sketches, which accompanied her on a trip around the world. Her experience and keen observation furnish unusually interesting material for her stories, of which she has now written seven, three before 1940. After 1940 came *Belinda Blue,* the story of a small stray kitten who assumed that dignified name, and *Pepper Moon,* which tells of a little Chinese boy who is so in need of a pet of his very own that his family begins to find snails in the teacups, mice in grandmother's sewing box, and frogs in everyone's shoes. When Pepper Moon turns up one day with a water buffalo, things begin to happen.

The next year Miss Wood produced *The House in the Hoo,* a picture-story book about three little chipmunks who did nothing at all to prepare for winter. They were helped out by rabbits, who had the reputation of having no sense. (The Hoo is a woodsy place, though the author nowhere says that in so many words.)

The backgrounds of several of Miss Wood's stories have been Oriental, but in *Silver Widgeon,* she returned to our own continent, to the rugged wilderness of Canada. Mr. Bickle, owner of the Silver Widgeon, invites Peter and Pudgy to fly with him to Canada. With them goes

Charlie May, the maid who declares fearfully every mile of the way: "Them as fly is long on ambition and short on common sense." When the plane is disabled on a lonely lake deep in the Canadian woods, the boys show Mr. Bickle what they really have in them. The climax comes when Pudgy is ill and is taken away by an Indian, leaving Peter, afraid of the dark all his life, to guard the Silver Widgeon alone.

Kathryn Worth

AUTHOR OF
They Loved to Laugh, The Middle Button, Etc.

Autobiographical sketch of Kathryn Worth:

I CAN never remember the time when I didn't write. My first recollections are of gathering shells by the surf of the Atlantic Ocean, off Wilmington, North Carolina, and of writing poems in my head as I ran barefoot along the sand. I had blue eyes and brown hair, and was very thin and very shy. I didn't play much with the other children. I still have blue eyes and brown hair and am very shy.

I went to school, and kept on writing poems. I traveled about a good deal with my family, went to boarding school in Switzerland, then continued my education at different colleges, including Radcliffe and Columbia University's Pulitzer School of Journalism. But always and forever I wrote poems and stories, never meaning to be anything but a writer. It took a lot of courage and persistence. Nothing ever came easy. No flowing angel descended from a cloud of fire to help me out. I just kept on working hard and sending manuscripts to editors. Finally I began to sell things.

Then I married Walter Clyde Curry, a professor of English at Vanderbilt University, in Nashville, Tennessee, and came here from North Carolina to live. We have a daughter. She has blue eyes, too, and her name is Josephine.

When Josephine was eight my first book was published, a volume of collected poems for grown people, called *Sign of Capricornus.* The poems were somewhat difficult to understand. Josephine memorized them without understanding what they meant. She was very proud of them since many

KATHRYN WORTH

were written about her. Finally she said, "Mother, why don't you write poems *I* can understand?" So I decided to write poems for Josephine.

I wrote about ducks and swans and elephants and geese and chickens and prunes and everything else under the sun. The poems were published in several magazines, including even the *Atlantic Monthly*. Josephine took pictures of ducks and swans and peacocks to go with them. When she was thirteen they came out as *Poems for Josephine*.

It was a natural step from writing poems for Josephine to writing novels for her. I started when she was ten. Josephine gave me her own prescription for what she wanted in a novel: "Have at least one death, preferably two; have at least one wild animal or dangerous snake; include a lot of animals of the tame kind; make part of the story funny; and if possible have a cataclysm near the end." In my books I have tried to live up to Josephine's directions.

Why do I usually write about North Carolinians? Because I was born in North Carolina, at Wilmington, and my ancestors settled there two hundred years ago. "I'm a Tar Heel born and a Tar Heel bred, and when I die I'll be a Tar Heel dead!" My great-grandfather, Jonathan Worth, was once governor of North Carolina. My ancestors were English Quakers and Scotch Presbyterians. My books are written about

those ancestors and about many other real people under fictitious names. Some of the characters are entirely fiction, of course.

N. C. Wyeth

October 22, 1882-October 19, 1945

ILLUSTRATOR

WHILE a student in the Massachusetts Normal Art School in Boston, N. C. Wyeth drew a picture of a fox's head. His instructor told him, he recalls, "that my drawing had the qualities made for illustration, and right there I jumped at a straw."

Before long he had landed a place in Howard Pyle's famous school of illustration and eventually he became one of Pyle's most distinguished pupils, rivaling the master in his own field.

He was born Newell Convers Wyeth at Needham, Massachusetts, on the estate of his grandfather Zirngiebel, a well-known horticulturist. His father had built a house next to his grandfather's and there he grew up. With his three younger brothers he did the farm chores, explored the River Charles, fished, and swam. Snowballing, skiing, and coasting were their winter pastimes. When still a small boy he began drawing pictures of the things about him.

The little district schoolhouse near his home and the Mechanic Arts High School in Boston, not far away, were the places of his schooling. His father wished him to be an architect or an engineer, but he preferred drawing. The rapid sketches of horses which he made at the polo grounds where Boston society people played brought him commissions from the owners to paint pictures of their horses. His parents then agreed to let him go to the Massachusetts Normal Art School in Boston and later to Howard Pyle's school in Wilmington, Delaware. In the summer the school moved to Chadds Ford in Pennsylvania, where Pyle had a country estate. Young Wyeth and several other boys boarded in a farmhouse, with an old gristmill near by for their studio. At the end of each week they were entertained at dinner in Pyle's home on the hill.

After about three years with Pyle, young Wyeth was granted a leave of absence to go out West. He was eager to experience the life of the frontier. In Colorado he took

From a self-portrait

N. C. WYETH

part in a great roundup and then, after recording on canvas his adventures, went to the Navajo reservations in New Mexico. There he was employed for a time as government mail rider, making lengthy trips on horseback between stations and settlements. He studied the life of the Indians and made numerous pencil sketches. Upon his return to Wilmington, these sketches attracted the attention of magazine editors, who came to him with manuscripts of Western stories to be illustrated. From that time his work was constantly in demand.

At twenty-three he married Carolyn Bockius, of Wilmington. They had five children, three girls and two boys. One of the boys, Andrew, is a well-known artist. Of the other four, only one is not an artist. He is an engineer. Two of the daughters, and the husband of one of them, paint. A third daughter writes music, and her husband is a painter. There are also nephews and nieces and cousins-in-law who paint.

The family started out in Wilmington, but later established their home at Chadds Ford, the village where Wyeth had studied with Pyle. There the artist's studio stood on the side of a wooded hill on the bank of the Brandywine.

N. C. Wyeth seldom took a vacation and when he did it usually lasted no longer than two or three days. He loved books and did a great deal of reading. Tolstoy, Thoreau, and Romain Rolland were among his fa-

vorite authors. The painters who impressed him most were Rembrandt, Millet, and Segantini. He loved to cut down trees or plough on his estate. He cared little for social events and wished the man who invented dress suits had been burned alive.

In later life he devoted himself mainly to mural decoration. The Federal Reserve Bank in Boston, the Missouri State Capitol, and the National Geographic Society in Washington, D.C., are among the many buildings where his work can be seen.

Mr. Wyeth was killed near his home at Chadds Ford three days before his sixty-third birthday, when a train hit the station wagon in which he and his three-year-old grandson were driving.

He is best known to boys and girls as the illustrator of books by Stevenson and James Fenimore Cooper. Most unforgettable are his pictures in color of hand-to-hand combats between men. Altogether he illustrated more than twenty books.

Elizabeth Yates

December 6, 1905-

AUTHOR OF

Amos Fortune: Free Man, Mountain Born, Patterns on the Wall, Once in a Year, Etc.

Autobiographical sketch of Elizabeth Yates:

IT was in Buffalo, New York that I was born and there I went to school; but the most memorable days of my childhood and youth were the long summers spent on my father's many-acred farm in the rich rolling country south of Buffalo. Next to the youngest of seven children, there were always playmates for me as well as horses and dogs; and there were always tasks—gardening, butter-making, caring for our animals.

The house was filled with books, and reading alone or being read to by my mother was part of our life. I used to go off on my horse for a day at a time, rambling through the countryside, a sandwich in my pocket and the knowledge that any fresh-running stream would give us both drink; but I was never lonely, for there was the horse to talk with and in my head I was writing stories. On the next rainy day, I would climb the ladder to an unused pigeon loft that was my own secret place and there write down in a series of copy books all that I had been thinking.

The winters were spent in Buffalo and there I attended the Franklin School from kindergarten through the twelfth grade. This school long had a wise and inspired principal who put special emphasis on the classics and English literature. I loved writing and got good marks in anything that had to do with writing, and when a poem of mine was published in the *Conning Tower* a few years later I knew that I wanted to be a writer.

A year at boarding school followed my graduation from the Franklin, a summer abroad, and then three years of work in New York. During those years I had various jobs, gradually working up to more and more writing. In the summers I taught riding at girls' camps.

At twenty-three I married William Mc-Greal, an American whose business was in London, and for the next ten years our life was rich and active. I kept writing, spending long hours in the British Museum and the London Library, and when, in 1938, my first book was published it seemed the culmination of a ten years' apprenticeship; years in which I had been doing book reviewing, article writing, interviewing, editorial work, some ghost writing. The achievements had been few and there had been many a heartache, but I never doubted during those years that my direction was

right. Our home was in London, but there were many months spent traveling in the British Isles, France and Germany, Switzerland, Spain, Iceland, and such travel was highlighted by adventures in mountain climbing and in meeting interesting people. I like travel, especially the kind that allows one to live in other countries long enough for the landscape and the people to become dear and familiar.

In 1939 we returned to the United States to live in Peterborough, New Hampshire. There we found an old farmhouse which adapted itself happily to our needs, and a farm of fields and woodland which we are endeavoring to bring back to usefulness and production. There are mountains near to climb, forest lakes to swim in, and lovely white villages strong with New England tradition. The garden is my joy; the vegetables especially, which grow in such abundance that there is always plenty to share with friends and neighbors.

I love good talk, I love the wide warm circle of friends which keeps expanding with the years, but I still love to be alone and it is the hours of working in garden or in the woods that help me to think out stories. A little loft in the far end of the house is where I work mornings from 8:30 to luncheon time. A wide table and two chairs take up most of the space and an oldfashioned wood stove keeps it cozy in winter. From the window I can look across the garden, across the small valley where a brook flows merrily, across the pine woods to the gentle slope of the East Mountains.

Except when the Scotty presents us with a new family of puppies requiring care for a few days, or some special guest comes to stay with us, my working hours are uninterrupted. The rest of the day goes in preparing meals, looking after the house, and various small oddments of activity.

Reading is still my joy—books about nature, biography, philosophy; while my mentors of earlier days—Traherne and Blake, Hardy and George Eliot—still have much to say to me. In the evenings we read aloud or listen to music, and it is then that another love of mine—knitting or rug-hooking or any such busyness with my hands—comes into play.

There are occasional trips to Boston and New York, to the seashore and the high mountains, to Durham every summer to teach at the Writers Conference of the Uni-

Elizabeth Yates

versity of New Hampshire, or to some city or town to give a talk on books or writing, but it is a quiet life we lead and in it there is time to think—time to enjoy the things that have always meant much: friends, books and the countryside.

*   *   *

In 1943 Elizabeth Yates won a New York *Herald Tribune* Spring Festival Award for *Patterns on the Wall*, and again in 1950 for *Amos Fortune: Free Man*. In 1951 the latter title was also awarded the American Library Association's Newbery Medal as "the most distinguished contribution to American literature for children" of the previous year. The narrative biography of a Negro slave who won his freedom and became a public benefactor in the 1700's, it was widely praised for its warmth and idealism. Wrote Ellen L. Buell in the New York *Times Book Review*: "It is a moving story, underlaid with deep religious feeling, which thoughtful young people will find absorbing and full of meaning today." Other critics have found in Elizabeth Yates' works "a gentle, serene faith which often transcends literary limitations" and a "deep belief in man's ultimate humanity to man." She has also written a number of books for adults, of which *Nearby* and *Beloved Bondage* were selections of the Peoples' Book Club and *Guardian Heart* of the Family Bookshelf.

In appearance, Elizabeth Yates is described as of medium height, with soft brown eyes and hair. Characteristically modest about her books, she prides herself on being a good farmer and enjoys riding, swimming, and mountain climbing. Her husband calls her a "super-cook" and says that "usefulness seems to be the yardstick of her philosophy."

Grace S. Yaukey

See *"Spencer, Cornelia"*

Ella Young

December 26, 1867-

AUTHOR OF

The Wonder-Smith and His Son, The Tangle-Coated Horse, The Unicorn with Silver Shoes, Etc.

Autobiographical sketch of Ella Young:

I HAVE always believed that the countryside where one is born leaves its mark on a person. I was born in the house of my grandfather, at Fenagh, County Antrim, Ireland. In Antrim my father's people and my mother's folk have called land their own for more than three centuries.

Antrim lifts itself above the sea level in rounded hills, purple with heather, green with bracken, bright-eyed with little lakes that have never a tree about them for an eyelash; they stare wide-open at the sky, blue with its blueness, silver-pale with its moon-glitter. These hills have no homesteads. Where the stone-walled fields begin by the thatched cottages, flax is grown (blue-flowered like the wild flax of America) and there are fields of beans to ripen as food for horses; beans all a-blossom in summertime, and filling the air with a honey-sweet fragrance. There is the salt tang of sea water too, for Antrim slips down to the sea in wooded glens; and prances down to the sea in cliffs that are hollowed into caves and carved by the wind into spires and pinnacles.

In the Northeast, where Scotland is only twenty miles away across the narrow sea, the Antrim coast stretches flatly out in the Giant's Causeway: a wonderful pavement of eight-sided rock slabs, so beautifully put together that it is no wonder the country folk say it was made by a giant who intended it for a pathway to Scotland. I saw these things as a child, and heard stories of Antrim giants and faeries when I was almost too young to listen.

My parents left Antrim when I was three years old, and I went with them to live in Limerick, a town in the southwest of Ireland. Here was the wide quick-flowing Shannon, with rich flat meadows and heavy-foliaged trees. I learned to climb trees and to row a boat. I read *Robinson Crusoe*, and with my sister and cousin played at desert island. We took turns being Robinson Crusoe.

School was a great adventure: I could have as many comrades as I wished to play my games. We played at being knights of King Arthur's Round Table; and spent our leisure reading Malory's *Morte D'Arthur*, when we were not making lances and helmets. My mother gave to my sister and myself a spare room in the house, and we turned it into a theatre. We wrote our own plays, and played them without an audience.

ELLA YOUNG

They were tragedies mostly, and the curtain rang down with the chief characters stretched cold, or rather warm, in death. We never thought how ridiculous it must have looked.

Almost as soon as I could read with ease I read Shakespeare, Milton, and Josephus. That was because my father would not allow Lamb's *Tales From Shakespeare* or children's magazines. At school, during sewing-hour, *Little Women* was read aloud: and Jo, Beth, and Amy were very real to me.

As I grew older, books dowered me with territories and centuries: Plato and the Greeks, Dante and the cities of Italy, Iceland and the Vikings, Egypt—and the world that is Egypt!

The Celtic Wonderland awaited me in Dublin. I had graduated at the Royal University (now merged in the National University) in political economy, history, and general jurisprudence, but as "AE" said once, in kindly fashion, when engaged in berating universities, "No one would have suspected it." Fresh from the country (I had lived for nine years in Queen's County, with trees and clouds and stretches of bog land, flooded fields that were sheets of ice in winter, and no one who thought as I thought) I suddenly found myself in company with poets, artists, writers, players, nationalists of the deepest dye. To have dreamed for years of brilliant groups and great movements, to find oneself in a dream come real. That is what happened to me when I came to Dublin.

I lived there through the most splendid period of the Celtic Renaissance, and through the Rising. I had part in these that were the flowering dream of a people, of a civilization, of a country, and then I came to America, its multitudinous mountain peaks, its prodigality of deserts, its new rich life.

I had written *Celtic Wonder-Tales* and *The Wonder-Smith and His Son*, before I left Ireland. In America I wrote more books, both prose and poetry. The *Wonder-Smith* had appeared as a serial, but it was first published in book form in America.

What else I have of poetry will appear in *Smoke of Myrrh*, at which I am working. *Flowering Dusk, Things Remembered Accurately and Inaccurately*, is my latest, and last, prose work.

If I have written about heroes and dragons and fantastic happenings, it is because these things delight me. I hope they may delight a few others, for it seems to me that the human mind is as full of fantastic imaginings as the sky is of stars; and this is good, for even as Hope remained in Pandora's box so Dream remains when things more prized slip through one's fingers.

What wish do I keep after eighty years of struggle, success, and failure? I think that I keep my first conscious wish to see beauty always with keener perception and subtler understanding.

Herbert S. Zim

1909-

AUTHOR OF

Elephants, Frogs and Toads, Snakes, Etc.

Autobiographical sketch of Herbert Spencer Zim:

SOME people, I suppose, set out to become authors, which is not the strangest thing people will do. But I suspect that most, like myself, find themselves writing books without ever having planned to become an author. In my case, I wanted to be a scientist —and still do. I don't remember exactly when this idea entered my head. I was born in New York, but soon we went to Santa Barbara, California, to live.

We returned East when I was ten and before I was twelve I was collecting leaves, flowers, minerals, chemicals, snakes, and every other specimen I could gather on local walks or longer week-end trips. My room at home overflowed with plants, growing and pressed; several aquaria; boxes of rocks; and cages of toads, salamanders, and snakes. When I was not busy caring for my specimens I had my nose deep in guidebooks, volumes on natural history, and whatever other science books the shelves of the local library would yield.

The details of what I did when I was young don't seem particularly exciting now, but they were then and if you have done anything like it, you know how much fun collecting and experimenting can be. If you have not, it's a secret you will never understand by reading. At any rate, when I got into high school I spent my spare time in the science laboratory. The teacher let me help him, and do my own experiments. I remember how calmly he took charge of things when he discovered I was on the verge of mixing some chemicals which might have blown us both through the laboratory walls. From him I learned of evening chemistry lectures which I attended at a local college.

To top all this, Dr. Michael Levine permitted me to assist him in his important biological research. I washed test tubes, looked up references, kept records, and assisted in experiments. I was well on the

HERBERT S. ZIM

way to a scientific career and I enjoyed every minute of it.

Perhaps because of the scientific information I picked up, I was offered a job to teach before I graduated from high school. And so, at the age of seventeen I started teaching and have kept it up ever since. I went right on teaching while I went through Columbia University and while I did my graduate study and research for my doctor's degree.

In the meantime I had become as much interested in teaching science as I was in doing science. I was first a teacher and then head of the science department of the Ethical Culture School in New York. So it was not surprising that I found myself doing research on the things that interested young people in science. For five years I studied to find the scientific things that concerned young people in junior and senior high school most: the things they really wanted to know and do. I couldn't help but pay special attention to those who wanted to become scientists when I discovered that they (as I) collected and experimented a great deal at home.

The first book I wrote for young people was on a subject I found interested boys and girls most—themselves. That book, *Mice, Men, and Elephants*, tells what makes people like and different from other animals, and why. After that I wrote a number of other scientific books for young people who were interested in understanding why and how things happen.

If you've seen any of these books, you know they are written for people twelve and over. Not so long ago an editor who believes younger children are scientific too, asked me to write a book for seven to nine year olds. I replied, truthfully, that I didn't know how, but she urged me to try. So I wrote a book on elephants which turned out to be pretty bad. I threw it away and tried again. By the third time I knew I was on the right track, and by the sixth time I had "Elephants" ready for publication. And just to make sure I could do it again, I wrote another on goldfish and still another on rabbits for the younger set.

Now I spend a good part of my time in a large, sunny room in Port Washington, New York, working on other books. I'm busy on a series of nature guides. I still teach and still do a bit of science research myself. I'm more interested than ever in young people who want to become scientists because we need scientists more than ever these days. We *all* have to think and act more scientifically if we want to solve the tremendous problems that face us. I hope my books will help those interested in science as many of the books I read years ago (and still read today) helped me.

Gulielma Zollinger

1856-1917
AUTHOR OF
The Widow O'Callaghan's Boys, Etc.

GULIELMA ZOLLINGER wrote from childhood. Her first story was published in the *Youth's Companion* when she was fourteen, and after that she often contributed to the magazines. It was not, however, until her second book, *The Widow O'Callaghan's Boys,* appeared in 1898, that she found herself established.

Gulielma Zollinger, who sometimes used the pen-name "William Zachary Gladwin," was one of three children. Her father, Jeremiah Rummel Zollinger, went with his parents as a boy from his birthplace, Hagerstown, Maryland, to Pennsylvania, thence to Illinois, and finally established his own home at Newton, Iowa, where he engaged in the occupations of contractor and builder, and later entered the grocery business. He served his city for three terms as sheriff and also in the council. Her mother, E. M. Randall Zollinger, came from Connecticut, which she often revisited with her daughter. Miss Zollinger was born in Illinois, one year before the family settled in Iowa.

A visit to England gave Miss Zollinger the idea for a series of stories with an early English background. She had written two of these when illness and the First World War prevented her return to England to gather material for the third book. Not long after that she died in Newton, where she had been making her home.

Miss Zollinger was described as a small person, "bright of eye, with fire and spirit radiating from her face." She was a good conversationalist and quick at repartee. She was a friend and college classmate of Jane Addams.

Dikken Zwilgmeyer

1859-1913
AUTHOR OF
What Happened to Inger Johanne, Four Cousins, Johnny Blossom, Etc.

Biographical sketch of Dikken Zwilgmeyer, noted Norwegian author of children's stories, written for THE JUNIOR BOOK OF AUTHORS by her American translator, Emilie Poulsson:

DIKKEN ZWILGMEYER (christened Hendrikke) was born in Trondhjem, Norway, and died in Christiania.

When Dikken was five or six years old, her family moved to Risor, on the southern coast of Norway, where her father was the town judge. This change was a fortunate one, for life in a small seacoast town, such as Risor, furnished a wholesome, stimulating environment for children. "So many places to play in," says Inger Johanne; and what chances for fun and adventure on sea as well as on land: islands, foreign ships, wharves, the market place, and the steep rocky hills overlooking all!

Dikken enjoyed these to the utmost, we may be sure, for even as Inger Johanne she missed no kind of pleasure they afforded—and has chronicled them in her own frank, vivacious, and amusing way, giving, in the Inger Johanne books a very realistic and vivid portrayal of herself, her playmates, the town, and the free life lived there by the sea.

These books were of an entirely new order in Norwegian child-literature (before that time few books had been written especially for children in Norway) and immediately won deserved popularity throughout the country. They are decidedly the best of all she wrote. Her books for grown-up people met with little favor; they lack the distinctive charm and freshness of her books for children.

Dikken Zwilgmeyer's publisher, F. Nygaard, tells of her first venture in authorship. She sent to a children's magazine a short story which he read with great interest and in which he saw much promise. (The story was "An Interrupted Celebration," a chapter of *What Happened to Inger Johanne.*) He urged Miss Zwilgmeyer to write more stories of this kind—to write a book, in fact—saying he would publish whatever she sent him.

Her prompt answer was: "I never thought I should write a book or be an author, but if you will risk your reputation as a publisher and your money, I can surely hide behind a name nobody knows and make the attempt." Some time after came a manuscript. It was *Vi Börn* "by Inger Johanne," the name she had chosen to hide behind.

To her these stories seemed trifling, but this was not the estimate the public placed upon them. The first book proved a great success and those which followed were equally successful. They were known and loved over the whole land and Dikken Zwilgmeyer had become a name in Norse literature.

To be sure, the critics found flaws in her writing—in fact these are quite obvious. But the worth of the diamond, despite the flaws, was indisputable. The children in these books see and feel and judge as real children do; and like them at times they lapse into cruelty entirely at variance with their usual kindheartedness and quick sympathy. But their sense of justice is keen enough to cause them to regret the cruelty and to try to make restitution. In this clear understanding of child nature lies the supreme value of Dikken Zwilgmeyer's work.

As to the personality of Dikken Zwilgmeyer, the testimony of those who knew her is that it was unusually interesting. Her conversation was full of flavor, "with the unmistakable Inger Johanne dash."

Indeed, there was not a little of child nature left in her, even when her childhood was long past, and with her goodness and warmheartedness, her originality, and sparkling humor, it was (said one of her friends) as if she scattered sunshine and warmth around, wherever she went.